The Essential Theatre

ENHANCED TENTH EDITION

The Essential Theatre

ENHANCED TENTH EDITION

OSCAR G. BROCKETT
Late of the University of Texas at Austin

ROBERT J. BALL
University of the Incarnate Word

WITH CONTRIBUTIONS BY
John Fleming, *Texas State University*
Andrew Carlson, *University of Texas at Austin*

WADSWORTH
CENGAGE Learning·

Australia • Brazil • Japan • Korea • Mexico • Singapore • Spain • United Kingdom • United States

WADSWORTH
CENGAGE Learning·

**The Essential Theatre,
Enhanced Tenth Edition**
Oscar G. Brockett and Robert J. Ball with
contributions by: John Fleming and
Andrew Carlson

Senior Publisher: Lyn Uhl

Publisher: Michael Rosenberg

Development Editor: Megan Garvey

Assistant Editor: Erin Bosco

Editorial Assistant: Rebecca Donahue

Media Editor: Jessica Badiner

Brand Manager: Ben Rivera

Senior Marketing Communications
    Manager: Linda Yip

Content Project Manager: Dan Saabye

Art Director: Linda May

Manufacturing Planner: Doug Bertke

Rights Acquisition Specialist:
    Mandy Groszko

Production Service: Integra

Text and Cover Designer: Chris Miller

Cover Image: Robbie Jack/©Corbis

Compositor: Integra

For product information and technology assistance, contact us at
Cengage Learning Customer & Sales Support, 1-800-354-9706

For permission to use material from this text or product,
submit all requests online at **www.cengage.com/permissions.**
Further permissions questions can be emailed to
permissionrequest@cengage.com.

Library of Congress Control Number: 2013930115

Student Edition:

ISBN-13: 978-1-133-30728-0

ISBN-10: 1-133-30728-0

Wadsworth
20 Channel Center Street
Boston, MA 02210
USA

Cengage Learning is a leading provider of customized learning solutions
with office locations around the globe, including Singapore, the United
Kingdom, Australia, Mexico, Brazil and Japan. Locate your local office at
international.cengage.com/region

Cengage Learning products are represented in Canada by Nelson
Education, Ltd.

For your course and learning solutions, visit **www.cengage.com.**

Purchase any of our products at your local college store or at our
preferred online store **www.cengagebrain.com.**

Instructors: Please visit **login.cengage.com** and log in to access
instructor-specific resources.

Printed in Canada
1 2 3 4 5 6 7 17 16 15 14 13

Brief Contents

Contents

PART 3: Theatrical Production — 295

Preface

Behind this edition lies more than forty years of publication. Although *The Essential Theatre* was first published in 1976, it began as an abridged version of another book, *The Theatre: An Introduction*, which first appeared in 1964. *The Essential Theatre* has since taken on an identity of its own and is now in its Enhanced Tenth Edition.

As in its earlier versions, this edition is divided into three parts. Part 1 addresses basic issues and features related to the nature of theatre, to the role of audiences, to the varied criteria for judging theatrical performances, and to dramatic structure and style. Part 2 looks at various theatrical experiences from theatre's past and present. These experiences suggest that, as a vital form of creative expression, theatre changes to reflect the dynamics of the cultures within which it exists. Part 3 provides an overview of theatre production today: the principles, practices, and procedures used in the creation of theatre.

The Essential Theatre is intended primarily to serve two kinds of courses: an introductory course in which an overview provides a foundation for those intending to major in theatre (future theatre-makers), and a theatre appreciation course in which an overview provides insights and understanding for audience members (future theatregoers). Although these two courses may address the same topics, they usually do so with somewhat different emphases. Because instructors often use the material in ways suited to their individual needs, we have sought to provide a logically organized, comprehensive overview of the theatre. But instructors need not follow the sequence we have

chosen nor use all of the material in the book. Some instructors may wish to use only some of the chapters in Part 2, for instance, while others may wish to assign Part 3 prior to or concurrently with Part 2. Regardless, our aim is to provide helpful discussions of topics pertinent to introductory and theatre appreciation courses rather than to prescribe how the courses should be organized.

This Enhanced Edition features more expanded versions of the "Theatre in a Broad Context" timelines; these help students situate theatrical events and developments within a larger historical context (see the final pages of Chapters 4 through 10). Chapters 13 through 17 include a series of questions to help students attending performances more fully consider and analyze the work of different theatre artists (directors, actors, and designers). Finally, an extensive bibliography is appended to the book as a guide to additional sources about the topics discussed in each chapter.

We have assumed that many of those who use this book will both read plays and attend theatrical performances. Ideally, students should be able to read a play and then see a performance of that play. This is often not possible, but reading plays and seeing performances illustrate the difference between text on the printed page and its production on stage—the difference between drama and theatre. Because students typically will not have read a wide variety of plays, fourteen examples cited in *The Essential Theatre*, Enhanced Tenth Edition, are also included in a companion anthology titled *Plays for the Theatre*, Eleventh Edition, originally edited by Oscar G. Brockett and Robert J. Ball and published by Wadsworth. These plays serve as foundations for discussions of various types of theatrical experience. The anthology includes three new plays. Plays retained from the previous edition include Sophocles's *Oedipus the King*, the anonymously composed *Noah and His Sons*, the Noh drama *The Shrine in the Fields*, William Shakespeare's *Hamlet*, Molière's *Tartuffe*, Henrik Ibsen's *A Doll's House*, Oscar Wilde's *The Importance of Being Earnest*, Tennessee Williams's *Cat on a Hot Tin Roof*, Wole Soyinka's *The Strong Breed*, Paula Vogel's *How I Learned to Drive*, and Octavio Solis's *Lydia*. The three new plays are Sam Shepard's *True West*, August Wilson's *Fences*, and Tony Kushner's *Angels in America*.

New to This Edition

As "contributors" to an enhanced edition, our goal has been to build upon a successful framework while enhancing the features we have found to be most instructive in our own teaching. Likewise, we have listened to users of this book in attempt to increase the clarity, content, and organization to fit the needs of different instructors.

As noted above, the "Theatre in a Broad Context" timelines have been expanded and a new one has been added for Chapter 10's coverage of Asian and African Theatre. In addition, the material in Part 2 has been reorganized to make the historical overview of theatre's many expressions more clear. The presentation of Chapter 7's examination of modernism's influence on theatre and drama from 1885 to 1960 has been amended. An examination of the differences between the early modernist movements of realism, symbolism,

expressionism, surrealism, futurism, and dada is now featured in a pull-out box that contrasts the distinctive features of each movement. In the second half of the chapter, the trends in post–World War I European theatre are now treated together, followed by the trends in American theatre, and concluding with a separate treatment of musical theatre during that era. Chapter 8's treatment of decentralization and subsidization now includes a consideration of Sam Shepard's play *True West* as it illustrates the back-and-forth movement between regional theatres and the different tiers of theatre production found in New York. Chapter 9's treatment of diversity now includes a discussion of August Wilson's *Fences* and Tony Kushner's *Angels in America*; its treatment of contemporary theatre retains Octavio Solis's controversial new play *Lydia* and is updated in its discussions of both plays and musicals. In addition, Chapters 7, 8, and 9 now feature increased attention to the major playwrights of the modern and contemporary periods and all plays include a date of first production, thereby offering a clearer sense of context.

In Part 3, updates have been made so that the discussions of theatre production reflect standard practices and terminology. There is also increased attention to the designer as artist and interpreter; Chapters 15, 16, and 17 now include pull-out boxes where designers discuss the artistry of their design process. In Chapter 17, the expanded treatment of sound design has been retained.

Throughout the text, the feature boxes, play summaries, and historical content have been subtly edited to sharpen the clarity or significance of the topic being discussed. Likewise, approximately eighty photos and illustrations are new to this edition, showing concepts and practices as vividly as possible.

Supplements

Resources for Students

- **Theatre CourseMate for *The Essential Theatre*.** Cengage Learning's Theatre CourseMate brings course concepts to life with interactive learning, study, and exam preparation tools that support the printed textbook including Theatre Workshop. **Theatre Workshop** is a series of short videos related to the Theatre world, accompanied by critical thinking questions. Make the most of your study time by accessing everything you need to succeed—online with Theatre CourseMate. You can access this tool and more at **http://www.cengagebrain.com**.

- *Theatregoer's Guide,* **Fourth Edition**. This brief introduction to attending and critiquing drama enhances the student's experience and appreciation of theatre as a living art. This essential guide can be packaged for free with this text.

Resources for Instructors

- **Theatre CourseMate for *The Essential Theatre*.** Cengage Learning's Theatre CourseMate brings course concepts to life with interactive learning, study, and exam preparation tools that support the printed textbook, including Theatre Workshop. Watch student comprehension soar as your class works with the printed textbook and the textbook-specific website. Theatre CourseMate goes beyond the book to deliver what you need! Learn more at **http://www.cengage.com/coursemate**.

- **Instructor's Resource Manual.** Save time, streamline your course preparation, and get the most from the text. This indispensable manual offers easy-to-use chapter-by-chapter outlines, as well as a listing of key terminology. It also provides discussion questions, sample quiz and essay questions, video and web resources, and suggested activities.

- **Instructor Companion Website.** This protected companion website provides exclusive instructor materials, including PowerPoint® presentations for the entire text, as well as a downloadable version of the Instructor's Resource Manual.

- **PowerLecture Featuring ExamView® Computerized and Online Testing.** Create, deliver, and customize tests and study guides (both print and online) in minutes with this easy-to-use assessment and tutorial system. PowerLecture featuring ExamView offers both a "Quick Test Wizard" and an "Online Test Wizard" that guide you step-by-step through the process of creating tests—you can even see the test you are creating on the screen exactly as it will print or display online. You can build tests of up to 250 questions using up to twelve question types. Using ExamView's complete word processing capabilities, you can enter an unlimited number of new questions or edit existing questions. This CD also contains an electronic version of the Instructor's Resource Manual, and predesigned Microsoft® PowerPoint® presentations. The PowerPoint presentations contain text and images that can be used as is or customized to suit your course needs.

Acknowledgments

It is impossible to list all the people to whom we are indebted. The bibliography indicates most of the sources we have used, and the captions indicate the people and organizations who have permitted us to include their illustrations. In addition to these, we wish to thank the following colleagues for their insightful and useful comments:

Pamela Cilek, *St. Charles Community College*

Nina LeNoir, *Chapman University*

Jeffrey Milet, *Lehigh University*

Simon Provan, *University of Wisconsin, Sheboygan*

Steve Reynolds, Ph.D., *Wittenberg University*

Sarah Maines, *Texas State University*

Michelle Ney, *Texas State University*

Finally, we thank the staff at Wadsworth Cengage: Michael Rosenberg, Publisher; Megan Garvey, Development Editor; Erin Bosco, Assistant Editor; Rebecca Donahue, Editorial Assistant; Dan Saabye, Content Project Manager; Jessica Badiner, Media Editor; Abbey Stebing, Permissions Project Manager at PreMediaGlobal; Michelle Dellinger, Sr Project Manager at Integra-Chicago; and Integra Software Services Pvt. Ltd.

John Fleming
Andrew Carlson

The Essential Theatre

ENHANCED TENTH EDITION

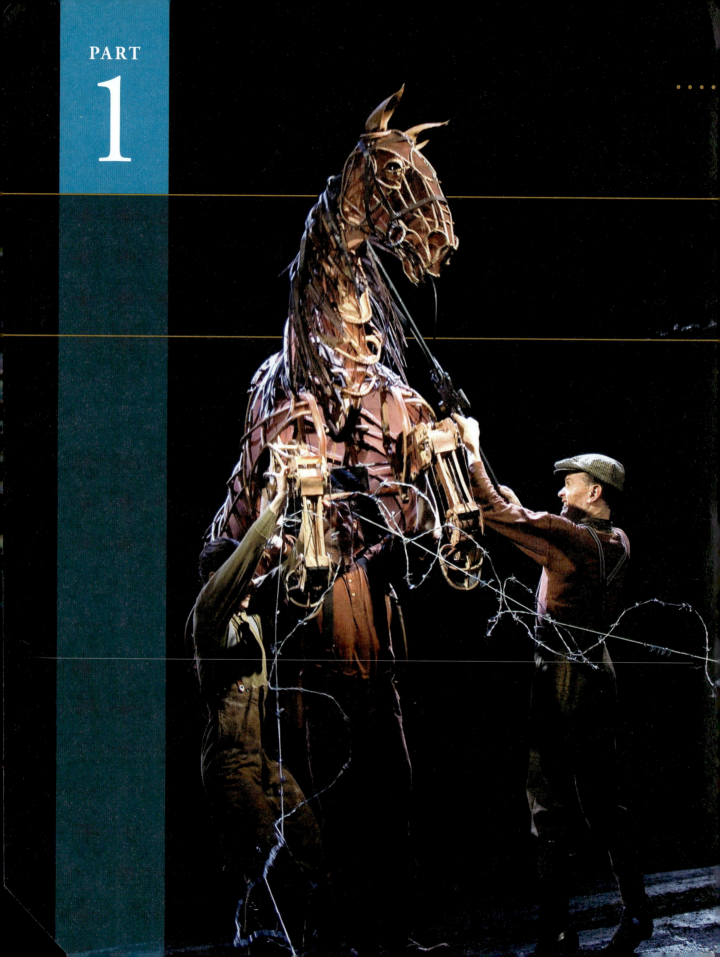

Foundations

Theatre is a complex art at least twenty-five hundred years old. Over such a long span, it has undergone many changes and followed diverse paths. When we attend the theatre today, we and a few hundred other people come together, usually in the evening, to see a performance that will last approximately two hours on an indoor stage illuminated by artificial light. But theatregoing has not always been this way. Our experience of theatregoing would have seemed strange indeed to Greeks living in the fifth century B.C. as they assembled at dawn in an outdoor theatre seating some seventeen thousand people to watch a series of plays that lasted all day under the bright sunlight. Our experience would have seemed equally strange to a fifteenth-century A.D. English audience that gathered at various places along a route to watch a series of short biblical plays performed on wagons that moved from one performance site to the next. These examples by no means exhaust the possibilities because theatrical experience has been as varied as the cultures in which it has appeared. The practices we are familiar with today encompass only a limited range of the theatre's immense possibilities.

Such diversity invites questions about what theatre's varied manifestations have in common and the significance of their differences. It also invites questions about the appeal of theatre: Why do people create theatre? What attracts audiences to it? What makes one production of a play seem better to us than another?

Let us begin our look at the theatre by examining some basic issues: the nature and function of theatre; the relationship of theatre to other forms of art; criteria for judging theatrical performances; how plays, the usual starting point of theatrical production, are structured; and other related topics. These initial explorations will help build the foundation for a fuller understanding and appreciation of theatre and the processes of theatrical production.

David Grimm's new play, *The Miracle at Naples,* treats the effects a traveling *commedia dell'arte* troupe has on a provincial town. Presented by the Huntington Theatre (Boston); directed by Peter DuBois; costume design by Anita Yavich; lighting design by Rui Rita; scene design by Alexander Dodge.

I regard the theatre as the greatest of all art forms, the most immediate way in which a human being can share with another the sense of what it is to be a human being.
—Oscar Wilde

The Nature of Theatre

It is uncertain just how and when theatre originated. As far back as we can trace human history, various kinds of rituals considered vital to the well-being of the tribe were already using the elements needed for theatre: a performance space, performers, masks or makeup, costumes, music, dance, and an audience. The function of these early rites was only incidentally theatrical; they were addressed to supernatural forces thought to control the return of spring, success in hunting and war, the fertility of human beings and the land, and the place of humans in the cosmic scheme. Other activities that contributed to theatre, such as storytelling and mimicry, also were already evident.

Although exactly how it emerged from these beginnings is unclear, theatre achieved its own distinct identity at least twenty-five hundred years ago. During its existence, it has at times been highly developed and highly prized. In ancient Greece, it was performed for the entire community at religious festivals financed by the state and wealthy citizens. At other times, theatre has existed on the fringes of respectability, as it did from the fifth to the tenth century A.D., when small bands of itinerant performers traveled around playing wherever they could for whatever they could collect from those who came to watch. In other times, theatre has been forbidden, as it was in England between 1642 and 1660 when the Puritans then in power considered it not only morally unacceptable but also an activity that tempted people away from more honest work. During its long life, theatre has as often been denounced as praised, and its value—even its right to exist—has frequently been questioned.

Such ambivalent response has been encouraged in part by theatrical terminology (*play, show, acting*) that suggests that theatre is the product of grown-ups who have prolonged their childhood by dressing up and playing games to divert themselves and others. Furthermore, because dramas are fictional, they have at times been denounced as a form of lying, as they were in colonial New England. Because they tend to emphasize human crises (often involving deception, violence, and socially reprehensible behavior), they have been accused of exerting dangerous influence on the young (as some claim much television drama does today). Nevertheless, in almost all periods at least some people have considered theatre not only an acceptable form of entertainment but also a truthful reflection of human behavior.

The theatre, then, has had its detractors and its advocates. Even so, those who value it often find themselves on the defensive with those who question whether it has a valid place in a college curriculum or whether a world dominated by film and television would miss theatre if it disappeared altogether.

The Basic Elements of Theatre

One reason for the varying responses can be found in the theatre's range and diversity, both of which are evident in its three basic elements:

- What is performed. (a play, scenario, or plan)
- The performance (including all of the processes involved in the creation and presentation of a production)
- The audience (the perceivers)

Each of these elements is essential and they affect not only each other but also the totality of what is expressed and how it may be perceived.

What is performed can be extremely varied—from a comic routine performed by a single entertainer to a Shakespearean tragedy performed by a large company of actors. Some people consider such events as street carnivals and parades types of theatre. Because of this great range, theatre is not easy to define. The critic Eric Bentley has argued that all of the many definitions of *theatre* can be reduced to: *A* performs *B* for *C*. That is, the most basic definition of *theatre* is someone performing something for someone else.

Though theatre is varied, typically it is thought of as the staged performance of a written text. But it is important to remember that theatre does not require a written text, dialogue, or conflict. Juggling and acrobatics, for example, have often been presented as theatrical entertainments. But even if we restrict our definition of *theatre* to performances that involve some degree of storytelling, we are still faced with great diversity because

improvised scenes, pantomimes, vaudeville sketches, musical plays, and spoken dramas are all theatrical entertainments. Furthermore, they may be brief or lengthy; they may deal with the everyday or the unusual, the comic or the serious.

With so much diversity, it is not surprising that some people think of theatre primarily as entertainment, whereas others find the essence of theatre to be its capacity to provoke thought or action about significant issues. John Millington Synge, one of the leading Irish dramatists of the twentieth century, argued that drama is at its best, not when it is dealing with social problems that will soon be forgotten, but rather when it feeds the imagination. Synge stated that "we should not go to the theatre as we go to a [pharmacy]…, but as we go to dinner, where the food we need is taken with pleasure and excitement…" Conversely, Peter Brook, one of the world's great directors, sees theatre as serving an important social and political role. According to Brook, "the basic function of theatre is to be anti-government, anti-establishment and anti-social. What we all recognize as feeble theatre is the theatre that enters into the public lie of pretending that everything's okay." If we are to understand the theatre, we must acknowledge its great range and recognize that its potential (like that of most human creations) can be developed in many ways, some of which we may like and some of which we may even consider dangerous.

Theatre's second ingredient, the performance, is equally complex. It translates the potential of a play, scenario, or plan into actuality. What the audience usually sees when it goes to the theatre is the fleshing out of a written text or plan through the application of theatrical processes. The performance takes place in a space that can vary from a building intended specifically for theatrical performances to a street, park, or nightclub. Spaces may vary from those that seat fewer than a hundred people to those (as in ancient Greece) that seat fifteen to twenty thousand. The arrangement of this space may also vary: It may permit the audience to surround the performers, require the audience to sit in rows facing a

Martin McDonagh's *The Pillowman,* a disturbing play about a writer of gruesome children's stories and their possible connection to actual crimes, at the George Street Theatre (New Brunswick, NJ); directed by Will Frears; scene design by Sandra Goldmark; costume design by Anne Kenney; lighting design by Paul Whitaker; sound design by Christopher J. Bailey.

© T. Charles Erickson

platform on which the performance occurs, or use other audience–performer configurations, each of which alters the total theatrical experience. (This subject is explored more fully in Chapter 11.)

Most performances require the creative efforts and cooperation of many people: playwright, director, actors, designers, and technicians. A musical involves even more people: composer, instrumentalists, singers, choreographer, and dancers. Any component of production (a play, acting, scenery, costumes, lighting, music, dance) can be manipulated to create varied effects. All of the components may be so skillfully integrated that the spectator is aware only of a single unified impression; or one or more of the components, such as acting or spectacle, may completely overshadow the others. Today, for example, many people argue that spectacular effects overwhelm the other elements in such popular musicals as *The Lion King, Miss Saigon,* and *Phantom of the Opera.*

The components may be handled in a way easily understood by almost everyone or in ways so strange that all but a few are puzzled. A performance may seem to one part of the audience original and entertaining and to another obvious and boring; conversely, what to one group may seem strange and incomprehensible may be judged insightful and brilliant by another. Although the possibilities and results of performance may be infinite, the beginning point of the theatrical experience has been reduced to its essentials by Peter Brook in his book *The Empty Space,* where he says, "I can take any empty space and call it a bare stage. A man walks across this empty space whilst someone else is watching him, and this is all that is needed for an act of theatre to be engaged."

The third basic ingredient of the theatre is the audience. All forms of theatre need an audience. A theatre performance is a communicative expression that is incomplete until an audience receives or experiences it. For all the arts, a public is imperative, but for some this public may be thought of as individuals—the reader of a novel or poem, the viewer of a painting or a piece of sculpture—each of whom may experience the work in isolation. But a theatre audience (as well as the audience for music and dance) assembles as a group at a given time and place to experience a performance. This group takes in a performance as a temporary community.

The Lion King, adapted for the stage from Disney's animated feature film (music and lyrics by Elton John and Tim Rice). Direction and design of costumes, masks, and puppets by Julie Taymor (aided by a number of others).

The audience affects the theatre in many ways, perhaps most clearly through the immediate feedback it provides the performers. Continuous interaction occurs not only between stage and auditorium, but also among spectators involved in a communal experience. For example, if one segment of the audience begins to laugh at what the director intended to be serious, the rest of the audience may come to respond in the same way; in turn, such unexpected response will probably disrupt the actors' concentration and alter their performance. Conversely, the shared enthusiastic laughter of an audience during scenes intended to be comic may lift the actors to greater effectiveness. This live three-way interaction is a distinctive characteristic of theatre and a major cause of variations in performances from night to night.

Audiences also affect the theatre through their expectations and motives for attending. Some members of the audience come to the theatre wanting only to be entertained, to be diverted from personal cares and the problems of their world. This group is likely to consider it the job of the playwright and director to make everything clear; it may see no need to make an effort to understand unfamiliar ideas or conventions. Such spectators may resent or avoid any production that questions conventional moral, political, or cultural values. Other members of the audience may prefer productions that challenge accepted values, raise provocative issues, advocate action about political or social issues, or use innovative theatrical means. Ultimately, various segments of the public make their preferences felt through attendance or nonattendance. They support what appeals to them and fail to support what they do not like or do not understand. Now that the cost of tickets to some Broadway productions is more than one hundred dollars, audiences understandably hesitate to attend the theatre unless they feel confident that a performance will suit their tastes. In turn, Broadway producers, who need to recover the large sums required to mount a play on Broadway, often avoid controversial subject matter or unfamiliar staging conventions that might reduce attendance. Off-Broadway and regional theatres, with lower costs and ticket prices, can afford to take greater chances and may seek a more restricted audience than that wooed by Broadway. Audience taste thus significantly influences what is performed, how it is performed, and where it is performed.

These three elements—play, performance, and audience—although they may be treated separately in discussion—interact and modify each other in practice. Playwrights may have specific intentions when they write, but they can seldom control how directors and others involved in production will interpret their plays. Therefore, different productions of the same play can vary drastically. Nor can directors dictate what audiences will get from their productions, and individual members of a single audience may have widely different reactions to the same performance. Because what is performed, how it is performed, and audience taste and perception are so diverse, not all theatre will appeal to all segments of the public. Responses to theatre are inescapably varied.

Whether the social context for a performance is formal or casual may affect how the audience as a group responds to the event. Here, the Royal Winnipeg Ballet performs at *Ballet in the Park*.

Ken Gillespie Photography/Alamy

Theatre as a Form of Art

Theatre should entertain. No one seriously questions that. But not everyone finds the same things entertaining. When a performance begins to violate our sense of propriety by presenting things we believe should not be put on the stage, we may be too offended to be entertained. But theatre is a form of art, and art is not always comfortable or comforting. It often insists on its right to look at the world in unpopular ways and to challenge our ways of looking at ourselves and the cultural standards that shape the way we view the world.

What is art? Probably no term has been discussed so frequently or defined so ambiguously. Until the eighteenth century, *art* always meant the systematic application of known principles to achieve some predetermined result. The word is still used in this sense when we speak of the art of medicine, politics, or persuasion. During the eighteenth century, critics began to divide the arts into two groups, "useful" and "fine." Into the latter category were placed literature (including drama), painting, sculpture, architecture, music, and dance. (Today, this list has been extended to include other forms, such as cinema and photography.) The reasoning was that the useful arts may be taught and mastered but the fine arts, as products of genius, cannot be reduced to rules or principles. It was reasoned further that, even if appropriate rules and principles could be codified and learned, few individuals possess the genius to create significant works of art. As a result, since about 1800 art has often been depicted as too complex to be fully understandable. Some critics have implied that only those with superior sensitivity can fully appreciate art and that the average person often mistakes an inferior product (usually some type of popular entertainment) for authentic artistic expression. Therefore, those who view the theatre as an art form are often contemptuous of those who think of it as "show business." Similarly, in the visual arts, a distinction is often made between works considered worthy of the museum or gallery and works created for advertisements or as illustrations; and in music, a clear line is sometimes drawn between compositions considered appropriate to a symphony orchestra and those played by a rock band.

Live theatre can include moments of intense realism. Shown here are Gordon Clapp, left, as Bill, Ethan Hawke as Travis and Ann Down as Margaret in a scene from Tommy Nohilly's *Blood From a Stone*, the story of a dysfunctional family.

Sara Krulwich/The New York Times/Redux

Society, Art & Culture

PRIOR CENSORSHIP AND SELF-CENSORSHIP

Although art may entertain us or illuminate various aspects of human experience, it may also offend some people when it includes subject matter they find morally offensive. Those offended often propose to control art through a form of prior censorship (forbidding the printing, performance, or display of works without prior approval). In the United States, even though the Constitution protects freedom of expression, there are periodic attempts to exert prior censorship, usually through threat or intimidation. The most common threat is the boycott. Groups may threaten not to buy the products of companies who sponsor works of which they disapprove. They may also mount campaigns against government subsidization or corporate support of specific arts organizations or artists or of art in general. More direct intimidation may also be used.

In 1998 the Manhattan Theatre Club announced that it was abandoning its planned production of a new play by Terence McNally, *Corpus Christi*, in response to a bomb threat made against the theatre. (Those condemning the play had not read it but were basing their objections on a report that the play included a Christ-like figure who is homosexual.) Athol Fugard, an internationally famous South African playwright who also had a play scheduled for presentation by the Manhattan Theatre Club, withdrew his work in protest against the theatre's decision, and TWA, one of the theatre's corporate sponsors, withdrew its financial support. Many theatre organizations in New York (and elsewhere) denounced the decision to cancel. The Manhattan Theatre Club later reinstated the production, but the implications of the cancellation remained: Threats of violence can be used to prevent the production of *any* play that one does not like.

Many theatre companies have been intimidated into adopting a kind of self-censorship under which they avoid presenting anything that might be interpreted as a challenge to some group's notions about religion, race, patriotism, or sexuality. Self-censorship is ultimately stultifying because if art never goes beyond what is already familiar, it risks being dull and predictable. Art may and does encompass the familiar, but it is crippled if it is not allowed to strike out in new directions as well. No one should be forced to accept art they consider offensive, but should they be able to prevent others who do not consider it offensive from experiencing this same art? Where should the line between acceptability and unacceptability be drawn? And who should draw it?

Some people are uneasy at the very mention of "art." Uncertain of what art is or how they should respond to it, they feel intimidated by it or resentful. This is probably one of the principal reasons why some people do not visit museums, attend concerts or theatrical performances, and perhaps discount altogether the value of these types of art. Their reluctance might be overcome if they could be convinced that there are no right or wrong responses to art: One responds as one does. Through multiple experiences we begin to perceive distinctions and patterns that permit us to develop our own standards. But we can never begin this process if we are unwilling to open ourselves to the unfamiliar.

We are faced less with distinctions between art and non-art than with two attitudes about what is worthwhile. All art is "made" (that is, art-works are not produced by nature the way human beings, animals, and plants are). Art comes into being through the application of certain processes, which are basically the same for all works in the same category. For example, in painting, all works, whether a sunset depicted on black velvet or a nonfigural composition on canvas, use the same basic elements: line, mass, color, light, and shadow, all of which are used to create spatial relationships. Unfortunately in modern times, the word *art* has come to be used as a value judgment. Consequently, though both works were created using the same process, artistic status would probably be denied the velvet painting but accorded the nonfigural composition.

Perhaps this will become clearer if we relate the issue to two broad categories used by cultural historians: popular culture and elitist culture. As the terms imply, popular culture is usually thought to reflect the tastes of a broad, general public, whereas elitist culture reflects the tastes of a smaller group whose members apply what they consider to be more demanding standards, often ones with which the general public is unfamiliar. Proponents of each category may speak contemptuously of the other using such terms as "low brow" for those who favor popular culture and "high brow" for those who take the elitist view. Although the boundaries are fluid, popular culture today would probably encompass such forms of expression as pop music, television sitcoms, advertising art, and musical comedy; elitist forms would encompass those kinds of music usually heard in concert halls, the visual art shown in galleries and museums, and many of the theatrical productions seen in not-for-profit or regional theatres. Nevertheless, no clear-cut distinctions exist between low and high art; they may and often do overlap or intermingle, and what was at one time looked upon as mere popular diversion (such as the plays of Shakespeare or the films of Charlie Chaplin) may later come to be considered significant art. Today the distinctions between high and low art have eroded as elements of each have increasingly been intermingled.

The type of theatre associated with popular culture seeks primarily to provide entertainment for a general audience by telling a story in a way that engages and builds interest. It employs easily recognizable character types, situations, and dramatic conventions, manipulating them with sufficient inventiveness to be entertaining but usually without raising disturbing questions that challenge the audience's values and assumptions. Perhaps the most obvious examples of this kind of entertainment are the prime-time, network-television series that, though they often show characters violating societal values, do so within a framework that ultimately reaffirms those values. These series are certifiably popular because the networks retain only those programs that attract audiences in sufficiently large numbers to please the advertisers who sponsor them. Anything so controversial as to alienate viewers is avoided. Such performances entertain, reaffirm values, divert audiences from their cares, and offer a change from the routine of existence. The majority of people feel most at ease with this type of art.

Dramatic performances share many characteristics with sports and games because all of these forms pit one side against another, build suspense, and reach an outcome. Games and theatre also share a dependence on conventions, that is, agreed-upon and understood rules, practices, and procedures. In football, the size and layout of the playing field, the number of downs and players, the uniforms, the system of scoring, and the length of the game are conventions that are understood by both players and spectators.

The theatre, too, depends on conventions, although more flexible ones: the stage as a place where fictional events occur, the use of scenery to suggest locales, the use in some periods of masks or of males to play female roles, and the singing (rather than speaking) of lines in opera. If we introduce new conventions or alter old ones, we are likely to confuse spectators, at least at first, although the changes may be accepted once understood. When Samuel Beckett's *Waiting for Godot* was first performed in the 1950s, many spectators were unable to relate to a play in which there was no discernible storyline beyond two tramps waiting for someone who never

Cirque du Soleil turns the music of The Beatles into theatrical extravaganza in *Love*. *Love* weaves together memorable music of The Beatles with eye-popping spectacle unified by The Beatles biography, a ringmaster (who looks as if he stepped off of the *Sergeant Pepper's Lonely Hearts Club* album cover), and a quartette of clowns ("nowhere men"). Above, "Here Comes the Sun" features classic Cirque du Soleil aerial acrobatics, while below the same stage space is converted through the use of trap doors and lighting effects into an undersea world for "Octopus's Garden." Note the elaborate costumes used to create the shape and movement of undersea creatures. Directed by Dominic Champagne; sets by Jean Rabasse; lighting by Yves Aucoin; costumes by Philippe Guillotel; musical directors George and Giles Martin.

CIRQUE DU SOLEIL

Although most forms of theatre use a play as the basis for performance, this is not always the case. Cirque du Soleil combines theatrical storytelling with breathtaking acrobatics, aerial stunts, circus acts, stunning visual effects, and contemporary music.

Cirque du Soleil began as a group of street performers walking on stilts, juggling, eating fire, and presenting other animal-free circus-style acts in Baie-Saint-Paul (a town north of Quebec). In 1984 some of these performers proposed that a circus show travel throughout Quebec province as part of the 450th anniversary celebration of Canada's discovery by Jacques Cartier. The Quebec government subsidized this endeavor called "Cirque du Soleil" (Circus of the Sun). Since then, Cirque du Soleil has transformed into a multibillion-dollar entertainment giant with nearly a dozen different shows touring across the world, with another seven shows being performed in Las Vegas and additional shows at resident theatres in Los Angeles and Disney World in Orlando, Florida.

Part of Cirque du Soleil's international appeal is that its performances rely more on eye-popping visual spectacle than they do on spoken dialogue, thereby making them accessible to audiences around the world. Cirque also uses contemporary circus clowns, humorous and adorable social misfits, who build an empathetic bridge between the audience and the world of the performance. As Cirque du Soleil has grown, so too has their use of spectacle to explore themes and tell simple stories. True to its roots, the group's early shows (1984–1992) were essentially collections of contemporary circus acts. Although the productions that followed did not attempt to develop a complicated, ongoing story, *Alegría* (1994) is organized around a general theme and uses a world of birdlike characters to explore the resiliency of the spirit even when oppressed. In 2005 Cirque premiered *KÀ*, which has the most fully developed storyline of any Cirque du Soleil show. Directed by Robert Lapage, an internationally famous Quebec-born theatre artist, *KÀ* tells a mythic story of the separation and reunion of a set of twins. The production maintains Cirque du Soleil's reputation for gravity-defying spectacle and uses a rectangular floating stage weighing approximately 50 tons, which can twist horizontally and vertically.

Cirque has continued to develop new extravaganzas, such as *Love* (2006), which is organized around the music of the pop-rock band The Beatles. Although some critics have dismissed Cirque du Soleil performances as "eye candy," few can deny its popular appeal. More than 100 million tickets have been sold to Cirque du Soleil performances since 1984.

arrived. The response of many to this innovative play was summed up in one of the play's speeches: "Nobody comes, nobody goes. It's terrible." But the conventions of this play, now considered one of the most important of the twentieth century, have become so familiar as to be commonplace.

Despite the similarities between games and theatre, we usually do not confuse them, not only because of differences in conventions but also because in most scripted drama the outcome is determined before the performance begins. For example, Hamlet always avenges the death of his father and dies himself because Shakespeare's text dictates these actions. In addition, the attitudes of audiences to the characters and their struggles are determined by information revealed during the performance. In games, loyalties that existed before the action begins usually determine which side spectators will root for.

Although much of the theatre's appeal lies in its ability to entertain, if it does not offer additional challenges, it may be (and often is) dismissed as an easily forgotten, momentary diversion—especially by those who consider the functions of art to include raising disturbing questions, challenging accepted values and assumptions, and searching for new types of theatrical expression, even though these often are the very elements that alienate the general

public. Elitists have so fully coopted the term *art* that the general public seldom applies it to the works it admires. Nevertheless, art (in the broad sense of something that is made and the process by which it is made) encompasses the whole range of theatre.

If no definition of *art* is universally accepted, some of its distinguishing characteristics can be explored by comparing it with other approaches to experience. First and most broadly, art is one way whereby human beings seek to understand their world. In this respect, it can be compared with history, philosophy, or science, each of which strives to discover and record patterns in human experience. All of these approaches recognize that human experience is composed of

AP Photo/Kirbin Doak Communications, Joan Marcus

Easily recognizable characters, a suspense-driven plot, and highly imaginative spectacle has helped *The Phantom of the Opera* appeal to a broad audience. Running since January 26, 1988, *Phantom* holds the record as the longest-running Broadway musical. Shown here is Brent Barrett as the Phantom in a 90-minute version created for Las Vegas.

innumerable happenings that have occurred to an infinite number of people through countless generations and that each person's life is made up of a series of momentary occurrences, many seemingly determined wholly by chance. One question these disciplines seek to answer is, What unifying patterns can be perceived behind the apparent randomness? The questions raised and the methods used to discover possible truths differ in each field, but they are always directed toward finding those relationships that reveal some pattern. As one approach, art shapes perceptions about human experience into forms (or patterned relationships) that help to order our views about humanity and the world in which we live. Some students of contemporary American culture have argued that our notions about love and marriage, for example, are determined much more by what we see in the media (both in dramatic programs and advertising) than by our real-life experiences with our own family and acquaintances. One may argue that some of the notions absorbed from television, film, and computer games are inaccurate or harmful, but they suggest nevertheless the power of art to shape or reflect perceptions.

The methods used in various approaches to human experience differ significantly. Historians, philosophers, and scientists isolate a limited problem, do their research or experiments, and then set down their conclusions in logical, expository prose; they direct their appeal primarily to the intellect. Artists, on the other hand, work primarily from their own perceptions and seek to involve the audience's emotions, imagination, and intellect directly. A play consequently shows events as though occurring at that moment before our eyes; we absorb them in the way we absorb life itself—through their direct operation on our senses. Art differs from life by stripping away irrelevant details and by organizing and telescoping events so that they compose a connected pattern. Thus a play illuminates and comments (though sometimes indirectly) on human experience even as it creates it. Nevertheless, a play often is not perceived to be a way

of knowing and understanding because we are aware that it is fiction.

How, then, can imagined experience be a way of knowing and understanding? Shakespeare offers one answer in *As You Like It* (Act II, Scene 7): "All the world's a stage, /And all the men and women merely players." This speech states not only that we may think of the world as a stage upon which each person plays a role but also, conversely, that the stage is a symbol of the world where it is possible to see reflected fundamental patterns of human behavior. Such representations, however, need not be realistic; they may represent experience in alternative ways. The stage can also serve as a magnifying glass through which we examine some aspect of human experience. What we see onstage, even though not factually real, are embodiments of types of human beings, situations, motivations, and actions. Thus, though fictional, plays may provide insights about human behavior that are as "truthful" as those obtained from a statistical study of actual human beings. What they show us also reflects basic assumptions of the society from which the plays have come. For example, the range of activities and values permitted female characters in the drama of any period reflects (by supporting or challenging) that period's cultural assumptions about women.

As spectators, our responses to a play differ from those to an actual event. Just as we do not mistake a statue for a real person, we do not mistake stage action for reality. We usually view a play with what Samuel Taylor Coleridge called a "willing suspension of disbelief"; although we know the events of a play are not real, we agree for the moment not to disbelieve them. We are nevertheless not moved to immediate action by what we see on the stage as we might be by real-life events. We watch one man seemingly kill another, but we make no attempt to rescue the victim or to call the police. We are aware that we are watching actors impersonate characters, but we acquiesce in granting them temporary reality. This state, in which we are sufficiently detached to view an artistic event semi-objectively, is sometimes called aesthetic distance. At the same time, the distance must not be so great as to induce indifference. Although a degree of detachment is necessary, involvement is of equal importance. This feeling of involvement is sometimes called empathy. Art lifts us above the everyday fray and gives us something like a "god's-eye" view of experience.

Art, then, is one method of discovering and presenting patterns that provide insights and perceptions or of raising questions about ourselves and our world. Thus, art may be viewed as one form of knowledge or way of knowing.

In addition, it is an imaginative reshaping of experience that operates directly on our senses in a way that involves us both aesthetically and empathically, allowing us to be simultaneously at a distance from and involved in the experience so that we participate in it emotionally even as we gain insights from it. Art lays claim to being serious (in the sense of having something important to communicate), but because its methods are indirect (it presents experience but does not attempt to explain all of its ramifications), it is often ambiguous and almost always open to multiple interpretations.

Geraint Lewis/Alamy

Shakespeare's Globe Theatre opened in London in 1997 near the site of the original theatre. The structure is a faithful replica of the original Elizabethan playhouse where many of Shakespeare's plays were first performed. Shown here is a 2008 production of *King Lear*, directed by Dominic Dromgoole.

Practices & Styles

THE FACTORY

Few theatre companies have taken as different an approach to standard theatrical practices and conventions as the London group, The Factory. Cofounded by University of London drama school graduates Alex Hassell and Tim Evans, The Factory group has performed classic plays with a different cast every performance; not even the actors know who will play a particular role until just before the performance begins. For example, when The Factory produced *Hamlet* in 2008 a large group of actors rehearsed the play for over a year. Different actors came together to rehearse as their schedules permitted and each actor prepared and memorized multiple roles. Then, dependent upon which actors were available for a given performance, the group determined just before beginning who would play specific roles for that performance. Rather than use carefully designed stage properties, they borrowed things the audience had with them and used those objects as properties during their performances. The Factory produced *Hamlet* in a number of locations; they sometimes performed on stages set up for other plays when those stages were not being used. Although normally such practices would spell disaster, most critics have praised the group and called their 2008 production of *Hamlet* "a theatrical coup," "unbearably poignant," and "unrepeatable." The group has not only won critical acclaim, but also some high-profile supporters including stage and screen actors Ewan McGregor, Bill Nighy, and Mark Rylance.

Behind it all is a basic desire to strip theatre of its accepted conventions and practices and embrace its immediacy. As Evans says, "We ask, what has become accepted as necessity in the theatre? And then scrape those things away, to see if you don't need them to put on great performances." Accepted necessities include having a set cast of performers, predictable stage properties, a set venue, and specific scene design for the performance. Rather than relying on traditional marketing and ticket sales, The Factory uses word of mouth and an e-mail announcement a few days before each performance to tell its growing group of friends, supporters, and the press where the performance will take place. The Factory likens its method of audience involvement to that of the rock band Radiohead (who escaped their major record label by distributing their albums online and announcing their gigs by e-mail on the day of the concert) as well as to the guerrilla graffiti art of Banksy.

It is uncertain how long The Factory will maintain this approach, but it demonstrates that theatre may be created in many different ways and that knowledge of accepted conventions and practices need not limit creative artists from exploring what is essential to theatre.

Special Qualities of Theatre

Within the fine arts, theatre holds a special place. It has a set of qualities that help to distinguish it from other arts:

- Lifelikeness
- Ephemerality
- Objectivity
- Complexity of means
- Immediacy

Although some of these qualities are present in other arts, theatre combines and manifests them in a special way.

Theatre is the art that comes closest to life as it is lived day by day. Shakespeare has Hamlet say (Act III, Scene 2), "the purpose of playing … is to hold … the mirror up to nature; to show virtue her own feature, scorn her own image, and the very age and body of the time his form and pressure." Not only is human experience its subject, but theatre also uses live human beings (actors) as its primary means of communicating with an audience. Often the speech of the performers approximates that heard in real life, the actors may wear costumes that might be seen on the street, and they may perform in settings that recall real places. Not all theatre attempts to be realistic, and at times it may approximate other arts (such as dance, music, or visual arts), but it remains the art (along with film and television) most capable of re-creating everyday human experience.

Such lifelikeness is one of the reasons theatre is often insufficiently valued: A play, a setting, and the acting may so resemble what is familiar to spectators that they fail to recognize how difficult it is to produce this lifelikeness skillfully. To a certain degree all people are actors; they vary the roles they play (almost moment by moment) according to the people they encounter and their relationship to them (parent, priest, friend, lover, enemy, and so on). In doing so, they use the same tools as the actor does: voice, speech, movement, gesture, and psychological motivation. Consequently, many people do not fully recognize or appreciate the problems actors face.

The theatre further resembles life in being ephemeral. As in life, each episode is experienced and then immediately becomes part of the past. When the performance ends, its essence can never be fully recaptured because—unlike a film, novel, painting, or statue, each of which remains relatively unchanged—when a theatrical production ends, it lives only in the play, program, pictures, reviews, and memories of those who were present.

Theatre resembles life also in presenting both outer and inner experience through speech and action. In this sense, it is the most objective of the arts. As in life, we come to know characters both externally and internally through listening and watching. What we learn about their minds, personalities, and motivations comes from what

they say and do and from what others tell us about them. But these are also conditions that make it necessary for each spectator to interpret what is seen and heard and, as in real life, interpretations may differ markedly. Thus, though theatre is objective in its presentation, it demands subjective response.

The theatre can be said to resemble life because of the complexity of its means and because like a scene from life itself it is made up of intermingled sound, movement, place, dress, lighting, and so on. Theatre draws on all of the other arts: literature in its play; painting, architecture, and sculpture (and sometimes dance) in its spectacle; and speech and music in its audible aspects.

Furthermore, theatre is psychologically the most immediate of the arts. Several contemporary critics have argued that the essence of the theatre (what distinguishes it from other dramatic media such as television and film) lies in the simultaneous presence of live actors and spectators in the same room. On the surface, the live nature of theatre may seem to have several drawbacks compared with other dramatic media. For example, more people often see a filmed or televised show on a single evening than attend the live theatre during an entire year. In fact, the theatre may be likened to a handcrafted product in an age of mass production because it must be re-created at each performance and for a relatively small group of spectators. Conversely, thousands of copies of a film may be printed and shown throughout the world simultaneously and year after year, and a televised program may be recorded and repeated at will. These media may make performers world famous almost overnight, whereas the actor who works only in the theatre may build up an international reputation only over a considerable period of time, if ever.

Nevertheless, the theatre has important attributes that television and film do not duplicate. The most significant of these are the three-dimensionality of the theatrical experience and the interactive relationship between performers and spectators. In film and television, the camera is used to select what the audience can see and to

Robbie Jack/Corbis

4:48 Psychosis by Sarah Kane explores lucidity and mental illness. Presented at St. Ann's Warehouse (Brooklyn, NY) as produced on tour by the Royal Court Theatre (London). Directed by James MacDonald; scene and costume designs by Jeremy Herbert; lighting by Nigel Edwards; sound by Paul Arditti.

ensure that it will see nothing more; the camera can frame the picture to restrict our view to a facial expression, the twitch of a hand, or a small object. In the theatre, the director uses various means to focus the audience's attention on a specific character or object, but—because the full acting area remains visible and close-ups are impossible—the audience may choose to watch something else. Perhaps most important, during a live performance, there is continuous interaction between performer and spectator; the pacing of a scene, for example, affects how the audience responds and, in turn, the audience response may stimulate the actors to alter the pace. Because of such interaction, each performance differs in many details. The audience thus plays a far more active role in the theatre than it does in film or television. Ultimately, there is an important difference in the psychological responses aroused in the spectator by electronic media and theatre because the former present pictures of events, whereas the latter performs the actual events in the same space as that occupied by the audience. This difference foregrounds one of theatre's unique characteristics: the simultaneous presence of live actors and audience. Film is also more literal than theatre; it usually seeks to show every detail of setting and action, whereas theatre requires the audience to imagine what it cannot show. Some critics have charged that film dulls the imagination, whereas theatre stimulates it.

These special qualities—lifelikeness, ephemerality, objectivity, complexity, and immediacy—define both the weaknesses and strengths of the theatre.

Art and Value

Art is valuable for its capacity to improve the quality of life—by bringing us pleasure, by sharpening our perceptions, by increasing our sensitivity to others and our surroundings, by suggesting that moral and societal concerns should take precedence over materialistic goals.

Of all the arts, theatre has perhaps the greatest potential as a humanizing force because much of it asks us to enter imaginatively into the lives of others so we may understand their aspirations and motivations. Through role-playing (either in daily life or in the theatre), we come to understand who and what we are and see ourselves in relation to others. Perhaps most important, in a world given increasingly to violence and tensions among ethnic and other diverse groups, the value of being able to understand and feel for others as human beings cannot be overestimated because violence depends on dehumanizing others so that we no longer think of their hopes, aims, and sufferings but rather treat them as objects to be manipulated or on whom to vent our frustrations. To experience (emotionally, imaginatively, and intellectually) what it means to be human in the broadest sense ought to be one of the primary goals of both education and life; few approaches have greater potential than theatre for reaching this goal because humanity is its subject and human beings its primary medium.

Theatre is also valued as a form of cultural expression. Every culture has some type of theatrical expression, the nature of which and the degree to which it is accepted tell us much about the society in which it exists. Greek tragedies and comedies, and the circumstances under which they were presented, reveal much about a culture that considered theatre its highest form of expression. Ancient Rome, whose theatrical activities were far more extensive and varied than those of Greece, favored entertainments such as mimes, chariot races, gladiatorial contests, and animal baiting, strong indicators that Rome valued popular-culture forms more highly than did Greece. We can gain insight into any culture by examining the range, prestige, and relative popularity of its entertainment forms. We can also measure the theatre's value to a culture by studying the relative emphasis it places on the theatre's capacity to provide diversion, recreation, or artistic expression.

Most people probably give little thought to the arts as an integral part of their lives. But try to conceive of life without any music, dance,

Performances of *Waiting for Godot* were given free of charge outdoors in New Orleans's neighborhoods badly damaged by Hurricane Katrina in 2007. The performances, which used abandoned homes and devastated areas as settings for the play, were part of a larger project that included art installations, a fund-raising drive for residents, and educational outreach programs. New Orleans's native, Wendell Pierce, and J. Kyle Manzay pictured; directed by Christopher McElroen in cooperation with the Classic Theatre of Harlem.

Lee Celano/The New York Times/Redux

drama (whether in theatre, television, or film), or visual art of any kind. Without these, the quality of our lives would be greatly diminished. Still, many people think of the arts as expendable "frills" that can be eliminated when financial stress occurs. Many also devalue the arts because they do not yield concrete benefits of the type derived from medicine or engineering. For these reasons, most artists have a difficult time making a living, although a few (including performers) win enormous fame and wealth. Parents typically try to discourage their children, especially as they approach adulthood, from viewing the arts as appropriate career choices. Because of such attitudes, many American adults have suppressed whatever artistic inclinations they may have had. They are thereby cut off from, or are only partly

using, one of the primary ways of knowing the world and understanding themselves.

Multiple Intelligences Theory and the Arts

Attitudes regarding the devaluation of the arts may (in part) be a by-product of a lack of understanding among educators and the general public regarding the nature of intelligence. Human intelligence long has been treated as a very narrow group of abilities measurable by I.Q. tests. The two clusters of abilities that education has sought to cultivate most are the linguistic/verbal and the logical/mathematical, and achievements or abilities in these two areas are the only ones addressed by the most commonly used standardized tests. In fact, the effectiveness of the educational system is often judged by how well students perform on standardized tests. However, psychologists have posited that there are many types of intelligence. Howard Gardner, a professor at Harvard University, argues that in addition to Linguistic (verbal) and Logical (mathematical), there are six types of intelligence:

- Musical—sensitivity to melody, rhythm, pitch, and tone
- Spatial—the ability to envision and manipulate spatial relationships
- Bodily kinesthetic—the ability to use the body and handle objects
- Interpersonal—the ability to understand others and human relationships
- Intrapersonal—the ability to use one's own emotions as a key to understanding oneself and others
- Naturalistic—sensitivity to the natural world and ability to interface with it

If Gardner is correct, much education has failed to cultivate major aspects of human intelligence and potential. Of these, most are related to one or more of the arts, especially music, dance, visual arts, and theatre. If education and society are to stimulate and develop the full range of human intelligence, the potential of the arts in this process and the value of the arts in society need to be more fully acknowledged and encouraged.

One purpose of this book is to affirm the value of theatre. The chapters that follow seek to acknowledge and encourage understanding and appreciation of the theatre by providing an overview of its various aspects: how plays are structured; varieties of theatre experience, both past and present; how the theatre functions today; and how each theatre artist makes use of available materials and techniques. Taken together, these discussions should provide a foundation for intelligent and sensitive reactions to the theatre and its role in its culture.

Theatre as an event must be experienced by an audience to be complete.

The audience is the most revered member of the theatre. Without an audience there is no theatre… They make the performance meaningful.
—Viola Spolin, *Improvisation for the Theatre*

The Audience and Criticism

All types of theatrical performance require an audience because it is in the mind and imagination of the spectator that the final step in the creative process occurs. No matter what the playwright or performers had in mind, audience members observing the theatrical event as it unfolds arrive at their own interpretations. Although shaping the theatrical medium to arouse the desired audience response is the primary challenge that the playwright, director, and performers seek to meet, there is no guarantee that a spectator's interpretation will accord with the playwright's or director's or that one spectator's interpretation will be the same as that of other spectators. The audience absorbs the developing action immediately and directly, taking in the relationships among the characters, the dialogue, rhythms, movements, and spectacle just as they would events in real life. However, they must watch and listen carefully to have the fullest possible experience and to understand the implications formed by the production as a whole.

During the theatrical performance, spectators are carried along at the pace the performers set. The spectator who fails to hear a line or to see a piece of business cannot go back and recover it; there are no instant replays or fast-forwards. Readers of plays may proceed at their own pace,

turn back, look ahead, or reread the entire play. The reader may decide that there are several possible interpretations of a line or scene and can leave all possibilities open, whereas the spectator in the theatre is offered only the one chosen by the director. What the spectator sees is one interpretation, but never the only possible interpretation, of a play. Productions of the same play by other directors may offer drastically different interpretations, resulting in drastically different visual and aural styles. Nevertheless, an effective performance can be far more satisfying than a reading because it translates words on a page into the sensual language of the stage, immediate and present in the living flesh and voices of the actors and the physical environment created by the designers.

Experiencing a Performance

Attending the performance of a play differs in several ways from going to a film. A live performance has more of a sense of special occasion. Except in large cities, live performances are not always readily available. One must usually buy tickets in advance and go to the theatre

25

at a specified time; usually there is only one performance a day, although some theatres offer afternoon matinees twice each week. Because tickets for a live performance usually specify the seat in which one is to sit, more attention is given to such matters as ushering spectators to their seats than at movie theatres. At live performances, spectators are usually provided with programs listing the author, director, designers, cast of actors, and the production staff—much like the on-screen credits shown at the end of movies. Unlike movies, most live performances also have one or more intermissions, during which audience members may leave their seats, mingle, and discuss what they have seen or what is to come. The audience at a theatre performance does more than watch images on a screen. They come together at a special time and place to experience a live event and their responses to that event have an effect upon it.

Theatres use various devices to prepare audiences in advance for experiencing performances in an informed and perceptive manner. Some of the most common are advance press releases, articles in newsletters sent to subscribers, lobby displays, and programs. Programs in some theatres are very elaborate, containing information about the play and the persons involved in the production as well as other information that places the production that the audience is about to see within an interpretive context. Because today the stage is seldom hidden by a curtain, the spectator can usually examine the stage and scenery and gain some idea of the production approach before the performance begins. Pre-show music is frequently used to get the audience into the appropriate mood.

There are no rules about how to experience a theatrical performance. Willingness to give one's full attention to what is happening onstage moment by moment is the prime requisite. As a performance unfolds, many questions that a reader can answer only in the imagination are given immediate form, at least in this production of the play: What is the appearance of the stage setting? How are the characters dressed? How do the characters move and relate to each other?

Unlike a film, in which the settings are usually realistic (often actual places), a live performance may use little scenery. The spectator may need to imagine much that is merely suggested by a few set pieces, projected images, lighting, or dialogue; and the same basic setting may be used to represent quite different locales. Costumes may be based on the dress of some historical period, or actors may wear ordinary street attire even though the characters are mythical, biblical, or historical personages. The audience may be asked to accept visual styles that alter ordinary modes of perception. These and other conventions may make great demands on the spectators' imagination.

In addition to using imagination, spectators need to concentrate. Unless they pay close attention, spectators may miss what is significant. Theatre requires more collaboration between director and audience than does film; in the theatre, although directors seek to focus audience attention on what is significant at any given moment, they cannot force attention as film directors can through such devices as close-ups and other camera shots that deny the audience the possibility of seeing anything other than what the director wishes. In the theatre, the entire stage space is visible and consequently each spectator may choose what to look at regardless of what the director may have established as the focal point through the placement of performers.

A number of factors may affect audience response. Although each audience member is free to respond as he or she wishes, individuals within a large group may be influenced by the responses of others to the performance. For example, if a sizable portion of the audience begins laughing at a character's behavior or a particular situation, others may quickly join in. Psychologists and sociologists have studied this group dynamic and have come to different conclusions about its cause. For the audience, a theatrical performance is a social event and conditions surrounding and defining that event play a role in how the audience responds. The size and configuration of the

The "Mousetrap" scene in *Hamlet* wherein Hamlet presents a play with a murder analogous to his father's to "catch the conscience of the king." Note the use of masks by the players and the makeup on Hamlet. Produced at the Alley Theatre (Houston); directed by Gregory Boyd; lighting by Chris Parry; costumes by Constance Hoffman; scene design by Neil Patel.

© T. Charles Erickson

auditorium and the stage may also affect audience response. A large auditorium may make seeing and hearing difficult, whereas a small auditorium may make it possible to see every detail and hear even the softest whisper. How the seating area is related to the acting area can also affect audience response. (The typical arrangements—arena, thrust, proscenium, and flexible stages—are explained at length in Chapter 11.)

Who Is the Audience?

Though we may speak of audiences as though they were all much the same, in actuality audiences vary widely in terms of tastes, education, economic status, race, age, and other factors. Those who produce theatre usually feel it necessary, in the choice of plays and production styles, to consider to whom they wish to appeal. Broadway, in part because of its elevated ticket prices, tends to cater to the well-to-do middle class, a large percentage of whom are tourists who, with limited time in town, must choose one or two shows from among the many available to them. The productions are usually tailored, polished, and marketed to appeal to the greatest number possible from this group. To this end, producers typically make blocks of discount tickets available to vendors who work with tour groups. Both the population of New York and the number of visitors to it encourage Broadway producers to aim for the longest

Society, Art & Culture

CULTURALLY CONDITIONED AUDIENCE RESPONSE

Although we tend to think of an audience's responses as immediate and spontaneous, they are conditioned by cultural expectations. Depending on the type of event and the expectations of the group for whom it is performed, audience behavior varies greatly. An audience's behavior is in part a product of cultural conditioning.

The quiet, sedate behavior of today's theatre audiences contrasts sharply with that of earlier times. In the eighteenth and early nineteenth centuries, audiences at plays were quick to let their responses be known. They often hissed and booed, threw things at the actors, and occasionally rioted—storming the stage or creating noise so intense and prolonged that no one could hear the actors. In an attempt to curb this behavior, English theatres during the late eighteenth century stationed a soldier with a bayonet-equipped rifle facing the audience on either side of the proscenium arch. In early nineteenth-century France, producers hired groups of people (*claques*) to applaud certain performer's entrances. Opposing claques sometimes tried to shout each other down in a battle over ideas and social standards. Theatrical performance served as a catalyst for heated debate over changing social mores—passivity was not expected.

Today, audiences of different cultural backgrounds show their approval in different ways. In the United States there is a fairly standard practice of applauding on a well-known or well-loved actor's first entrance. In London, this practice is generally frowned upon as disruptive to the flow of the performance. At Kabuki performances in Japan, audiences practice *kakegoe*, shouting out encouraging phrases to actors not only upon their initial entrance but throughout the performance. There is no curtain call for Kabuki performances so the only opportunity to express appreciation is during the performance itself.

Expectations regarding curtain calls have changed dramatically. In the early twentieth century, standing ovations were extremely rare, reserved for performances of the highest quality. Now it is rare to attend a theatrical event that is not greeted with a standing ovation. Peter Marks, writing in *The New York Times*, observes that "In the absence of standards shared by a wide range of informed theatregoers, it may be unsurprising that audiences stand to applaud anything, regardless of how mediocre."

possible run, and the success of plays is often judged by the number of performances they achieve. For example, *The Phantom of the Opera*, which has been performing on Broadway since 1988, holds the record as the Broadway musical with the greatest number of performances.

But many theatres exist in communities where long runs are not possible and may not be considered desirable. Most not-for-profit theatres in the United States stage plays for limited runs (usually no more than six weeks and often less). Over the course of a season, these theatres usually offer a series of plays of varying types drawn from both the past and present. They, too, have tended to attract primarily white, well-educated, middle-class (and, it is often said, middle-aged) spectators. In recent years, concern has grown about how to enlarge the theatre audience and especially how to attract the young and others who do not have a history of theatregoing.

Attracting new audiences is not easy and when successful sometimes alienates existing patrons. Plays that appeal to a new constituency may polarize audiences over artistic, racial, class, or gender

Disruptive audience behavior was common in eighteenth-century England, as illustrated here by the beginning of a riot at London's Covent Garden Theatre in 1763.

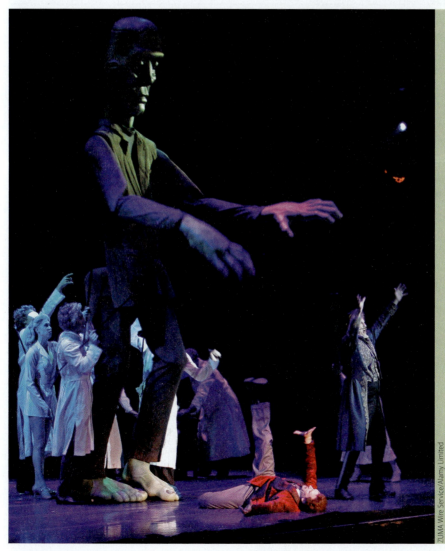

The musical *Young Frankenstein* closed after only a limited run on Broadway. It was reported that the producers overestimated its appeal and, hoping to maximize their profits by selling tickets at a premium, failed to make discount tickets available to tour groups, thereby reducing advance sales for the production. Book by Mel Brooks and Thomas Meehan; music and lyrics by Mr. Brooks; directed by Susan Stroman; sets by Robin Wagner; costumes by William Ivey Long; lighting by Peter Kaczorowski.

ZUMA Wire Service/Alamy Limited

issues. An increase in productions of interest to specific racial or minority groups has been encouraged by foundations and corporations through funding earmarked for this purpose. Such funding in many instances has become controversial. Minority theatres argue that these grants should have come to them (to strengthen their work) rather than being used to encourage mainstream theatres to broaden their repertories (and in doing so attract audiences away from minority theatres). This controversy, in turn, raises questions as to whether minority theatres should cater only to minority audiences and whether any theatre can adequately serve the needs of all members of a community or geographical area. Many theatres struggle with these ongoing questions: How many audiences are there? Of these, which ones do we wish to attract? How may the differing interests of multiple audiences be met?

Some theatres consider it important to challenge audiences to move beyond what they have become accustomed to and to enlarge their experience and appreciation of unfamiliar forms of theatre. Some theatres devote their entire program to these goals, but more typically theatres include one unusual piece among an otherwise traditional

Practitioners & Theorists

THEATRE FOR A NEW AUDIENCE

Founded in 1979 by Jeffrey Horowitz, Theatre for a New Audience is a nonprofit organization that produces modern and classical plays in New York (Off-Broadway) as well as for national and international tours. Some of its collaborators include London's Globe Theatre, the Royal Shakespeare Company, and Tony Award–winning director Julie Taymor (who has directed several productions for the group, including *The Tempest* and *Titus Andronicus*).

Perhaps no group has been more active in audience development, especially among a diverse population of young students, than the Theatre for a New Audience. Over the course of its more than thirty-year history, approximately 125,000 elementary, middle, and high school students have attended one of its performances or participated in one of its initiatives to make theatre and drama more accessible. Its "World Theatre Project" introduces young students to Shakespeare and other world-renowned playwrights by bringing artist-teachers into the classroom to help students and their teachers read, interpret, and perform one of these plays. Its "New Voices Project" brings professional actors into the classroom to help students write and rehearse their original plays and to perform some of the students' completed plays in staged readings before an invited audience. Both programs attempt to build appreciation by getting students creatively involved in writing or performing plays.

Richard Feldman

The Theatre for a New Audience produces bold treatments of new and classical plays. In their production of Shakespeare's *The Tempest*, directed and designed by Julie Taymor, Caliban (played by Avery Brooks and pictured here) begins the performance imprisoned in a mask, because of which he is considered to be a monster. Eventually the mask is broken, freeing the man within.

repertory. For most, the goal is not merely to follow but to lead audiences. Some theatres pursue this goal more aggressively than others.

Because the majority of the theatregoing public in America is middle-aged or older, and because relatively few spectators have come from lower economic classes and from racial minorities, how can theatres attract young audiences, and how can they increase attendance from groups for whom theatregoing has not been customary? A number of different approaches to this issue have been taken. One approach involves outreach programs designed to bring school children to the theatre or take productions to schools or to community centers. Similarly, the Theatre Communications Group, Inc., has partnered with state and civic arts agencies to sponsor a nationwide program called "Free Night of Theatre." The program offers free tickets on a selected night to a broad range of performances at over 600 theatres in over 100 cities. The program not only attracts new audiences but attempts

to assist individual theatres by providing tools, training, and suggestions on how best to work with "Free Night" patrons to encourage them to return, thereby increasing the number of future paying customers and reaching groups that are currently underrepresented in theatre audiences across the country. The hope is that once new audiences become familiar with theatre, they will continue to attend. Some theatres have developed expansive websites for today's online culture to provide information, particularly of a visual nature, about the plays they are producing. Many of these websites also make tickets available for purchase online and may offer special discounts. There have been some indications of success. The number of under-twenty ticket holders more than doubled for Broadway productions during the 1990s, but today they still make up less than 20 percent of the audience.

A theatre's attempts to identify its potential audience (or audiences) and its concerns as well

© T. Charles Erickson

Suzan-Lori Parks writes intellectually challenging and emotionally charged plays that often draw a younger and more diverse audience. Pictured here is her Pulitzer Prize–winning play *Topdog/Underdog*, which treats (among other things) the sibling rivalry of two brothers, Lincoln and Booth; produced by the Hartford Stage Company.

as to devise means of reaching them are important because the theatre cannot exist without audiences. Sensitivity to varying audience tastes and interests is essential to achieving a diversified theatre.

The Audience and Critical Perspective

Do we need a critical perspective to enjoy theatre? Most of us go to the theatre hoping to be fully caught up in the performance. When this happens, we are too involved to pass judgment on what we are seeing, although our involvement itself may be an acknowledgment of the production's power. Only after the performance has ended can we fully process our response to it. At an ineffective performance, however, we are likely to pass judgment even as we watch, largely because we are not able to become absorbed in it. Even if we have liked a production, we may have trouble formulating our responses to it when it is over. Most of us restrict ourselves to such generalized responses as "I really enjoyed it" or "I thought the actors did a good job with a weak play." If we are to be more articulate, we must not only examine our overall response but also look more analytically at the elements that went into the production (the play, the directing, acting, scenery, costumes, lighting) and develop criteria for judging the individual elements as well as the overall achievement. This can be viewed as a three-step process: One has an experience, one analyzes the experience, and then one communicates one's response to another. If we can reason through our subjective response to art, we may discover more about our own thoughts and feelings as well as express ourselves in a more coherent way. Although a critical perspective is not required to enjoy theatrical performance, it increases our understanding of the experience and helps us to communicate our response to others. This book, taken as a whole, seeks to assist in this process.

Although every member of the audience is in some sense a "critic," this title is usually reserved for those who formulate their judgments for dissemination. Such critics should have had considerable theatregoing experience (an inexperienced theatre critic is comparable to a sports columnist who has never seen a baseball game); they need to understand what goes into a production (the potentials and limitations of the various theatre arts) so they can assess the contributions of each element of a production. Critics need to be aware of the audience for whom they are writing so they can express themselves in terms meaningful to it.

Usually, the critic has a particular type of audience in mind. The production reviews published in daily newspapers are addressed to a general public that may have no extensive knowledge of theatre, whereas the critical articles written for literary quarterlies or scholarly journals are addressed to a more restricted, often an academic, audience. A single piece of criticism seldom serves the needs of all audiences.

Critics who write reviews for newspapers often think of themselves as consumer guides, alerting readers to which productions are worth their time and money and which are not. Some television stations review plays, though only in short spots of two to five minutes. Bloggers with large followings also review plays. Whether through newspapers, television, or Internet blogs, reviews often have a substantial impact on ticket sales.

To many, criticism means adverse response, but the true meaning of the word is "the act of making judgments." The best criticism requires attention to both excellence and shortcomings. Not all critics provide balanced discussions. Benedict Nightingale, theatre critic for the *London Times*, states: "So often criticism seems to be a courtroom in which theatre practitioners are arraigned. If that is so, then perhaps the critic should think of himself as court recorder and defense attorney at least as much as a prosecutor and judge."

Society, Art & Culture

INFLUENCE OF CRITICISM

Although many people insist that published critiques of plays have no influence on their reactions, this certainly is not true for everyone. It used to be said that a negative review in *The New York Times* spelled failure for a Broadway production. This is not necessarily true anymore, if it ever was, but newspaper reviews do serve as a kind of shopping guide, and theatregoers are understandably reluctant to pay high prices to attend a production that has been panned by reviewers. In several instances, however, positive "word of mouth" passed along by those who have seen the production has overcome negative reviews and has led to long runs. Initially, many theatre critics gave *Les Misérables* (1985), a musical based on Victor Hugo's novel, unfavorable reviews. Some reported that the musical cheapened Hugo's novel by treating it too sentimentally. Others said that a Victor Hugo novel was not appropriate source material for a musical. Despite less than rave reviews, which normally might close a production then and there, audiences flocked to see it and in a few days the production was sold out for months in advance. *Les Misérables* played for long runs in London and New York as well as on tour and in cities throughout the world for several years.

Reviewers may influence in other ways how audiences respond in the theatre. Michael Gambon, one of England's most admired actors, tells of his experience of performing in David Hare's *Skylight* (1995) in New York after a long and much praised run in London, where audiences laughed appreciatively during performances. The same response greeted the production in New York during preview performances, but once the play was reviewed by critics, the laughter largely ceased. According to Gambon, audiences "were told it's a serious play," and they seemed thereafter to feel it in bad taste to laugh.

Despite the initial mixed reviews *Les Misérables* has become London's longest running musical. The musical was adapted by Alain Boublil and Claude-Michel Schönberg from the Victor Hugo novel; lyrics by Herbert Kretzmer (additional lyrics by James Fenton); directed by Trevor Nunn and John Caird; scene design by John Napier; costumes by Adreane Neofitou; lighting by David Hersey.

John Marshall/JME Enternational/AP Photos

Some critics may provide less-than-balanced discussion either because they lack the space or because they believe a play or a production is so good or so inadequate that nothing of importance need be said on the other side. However, one-sided criticism of the "thumbs-up" or "thumbs-down" variety is generally unhelpful; it fails to provide readers enough information to determine for themselves whether they might enjoy or deplore the event. Likewise, a review that concentrates on only one aspect of the event (for example, the acting or the playwriting) and ignores the other aspects of it does little to communicate the total experience.

Some commentaries on productions are almost wholly descriptive. A critic may explain how a play is structured or may provide information about certain aspects of the production (the visual appearance of the costumes, the use of lighting, the innovative conventions, how the production differs from previous ones of the same play, and so on) without passing any judgment on these features. Such descriptive pieces can help an audience appreciate a production or a play that it might otherwise find baffling because of unfamiliar conventions or a controversial directorial interpretation.

Some reviewers have a tendency to be flippant or condescending. Legendary examples of flippancy are Dorothy Parker's comment that Katharine Hepburn's performance ran the gamut of emotion from A to B (in a Broadway production of *The Lake* in 1933) and John Mason Brown's statement, "Tallulah Bankhead barged down the Nile last night and sank" (in his review of her performance in a 1937 Broadway production of Shakespeare's *Antony and Cleopatra*). Examples of condescension include John Simon's remarks on Jerzy Grotowski's production of *The Constant Prince* (1967)—"I was so dumbfounded by the infantilism and coarseness of the proceedings that sheer amazement kept me from even trying [to take notes]." Such quips may be amusing, but they can be infuriating and discouraging to theatre workers whose efforts are callously dismissed out of hand. Such reviews contribute significantly to the antipathy that sometimes exists between theatre artists and critics.

The Basic Problems of Criticism

The critic is concerned with three basic problems: understanding, effectiveness, and ultimate worth. What were the playwright,

director, and other theatre artists trying to do? How well did they do it? How valuable was the experience?

Critics follow any of several paths to answering the first question. If the play is available, they may study it carefully prior to attending its production. They may find out more about the author's life and other works and about what other critics have said about the dramatist's plays. They may refresh their memory of previous work by the director and production team or of previous productions of the same play. Some reviewers avoid any preparation for viewing a production on the grounds that they wish to attend it much as any other spectator might, so they may react without preconceptions about the play or how it should be performed.

By choice or necessity, many reviewers write about the production of plays they have not read and know only from a single performance. In such circumstances, reviewers are often guilty of damning a play rather than its inadequate production, or a performance rather than its inadequate play, because of the difficulty in judging the sources of strengths and weaknesses based on a single viewing or without prior knowledge of the play.

In dealing with effectiveness—How successful were the playwright, director, and other theatre artists in accomplishing what they set out to do?—the critic may focus on the play's intention or the director's interpretation. Rarely do playwrights state their intentions directly. Intention is indicated by the way conflicts, characters, and ideas are handled and by the look and sound of the production. Evidence of the director's interpretation usually comes from what one sees and hears during the performance, although sometimes the director explains his or her approach in notes printed in the program, in interviews before the opening, or in publicity releases. Many directors try to embody the play's intention as faithfully as possible. But some directors use the written text (somewhat like acting, scenery, and lighting) as raw material to be shaped according to the director's vision. Contemporary directors often interpret plays in ways that are at variance with the playwright's apparent intentions on the grounds that by doing so one gains a new perspective on the issues dealt with in the play or that a close examination of the play reveals unconscious motives or biases that need to be brought out or that certain changes make a play from the past more relevant to today's world. For example, *Hamlet* has been set in contemporary corporate America with the introspective Dane played as an amateur videographer in an attempt to translate the play's characters and themes into more accessible terms for a modern audience. In evaluating such productions, the critic may assess how the director's interpretation is related to, or differs from, the play's apparent intention. Although the critic may believe that the director is misguided, this belief is irrelevant in the critic's assessment of whether the director has achieved what he or she set out to do.

Even though a play or production is understandable and effective, a critic may still consider it unsatisfactory when seeking to answer the third basic question: How valuable was the experience? Any response to this question assumes some standard against which value can be measured. Unfortunately, there are no universally accepted standards of worth, and no standard can be proven incontestably better than another. Often we are puzzled by other people's pronouncements because we do not know what criteria have been used in making them. Why do friends detest a play or movie we have greatly admired? If we discuss with them our conflicting responses, we often find that each of us is looking at the same work from a different perspective. One of us may praise a production's comic inventiveness, whereas another may find the work's treatment of women (or some other element) so appalling that nothing can compensate for this shortcoming.

Many contexts are used in evaluating the relative worth of plays or productions. Some critics consider the only meaningful context to be other plays or productions of the same type. Each critic may value a production for a different reason: its emotional power, its relevance to contemporary issues, its insights into human behavior, its innovations, its embodiment of the

In Shakespeare's *King Lear*, Lear loses the privileges of his position and ends up living in a "hovel." The Center Stage (Baltimore) production of the play represents the hovel as a discarded cardboard box to express Lear's homelessness in contemporary terms; directed by Irene Lewis with scene design by Robert Israel; costumes by Catherine Zuber; lighting by Rui Rita.

Richard Anderson; courtesy of Center Stage

written text, its ability to entertain. At times, critics seem to damn productions for failing to satisfy criteria that the playwright or director never intended to meet. Furthermore, critics do not necessarily adhere to a single context in making their judgments and often shift their ground within a single review. Examining carefully any review to uncover the stated or implied criteria that underlie the various value judgments expressed can be instructive. In turn, this may lead us to a greater awareness of the preconceptions and prejudices that underlie our own judgments.

We should define what, for us, makes a production satisfying or unsatisfying. Many believe that the most satisfying production is one that so fully absorbs their attention that they completely forget themselves. Others have argued that to enter so fully into a production makes it impossible to watch critically or to be aware of the ideology or prejudices implied by the action.

In assessing our own critical stance, here are some questions that may be helpful:

- Am I open to unfamiliar subjects, ideas, or conventions?
- In the theatre, am I uncomfortable with moral stances that differ from my own?
- Are there subjects I think should not be treated on the stage? If so, which?
- What standards do I use in judging a play or performance? Why?

Such questions suggest the need for each of us to understand our own convictions and biases because these influence (usually quite unconsciously) our critical judgments.

Critical responses, whether those of the casual spectator or the professional critic, ultimately involve the three major questions already posed:

- What was attempted?
- How fully was it accomplished?
- How valuable was the experience?

In addition, an informed and perceptive reviewer usually deals with elaborations on the following major questions:

- What play was performed? Who is the playwright? What information about the playwright or the play is important for understanding the production?
- Where and when did the performance take place? Will there be additional performances?
- Who was involved in the production—producer, director, actors, designers? (Not everyone need be named, and comments about those who are may be scattered throughout the reviews.)
- What were the apparent goals of the play or production?
- How effectively and fully were the goals realized (in the directing, acting, design elements)?
- Should others see it? Why?

A critic may not deal with all of these questions or in this order, and answers to each question may vary in length and complexity.

Qualities Needed by the Critic

Because the theatre is a composite art and because each of us is subject to many influences, it is difficult to become a good theatre critic. A reliable critic usually has had years of theatregoing on which to draw, as well as a firm foundation of studying and reading about the theatre, its processes, and its cultural context.

A critic should strive

- to be sensitive to feelings, images, and ideas.
- to become as well acquainted as possible with the theatre of all periods and of all types.
- to be willing to explore plays and production processes.
- to be tolerant of innovation.

- to be aware of his or her own prejudices and values.
- to be articulate and clear in expressing judgments and their bases.
- to be courteous.

Perhaps most important, the critic should avoid becoming dogmatic or unwilling to consider alternative views. The theatre is constantly changing, and critics must be willing to reassess their standards in light of innovations even as they seek to evaluate the changes.

David Catlin pressed together two prior literary works, Lewis Carroll's *Alice's Adventures in Wonderland* and *Through the Looking Glass*, to make a single play, *Lookingglass Alice*.

© T. Charles Erickson

Drama assumes an order. If only so that it might have—by disrupting that order—a way of surprising.

—Vaclav Havel (playwright and former president of the Czech Republic)

The Play

The play is both the typical starting point for a theatrical production and the most common residue of production, because it usually remains intact after its performance ends. It is useful to distinguish the play—the written text—from a theatrical production of it because the same play may serve as a basis for many different productions. A play has greater permanence than its theatrical representations and may come to be considered a literary work. Drama is consequently often taught apart from theatre; many people who read plays have never seen a live theatre performance, and most students get their first glimpse of theatre through reading plays in literature classes. But a play may seem unsatisfactory or puzzling, because it is essentially a blueprint demanding from both reader and performer the imaginative creation of much that is only implied on the printed page. Learning to read, understand, and fill out the play (either in the mind or on the stage) is essential if its power is to be fully realized.

On Reading a Play

There are no rules about how one should read a play. Nevertheless, some observations may be helpful to those who are new to play reading. First, one must accept that the ability to read imaginatively and perceptively is a basic skill that everyone needs; without this skill much of human experience is lost, and intellectually we suffer from historical and cultural amnesia.

Because all writers do not express themselves in the same form, all written works cannot be read in the same way. Each form has its own characteristics, and each makes distinctive demands on the reader. We cannot read a play in the same way we read a historical treatise, an essay, a biography, a novel, or a poem. To read a play adequately, we must adjust our minds to the dramatic form. A play is distinctive in part because it is made up primarily of dialogue constructed with great care to convey its intentions and to create the sense of spontaneous speech by characters involved in a developing action. A play is both a highly controlled structure and a simulated reflection of human experience. Consequently, drama requires readers to contribute more than most other forms of fiction do.

Play readers need to pay particular attention to several things:

- Stage directions
- Time and place of the action
- Implied meanings and "subtext"
- Character action and interaction

Novels and short stories often provide their readers narration that continuously describes settings, sounds, and character action, as well as the innermost thoughts and feelings of the characters. Plays do not usually provide such information so directly. Instead, some playwrights use stage directions to clarify their intentions. It has become common for playwrights to use stage directions that state where and when the action is taking place. But whether this information is provided directly or embedded in the dialogue of the characters, the time and place of the action—for a scene or for the play as a whole—may have significant implications. Stage directions may not only situate the action but also suggest things about characters' speech and behavior since these expressions are often situational. Stage directions may also help to establish the mood and desired atmosphere or even the tone in which the playwright imagines specific lines may be spoken. However, most playwrights primarily convey intentions through dialogue.

In reading a play, we should assume that what is written is what the writer wished to say. But because the dramatist must convey intentions through a likeness of conversation, we must be sensitive—as in life—to deeper meanings that may be implied. The term *subtext* is often used to refer to a character's true meaning beneath the surface level of their communication. Readers must not only understand what is explicitly said and done, but they must also be aware of all that is implied. What is left unspoken may in some instances prove even more significant than what is overtly said. Therefore, the reader must be especially alert to actions and the nuances of interactions among characters. Although it is not a simple undertaking to inwardly and imaginatively see and hear what a written text suggests, we can become adept with practice. Perhaps the best place to begin is with a look at how plays are constructed and how structure is related to dramatic effectiveness and meaning. (How playwrights function in today's theatre is discussed in Chapter 12.)

Dramatic Action

Broadly speaking, a play is, as the ancient Greek philosopher Aristotle wrote in his *Poetics*, a representation of human beings "in action." By *action* he did not mean mere physical movement. Rather, he was concerned not only with what characters do but also with why they do it. In turn, the actions of the individual characters relate to some question, problem, or theme that forms the central focus, or dramatic action, of the play as a whole.

Francis Fergusson, a twentieth-century American critic, has argued that a dramatic action builds through three steps: purpose, passion, and perception. By *purpose* he means awareness of some desire or goal; by *passion* he means the strength of desire or suffering that makes characters act to fulfill their goals, along with the emotional turmoil they undergo while doing so; and by *perception* he means the understanding that eventually comes from the struggle. In Ibsen's *A Doll's House*, for example, we see Nora attempt desperately to conceal that she has borrowed money without her husband's knowledge, the increasing anguish into which this attempt leads her, and her eventual discovery that her marriage has been a lie based on a misunderstanding of her husband's character.

The range of human motivation and behavior is so great that no single play can depict more than a small part of the totality. Because each playwright's view of the human condition differs, each drama is in some respects unique. Still, all plays share certain qualities that allow us to draw some conclusions about the characteristics of effective dramatic action. Effective dramatic action

- is complete and self-contained.
- is deliberately shaped.
- has variety.
- engages and maintains interest.
- is internally consistent.

dominic dibbs/Alamy Limited

Although Shakespeare's plays contain very few explicit stage directions, the lines of characters often contain descriptions of place, time, or action that function as implicit stage directions. Here the three witches meet in *Macbeth*.

Aristotle stated that a dramatic action should have a beginning, middle, and end. On the surface, this statement seems obvious, but it summarizes a fundamental principle: A dramatic action should be *complete and self-contained* (that is, everything essential for understanding it should be in or implied in the play). If this principle is not observed, the action will probably seem incomplete or unsatisfying. Effective dramatic action is *deliberately shaped* or organized to reveal its purpose and goal and to evoke from the audience specific responses (pity, fear, laughter, ridicule, and so on). Effective dramatic action, in addition to having purpose, must also have *variety*

(in story, characterization, idea, mood, spectacle) to avoid monotony. Effective dramatic action *engages and maintains interest*. The situation must be sufficiently compelling to arouse curiosity, the characters interesting enough to awaken sympathy or antipathy, the issues vital enough to provoke concern, or the spectacle and sound novel enough to attract attention. Effective dramatic action is *internally consistent*. Even if the events might be impossible in real life, they should be consistent with the "rules of the game" established within the play. For example, when during the opening speech of Eugene Ionesco's *The Bald Soprano* the clock strikes seventeen times and a character

Sara Krulwich/The New York Times/Redux Pictures

Few think that in real life chimney sweeps join together in the streets to sing and dance with a nanny who can travel through the sky with her umbrella, but given the conventions of musical theatre and the interior logic of *Mary Poppins*, such events can become believable within the fiction. Directed by Richard Eyre; codirected and choreographed by Matthew Bourne; sets and costumes by Bob Crowley; lighting by Howard Harrison.

announces that it is nine o'clock, we are warned that in this play we should be prepared for things to deviate from normal modes of perception—and they do. It is consistency within the framework of the particular play, not whether the events would have happened this way in real life, which leads us to accept events in drama as believable.

Methods of Organizing Dramatic Action

A play is composed of incidents organized to accomplish a purpose. This organization directs attention to relationships that create a meaningful pattern. In analyzing a play, it is helpful to pinpoint the source of unity; otherwise, the play may seem a collection of unrelated happenings rather than a whole. The most common sources of unity are cause-to-effect arrangement of events, character, and thought. (The following discussion uses a number of plays contained in *Plays for the Theatre* as examples.)

The majority of plays from the past are organized through cause-to-effect arrangement of events. This is the organizational principle used in *A Doll's House*. Using this method, in the opening scenes the playwright sets up the necessary conditions—the situation, the desires and motivations of the characters—out of which later events develop. The goals of one character come into conflict with those of another, or two

Practitioners & Theorists

ARISTOTLE'S POETICS

Probably no one has exerted greater influence on ideas about the nature of drama, dramatic structure, and dramatic form than the Greek philosopher Aristotle (384–322 B.C.). The son of a physician, he was sent to Athens at the age of eighteen to study at the Academy, the school headed by Plato, another of the great Greek philosophers. Aristotle remained for twenty years, becoming a teacher there. Beginning in 343, he was for the next seven years tutor to the future Alexander the Great. When Alexander succeeded to the throne in 336, Aristotle returned to Athens, where he founded his own school, the Lyceum. When Alexander died in 323, a reaction against those who had been associated with the ruler made it prudent for Aristotle to flee Athens. Aristotle died the next year at the age of sixty-two or sixty-three.

Aristotle was a biologist by training, but he studied and wrote in a number of other fields. His study of drama led to the *Poetics* (c. 335–323), the oldest surviving treatise on drama. After it was rediscovered in the fifteenth century A.D., the *Poetics* came to be considered authoritative on drama, especially tragedy. Although its influence began to decline in the nineteenth century, it continues to be one of the works most frequently referred to in discussions of the nature and structure of drama. It seems likely that only a part of the *Poetics* has survived, because although it divides drama into two basic types—tragedy and comedy—and promises to treat both, it discusses only tragedy at length. While describing tragedy, it outlines several principles of dramatic writing. It recommends the cause-to-effect arrangement of incidents, progressing through complications and resolution, as the most effective means of unifying action. It also considers internal consistency to be the basis of believability. The *Poetics* is too complex to summarize briefly, especially because the meaning of almost every line has been heatedly debated. Because it has been so influential, it is a work with which serious students of drama should be familiar.

conflicting desires within the same character lead to a crisis. Attempts to surmount the obstacles make up the substance of the play, each scene growing logically out of those that precede it. Any organizational pattern other than cause-to-effect is likely to seem loose, often giving the effect of randomness.

Less often, a dramatist uses a character as the source of unity. Such a play is held together primarily because all of the events focus on one person. Few plays are unified predominantly through character, however, because, to create a sense of purpose, more is required than that all the incidents involve one person. They must also either tell a connected story or embody a theme. Eugene O'Neill's *The Hairy Ape* is unified in part through the character of Yank, but mostly through its central theme of humanity's frustrated search for identity in a hostile environment. Similarly, *A Doll's House* gains much of its sense of purpose from Nora Helmer, but the play is organized mainly through the structure of its incidents. Plays with primary emphasis on character are usually biographical, as, for instance, George Stevens Jr.'s recent play about former U.S. Supreme Court Justice Thurgood Marshall.

Some contemporary dramatists organize plays around thought, with scenes linked through a theme or set of ideas. Vogel's *How I Learned to Drive* shows its central character in various moments in the protagonist's life, moving easily back and forth from one time period to another as they become relevant to her feelings or anxieties. It is organized somewhat like a musical composition, in which a theme or motif is introduced and then elaborated upon in a series of variations; ultimately, these variations fuse to create a vision of human existence and illuminate a central thought.

Although a play usually has one major source of unity, it also uses secondary sources because every play involves a sequence of incidents, uses characters, and implies a theme or set of ideas. Other sources of unity are a dominant mood, visual style, and distinctive use of language.

The organization of dramatic action may also be approached through the parts of drama, which, according to Aristotle, are plot, character, thought, diction, music, and spectacle.

James Earl Jones as Thurgood Marshall in *Thurgood* **by George Stevens Jr. at the Westport County Playhouse.**

© T. Charles Erickson

Plot

Plot is often considered merely the summary of a play's incidents, but it also refers to the organization of all the elements into a meaningful pattern. Thus, plot is the overall structure of a play. The plot of a play may be structured in many different ways, but two of the most common plot structures are *episodic* and *climactic*. Climactic plots normally follow the action in a cause-to-effect manner to its conclusion, and, because they frequently enlist a late point of attack, they are often successful in creating a sense of compression or dramatic tension. Episodic plots jump from one scene to the next, often separated by time or place, without necessarily building cause-to-effect relationships between them. Because episodic plots usually treat some central character or concern over time or through a number of variations, they are often successful in creating a broad perspective.

The Beginning

The beginning of a play establishes some or all of these: the place, the situation, the characters, the mood, the theme, and the internal logic (the rules of the game) that will be followed. Viewing a play is like coming upon previously unknown places and persons. Initially, the novelty may excite interest, but as information about the place and people unfolds, interest either wanes or increases. The playwright is faced with a double problem: to give essential information and at the same time to make the audience want to stay and see more.

The beginning of a play usually involves *exposition*, or the setting forth of information about earlier events, the identity and relationship of the characters, and the present situation. Although exposition is a necessary part of the opening scenes, it is not confined to those scenes because information is gradually revealed throughout most plays. Normally, the storyline of a play is longer than its plot. For example, one may view the story of *Oedipus Rex* as beginning, long before the play starts, with the prophesy that the child of Laius and Jocasta would kill his father and marry his mother. Yet, the play begins long after these events have taken place. This choice, to begin the action late in the storyline (known as a late point of attack), compresses events and creates dramatic tension.

The amount of exposition required about past events is partly determined by the *point of attack*: the moment at which the story is taken up. Shakespeare typically uses an early point of attack (that is, he begins the play near the beginning of the story and tells it chronologically). Thus, he needs relatively little exposition. Greek tragic dramatists, on the other hand, use late points, which require that many previous events be summarized for the audience's benefit. Thus, Greek tragedies actually show only the final parts of their stories. In *Oedipus Rex*, all of the action seems to take place in one day, but to uncover the truth on which the action turns, we must be told about events that begin before Oedipus' birth. Some modern plays have a late point of attack but show, in flashbacks, events that range through many years.

Playwrights motivate the giving of exposition in many ways. Ibsen, as in *A Doll's House*, frequently introduces a character that has returned after a long absence; questions about happenings while the character was away motivate the giving of background information the audience needs to understand the situation. On the other hand, some plays offer exposition without attempting to make it seem natural. Many of Euripides' Greek tragedies open with a monologue-prologue that summarizes events up to this time. In a musical play, exposition may be given in song and dance.

In most plays, attention is focused early on a question, potential conflict, or theme. The beginning of such plays includes what may be called an *inciting incident*, an occurrence that sets the main action in motion. In Sophocles' *Oedipus Rex*, a plague is destroying the city of Thebes; the oracle at Delphi declares that the murderer of the former king, Laius, must be found and punished before the plague can end. This is the event (introduced in the prologue) that sets the action in motion.

Oedipus the King, as produced by the Hartford Stage. Directed by Jonathan Wilson; scene design by Scott Bradley; costume design by Susan Hilferty; lighting by Kevin Snow; sound by Stephen Baker, with original music by René McLean.

© T. Charles Erickson

The inciting incident usually leads directly to a *major dramatic question* around which the play is organized, although this question may change as the play progresses. For example, the question first raised in *Oedipus Rex* is, Will the murderer of Laius be found and the city saved? Later, this question changes as interest shifts to Oedipus's involvement in the crime. *A Doll's House* asks, Can Nora conceal her criminal act from Torvald, and if not, what will he do?

Not all plays include inciting incidents or clearly identifiable major dramatic questions. All have focal points, nevertheless, frequently a theme or controlling idea around which the action is centered. *How I Learned to Drive* exemplifies this alternative pattern as Li'l Bit seeks to cope with having been sexually abused.

The Middle

The middle of a play normally consists of rising action composed of a series of *complications*. A complication is any new element that changes the direction of the action—the discovery of new information, for example, or the arrival of a character. The substance of most complications is discovery (any new information of sufficient importance to alter the direction of action). Discoveries may involve objects (a wife discovers in her husband's pocket a weapon of the kind used in a murder), persons (a young man discovers that his rival in love is his father), facts (a young man about to leave home discovers that his mother has cancer), values (a woman discovers that self-esteem is more important than marriage), or self (a man discovers that he has been acting from purely selfish motives when he thought he was acting out of love for his children). Each complication normally has a beginning, middle, and end—its own development, climax, and resolution—just as the play as a whole does.

Other means than discoveries can be used to precipitate complications. Natural or mechanical disasters (earthquakes, storms, airplane crashes, automobile accidents) are sometimes used, but these are likely to seem contrived if they resolve the problem (for example, if the villain is killed in an automobile accident and as a result the struggle automatically ends).

The series of complications culminates in the *climax*, the highest point of interest or suspense. It is often accompanied by the *crisis*, the discovery or event that determines the outcome of the action. For example, the title character in *Oedipus Rex* sets out to discover the murderer of Laius; the interest steadily grows as events increasingly focus attention on Oedipus, and the turning point comes when Oedipus realizes that he himself is the guilty person and becomes the pursued rather than the pursuer. Not all plays have a clear-cut series of complications leading to climax and crisis. Nevertheless, usually interest is maintained by the frequent introduction of new elements and an ongoing pattern of tension and relaxation. One way of analyzing such plays (and all others as well) is to divide them into beats, or units, the beginnings and endings of which are indicated by shifts in motivation or the introduction of some new element. One can then examine the function of each of these units both at that point in the action and in the overall development of the play.

The End

The final portion of a play, sometimes referred to as the *resolution* or *denouement* (unraveling or untying), extends from the crisis to the final curtain. It may resolve the conflict, make sense of the various strands of action, answer the questions raised earlier, or solidify the theme. It typically returns the situation to a state of balance and satisfies audience expectations.

Plays may also have *subplots*, in which events or actions of secondary interest are developed, often providing contrast to or commentary on the main plot. In *A Doll's House*, the relationship of Krogstad and Mrs. Linde contrasts sharply with that of Nora and Torvald. Often a subplot becomes a major factor

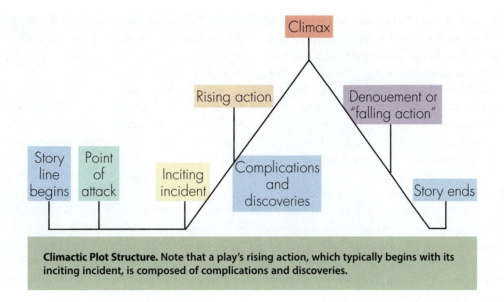

Climactic Plot Structure. Note that a play's rising action, which typically begins with its inciting incident, is composed of complications and discoveries.

in resolving the main plot, as in *Hamlet*, when Laertes, a morally upright character, is provoked by the death of his father and the madness of his sister to agree to help the king in his plan to kill Hamlet.

Character and Characterization

Character is the primary material from which plots are created, because incidents are developed through the speech and behavior of dramatic personages. *Characterization* is anything that delineates a person or differentiates that person from others. It operates on four levels:

- Physical or biological—defining gender, age, size, coloration, and general appearance

- Societal—defining economic status, profession or trade, religion, family relationships, and all of the factors that place a character in a particular social environment

- Psychological—defining a character's habitual responses, desires, motivation, likes, and dislikes (the inner workings of the character's mind)

- Moral—defining a character's value system (through choice and action, revealing what characters are willing to do to get what they want)

A playwright may emphasize one or more of these levels and may develop many or few traits, depending on *how the character functions in the play*. For example, the audience needs to know very little about a maid who appears only to announce dinner, whereas the principal characters need to be drawn in considerable depth. Even the major characters in a play may be depicted more through certain levels of characterization than others due to the nature of the play or the playwright's intentions. For example, Sophocles gives only very basic information regarding the physical level of characterization for his characters in *Oedipus Rex*. Because drama most often arises from conflicting desires, the psychological and moral levels of characterization are often the most essential. The moral level is developed most fully in serious plays because it shows what characters actually do when faced with making a difficult choice (as opposed to what they have said they or others should do in such situations). Moral decisions differentiate characters more fully than any other type because deliberating about such decisions causes

Nora (Hattie Morahan) and her husband Torvald (Dominic Rowan) in a 2012 production of *A Doll's House* at London's The Young Vic Theatre, as directed by Carrie Cracknell.

Geraint Lewis/Alamy Limited

characters to examine their values and motives, in the process of which their true natures are revealed to themselves and to the audience. (Analyzing Nora in *A Doll's House* or Misha in *Lydia* in terms of the four levels will reveal much about these characters and the plays in which they appear.)

A character is revealed through:

- Descriptions in stage directions, prefaces, or other explanatory material not part of the dialogue
- What the character says
- What others in the play say about the character
- What the character does

Dramatic characters are usually both *typified* and *individualized*. On the one hand, spectators would be unable to relate to a character who was totally unlike any person they had ever known. Therefore, characters can usually be placed in one of several large categories of people. On the other hand, audiences may be dissatisfied unless the playwright goes beyond this to give characters individualizing traits that set them apart from other characters of the same type. The most satisfactory dramatic characters are usually easily recognizable types with some unusual or complex qualities.

A playwright may be concerned with making characters *sympathetic* or *unsympathetic*. Normally, sympathetic characters are given major virtues and lesser foibles, whereas the reverse is true of unsympathetic characters. A character that is either completely good or bad is likely to seem unconvincing as a reflection of human behavior. Acceptability varies, however, with the type of play. Melodrama, for example, oversimplifies human psychology and clearly divides characters into good or evil. Tragedy, on the other hand, normally depicts more complex forces at work both within and without characters and requires greater depth and range of characterization.

Thought

The third basic element of a play is *thought*. Thought includes the themes, arguments, and overall meaning of the action. Thought is present in all plays, even the most lighthearted farce, because

- playwrights write from a point of view.
- playwrights react in some respect to the broader social point of view from which they emerge—though this reaction may be expressed in many different ways.

A playwright cannot avoid expressing some attitudes because events and characterization always imply some view of human behavior.

Meaning in drama is usually implied rather than stated directly. It is suggested by:

- Character relationships
- Ideas associated with unsympathetic and sympathetic characters
- The conflicts and their resolution
- Spectacle, music, and song

Playwrights often use their characters to advocate a certain line of action, point of view, or specific social reform. Dramatists in different periods have used various devices to project ideas. Greek playwrights made extensive use of the *chorus*, a group representing some segment of society, just as those of later periods employed such devices as *soliloquies*, *asides*, and other forms of statement made directly to the audience. Other tools for projecting meaning are *allegory* and *symbol*. In allegory, characters are personifications of abstract qualities (mercy, greed, and so on), as in the medieval play *Everyman*. A symbol is an object, event, or image that, although meaningful in and of itself, also suggests a concept or set of relationships. In *Lydia*, Ceci's quinceañera dress is a reminder of her and her family's shattered hopes and dreams. The dress serves as a powerful symbol that visually contributes to the play's thought.

Just because plays imply or state meaning, we should not conclude that there is a single correct interpretation for each play. Most plays permit multiple interpretations, as different productions of, and critical essays about, the same play clearly indicate. Nevertheless, each interpretation should be supported by evidence found in the play.

Sound and Spectacle

Plot, character, and thought are the basic subjects of drama. To convey these to an audience, playwrights have at their disposal two means: sound and spectacle. Sound includes language, music, and other aural effects; spectacle includes the visual elements of a production (the physical appearance and movement of performers, the costumes, scenery, properties, and lighting).

Lydia in its premiere production at the Denver Center Theatre, as directed by Juliette Carrillo with Onahoua Rodriguez (Ceci), Christian Barillas (Alvaro), and René Millán (Rene).

Terry Shapiro; courtesy of the Denver Center Theatre

Diction

Language is the playwright's primary means of expression. When a play is performed, other expressive means (music, sound effects, and spectacle) may be added; but to convey intentions to others, the dramatist depends almost entirely on dialogue and stage directions. Thus, language (diction) is the playwright's primary tool.

Diction serves many purposes:

- It imparts information.
- It characterizes.
- It may direct attention to important plot elements.
- It may reveal the themes and ideas of a play.
- It helps to establish tone or mood and internal logic.
- It may be used to establish tempo and rhythm.

The diction of every play, no matter how realistic, is more abstract and formal than that of normal conversation. This is because a dramatist always selects, arranges, and heightens language. In a realistic play, although the dialogue is modeled after and may retain the rhythms and basic vocabulary of everyday usage, the characters are usually more articulate and state their ideas and feelings more precisely than their real-life counterparts would.

The dialogue of nonrealistic plays (such as Greek and Shakespearean tragedies) deviates markedly from everyday speech. It employs a larger vocabulary, abandons the rhythms of conversation, and makes extensive use of imagery and meter. Other types of nonrealistic plays may emphasize the clichés and repetitiveness of conversation as a means of commenting on the mechanical quality and meaningless exchanges that pass for communication.

The basic criterion for judging diction is its appropriateness to characters, situation, internal logic, and type of play.

Music

Music, as we ordinarily understand the term, does not occur in every play. But if the term is extended to include all patterned sound, it is an important ingredient in every production, except those wholly silent.

Language has been described as the playwright's principal means of expression. But a play is not fully realized until the performers transform words into sound. The elements of pitch, stress, volume, tempo, duration, and quality convey meaning. For example, though the words of a sentence may remain constant, its meaning can be varied by manipulating emphasis or tone ("You say *he* told her?" as contrasted with "You say he told *her*?" or the differences that result if the tone in the same speech is shifted from joy to sarcasm). Because written language is imprecise in emphasis and tone, actors and directors may interpret a passage in ways the playwright did not intend. The spoken aspect of language also varies in its formal qualities. In some plays, among them *A Doll's House*, it simulates the loose rhythms of everyday speech; in others, such as Shakespeare's *Hamlet*, it is shaped into formalized metrical patterns.

In addition to the sound of the actors' voices, a play may also use music in the form of incidental songs and background music, or it may use song and instrumental accompaniment as integral structural means, as in musical theatre and opera. Music (especially in combination with lyrics) may serve many functions. It may establish mood, it may characterize, it may suggest ideas, it may compress characterization or exposition (by presenting information, feelings, or motivations in a song), it may lend variety, and it may be pleasurable in itself.

Spectacle

Spectacle encompasses all the visual elements of a production: the movement and spatial relations of characters, the lighting, settings, costumes, and properties. Because others normally supply these elements, the playwright does not have full control over them; and because playwrights seldom describe the spectacle precisely, other theatre artists must carefully study the text and consider all the implications their creative choices may have upon the play's meaning in performance. Similarly, the reader of a play must try to envision the spectacle in order to grasp a play's full power. This is true even of subtle visual signals. The visual image of Nora and Torvald sitting down to have their discussion near the end of *A Doll's House* is a powerful choice by the playwright, which focuses our attention on what they say as well as suggests that this is

a rational, rather than flamboyantly emotional, exchange.

Some playwrights give the reader more help than others. Many older plays (including Greek and Shakespearean tragedies) contain almost no stage directions, and most clues to spectacle must be sought in the dialogue. When place or action is important, such plays usually have a character describe them. Beginning in the nineteenth century, when visual elements were given added prominence, stage directions became usual. Since that time, the printed texts of plays have typically included many aids designed to help the reader visualize the action. In evaluating spectacle, the characteristics we should be most concerned with are appropriateness and

Sara Krulwich/The New York Times/Redux

Director John Doyle reconceived Stephen Sondheim's *Sweeney Todd* in a 2005 Broadway revival starring Patti LuPone (right center). In Doyle's production, every actor also played at least one musical instrument to provide the accompaniment. This added an element of spectacle not inherently in the musical as sometimes actors played an instrument during scenes as not only accompaniment but as an extension of their characters' action.

Practices & Styles

ANALYZING PLAYS

Dramatic structure can best be understood by analyzing specific plays. Here is a list of questions useful in that process.

1. What are the given circumstances? (Location? Period? Time of day? Socioeconomic environment? Attitudes and relationships of the characters at the beginning of the play? Previous action?) How is this information conveyed?

2. Where in the overall story is the play's point of attack? What sets the dramatic action in motion? How is the action resolved?

3. What is the major conflict, dramatic question, or unifying theme? Are there subplots? If so, how is each related to the main plot? How is the dramatic action unified?

4. Are the play's characters typified or individuated? What is each character willing to do to achieve his or her desires?

5. What is the dominant tone of the play? Serious? Comic? Ironic? Is the tone consistent throughout or does it change often? How is its tone established?

6. What are the major ideas/themes/implications of the dramatic action? Are there a number of possible interpretations of the play? If so, which seems most valid based on the play's action, characterizations, and other elements?

7. To what extent do the vocabulary, rhythm, and tempo of speeches follow or deviate from everyday colloquial usage? What information is given or implied about sound, music, settings, costumes, makeup, and lighting? Is this information significant to the dramatic action? If so, how?

8. For what kind of theatrical space was the play written? What characteristics of the play are explained by the theatrical or dramatic conventions in use at the time the play was written?

Not all of these questions need be answered for every play. Additional questions may be needed for some plays or for specialized interests (to meet the needs of actors, designers, and others) or for atypical plays.

distinctiveness. (The chapters that make up Part 3 treat the process of transferring the play to the stage more fully.)

Form in Drama

Plays are frequently classified according to form: tragedy, comedy, tragicomedy, melodrama, farce, and so on. Considerable emphasis is sometimes placed on understanding the essential qualities of each dramatic form and the proper classification of each play. Since the 1960s concern over dramatic form has lessened, in part because much recent drama defies formal classification. Nevertheless, one cannot read plays without encountering formal labels. Consequently, some understanding of dramatic form is helpful.

Basically, *form* means the shape given to something for a particular purpose. A sentence is

Richard Hein

Lee Breuer and Bob Telson's *Gospel at Colonus* is a retelling of Sophocles' *Oedipus at Colonus* through American gospel music and preaching. Pictured here in a production at the Goodman Theatre (Chicago) is Martin Jacob (a member of the gospel group "Soul Stirrers") separating the Balladeer at left (Sam Butler Jr.) and Polyneices at right (Terrence A. Carson).

a form created by words arranged in a particular order to convey a thought. Similarly, a play is a form created by arranging incidents in a particular order to create a dramatic action. Most plays have in common certain formal elements that permit us to recognize them as plays rather than as novels, epic poems, or essays. Still, those works we recognize as plays are not all alike. Critics have divided them into a number of dramatic forms on the basis of certain characteristics, the most important of which are type of action, overall tone, and basic emotional appeals. Through-

out much of history, tragedy and comedy have been considered the two basic forms.

Tragedy

The oldest known form of drama, tragedy, presents a genuinely serious action and maintains a serious tone throughout, although there may be moments of comic relief. It raises significant issues about the nature of human existence, morality, or human relationships. A tragedy's

THE POSSIBILITY OF WRITING TRAGEDY TODAY

I s it still possible to write tragedy? This question has been debated frequently during the past century. Few dramatists since the mid-nineteenth century have called their serious plays tragedies, and today, though we still study tragedy and talk about tragic form, when we do so we usually look back to the Greeks or to Shakespeare for our examples. Joseph Wood Krutch, a university professor and critic, argued in his essay "The Tragic Fallacy" (1929) that it is impossible to write tragedy in modern times because we consider human beings too petty to be capable of tragic action: "the idea of nobility is inseparable from the idea of tragedy, which cannot exist without it. … [A] tragedy…must…have a hero, and from the universe as we see it both the Glory of God and the Glory of Man have departed. Our cosmos may be farcical or it may be pathetic but it has not the dignity of tragedy. … The death of tragedy is, like the death of love, one of those emotional fatalities as the result of which the human as distinguished from the natural world grows more and more a desert."

Not everyone agrees with Krutch's conclusions. Arthur Miller was driven to offer a different point of view when *Death of a Salesman* (1949), following its original production, became the subject of a lengthy debate over whether it could be considered a "true tragedy." In an essay entitled "Tragedy and the Common Man" (1949) Miller responded, "For one reason or another, we are often held to be below tragedy—or tragedy above us. … I believe that the common man is as apt a subject for tragedy in its highest sense as kings were. … [T]he tragic feeling is evoked in us when we are in the presence of a character who is ready to lay down his life, if need be, to secure one thing—his sense of personal dignity."

protagonist, or leading character, is usually someone who arouses our sympathy and admiration but who encounters disaster through the pursuit of some goal, worthy in itself, that conflicts with another goal or principle. The emotional effect of tragedy is the arousal of a strong empathy for those who strive for integrity and dignity.

Tragedy is a form associated especially with ancient Greece and Elizabethan England. (Two of the world's greatest tragedies, Sophocles' *Oedipus Rex* and Shakespeare's *Hamlet*, are discussed in detail in Chapters 4 and 5, respectively.) Few modern plays have been called tragedies, perhaps because, as some critics have argued, we no longer consider human beings capable of the kind of heroic action associated with the great tragic heroes.

Comedy

A dramatic form that had its origins in ancient Greece, comedy is based on some deviation from normality in action, character, or thought. It must not pose a serious threat, and an "in-fun" tone is usually maintained. Comedy demands that an audience view the situation objectively. Henri Bergson argues that comedy requires "an anesthesia of the heart" because it is difficult to laugh at anything about which we feel deeply. We may find it funny to see a person slip on a banana peel, but if we discover that the person is a close relative who is just recovering from a serious operation, our concern will destroy the laughter. Similarly, we may dislike some things so intensely that we cannot see their ridiculous qualities. Nevertheless, any subject, however trivial or important, can become the subject of comedy if we place it in the right framework and distance ourselves sufficiently from its serious implications. Comedy arouses emotions ranging between joy and scorn, with laughter as their common response.

Other Forms

Not all plays are wholly serious or comic. The two are often intermingled to create mixed effects, as in tragicomedy, a serious play that ends happily. Perhaps the best known of the mixed types is *melodrama*, the favorite form of the nineteenth century and still the dominant form among television dramas dealing with crime and danger. A melodrama develops a temporarily serious action that is initiated and kept in motion by the malicious designs of a villain; a happy resolution is made possible by destroying the villain's power. Melodrama depicts a world in which good and evil are sharply differentiated; there is seldom any question where the audience's sympathies should lie. The appeals are strong and basic, creating a desire to see the "good guys" triumph and the "bad guys" punished. This desire is usually met in a double ending, one outcome for the good, another for the bad. Melodrama is related to tragedy through its serious action and to comedy through its happy ending. It is a popular form, perhaps because it assures audiences that good triumphs over evil.

As mentioned previously, concern for giving formal labels to plays has greatly diminished. Today, many people no longer consider it possible to categorize situations and people precisely. Boundaries have come to seem so fluid that a single event might be viewed almost simultaneously as serious, comic, threatening, or grotesque. Thus, tone in contemporary drama may shift rapidly and elements that were previously associated with tragedy or comedy might be intermingled or be transformed into their opposites. As a result, the old formal categories have lost much of their significance. But we still need to recognize that each play has a form. It is perhaps best to remember that the form of each play is in some respects unique—no two plays are exactly alike—but that there are sufficient similarities among certain plays to group them into a common category. Whether or not we have precise notions about tragedy, comedy, or other forms, we are aware of distinctions between the serious and the funny, and most of us freely use "tragic," "comic," and "melodramatic" to describe events in the world around us. Basic awareness of dramatic form will be helpful in many of the subsequent discussions in this book.

Style in Drama

Even plays of the same form vary considerably. One reason for this variety is *style*. Like form, the word *style* is difficult to define because it has been used to designate many things. Basically, however, style results from a distinctive mode of expression or method of presentation. For example, style may stem from traits attributable to a period, a nation, a movement, or an author. In most periods, the drama of all Western nations has certain common qualities caused by prevailing cultural concepts (religious, philosophical, psychological, economic) and by then-current theatrical conventions. Thus, we may speak of an eighteenth-century style. Within a period, national differences permit us to distinguish a French from an English style. Furthermore, the dramas written by neoclassicists have qualities that distinguish them from those written by romantics, expressionists, absurdists, or postmodernists. Finally, the plays of individual authors have distinctive qualities that set them off from the work of all other writers. Thus, we may speak of Shakespeare's style.

Style in theatre stems from three basic influences and may be thought of in three basic ways:

- Style stems from assumptions about what is truthful and valuable.
- Style stems from the manner in which a playwright uses the elements of drama.
- Style stems from the manner in which a play is presented.

Dramatists of all movements and periods have sought to convey truthful pictures of humanity, but they have differed widely in their answers to the following questions: What is ultimate truth? Where is it to be found? How can we perceive reality? Some have argued that surface appearances only disguise truth, which is to be found in some inner or spiritual realm. Others have maintained that truth can be discovered only by objective study of things that can be felt, tasted, seen, heard, or smelled. To advocates of the latter view, observable details hold the key to truth; to advocates of the former view, the same details only hide the truth. Although all writers attempt to depict the truth as they see it, the individual playwright's conception of truth is determined by basic temperament and by the culture in which he or she lives.

All dramatists have at their disposal the same basic elements—plot, character, thought, diction, music, and spectacle. Nevertheless, the work of each playwright is distinctive because each perceives the human condition from a unique point of view, and these perceptions are reflected in situations, characters, and ideas; in manipulation of language; and in suggestions for the use of spectacle. In the process of writing, playwrights set their distinctive stamp (or style) on their plays.

Finally, the directing, acting, scenery, costumes, lighting, and sound used to translate the play from a written text to the stage can each be manipulated in many ways; the distinctive manner in which these elements are handled in a production characterizes its style. Many people are involved in producing a play and have an impact on the production's style. Traditionally, unity is the common artistic goal. Each theatre artist usually seeks to create qualities analogous to those found in the play, and the director then coordinates all of the parts into a unified whole. In recent times, postmodernism has intermingled different styles, although this intermingling may itself be considered a style. Ultimately, style results from the way in which means are adapted to ends.

Different Styles of Production Applied to the Same Play

Hamlet as produced in 2007 by the Shanghai Peking Opera Ensemble. This production used the costuming and staging conventions of Beijing Opera, a form of theatre developed in the 1790s in China. (Chapter 10 discusses this and other Asian theatre forms.)

Paul van Riel/Hollandse Hoogte/Redux

Hamlet as produced by the McCarter Theatre (Princeton, N.J.) under the direction of Daniel Fish. The scene design by John Conklin (complete with mirrored side wall, folding metal table, and chairs) and contemporary dress costumes by Kaye Voyce characterize the performance space as a rehearsal hall rather than Gertrude's bedroom. Seen here is Hamlet after killing the eavesdropping Polonius, who, in this production of the play has been eavesdropping along with the audience on their side of the theatre's proscenium curtain.

T. Charles Erickson

Hamlet as directed by Brian MacEleny for the Trinity Repertory Theatre Company and performed on a modern modified thrust stage. The costumes, scenery, and properties place the action in a 1930s manor house. The production foregrounds the social class distinctions in Shakespeare's play by portraying Laertes (pictured holding a tray) and Ophelia as servants in this *Upstairs/Downstairs, Gosford Park–styled Hamlet*.

© T. Charles Erickson

Epilogue to Part 1

Part 1 has introduced and discussed several basic issues related to the nature of theatre, to the role of audiences, to varied criteria for judging theatrical performances, and to dramatic structure, form, and style. Such discussions remain somewhat abstract, however, until they are made concrete through specific examples. Consequently, the chapters that follow explore how these issues have been manifested in the theatrical practices of diverse times and places, both past and present.

Varieties of Theatrical Experience

Since the very earliest times, some form of theatrical activity has existed, although surviving records permit us to trace it back with any certainty for only about twenty-five hundred years. When we look at today's theatre, we see only a small part of what the theatre is capable of. If we are to appreciate the full range of possibilities, however, we need to be aware of its multiple manifestations and the transformations it has undergone. This awareness of the diverse forms theatre has taken can alert us to possibilities for reshaping theatre in the present and future. Creative artists do not repeat past forms so much as reshape them by exploring alternative possibilities.

In the theatre, awareness of the past is important for other reasons as well. Many plays from the past are still performed regularly. Each of these plays was written with a particular kind of theatre structure, set of theatrical conventions, and audience in mind. Each also reflects the cultural assumptions and values of its time; theatre both reflects and shapes the culture from which it derives. Although plays may transcend the conditions of time and place (otherwise they would not communicate with us today), we can perhaps understand them most fully in the context within which they originated. Plays are among the best indicators we have of the culture out of which they came. They are simultaneously specific to a particular context and universal in their ability to speak to us in the much broader context of human experience.

In a book of this length, it is impossible to treat every form the theatre has taken in the past and present. Therefore, only representative types of theatrical experience will be discussed. Those chosen do not provide a comprehensive survey of the theatre's development, but they do touch on most major periods. Taken all together, these discussions should contribute to a fuller understanding of today's theatre.

Euripides's tragedy, *Iphigenia at Aulis*, is given a contemporary twist in Charles Mee's *Iphigenia 2.0* as produced by the Signature Theatre Company (New York).

The second phase [in the development of theatre brings it] to as elaborate a scale of great festival performance as one can reach, but still acted under the...open sky. ... [The offerings] are performed only on special, ritual occasions in the year. There is still a dominating...religious element. There is no, or very little, professionalism. ..."

—Richard Southern, *The Seven Ages of the Theatre*

Festival Theatre

Greek, Roman, and Medieval Theatre Experiences

During the first two thousand years of its existence, Western theatre was markedly different from the professional and commercial theatre that we know today and that has flourished only during the past four hundred years. Until the sixteenth century A.D., theatre in the Western world was performed primarily as part of festivals. Financed by the community and performed for the community, it was available only for brief periods each year when theatrical performances were presented as offerings to a god and for the enjoyment of the general populace. This type of theatre flourished in ancient Greece, Rome, and medieval Europe, although in each the differences were as important as the similarities.

The Theatre of Ancient Greece

Theatre in the Western world can be traced back to ancient Greece, and especially to Athens, usually considered the cradle of Western civilization. The Athenians, inventors of democracy, were the first to have sufficient faith in humanity to let citizens be responsible for making the laws that governed their lives. Nevertheless, the Greeks did not consider everyone equal: Their economy depended on slave labor, and women were permitted no voice in political affairs.

The belief in the ability of human beings to make significant decisions contrasted sharply with the beliefs of earlier societies that people are at the mercy of supernatural forces or all-powerful tyrants. This new attitude may have been a major factor in the development of Greek drama, which usually emphasized the attempts of human characters to control their own destinies. The Greeks nevertheless considered happiness to depend on harmony between human and supernatural forces and believed that this harmony could easily be broken. Greek tragedy often shows the results of human attempts to escape fate or the will of the gods. From the beginning, Greek drama was presented exclusively at festivals honoring Dionysus, one of the many gods worshiped by the Greeks, who conceived of their gods essentially as immortal human beings. Each god had power over a limited sphere of activity. Like human beings, these gods had many failings: They were jealous of each other, bickered among themselves, were vindictive when slighted, took sides in both human and divine quarrels, indulged frequently in adulterous affairs, and generally made mortals' lives unpredictable. The Greeks did not observe a holy day comparable to the Sabbath but had a series of religious festivals throughout the year, one or more dedicated to each of the gods.

Dionysus, the god in whose honor plays were presented, was the god of wine (one of the principal products of Greece) and fertility. His blessing was sought in order to ensure fertility of both human beings and the land. The son of Zeus (the greatest of Greek gods) and Semele (a mortal), Dionysus was killed (allegedly at the behest of Zeus's jealous wife Hera), dismembered, resurrected, and deified. The myths associated with him were closely related to the life cycle (birth, growth, decay, death, and rebirth) and seasonal changes (summer, fall, winter, and especially spring, the season of rebirth and the return of fertility). As the god of wine and revelry, he was also associated with a number of irrational forces.

By the fifth century B.C., Athens held four festivals in honor of Dionysus each year; theatrical performances were offered at three of the festivals. Plays were not presented at the festivals of other gods. The major Dionysian festival in Athens was the City Dionysia. Extending over several days near the end of March, it was one of the most important occasions of the year and a major showcase for Athenian wealth and power. The festival was both a religious and civic celebration under the supervision of the principal state official. Theatrical performances were viewed in a radically different light than they are today. They were offerings of the city to a god. At the same time, they were expressions of civic pride—indications of the cultural superiority of Athens over the other Greek states, which only later developed their own theatres. (Eventually there were theatres throughout the eastern Mediterranean in areas now parts of Turkey, Lebanon, Syria, Israel, southern Italy, and elsewhere.)

Our first record of a theatrical event in Athens is the establishment in 534 B.C. of a contest for the best tragedy, a form that also originated in Athens. The first winner was Thespis, the earliest playwright and actor whose name has come down to us. From his name we derive the term *thespian*, still used in reference to actors. During the fifth century, three tragic dramatists competed at each City Dionysia, each writer presenting a group of four plays: three tragedies and one satyr play.

A *satyr play* was short and comic in tone; it typically poked fun at some Greek myth using

From Baumeister, *Denkmäler der Klassische Alterturns*, 1888

Actors of a satyr play as depicted on a Greek vase of the late fifth century B.C. **The embroidered robes resemble those thought to have been worn by some tragic actors. Notice at bottom center the flute player who provided the musical accompaniment for dramatic performances.**

Society, Art & Culture

PERFORMANCE IN ANCIENT EGYPT

Theatrical performances may have taken place in Egypt long before the Greeks held their first City Dionysia Festival in Athens. At Abydos, the most sacred spot in Egypt, some kind of event relating to the myth of the Egyptian god Osiris occurred annually from around 2500 to 550 B.C. But it is unclear if this was a ceremonial rite, a theatrical performance, or some combination of the two.

According to the myth, Osiris, son of Geb (the earth) and Nut (the sky), succeeded his father as ruler and married his sister, Isis. His brother, Set, was jealous of Osiris's power. Set killed and dismembered Osiris, burying parts of his body throughout Egypt. However, Isis found these parts and Osiris was resurrected. Osiris went to dwell in the afterworld, where he became the judge of souls. His body was buried at Abydos, and Horus, Osiris's son, defeated Set and won back his father's kingdom. This is the most revered of all the Egyptian myths. Osiris is associated with the life-giving power of the Nile (water), fertility, and everlasting life.

No text for any play or plays (dating back to ancient Egypt) connected with the myth exists. Most of what scholars know about the event has been deduced from an account by one of its participants, Ikhernofret, who carved what he did on a stone in (approximately) 1868 B.C. However, scholars disagree on how to interpret Ikhernofret's account.

Some scholars argue that each major event of Osiris's life was reenacted in an enormous spectacle staged at different locations over a period of weeks or months. Ikhernofret's account tells of ships sailing, battles, processions, and burial ceremonies. These scholars suggest the principal roles were taken by priests and that the spectators would also participate by representing crowds whenever crowds were called for by the events. If they are correct, this was perhaps the most spectacular form of festival theatre ever performed.

Other scholars argue that the evidence does not indicate that the life or death of Osiris was reenacted. They see the event as a rite commemorating all of the dead pharaohs, each of whom was symbolized in Osiris, and believe that this ritual consequently took on the character of a royal funeral. Scholars who argue that the events were commemorated rather than reenacted reason that equating the Egyptian ritual with the Christian passion plays of the medieval period suggests a projection of one culture upon another without taking into account their many differences or the scarcity of evidence.

Because so many things may be deemed "performance," the debate over whether the event at Abydos was ritual or theatre is likely to continue.

a chorus of satyrs (beings that are half-man/half-goat), and was presented following the tragedies. Nine tragedies were produced at each City Dionysia, a total of nine hundred during the fifth century. Of these, only thirty-two have survived, all written by three dramatists—Aeschylus (523–456 B.C.), Sophocles (496–406 B.C.), and Euripides (480–406 B.C.)—who are ranked among the world's greatest playwrights.

Of the surviving tragedies, some of the best include the *Oresteia* (458 B.C.) by Aeschylus, *Antigone* (c. 441 B.C.) and *Oedipus Rex* (c. 430–425 B.C.) by Sophocles, and *Medea* (431 B.C.), *The Trojan Women* (415 B.C.), and *The Bacchae* (405 B.C.) by Euripides. Before we look more closely at *Oedipus Rex* and its performance, let us examine some features of the Greek theatre building and other conventions that affected staging.

The Theatre of Dionysus

Plays were performed in the Theatre of Dionysus, on the slope of the hill just beneath the Athenian Acropolis (a fortified area including the Parthenon, the city treasury, and other buildings considered essential to the city's survival). The theatre was located within a compound that included a temple and a large outdoor altar dedicated to the worship of Dionysus. Originally, the slope (without any seating) served as the *theatron* ("seeing place," the origin of our word *theatre*). A flat terrace below the slope served as the *orchestra* (dancing place), in the middle of which was placed an altar (*thymele*) dedicated to Dionysus.

The Athenians gradually converted this arrangement into a permanent structure and shaped the auditorium into a semicircle of stadium-like stone seats extending up the hill to the retaining walls of the Acropolis (the structure was not fully completed until the late fourth century B.C.). It held between fourteen thousand and seventeen thousand spectators. This seating curved about halfway around a circular orchestra, measuring about sixty-five feet in diameter, which was used as performance space, especially for the chorus. On the side of the orchestra opposite the audience was the *skene* ("hut" or "tent," the origin of our word *scene*). The term suggests that the original structure was used as a place to which the actors could retire or where they could change costumes. Once its possibilities as a background for the action were recognized, the *skene* was elaborated into a structure seventy-five to a hundred feet long and probably two stories high. It is thought that this *skene* had three doors—a large central doorway flanked on either side by smaller doors—all opening onto the acting area. The roof of this structure could be used as an acting area to represent high places or for the appearance of gods. The *skene* was

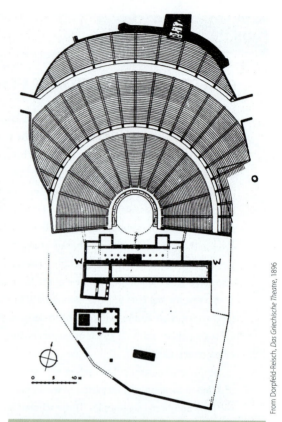

From Dörpfeld-Reisch, *Das Griechische Theatre*, 1896

Plan of the precinct devoted to the worship of Dionysus in Athens: at bottom, the temple and altar; at top, the theatre. Notice the rectangular structure (the *skene*, or scene house) immediately below the circular area (the *orchestra*) and the passageways (the *parodoi*), used for the entrance of the chorus and others, between the ends of the *skene* and the auditorium.

not architecturally joined to the auditorium; the spaces (called *parodoi*) at either side between the *skene* and the auditorium were used as entrances and exits for performers (especially the chorus) and perhaps by spectators before and after performances. Because the original *skene* has long since disappeared, no one knows exactly how it looked. (Some possibilities are shown in the illustrations on page 68.)

The *skene*, or scene house (as, later, in Shakespeare's theatre), probably served as a formalized

The theatre at Epidaurus, the best preserved of all ancient Greek theatres, is still used for festival performances. A tragic chorus of fifteen is performing in the orchestra. Notice the large size of the theatre and the audience–performer relationship.

Bettmann/Corbis

architectural background for all plays, even those set in woods, on seashores, or outside caves. This convention meant that dialogue, not representational scenery, probably established locale. The action in Greek plays usually took place outdoors, but occasionally the outcome of events that occurred indoors was shown. Most of the latter scenes involved the corpses (effigies) of characters slain offstage that were then shown onstage. To show the corpses, the large central doorway was probably opened and a wheeled platform (the *eccyclema*) pushed out. Another common occurrence in Greek plays was the appearance of a god. Sometimes the roof was used, but in many plays the god had to descend to ground level or to be lifted from the orchestra to roof level. For this purpose, a crane-like device (the *machina*) was used. (The overuse of gods to resolve difficult dramatic situations led to any contrived ending being labeled a *deus ex machina*—god from the machine—ending.) Probably nothing better illustrates the nonrepresentational conventions of the Greek theatre

than the *machina* because its fulcrum arm, ropes, and pulleys were visible to the audience. It was not intended to fool anyone; rather, it was used to suggest the idea of flying, a power possessed by the gods and denied to human beings (except for a few who had been granted special powers by the gods).

From our standpoint, one of the most remarkable things about the Theatre of Dionysus is its size. Today, a theatre with an audience capacity of even three thousand is considered almost unusable for drama because of the difficulty of seeing and hearing. We expect realistic visual effects and acting, and we feel cheated if we cannot see every detail as we do on the movie or television screen. Obviously, the Greeks had expectations that differed from ours, as is clear from the conventions they developed and accepted. The structures today that most resemble Greek theatres are sports arenas. (Keeping in mind the scale of such structures will help us understand many other conventions of the Greek theatre.)

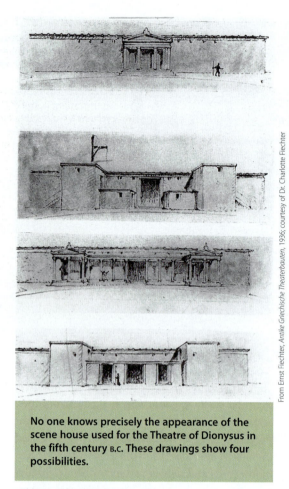

From Ernst Fiechter, *Antike Griechische Theaterbauten*, 1936; courtesy of Dr. Charlotte Fiechter

No one knows precisely the appearance of the scene house used for the Theatre of Dionysus in the fifth century B.C. These drawings show four possibilities.

The Performers

One may divide performers in the Greek theatre into four categories: actors, chorus, supernumeraries, and musicians. All were male.

By the time *Oedipus Rex* was produced, around 430 B.C., the rules of the contests restricted the number of speaking actors to three for each author. This rule did not restrict the number of roles to three; rather, all speaking parts had to be played by three actors, which meant that the same actor might have to play several roles and that the same three actors appeared in all three of the tragedies presented by a competing dramatist. *Supernumeraries* (extras) could be used but they were not permitted to speak lines. This convention probably developed to ensure fairness in the competition. A principal actor was assigned by lot to playwrights, who usually staged their own plays. The playwright and the leading actor then probably chose the other two. A prize was offered for the best tragic actor at each festival, but only the leading actors were eligible to win.

The general view is that the tragic chorus was composed of fifteen men. A playwright wishing to present his plays at the City Dionysia had to apply to the principal government official for a chorus. We do not know how this official decided which playwrights would be granted choruses, but it is clear that being granted a chorus was the mark that a playwright had been accepted as a competitor. This official also paired the dramatist with a *choregus*, a wealthy citizen who bore the expense of training and costuming that dramatist's chorus and of the musicians who accompanied the chorus during their training and performances. The well-to-do citizens of Athens were required to take turns serving as *choregoi*, and most seem to have done so willingly. Thus, the state and a few wealthy citizens financed the productions. The playwright and his *choregus* shared the prize awarded for the best group of plays. We are not sure what the prizes consisted of; they may have included money, but the honor of winning seems to have mattered most, just as winning an Oscar or an Olympic medal does today.

Choruses were assigned approximately eleven months prior to the next festival. How much time was spent in training is unknown, but apparently the routine was not unlike that today in training athletes. Exercises and diets were controlled, and the chorus worked under the strict and strenuous supervision of a trainer. A great deal of emphasis was placed on singing and dancing because the fifteen members both sang and danced the choral passages. Thus, much of their training resembled that of opera singers and dancers. Usually they performed in unison, but at times they were divided into semi-choruses of seven members. The chorus leader sometimes had solo lines, but the rest of the chorus usually responded as a group or as two subgroups that performed and responded to each other alternately.

In Greek theatre all of the actors and chorus members wore masks. Since the masks were made of perishable linen, cork, or lightweight wood, none of the actual masks have survived. However, there are many stone carvings, such as those pictured here, that provide visual evidence of the different looks that the masks may have provided.

Theatre masks/Hermitage, St. Petersburg, Russia/De Agostini Picture Library/
E. Lessing/The Bridgeman Art Library

The chorus was one of the distinctive conventions of the Greek theatre. It usually made its entrance following the prologue and was present thereafter until the end of the play. The choral odes, performed between episodes, divided the action into segments something like the acts of a modern play. The chorus served several functions in Greek drama:

- It formed a collective character who expressed opinions, gave advice, and occasionally threatened to interfere in the action.

- It often seemed to express the author's point of view and establish a standard against which the actions of the characters could be judged.

- It frequently served as the ideal spectator, reacting to events and characters as the author would like the audience to react.

- It helped to establish mood and heighten dramatic effects.

- It added color, movement, and spectacle as it sang and danced the choral interludes.

The principal musical accompaniment in Greek tragedy was provided by a flute player, who preceded the chorus as it made its entrance and then (like the chorus) remained onstage throughout. The source of the musical accompaniment was thus visible to the audience and not kept offstage, as in most modern productions. The flute player wore sandals, one with a clapper on its sole for beating time. Both percussionist and flutist, he also likely composed the music he played.

Although much music was used in Greek theatrical performances, almost none of it has survived; the texts of Greek plays do little to make us aware that we should be hearing certain passages sung or recited to musical accompaniment. (Attempts to unite music and text as they had been in Greek tragedy gave rise to opera in Italy during the late sixteenth and early seventeenth centuries.) Greek music had a great variety of musical modes, each with a particular tonal quality that was thought appropriate to certain kinds of subjects or emotions. It probably more nearly approximated the sounds of traditional music from the Near East than that of western Europe or America. In Greek theatre, music may have had much in common with film music, enhancing the mood and emotion of the action it accompanied.

All of the performers, except the musician, wore masks of lightweight wood, cork, or linen.

Practitioners & Theorists

GREEK TRAGIC DRAMATISTS

Aeschylus, Sophocles, and Euripides are the only tragic authors whose plays have survived. Aeschylus (523–456 B.C.), a member of the Athenian nobility who distinguished himself in the wars against Persia, wrote approximately eighty plays, of which seven survived: *The Persians* (472 B.C.), *Seven Against Thebes* (467 B.C.), *The Suppliants* (c. 463 B.C.), *Prometheus Bound* (unknown), and the *Oresteia* (458 B.C., a trilogy of plays: *Agamemnon*, *The Libation Bearers*, and *The Eumendies*). Some scholars believe that all of Aeschylus's surviving plays were parts of trilogies (three plays based on a single story or theme) treating philosophical issues. The *Oresteia*, for example, shows the evolution of the concept of justice as personal revenge is replaced by the impersonal judgment of the state. Aeschylus's plays, the oldest that have survived, are not as refined as Sophocles's, but they show heroic figures wrestling with significant philosophical issues.

Sophocles (496–406 B.C.) was from a wealthy family, well educated, handsome, and popular. For a time, he served as one of ten generals, the highest elective office of the Athenian state. Sophocles wrote more than 120 plays and won 24 contests, more than any other Greek dramatist. Of his plays, only seven have survived: *Ajax* (c. 450–440 B.C.), *Antigone* (c. 441 B.C.), *Oedipus Rex* (c. 430–425 B.C.), *Electra* (c. 418–410 B.C.), *Trachiniae* (c. 413 B.C.), *Philoctetes* (409 B.C.), and *Oedipus at Colonus* (406 B.C.). Sophocles wrote his final play, *Oedipus at Colonus*, when he was almost ninety years old and it was produced the year after his death. His reputation as one of the world's great dramatists has remained constant since his lifetime, probably because of his masterful dramatic structure, moving stories, complex characters, beautiful poetry, and universal themes.

Euripides (480–406 B.C.), the last of the great Greek tragic dramatists, wrote about ninety plays, of which eighteen have survived. His best-known plays are *Alcestis* (438 B.C.), *Medea* (431 B.C.), *Hippolytus* (428 B.C.), *The Trojan Women* (415 B.C.), *Electra* (c. 420 B.C.), *The Bacchae* (405 B.C.), and *Iphigenia at Aulis* (405 B.C.). He is also author of *Cyclops* (unknown), the only complete surviving satyr play. Because he questioned many Athenian beliefs and customs, he was rarely honored during his lifetime but later became the most popular of tragic writers. Often denounced for writing about subjects considered unfit for the stage (such as Medea killing her children and Phaedra falling in love with her stepson), he was also disliked for suggesting that the gods of Greek myth were morally corrupt. Writing at the end of the fifth century, Euripides raised doubts about many of the values that Aeschylus had championed at the beginning of that century.

The use of masks, another of the Greek theatre's distinctive conventions, served several purposes:

- It facilitated the rapid change of roles when three actors had to play all of the parts.
- It made it easier for male performers to embody female roles.
- It helped the actor in assuming roles that differed widely in age or character type.
- It assisted communication in the large theatres by capturing and emphasizing the essential qualities of each character.

Because each mask covered the entire head and included the appropriate hair and headdress, the actor's appearance could be changed instantaneously with a change of mask.

A variety of clothing was used for stage purposes. Some characters wore a long-sleeved, heavily embroidered tunic, but because there are

Euripides's plays challenged the prevailing social and religious standards of his time. Pictured here is *The Bacchae* as presented by the Guthrie Theatre (Minneapolis). Agave has just discovered that while possessed she killed her son. Direction and scene design by Liviu Culei; costumes by Patricia Zipprodt; masks by Mary Walker; lighting by Marcus Dillard.

Courtesy of the Guthrie Theatre

references in the plays to characters in rags, in mourning, and in Greek or in foreign dress, it seems unlikely that all characters were dressed alike. The selection of costume was probably determined by its appropriateness to the role. The sleeved, embroidered tunic, which was not a garment worn in Greek daily life, may have been reserved for supernatural or non-Greek characters, whereas native dress was used for Greeks. The usual dress in Greece was an ankle-length or knee-length garment called a *chiton*. On his feet the tragic actor wore soft, flexible, high-topped boots in common use at that time.

These conventions suggest that performance in the Greek theatre was highly formalized:

- A group of performers formed a chorus.
- One actor often played several roles in a single play.
- Men played both male and female roles.
- Performers wore masks and character-appropriate dress.
- Performers sang, chanted, and danced much of the text.

- The scale of the theatre prevented small details from being seen.

Overall, it is a performance mode quite different from that of the present day. That this mode was pleasing to the Greeks emphasizes a simple truth: What any group accepts as effective theatrical performance depends to a great extent upon the group's familiarity with, and acceptance of, a particular set of conventions and upon the skill with which those conventions are handled.

OEDIPUS REX AND ITS PERFORMANCE

The City Dionysia included five days of performances. In addition to the tragedies, there were comedies and dithyrambs (hymns to Dionysus sung and danced by groups of fifty men or boys). At the end of the festival, prizes were awarded. The performance of *Oedipus Rex* was thus embedded in a much larger festival framework.

The performances were open to everyone, but the audience was composed primarily of men and boys, although some accounts suggest that women, children, and even slaves attended. Officials were responsible for keeping order, and violence in the theatre was punishable by death. Performances lasted many hours because several plays were presented. The audience at times expressed itself noisily and occasionally hissed actors off the stage. The atmosphere probably resembled a mixture of religious festival and athletic event.

Performances seem to have begun near dawn. There was no artificial lighting in the theatre, no proscenium arch or curtain. The auditorium rose sharply up the hill, so that most of the spectators looked down on the acting areas and could see over the stage house across a plain to the sea. The total visual context was immense.

The beginning of *Oedipus Rex* was signaled by the entrance through one of the *parodoi* of a group of people of all ages carrying branches, the symbol of the suppliant. Oedipus, masked and in full-length *chiton*, appeared through the central doorway of the stage house (which in this play represented a palace) to hear their petition that something be done to end the plague that

had been ravishing Thebes for some time. Then Creon, returning from Delphi—where he had been sent to consult the oracle about how to end the plague—arrived through the other *parodos*. After the suppliants left, the chorus of fifteen elderly Thebans, all as nearly identical in appearance as possible and preceded by the flute player, marched into the orchestra and performed the first choral song. As this description of the performance's opening suggests, spectacle played an important role throughout.

The skill with which *Oedipus Rex* is constructed can be appreciated if we compare the complex story (which actually begins with a prophecy prior to the birth of Oedipus) to Sophocles's ordering of the events. In the play, there is a simultaneous movement backward and forward in time during which the revelation of the past moves Oedipus ever nearer to his doom in the present.

The division of the play into a prologue and five episodes or scenes separated by choral passages is typical of Greek tragedy. The prologue is devoted principally to exposition: A plague is destroying the city of Thebes; Creon returns

Sophocles's *Oedipus the King* at the Stratford Shakespearean Festival (Canada). Oedipus (on right), played by Douglas Campell, and Creon (on left), played by Robert Goodier, surrounded by the chorus. Directed by Tyrone Guthrie; designed by Tanya Moiseiwitch.

from Delphi with a command from the oracle to find and punish the murderer of Laius, the former king; Oedipus promises to obey the command. All of the necessary information is given in this very brief scene, and the first important question—Who is the murderer of Laius?—is raised. The prologue is followed by the entry of the chorus, and the first choral song, which offers prayers to the gods for deliverance from the plague.

The first episode begins with Oedipus's proclamation demanding that anyone with knowledge of the crime come forward and placing a curse on the murderer. This proclamation has great dramatic power because Oedipus is unknowingly pronouncing a curse on himself. Then Tiresias, the blind seer, enters. His refusal to answer questions about the past provokes Oedipus's anger, the first display of a response that is developed forcefully throughout the first four episodes. Oedipus's quick temper, we later discover, has caused him to kill Laius. When Tiresias suggests that the truth is too painful to reveal, Oedipus suspects some trickery. The scene ends in a stalemate of accusations.

It is interesting to note that while the first four episodes move forward in the present, they go successively further back in time. This first episode reveals only that part of the past immediately preceding Oedipus's arrival at Thebes. The choral passage that follows the first episode reflects upon the previous scene, stating the confusion that Sophocles probably wished the audience to feel.

The second episode builds logically upon the first. Creon returns to defend himself against Oedipus's accusation that he is involved in a conspiracy with Tiresias. Queen Jocasta is drawn to the scene by the quarrel, and she and the chorus persuade Oedipus to let his anger cool. This quarrel illustrates Oedipus's complete faith in his own righteousness. Ironically, Jocasta's attempt to placate Oedipus leads to his first suspicion about himself. She tells him that oracles are not to be believed and as evidence points to Laius's death, which did not occur in the manner prophesied. But her description of how Laius was killed recalls to Oedipus the circumstances under which he killed a man. He insists that Jocasta send for the sole survivor of Laius's party. This scene continues the backward exploration of the past; in it Oedipus tells of his life in Corinth, his visit to the oracle of Delphi, and his killing of a man who is later discovered to have been Laius. The choral song that follows concludes that if oracles are proved untrue, then the gods themselves are to be doubted.

Though Jocasta has called oracles into question, she seems to believe in the gods, for at the beginning of the third episode she makes offerings to them. She is interrupted by the entrance of the Messenger from Corinth, who brings news of the death of Oedipus's supposed father, Polybos. But this news, rather than arousing grief, as one would expect, is greeted with rejoicing, for it seems to disprove the oracle's prediction that Oedipus would kill his father. Oedipus still fears returning to Corinth because the oracle also has prophesied that he will marry his own mother. Thinking that he will set Oedipus's mind at ease, the Messenger reveals that he himself brought Oedipus as an infant to Polybos. The circumstances under which the Messenger acquired the child reveal the truth to Jocasta. This discovery leads to a complete reversal for Jocasta; the oracles she cast doubt upon in the preceding scene have suddenly been vindicated. She strives to stop Oedipus from making further inquiries, but he interprets her entreaties as fear that he may be of humble birth. Jocasta goes into the palace; it is the last we see of her.

The scene not only reveals the truth to Jocasta, but it also diverts attention from the murder of Laius to the birth of Oedipus. The scene goes backward in time to the infancy of Oedipus. The choral song that follows speculates on Oedipus's parentage and suggests such possibilities as the god Apollo and the nymphs. The truth is deliberately kept at a distance to make the following scene more powerful.

The fourth scene begins with the entry of the Shepherd (the sole survivor of Laius's party at the time of the killing and the person from whom the Corinthian Messenger had acquired the infant). The Shepherd does not wish to speak, but Oedipus's servants force him to do so. In this very rapid scene, everything that has gone before is brought to a climax. We are taken back to the beginning of the story (Oedipus's birth). We learn that he is the son of Laius and Jocasta, that Oedipus killed Laius, and that Oedipus is married to his mother. The climax is reached in Oedipus's cry of despair and disgust as he rushes into the palace.

The final episode is divided into two parts. A Messenger enters and describes what has happened offstage. The "messenger scene" is a standard part of Greek drama. Because Greek sensibilities dictated that acts of extreme violence take place offstage, a messenger often appears to tell of these acts. The results of the violence (the bodies of the dead, or in this case Oedipus's self-inflicted blindness) might be shown. Following the Messenger's part of the scene, Oedipus returns to the stage and seeks to prepare himself for the future.

Oedipus Rex is structurally unusual, for the resolution scene is the longest in the play. Sophocles was not solely concerned with discovering the murderer of Laius, for in this lengthy final scene interest shifts to the question: What will Oedipus do now that he knows the truth? Up to this scene, the play has concentrated upon Oedipus as the ruler of Thebes, but in the resolution, Oedipus as a man and a father becomes the center of interest. At this point, he has ceased to be the ruler of Thebes and has become the lowest of its citizens.

Oedipus's act of blinding himself grows believably out of his character, for his very uprightness and deep sense of moral outrage cause him to punish himself by thrusting pins into his eyes. Although he is innocent of intentional sin, he considers the deeds themselves (killing a blood relative and incest) to be so

Courtesy of the Guthrie Theatre

Oedipus (standing center), flanked by Guards, forces the Shepherd (kneeling) to tell him the truth. Oedipus does not realize that the truth he seeks will eventually implicate him as the killer of King Laius.

horrible that ignorance cannot wipe away the moral stigma. Part of the play's power resides in the revulsion with which people in all ages have viewed patricide and incest. That an essentially good man might commit these acts only makes them more terrible.

In drawing his characters, Sophocles pays little attention to the physical level. The principal characters—Oedipus, Creon, and Jocasta—are mature persons, but Sophocles says almost nothing about their age or appearance. One factor that is likely to distract modern readers—the relative ages of Jocasta and Oedipus—is not even mentioned by Sophocles. When Oedipus answered the Sphinx's riddle, his reward, being made king, carried the stipulation that he marry the queen, Jocasta. Sophocles never questions the suitability of the marriage on the grounds of disparity in age.

On the sociological level of characterization, Sophocles again indicates little. Oedipus, Creon, and Jocasta hold joint authority in Thebes, although the power has been delegated to Oedipus. Vocational designations—priest, seer, shepherd, servants—are used for some of the characters.

Unlike a modern play, then, in which characterization is usually built from numerous realistic details, here the characterization is drawn with a few bold strokes. For example, Oedipus's quick temper, his arrogance, his love for his children, and his willingness to take responsibility for his actions once they have been made clear to him are all qualities that help us to understand Oedipus. Jocasta is similarly restricted. She strives to help and comfort Oedipus, to mediate between him and Creon, and to stop Oedipus when she suspects that his quest may bring about his ruin. She commits suicide when the truth becomes clear. We know nothing of her as a mother, and the existence of the children is not mentioned until after her death. In Sophocles's play, characterization is pared down to essential attributes and the most important traits are psychological and moral.

All of the speaking roles had to be played by three actors. Examining which actor played which roles is revealing. The first actor played Oedipus throughout because he is present in every scene. The second actor probably played Creon and the Messenger from Corinth; the third actor probably played the Priest, Tiresias, Jocasta, the Shepherd, and the second Messenger. The greatest range is required of the third actor, whereas the greatest individual power is required of the first.

In addition to the three speaking actors, many supernumeraries are required, many of whom no doubt appeared in more than one scene. For example, the band of suppliants in the prologue includes children, two of whom could

later appear as Antigone and Ismene. Some who portrayed suppliants probably also later appeared as servants and attendants. To the actors must be added the chorus of fifteen members. The total number in the cast of *Oedipus Rex* was probably no fewer than thirty.

In reading the play, it is sometimes difficult to perceive that there were so many participants and that the visual and aural appeals were so numerous and continuous. The power of the play and of the production was so great that *Oedipus Rex* became one of the most admired plays in ancient Greece. It is still among the most frequently performed Greek plays.

Why has *Oedipus Rex* continued to attract audiences? We have already looked at its skillful construction and its concern with the moral taboos of incest and patricide. In addition, it develops themes of universal relevance. The fall of Oedipus from the place of highest honor to that of an outcast demonstrates the uncertainty of human destiny. This is related to another theme: the limited ability of human beings to control their fate. Oedipus has done everything he can to avoid the oracle's prediction that he will kill his father and marry his mother but, in doing so, he unknowingly fulfills the oracle. The contrast between human beings seeking to control their destiny and external forces shaping destiny is clearly depicted.

It is significant that no attempt is made in the play to explain why destruction comes to Oedipus. It is implied that human beings must submit to fate and that in struggling to avoid it, they only become more entangled. No one in the play asks who or what has determined Oedipus's fate. The truth of the oracle is established, but the purpose is unclear. It is possible to interpret this play as suggesting that the gods, rather than having decreed the characters' fates, have merely foreseen and foretold what will happen. Such an interpretation shifts the emphasis, but it does not contradict the picture of humanity as a victim of forces beyond its control.

Oedipus leaves Thebes in exile at the end of *Oedipus Rex*. Pictured here is Ellen McLaughlin's new version of Sophocles's play at the Guthrie Theatre. Directed by Lisa Peterson; scene design by Riccardo Hernandez; costume design by David Zinn; lighting by Christopher Akerlind.

Greek Comedy

In addition to tragedy and satyr plays, Athens developed a distinctive comic drama. Comedy became an official part of the Dionysian festivals about fifty years later than tragedy. Although comedy was performed at the City Dionysia with the tragedies, it eventually found its most sympathetic home at another Dionysian festival, the Lenaia, which was held during the winter, when few outsiders were present and at which the playwrights were allowed to ridicule Athenian events more pointedly.

Five comic dramatists competed each year at the Lenaia, but each presented only one play. The conventions of comedy differed significantly from those of tragedy. Greek comedy was usually concerned with current issues in society or politics, with questions of war and peace, or with persons or practices disliked by the author. Occasionally playwrights used mythological material as a framework for satire, but usually they invented their own stories. Comedy used a chorus of twenty-four members, not always identical in appearance or all of the same sex. Sometimes the choruses were depicted as everyday citizens but often as nonhuman (birds, wasps, frogs, clouds). Many of the male characters wore a very tight, too-short *chiton* over flesh-colored tights, creating a ludicrous effect of partial nakedness. This effect was emphasized by an enormous phallus attached to the costumes of most male characters. This not only was a source of humor but also was a constant reminder of the purpose of the Dionysian festival: the celebration of fertility. Masks contributed to the ridiculous appearance of the characters.

Numerous authors wrote Old Comedy, as the plays written prior to 404 B.C. are called, but only eleven comedies have survived and all of these are by Aristophanes (448–380 B.C.). His plays mingle slapstick, fantasy, lyrical poetry, personal abuse, literary and musical parody, and serious commentary on contemporary affairs. The plot of an Old Comedy revolves around a "happy idea" (a far-fetched premise) and the results of putting it into practice. For example, in *Lysistrata* (411 B.C.), probably the best known of all Greek comedies, the women of Greece successfully use a sex strike to end a war. Old Comedy has several typical features:

- A *prologue* introducing the happy idea
- A *parodos*, or entry of the chorus
- An *agon*—a debate over the merits of the happy idea, ending in its adoption
- A *parabasis*—a choral passage addressed to the audience, most frequently filled with advice on civic or other contemporary problems
- A series of episodes showing the happy idea in practice
- A *komos*—an exit to feasting and revelry

A figure from Old Comedy.

From Robert, *Die Masken der Neueren Attischen Komedie*, 1911

The unity of Old Comedy is found in its ruling idea rather than in a series of causally related events. Sometimes days or weeks are assumed to have passed in between scenes, and place may change often. Stage illusion is broken frequently as characters make comments about or to the audience.

After the fifth century, Greek drama declined in quality, although not in quantity. During the fourth century B.C., especially after Alexander the Great conquered most of the Middle East and Egypt, Greek theatres were built throughout the eastern Mediterranean areas, and plays began to be performed at festivals other than those in honor of Dionysus. Comedy underwent the most drastic change, no longer treating major political, artistic, or social issues, turning instead to the intrigues of everyday domestic life. Although Old Comedy (the type written by Aristophanes) is now considered superior to the New Comedy that replaced it, Old Comedy exerted little influence after its own time. New Comedy, especially after it was taken over, adapted, and expanded by the Romans, set the pattern followed by most popular comic drama down to the present.

The Roman Theatre Experience

Around two hundred years after the first performance of *Oedipus Rex*, Rome became a major power, eventually gaining control of Greece, the entire eastern Mediterranean, and most of western Europe and northern Africa.

For seven hundred years, the Romans reigned over an extensive empire.

As in Greece, theatrical performances were part of religious festivals, although in Rome they might be for any of several gods. The Roman term for these festivals was *ludi* ("games"). At the *ludi*, in addition to religious ceremonies and sacrifices, many other activities were offered for the pleasure of the god being honored—as well as for the diversion of the Roman people whose tastes were considered to coincide with those of the gods. Such attitudes led increasingly to theatrical offerings that appealed to the greatest common denominator. The activities (other than the ceremonies and sacrifices) varied from festival to festival and from year to year, but all involved tests of skill, frequently with prizes for the most skillful or popular competitors. The theatrical company that won the greatest favor with the audience received extra payments, as did the winners of chariot races, horse races, animal baiting, acrobatic feats, and other activities. In general, the Romans placed their theatrical performances in the same category as sports and other forms of diversion.

The Romans were great assimilators, accepting, borrowing, or changing those things that seemed useful or desirable. When they encountered Greek drama in the mid-third century B.C., they imported a Greek writer, Livius Andronicus, to adapt Greek drama to Roman tastes. The first of his plays was produced in 240 B.C., and soon native Romans began to write plays. But the taste for this Greek-style drama seems to have peaked quickly because the major period of this type of Roman drama was over by about 150 B.C. Roman taste favored novelty and variety. When Greek-style plays were introduced in 240 B.C., they were novelties to be elaborated and exploited. When their appeal faded, they were displaced by other kinds of entertainment, although they did not disappear altogether.

Although the taste for full-length scripted drama sharply declined after the mid-second century B.C., the demand for other types of theatrical entertainment steadily increased. These entertainments included: short comic plays, dancing, singing, juggling, tightrope-walking, acrobatics, trained animals, gladiatorial contests, animal baiting, water ballets, mock sea fights, and a host of other events. From a single day given over to theatrical entertainments in 240 B.C., the number had grown to 100 by A.D. 354, with another seventy-five days devoted to chariot racing and gladiatorial events.

Because plays, as written texts, survive and artifacts relating to other kinds of theatrical entertainment often do not, accounts of theatrical activities usually emphasize performances based on full-length written plays. Accounts of Roman theatre typically concentrate on theatrical production between 205 and 159 B.C., when Plautus (c. 254–184 B.C.) and Terence (c.195–159 B.C.) wrote the twenty-six surviving Roman comedies. Nine tragedies by Seneca (5 B.C.–A.D. 65) have survived, but they apparently were not intended for public performance. Let us look at the theatrical experience in the age of Plautus and Terence.

Roman Theatrical Context

The Roman theatre resembled that of Greece in many ways, but it also differed in significant ways. All of the surviving Roman comedies are adapted from Greek plays. In these adaptations, the setting and characters remain Greek, even though the manners and customs depicted in the plays are far more Roman than Greek. When the Roman comedies were written, Rome placed great emphasis on seriousness of purpose (*gravitas*) in its citizens. Historians have suggested that the Greek setting was retained in the comedies so as not to offend the Roman authorities that controlled the festivals and their contents.

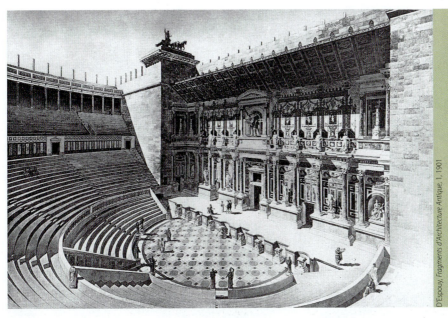

A conjectural reconstruction of one of the oldest Roman theatres (in Ostia, near Rome), built between 30 and 12 B.C.

As in Greece, the state assumed the expenses of theatrical production. The government made an appropriation for each festival as a whole; the officials in charge, usually wealthy citizens who often used the occasion to curry favor with the Roman populace, frequently contributed additional funds. Rather than choosing the plays, as seems to have been the rule in Greece, these officials contracted with the heads of theatrical companies for productions. The officials probably viewed the productions before they were presented, more for the sake of guarding against unacceptable material than for judging artistic merit.

In addition to underwriting production expenses, the Roman state also supplied the theatre in which the plays were presented. In the time of Plautus and Terence, all theatres were temporary structures (no permanent theatre was built in Rome until 55 B.C.). We cannot be certain about the appearance of these temporary structures, but it is usually assumed that they were less elaborate versions of the one depicted in the illustration above. Tiered seating for several thousand people apparently surrounded a semicircular orchestra (half of the Greek full-circle orchestra). The orchestra area seems never to have been used in the Roman comedies, which did not include a chorus. The stage was long, probably more than one hundred feet long and twenty or more feet deep, and rose five feet above the orchestra. The stage was also enclosed at both ends and across the back by a facade called the *scaenae frons*. The *scaenae frons* apparently had three to five doors in the back wall and one at each end. Roman comedies take place outdoors, most frequently on a street in front of one or more houses. The stage was treated as a street, with the doors in the back wall serving as entrances to houses fronting on the street, and the doors at the ends serving as continuations of the street. The facade also had windows and a second story that could be used as needed by the action. The scale of the Roman theatre was comparable to that of the Greek. It, too, was an outdoor structure, but the stage house and the auditorium were joined.

Admission to this theatre was free and audiences were often so unruly that guards were present to enforce order. In the prologue to his *The Carthaginian* (date unknown), Plautus lists

The Romans built theatres both in Italy and abroad. Shown here are the surviving remains of a Roman-style theatre still being used for performance purposes in Merida, Spain.

several types of distracting behavior that apparently were common among Roman audiences: "Let no worn out prostitutes sit in the front part of the auditorium, nor the guards make any noise with their weapons, nor the ushers move about in front of spectators or show anyone to seats while the actors are onstage. ... Don't let slaves take up seats meant for free men..., let nursemaids keep little children at home." The Romans presented a series of plays that had to compete with other attractions; the actors had to satisfy a mass audience or risk them leaving to attend other entertainments. Terence states in the prologue to one of his plays that it is the third attempt to present the play; the earlier two attempts had been abandoned because one time the audience left to see rope dancers and another time to see gladiators. The total context of attractions was akin to the multiple channels on our television sets, which permit us to move from one attraction to another, seeking the most entertaining.

By the time of Plautus and Terence, there seems to have been a number of theatre companies. We do not know what they did when they were not performing at the festivals, but probably they traveled about or gave private performances for wealthy Romans. In any case, more than one company was hired to give performances at the festivals. Once hired, they were responsible for all details of production: finding plays, providing the actors, costumes, musicians, and so on. Although each company was assured a certain payment, special incentives were offered to those companies receiving the most favorable audience response.

The actors wore Greek costumes similar to those of Greek daily life, although there may have been some exaggeration for comic purposes. Because most of the characters were types, certain colors came to be associated with particular groups, such as red with slaves and yellow with courtesans. This conventional use of color extended to wigs as well, making distinctions among the types of characters instantly visible to audiences. All of the performers were male and wore masks.

Roman comedy does not deal with political or social issues but rather with everyday domestic affairs. Almost invariably, the plots turn on misunderstandings of one sort or another: mistaken identity (frequently involving long-lost children), misunderstood motives, or deliberate deception. They show the well-to-do middle class (the older man concerned with his wealth or children; the young man who rebels against authority) and those around them (slaves, slave dealers, hangers-on, courtesans, cowardly soldiers). Of all the characters, the most famous is perhaps the "clever slave" who, to help his master, devises all sorts of schemes, most of which go awry and lead to further complications. Very few respectable women appear in Roman plays, and although love affairs may be the source of a play's intrigues, the women involved seldom appear onstage.

Brilliant Pictures, Inc

The plays of Plautus serve as the basis for many later comedies, including some of those by Molière and Shakespeare. Shakespeare used *The Menaechmi* as the basis for his play, *Comedy of Errors*, pictured here as produced by Boston's Commonwealth Shakespeare Company.

While reading a Roman play, we should try to remember the musical element. In Plautus's plays, about two-thirds of the lines were accompanied by the flute. The flute player remained on stage throughout the play, although the actors ignored his presence. There were a number of songs by the characters (rather than by the chorus, as had been the practice in Greek drama). In performance, a Roman comedy closely resembled a modern musical.

THE MENAECHMI

Of all Roman comedies, Plautus's *The Menaechmi* (date unknown) has perhaps been the most popular. As in most of Plautus's plays, *The Menaechmi* begins with a prologue that carefully lays out the background of the action and goes over important points more than once. By the time the play begins, the audience has been given a summary of the prior action: twin brothers (both known as Menaechmus) were separated when very young, and one (Menaechmus II) has been looking for the other and arrives in Epidamnus without knowing that this is where his twin (Menaechmus I) now is. The introductory scenes are used to establish the present conditions out of which the comedy will grow: the dispute between Menaechmus I and his wife; the visit of Menaechmus I to the courtesan Erotium, his gift to her of a dress stolen from his wife, their plans for an elaborate meal and party later in the day, and the departure of Menaechmus I to the Forum followed by the entrance of Menaechmus II and his slave, Messenio. When Menaechmus II is addressed by name by Erotium and her servants, he and Messenio assume that they are being set up for some con game by people who have learned Menaechmus's name at the dock where their ship has just put in. The remainder of the play presents a series of scenes in which the two Menaechmi are in turn mistaken for each other, and each is mystified and maddened

by being accused of doing things that the other has done. The two are kept apart until the final scene, when their meeting solves the mystery and resolves the complications.

Plautus has little interest in social satire. Instead, he concentrates on the ridiculous situation growing out of mistaken identity. Consequently, when his characters indulge in adultery, stealing, or deception, they merely contribute to the overall tone of good-humored cynicism, with a considerable touch of misogyny.

As in most Roman comedy, the characters in *The Menaechmi* are types rather than individuals. Some roles are summed up in their names: Peniculus ("Brush") suggests the parasite's (or flattering sponger's) ability to sweep the table clean; the cook is called Cylindrus ("Roller"); and the courtesan is named Erotium ("Sexy"). Each character has a restricted number of motivations: the twins wish to satisfy their physical appetites; the wife wants to reform her husband; the father-in-law desires to keep peace in the family; and the quack doctor, who is sent for when the wife decides that Menaechmus I has gone mad, is seeking a patient on whom he can practice a lengthy and costly treatment.

A company of six actors could easily perform the ten speaking roles in *The Menaechmi*. Doubling of roles was common in the Roman theatre and in changing roles, all of the actors had the advantage of masks and conventionalized costumes and colors of garments and wigs. The play does not require actors who are skilled in the subtle portrayal of a wide range of emotions; rather, they need that highly developed comic technique that produces precision in the timing of business and dialogue. The scenes of quarreling, drunkenness, and simulated madness indicate that physical nimbleness is essential. Most of the actors also must be skilled singers because the main characters have "entering songs" when they first appear and sometimes additional songs later in the action. The musical accompaniment was

Roman civilization. Mosaic depicting staging of show in theatre. From House of Tragic Poet in Pompeii/De Agostini Picture Library/A. Dagli Orti /The Bridgeman Art Library

A mosaic from Pompeii shows Roman actors preparing for a performance. Note the use of masks and musical instruments.

played on a flute with two pipes, each about twenty inches long. Sometimes it was bound to the player's head to free his hands for playing the instrument. Its sound resembled that of a modern oboe.

Other Roman Drama and Theatre

By the beginning of the Christian era, Rome seemed to have forgotten its earlier emphasis on *gravitas*. As power came to rest almost wholly with emperors and armies, the people were offered increasing numbers of public entertainments, many of them bloodthirsty. During this time, theatres and amphitheatres were built throughout the empire, which included most of western Europe, northern Africa, and the Middle East.

In addition to comedy, the Romans also wrote tragedy. The only surviving examples of Roman tragedy, nine plays by Seneca, are from this period, but they were probably not intended for production. Like Greek tragedies, Seneca's are based on myths but emphasize exaggerated emotions and onstage violence, features that centuries later would influence the writers of tragedy in Shakespeare's age.

The Roman preference for variety entertainment and short plays drove regular comedy and tragedy from the stage. The favorite form in late Rome was the mime, a short, topical, usually comic, often improvised playlet. (It was not silent, as today's mime is.) Women played the female roles in the mime, perhaps the first form in which female performers were permitted to appear. (There were also Greek mimes that likely included females.) None of the mime actors seem to have worn masks. Mime used more realistic conventions than

Practices & Styles

ROMAN PARATHEATRICAL ENTERTAINMENTS

Roman religious festivals included entertainments—many of them quite violent and bloodthirsty—extending far beyond theatrical performances. The oldest and most popular of these was chariot racing, for which structures (circuses) were built that allowed twelve chariots to race abreast of each other. One of these, the Circus Maximus, held sixty thousand people. The circuses also were used for other forms of entertainment: horseracing (sometimes with trick riding), cavalry battles, footraces, acrobatics, prizefighting, wrestling, exhibitions of wild and trained animals, and fights between animals or between animals and men.

Another popular form of entertainment was gladiatorial contests. Originally gladiatorial combat was confined to funeral games and did not become part of state religious festivals until 105 B.C. The number of combatants steadily increased. In A.D. 109, five thousand pairs were featured at one festival. Used primarily as places for gladiatorial contests and animal fights, amphitheatres were built, the most famous of which is the Colosseum (seating fifty thousand), which opened in A.D. 80 when nine thousand animals were killed during the hundred-day inaugural program. It was also here that Christians were placed in the arena with lions, for which they quickly became prey, as a form of entertainment and religious persecution.

Among the most spectacular of all of the entertainments were the *naumachiae*, or sea battles. Sometimes these were staged on lakes, but amphitheatres also were sometimes flooded for such events. The largest *naumachia* was given in A.D. 52 on the Fucine Lake east of Rome; many of the nineteen thousand participants it involved perished in the battles.

tragedy or comedy did. The dramatic action of mimes in late Rome often centered on sexual encounters, and the dialogue was often obscene. As Christianity grew, its sacraments and beliefs were frequently ridiculed in the mimes.

In addition to the mimes, late Roman festivals increasingly emphasized blood sports, which, along with mimes and variety entertainment, remained integral parts of religious festivals until around A.D. 400. Perhaps not surprisingly, the emerging Christian church became a strong opponent of the theatre—not only because of what was performed but also because it was associated with the worship of pagan gods.

The Roman Empire rapidly disintegrated after being overrun by invaders in A.D. 476. One consequence was the loss of the official and financial support that had sustained the theatre for more than a thousand years. During the following five hundred years, theatrical activity in western Europe was reduced to small bands of players or individuals who traveled about performing wherever they could. These performers were often denounced by the Christian church (by then the dominant and most stable institution) and denied its sacraments. It is ironic, therefore, that the revival of the theatre owed most to the church's discovery (during the last half of the tenth century) that the dramatization of biblical episodes was an effective means of teaching.

A conjectural drawing of a Roman *naumachia* (a staged sea battle) in the late first century A.D. (drawn during the Renaissance).

The Revival of Drama in the Medieval Period

Historians usually divide the medieval period into three broad phases:

- Early— A.D. 900 to A.D. 1050
- High or mid— A.D. 1050 to A.D. 1300
- Late— A.D. 1300 to A.D. 1500

Although these divisions are indicative of changes in society, all three phases shared a relatively stable set of beliefs and values that permit them to be grouped together and labeled medieval. During the first two phases, drama was performed primarily within churches or monasteries; it is usually called liturgical drama. During the third, it flourished in elaborate outdoor productions, some of which continued even after 1500 (when the medieval period is usually said to have ended). This type is usually referred to as vernacular religious drama. Most of the plays and productions discussed here are from the late medieval period. But before we turn to them, we need briefly to consider liturgical drama—drama performed within the church as a part of the religious service, or liturgy.

The earliest known example of a liturgical play, the *quem quaeritis* trope, dates from about A.D. 970. It dramatized the arrival of three women at the tomb of Christ, the announcement by an angel that Christ has risen, and the subsequent rejoicing. This short play (only four lines of sung dialogue) was performed as part of Easter services. Subsequently, many other biblical episodes were dramatized, but all remained short so as not to interfere with the regular services. These short plays shared the following characteristics:

- They were written in Latin (the language of the church throughout western Europe).
- They were chanted or sung.
- They were performed by choirboys or members of the clergy.
- They were financed by the church.

Around 1200, some religious plays began to be performed outside the church, and by around 1375 a religious drama had developed independent of the liturgy. Plays of this new type were performed throughout most of western Europe until the sixteenth century, when controversy over religious beliefs and practices (exemplified in the Protestant secessions from the Roman Catholic Church) led to the suppression of these plays almost everywhere. But by that time these religious plays had for almost two hundred years been the major theatrical expression of western Europe. These plays came to be called vernacular religious drama and they differ from liturgical drama and its presentation in several ways:

- They were written in the vernacular (or common) language of a region.
- They were written to be spoken rather than chanted or sung.

From *Romanesque Art in Italy*, 1913

The interior of a church like those in which plays may have been performed during the medieval period. Notice the absence of fixed seating, which would have left space for scenic units, performers, and spectators. In the background is the raised apse that might be used for scenes in heaven or high places, and beneath it is the crypt that might be used to represent the descent into the grave or Hell.

- They were performed primarily by laymen rather than clergy.
- They were financed by the community rather than by the church.

The medieval religious theatre that developed resembled the festival theatre of Greece and Rome in its general purpose: It celebrated religious belief in the form of community-wide festivals connected to a special occasion. But, though similar in purpose, these medieval festivals differed from those of Greece and Rome in how they were organized, financed, and presented.

Trade Guilds and the Corpus Christi Festival

The production of the outdoor religious dramas in England is usually associated with trade guilds that flourished beginning in the thirteenth century. The return of relative stability after centuries of warfare and general uncertainty had by around 1200 encouraged increased trade among various parts of Europe, which in turn encouraged an increase in manufactured goods to satisfy the growing demand. Eventually, the need to regulate working conditions, wages, the quality of products, and other matters led craftsmen in various trades—bakers, brewers, goldsmiths, tailors, and so on—to establish guilds to promote the common good of those in each trade. Guilds were organized hierarchically: Masters, Journeymen, and then Apprentices.

Each trade guild was governed by a council of masters. A master owned a shop, supervised the work of others within it, and took the risks and rewards of being a business owner. Under each master were a number of journeymen (those skilled in the trade but who worked for wages), and apprentices (boys or young men who received room and board while learning a trade, usually over a period of seven years). The forces that gave rise to the guilds also encouraged the

Society, Art & Culture

THE FIRST FEMALE DRAMATIST

The first female dramatist of whom we have any record wrote her plays at about the same time liturgical plays began to be performed. Hrosvitha (c. A.D. 935–c. 975), canoness of a nunnery at Gandersheim (Germany), was, according to her own account, drawn to the comedies of the Roman playwright Terence but, fearing their adverse influence, decided to write others that would show Christian virgins and martyrs triumphing over earthly temptations. It is unclear whether her six plays, *Pafnutius*, *Dulcitius*, *Gallicanus*, *Abraham*, *Callimachus*, and *Sapientia* (all probably written between 963 and 973), were performed during her lifetime. Written in rhymed Latin, most of these plays deal with characters martyred for their Christian faith or with young women who overcome the temptations of the flesh. After they were published in 1501, they exerted considerable influence on the didactic drama written during the sixteenth century for performance in schools. Hrosvitha, the first dramatist of the postclassical period whose name we know, is a figure of special interest to those seeking to recover the history of women in theatre.

Hrosvitha's uniqueness also reminds us that the theatre prior to the Renaissance was essentially a male preserve. The plays, even those that focus on female characters, were not only written by men but also acted by them. In general, women were viewed as significantly inferior to men. In the Christian era, women were usually viewed as daughters of Eve—weak, easily tempted, and themselves temptresses—requiring guidance and discipline from a father or husband. The Virgin Mary was, of course, always treated as an exception.

growth of towns. As the towns and guilds grew, power within each town came to rest primarily with the guilds because they usually elected the mayor and the council from among their members.

The increased prominence of secular groups seems also to have been at least partially responsible for the church's desire to incorporate ordinary people more fully into its activities. One result was the creation of a new feast day, Corpus Christi ("Body of Christ"). This festival, officially approved in 1311 and observed throughout Europe by about 1350, celebrates the redemptive power of the sacraments of bread and wine (the body and blood of Christ), the mystery that gave meaning to existence: the union of the human and divine in the person of Christ and the promise of redemption through his sacrifice. All biblical events could be related to this festival, and eventually Corpus Christi

became the occasion for dramas encompassing everything from the Creation to the Last Judgment. (Previously, plays about the birth of Christ had been done at Christmas, about His resurrection at Easter, and so on according to the church calendar.) Corpus Christi, observed sixty days after Easter, fell variously from May 21 to June 24. Coming during warm weather and when the days were near their longest, it was favorable to outdoor performance.

The central feature of the Corpus Christi festival was a procession through the town with the consecrated bread and wine. The church sought to involve everyone in the festival by including in the procession representatives from every rank and profession (churchmen, nobles, merchants, craftsmen). This cooperative venture marked the beginning of an association that would eventually lead to the guilds' assumption of a dominant role in the staging of outdoor religious plays. The procession may also be the forerunner of the type of staging eventually adopted in some English towns: mounting plays on wagons and performing them at various stops—a combination of procession and performance.

In the British Isles, about 125 towns produced plays at some time during the medieval period. Nevertheless, only a few plays have survived. Most of these are parts of cycles (a number of short plays that, taken together, dramatize the Bible from Creation to Doomsday). The surviving cycles come from four towns: York (whose cycle includes forty-eight plays), Chester (twenty-four plays), Wakefield (thirty-two plays),

and an unidentifiable town (forty-two plays). All of these date originally from about 1375 and were performed at intervals (that is, regularly but not every year) over the next two centuries. During that time, the cycles underwent many changes as individual plays were rewritten, new ones added, others dropped. The surviving texts show the cycles as they existed near the end of their active production life. All of the plays dealt with the same basic subject: Christian views of God's ordering of existence as revealed in the Bible and in other church writings. Regardless of where they were written, they had many common characteristics and shared conventions.

A double page from the manuscript of the medieval outdoor drama staged at Valenciennes (France) in 1547. At bottom, the play; above, simultaneous drawings of several scenes, including Christ being nailed to the cross, the crucifixion, and the entombment.

Conventions of Medieval Theatre

A major convention of medieval drama involves the way time is handled. Throughout the medieval period, humanity was thought to participate in two kinds of time: eternal and earthly. God, Satan, and human souls exist in eternity—which, unlike physical being, has neither beginning nor end. Thus, earthly existence is a short interlude during which human beings must make choices that will determine how they will spend eternity—in Heaven or Hell. Medieval staging often made the human dilemma visible by using a stage that depicted Heaven at one end of a long platform and Hell at the other end (see the illustration on page 90).

The plays illustrated this situation, especially in the Doomsday (or Last Judgment) play. Because earthly time and place were relatively unimportant, the historical period or geographical location of an event was insignificant. There was little sense of historicity in the plays: Ancient Israelites were dressed in medieval garments, and Old Testament characters referred to Christian saints.

The fluidity of time is also reflected in the structure of the cycles. Rather than treating one of many myths or a restricted story (as the Greeks and Romans did), the medieval cycles encompass the biblical story of humanity from Creation to Doomsday. Seldom was any causal relationship established among the various plays of a cycle. Events were thought to happen simply because God willed them. Both time and place were telescoped or expanded as needed.

Practices & Styles

SPECIAL EFFECTS IN RELIGIOUS PLAYS

Far greater marvels could be shown on fixed stages than on pageant wagons. Miraculous events proliferated because they reinforced belief in biblical accounts of the life of Christ. One of the most elaborate of these fixed-stage productions was mounted at Valenciennes, France, in 1547. An account (by H. d'Outreman) published almost one hundred years later gives many details, of which the following are only a few:

> The production lasted 25 days, and on each we saw strange and Wonderful things. ... we saw Truth, angels, and others descend from very high up, sometimes by visible and sometimes by invisible means. Lucifer flew out of Hell on a dragon without anyone being able to tell how. ... Jesus was carried to the top of a wall forty feet high by the Devil. ... The fig tree, when cursed by Our Lord, dried up and its leaves withered in a minute. Other marvels shown at the death of Our Lord included the eclipse, the earthquake, and the splitting of rocks.

Another account of a play staged at Mons in 1501 tells how water was stored in wine barrels on the roofs of buildings so that during a Noah play the flood could be represented by channeling water through perforated pipes (mounted above the playing area) to create five minutes of continuous rain.

Bibliothèque nationale de France

The stage set up for the Passion play at Valenciennes (1547) used several mansions to represent different locations. Note that the most vividly characterized location is Hell, depicted as the mouth of a giant beast. The Hell mansion frequently was depicted in such a manner, complete with the burning of sulfur, and actors dressed as demons who might very well have accosted unruly audience members and dragged them into the "Hell mouth."

Staging also involved a number of conventions. There were no permanent theatres, so theatrical spaces were improvised. The principal requirement was an open space sufficient to accommodate a large audience. The stages might be fixed or movable. Fixed stages were most typically set against buildings on one side of a town square or large courtyard, but they sometimes extended down the middle of a square (and were viewed from two or three sides) or were set up in the ruins of a Roman amphitheatre or other circular space (and were viewed in the round). A movable stage was a wagon that could be moved from one location to another.

Regardless of the type of stage or its location, the staging conventions were the same everywhere. There were two parts to the stage space: *mansions* and *platea*. Mansions, used to represent locales, were scenic structures, sufficient to indicate place but not meant to do so fully. A single play might require more than one mansion, and an entire cycle might require as many as seventy.

The *platea* was undifferentiated stage space. Once the location of the action was established by relating it to a mansion, the actors could move out and appropriate as much of the adjacent stage space as the action required; this appropriated space then was considered to be part of the place represented by the mansion. Thus, the same space might change its identity merely by being associated with a different mansion. Place, then, was almost as fluid as time. There was no proscenium arch or other framing device. The overall setting ultimately symbolized (as the total cycle indicates) the entire universe—human and earthly existence framed by Heaven and Hell.

Costumes were used to distinguish among the inhabitants of Earth, Heaven, and Hell. Secular, earthly characters (no matter the period or place of the action) wore contemporary medieval garments appropriate to their rank, profession, or gender, because no attempt was made to achieve historical accuracy. God, the angels, the saints, and certain biblical characters wore church garments, usually differentiated by adding accessories: Angels wore church robes with wings attached, whereas God was dressed as a high church dignitary and often had his face gilded. Many saints and biblical personages were associated with specific symbols. For example, St. Peter carried the "keys to the Kingdom of Heaven," and the Archangel Michael wielded a flaming sword. Because such visual symbolism was common and well understood in the medieval period, it quickly identified characters for the audience. The greatest design imagination went into the costumes of devils, who were fancifully conceived with wings, claws, beaks, horns, or tails. The devils also often wore masks to emphasize their deformities.

There were frequently a number of spectacular special effects. Hell with its horrors was depicted with great care to make it as gruesome as possible. The entrance to Hell was often represented as the mouth of a fire-breathing monster (the "Hell mouth"). Many miracles described in the Bible were staged as convincingly as possible to reinforce faith. Nevertheless, the illusion of actuality was not always a goal because several widely separated places were usually juxtaposed within a limited stage space and represented by fragmentary scenery. Thus, medieval staging ranged between illusionistic and symbolic devices. Overall, conventions permitted rapid switches from broad outline to specific detail, asking the audience to use its eyes in a way analogous to present-day cinematography—focusing in, pulling back, and cutting from one locale to another. Much in medieval staging may now seem naive, but in its time it made efficient use of conventions that evoked the human condition as the medieval mind understood it.

The Wakefield Cycle

Let us look at the English cycle staged at Wakefield, a town in central England. The surviving manuscript of this cycle contains thirty-two plays, beginning with the Creation and extending through the Last Judgment. As with all of the cycles, the authors (there appear to have been several) are anonymous. Most medieval artists did not strive for individual glory and recognition but rather contented themselves with serving God, the church, and the community. Some of the Wakefield plays are borrowed from other cycles, whereas others have qualities suggesting varied origins. Five of the plays are by the same unknown author, usually referred to as "the Wakefield Master." His plays are noted for their details of everyday life and their comic scenes. One of these, *Noah and His Sons* (c. 1425–1450), will be examined more fully later.

The production of the Wakefield cycle was a community effort involving the town council, the church, and the guilds. The council proposed whether the plays would be performed in a given year, subject to the church's approval because the plays were part of a church festival. The church also had to approve the play texts to ensure that they did not distort church doctrine. There was an official copy of the cycle, which had to be adhered to in performance. The usual rationale for presenting the plays was "to honor God, to edify man, and to glorify the city." Most of the actual work of production was undertaken by the guilds.

The decision to perform the plays apparently was made several months prior to Corpus Christi. One official document is dated September 29, thus permitting nine months of preparation, although it is not certain how much of this time was devoted to preparation. Individual plays apparently were assigned according to a perceived relationship between the guild's specialty and the events of a play. The assignments at Wakefield have not survived, but we know that at other places the Shipwrights, Fishers, or Mariners were assigned plays dealing with Noah (the ark and the Flood), whereas the Goldsmiths were usually given the play in which the Three Kings bring gifts to the Christ child. Each guild was expected to assume the costs of producing its play, and the city council levied fines against those who failed to fulfill their obligations adequately.

At Wakefield, processional staging appears to have been used. Each play was mounted on a pageant wagon (similar to a modern parade float) and drawn through the streets from one playing place to another in the order indicated in the script. No reliable description of a pageant wagon has survived. The wagons were probably as large as the narrow streets would accommodate and were probably designed to meet the requirements of specific plays. The wagons could be stored and refurbished as needed for subsequent festivals. Each wagon usually had to carry one or more mansions and might require some machinery for special effects. Some scholars believe that at each playing place the wagon was drawn up alongside a stationary platform that served as the *platea*. The actors sometimes performed scenes in the street.

In addition to providing the pageant wagon and its equipment, each guild had to supply performers and someone to oversee the production. All of the personnel involved in production were amateurs, but as time went by some became quite skilled and seem to have approached the status of professionals. Surviving records show that sometimes one actor was paid much more than the others; thus, it seems likely that he was in charge of the total production (that is, served as director). Some guilds put the same person under contract for several years to stage their part of the cycle. Actors were recruited from the local populace and were not restricted to members of the guild producing that play. We do not know how many rehearsals were held, but the plays were relatively short, and often the same actor played the same role at many different festivals. All of the actors were male, female roles being played by boys or young men.

Costumes, for the most part, consisted of clothing in common use in medieval England and were usually supplied by the actors or borrowed. Church robes, the starting point for ecclesiastical and angelic costumes, could be borrowed or rented from the church, but the costumes of devils had to be made.

Each guild rehearsed and prepared its play separately from the others. No dress rehearsal of the entire cycle was needed because coordinating the individual plays merely required that the pageant wagons be lined up in the correct order.

The council specified the places at which the plays would be performed; at Wakefield there probably were two or three sites. Actors were required to be in their pageant wagons by 5 A.M., presumably the starting time. When all was ready, the first wagon moved to the first

The pageant wagon for a Noah play in performance (England, 1966) gives an idea of how the size of a pageant wagon related to the narrow streets.

Eileen White/Stewart Lack, New York Mystery Plays Archive, The National Center for Early Music

performance place, where the actors performed the play, and then moved on to the next. Thus, all of the plays were performed in the prescribed order at each of the designated places.

On the day of performances, all normal work was suspended; most of the town's residents must have crowded into the places designated for the performances. Word about the performances was usually sent to neighboring towns, and a large number of spectators probably came from outside Wakefield. Provisions for the audience were not extensive, other than choosing sites that permitted a crowd to assemble. The majority of spectators stood, although some seating may have been erected. The windows and roofs of houses overlooking the performance place were in great demand and probably were rented. The council's proclamation provided that sizable fines be levied against anyone who disturbed the plays or hindered their procession; carrying weapons was forbidden. Even if the performances began at 5 A.M., they probably required all of the daylight hours (at that time of the year in central England until around 10 P.M.) to complete the full cycle at each of the prescribed stops. That would have made for a very long day, but spectators were as mobile as the wagons and could move from one viewing place to another, watch only some of the plays, move forward or back along the route, and choose how long they wanted to stay. The atmosphere may have been as festive as it was reverential. It was both a holiday and a holy day.

It is impossible here to examine in detail a performance of the entire Wakefield cycle. Therefore, we will look at one play, considered by many to be one of the best of all of the English cycle plays. It is the cycle's third play, *Noah and His Sons*.

NOAH AND HIS SONS

Before the spectators saw *Noah and His Sons* they had already viewed two other plays, *The Creation* and *The Killing of Abel*. *Noah and His Sons*, then,

comes very early in the overall cycle of thirty-two plays. This 558-line play is an elaboration of biblical passages from Genesis (chapters 6 through 10).

The play begins with Noah praying to God and comparing God's goodness toward all creatures with the ungrateful responses of those he has created, not only human beings but also Lucifer, whose rebelliousness has caused him to be cast out of Heaven. God, unseen by Noah, continues this lamentation, condemning the wickedness of human beings and promising to destroy them all—except faithful Noah and his family. He then appears to Noah and orders him to build a ship, giving him precise directions about its size and layout. He also orders Noah to take his family and a pair of every known beast into the ship so they may be saved from a flood that will destroy all creatures not on the ship.

The solemn tone of this opening expository scene, which takes up approximately one-third of the play, is abruptly broken when Noah returns home to his wife, who immediately begins to berate him for being an incompetent provider. Their dispute rapidly escalates into an exchange of blows. This scene redirects the play's tone toward domestic comedy and relocates the biblical action within the familiar world of the English audience.

Noah then turns to carrying out God's orders and, without assistance and within a space of twenty-five lines, builds the ship. There follows a lengthy segment during which Noah's three sons and their wives board the ship and seek to persuade Noah's wife to do likewise. Another comic fight occurs between husband and wife, during which they seemingly beat each other thoroughly, before the wife agrees to come aboard (and then only because the water is rising around her). The remainder of the play takes place on the ship, where a year of domestic harmony passes in the midst of anxiety about their plight, as they measure the depth of the water and send out birds in search of signs that land has reappeared. Eventually, the waters recede, and the play ends with prayers that human beings will profit from Noah's example and reconcile themselves to the will of God.

The action of the play is almost equally divided among three parts: One third is devoted to the opening expository scene; one third to the two scenes of bickering between Noah and his wife; and one third to the ship-building and onboard scenes. Time is severely telescoped in the third part. No clues are given as to how much time elapses during the building of the ship, but in the final scene Noah speaks of having endured forty days of rain and of having been on board for 350 days.

There are nine roles, of which six are very minor—those of Noah's sons and their wives, who have few lines and serve little dramatic function. They seem to be there only because the biblical source includes them. Characterization of the three main roles is simple. God magisterially voices feelings of having been betrayed by his ungrateful creations and announces his decision to destroy them. His benevolence is seen only in his attitude toward Noah and his family. Noah, who claims to be more than six hundred years old, is pious and obedient. His life apparently has been tranquil except where it involves his wife. Comedy in the play is derived from Noah's inability to control his headstrong and independent wife. Noah's wife (she is given no name in the play) resists being bossed about by anyone and insists on her right to gossip, but she is industrious, always spinning, and once aboard shares responsibility equally with Noah. All of the roles would have been played by men; having Noah's wife played by a man probably contributed to making the quarreling and fighting more acceptably comic. The realistic bickering and highly physical fights help to balance the necessarily nonrealistic scenes—building the ship, enduring forty days of rain, and floating for a year on the flood water.

The play seems to demand stylized speech. It is written in sixty-two nine-line stanzas, each

Noah releases a bird in hope that the waters have receded in *Noah*, one part of *The Mystery Plays*, as performed at the Hartford Stage. Adapted by John Russell Brown; directed by Mary B. Robinson.

Lanny Nagler Photography; courtesy of the Hartford Stage Company

using the same structure. The first four lines use a double rhyme scheme: The final words of the lines rhyme, as do words halfway through those lines. The fifth and ninth lines are short and rhyme, and lines six through eight, somewhat longer than five and nine, also rhyme. Thus, rhythmical speech is a basic structural element.

Only one mansion is required—the ship. It seems likely that a pageant wagon was fitted out to represent a ship and that the ship was initially concealed in some manner (perhaps by a cloth) and then was gradually revealed during the short scene in which Noah supposedly builds it. It also seems likely that the ship was supplied with cut-outs or painted cloths representing animals because only one line mentions getting "gear, cattle, and company" on board. The initial scene and the scenes with Noah's wife require no mansions. When Noah leaves to build the ship, he declares that he must take his tools along. These tools, along with the spinning wheel, the straps that figure in the beating scenes, and a plumb line that is lowered to measure the depth of the water are the only stage properties mentioned in the play. The raven and doves sent out to search for signs of life may have been actual birds. The costuming was simple. All of the characters except God would have worn contemporary working-class dress. God would have been costumed in garments associated with the pope or some other high church official.

Because the spectators crowded around the performance space, many spectators saw the actors at close range, and the total configuration of the playing places meant that the performance was viewed from a variety of angles. Thus, the spatial relationship between audience and performer and the overall scale differed markedly from those of the Greek and Roman theatres. In addition, the degree of formalization apparently was less than in classical theatres because most elements of performance in *Noah and His Sons*, though perhaps somewhat exaggerated, were variations on things familiar to the audience.

Fair with Theatrical Presentation (oil on panel), c1600, Brueghel, Pieter the Younger (c.1564–1638)/Hermitage, St. Petersburg, Russia/The Bridgeman Art Library

Pieter Brueghel the Younger's painting *Fair with Theatrical Presentation* (c. 1600) shows a temporary stage erected on a village street. Notice the raised platform stage and the hanging curtain that helps to create a backstage area. A prompter stands behind the curtain, while another backstage helper passes out a stool to an audience member.

As the play ended, the wagon moved on to another site and was replaced by the next wagon, bearing a play about Abraham and Isaac. Twenty-nine more short plays would be performed before the day ended.

Other Medieval Theatre and Drama

In addition to religious plays, several other dramatic types were popular during the medieval period, among them moralities, farces, and interludes. Morality plays flourished between 1400 and 1550. Unlike the religious plays, which treated biblical or saintly characters, morality plays treated the spiritual trials of ordinary persons. They were allegories about the moral temptations that beset all human beings. The protagonist (often called Everyman or Mankind) was advised and cajoled by personifications of good and evil; most frequently the protagonist succumbed to temptation but was eventually recalled to the path of righteousness by a character called Faith or Mercy or by the grace of God. The most famous morality play is *Everyman* (c. 1500) in which God orders Death to summon the title character. Everyman, who has been too busy leading a carefree existence to think about death, now seeks among his companions (Kindred, Cousin, Goods, Knowledge, Five Wits, Beauty, Strength, and so on) for one that will accompany him on his journey, but once they know his destination, they decline his invitation. Ultimately only Good Deeds goes into the grave with him. Through this search, Everyman comes to understand the relationship of his earthly life to salvation.

During the sixteenth century, the morality play was gradually secularized as its original moral concerns were replaced by new ones such as the ideal training of rulers and the content of a proper education. Then, when religious controversies erupted, moralities were used to attack one's opponents, Protestants or Catholics, by associating one's own side with good and one's enemies with evil. Such changes moved the morality play increasingly toward a wholly secular drama; thus, it served as a transition between the medieval religious drama and the secular drama of Shakespeare's time.

Farce, a form of comic secular drama, began to emerge around the thirteenth century, but because the form was not officially encouraged,

Everyman as produced by the Royal Shakespeare Company. Directed by Kathryn Hunter and Marcello Magni; sets by Rosa Maggiora; lighting by Chris Davey.

Sara Krulwich/The New York Times/Redux

it remained a minor though highly entertaining type, emphasizing the ridiculous and comically depraved aspects of human behavior. One of the best examples is *Pierre Patelin* (c. 1470), an anonymous French farce that dramatizes the story of an impoverished lawyer who buys a piece of cloth from a merchant, whom he invites to dinner to receive his payment. When the merchant arrives, Patelin is in bed, and his wife swears that he has not been out of the house. Patelin pretends madness, beats the merchant, and drives him away without payment for the cloth. This story is loosely joined to a second one in which Patelin agrees to defend a shepherd against a charge of stealing sheep. He counsels the shepherd that during the trial he should answer only "Baa" no matter what anyone says to him. The accuser turns out to be the merchant, who creates total confusion during the proceedings by his alternating charges against the shepherd and Patelin. In view of this confusion and the shepherd's seeming feeblemindedness, the judge dismisses the case, but when Patelin tries to collect his fee, the shepherd runs away, calling "Baa." Like many farces, *Pierre Patelin* shows clever knaves outwitting each other, but it adds a comic twist by having the seemingly stupid shepherd outwit the experienced lawyer.

The interlude was a nonreligious play, serious or comic, that was performed between the parts of a celebration (such as the courses of a banquet, usually for some festival or special occasion). It was associated with the rise of professional performers, who developed their art in the specialized entertainments presented in the households of kings and nobles. Eventually these servants were permitted, when not needed at home, to travel about and perform for pay. Thus, the interlude is associated with the rise of both the professional actor and the professional theatre.

Because the medieval period was a time when religious and secular ceremony played an important role in people's lives, many other celebrations utilized theatrical elements. Amidst the diversity, the religious drama was the most important and characteristic. More than any other type, it appealed to (and actively involved) the largest cross section of the populace and most fully embodied those concerns that the age idealized—the biblical vision of human history and destiny.

An interlude performed during a medieval banquet. In the background St. George is on his horse; he will fight and slay the dragon (center right). The ruler's table is center back. Notice the spectators in the gallery (upper left).

From Pougin, *Dictionnaire du Théâtre*, 1885

Comparing Greek, Roman, and Medieval Theatre

The Greek, Roman, and medieval theatre experiences, then, were alike in some ways and quite unlike in others. For the most part, they were occasional (that is, performances were given on special occasions and not on a continuing, everyday basis, as in modern times); ceremonial (performances were parts of religious festivals and considered offerings to gods); financed by the state, religious or secular organizations, or wealthy citizens; and open to all. They also used many similar conventions: male performers only, musical accompaniment, large audience spaces, and formalized scenic backgrounds. Greek and Roman theatre used masks for all characters (except in mime); medieval theatre used masks for devils and sometimes for allegorical characters.

There were many differences. In Greek theatre, the chorus played a large role, as did dance. In Roman theatre, the musical element was more equally distributed throughout the play and was associated with the actors more than with the chorus. In medieval theatre, music was plentiful but followed no fixed plan. The theatre structures also differed. But the most important differences were those reflecting basic values. The Greeks seem to have placed great emphasis on moral values and significant issues, whereas the Romans were more concerned with popular, diversionary entertainment, and medieval theatre was tied to Christian teaching.

THEATRE IN A BROAD CONTEXT

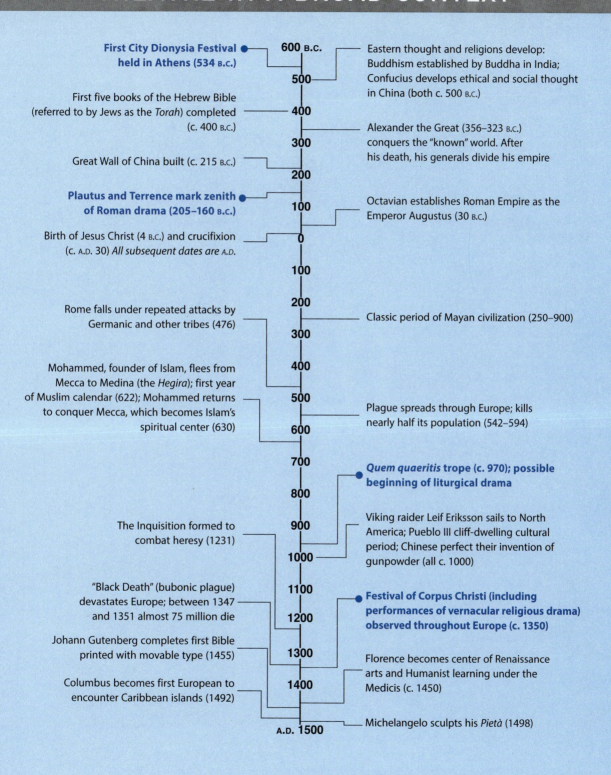

First City Dionysia Festival held in Athens (534 B.C.) — 600 B.C.

Eastern thought and religions develop: Buddhism established by Buddha in India; Confucius develops ethical and social thought in China (both c. 500 B.C.)

500

First five books of the Hebrew Bible (referred to by Jews as the *Torah*) completed (c. 400 B.C.) — 400

300

Alexander the Great (356–323 B.C.) conquers the "known" world. After his death, his generals divide his empire

Great Wall of China built (c. 215 B.C.) — 200

Plautus and Terrence mark zenith of Roman drama (205–160 B.C.) — 100

Octavian establishes Roman Empire as the Emperor Augustus (30 B.C.)

Birth of Jesus Christ (4 B.C.) and crucifixion (c. A.D. 30) *All subsequent dates are A.D.* — 0

100

200

Rome falls under repeated attacks by Germanic and other tribes (476) — 300

Classic period of Mayan civilization (250–900)

Mohammed, founder of Islam, flees from Mecca to Medina (the *Hegira*); first year of Muslim calendar (622); Mohammed returns to conquer Mecca, which becomes Islam's spiritual center (630) — 400 / 500

Plague spreads through Europe; kills nearly half its population (542–594)

600

700

***Quem quaeritis* trope (c. 970); possible beginning of liturgical drama**

800

The Inquisition formed to combat heresy (1231) — 900

Viking raider Leif Eriksson sails to North America; Pueblo III cliff-dwelling cultural period; Chinese perfect their invention of gunpowder (all c. 1000)

1000

1100

"Black Death" (bubonic plague) devastates Europe; between 1347 and 1351 almost 75 million die — 1200

Festival of Corpus Christi (including performances of vernacular religious drama) observed throughout Europe (c. 1350)

Johann Gutenberg completes first Bible printed with movable type (1455) — 1300

Florence becomes center of Renaissance arts and Humanist learning under the Medicis (c. 1450)

Columbus becomes first European to encounter Caribbean islands (1492) — 1400

A.D. 1500

Michelangelo sculpts his *Pietà* (1498)

Shakespeare's *Macbeth*, directed by Teller (of the magic duo Penn & Teller) and Aaron Posner with Magic designed by Teller, at Two River Theater Company; scene design by Dan Conway; lighting design by Tom Weaver; costume design by Devon Painter; sound design by Karen Graybash.

T. Charles Erickson

[The third phase in the development of theatre brings] an incursion of the secular; the shows decrease in scale, the performers decrease in number,... but a more specialized note creeps in. Professionalism begins. The seasonal element recedes; the religious gives place to the satirical or the philosophical.... And the show is designed for a far smaller and more particular audience, an audience which is sometimes indoors.

— Richard Southern, *The Seven Ages of the Theatre*

Creating a Professional Theatre

Elizabethan England, Italian Commedia dell'Arte, and Seventeenth-Century France

The theatrical experiences we have examined so far were parts of festivals sponsored by governmental or religious authorities, performed on special occasions, and financed by the state or wealthy citizens. Although there were other types of performance, they were considered inferior. Then, during the sixteenth and seventeenth centuries, the role of theatre in European society was redefined.

Creating a Professional Theatre

Among the forces that brought about change was a growing secularization of thought as people became more interested in life here and now and less preoccupied with preparing for the life hereafter. While religion remained important, an interest in earthly concerns increased, and a rebirth of learning occurred in many fields that had long been neglected. This period of rebirth is often referred to as the Renaissance. Scholars, artists, and others turned their attention once more to Greece and Rome, both of which had played a relatively minor role during the medieval period, in part because so many classical works had been lost or destroyed, while others were ignored because, as pagan creations, they were considered dangerous. Those that had continued to be used were interpreted in ways that obscured their pagan origins. Revived interest in the classical world included Greek and Roman plays and theatrical practices, even though during the Renaissance understanding of the classical theatre was severely limited and often distorted. Nevertheless, educated people began to perceive alternatives to medieval practices, and across Europe playwrights began to write plays that imitated or adapted classical subjects and forms or that mingled medieval and classical elements.

The Renaissance spirit of inquiry also extended to religion. During the sixteenth century disputes over church doctrine and practice led to secessions from the Roman Catholic Church and the formation of several Protestant sects. Various factions soon found theatrical performance a good propaganda medium (especially because the majority of the audience could not read), and they exploited it in plays that ridiculed their opponents and upheld their own views. Disputes often erupted into violence, even wars. In England, the official state religion changed four times during the sixteenth century, and each time many people were executed because of their refusal to accept the changes. In France, religious disputes between Catholics and Huguenots resulted in violent attacks that lasted throughout most of the sixteenth century. Most European rulers were under enormous pressure to choose sides in these religious controversies. Under these circumstances, it is not surprising that by the mid-1500s both church and state had begun to look for ways to reduce disturbances. In 1548 King Henri II banned the performance of religious drama in France. In England, Elizabeth I succeeded to the English throne in 1558, and the following year she, too, decreed a ban on plays dealing with religious and political subjects. These decrees, in effect, sounded the death knell for the public performance of religious drama. Across most of Europe a type of theatrical experience—the outdoor religious play—that had enjoyed enormous popularity for more than two hundred years was now forbidden by the same institutions (church and state) that had encouraged and supported it.

Forbidden to perform plays on religious subjects, theatre became secular, and for its subjects, it turned to classical literature, historical chronicles, and legends. In part out of necessity, a new kind of drama was born and theatre reinvented itself as a commercial enterprise. Rather than remaining occasional (part of a religious festival), officially supported (by church or state), and essentially amateur, it became continuous, secular, and professional.

Those who had been the most enthusiastic supporters of religious drama were the most vehement opponents of a professional theatre. To them, the presentation of plays for the glory of God, the honor of the city, and the edification of citizens seemed worthy goals, but devoting one's life to performing plays for money was considered wasteful and sinful. The guilds that had produced many of the cycle plays in England sought to have professional theatre banned on the grounds that it took people away from work, encouraged immoral behavior, spread diseases, and offered cover for seditious activities. In short, guilds saw the professional theatre in a different light than they had viewed the largely amateur theatre of the medieval period.

To survive, professional groups had to be able to perform often, had to have a stock of plays sufficiently large and varied to keep the limited available audience coming back, and had to have a performance space large enough to accommodate a sizable number of paying customers and sufficiently enclosed to permit the company to control access and collect entrance fees. They also had to own or control their costumes, scenery, and other production elements and had to assemble a company of actors and production personnel who could devote full time to theatrical production and performance.

Accomplishing these tasks was difficult because in the sixteenth century acting was not an accepted profession. It did not fit into the then-dominant trade-guild scheme in which there was a clear-cut hierarchy of responsibility wherein each master was held responsible for the journeymen and apprentices who worked for him. Because actors did not belong to a guild, they were seen as "masterless men," meaning that no one was considered to be responsible for them; they fell into the category of vagrants who, because of their threat to the social order, were subject to arrest and punishment. To get around this difficulty, acting companies petitioned noblemen to serve as their patrons; technically, actors became "servants" of these patrons and therefore were no longer masterless. For this reason, during the time of Shakespeare and Molière, acting companies had such titles as the Lord Admiral's Men, the Lord Chamberlain's Men, and the King's Men as indications of their legal status. Acting companies that were associated with a noble patron gained not only a measure of protection but also a degree of status that helped sell tickets. Molière's company, for example, increased in popularity once Louis XIV became its patron and allowed it to be called *Troupe du Roi* (the King's Players or Company of the King). Without the patronage

The School for Husbands by Molière, translated by Richard Wilbur, directed by Doug Hughes at the Westport Country Playhouse; scene design by Hugh Landwehr; costume design by Linda Fisher; lighting by Jane Cox; original music by Louis Rosen.

T. Charles Erickson

of rulers and noblemen, the professional theatre would have had difficulty surviving even though patronage brought little direct financial support.

If this system protected the companies, it also imposed restrictions; rulers eventually insisted that every company have a license from the crown and that every play be approved before being performed. Such licensing made it possible for the ruler to ensure that the companies did not perform plays that might stir up political or religious controversy. Despite these problems, by the 1600s professional acting companies across Europe were creating one of the greatest theatrical eras the world has known. Nowhere was this truer than in England.

Shakespeare and the Globe Theatre

The reputation of the Elizabethan theatre rests above all on the work of William Shakespeare (1564–1616), perhaps the greatest playwright of all time, and the company of which he was a member (the Lord Chamberlain's Men, later the King's Men). Other significant drama-tists of Shakespeare's time included: Thomas Kyd, Christopher Marlowe, Ben Jonson, John Fletcher, and John Webster. All of these playwrights (and others) contributed to the astonishing growth of English drama between 1585 and 1642.

Theatrical conditions favored the develop-ment of playwriting. From the 1580s until 1642, there were always at least two (and sometimes as many as four) companies playing in or around London. Because they performed six times a week (every day except Sunday) in the after-noon (beginning around 2 P.M.) during normal working hours, and because London was still a relatively small city (growing from 100,000 to 400,000 during this period), the companies were in strong competition for audiences. They could not rely on long runs; normally, they changed the bill every day. New plays were performed once and then added to the theatre's repertory to be revived from time to time until they lost their appeal. In the 1590s, a London company produced a new play about every seventeen days. Ten performances was the average life of a play (that is, the total number of times played—spread over one or more seasons—before it was dropped from the repertory). To entice the same basic audience group to return to the theatre, new plays were in constant demand, a situation favorable to playwrights. Because Shakespeare and his contemporaries considered their plays popular entertainment rather than literary works, they did not initially seek to publish them. It was not until 1616, when Ben Jonson collected and published all of his own dramas, that plays began to gain the status of literature. Shakespeare's plays were not collected and published until several years after his death.

Playwrights had an incentive to be prolific. Once a company had paid the dramatist for a play, it belonged to the company and the author received no further income from it. A writer who depended entirely on plays for a living had to sell four or five a year. Shakespeare seems to have written about two a year, but he was also an actor and a major shareholder in his company (that is, he was a part owner of the company's assets and was involved in running the company) and after 1599 was a part owner of the Globe Theatre, in which the company performed. Thus, he was involved in almost every aspect of the theatre and became wealthier than most of his fellow dramatists.

In addition to a steady supply of new plays, a company needed a performance space. Despite the legal status that acting companies achieved in England through the patronage of nobles and the licenses issued by the crown, the London city council (composed of guild members who opposed theatre) sought to forbid performances within the city. Consequently, when permanent theatres were built, they were erected outside the city limits. Between 1567 and 1625 more than a dozen playhouses were built. Although the English public theatres varied in details, all had similar features that drew on medieval conventions but transformed them.

Let us look at the Globe, the theatre used by Shakespeare's company after 1599 and of which Shakespeare was part owner. Basically round with an exterior diameter of approximately ninety-nine feet, the Globe had three levels of roofed galleries, each about twelve feet six inches deep. These galleries enclosed an unroofed open space (the yard) approximately seventy-four feet in diameter. The stage extended to the middle

of the yard. Approximately forty-one feet three inches wide and twenty-four feet nine inches deep and raised five to six feet above the yard, the stage was viewed from three sides by spectators sitting in the galleries or standing in the yard. The stage was sheltered by a roof ("the heavens" or "the shadow") supported by two posts near the front of the stage platform.

At the back of the stage platform was the "tiring house," a multilevel facade. On the stage level, at least two large doors permitted exits and entrances and served as openings through which stage properties could be moved on and off the stage. These doors were very important because changes of locale were often indicated by the exit of characters through one door, followed by the entrance of different characters through another door. Usually, the doors remained unlocalized,

The Swan Theatre, London, 1596. This is the only surviving drawing of an English public theatre during Shakespeare's lifetime. It shows three levels of seating in galleries, a stage jutting to the middle of an unroofed yard, a roof canopy over part of the stage, and two doors at the rear of the stage (but no "discovery space" between the doors).

Bapst, Essai sur l'Histoire du Théâtre, 1893

but at times they were used to represent houses, city gates, castles, or other places (what they represented, if important, was indicated in the dialogue). There may have been a larger space between the doors that could be used to make "discoveries" (reveal objects or persons hidden until the crucial moment), common occurrences in the plays of Shakespeare and other dramatists of the time. Some believe the stage doors were used for this purpose, but others argue that there was something like a small inner stage that could be concealed or revealed by a curtain. There is debate over the exact layout of the second and third levels of the "tiring house." These levels included an acting space used to represent balconies (as in *Romeo and Juliet*), windows, battlements, or other high places. They also included the "Lords' Rooms," the most expensive seats, and the musician's gallery, which may have been on the second or third level.

Overall, then, this stage was an adaptation of medieval conventions. The facade served the function of mansions in the medieval stage, while the stage platform served as *platea*. Stage properties, such as tables, thrones, tents, beds, altars, and scaffolds, were sometimes brought onto the stage, usually to meet the demands of the action rather than to localize a scene. This stage also had some things in common with those of Greece and Rome. The background for all scenes was the formalized facade, and the specific location of a scene was established primarily through dialogue. When place was important, the characters named or described it; this convention is called "spoken decor." This Elizabethan structure and the conventions governing its use greatly facilitated staging because one scene could flow into another without a pause for changing scenery. The playwright had almost unlimited freedom in handling time and place.

A performance at Shakespeare's Globe Theatre in London. This theatre attempts to duplicate as much as possible both the theatre building/stage and the performance conditions used in Shakespeare's time.

Andrea Pistolesi/The Image Bank/Getty Images

Society, Art & Culture

THE NEW GLOBE THEATRE

In 1997, a reconstructed Globe Theatre opened in London at a site only two hundred yards from the place where the original structure had stood. The theatre is a twenty-sided polygon, one hundred feet in diameter, with whitewashed, half-timber walls and a thatched roof. The stage is raised five feet above ground level; two pillars, painted to look like marble, support the "heavens" decorated with figures of the zodiac. At stage level, the background facade has a large door at either side and a still larger opening at the center. On the second level, there is a large open space that may be used by actors, musicians, or (sometimes) spectators. Plays are staged without scenery, microphones, or spotlights (although floodlights are used to simulate daylight during evening performances). In addition to Shakespeare's plays, others from the same time period are presented. The theatre holds about fifteen hundred people: five hundred standing in the roofless yard and one thousand sitting on benches in the three levels of balconies.

Actors performing in the new Globe have remarked on the amount of audience participation the setting (in combination with plays) inspires. As one actor stated, "I have never performed in any play where the audience became so vocally and physically involved." Another said, "If the audience wasn't saying, 'Oh come on, give her a kiss,' they were booing or hissing at the sexual innuendos." Sir Peter Hall, former director of the Royal Shakespeare Company and the Royal National Theatre, has said about performances at the new Globe: "The essence of Shakespeare's drama is live interaction with a packed audience in a very small space in daylight, challenged to use their imaginations. There's nowhere else in Britain where that's happening."

The conventions that governed costuming and lighting also resembled those of the medieval theatre. Most characters, regardless of the historical era of the action, were clothed in contemporary Elizabethan garments appropriate to their rank, age, and profession. Other kinds of costumes were used sparingly: Greek and Roman characters were often identified by drapery superimposed on Elizabethan dress; ghosts, witches, fairies, and allegorical figures were dressed in fanciful garments corresponding to accepted ideas of the appearance of such creatures; sometimes racial or national stereotypes (Jews, Moors, Turks) were indicated by dress. Costumes and banners accounted for much of the color and pageantry of Elizabethan theatre because there were many processions, battles, and celebrations. Maintaining an adequate wardrobe was one of a company's greatest expenses.

Lighting was not a major problem because performances took place in unroofed structures during daylight hours. Darkness was indicated either in dialogue or by torches, lanterns, or candles carried by characters.

Most important was the acting company itself. It was made up of about twenty-five persons, of whom about half were shareholders (part owners of the company's assets). The shareholders made all of the important decisions, played most of the major roles, and shared any profit. A number of hired men were paid weekly wages as actors, prompters, musicians, stagehands, or wardrobe-keepers. There were also four to six apprentices, boys who played female roles. All members of the company were male. (There were no English actresses until 1661.) Because the plays often included a large number of characters, there was much double casting, and because a company usually performed a different play each day, each actor was responsible for a large number of roles. Although the overall performance style was probably not realistic in the modern sense, it was considerably closer to everyday behavior and appearance than that of a Greek performance. For example, Elizabethan actors did not wear masks (except as disguises), there was no chorus, and all lines were spoken without the musical accompaniment often found in the classical theatre.

The conventions that most removed the performances from realism were the verse in which much of the dialogue was written, the use of males to play female roles, and the formalized background.

Elizabethan theatre included a considerable musical element. Trumpets sounded flourishes to mark the entrances of kings, to call attention to important announcements, and to serve as signals in battles. Music accompanied songs and dances in plays; often performances concluded with a jig (a short, lively music-and-dance piece).

Elizabethan acting companies learned quickly how to make the theatre fully professional and sufficiently attractive and remunerative to support a large number of persons. The other important ingredient was the paying audience, among whom backgrounds and tastes varied considerably. The plays usually included something for everyone. Shakespeare's plays have plots as complex as a modern soap opera and often have as much violence as a television police series, but they also use poetic language and other devices that direct attention to the significance of events and provide insights into human behavior so profound that the plays have retained their appeal.

A small general-admission fee permitted one to stand in the yard. Those who wished to sit had to pay a larger fee for admission to the galleries, while for a third penny one could get a cushioned seat in a box. A limited number of seats in the "Lords' Rooms" cost six pennies, and entrance fees might be increased for new plays. The Globe probably held about three thousand persons, although seldom did that many attend. The configuration of the theatre (with the stage jutting to the middle of the yard) meant that no one was very far

The Art Archive/Alamy

Sketch (supposedly made in 1595) showing characters from Shakespeare's *Titus Andronicus*. Notice the variety of costumes. The male character standing at center wears drapery suggesting Roman times; the character at extreme right also has some features suggesting the classical era. The others wear Elizabethan costume. Some scholars consider this drawing a forgery.

Society, Art & Culture

ATTITUDES TOWARD WOMEN ON STAGE

Shakespeare wrote his female roles for boy actors. Although we are inclined to think the playgoer of Shakespeare's day must have regretted not seeing female roles played by actresses, the English not only considered it immoral for women to appear on a public stage, but some may have believed that boys played female roles more effectively than women could. Thomas Coryat, an Englishman who witnessed some theatrical performances in Venice in 1608, recorded in *Coryat's Crudities* his wonder both at seeing actresses and at their skill: "I saw women act, a thing that I never saw before,… and they performed it with as good a grace, action, gesture, and whatsoever convenient for a Player, as ever I saw any masculine Actor."

Although women were not allowed to act in public, women of the court sometimes appeared in nonspeaking roles in the lavish Stuart Court Masques and performed in speaking roles in private plays put on at court. England's Puritans took a dim view of such behavior. In 1633 William Prynne—a Puritan lawyer—sent to press a thousand-page work, *Histriomastix*, in which he basically denounced all actresses as whores. Queen Henrietta Maria, wife of Charles I, had performed in court plays. She was outraged at being labeled, through association, a whore. Prynne was indicted and convicted of seditious libel; he was disbarred from ever practicing law again, fined £5,000, sentenced to life imprisonment, and had both his ears cut off.

After Charles II was restored to the throne, following the English Civil War, women were finally allowed to perform publicly on the English stage. But many people still considered actresses to be little more than glorified prostitutes. Restoration actresses Moll Davies and Nell Gwynne, who were each at one time mistresses of Charles II, did little to dispel this notion. Moreover, male audience members were even more astonished by the ability of actresses to play female characters pretending to be men. Samuel Pepys's diary records his experience seeing Nell Gwynne impersonating a man: "… then most and best of all when she comes in like a young gallant; and hath the motions and carriage of a spark the most that ever I saw any man have. It makes me, I confess, admire her."

from the stage. There were no intermissions, and wine, beer, ale, nuts, and playing cards were sold in the theatres by vendors who circulated during performances. The atmosphere must have been somewhat like that of a modern sports event. Keeping the audience quiet and attentive depended on the power of the play and the skill of the performers.

Let us look at *Hamlet* (1600–1601), one of the thirty-eight plays by Shakespeare that have come down to us. It is representative of Elizabethan drama in its story, structure, and conventions, but it is superior to most plays of its time.

HAMLET

Like *Oedipus Rex*, *Hamlet*, one of the world's great tragedies, concerns a man charged with the duty of punishing the murderer of a king. But Shakespeare uses a broader canvas than Sophocles and includes within his drama more facets of the story, more characters, and a wider sweep of time and place.

Shakespeare organizes his action with great skill. The opening scene, in which the Ghost of Hamlet's father appears at midnight on the castle ramparts, quickly captures attention and establishes a mood of mystery as well as expectation

Twelfth Night is given a spectacular production at the McCarter Theatre (New Brunswick, N.J.). Olivia falls in love with Viola while Viola is disguised as a man. In Shakespeare's theatre, both Olivia and Viola would have been played by male actors.

T. Charles Erickson

of revelations to come. The remainder of Act I introduces the main characters and establishes the dramatic situation—that Hamlet's father, the former king, has been murdered by his brother Claudius, the present king and new husband to Hamlet's mother, but that no one, other than the Ghost, Claudius, and Hamlet, knows this. The Ghost's revelation of the murder to Hamlet coupled with the Ghost's demand that Hamlet revenge his murder (at the hands of Claudius) is the inciting incident that sets the central action of the play in motion. Hamlet, though he wishes to believe the Ghost's charge,

cannot be certain that the Ghost has not been sent by the Devil to tempt him into a deed that will damn his soul. Therefore, he seeks confirmation of the Ghost's accusations. He is so torn that in Act II others question whether he has lost his sanity, and he is so disillusioned by his mother's behavior that he rejects Ophelia, the woman he loves. Hamlet's search for confirmation of the Ghost's charge reaches its climax in Act III, Scene 2, when Claudius's response to a play, whose action parallels the murder of Hamlet's father, establishes his guilt. But this scene also reveals to Claudius that Hamlet is aware of the murder; consequently, Hamlet—who until this point has been the pursuer—now becomes the pursued. The remainder of the play shows Claudius plotting to have Hamlet killed in ways that will not draw suspicion on himself. Hamlet kills Polonius, thinking it is Claudius eavesdropping on him and his mother; Claudius uses this as an excuse to send Hamlet to England, accompanied by Hamlet's supposed friends Rosencrantz and Guildenstern, with a letter commanding the ruler there to kill Hamlet. But Hamlet escapes and returns to Denmark just in time for Ophelia's funeral.

Shakespeare skillfully interweaves this main plot with the subplot concerning Polonius and his family. The two strands of action are related through Hamlet's love for Polonius's daughter, Ophelia, Polonius's relation to the king as his principal advisor, and Laertes's wish to revenge his father's death after Hamlet kills Polonius and after Ophelia goes mad. The final scene, during which Claudius's plan to have Hamlet killed by Laertes (in a fencing match for which Laertes uses a poisoned foil) ends not only in Hamlet's death but also in that of Gertrude, Laertes, and Claudius, thereby resolving both the main plot and the subplot.

All of the main characters in *Hamlet* are drawn from the nobility or aristocracy. Shakespeare does not tell us the age of his characters or reveal much about their physical appearance. Nevertheless, age and contrast are important. The young and innocent—Hamlet, Ophelia, and Laertes—suffer most.

Many people consider *Hamlet* to be among the most demanding roles ever written for a tragic actor, in part because the actor must project one set of attitudes and responses to the characters and another to the audience. So carefully balanced are the demands that an ongoing debate has developed over questions of interpretation:

- Does Hamlet feign madness in Acts II and III or, for a time, is he actually insane?

- What are Hamlet's feelings toward his mother?

- Why does Hamlet delay so long in avenging his father's murder?

These questions have been answered differently in particular productions of the play by various actors who have played Hamlet. Perhaps one of the hallmarks of the role is its ability to sustain different interpretations and remain

The Royal Shakespeare Company's production of *Hamlet*, featuring Patrick Stewart as Claudius and David Tennant as Hamlet; directed by current RSC Artistic Director, Gregory Doran.

Robbie Jack/Corbis

compelling and cohesive. The actor playing this role is faced with enacting a range of complex emotional responses, delivering ambiguous speeches and actions, and maintaining enormous energy through the final scene wherein additional physical demands (fencing and fighting) are required.

Like Hamlet, Ophelia is sensitive. She has little knowledge of the world and is easily led by her father, Polonius. Hamlet's seeming rejection of her and his killing of her father come as such shocks that she becomes truly mad and apparently commits suicide. Her brother, Laertes, who is near Hamlet in age, rushes into action instead of hesitating when faced with a situation comparable to that with which Hamlet must deal. Claudius, playing on Laertes's impulsiveness, is able to talk him into a deception (the use of the poisoned foil) contrary to his nature—which he repents, although too late. One may conclude that, whereas Claudius, Gertrude, and Polonius deserve their fates, the young people are victims of their elders' weaknesses.

Claudius is doubtless suave and charming; otherwise, it would be difficult to understand how he is able to deceive so many people. He has won the support of the court, he has seduced Gertrude (who apparently is unaware that he has murdered her husband), and he easily takes in Laertes. Not until the final scene do most of the characters perceive Claudius's villainy. Claudius's surface respectability also provides an explanation for Hamlet's hesitation to act hastily or openly; Hamlet probably would not have been believed had he accused Claudius of murder (his knowledge of the murder depends on the Ghost whose accusations only Hamlet has heard).

Hamlet's mother, Gertrude, is still relatively young; she has married Claudius hastily following her husband's death. Polonius is a pompous, self-important, verbose politician who gives unsolicited advice and reaches unwarranted conclusions. He is often played as a buffoon, but there is danger in exaggerating his ridiculousness because this diminishes the obstacles Hamlet must overcome.

Shakespeare's dramatic poetry is generally recognized as the finest in the English language. The usual medium is blank verse, which retains much of the flexibility of ordinary speech while elevating and formalizing it. But many passages are in prose, especially those involving such lower-class characters as the gravediggers and the actors; because these passages often play on words or use slang, the prose is often more difficult to comprehend than the poetry.

Probably the most important element in Shakespeare's dialogue is figurative language. The principal purpose of a figure of speech in dramatic poetry is to set up either direct or indirect comparisons. Shakespeare's superiority over other writers of dramatic poetry lies in his use of comparisons that enlarge the significance without distracting attention from the dramatic situation. His poetic devices partially fulfill the same function as the visual representation of Heaven and Hell on the medieval stage: They relate human actions to the divine and demonic forces of the universe and treat human affairs as significant to all creation.

Shakespeare's language makes special demands on the actor. Figures of speech are likely to seem contrived and bombastic if the actor does not appear to be experiencing feelings strong enough to call forth such language spontaneously. Shakespeare's plays may be damaged in performance if actors do not rise to the emotional demands of the poetry. Therefore, the very richness of expression can be a stumbling block for both performer and reader.

The action of *Hamlet* occurs in many places, but Shakespeare envisioned them all in terms of stage properties, costumes, and the movement of the actors. Scenery was not important, but change of place was. The main stage, discovery space, and upper stage facilitated the flow of one scene into the next. The relatively bare stage was constantly varied by such scenes as the sentry patrols and the appearance of the Ghost in the opening scenes, the elaborate procession and court ceremony in Act I, the play-within-the-play in Act III, the burial of Ophelia and the

This scene from *Hamlet*, directed by Ingmar Bergman, shows the fencing match between Hamlet and Laertes in Act V. Performed at the Brooklyn Academy of Music.

Courtesy of Martha Swope

fight between Hamlet and Laertes in her open grave (a trapdoor in the stage floor) in Act V, and the fencing match that leaves the stage littered with corpses.

Costumes added to the visual effect. Though most of the characters were probably dressed in the garments of Shakespeare's own time, Hamlet was set off from the others by his black mourning clothes amid the bright colors the others wore, the period of mourning for the dead king having been replaced by rejoicing at the marriage of Claudius and Gertrude.

Sounds also added to the overall effect. They include trumpet flourishes, cannons, and, in Act IV, the offstage crowd. But most important was the sound of the actors' voices speaking Shakespeare's poetry.

Hamlet is rich in implications, the most important of which concerns the shock of betrayal by those one has most trusted. The betrayals are pervasive—brother of brother, wife of husband, parent of child, friend of friend. After an apparently uneventful youth, Hamlet is suddenly faced with a series of shocking revelations: his father has been murdered by his uncle; his mother has been unfaithful to his father; his mother has accepted his uncle's usurpation of the throne that should have been Hamlet's; and his supposed friends (Rosencrantz and Guildenstern) have become his uncle's spies. It is not surprising that these discoveries make Hamlet suspicious of almost everyone, even of Ophelia, the woman he loves. Considering the nature of the betrayals and the rapidity with which they come, it also is not surprising that both Hamlet and others wonder if he has gone mad. A second theme is the opposing demands made on Hamlet—to avenge his father's death (which seemingly requires him to murder his uncle) and to adhere to Christian teaching (under which the murder of his uncle would be a deadly sin). A third theme concerns the way one crime sets off a chain of evil as the wrongdoer tries to conceal the crime. Everything in *Hamlet* can be traced to Claudius's murder of his brother and the series of deceptions he devises to hide it. It is this deed that leads to the total destruction of two families.

Horatio (Scott Plate) holds the dying Hamlet (Steve Tague) in the Great Lakes Theater Festival's production of Shakespeare's *Hamlet* at the Ohio Theatre, Playhouse Square Center in Cleveland, Ohio.

Roger Mastroianni, Courtesy Great Lakes Theatre Festival

Another set of implications concerns the nature of kingship and the need to rule oneself before attempting to rule others. This motif is seen especially in the conduct of Claudius and is suggested through the contrasts drawn between Claudius and his dead brother and between Hamlet and Fortinbras (the forceful, uncomplicated prince who is left to return order to the state). These are some implications of the dramatic action, but many others could be suggested because a play as rich as *Hamlet* cannot be wholly exhausted. Perhaps for that reason, *Hamlet* has transcended its time and place and has appealed to all succeeding generations. It is one of the few plays that has never been out of the active performance repertory.

The Theatre Experience in Renaissance Italy

Another of the theatre's great eras occurred in Italy during the Renaissance. It represents a different kind of experience using conventions that would eventually displace those of Shakespeare's theatre and dominate Western theatrical practices until the nineteenth century. The reawakened interest in Greek and Roman thought, literature, and art, which began in the fourteenth century, had by the late fifteenth century led to occasional performances of Roman comedies at the courts of the many small states into which Italy was then divided. In the early sixteenth century, plays imitating classical forms began to be written in Italian. To present such plays was considered a mark of a ruler's cultural enlightenment, and theatrical entertainments soon became standard features of court festivals given to celebrate betrothals, weddings, births of royal children, visits of emissaries from other states, and similar events. Thus, theatre played a role somewhat like that in the classical and medieval periods; the difference was that the occasions were secular and were intended to reflect glory on the ruler. The subject matter of plays and the themes developed in the many events of a festival were usually drawn from classical mythology.

In mounting these festivals, the Italians drew on classical sources, especially *De Architectura* by Vitruvius (a Roman architect of the first century B.C.), who described how a theatre is laid out, as well as the settings appropriate to three kinds of plays: tragedy, comedy, and pastoral. Italian artists sought to re-create what they found in Vitruvius's treatise, but in doing so they transformed it radically, thereby creating the theatre structure and scenic practices that would dominate the European theatre into the twentieth century.

Because they had no permanent theatres, the Italians at first set up temporary performance spaces, usually in large halls of state (comparable in size and shape to the ballrooms of modern hotels). In 1545, Sebastiano Serlio published *Architettura*, in which he showed how to create a performance space within an existing room. He included drawings showing his version of Vitruvius's tragic, comic, and pastoral settings (see illustrations). These drawings fuse classical theatre architecture with Renaissance perspective painting.

The principles of perspective drawing had been developed during the fifteenth century. It is difficult today to appreciate the Renaissance excitement over perspective, which was sometimes viewed almost as a form of magic, because with it the artist seemed to create space and distance on a two-dimensional surface. Given this enthusiasm, it is not surprising that by the sixteenth century perspective had been adapted to stage use.

The acceptance of perspective scenery is of profound importance because it signaled a movement away from the formal and architectural stage toward the representational and pictorial stage. The Greek, Roman, and Elizabethan stages all used a formalized architectural facade as the basic background for all plays; in these theatres, the facade could be modified by the addition of small elements, but no stage property or pictorial element could ever disguise the fixed facade. Any added elements merely suggested (rather than represented realistically) a scene's locale. The mansions of the medieval theatre lay somewhere between the formal and pictorial traditions. Still, no place was represented in its entirety, and the gaps between places were telescoped. With the coming of perspective, each place was represented in its entirety as seen from a fixed viewpoint. If more than one place was involved, they were shown sequentially, not simultaneously. During the seventeenth century, pictorial representation of place would become

Serlio, Architettura, 1545

In Serlio's design for the comic scene, one sees the squares on the raked stage, diminishing in size from front to back, that help create apparent depth, as does the downward slope of the upper portions of buildings.

Serlio, Architettura, 1545

In Serlio's design for the tragic scene, note that the buildings represent those associated with the ruling classes. This is unlike the comic scene where the buildings are shops and dwellings of the middle class.

the standard for stage scenery throughout Europe, remaining so into the twentieth century.

How to transform a two-dimensional drawing into a stage setting that occupies three-dimensional space was a problem that Renaissance artists had to solve. The solution eventually accepted everywhere was to break up the picture and paint the parts on one of three scenic elements: side wings, backdrops, and overhead borders. Everything painted on the wings, drops, and borders was drawn as seen from a fixed viewpoint located somewhere in the auditorium (originally the seat of the ruler). The floor of the stage raked upward toward the back, giving us our terms *upstage* and *downstage*, and the height of the side wings diminished as they receded from the audience; both of these features helped perspective achieve apparent depth within a restricted space. The goal was to create a complete and convincing picture.

A pictorialized setting demanded a frame because otherwise spectators would see around or over the setting, and the apparent scale would be negated. From this need came the *proscenium arch*, used to frame the stage opening (the "picture-frame stage"). Originally, the frame was a temporary structure like the scenery itself, but eventually the advantage of a permanent architectural frame was recognized. The oldest surviving theatre with a permanent proscenium arch is the Teatro Farnese, built in 1618 in Parma, Italy. The proscenium arch soon became a standard feature of theatres and remained so until recently; even today, the picture-frame stage is the most common type.

A setting that depicted a single place in its entirety created another problem: how to move from one locale to another. The eventual solution was to use two-dimensional *wings* set up parallel to the front of the stage and in a series from front to back. At each wing position, as many different flats were used (one immediately in back of another) as there were scenes to be depicted during the performance. To change from one set to the next, the visible wings were pulled offstage, revealing others that represented the next scene. The set was enclosed at the back by painted flats, which met at the center of the stage. Several back-scenes (or *shutters*) could be set up and shifted in the same way as the side wings. (Eventually, *drops* that could be lowered and raised replaced the back-scenes.) *Borders* (two-dimensional cloths, most often representing clouds or the sky) hung above each set of wings and enclosed the scene overhead. Until the nineteenth century, scene changes were usually made in full view of the audience. The front curtain was raised at the beginning of a performance and not lowered until the end. Thus, scene shifts were part of the overall visual experience.

The desire to shift scenery was inspired by the love of spectacle and special effects, which the Italians exploited primarily in *intermezzi* (interludes) between the acts of regular plays (which usually did not require any changes of place or special effects). *Intermezzi* were elaborate compliments that suggested parallels between some mythological figure and the person in whose honor the festival was being given; usually the mythic protagonist routed the forces of chaos through magical feats involving elaborate special effects. Music and dance were major features. More effort usually went into the staging of *intermezzi* than the plays they accompanied.

The appeals of *intermezzi* were eventually absorbed into opera, a new form that originated in the 1590s out of attempts to re-create the relationship between music and speech found in Greek tragedy. Opera soon became a popular form, combining drama, music, dance, spectacle, and special effects. Opera became the primary medium for popularizing perspective scenery and the picture-frame stage, both of which had developed in the rarefied atmosphere of the Italian courts, where performances were not open to the general public. In 1637, a public opera house in Venice made the pleasures of the court theatres available to the general Italian public. It was so successful that soon there were four public opera houses in Venice.

The Venetian opera houses were in many ways the prototypes of subsequent theatres, not only for opera but also for drama, because they

Act II, scene X: the courtyard of the King of Naxos (oil on canvas), Torelli, Giacomo (1608-78)/Pinoteca Civica di Fano, Fano, Italy/The Bridgeman Art Library

Setting by Giacomo Torelli for *Jealous Venus*, produced at an opera house in Venice in 1643.

not only incorporated the proscenium arch and perspective scenery but also divided and arranged auditoriums in the way that would remain typical until the late nineteenth century. The division of the auditorium into *box, pit,* and *gallery* reflected the class structure of Europe; it permitted each class to attend the theatre without having to mingle with another class. The auditorium was surrounded by two or more levels of boxes (which permitted well-to-do or snobbish spectators to be more or less private while in a crowded place); on the ground floor was the pit (today's orchestra), less expensive than the boxes and favored by those unconcerned about reputation; above the boxes was the gallery, the least desirable and cheapest seats, usually inhabited by working-class patrons. The popularity of opera, which burgeoned during the seventeenth century, spread throughout Europe, bringing with it the staging practices of Italy.

Commedia dell'Arte

Although much of the theatrical activity in Renaissance Italy was neither professional nor open to the public, one form—*commedia dell'arte*—was both. *Commedia dell'arte* (comedy of professional artists) and *commedia all'improvviso* (improvised comedy) are terms used to distinguish the plays performed by certain professional troupes from those performed by amateur actors at court (*commedia erudita*, or learned drama). No one knows precisely how or when *commedia dell'arte* came into being. Some trace it to the mimes and other entertainers of Roman times, whose traditions were supposedly continued thereafter by small wandering troupes. Others see the form as evolving out of improvisations based on the Roman comedies of Plautus and Terence. Still others trace it to medieval farce.

Practices & Styles

ITALIAN INTERMEZZI *AND ENGLISH MASQUES*

The English developed their own variation on the Italian *intermezzi*, "masques," which were first performed at the court of Henry VIII. They were most fully developed under the Stuart rulers James I and Charles I between 1605 and 1640. Masques, performed solely for court audiences, were similar in all important respects to Italian *intermezzi*, except that masques were independent productions, not being inserted between the acts of plays. Like the Italian *intermezzi*, Stuart masques took their subjects primarily from classical mythology or historical legend; the subjects were developed to draw parallels between some mythical or legendary character and the person who was being honored by the performance. Masques developed an idealized vision of monarchy and nobility because within the masques the action moved from disorder to order, usually with the ruler or a noble as the transforming agent. Thus, masques served not only as an entertainment but also as a justification of the political system.

These spectacular pieces, requiring enormous sums to mount, emphasized music, dance, costumes, scenery, and elaborate special effects. While actors and musicians performed the speaking and singing roles, the many dancing roles were filled by courtiers. Ben Jonson, a major playwright of the day, wrote the majority of the short English texts for the masques, which served primarily to establish a mythical framework. But the principal appeal of the pieces lay in the spectacle created by Inigo Jones, the court architect, who had studied in Italy, where he observed the staging of *intermezzi*. It is primarily through Jones's work that Italian scenic practices were brought to England, although they were confined to court productions until after 1660.

Whatever its origin, *commedia dell'arte* is first definitively mentioned in historical records in the 1560s. By 1600 companies were playing not only throughout Italy but also in France, Spain, and other European countries. Wherever they went, they easily found audiences among both the common people and the ruling classes.

The actor was the heart of *commedia dell'arte* and almost the only essential element. The *commedia* companies could play almost anywhere: in town squares or at court, indoors or out, on improvised stages or in permanent theatres. If elaborate scenery was available, they used it, but they could function as well against the background of a simple curtain (with slits for entrances and exits). Adaptability was one of their major assets.

The script was a *scenario* merely summarizing the situations, complications, and outcome. The actors improvised the dialogue and fleshed

out the action. Although the broad outlines of a script remained the same, the details differed at each performance, depending on the inspiration of the moment and the response of the audience. Many scenarios have survived. A few are tragic, melodramatic, or musical, but the greatest number are comic, revolving around love affairs, intrigues, disguises, and cross-purposes.

In Italian *commedia* troupes an actor played the same character (with its standard attributes and costume) regardless of the scenario in which that character appeared. Therefore, performers became very familiar with their characters. This facilitated improvisation, a distinguishing feature of *commedia*. Over the years, the actors must have developed sure-fire dialogue and stage business that they could call on as needed. Some pieces of comic business (*lazzi*) became sufficiently standardized to be indicated in the plot outlines as

Interior of the Theatre Royal, Turin (Italy) in the 1740s. Notice that the proscenium arch is so thick that it is able to contain a box for spectators on each of three levels. The male actors at left and center are wearing the *habit à la romaine*; the actress between them is dressed in the fashion of the eighteenth century. In the auditorium a vendor is selling fruit and drink, and a soldier is posted to keep order. The setting is by Giuseppe Bibiena, noted for his monumental painted scenery. Despite the setting's apparent realism, all of the details are painted on wings, drops, and borders.

Gianni Dagli Orti/The Art Archive/Alamy

lazzi of fear, sack *lazzi*, fight *lazzi*, and so on. When we read about *commedia dell'arte*, we can easily get the impression that the performers made everything up as they went along. However, improvisation occurred within a rehearsed framework. For the improvisation to be effective, the performers had to always keep in mind where each scene was headed and what had to be done to make the plot as a whole work. They had to know the outline of the action and, when they inserted *lazzi*, they had to make sure they did not let the pieces of comic business get so out of hand as to obscure the plot line. In addition, actors who played the fashionable young men and women were encouraged to keep notebooks in which to record appropriate sentiments from poetry and popular literature, and many lines and actions were probably repeated in various plays. Nevertheless, performances created the impression of spontaneity because no actor could be certain what the others would say or do, and each had to concentrate moment by moment on the unfolding action and respond appropriately.

The *stock characters*, *commedia*'s best-known feature, can be divided into three categories: lovers, masters, and servants. The lovers' roles were the most realistic. Young and handsome, they did not wear masks and were usually dressed in the latest fashions. Each company had at least one pair of lovers, and most had two. The lovers were often the children of those characters who fell into the category of masters, and their love affairs were typically opposed by their fathers and aided by their servants.

Three masters recurred most often: Pantalone, Dottore, and Capitano. Pantalone was an

Mary Evans Picture Library/Alamy

Photos 12/Alamy

Pantalone and Dottore, two of the "master" characters of *commedia dell'arte*.

elderly Venetian merchant, often the father of one or more of the young lovers or a would-be lover himself. His costume consisted of a tight-fitting red vest; red breeches and stockings; soft slippers; a black ankle-length coat; a soft, brim-less cap; a brown mask with a large hooked nose; and scraggly gray beard. Dottore, usually Pantalone's friend or rival, was a lawyer or doc-tor who loved to show off his spurious learning in speeches filled with Latin (often ludicrously incorrect). Despite his supposed wisdom, he was credulous and easily tricked. His dress was the academic cap and gown of the time. Originally the Capitano was one of the lovers, but eventu-ally he was transformed into a braggart and cow-ard who boasted of his prowess in love and war, only to be discredited in both. He usually wore a cape, sword, and feathered headdress, often

greatly exaggerated to indicate his braggadocio. He typically was an unwelcome suitor to one of the young women.

The most varied of the commedia types were the servants (the *zanni*—the origin of the Eng-lish word *zany*). Most companies included at least two, one clever and one stupid, but there might be as many as four. They figured prominently in the action; their machinations kept the plots mov-ing as they sought to help or thwart their masters. Most of the servants were male, but there might be one or more maids (*fantesca*) who served the young women. Typically young, coarsely witty, and ready for intrigue, the female servants carried on their own love affairs with the male servants while helping their mistresses. Occasionally, one was older and served as hostess of an inn or as the object of the older men's affections.

Of the *zanni*, Arlecchino (Harlequin) eventually became the most popular, although originally he was of minor importance. A mixture of cunning and stupidity and an accomplished acrobat and dancer, he was usually at the center of any intrigue. His costume, which began as a suit with irregularly placed multicolored patches, evolved into one with a diamond-shaped red, green, and blue pattern. He wore a rakish hat above a black mask and carried a wooden sword or slapstick (so called because it was slit down the middle so it would make a sharp sound when struck against someone; it is the source of our term *slapstick comedy*). The slapstick figured prominently in the many fights and beatings. Although each company had a Harlequin-like character, not every company used that name for the character. Name variations include Truffaldino and Trivellino.

Harlequin's most frequent companion was a cynically witty, libidinous, and sometimes cruel servant. His mask had a hooked nose and moustache, and his jacket and trousers were ornamented with green braid. He was variously called Brighella, Scapino, Mezzetino, and Flautino. Another character, Pulcinello, was always a Neapolitan, but his function in the scripts varied. Sometimes he was a servant, but he also might be the host of an inn or a merchant. He had an enormous hooked nose, a humped back, and wore a pointed cap. He was the ancestor of the English puppet character Punch. There were many variations, both in name and attributes, on these *zanni*, because each company developed its own version of these types.

A *commedia* troupe averaged ten to twelve members (seven or eight men and three or four women). Most companies were organized on the sharing plan, although some of the younger actors and assistants may have been salaried. Most troupes traveled frequently, but some were able to settle in one place for considerable periods of time. For example, Molière shared his theatre in Paris with a *commedia* troupe and alternated days of performance with it. (Molière, like many other dramatists of his era, learned much of his comic technique from *commedia*,

ARLECHINO
(1671)

Arlecchino (Harlequin), one of the *zanni* characters of *commedia dell'arte*. Note the slapstick he carries to create the sound effects of comic stage violence.

and a number of his plays incorporate *commedia* characters and situations.)

Commedia was most vigorous and popular between 1575 and 1650, but it continued into the last half of the eighteenth century. Its last stronghold was Venice, where two playwrights, seeking to reform and preserve it, contributed to its destruction. Carlo Goldoni (1707–1793), Italy's most famous comic dramatist, began writing scenarios for *commedia* companies in Venice around 1734. Because he believed the situations in *commedia* had become hackneyed and vulgar, he refined and sentimentalized the characters and situations. He also believed the usual level of improvisation was inadequate, and he was able to persuade companies to accept scripts with most of the dialogue written out. In addition, he campaigned for the abandonment of masks because he felt they handicapped the actors by hiding facial expressions. Goldoni wrote a number of plays (many of them still performed) using *commedia* characters. Had all of the changes he championed been implemented, they would have done away with most of the basic conventions of *commedia*. He was bitterly opposed by another dramatist, Carlo Gozzi (1720–1806), who emphasized fairy-tale stories and improvisation in his scripts. For a time their battle aroused new interest in *commedia*, but by about 1775 this theatrical mode had largely faded. Its death may have been due to over-familiarity after two hundred years or because its rather broad, often coarse, farcical humor had lost its appeal in the more refined atmosphere of the eighteenth century. *Commedia* would resurface during the second half of the twentieth century.

Although numerous scenarios have survived from the period when *commedia* was at its peak, they are too bare in outline to convey the flavor of a *commedia* performance. Goldoni's *The Servant of Two Masters* (1743), though it comes from the last days of *commedia* and lacks most of the improvisational element, probably brings us as near to the *commedia* experience as we can come today.

THE SERVANT OF TWO MASTERS

Goldoni wrote *The Servant of Two Masters* for a Venetian *commedia dell'arte* troupe that permitted him to write out the dialogue. Although this written text eliminated much of the improvisational element, it did not do away with it altogether because the actors were allowed to improvise comic business, and the lead actor playing Truffaldino was initially allowed to improvise his lines. When the script was published in 1753, all the dialogue was scripted. The script incorporates other of Goldoni's reforms, including taking away the more exaggerated qualities of certain characters. For example, Goldoni's Pantalone has none of the miserly traits typical of the character in earlier scenarios, and Brighella has been deprived of his libidinous and cruel traits. In fact, both have become solid citizens with virtually no ridiculous aspects. As in Goldoni's non-*commedia* scripts, in *The Servant of Two Masters* middle-class characters are treated with respect, and the women are far more sensible than the men. Goldoni has also avoided the coarse, often smutty humor and sexual innuendo of earlier *commedia*.

Nevertheless, the cast of characters (and the basic traits of each) clearly belongs to commedia. There are two pairs of lovers (Clarice and Silvio, Beatrice and Florindo), two masters (Pantalone and Dottore), and three servant types (Truffaldino, Brighella, and Smeraldina), although Brighella has been elevated to innkeeper. Silvio has also been given some traits (his exaggerated threats and his easy defeat in the fight with Beatrice) that relate him to the Capitano of other scripts. There are four minor roles (two porters and two waiters), but two actors could easily play the four roles. Thus, the company size is probably eleven or twelve—typical for a *commedia* troupe.

The plot of *The Servant of Two Masters* relies on disguise, coincidence, misunderstanding, and withheld information. When the play opens, Pantalone, believing that his daughter Clarice's fiancé, Federigo Rasponi, is dead, agrees to marry her to Silvio, son of Dottore. Just as this agreement is concluded, Federigo arrives. (It is actually Federigo's sister Beatrice, who has taken on his identity so she may follow her own fiancé Florindo, who supposedly has killed Federigo in a duel and has fled to Venice from Turin.) Both Silvio and Federigo/Beatrice state their intention to hold Pantalone to his agreement.

Geraint Lewis/Alamy Limited

Richard Bean's *One Man, Two Guvnors* has been a popular, modern adaptation of Goldoni's *The Servant of Two Masters*.

Beatrice and Truffaldino, the servant she has hired along the way, take up residence in the inn run by Brighella. Florindo is also staying there and, needing a servant, he, too, hires Truffaldino, who wants the financial profit as well as the challenge of serving two masters without either knowing about the other. The remainder of the play is taken up with Truffaldino's attempts not to be found out. Eventually the truth is revealed, Beatrice and Florindo are reunited, as are Silvio and Clarice, and Truffaldino and Smeraldina (Clarice's maidservant).

Goldoni is a master of plot development. Everything is neatly set up in the opening scene, and each complication is carefully prepared for and clarified for the audience, even as the play's characters become more confused. Goldoni further demonstrates his skill by making many complications grow out of the characters: Pantalone's haste in arranging another marriage for Clarice is the source of one chain of complications; another grows out of Beatrice's decision to adopt a disguise that serves only to delay her search for Florindo; and others come from Silvio's and Dottore's habit of leaping to conclusions. Coincidence is an equally important ingredient: Beatrice arrives at Pantalone's just as the betrothal is concluded; Beatrice and Florindo take up residence at the same inn and employ the same servant; Truffaldino, while unpacking and repacking his masters' trunks, switches items that lead them to discover each other.

The most important character is Truffaldino, who has all of the characteristics of Arlecchino—

being both clever and stupid, wearing a black mask and parti-colored costume, and carrying a slapstick. Though the storyline concerns the lovers, it is Truffaldino's stupidity that creates many of the difficulties, just as it is his cleverness that often resolves them. He is the principal source of humor and is onstage more than any other character. He also has the greatest number of opportunities to improvise *lazzi*: trying to reseal letters with chewed bread but always swallowing it because he is so hungry; unpacking and mixing up the contents of his two masters' trunks; and, above all, simultaneously serving dinner to two masters (who are in two separate rooms and unaware of each other's presence). Opportunities to improvise comic business are also provided other characters, including an argument between Pantalone and Dottore (a traditional feature of *commedia*); a sword fight between Beatrice and the disappointed lover, Silvio (in which Beatrice wins); and the beating of Truffaldino by both Beatrice and Florindo over his mix-ups.

Goldoni wrote for a company that performed in a public theatre of the kind then typical: box, pit, and gallery arrangement of the auditorium, and picture-frame stage with wing-and-drop, perspective scenery. *The Servant of Two Masters* is divided into three acts with a total of ten scenes, although it requires only five settings: a room in Pantalone's house, the courtyard of Pantalone's house, the street in front of Brighella's inn, a room in Brighella's inn, and a street. None of these has great specificity. No furniture is mentioned for Pantalone's house (and probably none was present); a sign identifying it and an entrance to Brighella's inn are the only requirements of that set; four doors are the only practical features of the room in the inn; and no details are noted for either the courtyard or the street. Except for the inn's sign, all of the scenic requirements could have been met from the stock scenery of any theatre of the period. Lighting would have depended on candles or oil lamps.

The Servant of Two Masters does not achieve a high level of characterization or social

Richard Feldman

Truffaldino hangs from a yardarm bundled with ropes to look like a giant fork wrapped in spaghetti in the American Repertory Theatre's production of *The Servant of Two Masters*. Directed by Andrei Belgrader; scene design by Anita Stewart; costume design by Catherine Zuber; lighting by Natasha Katz.

commentary, but Goldoni was not seeking profundity. He was concerned with providing entertainment for a popular audience by reworking the conventions of a long-familiar form. That he achieved his goal is indicated by the popularity of his play, which has continued to the present day. In addition to productions of Goldoni's script, Richard Bean created an English adaptation called *One Man, Two Guvnors* (2011), with the action moved to Brighton, England, in 1963. That play has enjoyed critical and commercial success in London and New York.

PROFESSIONAL THEATRE IN SPAIN

Until the 1490s, what we now consider Spain was divided into Christian territory in the north and Moorish territory in the south. By 1500, Spain was united under the rule of Ferdinand and Isabella, who conquered the southern territories. The new rulers instituted The Inquisition to ensure religious purity in Spain. Although religious and political controversies led to a ban on religious drama across Europe in the mid-sixteenth century, in Spain the suppression of potential disputes allowed religious drama to flourish in a particular form of plays called *auto sacramentales*.

The *auto sacramentales*, or *autos*, were associated with the Corpus Christi festival and combined characteristics of morality and cycle plays. Characters included human, biblical, supernatural, and allegorical figures (Fortune, Grief, Beauty, Sin, etc.), who at times intermingled in stories that could be drawn from any source as long as they supported the value of the sacraments and church doctrine. The *autos* were performed on pageant wagons (*carros*) sometime after a procession that opened the celebration of the Corpus Christi festival. As part of the procession, the wagons were pulled through the city by bulls with gilded horns. By the mid-1630s these wagons were quite large: about twenty feet long, ten feet wide, and holding a two-story structure that was often rigged to provide special effects required by the plays.

The *autos* were initially produced by trade guilds in association with the church and civic authorities, but by the late 1500s financing for the *autos* had been assumed by city councils. The city councils then hired professional theatre troupes to stage and perform the *autos*, providing the troupe with the wagons and other necessities for the performance except costumes and hand properties.

The earliest historical records documenting professional troupes in Spain link them to the performance of religious drama and the *autos*. In addition to performing the *autos*, these troupes were allowed to perform secular works. Therefore, unlike the rest of Europe, the emergence of professional theatre in Spain is linked directly to its religious drama.

The French Background

Civil wars, which grew out of religious controversy, interrupted the development of the French theatre during the sixteenth and seventeenth centuries. Stability did not return until the 1620s, by which time Cardinal Richelieu, Louis XIII's prime minister, having secured absolute power for the king, set out to make France the cultural center of Europe. Up to that time, France's theatre had remained under medieval influence. Although religious plays were outlawed in Paris in 1548, the theatre had continued to use simultaneous settings for its plays, most of which required numerous locales. (See the illustration on page 125 for a typical stage setting around 1635.)

Richelieu believed that the French stage needed drastic reform and looked to Italy for guidance. He advocated adoption of the proscenium stage and perspective scenery and a drama that would adhere to theoretical principles articulated in Italy during the sixteenth century. These principles make up what came to be called the neoclassical ideal:

- Genres should be firmly restricted to tragedy and comedy, which should not be mixed.

- Tragedy should treat royalty and nobles; comedy should treat middle and lower classes.

- Characters should behave in a manner appropriate to their social status, gender, and ethnicity (*decorum*).

- All plays should be written in five acts.

- All plays should observe the unities of time (take place within twenty-four hours), place (one location), and action (only one plot).

- All plays should uphold "poetic justice" (punish the wicked and reward the good).

There were other demands, but these were the most important. Neoclassicists believed that the purpose of all drama is to teach and to please.

Although Richelieu and others favored them, these rules were not widely known or accepted in France until 1636, when *The Cid* by Pierre Corneille (1606–1684) became the most popular play yet written in France. Despite its popularity, the play was viciously attacked because it failed to adhere to some of the neoclassical rules. To settle this controversy, Richelieu asked the recently formed French Academy (whose membership was restricted to the forty most eminent literary figures of the day) to deliver a verdict on the play. The Academy praised the play for many of its qualities but faulted its deviations from neoclassical rules. For example, although the play observed the unity of time, too many events (including an entire war) had occurred within a twenty-four-hour period. The play failed to observe decorum because the aristocratic heroine agreed to marry the man who had killed her father a few hours earlier. The French Academy's ruling on *Le Cid* is a watershed event in French drama, because it effectively legitimized the neoclassical view. After 1640, Corneille adopted the new mode, which was later perfected by Jean Racine (1639–1699), especially in his *Phaedra* (1677). The tragedies of Corneille and Racine were to set the standard for serious playwriting throughout Europe until the nineteenth century. On the European continent, these French tragedies were, until around 1800, thought superior to those of Shakespeare.

The transition to the new ideal also required a new theatre structure. To set an example, Richelieu had the first theatre in France with a proscenium arch erected in his own palace in 1641. By 1650, all of the Parisian public and court theatres had been transformed into picture-frame stages of the Italian type. Thus, by the mid-seventeenth century, the Italian order had replaced the medieval heritage.

Design by Laurent Mahelot for *La Prise de Marsilly*. Notice that several locales are represented simultaneously.

Bibliothèque nationale de France

Molière and Seventeenth-Century French Theatre Practice

Just as Corneille and Racine set the standard for tragedy, Molière (1622–1673) set the standard for comedy. Molière began his career as an actor in 1643. Meeting little success in Paris, his company toured the provinces for many years, often competing with *commedia* companies, from which he learned much about playwriting and how to please an audience. Upon returning to Paris, his company performed in the theatre that Richelieu had built and that had become the property of the crown upon the cardinal's death. Usually referred to as the Palais Royal, this theatre had a picture-frame stage and a box, pit, and gallery auditorium. Thus, Molière performed in a theatre owned by the king but open to the general public. He also shared this theatre (alternating playing days) with a *commedia* company.

Despite the differences between the Elizabethan and French stages, their acting companies had many features in common. French companies, like the English, were organized on the sharing plan. They usually included ten to fifteen sharing members, but others were hired as actors, musicians, stage assistants, and so on. After the costs of production were deducted from the receipts, the remainder was divided among the shareholders. A major difference between the French and English companies was that French companies included women, who had equal rights with the men and received comparable pay. Additionally, all of the leading companies in Paris (usually two or three) received a subsidy from the crown, but the sum was not sufficient to guarantee them against loss.

Plays were selected by a vote of the shareholders after hearing a reading of the play. Until the 1650s, authors were paid a fixed sum; subsequently the method of payment was to give the author a percentage of the receipts for the initial run, after which the play belonged to the company. An acting company usually had in its active repertory fifty or more plays, which were alternated in order to keep the audience coming back.

The first proscenium-arch theatre in France, built by Cardinal Richelieu in his palace in 1641. Seated in the foreground (from right to left) are Cardinal Richelieu, Louis XIII, and the queen. After Richelieu's death, this theatre was called the Palais Royal. It was used by Molière's company from 1660 until his death in 1673.

Archives Charmet/The Bridgeman Art Library

Casting was simplified because each actor played a limited range of roles. By the eighteenth century, actors were being hired according to "lines of business" (according to the type of characters they played) and remained in those lines throughout their careers. A new actor in the company usually learned roles from the person he or she was understudying or replacing, and therefore, many roles came to be played in a traditional manner handed down from one generation to the next. Such practices continued well into the nineteenth century, not just in France but also throughout Europe.

In France, actors were expected to furnish their own costumes, a major expense for the actors. As on the Elizabethan stage, most costumes were contemporary garments, although there were exceptions, especially for Near Eastern, Moorish, and classical characters. Because so many French plays were based on classical myth or history, the costumes for classical characters were of special concern. The typical dress for classical heroes was the *habit à la romaine* (Roman costume), an adaptation of Roman armor, tunic, and boots, which by the late seventeenth century had become highly stylized. Classical female characters, however, wore the fashionable dress of France but with such added exotic touches as ostrich-feather headdresses.

The scenic demands of regular comedy and tragedy were simple. Ordinarily, in compliance with the neoclassical rules, the plays were set in one place and required no scene changes. (Opera and other "irregular" forms were permitted many scene changes and elaborate effects.) Most settings were so generalized in their features (appropriate to a particular kind of play but without individualizing details) that the same set could be used for several different plays. The setting was removed from specificity by using only those stage properties (chairs, tables, beds, and the like) absolutely demanded by the action; thus, the stage was largely bare. This emphasis on generalized place served as well to keep down the cost of scenery.

Because the theatre performances now took place indoors, lighting was a concern. The

Margaret Mitchell

This drawing conveys the costuming convention, the *habit à la romaine*, that the French used for classical characters.

available illuminants were candles and oil lamps. The auditorium was usually lighted by chandeliers, those hung just forward of the stage being of special importance because they, along with a row of footlights at the forward edge of the stage, were the primary lighting sources for the actors, who usually played near the front of the stage. Audiences as well as actors were lighted throughout performances, promoting considerable interaction between auditorium and stage. Sometimes chandeliers were also hung above the stage, but more often overhead or side masking concealed the onstage lighting sources. Along the sides, behind the proscenium arch and each wing position, were vertical poles on which oil lamps were mounted, one lamp above the other. Lamps could also be mounted on horizontal pipes above the proscenium and behind the overhead borders. Reflectors were sometimes used to increase the amount of light that reached the stage. At least three methods were used to darken the stage: Lights were extinguished (although this was awkward if they had to brighten again); open cylinders were suspended above the lamps and lowered over them to darken the stage, then raised to brighten it; or lamps were mounted on rotating poles that could be turned either toward or away from the visible portions of the stage. Because the intensity of lamps and candles was so limited, providing an adequate level of illumination took precedence over all other functions of stage lighting. By modern standards, the level of illumination was very low.

Between 1636 and 1759 the seating arrangements for audiences in Paris were much like those in Italian theatre with one notable exception: Some audience members were seated on stage during performances. This practice apparently originated during the controversy over Corneille's *The Cid*, when the demand to see that play was so great that spectators were allowed to sit or stand in the wings. Sitting on stage soon became fashionable for those who came to the theatre more to be seen than to watch the performance. French acting companies permitted this practice because they could charge more for onstage seats than for any others in the theatre.

These were the prevailing practices during the years 1658 through 1673, when Molière performed in Paris. Molière (like Shakespeare) was involved in every aspect of the theatre. He was head of his own company, its principal actor, and its principal playwright. Molière wrote several kinds of plays, many of them resembling *commedia* and using *commedia* characters. But his best-known works are comedies of character, among which the most popular is *Tartuffe* (first version 1664, final version 1669).

TARTUFFE

Tartuffe is concerned with religious hypocrisy. The play's title character denounces others for their pursuit of worldly pleasures while privately seeking those pleasures for himself. The most likely target of Molière's satire was the Company of the Holy Sacrament, a secret society of the time, whose purpose was to improve morals by acting as "spiritual police" who spied on the private lives of others. Molière's troupe performed a version of *Tartuffe* at court in 1664. The Company immediately organized an attack upon it. The controversy became so heated that Louis XIV forbade further performances. Molière revised the play in 1667 and attempted to perform it while Louis XIV was in Flanders preparing for war. However, the president of Parliament quickly banned this new version of the play and the archbishop of Paris threatened to excommunicate anyone who recited or performed the play in public or private. But by 1669, the opposition was largely gone, and the play was performed frequently thereafter.

Whether or not Molière had the Company in mind, he was clearly thinking of groups like the Company, who feel that they alone can discern true piety from false, creating conditions under which hypocrites flourish. As in all of Molière's works, in *Tartuffe* the balanced view of life is upheld. To Molière, true piety demands not the abandonment of pleasure but rather the right use of it. The truly devout try to reform the world by actions that set a good example, rather than by pious speeches.

The conflict in *Tartuffe* is established quickly in the opening scene, as Madame Pernelle, Orgon's mother, storms out of the house while denouncing the entire household for failing to appreciate Tartuffe's piety. The conflict is clarified when Orgon, the head of the household, returning home after an absence, demonstrates more concern for the welfare of Tartuffe than for his own wife. When Orgon's brother-in-law, Cléante, tries to reason with him, Orgon asserts his power by announcing his intention of marrying his daughter, Mariane, to Tartuffe, even though he has promised her to Valère. The news of this proposed marriage leads Valère to start a quarrel with Mariane because he assumes that Mariane has not opposed the plan. But the rift is finally healed through the intervention of Dorine, the outspoken maid. Orgon's son, Damis, also tries to bring his father to his senses by reporting that he has witnessed Tartuffe trying to seduce Orgon's wife, Elmire. When Tartuffe, with an air of injured humility, refuses to defend himself, Orgon denounces Damis and, to protect Tartuffe from such attacks in the future, signs over all of his property to Tartuffe.

Elmire, at last recognizing how deceived Orgon is, seeks to show him his mistake by hiding him under a table to witness Tartuffe's assault on her virtue. Finally convinced, Orgon orders Tartuffe from the house, but Tartuffe, now the owner of the property, declares that, rather than moving out, he will have the family evicted. Just as Tartuffe seems triumphant, officers arrest him as a notorious deceiver on whom the king has been keeping watch and return the property to Orgon.

The plot of *Tartuffe* can be divided into five stages: the demonstration of Tartuffe's complete hold over Orgon; the unmasking of Tartuffe; Tartuffe's attempted revenge; the foiling of Tartuffe's plan; and the happy resolution. There are three important reversals. The first (the unmasking of Tartuffe) brings all of the characters to an awareness of the true situation. The resulting happiness is quickly dispelled, however, when Orgon is shown to be at the mercy of Tartuffe. The first two reversals (Orgon turning the tables on Tartuffe; Tartuffe turning the tables on Orgon) have been carefully foreshadowed, but the final one and the play's resolution have not. The contrived (*deus ex machina*) ending (in which Tartuffe is discovered to be a notorious criminal) is emotionally satisfying in the sense that justice triumphs, but the contrivance is totally unprepared for in the preceding dramatic action.

To prevent any confusion about Tartuffe's nature, Molière uses two acts to prepare for his entrance. The first act includes a lengthy argument by Cléante, the character who apparently represents Molière's point of view, in which true piety is distinguished from false. The structure of *Tartuffe* may be clarified by examining the use of various characters. Cléante appears in Act I, where he performs his principal function: to present the commonsense point of view. He does not appear again until Act IV, in which, as well as in Act V, he merely reinforces the ideas he set forth in Act I. Cléante does not influence the action; rather, he clarifies the theme.

Madame Pernelle, Orgon's mother, defends Tartuffe and criticizes Orgon's family for their loose behavior in the opening scene from *Tartuffe* by Molière, English translation by Richard Wilbur. Directed by Daniel Fish at the McCarter Theatre; scene design by John Conklin; costume design by Kaye Voyce; lighting design by Jane Cox; sound design by Karin Graybash.

T. Charles Erickson

Although Dorine, the maid, appears in every act, her role is virtually completed after the beginning of Act III, though she has been a major character up to that point. Her frankness and outspokenness serve to show up Orgon's credulity, the lovers' petulance, and Tartuffe's false piety. Her wit and common sense put the exaggerated behavior of others in proper perspective.

Even Tartuffe is given strange treatment when he finally makes his appearance after two acts of preparation. Most of his time onstage is given over to his two "love scenes" with Elmire. Molière seems to take it for granted that the audience will accept the picture of Tartuffe painted by the other characters and that the play need only emphasize one aspect of his hypocrisy. Tartuffe displays his wiles most fully when he is denounced by Damis. Rather than defend himself, he endures the accusations with apparent humility. This scene, more than any other, shows how Orgon has been taken in by Tartuffe.

The lovers, Valère and Mariane, first appear in Act II and are unimportant thereafter. They serve to show the depth of Orgon's credulity and the consequences of it to others because he plans to marry his daughter to Tartuffe. Their lovers' quarrel that ensues is a source of amusement largely unrelated to the rest of the play.

Although Elmire appears in earlier scenes, most of her lines come in Act IV, where she serves as the instrument for unmasking Tartuffe. This uneven distribution of the role has led some critics to argue that Elmire's moral character is questionable because she originally seems undisturbed by Tartuffe's advances. Molière probably meant to show Elmire as a reasonably worldly but upright woman who is capable of defending herself without making a fuss about it.

Orgon's role is the one most evenly distributed throughout the play. Although the Tartuffes of the world are dangerous, they can exist only because of the Orgons; the success of the wicked depends on the gullibility of the foolish. Just as Molière emphasizes Tartuffe's calculated piety, so, too, he emphasizes Orgon's impulsiveness

Elmire (Carie Yonekawa) tries to trick Tartuffe (Steve Tague) in the Great Lakes Theater Festival's production of *Tartuffe* at the Ohio Theatre, Playhouse Square Center in Cleveland, Ohio.

Roger Mastroianni, Courtesy Great Lakes Theatre Festival

and stubbornness. Orgon errs largely because he acts without considering sufficient aspects of a question. When Tartuffe is finally unmasked, Orgon's character remains consistent; failing to see the difference between hypocrisy and piety, he says, "I'm through with pious men: Henceforth I'll hate the whole false brotherhood." Instead of returning to middle ground, he assumes an equally exaggerated (though opposite) position.

Little indication is given of the age or physical appearance of the characters. Because Molière wrote with his own company in mind and directed them, he did not need to specify every detail in his play. The role of Tartuffe was written for DuCroisy, a large man with a ruddy complexion. No doubt this was one of the sources of humor. All of Tartuffe's talk about scourges and fasting was contradicted by his obvious plumpness and lecherousness. Molière, noted for his expressive face and body, played

Practitioners & Theorists

MOLIÈRE

Molière, born Jean-Baptiste Poquelin (1622–1673), was the son of a prosperous upholsterer and furniture maker. After receiving an excellent education, he abandoned a promising future with his father at the age of twenty-one to join nine other young people in founding the Théâtre Illustre. At this time he took the stage name Molière. After the company failed in Paris, it toured the provinces for fifteen years, polishing its skills and learning to please audiences, often in competition with *commedia dell'arte* companies.

In 1658, the company was invited to play for the king, who was sufficiently pleased to let it use a court theatre for public performances. Molière remained in Paris thereafter, often stirring up controversy with plays that satirized obsessive behavior and repressive customs, but enjoying the favor of the king, for whose festivals he wrote entertainments and who awarded the company an annual subsidy. Molière's enemies were often vicious, even spreading the rumor that his wife, some twenty years younger than he, was actually his illegitimate daughter. Molière virtually died on stage, having taken ill while performing the title role in his *The Imaginary Invalid* (1673) and surviving only a few hours. Initially denied a Christian burial because he was an actor, he was permitted minimal ceremony and burial in consecrated ground only after the king intervened.

Orgon; Molière's wife, who was twenty-seven years old in 1669, played Elmire. As was often the case with comic old women, a man played Mme. Pernelle; thus, the character was no doubt intended to be seen as ridiculous in her denunciation of pleasure. All of the characters are drawn from the middle or lower classes (in accordance with neoclassical theories of comedy).

In *Tartuffe*, Molière uses the verse form that by that time had become standard in French drama, the *alexandrine* (twelve-syllable lines, with each pair of adjacent lines rhyming). The nearest equivalent in English is the rhymed couplet, although this form seems far more unnatural than the French alexandrine. English verse, unlike French verse, uses repeated heavy-stress patterns within lines, and these, in combination with rhymed line endings, encourage a singsong quality in English. In French verse, in which these internal stress patterns are absent, rhymed endings are far less intrusive. Molière, like most French dramatists until modern times, started a

new scene each time a character entered or exited in order to indicate an alteration in motivations or focus created by the change of characters on stage. Thus, although the action may be continuous, the printed text is divided into numerous scenes. (Such divisions are usually referred to as *French scenes*.)

The unities of time and place are strictly observed in *Tartuffe*. Only a single room is used, and even that requires only a table, under which Orgon can be concealed, and a closet, in which Damis can hide, both used to witness Tartuffe trying to seduce Elmire. No specific use is made of the setting except in these two instances. The action is continuous, or nearly so, and occurs in a single day. All of the episodes, with the possible exception of the lovers' quarrel, are directly related to the main theme of the play. *Tartuffe* is clearly within the neoclassical tradition. It has remained in the repertory almost continuously and has been performed more often than any other play by Molière.

The Elizabethan, Italian, and French Traditions

Although Shakespeare and Molière are among the world's great dramatists and were separated in time by only a few decades, they worked within different theatrical traditions. Shakespeare's offered greater flexibility, but before the end of the seventeenth century, it had been replaced by Molière's, probably because the tide of taste was moving steadily toward a preference for representationalism.

While the English public theatre continued most of the practices of Shakespeare's day until 1642, a civil war brought the forced closure of all theatres until 1660. When the English theatres reopened in 1660, English theatre more nearly reflected the practices introduced in Italy and then popularized in France during the seventeenth century; i.e., they accepted actresses for the first time in England and adopted the picture-frame stage, perspective scenery, and the neoclassical vision (although never so completely as elsewhere in Europe). During the Restoration, several of Shakespeare's plays were adapted to make them conform more nearly to the neoclassical ideal. For example, at the end of Nahum Tate's adaptation of *King Lear* (1681) only the wicked people died; Lear, Gloucester, and Kent retired to the country, and Cordelia and Edgar married and became the rulers of England. This is the version of *King Lear* that was performed in English theatres until the 1840s.

English theatre between 1660 and 1700, a period usually referred to as the Restoration, was noted principally for its comedy of manners, which focused on the amoral behavior and witty verbal exchanges of the rich and idle upper class. Restoration comedy was concerned above all with sexual conquests, advantageous marriages (in which love played little part), the latest fashions, and a seeming determination to be shocked at nothing. The butts of ridicule included the fop, the old man who marries a young wife, the old woman who tries to appear young, the pretender at wit and sophistication, and the self-deceived. The amoral tone of these plays has made them controversial ever since they were written. Restoration comedy originated with such works as Sir George Etherege's *She Would if She Could* (1668) and *The Man of Mode* (1676) and reached its peak in the plays of William Congreve, especially *Love for Love* (1695) and *The Way of the World* (1700).

Commedia dell'arte influenced many European playwrights. The degree of its influence on English writers of Shakespeare's day is still debated, but it was clearly evident in eighteenth-century English theatre, especially in pantomimes. *Commedia*'s influence on Molière and other French playwrights is undeniable, and this influence continued throughout the eighteenth and into the nineteenth century, even after *commedia* had ceased to be a separate form.

By the eighteenth century, although there were still obvious differences among the theatres of various European countries, they shared the same basic conventions, the ideas of neoclassicism. The theatre had made the transition from festival offerings to professional, secular entertainment.

THEATRE IN A BROAD CONTEXT

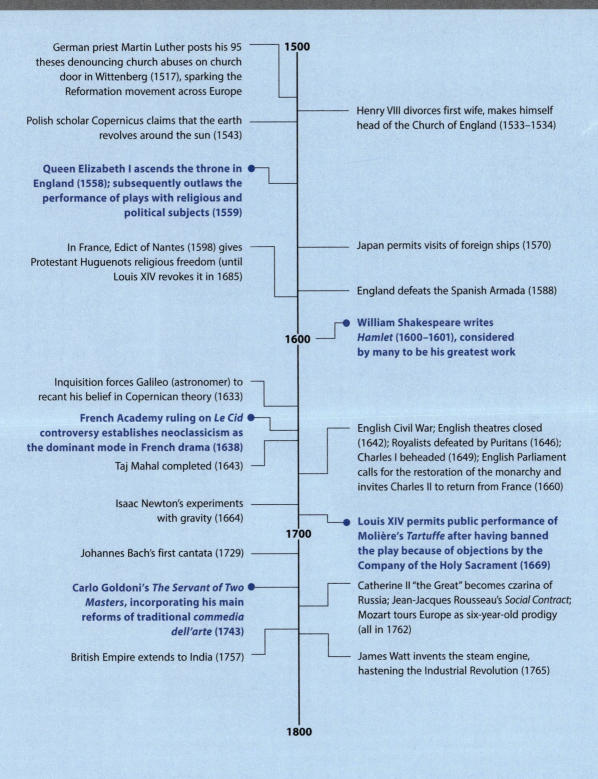

German priest Martin Luther posts his 95 theses denouncing church abuses on church door in Wittenberg (1517), sparking the Reformation movement across Europe

1500

Henry VIII divorces first wife, makes himself head of the Church of England (1533–1534)

Polish scholar Copernicus claims that the earth revolves around the sun (1543)

Queen Elizabeth I ascends the throne in England (1558); subsequently outlaws the performance of plays with religious and political subjects (1559)

In France, Edict of Nantes (1598) gives Protestant Huguenots religious freedom (until Louis XIV revokes it in 1685)

Japan permits visits of foreign ships (1570)

England defeats the Spanish Armada (1588)

William Shakespeare writes _Hamlet_ (1600–1601), considered by many to be his greatest work

1600

Inquisition forces Galileo (astronomer) to recant his belief in Copernican theory (1633)

French Academy ruling on _Le Cid_ controversy establishes neoclassicism as the dominant mode in French drama (1638)

Taj Mahal completed (1643)

English Civil War; English theatres closed (1642); Royalists defeated by Puritans (1646); Charles I beheaded (1649); English Parliament calls for the restoration of the monarchy and invites Charles II to return from France (1660)

Isaac Newton's experiments with gravity (1664)

1700

Louis XIV permits public performance of Molière's _Tartuffe_ after having banned the play because of objections by the Company of the Holy Sacrament (1669)

Johannes Bach's first cantata (1729)

Carlo Goldoni's _The Servant of Two Masters_, incorporating his main reforms of traditional _commedia dell'arte_ (1743)

Catherine II "the Great" becomes czarina of Russia; Jean-Jacques Rousseau's _Social Contract_; Mozart tours Europe as six-year-old prodigy (all in 1762)

British Empire extends to India (1757)

James Watt invents the steam engine, hastening the Industrial Revolution (1765)

1800

Anton Chekhov's *The Cherry Orchard* performed using a new translation by Richard Nelson at the Huntington Theatre (Boston); directed by Nicholas Martin; scene design by Ralph Funicello; costumes by Robert Morgan; lighting by Donald Holder; sound by Drew Levy; original music by Michael Friedman.

T. Charles Erickson

We should not be surprised if, in the course of the journey, at some point we cannot today ascertain,
the road should suddenly turn and astonishing new vistas in art and life should emerge.
For human culture is bound by no formula, not even the most recent.

—Otto Brahm, *Freie Buehne für Modernes Leben*

From Romanticism to Realism

The late eighteenth and early nineteenth centuries brought a reaction against the neoclassical rules that had dominated dramatic writing since the mid-seventeenth century. These rules, although not always followed, had attempted to restrict the action of each drama to a span of twenty-four hours, to one place (additional places were permitted as long as they could be reached without stretching the twenty-four-hour limit), and to one plot (subplots were tolerated only if they were clearly offshoots of the main plot). Neoclassicism also sought to rule out fantasy and supernatural elements. And, because neoclassicism was grounded in the belief that human nature is the same in all times and all places, it sought to depict universal (rather than historically accurate or individualized) traits, behavior, and visual elements. Settings were so generalized that they could be used in many different productions. For example, if the place of action was a prison, the goal was to depict the essence of a prison rather than any particular prison; therefore, the same set could be used for any prison scene. Similarly, characters were usually dressed in clothing of the period of the performance, no matter what the historical period of the action, because to place characters in a specific historical milieu might suggest that the play's depiction of human behavior was true only for that earlier time and place. Therefore, in the eighteenth century Hamlet wore fashionable eighteenth-century dress, and Macbeth was dressed in the uniform of a British general.

Most of the strictures of neoclassicism were applied only to "regular" drama (that is, comedy and tragedy written in five acts). Perhaps for this reason a number of "irregular" forms gained popularity during the eighteenth century. Many were probably influenced by opera, which had never been subjected to the rules and included numerous special effects, changes of scene, music, dance, and other appeals that were kept to a minimum in regular drama. But by the eighteenth century opera had become an elitist entertainment in most of Europe because of high ticket prices. Consequently, many of its features, in modified form, were brought into the popular theatre through new types of musical drama. England developed the *ballad opera*, which incorporated in an otherwise spoken drama numerous lyrics set to the tunes of well-known popular songs or ballads. The most famous example is John Gay's *The Beggar's Opera* (1728). In France, comparable pieces were called *opéra comique* and in Germany and

Austria *Singspiele* (of which Mozart's *The Magic Flute* (1791) is the best-known example, though it is now performed as an opera). Another popular form was pantomime, in which Harlequin was usually the main character. Harlequin's slapstick became a magic wand, permitting spectacular transformations of people and places; the action was accompanied throughout by music, and there were usually several dances. Thus, "irregular" pieces overcame the restrictions imposed by the neoclassical rules, although they were considered inferior to the "regular" dramas.

The Emergence of Romanticism

Toward the end of the eighteenth century, the attitudes that had supported neoclassicism began to change, and several playwrights in Germany, especially members of the *Sturm und Drang* (Storm and Stress) school, began to write serious plays that experimented with both bold subjects and dramatic form. By the early nineteenth century, ideas about appropriateness in dramatic writing had undergone an almost complete reversal, ultimately coalescing to create *Romanticism*. The earlier belief that truth is to be found in "norms" gave way to the conviction that truth is to be found in the infinite variety of creation. According to the romantics, God created the universe out of himself so that he may contemplate himself. Therefore, everything has a common origin and is part of a greater whole. Thus, rather than eliminate details to arrive at norms, one should welcome them in all of their variety. Romantics also believed that the more unspoiled a thing is—the less it deviates from its natural state—the more truthful it is; writers showed a marked preference for poetry about nature and drama about unspoiled human beings living in primitive times or in rebellion against restraints imposed by society. Romantics glorified the writer-genius, who, grasping intuitively the complexity of the universe, rejected the strictures imposed by neoclassicism.

Perhaps the changes in critical attitudes are best summed up in relation to Shakespeare. Although Shakespeare's plays had always been popular in England, they were rarely performed in other European countries until the late eighteenth century. In continental Europe, Shakespeare was ignored because his plays did not adhere to

Macbeth as costumed about 1775. Macbeth (played by David Garrick, one of England's greatest actors) is dressed as an eighteenth-century British general, and Lady Macbeth (played by Mrs. Pritchard) wears the fashionable dress of that time. In this scene, Lady Macbeth holds the daggers with which she urges Macbeth to kill King Duncan.

COMPARING NEOCLASSICISM AND ROMANTICISM

Neoclassicism	Romanticism
Favors socially accepted norms	Favors the variety of nature and its particular manifestations
Supernatural elements in drama frowned upon as improbable products of fantasy rather than reason	Mystical and supernatural elements embraced as aspects of existence beyond the confines of rationality
Character behavior according to socially accepted norms pertaining to age, social status, occupation, ethnicity, and gender	Character behavior frequently defiant of socially accepted norms; leading characters often possessing opposing qualities
Unities of time, place, and action followed	Unities of time, place, and action not followed
Generic scenery and costumes emphasizing the essential rather than the particular	Particular scenery and costumes, often details from real-life locations and costumes beginning to individualize characters

the neoclassical rules. Even in England, many of Shakespeare's plays were rewritten to bring them more nearly into accord with neoclassical demands. English critics tried to explain Shakespeare's appeal by labeling him a natural genius who, despite his ignorance of the rules, had managed to write effective, though flawed, dramas. Nevertheless, they implied, he would have been even better had he known and followed the rules.

During the last quarter of the eighteenth century, Shakespeare's plays began to be translated into other European languages and staged, although at first only in heavily adapted versions. As Shakespeare's reputation grew, his plays were altered less and less, and by the early nineteenth century his works were becoming the standard against which plays were judged throughout Europe. During the nineteenth century, Shakespeare achieved the reputation he has been accorded ever since as the greatest dramatist of all time. Because he had written without regard for the neoclassical rules, he became an argument for ignoring them, and the unities of time, place, and action gave way to stories occurring over many years, in numerous places, and through a tangle of plots. Variety often took precedence over unity. The mysterious and supernatural, which had been deplored by the neoclassicists, became common occurrences in the new drama, as did concern for the characteristic features of specific times and places. Historical accuracy in settings and costumes began to be favored, although it was not consistently realized until around 1850. The critical reception of Shakespeare's plays evinces the wane of neoclassicism and the rise of romanticism as an aesthetic.

Although romanticism was not without appeal to the masses, it was melodrama—with its easily identifiable characters, its suspenseful action, its moral clarity, and its inclusion of spectacle—that provided the general public a theatre that embraced variety over unity.

Melodrama

Melodrama was the popular-culture manifestation of romanticism and it became the most popular dramatic form of the nineteenth century. Melodrama emphasized clear and suspenseful plots in which a villain hounded a virtuous protagonist who overcame seemingly insurmountable difficulties after undergoing a series of threats to life, reputation, or happiness. All important events occurred on stage; typically, there was at least one elaborate spectacular happening (earthquake, burning building, explosion, or the like) and/or scene of local color (festivals or dances using the picturesque customs or conditions of a specific country or city). Typical plot devices included concealed or mistaken identity, abductions, strange coincidences, and hidden documents. Comic relief was often provided by a servant, ally, or companion of one of the principal characters. Perhaps most important, strict poetic justice was meted out: The evil people were punished, and the good were rewarded. The villain might seem triumphant until the final scene, but ultimately he was unmasked and defeated.

Melodrama literally means "music drama" and the productions had a large musical element. Originally, there were a number of songs in each play; more importantly, the action was accompanied by a musical score (every theatre in the nineteenth century employed a pit orchestra) that enhanced the action and the emotional tone of scenes. With its simple, powerful stories, unequivocal moral tone, spectacle, and music, melodrama offered compelling, escapist entertainment to the mass audiences of the nineteenth century. Many of melodrama's features have been taken over by film. [Examples include *Raiders of the Lost Ark* (1981) and *Tomb Raider: The Cradle of Life* (2003).]

The popularity of melodrama in the nineteenth century is explained in part by fundamental changes

Besnard, Paul Albert (1849-1934)/The Art Gallery Collection/Alamy

This painting depicts the riotous confrontation over Victor Hugo's *Hernani* at the Comédie Française in 1830. Hugo's tragedy broke the neoclassic rules governing language and character behavior as well as the unities of time and place. This enraged supporters of traditional drama and delighted those who supported romanticism's call for a lifting of restrictions and rules.

in social and economic conditions stemming from the Industrial Revolution. As inventions such as the steam engine, power loom, steamship, and locomotive were exploited, the factory system of mass production gradually replaced individual craftsmen, who had been the major producers of goods since medieval times. Because workers had to live near the factories, urbanization accelerated rapidly and created large potential audiences for theatrical entertainment. The largest city in Europe, London, had supported only two or three theatres during the eighteenth century, but between 1800 and 1850, its population doubled and the number of its theatres grew to more than twenty. Its population and number of theatres continued to grow through the remainder of the century. As in television programming today, theatres sought to attract the largest possible audiences. Melodrama and variety entertainment proved to be the answer. Many critics argue that catering to mass taste led to a decline in the quality of theatrical offerings. But eventually theatre managers discovered that they did not have to appeal to everyone, and, during the last half of the nineteenth century, each theatre began to aim its programming at a specific segment of the population or a particular taste.

Because the pattern of melodrama is always the same (good threatened by evil, with the eventual triumph of good), variety was gained through such novelties as exotic locales, ever-more-spectacular effects, incorporation into the action of the latest inventions, and dramatizations of popular novels or notorious crimes. A few melodrama theatres included facilities for horseback riding and featured plays with spectacular feats of horsemanship and last-minute rescues by mounted riders. Others installed water tanks to accommodate "aquatic" melodramas. The first important writer of melodramas, the Frenchman Guilbert de Pixérécourt, resolved one of his plays by having the villain destroyed as lava from a volcanic eruption inundated the stage. Dion Boucicault, one of the most popular playwrights of the English-speaking stage between 1840 and 1890, used the newly invented camera to reveal the identity of a murderer in *The Octoroon* (1859). American playwright Augustin Daly's *Under the Gaslight* (1867) included a thrilling scene where a character was tied to a railroad track in the path of an oncoming locomotive only to be rescued at the last moment.

A contemporary engraving

The Octoroon, a melodrama by Dion Boucicault, first performed in 1859. Here a man is seeking to save the mixed-blood woman he loves from being sold to the highest bidder at a slave auction.

A publicity poster for Augustin Daly's *Under the Gaslight*, the first of many plays to place a character in imminent danger of destruction by an oncoming locomotive.

A contemporary engraving

After electricity became common in the 1880s, electric motors were coupled with treadmills to stage horse or chariot races. To make the race realistic, moving panoramas (long cloths on which a continuous scene was painted) were suspended at the rear of the stage in overhead tracks and pulled between upright spools on either side of the stage. The movement of these panoramas was synchronized with the treadmills so that the horses were kept onstage by the treadmills while the scene painted on the panorama rushed by behind them, creating the effect that the horses were racing around a track (see illustration below). The trend was toward ever-more-realistic

effects. In the early twentieth century, film inherited this tradition and continued to exploit it. Once the potential of film was established, the theatre largely abandoned such productions.

In melodrama, realistic spectacle, thrilling effects, novelty, suspense, and the vindication of virtue were the major appeals. Melodrama encouraged the development of realism in the visual aspects of theatre while clinging to recognizable and comforting stereotypes in characterization and morality. Let us look more closely at *Monte Cristo*, as an example of nineteenth-century melodrama, both as a play and in terms of the production practices it required.

A drawing showing an onstage horse race in *The County Fair*, staged at the Union Square Theatre, New York, 1889, using a moving panorama and treadmills connected to electric motors, the speed of which was controlled by the man at upper right.

Scientific American, 1889

MONTE CRISTO

Monte Cristo is a dramatization of Alexandre Dumas *père's The Count of Monte Cristo* (1845), one of the world's most popular novels. Dumas himself dramatized the work in 1848, but it was in twenty acts and required two evenings to perform. Several other dramatizations were made, but the one that eventually held the stage was by Charles Fechter, a French actor who had a long and distinguished career on the stages of France, England, and America. In 1885, James O'Neill (1847–1920) purchased the rights to this version and subsequently made numerous revisions. The text as it now stands is the work of at least several persons. O'Neill became so identified with the role of Edmund Dantès that the public would go to see him in no other play; he toured the United States for thirty years in the production. His plight was like that of many actors of recent times who have become so identified with their roles in television series that they have no subsequent careers or are always cast in the same type of role. O'Neill's sense of being trapped by the role is forcefully stated in *Long Day's Journey into Night* (1956) written by his son, Eugene O'Neill.

Reducing a novel of several hundred pages into a play that could be performed in two or three hours was a formidable task, but not unusual in the nineteenth century, because popular novels were typically dramatized soon after their publication. Almost all of Charles Dickens's novels were adapted for the stage, and Aiken's *Uncle Tom's Cabin* (1852), was adapted from Harriet Beecher Stowe's novel. Film and television have continued this practice.

The sweep of *Monte Cristo* is nearer to that of Shakespeare's plays than to that of plays by Sophocles or Molière. There are many incidents, though the basic pattern is relatively simple.

Practices & Styles

SCENES OF SUSPENSE AND SPECTACLE IN MELODRAMA

Much of the appeal of melodrama during the nineteenth century lay in the suspense created by placing sympathetic characters in great physical danger and by their last-minute rescue. These scenes were made even more attractive by spectacular scenic contrivances that made the danger seem real and present. One of these occurs in George Aiken's adaptation of Harriet Beecher Stowe's novel *Uncle Tom's Cabin* (1852), the most popular stage melodrama of the nineteenth century. The enslaved Eliza, learning that her child, Harry, is to be taken from her and sold, runs away with him. She finds someone who will help her, but she must first get out of Kentucky (where slavery is legal) across the Ohio River (to territory free from slavery). While Eliza waits at an inn for the ferry that will take her across the river, villainous bounty hunters arrive, unaware of her presence. Overhearing their plan to capture her, she slips out through a window, but they see her and give chase. (In some productions, Eliza's pursuers used live bloodhounds and horses to track her.) The Ohio River has been frozen over, but the ice has broken into pieces. In desperation, Eliza, clutching Harry, leaps onto a large piece of ice and, as her pursuers look on helplessly, floats across the river where the man who will rescue her is seen waiting. This scene was so popular and well known that it became legendary. Even in the twentieth century, it was not uncommon for people, when circumstances seemed to be closing in on them, to say they felt like Eliza fleeing the bloodhounds.

The hero, a ship's officer named Edmund Dantès, returns from a voyage prepared to marry his fiancée, Mercedes. He runs afoul of three villains: Danglars (the ship's cargo officer), Fernand (who loves Mercedes), and Villefort (a government prosecutor who fears that his brother, Noirtier, will ruin his career if he obtains a letter Edmund is bringing from the deposed emperor Napoleon). These three arrange for Edmund's arrest as a traitor, and he is imprisoned on the notorious penal island, the Chateau d'If. Edmund remains in prison for fourteen years, but during that time an elderly prisoner, Faria, befriends him and reveals the location of his family's vast fortune—the island of Monte Cristo. When Faria dies, Edmund takes the corpse's place in the sack, which—in the prison's burial practice—will be thrown into the sea. Through this ruse, Edmund escapes, recovers the Faria fortune, and sets out to punish those who have wronged him. While Edmund has been in prison, his betrayers have prospered: Villefort has become minister of justice; Danglars, a major financier; and Fernand, a general, a peer of France, and Mercedes's husband (after she has been persuaded that Edmund is dead). As the Count of Monte Cristo, Edmund relentlessly tracks down his persecutors and punishes each in turn. By the story's end, all of the villains have been publicly disgraced and are dead.

Like other melodramas, *Monte Cristo* shows goodness victimized and evil triumphant for a time, but ultimately evil is exposed and punished and goodness is vindicated. It differs from most melodramas in rescuing the hero early from danger (at the end of Act II) and in the great amount of time devoted to punishing the villains. By actual time, of course, the hero languishes in prison for fourteen years, but in the play, those years are passed over in the interval between Acts I and II. Edmund is actually seen in prison in only one scene (whereas the novel devotes many chapters to his sufferings). Many of the events (especially the way in which Villefort is punished) and character relationships (most importantly in making Albert the son of Edmund and Mercedes rather than of Fernand and Mercedes) differ from those in the novel.

The turning point, Edmund's escape, has a miraculous quality both in the event itself and in Faria's legacy of enormous wealth, which makes Edmund's revenge possible. In this scene, Edmund proclaims himself an instrument of revenge. Reading the script fails to convey the effect created in performance by Edmund rising from the sea, climbing onto a rock, and proclaiming, "The world is mine." This scene became one of the best-loved moments of nineteenth-century theatre. Following this powerful scene, the villains are punished in the reverse order of

Uncle Tom's Cabin as produced by William Brady in 1901. Eliza (right rear) is about to cross the Ohio River on a piece of ice. The use of dogs and horses by Eliza's pursuers had become common by this time. Note the use of painted two-dimensional scenery (the trees) and the shadows it casts on the rear wall.

their betrayals (Villefort first, then Fernand, and finally Danglars). As each is punished, Edmund announces the score— "One," "Two," "Three"— an accounting so satisfying to O'Neill's audiences that they often counted aloud with him. At the end, the play achieves additional symmetry by implying the possibility of achieving the happiness promised in the opening scene. Though the plot is intricate, the underlying pattern is simple—and deeply reassuring in its inexorable meting out of just rewards and punishments.

Characterization is far simpler than plot in *Monte Cristo*. The main characters are types with minimal individualizing traits. Edmund seems almost entirely good. Near the end, when he discovers that Albert, with whom he has arranged a duel, is his son and not Fernand's as he had thought, he abandons his murderous plan and resigns himself to let Albert kill him. Most of the

characters are at some point torn briefly between acting honorably and acting out of self-interest; the bad always choose self-interest, and the good choose to act honorably. Melodrama seldom suggests that moral choices are determined by environmental forces; rather, awareness of good and evil is innate, and each character is free to choose right or wrong. Values are viewed as absolute rather than relative (as they are in most current drama).

The characters are always wholly conscious of their motives and feelings and state them to the audience. To prevent any misperception, they use asides to inform the audience (or another character) of reactions they do not wish to share with all those onstage. (The aside, a convention almost as old as drama itself, came under attack in the late nineteenth century as being unrealistic and was eventually abandoned except in self-consciously nonrealistic plays.)

Albert Davis Collection, Hoblitzelle Theatre Arts Library, Harry Ransom Humanities Research Center, University of Texas at Austin

Pictured here is James O'Neill (center, without coat) in the final scene from *Monte Cristo*. The acting area is very shallow, but the set is made to seem deep by the use of cut drops—that is, by cutting away portions of each drop so another can be seen through the openings.

Next to suspenseful and morally satisfying plots, melodrama owed its appeal most to spectacle. By the late 1800s, producers were priding themselves on the realism and authenticity of their costumes and settings. The first act of *Monte Cristo* takes place in 1815 (when Napoleon was in exile on Elba), whereas the other acts occur in the 1830s. Costumes played a major role in marking both passage of time and alteration in the economic and social status of the characters. Much of the "local color" of time and place was created through the dress of sailors, policemen, tavern patrons, and partygoers.

Monte Cristo requires eight sets, two of which were probably simple and very shallow, permitting more complex sets to be erected behind them while a scene was in progress. For example, the Act II scene in Fernand's house involves only a few characters and no unusual physical action. It was probably set up in front of the Chateau d'If setting, the most elaborate of the play, which comes right after it. The Chateau d'If prison setting requires two levels, one of which sinks, concealing the prisoners' cells and revealing the water into which Edmund's body is thrown and the rock onto which he climbs triumphantly.

The demands of the Chateau d'If scene illustrate the changes that had occurred in scenic practices by the late nineteenth century. O'Neill first played his version of *Monte Cristo* at Booth's Theatre in New York. This theatre, opened in 1869, had been built by one of America's greatest actors, Edwin Booth, and probably was the first stage in modern times to have a flat floor and to eliminate the traditional arrangement of wings. Wings had become increasingly unsatisfactory because they were two dimensional, parallel to the front of the stage, and arranged in pairs from front to back. In combination with a raked stage floor, wings made it difficult to move large three-dimensional pieces on and off the stage. The design of Booth's Theatre provided for new ways of handling three-dimensional practicable scenery, furniture, and other details found in real-life places. The flat floor and the absence of wing positions in Booth's Theatre permitted scenery to be erected wherever desired and to be moved on and off without hindrance. This theatre also had a number of elevator traps that raised and lowered heavy set pieces hydraulically.

By the late nineteenth century, the stage floor in most theatres was divided into sections a few feet wide, any of which could be removed to create an opening ("bridge") extending completely across the stage. In the second act of *Monte Cristo* the sinking of one part of the setting probably utilized one or more bridges. Upstage was the sea and the rock, both of which became visible as the cells sank. The sea was represented by a painted cloth moved up and down rhythmically by ropes attached to the underside. The sack (containing a dummy) was thrown into the water (no doubt with accompanying splash), and then, after a time, a soaked Edmund rose, probably through a trapdoor, climbed onto the rock, and uttered his triumphant "The world is mine." Such complex spectacle was typical of melodrama. The sets for the final three acts (an inn, ballroom, and forest), though elaborate, could be changed during the intervals between acts. The settings, which provided great variety, had to be designed and constructed with care because O'Neill toured this production throughout the country for thirty years, beginning in the 1880s.

Touring such complex productions was made possible by the development of dependable transportation, which became a reality with the spread of railroads. The first transcontinental line in the United States was completed in the 1860s; by the late 1870s, it was possible to reach almost any area of the country by rail, and numerous theatrical productions were touring with sets, costumes, properties, and actors. Such companies soon became the major purveyors of theatrical entertainment in most of America and remained so until displaced by sound motion pictures in the 1930s.

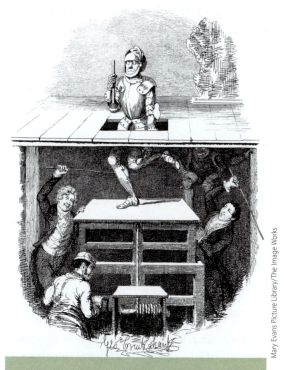

Pictured here is a trapdoor in the stage floor, circa 1843. Beneath the stage, one man winds the trap up, while two others make appropriate sound effects.

Mary Evans Picture Library/The Image Works

we get the expression "being in the limelight"). The limelight was made by placing a column of calcium (lime) inside a hood equipped with reflector and lens. Onto the lime were directed compressed hydrogen and oxygen along with a gas flame; the lime was heated to incandescence until it gave off an extremely bright light used to create such atmospheric effects as rays of moonlight or sunlight or to focus attention on a character or object. At the end of Act II in *Monte Cristo*, the stage direction reads: "The moon breaks out, lighting up a projecting rock. Edmund rises from the sea, he is dripping, a knife in his hand, some shreds of sack adhering to it." The effectiveness of this scene was greatly enhanced by the limelight.

O'Neill's production of *Monte Cristo* calls attention to another change then underway: long runs of single plays performed by actors hired for that production only were replacing a repertory of plays performed in rotation by a permanent company (the system that had prevailed since Shakespeare's day).

With melodrama, theatre in the nineteenth and early twentieth centuries achieved its greatest mass appeal. It developed the audience and many of the conventions taken over by film, which gradually displaced it as the prime medium of popular entertainment, especially after sound was added in the late 1920s and then color in the 1930s. Through film this legacy was subsequently passed on to television. Film forced theatre to reassess what it could do most effectively; as a result, by the 1920s theatre largely abandoned attempts to create the kind of realistic spectacle seen in *Monte Cristo*, which could be achieved much more convincingly by film. With their capacity to replicate their products endlessly, film and television were analogous in their effects on theatre to the influence of factories on individual craftsmen in the nineteenth century; theatre is the equivalent of a handcrafted product, one that has difficulty competing in a world attuned to mass production. Theatre has tried to meet the demand for mass production

Melodrama's visual appeal was further enhanced by lighting, the potential of which had increased greatly after gas replaced candles and oil during the first half of the nineteenth century. For the first time, the stage could be lit as brightly as desired. Equally important, control over intensity became possible through a "gas table," a central location from which all the gas lines ran and from which the supply of gas to any part of the theatre could be controlled. Lights could be dimmed or brightened as desired by one person operating the gas table. It was now possible to darken the auditorium and brighten it again when needed. These improvements encouraged increased concern for atmosphere and mood in stage lighting. Gas also made possible the development and use of the "limelight," a type of spotlight (from which

by mounting elaborate productions and sending them throughout the country by the most efficient means of transportation available. But theatre ultimately is not a medium adaptable to mass production; film is. The popular entertainment of the late nineteenth and early twentieth centuries, especially melodrama, was the meeting ground for theatre and film and was crucial in the subsequent history of both.

The Advent of Realism

Even as *Monte Cristo* was achieving great popular success, new theories and ideas were undermining the absolutist moral values on which melodrama had depended. Although unanimity of belief was never an actuality, Western civilization throughout the Christian era had looked to the Bible as the ultimate authority on values and moral principles. The biblical version of Creation and subsequent events was often accepted literally. Until the late nineteenth century, the earth was thought to be about six thousand years old, the date of the Creation having been calculated by counting back through the generations that, according to the Bible, had preceded the birth of Christ.

In the late nineteenth century, a number of intellectual and scientific developments (especially in the fields of geology and anthropology) called many biblical passages into question. When geologists began to suggest that the earth is millions (and eventually billions) of years old, and when anthropologists began to discover animal and human remains thousands of years older than the supposed date of the world's creation, heated controversies resulted. The greatest controversy was provoked by Charles Darwin's *The Origin of Species* (1859), in which he argued (1) that all forms of life have developed gradually from a common ancestry, and (2) that this evolution of species involves the natural selection of those best adapted to specific environmental conditions. This theory was, and remains,

anathema to those who interpret literally the biblical account of Creation.

Apart from their scientific impact, Darwin's theories influenced other late nineteenth-century beliefs that:

- Heredity and environment have enormous influence on human behavior.

- Society must accept some responsibility for learned behavior.

- Progress or change is a natural process involving trial and error toward improvement or refinement.

- The Bible, at least in terms of the dating of the world and its creatures, is fallible if interpreted literally.

- Humanity is as fit for scientific study as any other species.

These implications were crucial in the development of the modern temperament because they suggested that change (rather than fixity) is the norm. Late nineteenth-century thought began increasingly to support the belief that moral standards are relative to each culture and that concepts of right and wrong may vary widely from one society to another.

The new ideas about human conscience were stated most comprehensively in the writings of Sigmund Freud (1856–1939), the most influential psychologist of the twentieth century. Freud argued that the basic human instincts are aggression and sexuality—self-preservation and procreation. Left alone, human beings would seek to satisfy their instincts without regard for others; therefore, if they are to be integrated into a community, they must undergo socialization. Through rewards and punishments, they learn early what is acceptable and what is unacceptable, and in this process they develop a superego (an interior, subconscious censor or judge), what had previously been called a conscience. Throughout the Christian era, most people had believed that conscience is innate—that human beings have an instinctive grasp of the difference between right and wrong. (Melodrama was built on this premise.) With Freud, a sense of right and wrong is not absolute and does not come from God; it is relative to the individual, family, and societal environment that have produced it. Freud further argued that the process of socialization causes us to suppress many desires and urges (bury them in the unconscious mind) and to find socially acceptable substitutes that the conscious mind can openly acknowledge. Freud's view of human psychology implies not only that we can never fully understand others but also that we can never be certain of our own motives. To assess people and situations, in addition to noting what is consciously said and done, we must also be aware of the subtext—what is not openly said and done. According to this view, then, not only are moral values relative, but also language and behavior are only partially reliable indicators of a person's state of mind and motives.

Relativity eventually affected every area of thought and action. It initially entered the theatre through realism and naturalism, even though these movements were seeking objective, scientific explanations of human behavior.

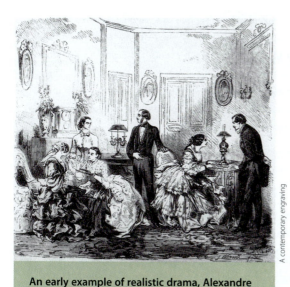

A contemporary engraving

An early example of realistic drama, Alexandre Dumas fils' *The Demi-Monde* as staged at the Théâtre du Gymnase in Paris in 1855.

Realism and Naturalism

Realism was first recognized during the 1850s, naturalism (a more extreme version of realism) during the 1870s. In theatre, these movements seemed in some ways extensions of already common practices, especially in the area of spectacle. Since around 1800, emphasis on visual accuracy in scenery and costumes had steadily increased, and one type of realism (illusionism in staging) had already been achieved. Nevertheless, this realism, as demonstrated by *Monte Cristo*, was exploited primarily as spectacular or picturesque background. In contrast to all preceding movements, realism and naturalism believed that character is determined in large part by heredity and environment, and they demanded that settings play an enlarged role—as representations of the environmental forces that have shaped the characters and (consequently) the dramatic action. In other words, setting was conceived as environment and not merely as appropriate or impressive background. One consequence was the belief that each play's scenic needs are unique because each play's environment is unlike that of any other. Perhaps more important, this approach to setting implies that what a character is and does is relative to specific environmental forces.

The views of realists and naturalists were grounded in the scientific outlook: the need to understand human behavior in terms of natural cause and effect. They restricted their pursuit of truth to knowledge that can be verified through the five senses. They argued that because we can know the real world only through direct observation, playwrights should write about the society around them and should do so as objectively as possible. Given these premises, it was logical that realists and naturalists would write primarily about contemporary subjects (unlike earlier serious dramatists who usually chose historical or mythical subjects) and introduce behavior not previously seen on the stage. Because many of the plays dealt with unsavory social conditions such as poverty, disease, prostitution, and the plight of illegitimate children, conservative critics charged that the theatre had become little better than a sewer. Realists replied that because they were depicting conditions truthfully, they were acting morally, truth being the highest form of morality. Furthermore, the realists argued that what their critics were demanding was an idealized, nonexistent vision of truth; instead, they declared, if audiences did not like the life portrayed on stage, they should change the society that furnished the models rather than denounce the playwrights who had

the courage to portray life truthfully. The real issue was the role of art in society. Should art, as in melodrama, always show good triumphant? If art shows deviations from accepted morality and behavior, should it reaffirm traditional values even though they have not triumphed in this instance? Or should art, as the realists and naturalists argued, follow truth wherever it leads without concern for conformity to social codes and moral values? Ultimately, it was a controversy over absolute versus relative values.

These issues were brought into focus by Henrik Ibsen (1828–1906), a Norwegian playwright often called the founder of modern drama. Ibsen had begun his playwriting career around 1850

Society, Art & Culture

CRITICAL REACTION TO IBSEN

It is difficult for us to understand how violent a response Ibsen's plays evoked when they first appeared. The reaction to *Ghosts* (1881) was extreme because, although the disease is never named in the play, both the husband and son of the principal character, Mrs. Alving, are victims of syphilis. This was a subject considered not only wholly inappropriate in the theatre but also unmentionable in polite society. In addition, the play suggests that her son might have escaped this curse had Mrs. Alving been permitted to leave her husband, as she wished. To many, Ibsen, in introducing into his play both syphilis and divorce, seemed to be attacking the family as an institution and to be violating all standards of decency. The response of some critics and censors was comparable to what might be expected today if one were to propose showing an X-rated movie to children.

When London's Independent Theatre produced *Ghosts* in 1891, though only for members of the organization, many critics wrote scathing reviews. George Bernard Shaw, a strong supporter of Ibsen, quotes excerpts from many of these responses in his *The Quintessence of Ibsenism* (1891):

"An open drain; a loathsome sore unbandaged; a dirty act done publicly…" "Garbage and offal."
"A piece to bring the stage into disrepute and dishonour with every right-thinking man and woman."

Ibsen's perception of women's role in society was also out of step with the time, when women were wholly subservient to fathers or husbands. In his notes on *A Doll's House* (1879), Ibsen wrote:

A woman cannot be herself in the society of the present day, which is an exclusively masculine society, with laws framed by men and with a judicial system that judges feminine conduct from a masculine point of view.

with verse dramas about Scandinavian legends, but in the 1870s he abandoned verse and turned to contemporary subjects. His plays stirred worldwide controversy because the endings of his plays did not reaffirm accepted values. These plays were denied production in many places because they were thought to be immoral and corrupting.

Nevertheless, these plays were widely read and discussed, especially because they were thought to challenge moral values and social norms long considered absolute. Let us look more closely at one of Ibsen's plays.

Initially banned because it was thought too scandalous for public performance, Ibsen's *Ghosts* has become a classic of the modern theatre. Seen here is the Royal Shakespeare Company's production of *Ghosts*; directed by Katie Mitchell and featuring Jane Lapotaire as Mrs. Alving.

Robbie Jack/Corbis

A DOLL'S HOUSE

In *A Doll's House* (1879), Nora Helmer is faced with the consequences of having (several years earlier) forged her father's name to borrow the money needed to restore her husband's health (although by law she could not borrow money without her husband's consent). Now, just as happiness seems assured (her husband Torvald is fully recovered and has just been appointed director of a bank), the man from whom Nora borrowed the money (Krogstad) threatens to expose her as a criminal if she does not help him keep the job he is about to lose at Torvald's bank.

Much of the remainder of the play is taken up with Nora's attempt to conceal the truth from her husband because she is convinced that, because of his deep love for her, Torvald will assume responsibility for the crime and thus be ruined. When Torvald learns the truth, he reacts quite differently than Nora had expected. Concerned only for his own reputation, Torvald declares her so morally corrupt that she will no longer be allowed to raise their three children. When Krogstad unexpectedly withdraws the threat of public scandal, Torvald is jubilant about his escape from ruin and, once certain of his safety, seeks to restore his previous relationship with Nora. She, however, now feels alienated not only from her husband but also her society. She chooses to leave her husband and children because, finding herself in disagreement with both law and public opinion and not yet certain of her own convictions, Nora does not believe herself capable of meeting her responsibilities as wife and mother. She leaves, an action that defies social standards, to assert herself as a person.

It is this ending that caused outrage and controversy because to many it seemed an attack on the family itself, the very basis of society. The outrage also stemmed from Ibsen's refusal to allow the audience the escape that Torvald had sought—the pretense, following a moment's anxiety, that the old social order was secure. The ending forced consideration of the status

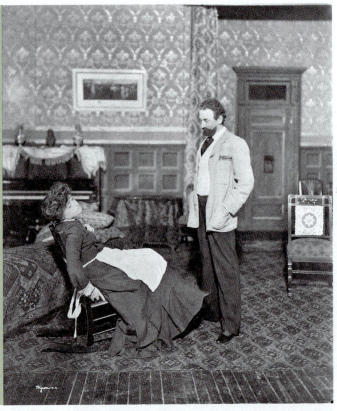

Minnie Maddern Fiske as Nora in a production of *A Doll's House* staged in New York in 1894.

of women who, by law, were defined as inferior because a wife was required to have her husband's consent in all matters, whereas he could act wholly independently, even dispose of property that originally belonged to her, without her consent or knowledge.

Mrs. Linde and Krogstad serve as contrasts to Nora and Torvald. Mrs. Linde has considerable experience, having had to work for a living, though always in positions subordinate to men. She accepts her lot, but what she craves most is someone to look after. Nora, as she herself eventually realizes, has spent her life being treated like a doll, protected from harsh realities but having learned to manipulate men by feeding their fantasies about female helplessness. The mistake for which Krogstad has paid so dearly (forging a signature) is the same one made by Nora, but because women are to be governed by men, her mistake, if revealed, will be attributed to the husband's failure to control his wife. Krogstad is shunned by society as morally corrupt, in contrast with Torvald, who

is considered a pillar of the community. Despite (or perhaps because of) their experiences, Mrs. Linde and Krogstad (who when young were in love but were separated by circumstances) appear at the play's end much more likely than Nora and Torvald to achieve a satisfying relationship. It is Mrs. Linde who insists that Krogstad not retrieve his letter (revealing to Torvald what Nora has done) because she believes it essential that Nora and Torvald cease their childish games so they can build a mature relationship based on truth and trust. Torvald embodies the attitudes and standards of his society. His condescension toward women, his smug conviction of his own moral superiority, his concern for public opinion and appearances, his fear of scandal are the qualities against which Nora's situation is measured.

The fifth major character, Dr. Rank, also serves as a contrast to Torvald. Nora can talk freely and share confidences with Rank about things that Torvald would find shocking. Rank probably would have made an excellent husband for Nora (a role he obviously covets) were it not for the congenital disease (probably syphilis) he has inherited from his father. Rank ultimately faces his unavoidable death with dignity.

Undergirding the characters and action of the play is a basic assumption that character and action are determined by hereditary and environmental forces. What each character is and does is explained by information about background, upbringing, and experience. All of the characters are products of their environment, although Mrs. Linde and Krogstad, having achieved understanding of their circumstances, ultimately seem capable of rising above them. Ibsen could have made his play melodramatic by depicting Krogstad as villain and Nora as heroine. Instead, all of the characters strive for what they consider to be right; the complications arise from their differing conceptions of proper goals and means for attaining them. Thus, they appear to be complex, fallible human beings.

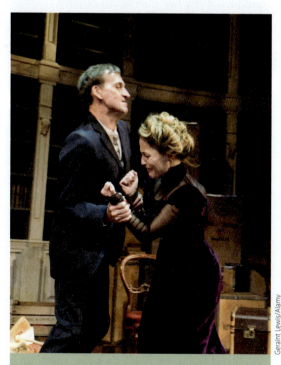

Nora (Gillian Anderson) battles Kelman (the Krogstad character, played by Christopher Eccleston) in Zinnie Harris's Edwardian England adaptation of Ibsen's *A Doll's House*.

A Doll's House could serve as a model of cause-to-effect dramatic construction. Like most of Ibsen's realist plays, this one uses a late point of attack. Mrs. Linde, because of her long absence, can believably inquire about the past and thereby motivate revelation of the complex circumstances that have preceded the play's beginning. The first act, then, sets up with seeming naturalness all of the conditions out of which the subsequent action develops logically, though not necessarily predictably.

A Doll's House uses a single setting throughout. It is a box set (that is, one that fully encloses the acting space on three sides like the walls of a room, with one side removed). Box sets permitted far more realistic representations of indoor spaces than could be achieved with wings, drops, and borders. The realistic effect was further enhanced by the addition of those furnishings, pictures, drapes, rugs, and bric-a-brac typically found in a real room of the period. Furthermore, instead of standing throughout on a stage largely devoid of furnishings, as had been typical prior to the late nineteenth century, actors now sought to behave as they would in real rooms, rather than letting the sets serve merely as visual backgrounds. In *A Doll's House* the characters seem to live in the setting. Action, character, and environment are intertwined.

Zola and Naturalism

Naturalism, unlike realism, had little success in the theatre, probably because it was too extreme in its demands. Its chief advocate, Emile Zola (1840–1902), thought many realists were more concerned with theatrical effectiveness (building complications, crises, and resolutions) than with truth to life. One of Zola's followers suggested that these temptations could be overcome by thinking of a play as "a slice of life," a segment of reality transferred to the stage. The naturalists were far more rigorous than realists in their demands for "truth in art" and for drama that demonstrated the inevitable laws of

The Earth, a play adapted from Emile Zola's novel of the same name. Directed by André Antoine at the Théâtre Antoine, Paris, 1902. Zola's play offers a compelling exploration of the destructive nature of human ignorance and greed. Notice the many naturalistic details, including the hayloft in the background and the chickens in the foreground.

Le Theatre, 1902

heredity and environment. In practice, naturalism emphasized the deleterious influence of poverty and other deprivations on the lives of the lower classes, a subject rarely treated seriously in earlier drama. Zola, who often compared naturalistic art with medicine, believed that, just as the medical pathologist seeks to discover the cause of a disease so it can be treated, the dramatist should expose social ills so their causes can be corrected. With such rigorous (and often unattainable) goals, it is not surprising that naturalism had a short life and was soon absorbed into realism.

Although naturalism produced few plays of importance, the underlying principles of realism and naturalism struck major blows against rigid social codes and absolute values. They laid the foundations on which modernists built.

The Emergence of the Director

Throughout history, someone has assumed responsibility for staging plays. In the Greek theatre, the playwright usually staged his own works. In later times, the heads of companies or someone appointed by them had that responsibility. The present-day director, who assumes responsibility for interpreting the script and for approving and coordinating all of the elements that make up a production, is primarily a product of the late nineteenth century.

A convergence of several complex developments led to the emergence of the modern director. One of these developments involved the growing need for someone to coordinate and unify all the elements of a production. From the Renaissance to the nineteenth century, the elements of production, though representational, had been so generalized as to require little attention. Each theatre had a stock of sets (prison, palace, street, country landscape, and so on) that was reused often. To achieve variety, prosperous theatres acquired two or more sets for each general type of scene. Costumes were typically clothing worn in contemporary life, usually chosen or supplied by the actors; some categories of characters (such as classical or Near Eastern) appeared in noncontemporary dress, but these costumes were so formalized that the same ones could be used for all characters in the same category.

Acting was also conventionalized during the period prior to the nineteenth century, in that actors were hired according to lines of business and always played the same limited range of roles. The actors usually stood near the front of the stage (in part so they would be more visible in the low-intensity lighting of the pre-gas era) and directed their lines as much to the audience as to the other characters. (The auditorium, like the stage, was lighted.) Because there was seldom any furniture on stage, the actors used a pattern of movement that gave the downstage-center position to whichever character had an important speech at that point; when the speech was over, the actor moved away from center stage so the next actor could have that position. Thus, there were frequent changes of place determined by a pattern so well understood that the actors did not need to be told when and where to move. Consequently, rehearsals were restricted largely to establishing where entrances and exits were to be made and to such complex action as duels. The person in charge of staging had little to do other than to make sure that all of the elements were assembled and to settle any disputes that arose. There were usually no more than seven to ten rehearsals.

As the nineteenth century progressed and the theatre became more complex, the number and specificity of sets and costumes increased, especially as elaborate spectacle and special effects multiplied. Much of the effect of melodrama depended on split-second timing and precise stage business. The introduction of box sets with furniture also served to alter the movement patterns typical of earlier times. These changes required increased supervision, coordination, and rehearsal. Nevertheless, each area of theatrical production continued for a time to work in relative isolation—scene painters did the sets, seamstresses and tailors the costumes, and so on—with little consultation. Even within an area, the work was often parceled out to several persons (for example, each set for a five-set production might be done by a different scene painter). As each element of production became more specific and complex, the need for greater unity and more control became increasingly evident in the late nineteenth century.

The acceptance of the modern director owes most to two influences: the theory of Wagner and the practice of Saxe-Meiningen. Richard Wagner (1813–1883), a German now known primarily as a composer of operas, sought to create a "master

Wagner envisioned a theatre in which the seamless unity of production would create a believable (although not realistic) world that the audience, moved by his mythic tales and powerful music, could easily accept and imaginatively enter. Pictured is Wagner's *Die Walküre* as performed at New York's Metropolitan Opera.

artwork" (*Gesamtkunswerk*) through a fusion of all the arts. Opposed to realism, he chose most of his stories from German myth and set his dramas to music, not only to avoid the realistic mode but also to control the way the text was performed. He argued that spoken drama is at the mercy of actors, who are free to speak the lines however they choose, whereas singers are forced to follow the tempo, pitch, and duration dictated by the musical score. He also wished through his music-dramas to create a theatrical experience so over-poweringly empathetic that the audience would be drawn out of its everyday, mundane existence into an idealized, communal, near-religious experience.

To realize his goal, Wagner erected a new kind of theatre building, opened at Bayreuth in 1876. This theatre was the first in the West to do away with the box, pit, and gallery arrangement in favor of a "democratic" configuration, with seating laid out in a fan-shaped pattern that supposedly created equally good seeing and hearing conditions for all. This new auditorium design set the pattern for many twentieth-century theatres. It was also one of the first in which the auditorium was always darkened during performances. Wagner adopted this convention to distinguish between the everyday world (the auditorium) and the ideal realm (the stage), into which the performance sought to pull the audience. Wagner's contribution to the development of the director came from his

strong demand for "unity of production"—that is, for productions in which everything has been filtered through a single consciousness to achieve a unified artistic effect. This theoretical position was fundamental to most twentieth-century ideas of staging.

Georg II, Duke of Saxe-Meiningen (1826–1914), is now usually considered the first director in the modern sense. Ruler of a small German state, Saxe-Meiningen gained international renown between 1874 and 1890 with his company's tours throughout Europe. The fame of the company did not stem from a new repertory, innovative design, or star actors, but rather from its directorial practices. Saxe-Meiningen exerted complete control over every aspect of production. He designed the scenery, costumes, and properties himself and insisted that they be constructed to his precise specifications both in materials and appearance. Unable to afford well-known actors, he depended on long rehearsal periods (sometimes extending over several months) to achieve the ensemble effects he sought. His company was known especially for its crowd scenes, which (unlike those in other companies) were staged with great precision, variety, and emotional power. In Saxe-Meiningen's productions, the total stage picture was worked out carefully moment by moment, and the superior results were seen as convincing arguments for a strong director who can impose his authority and

Shakespeare's *Julius Caesar* as produced by Saxe-Meiningen. Shown here is Antony's oration over Caesar's corpse.

Die Gartenlaube, 1879

implement his vision. The Meiningen Company validated many of Wagner's views, and the need for unified production (to be achieved primarily through the authority of the director) soon became a basic tenet of theatrical production.

The Independent Theatre Movement

By the 1880s, innovative plays by realists and naturalists had appeared, but censorship had kept most of them from production. Similarly, Wagner and Saxe-Meiningen had established the importance of the director, but Wagner had devoted his attention to opera, and Saxe-Meiningen's company was staging mostly poetic drama (by Shakespeare or nineteenth-century playwrights). The new drama and the new staging had remained isolated from each other. They were finally to meet in "independent" theatres.

Throughout most of Europe, plays could not be performed for public audiences until they had been approved by a censor. Some of Ibsen's prose plays were not performed in the 1880s because censors would not license them. On the other hand, "private" performances (those done by a group for its members only) were not subject to censorship. Beginning in the late 1880s, this loophole was exploited by a number of small, "independent" theatres, which were open only to subscribing members and therefore were not subject to censorship. These theatres were able to accomplish what more established theatres had not: the uniting of the new drama with the new staging techniques.

The first independent theatre was the Théâtre Libre, founded in Paris in 1887 by André Antoine. An enthusiastic follower of Zola and Ibsen, Antoine produced their plays and those of similar writers in settings that reproduced every detail of an environment (in one instance, he hung carcasses of real beef in a butcher-shop set). Like Saxe-Meiningen, he exerted control over every element of production.

Antoine's was only the first of numerous independent theatres. In 1889, the Freie Bühne was founded in Berlin. It was less interested in staging than in providing a hearing for new playwrights. It is credited with launching the careers of playwrights (such as Gerhardt Hauptmann) associated with the inauguration of modern drama in Germany. In 1891, the Independent Theatre was established in London. Its inaugural production, of Ibsen's *Ghosts*, created an enormous scandal that did much to call public attention to a new type of drama.

Mrs. Warren's Profession by George Bernard Shaw as directed by Emily Mann at the McCarter Theatre (Princeton, N.J.); sets by Eugene Lee; costumes by Jennifer von Mayrhauser; lighting by Jeff Croiter.

T. Charles Erickson

The Independent Theatre made its greatest contribution by inducing George Bernard Shaw (1856–1950) to begin writing plays. Unlike most dramatists of the new school, Shaw chose to write comedies through which he sought to puncture popular prejudices and provoke audiences into reassessing their values. In *Arms and the Man* (1894) he ridiculed romantic notions about love and war. In *Major Barbara* (1905) he suggested that a munitions manufacturer is a greater benefactor than the Salvation Army because the manufacturer provides his employees the financial means for bettering their lives, whereas the Salvation Army provides only momentary relief. In *Pygmalion* (1913), later adapted into the musical *My Fair Lady* (1956), he shows how the English class system is related to speech. His other plays include *Man and Superman* (1903), *Heartbreak House* (1919), and *Saint Joan* (1923). Shaw is considered one of the major playwrights of the twentieth century.

Society, Art & Culture

CENSORING SHAW

Out of the eight thousand plays submitted to the British censor between 1895 and 1909 only thirty were banned from public performance, and three of those were by George Bernard Shaw. One of those plays was *Mrs. Warren's Profession* (1902), which, like most of Shaw's early plays, had its first performance in a private, independent theatre. The play was banned in England because the profession of its title character is prostitution. Although other plays had treated "fallen women," those women either repented their sordid past or were punished. Shaw's prostitute not only refuses to apologize for her past, she has a clergyman as one of her former clients, and (perhaps most shocking) has prospered. Shaw states his purpose in his preface to the play:

> *Mrs. Warren's Profession* was written to draw attention to the truth that prostitution is caused, not by female depravity … but simply by underpaying, undervaluing, and overworking women so shamefully that the poorest of them are forced to resort to prostitution.

When Arnold Daly announced plans to produce the play in New York, Anthony Comstock, secretary and special agent of The Society for the Suppression of Vice, warned him not to produce "Bernard Shaw's filthy product." Daly responded by inviting Comstock to read the play or attend a rehearsal, but Comstock refused. Their correspondence was leaked to the newspapers and the production's opening night (1905) was jammed with spectators. Police were called for crowd control, two to three thousand people wanting to buy tickets were turned away at the door, and tickets were scalped for the then almost unheard-of price of $40 each. Following the performance, warrants were issued for the entire cast and crew, charging them with "offending public decency."

Reviews in leading newspapers damned the play: *The New York Times* deemed it "Unfit"; *The New York Herald*, "morally rotten"; and *The American* labeled it "illuminated gangrene." (Shaw later pointed out that one of the newspapers most righteous in its condemnation of the play derived considerable revenue by publishing advertising for houses of prostitution.)

Eight months later, those involved with the New York production of *Mrs. Warren's Profession* were cleared of all charges. However, the production was effectively killed after its single Manhattan performance. Shaw later remarked, "to prohibit the play is to protect the evil which the play exposes."

The final act of Chekhov's *The Three Sisters* as performed at the Moscow Art Theatre.

Photo by Fred Fehl; courtesy of the Hoblitzelle Theatre Arts Collection, Harry Ransom Humanities Research Center, University of Texas at Austin

Not only did these independent theatres meet an important need, they also established a significant precedent: Since that time, whenever established theatres have become insufficiently responsive to innovation, small companies (variously called "art" theatres, "little" theatres, Off-Broadway, or "alternative" theatres) have been formed to meet the need.

Another organization that emerged from the independent theatre movement—the Moscow Art Theatre—was to be of special importance. Founded in 1898 by Konstantin Stanislavsky (1863–1938) and Vladimir Nemerovich-Danchenko (1859–1943), it achieved its first major success with the plays of Anton Chekhov (1860–1904), known primarily for *The Sea Gull* (1896), *Uncle Vanya* (1897), *The Three Sisters* (1901), and *The Cherry Orchard* (1904), all of which are set in rural Russia and depict the monotony and frustrations of provincial life. All the characters in these plays aspire to a better life but do not know how (or do not have the initiative) to achieve their goals. They often do not understand their own feelings, and they seek to conceal as much as to reveal their responses. In these plays, subtext is often as important as text. Chekhov does not pass judgment on his characters; rather, he treats all with tolerance and compassion. The plays intermingle the comic, serious, pathetic, and ironic so thoroughly that they do not fit comfortably into any dramatic type (tragedy, comedy, tragicomedy). Chekhov's plays continue to hold a firm place in the repertory, not only in Russia but also throughout the world. Following the Russian Revolution in 1917, the Moscow Art Theatre faltered, but by the 1930s, Soviet authorities considered it the model that other companies should emulate. It retained this status into the disintegration of the Soviet Union. Today, the Moscow Art Theatre's legacy is most widely associated with its realistic productions of Chekhov's plays and with the systematic approach to acting created by its cofounder Stanislavsky.

The Stanislavsky System

Stanislavsky was the adopted stage name of Konstantin Sergeyevich Alekseyev, the Russian creator of an approach to acting that arguably had the greatest impact on acting in the twentieth century. After extensive experience as an actor, Stanislavsky came to recognize that many of his shortcomings as a performer and those of the Russian theatre of the time were due to the lack of a systematic approach to acting. His goal was to formulate a system that would achieve the highest level of ensemble playing in productions, clarify the dramatic action, and emphasize the inner truth and life of a character rather than call attention to the virtuosity of the performer. He wanted performers to act truthfully and not mechanically or in a manner designed purely for its sensational effect. These were the basic premises of Stanislavsky's system:

1. The actor's body and voice must be trained and flexible so they can respond to all demands.

2. Truthful acting requires that the actor be a skilled observer of human behavior and understand the relationship between a character's inner life and its external manifestation.

3. Actors must project themselves into the world of the play and may learn to do so through the *magic if* (that is, through imagining how one would feel or act if one were this specific character in this specific situation).

4. If actors are not merely to play themselves, they must understand a character's motivations and goals in each scene and in the play as a whole, as well as each character's relationship to all the other roles and the dramatic action.

5. Onstage, the actor should concentrate moment by moment, as if the events were happening spontaneously and for the first time.

Stanislavsky and his company at the Moscow Arts Theatre were successful in achieving most of these goals, but he never viewed his system as complete. He recorded the first outlines of his system in 1909, and in 1912 he established the Moscow Art Theatre's First Studio to explore the system through training and performances by young actors. He created additional studios to explore alternative approaches, but he was never fully satisfied with the results. Stanislavsky sought to deal with all aspects of acting in his system, and he continued to adapt and refine it until his death in 1938.

Several books have been published describing features of Stanislavsky's system: *My Life in Art* (1924), *An Actor Prepares* (1936), *Building a Character* (1949), and *Creating a Role* (1961). What Stanislavsky wrote has been interpreted in different ways by different people, but criticism of his system usually focuses on one of two main points: that the system is overly analytical or that the system is ineffective for acting in nonrealistic dramas. Stanislavsky was perhaps personally most comfortable with realistic acting, but he recognized the need to master other styles and never stopped exploring alternative techniques as well as freely acknowledging mistakes in his earlier work. His later work emphasized the "Method of Physical Action," through which he sought to simplify portions of his earlier analytic and psychological efforts by focusing on physical action. Despite its detractors, Stanislavsky's system continues to be the best-known attempt to describe what is involved in effective acting.

Summary

By the late nineteenth century, realism in the theatre was well established. In some respects, it was the logical culmination of developments that began in the Renaissance, when the picture-frame stage and perspective scenery were introduced. At that time, the stage became essentially representational, and subsequent trends were toward ever-more-convincing pictures. As the nineteenth century progressed, the demand for realistic detail reached a peak. It can be seen in melodrama first and then in realism/naturalism.

Melodrama and realism differed, not so much over realistic staging, but over their views of truth and values. Melodrama was grounded in the assumption that human beings innately know the difference between right and wrong and that moral behavior has little to do with environment, class, or wealth. It taught that if one remains faithful to moral principles, everything will eventually work out satisfactorily—that good will win and evil will lose. Realism and naturalism, on the other hand, tended to view the world scientifically rather than morally and to believe that the forces of heredity and environment are the determinants of human behavior. They did not believe that providence intervenes on the part of moral goodness, but rather that it is up to human beings to analyze and discover the causes of undesirable behavior and to alter those causes to achieve the desired results. By challenging melodrama's metaphysical foundations, realism and naturalism undermined the absolutist values that had dominated art since the medieval period. A pathway was thereby opened for those ideas and practices that have come to be labeled "modernist."

THEATRE IN A BROAD CONTEXT

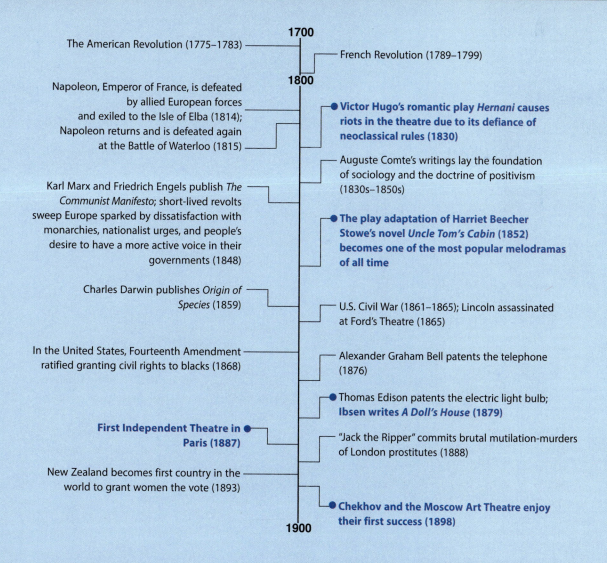

1700

The American Revolution (1775–1783)

French Revolution (1789–1799)

1800

Napoleon, Emperor of France, is defeated by allied European forces and exiled to the Isle of Elba (1814); Napoleon returns and is defeated again at the Battle of Waterloo (1815)

● **Victor Hugo's romantic play *Hernani* causes riots in the theatre due to its defiance of neoclassical rules (1830)**

Auguste Comte's writings lay the foundation of sociology and the doctrine of positivism (1830s–1850s)

Karl Marx and Friedrich Engels publish *The Communist Manifesto*; short-lived revolts sweep Europe sparked by dissatisfaction with monarchies, nationalist urges, and people's desire to have a more active voice in their governments (1848)

● **The play adaptation of Harriet Beecher Stowe's novel *Uncle Tom's Cabin* (1852) becomes one of the most popular melodramas of all time**

Charles Darwin publishes *Origin of Species* (1859)

U.S. Civil War (1861–1865); Lincoln assassinated at Ford's Theatre (1865)

In the United States, Fourteenth Amendment ratified granting civil rights to blacks (1868)

Alexander Graham Bell patents the telephone (1876)

● Thomas Edison patents the electric light bulb; **Ibsen writes *A Doll's House* (1879)**

First Independent Theatre in Paris (1887) ●

"Jack the Ripper" commits brutal mutilation-murders of London prostitutes (1888)

New Zealand becomes first country in the world to grant women the vote (1893)

● **Chekhov and the Moscow Art Theatre enjoy their first success (1898)**

1900

The Yale School of Drama production of August Strindberg's *The Ghost Sonata* celebrates the one-hundredth anniversary of this modernist drama. Directed by Shana Cooper; scene design by Scott Dougan; costume design by Katherine O'Neil; lighting design by Marie Yokoyama; sound design by Phillip Owen.

[I]n the years following…1885, all the arts changed direction as if they had been awaiting a signal. … In all the arts, 1885 is the point from which we must reckon the meaning of the word "modern."
—Roger Shattuck, *The Banquet Years*

Modernism and Its Effect: 1885–1960

By the time the independent theatre movement got underway in the late 1880s, another strand of performance—in rebellion against realism—was emerging. This new strand can be viewed as an alternative reaction to many of the same impulses that had led to realism and naturalism. The belief that art should seek to represent human behavior and the physical world (as normally perceived) had dominated theory and practice since the Renaissance. It was a fundamental premise of realism and naturalism. Beginning in the 1880s, however, one group of artists increasingly rejected this premise and substituted its own subjective visions (usually involving some degree of abstraction and distortion) for the traditional approach that had allowed the audience to compare a subject with its artistic rendering. This rejection of the long-standing relationship between perception and representation is often considered the true beginning of the modernist temperament. No longer shackled to the natural world, artists could now be valued for imaginative perception and formal innovation rather than accurate renditions of recognizable subjects. A dizzying array of artistic movements and styles arose almost simultaneously, providing different views of the human experience.

Symbolism

The first artistic movement to reject representationalism was *symbolism*, launched in 1885. It denied the claims made by realists that ultimate truth is to be discovered through the five senses, arguing instead that truth is beyond objective examination. Because it can be only intuited, it cannot be expressed directly or through wholly rational means; truth can be only hinted at through a network of symbols that evokes feelings and states of mind corresponding imprecisely to our intuitions. Maurice Maeterlinck, author of *Pelléas and Mélisande* (1892), the best known of all the symbolist plays, wrote that the most important element of great drama is the "idea which the poet forms of the unknown in which float about the beings and things which he evokes, the mystery which dominates them."

Unlike the realists, the symbolists chose their subjects from the past, the realm of fancy, or the mysterious present and avoided any attempt to deal with social problems or environmental forces. They aimed to suggest a universal truth independent of time and place that cannot be logically defined or rationally

Susan Sontag's play *Alice in Bed* as produced by the American Repertory Theatre evoked the theatrical style of symbolism with its use of scrims and haze to separate the onstage world as a mythic realm quite apart from our physical reality. Directed by Bob McGrath; scene design by Laurie Olinder and Fred Tietz; costume design by Susan Anderson; lighting by John Ambrosone; with interactive films by Bill Morrison.

Richard Feldman

expressed. Thus, their drama tended to be vague and mysterious.

Established theatres, finding symbolist drama incomprehensible, were even less inclined to produce it than the works of Ibsen and Zola. Consequently, the symbolists, like the realists and naturalists, established independent theatres in which to perform their plays. The most influential was the Théâtre de l'Oeuvre, founded in Paris in 1893 by Aurélien-Marie Lugné-Poë. The symbolists believed that the most important aspect of a production is mood or atmosphere. They used little scenery, and even that was vague in form and almost devoid of detail. They often placed a gauze curtain (*scrim*) just back of the proscenium so the action would appear to be taking place in a mist or timeless void. Color was chosen for its mood value rather than for representational accuracy. The actors often chanted their lines and used unnatural gestures. The goal was to remove the action from the immediate, everyday world. One can scarcely conceive of productions more unlike those of the realists and naturalists. They so differed from what audiences had become accustomed to that many spectators were baffled. As a movement in the theatre, symbolism soon lost its appeal, and by 1900 had largely ceased. Nevertheless, symbolism is important as the first of the nonrealistic movements that would proliferate in the twentieth century.

"Art for Art's Sake"

Symbolism was not alone in challenging realism and naturalism during the late nineteenth century. In England, Walter Pater set forth the basic ideas of English aestheticism, which advocated that the only functions of art were to intensify experience and to provide sensuous pleasure. The movement came to be called "art for art's sake," and it was Oscar Wilde who became its best-known playwright and its most eloquent spokesman. In his 1889 essay, "The Decay of Lying," Wilde expresses the basic principles of the movement. Rather than focusing on contemporary subjects and problems, as the realists and naturalists advocated, Wilde claimed that art has an independent life and that its imaginative power must remain free from the concerns of its time. Instead of art imitating life, he proposed that life imitates art. Wilde argued that nature is not a model to be replicated but raw material to be fashioned and improved upon by fancy. Whereas realism and naturalism strove to use art to expose "the truth," Wilde claimed that "Lying, the telling of beautiful untrue things, is the proper aim of art." Wilde was not advocating dishonesty; he was freeing art from a responsibility to express anything but itself. This stance has important implications in respect to the mushrooming of artistic styles within the twentieth century. It implies that art should be judged on the creativity of artists to express new vistas rather than to replicate old ones. As such, the stance breaks from adherence to conventional standards regarding both subject and method. We may gain a fuller understanding of Wilde's ideas by looking at the play generally considered his comic masterpiece, *The Importance of Being Earnest* (1895).

THE IMPORTANCE OF BEING EARNEST

Written in 1895, the play makes use of the standard devices of the three-act, "well-made play": carefully constructed exposition, cause-to-effect arrangement of events, skillful manipulation of withheld information, and startling reversals accomplished by last-minute revelations. Wilde lifts these devices to ridiculous levels, making the inherent artifice of the formulaic pattern laughably evident. He uses stock characters to embody the action: two fashionable bachelors matched with two proper young ladies (one from the city and one from the country), a stern English matron, a governess, an erudite churchman, and appropriately dry servants. The artificiality of the play's language and the self-conscious style called for on the part of its performers resembles Restoration comedy more than realism.

The play begins in the London flat of the fashionable bachelor, Algernon Moncrieff. During a conversation between Algernon and his friend Mr. Worthing, we learn that Worthing wishes to marry Algernon's cousin Gwendolen. But before Algernon will give his consent, he wants to know why his friend has a cigarette case engraved, "from little Cecily, with her fondest love to her dear Uncle Jack." After all,

Algernon knows Worthing's name to be Ernest, not Jack, and he has never heard of this Cecily before now. Worthing explains that he goes by the name Jack in the country and Ernest in town. In the country, he feels he must play the role of a high-minded moral guardian. He therefore invented a wicked younger brother named Ernest, who lives in London, so that he might have a ready excuse to visit London in order to rescue Ernest from the dreadful scrapes he gets into. Algernon understands all too well. He has invented an imaginary friend, an invalid named Bunbury, whom he uses as an excuse to avoid his social obligations in town. Both men have invented personas that free them from social responsibilities and expectations. Lady Bracknell, Algernon's aunt, and her daughter Gwendolen arrive. Worthing proposes to Gwendolen and she accepts, but specifies she could only love and marry him because his name is Ernest; the name of the man she believes she was destined to marry. However, Lady Bracknell reminds Gwendolen that she and her father will decide whom Gwendolen should marry. Lady Bracknell interviews Worthing and, discovering that he is a foundling, refuses her consent.

This synopsis of the events in Act I recounts Wilde's story but lacks the essence of his style. It is Wilde's use of language (puns, epigrams, hyperbole, etc.) that comically reveals the hypocritical attitudes, capricious behavior, and twisted logic of his characters who consistently value artifice over reality and appearances over substance. For example, after Gwendolen agrees to marry Worthing, she remarks, "I hope you will always look at me just like that, especially when there are other people present." Lady Bracknell is pleased to discover that Worthing knows "nothing" because she does "not approve of anything that tampers with natural ignorance" and purports that the "whole theory of modern education is radically unsound. Fortunately in England, at any rate, education produces no effect whatsoever." Lady Bracknell is also almost devoid of sentimentality and flippantly characterizes Worthing's having lost his parents as "careless" and advises him to "acquire some relations as soon as possible."

Wilde loads the second act with complications and discoveries that sustain the comedic action. In order to get to know "little Cecily," Algernon arrives at Mr. Worthing's country home pretending to be his brother Ernest, and Worthing arrives dressed in mourning declaring that his brother Ernest has died. Cecily brings the two men together and attempts to reconcile their differences, but the fiction of their being at odds has now become true. Worthing orders Algernon/Ernest to leave and storms off. Algernon proclaims his love for Cecily, which she takes as a matter of fact because she has already created a love affair between them months ago in her diary. Far from being a factual record of daily events, her diary is a work of imaginative fiction. She recounts from her diary their engagement, break-up, and reconciliation. She produces letters from him, and when he exclaims that he never wrote her any letters she retorts, "You need hardly to remind me of that. I remember only too well that I was forced to write your letters for you…the three you wrote me after I had broken off the engagement are so beautiful, and so badly spelled, that even now I can hardly read them without crying a little." Algernon discovers that she, too, finds Ernest the only acceptable name for a prospective husband. Wilde further complicates matters by having Gwendolen arrive expecting to see her fiancé Ernest. Gwendolen meets Cecily and the two women learn that each is engaged to "Ernest Worthing." They have tea, but the etiquette of this social ritual barely masks their antipathy. When Worthing and Algernon reappear and clarify who is engaged to whom, the ladies discover that neither man is truly Ernest. The women close ranks and firmly assert that they are not engaged to anyone if they are not engaged to Ernest. The men console themselves by eating muffins and reaffirming their intentions to be rechristened as Ernest.

In Act III, the conflict reaches its crisis. Lady Bracknell arrives and recognizes Cecily's governess, Miss Prism, as the nanny who many years ago lost a baby in her charge. Miss Prism had mistakenly

Paper Mill Playhouse's production of *The Importance of Being Earnest* featuring Lynn Redgrave as Lady Bracknell. Directed by David Schweizer; costumes and millinery by David Murin; sets by Alexander Dodge; lighting by Matt Frey.

Gerry Goodstein

deposited a novel she had written in the baby carriage and the baby in her handbag, inadvertently leaving the bag at Victoria Station. Worthing produces the handbag which Prism identifies, implicating him as the long-lost baby. Lady Bracknell then reveals that Worthing is her sister's child, General Moncrieff's son, and Algernon's older brother. Furthermore, it happens that Worthing was actually christened "Ernest." Wilde has brought us full circle; the characters' lies have become truths.

The Importance of Being Earnest has been viewed by some as a farcical excuse for clever dialogue and by others as an insightful comic critique on Victorian society. Both views have some validity. Wilde subtitled *The Importance of Being Earnest* "a trivial play for serious people," and it is a rollicking verbal comedy enlisting contrived complications, discoveries, and startling last-minute revelations. Conversely, if one views the play as a critique of Victorian hypocrisy and shallowness, it may appear that Wilde directly treats the concerns of his time despite his "art for art's sake" stance. However, inasmuch as the characters create fictions (lies), which become true, the play supports his essential critical stance—life imitates art.

The Modernist Influence on Theatrical Visionaries

Modernism influenced all of the arts. From the Renaissance to the twentieth century, the visual arts (including theatrical scenery) had depicted everything in relation to a fixed eye-point. In the early twentieth century, however, the visual arts no longer always depicted all details of the same picture as seen from one eye-point. The best-known examples are some of Picasso's paintings, in which various parts of the same subject are painted as though seen from different eye-points. Attention shifted from subject matter to the elements of art forms. In painting, recognizable subjects were some-times abandoned altogether, resulting in wholly abstract works. Such painting had to be judged by formal criteria (effectiveness in manipulating line, color, and composition) rather than by the accuracy with which it represented its subject. Similar developments in music displaced melody, so that a composition could be valued not for its melodic and harmonic patterns but rather for its handling of time and atonal relationships. The theatre also participated in these modernist trends. During the early twentieth century, two theorists—Appia and Craig—were especially successful in reshaping ideas about the "art of the theatre."

Born in Switzerland, Adolphe Appia (1862–1928) began with the idea that artistic unity in

This design for the opera *Orpheus and Eurydice* shows the influence of Adolphe Appia, who advocated the use of steps, ramps, and platforms to create transitions from horizontal to vertical planes.

Bettmann/Corbis

theatre is fundamental but difficult to achieve because of conflicting elements: the moving actor, the horizontal floor, and the vertical scenery. He sought to replace flat, painted scenery (as well as all decorative detail) with three-dimensional structures as the only proper environment for three-dimensional actors. To overcome the limitations of the flat stage floor, he advocated the use of steps, platforms, and ramps to create transitions from horizontal to vertical planes, thereby making possible greater compositional variety in the total stage picture and the movement of actors.

Appia was also a major theoretician of stage lighting. To reveal the shape and dimensionality of the setting and actor, Appia advocated the use of light from various directions and angles. He considered light the most flexible of all theatri-

cal elements because, like music, it can change moment by moment to reflect shifts in mood and emotion and because it unifies all other elements through its intensity, color, direction, and movement. Appia's views on lighting came at a crucial time—just as the technology needed to implement his theories was becoming available. The incandescent electric lamp was invented in 1879, and as the first medium that did not use an open flame, it gained acceptance rapidly because of its safety. Initially, the wattage of electric lamps was very small, and not until 1911 were lamps available with a concentrated filament of sufficiently high wattage to permit the development of spotlights. By around 1915, most of the technology (electric lamps, spotlights, color filters, and dimmers) needed to implement Appia's theories was available and in use.

Edward Gordon Craig's 1926 design (watercolor and pastel on paper) for *Hamlet,* showing the scene in Act III when Hamlet meets the acting troupe that has arrived at Elsinore.

Edward Gordon Craig (1872–1966) began his career as an actor in the English theatre. Much more militant than Appia, he was always in the public eye because of his controversial views. Craig denied that the theatre is a fusion of other arts; he saw it as a wholly autonomous art whose basic elements—action, language, line, color, and rhythm—are fused by a master artist. He once suggested that actors should be replaced by large puppets (*übermarionetten*) because they, unlike actors, could not impose their own personalities on a production and undermine the master artist's intentions. Like Appia, Craig advocated simplicity in scenery, costumes, and lighting. Both sought to replace the representational approach to visual elements with one concerned with abstract structures that embodied the line, mass, color, texture, and mood appropriate to the dramatic action. Appia and Craig also promoted the concept of the director as the supreme, unifying theatre artist.

The influence of Appia and Craig was reinforced by the German director, Max Reinhardt (1872–1943), who was then amending earlier conceptions of the director. During the late nineteenth century, Wagner, Saxe-Meiningen, Antoine, Lugné-Poë, and others had won acceptance for the director. Although each of these men differed in their approaches to staging, they used basically the same mode for every production they staged. As new artistic movements appeared, each movement was faced with the need to establish a theatre specializing in its distinctive style because each existing theatre was devoted to a single approach in theatrical production.

A breakthrough was achieved around 1900, when Reinhardt began to treat each production as a new challenge demanding its unique stylistic solution. Using this approach, the plays of all movements and periods could be accommodated in the same theatre. For the first time, theatre history became important to directing because Reinhardt frequently built productions around elements significant to the theatrical context in which a play had originally appeared. Often he tried to re-create the audience-performer spatial relationship. (As examples, he remodeled a circus building to accommodate Greek plays; for a medieval play, he transformed a theatre into a cathedral; and he presented many eighteenth-century plays in a hall of state in an eighteenth-century palace.) He unified some productions around dominant visual motifs and others around theatrical conventions typical of the period when the play was written. Thus, knowledge of the theatre's past was crucial in many of his productions.

Reinhardt's method further enhanced the role of the director. Because the stylistic approach to be used in any production was optional, the choice was the director's to make; as the one who chose the vision that would undergird the production, the director was also the arbiter of all

Reinhardt's production of *Oedipus the King* in the Circus Schumann, Berlin, 1910.

Le Theatre, 1911

choices made by those who worked to implement his vision. Although Reinhardt considered the director's the primary artistic consciousness, he did not, as many of his successors were to do, alter the time or place of a play's action. He believed that the production should serve the script (rather than the script serve the production, as has become common in more recent times). His productions, viewed from today's perspective, do not seem stylistically as varied as they did to his contemporaries because most of his productions were still largely representational. Nevertheless, Reinhardt established eclecticism as the dominant directorial approach. Once accepted, eclecticism was (and continues to be) elaborated and extended by others, frequently in ways never envisioned by Reinhardt. With Reinhardt, relativism triumphed in directing (as it already had in many other areas); instead of applying the same approach to all plays (the absolutist's way), the approach was altered to suit each play (the relativist's way).

Futurism, Dada, and Expressionism

The decade between 1910 and 1920 was one of unrest and upheaval, epitomized by World War I. Not surprisingly, this decade saw the emergence of numerous artistic movements, each championing a new perspective on human experience and new ways of expressing this perspective. Three of the most important of these movements were futurism, dada, and expressionism.

Futurism was launched in 1909 by Filippo Tommaso Marinetti (1876–1944), an Italian who glorified the speed and energy of the machine age, which he saw as the key to an enlightened future. Because he thought veneration of the past stood in the way of progress, he declared that all libraries and art museums should be destroyed. The futurists sought to replace old art forms with a number of new ones, among them collage, kinetic sculpture, and *bruitisme* ("noise music" based on the sounds of everyday life). Especially contemptuous of drama that developed leisurely and required no active involvement from its audience, the futurists issued a number of manifestos demanding change. In one of these manifestos, "The Variety Theatre," Marinetti argued that the theatre of his day was devoted almost entirely to historical drama or photographic reproductions of daily life. He considered such drama to be remnants from "the age of the oil lamp." To reform this theatre, he proposed as a model the variety theatre with its vaudeville acts, jugglers, dancers, gymnasts, and the like because of its dynamic energy and audience involvement. "The Variety Theatre is alone in seeking the audience's collaboration. It doesn't remain static like a stupid voyeur, but joins noisily in the action. …" Marinetti went on to suggest ways of disrupting the refined and detached behavior of theatre audiences: "Spread a powerful glue on some of the seats. … Sell the same seat to ten persons… Sprinkle the seats with dust to make people itch and sneeze."

The futurists proposed to replace existing drama with a synthetic drama that would compress into a moment or two the essence of a full-length play. Their desire to speed up life also led them to champion simultaneity and multiple focus. In their performances, several scenes or different kinds of events (musical, pictorial, dramatic) proceeded simultaneously in different parts of the performance-audience space. The futurists sought confrontations with audiences, whose prejudices about what art is or can be they challenged so strongly that their performances often provoked near-riots. Futurism lost much of its appeal during World War I because it praised war as the supreme expression of the aggressive life it championed.

Dada was grounded in rejection of the values that had provoked World War I. When that war broke out, many artists sought refuge in neutral Switzerland, where in 1916 dada was born.

Its principal spokesman was Tristan Tzara (1896–1963). Because insanity seemed the world's state, the dadaists sought in their art to replace logic, reason, and unity with chance and illogic. They presented a number of programs in which, like the futurists, they used simultaneity and multiple focus. Among their favorite forms were "chance poems" (created by placing words in a hat, drawing them out at random, and reciting them) and "sound poems" (composed of nonverbal sounds). They also performed short plays, dances, and music. They recognized no barriers between art forms. Dada was essentially anarchistic, thumbing its nose at a hypocritical, discredited society and the art forms it venerated.

Dada lost much of its energy when the war ended, but some of the most interesting examples occurred after the war. For example, in Cologne, Germany, in 1920 Max Ernst, Hans Arp, and Theodor Baargeld staged a dada event in a glassed-in courtyard entered through a men's toilet. The event included several unrelated features, among them a young woman, dressed as if for her first communion, reciting obscene poems, a pool of blood-red liquid from which a skull and a hand projected, and a wooden sculpture to which a hatchet was attached for the convenience of anyone wishing to attack it.

Much of what the futurists and dadaists did seems prankish, intended deliberately to provoke.

Practices & Styles

CHICAGO'S NEO-FUTURISTS

The variety, speed, immediacy, and audience interaction of futurism can be experienced at a performance of the Neo-Futurists in the longest running play in Chicago today, *Too Much Light Makes the Baby Go Blind*. *TMLMTBGB* is a collection of very short, comedic plays written and produced by Neo-Futurist company members. In every performance since its premiere in 1988, the Neo-Futurists have performed thirty plays in sixty minutes. More than six thousand of these short plays have been written and performed since 1988 in the group's theatre space located above a funeral parlor in suburban Chicago.

The Neo-Futurists have adopted a number of practices inspired by the futurism movement. Among these is a very interactive relationship with the audience. For example, audience members roll dice to determine part of their admission price. The audience chooses which plays they'll see next by shouting out a number that corresponds to a particular play. These numbers, identifying the plays, are listed on the audience's program (the Neo-Futurists call it a "menu") and also hang above the stage on makeshift placards. As audience members call out a number, the performers leap up to grab the audience's selection—whichever number a performer comes down with first is the play performed next. The performance as a whole takes shape as a randomly formed collage. Variety and immediacy are the fundamental principles guiding the performance. Their intention is to create an experience for their audience that cannot be reproduced, one that moves at a dizzying pace that matches that of today's world.

Over the more than twenty years *TMLMTBGB* has been running, the members of the Neo-Futurists have changed considerably. Some former members include Greg Kotis, who went on to win the 2002 Tony Award for "Best Book of a Musical" for *Urinetown*, and Stephen Colbert, who was with the group for only three days before leaving to perform with Second City, also in Chicago.

It is difficult to assess their immediate influence, but the challenges they posed aroused strong emotion and heated debate about such topics as how to define a work of art, the role of audience response, art as an instrument of change, the need for innovation in art, and the relationship of art to its culture. Their influence would resurface strongly after 1960.

Expressionism emerged around 1910 in Germany. It sought to counter materialism and industrialism, which it saw as distorting the human spirit. Unlike futurism, which glorified the machine age, expressionism charged that the industrial age had turned human beings into machines with conditioned responses and souls shriveled by materialistic values. Its proponents wished to reshape the world to make it conform to what is best in the human spirit and thereby to achieve "the regeneration of man." Unlike futurism and dada, whose theatrical programs were forerunners of today's performance art, expressionism, with its emphasis on text, was more easily assimilated and had a greater immediate impact on theatre than did futurism or dada.

Most expressionist drama focuses on how the human spirit has been distorted by false values. It usually shows the protagonist searching for identity, fulfillment, or a means to change the world. Because these protagonists have usually been warped by materialism and industrialism, the external world that they see (and that we see through their eyes) is also distorted. The walls of buildings or rooms may lean in threateningly, color may reflect emotion (for example, the protagonist's jealousy may make the sky green rather than blue), movement and speech may be robotlike, or several persons or objects may be identical in appearance (as if machine made). Expressionism typically presents a nightmarish vision of the human situation.

Some of August Strindberg's (1849–1912) plays are often seen as forerunners of expressionism. Perhaps the most important of these is *A Dream Play* (1902), in the preface to which Strindberg wrote:

> The writer has tried to imitate the disconnected but seemingly logical form of the dream. Anything may happen; everything is possible and probable. Time and space do not exist. On an insignificant background of reality, imagination designs and embroiders novel patterns: a medley of memories, experiences, free fancies, absurdities, and improvisations.

The Cabinet of Dr. Caligari, a music theatre performance piece by composer/author John Moran, inspired by the 1919 German expressionist silent film of the same name. Note the sharp contrasts and nightmarish reality conveyed through the production's combination of live action with stylized costumes, slides, film, and a computer-generated landscape. Directed by Bob McGrath; costumes by Catherine Zuber.

Richard Feldman

Practices & Styles

MODERNIST MOVEMENTS

The modernist era is marked by a shift from absolute to relative values. One of the hallmarks of modernist art is a continuing search for a set of values that can serve as the basis for action and that can attract a widespread following. During the twentieth century there were more artistic movements than all the previous centuries combined; the elimination of an absolute standard meant there were many different views as to what constitutes truth and how art/theatre should deal with the truth. One way to understand the different modernist movements is to examine their competing philosophies; each movement's worldview helped dictate their staging style. (The specifics or their distinctive staging style are discussed in the body of the chapter corresponding to each movement.)

	Realism/Naturalism	Symbolism	Expressionism	Surrealism
Where is truth located?	Truth is in the physical world, in science	Truth exists in a spiritual or mystical realm	Truth is located within the individual spirit or soul	Truth is located in the unconscious mind
How does one get to the truth?	Get to the truth through the five senses and direct observation	Get to truth via intuition	Truth is personal and subjective	Get to truth via illogical associations and metaphorical thinking
How does one represent truth on stage?	Present events as lifelike and objectively as possible	Use symbols and abstraction that evoke feelings and states of mind that correspond to our intuitions	Externalize the inner vision of the artist; use distortion and present world through protagonist's eyes	Put familiar objects in unfamiliar combinations; use dreams and automatic writing

Another way to understand the various modernist movements is to look for their points of difference. For example, futurism looked to technology as the source of progress, while expressionism viewed technology and materialism as dehumanizing the individual. Likewise, while both futurism and dada shunned traditional scripted drama in favor of a variety theatre format that might include "noise music," simultaneity, and collage, they had fundamentally different worldviews. For example, the futurists embraced war and their artists went and fought in World War I, whereas dada was disgusted by war (and a world that had seemingly gone mad) and their artists fled the war, founding their movement in neutral Switzerland.

Overall, the shift to a more relativist perspective has resulted in continuing artistic experimentation as individuals use art and theatre as a means of trying to understand and express the world around them and the varying perspectives of the human condition. The implications of the modernist era continue to ripple through the world of theatre and contemporary society.

Strindberg overcame the limitations of time, space, logical sequence, and appearance by adopting the viewpoint of the dreamer. In *A Dream Play*, one event flows into another without logical transition, characters are transformed into others, and widely separated places and times are telescoped in a story about tortured and alienated human beings. From Strindberg the expressionists borrowed many of their techniques.

Expressionism flourished in Germany, especially immediately after World War I, when optimism over the establishment of Germany's first democratic government made the realization of expressionist goals seem possible. The most important German expressionist playwrights were Georg Kaiser (1878–1945) and Ernst Toller (1893–1939). By the mid-1920s disillusionment had replaced optimism, and the popularity of expressionism faded rapidly. Nevertheless, expressionism had attracted a number of writers in various countries. In the United States, several noteworthy expressionist plays were written, the best known of which are *The Adding Machine* (1923) (whose accountant-protagonist is little more than an adding machine himself) by Elmer Rice (1892–1967) and *The Hairy Ape* (1922) by Eugene O'Neill.

Eugene O'Neill (1888–1953), son of James O'Neill, was the first American dramatist to win wide and lasting international recognition. Like many American playwrights of his day, O'Neill was aided in his early career by groups modeled after Europe's independent theatres. In the United States these companies, which began to appear around 1912, were usually called "little" or "art" theatres. O'Neill was discovered by the Provincetown Players, a group that between 1915 and 1929 was concerned with promoting American playwriting. O'Neill explored a wide variety of dramatic styles and techniques in his plays. For example, *The Emperor Jones* (1920) and *The Hairy Ape* owe much to expressionism. *Desire Under the Elms* (1924) and *Mourning Becomes Electra* (1931) take on subjects that seem appropriate for classical Greek tragedy and then develop them through modern psychology. *Strange Interlude* (1928) uses the technique of inner monologue as external expression. Toward the end of his career, O'Neill wrote a trilogy of realistic, autobiographical plays: *The Iceman Cometh* (written 1939, produced 1946), *Long*

August Strindberg's *A Dream Play* produced in 2005 in London at the National Theatre; directed by Katie Mitchell.

Tristram Kenton/Lebrecht Music & Arts

Day's Journey into Night (written 1941, produced 1956), and *A Moon for the Misbegotten* (written 1943, produced 1947). These works cemented O'Neill's reputation as one of the greatest playwrights the United States has produced. O'Neill won the Pulitzer Prize for drama four times and is the only American playwright to receive the Nobel Prize for Literature. Let us examine *The Hairy Ape* and O'Neill's use of expressionism in that play.

THE HAIRY APE

The Hairy Ape derives its unity from its central theme: humanity's frustrated search for identity in a hostile environment. When the play begins, the protagonist, Yank, is confident that he and his fellow stokers on an ocean liner are the only ones who "belong" because they make the ship go (and, by extension, the factories and machines of the modern, industrialized society). They do not recognize that their quarters resemble "the steel framework of a cage" or that they themselves resemble Neanderthal men.

The second scene introduces Mildred Douglas, the spoiled daughter of a wealthy steel and shipping magnate. In Scene 3, she insists on visiting the stokehole to watch the men shovel the coal that makes the ship's engines run. When she sees Yank, she is so horrified that she faints and must be carried away. This is the catalytic moment for Yank because Mildred's revulsion makes him begin to question all of his beliefs. According to O'Neill, from Scene 4 onward, Yank "enters into a masked world; even the familiar faces of his mates in the forecastle have become strange and alien."

In Scene 5, seeking to reestablish his sense of worth, Yank goes to New York's Fifth Avenue, where the shops catering to the rich and powerful display "magnificence cheapened and made grotesque by commercialism." O'Neill also indicates that the people, dressed identically, look like "gaudy marionettes [with] detached, mechanical unawareness." When Yank tries to get their attention, they ignore him; resorting to force, he strikes at the men, but they remain oblivious to his existence and give their full attention to a monkey-fur coat in the shop window.

O'Neill's *The Hairy Ape* (Scene 1), in its first production, 1922, at the Provincetown Playhouse, New York. Directed by James Light; designed by Robert Edmond Jones and Cleon Throckmorton.

Courtesy of The National Theatre of Norway

In Scene 6, Yank is in jail (called "the zoo"). O'Neill's stage direction indicates the cages should appear to run on "numberless, into infinity." Yank decides that he will get his revenge by destroying the steel and machinery over which he originally thought he had power. Having learned that the IWW (International Workers of the World) opposes the owners of factories and ships, Yank goes to an IWW office upon his release from jail and offers to blow up its enemies. His offer is greeted with contempt, and he is thrown into the street. In the final scene, Yank arrives at the zoo, where he identifies with a caged gorilla. But when he frees the gorilla, it crushes him and throws him into its cage. Yank dies without achieving the sense of belonging that he has so desperately sought.

Emblematic of expressionist thought, Yank symbolizes modern humanity in an industrialized society. Cut off from a past when human beings were an integral part of the natural environment, he is trapped in an existence where he is little better than a cog in the industrial machine.

Only a few of the characters in *The Hairy Ape* have names. Most are representative types or members of groups. O'Neill's stage directions indicate that, except for slight differentiations in size and coloration, the stokers are all alike. Overall, O'Neill seems to suggest that human beings in the modern, industrialized world have been distorted—the workers having been reduced to the level of animals, the rich having become useless puppets. These conceptions are embodied in speech and appearance. In Scene 4, almost all of the speeches are described as having a "brazen metallic quality as if [the characters'] throats were phonograph horns," and much of what Yank and others say in this scene is greeted with "a chorus of hard, barking laughter." In the scene set on Fifth Avenue, the rich characters speak in "toneless, simpering voices," and they are masked and dressed to make them look like puppets. In comments on the appropriate performance style for the play, O'Neill suggests that, beginning with Scene 4, everyone whom

Yank encounters, "including the symbolic gorilla," should wear a mask. Yank is set off from the other characters because he is the only one who recognizes the need to seek a coherent relationship between himself and his environment. In his search, he meets no one who understands his need, but O'Neill seems to have hoped that Yank's plight would illuminate for the audience an aspect of modern existence.

The Hairy Ape is representative of both the outlook and the techniques of expressionism. The episodic structure and distorted visual elements are typical, as is Yank's longing for fulfillment, with its suggestion that society be changed so the individual can achieve a sense of belonging.

The Hypocrites Theatre Company's 2009 production of *The Hairy Ape* presented as part of the Goodman Theatre's "A Global Exploration: Eugene O'Neill in the 21st Century."

Chicago Tribune

American Theatre and Drama Between the Wars (1917–1940)

By the 1920s the modernist temperament was prominent in all the arts. Yet, many persons still believed in absolute values and considered much of twentieth-century thought and art misguided or dangerous. The modernist and more traditionalist points of view coexisted; perhaps this was a sign that the fragmentation of standards and values (in both life and art) had become the norm rather than the exception. In this atmosphere of competing values and viewpoints, the varieties of theatrical experience multiplied, and several styles existed simultaneously.

If modernism dominated "high" art both in Europe and America during the 1920s and 1930s, popular culture still preferred less complicated types of entertainment: music halls, vaudeville, burlesque, and film. Film became increasingly popular at this time and audience attendance shifted away from the theatre. This shift was accelerated by the almost simultaneous advent around 1929 of sound in films and a major economic depression; not only was film's entertainment potential greatly increased by sound but also its ticket prices were a fraction of those for live theatre. Between 1929 and 1939 approximately two-thirds of all live-entertainment theatres in the United States closed.

In the United States, the majority of those who continued to attend live theatre still preferred some version of realism. New theatrical movements were welcomed first (and often only) by "art" or "little" theatres (the counterparts of European independent theatres). Broadway audiences were not typically accepting of stylistic innovation in extreme forms. However, Broadway audiences flocked to see Thornton Wilder's *Our Town* (1938) despite its incorporation of nonrealistic techniques: the use of an onstage assistant to facilitate the action (the "Stage Manager"), visual emphasis on costume rather than on scenery, and the use of pantomimed props and abstraction in establishing location. While Wilder uses nonrealistic theatricalism, he applies it to clearly understandable subject matter. Set in small-town America, *Our Town* depicts the archetypal patterns and life cycles that underlie human experience. In the process, this stylistically innovative play found, and continues to find, a wide audience. Overall, by 1940 American theatre and drama had assimilated influences from European modernism into

T. Charles Erickson

Thornton Wilder's *Our Town* as produced by the Acting Company. Directed by Claudia Zelevansky; scene design by Erik Flatmo; costume design by Melissa McVay; lighting by Scott Bolman; sound design by Fritz Patton. When first produced in 1938, *Our Town* seemed much more radical than it does today. The play's nonrealistic staging conventions and nonlinear treatment of time have been assimilated into mainstream theatre, like many conventions and practices of the modernist period, so that today they seem commonplace.

Practices & Styles

THE NEW STAGECRAFT

The forces that created modernism in Europe had little impact on theatre in America until around World War I. Significant change began around 1912 when Americans who had studied and traveled abroad began to adopt the tactics of European independent theatres. Important "little theatres," as they were called in the United States, included the Toy Theatre (founded 1912) in Boston; the Chicago Little Theatre (1912); and the Neighborhood Playhouse (1915), the Washington Square Players (1915), and the Provincetown Players (1915), all in New York. In the beginning, these were amateur groups, although some later became professional.

The first important professional work by an American in the European mode came in 1915 with the production of Anatole France's *The Man Who Married a Dumb Wife* (1908). Designed by Robert Edmond Jones (1887–1954), who had traveled through Europe and spent a year at Reinhardt's theatre in Berlin, this set is usually called the first American expression of the "new stagecraft" (the term used in the United States for the European innovations). Jones, along with Lee Simonson (1888–1967) and Norman Bel Geddes (1893–1958), popularized the new mode in America. He designed sets for many of Eugene O'Neill's plays, both on Broadway and at the Provincetown Playhouse, and he was the principal designer of Arthur Hopkins's Broadway productions.

Simplification and suggestion (rather than detailed reproduction of the real world) were the hallmarks of new stagecraft design. Jones wrote, "Stage designing should be addressed to the eye of the mind," stimulating the imagination to perceive the underlying feeling of a play rather than stifling the imagination by providing too much. Perhaps more than any other designer, Jones established the style that dominated the American theatre between the two world wars. His influence is still felt through his book, *The Dramatic Imagination* (1941).

a form of modified (or simplified) realism that was much less detailed than nineteenth-century realism but still basically representational.

The economic depression of the 1930s brought a unique development in American theatre, the Federal Theatre Project, the government's first financial support of theatre in the United States. As the depression deepened and unemployment grew, Congress created the Works Progress Administration to provide jobs in many fields, including theatre. The Federal Theatre Project, which existed from 1935 to 1939, was most active in New York, although it had units in forty states. Its primary task was to provide "free, adult, uncensored theatre." As it pursued this task, it also helped to encourage theatre among minorities that had received little prior encouragement,

particularly African Americans. The Federal Theatre Project is perhaps best remembered for the *Living Newspaper*, a form that aimed at achieving in the theatre something comparable to the printed newspaper. In actuality, it more nearly resembled the documentary film. The most famous Living Newspapers are *Triple-A Plowed Under* (1936, on the government's farm-subsidy program), *Power* (1937, on rural electrification and flood control), and *One Third of a Nation* (1938, on slum housing). Each of these plays explored a specific problem, along with its causes and proposed solutions. They alternated dramatic scenes (illustrating the effect of existing social conditions on human lives) with narrative sequences (providing factual information through statistical tables, still photographs, and motion pictures, all projected onto screens). Collaborative creations of many authors, the plays advocated social reform and corrective legislation. This aggressive advocacy eventually contributed to the discontinuance of the Federal Theatre, when in 1939 Congress refused to appropriate funds to continue it.

During the years between the two world wars, Konstantin Stanislavsky became a major influence on American acting after the Moscow Art Theatre toured the United States in the early 1920s. Following that visit, two of Stanislavsky's former students, Richard Boleslavsky and Maria Ouspenskaya, founded the American Laboratory Theatre in New York, where from 1923 to 1930 they taught his approach to acting. But the upsurge in Stanislavsky's influence owed most to the Group Theatre, founded in 1931 by former students of the American Laboratory Theatre and modeled on the Moscow Art Theatre. For the next ten years, it was the most respected theatre in the United States. Among its members were Lee Strasberg, Harold Clurman, Stella Adler, Elia Kazan, Cheryl Crawford, Robert Lewis, Lee J. Cobb, and Morris Carnovsky—the directors, actors, teachers, and producers who

most actively promoted Stanislavsky's system in the United States. During the depression years, the Group Theatre presented many of the best productions on Broadway, most dealing with the pressing economic and social issues of that time. Among its most memorable productions were the plays of Clifford Odets, including *Waiting for Lefty* (1935), *Awake and Sing* (1935), and *Golden Boy* (1937). The fame that Odets and other Group Theatre members gained fed internal dissension within the company, and ultimately the Group Theatre disbanded in 1941.

A number of American playwrights in addition to O'Neill (whose work has been previously discussed) made significant contributions to American drama between 1917 and 1940. Among them were Maxwell Anderson, Susan Glaspell, Paul Green, Lillian Hellman, Clifford Odets, Elmer Rice, Robert Sherwood, and Thornton Wilder.

While simplified realism and musicals (discussed later) dominated the theatre in the United States, innovations were common in Europe after World War I. Many made little impact, but a few eventually exerted significant influence. One of the most important was *epic theatre*.

Power, a Living Newspaper, presented by the Federal Theatre Project. The scene shows an argument before the Supreme Court over the constitutionality of the Tennessee Valley Authority.

Epic Theatre

Epic theatre developed in Germany during the 1920s in the wake of expressionism. It is associated above all with Bertolt Brecht (1898–1956), who shared the expressionists' desire to transform society but thought their methods vague and impractical. Brecht's ideas lacked focus at first, but around 1926 he embraced Marxism and its belief that values are determined by the prevailing economic mode of production. Brecht came to view many of the world's problems as the result of capitalism and to believe that they could be solved by the adoption of socialism or communism. Thereafter, he sought to make audiences evaluate the socioeconomic implications of what they saw in the theatre; he was convinced that, if this was done effectively, audiences would perceive the need to alter the economic system and would work to bring about appropriate changes. He was also convinced that his goals could not be attained in the kind of theatre then dominant—one that sought to evoke an empathetic response so overwhelming that the spectators suspended their critical judgment, letting themselves be carried along passively by the performance. Brecht referred to such a theatre as the "dramatic theatre," wherein all the problems raised are solved at the end of the play and the audience has no need to relate what it has seen to the real world. Brecht wished to alter the audience's relationship to the production by encouraging spectators to watch actively and critically. Brecht did not see the theatre as a place to escape one's problems but rather as a place to recognize problems that are then to be solved outside the theatre.

As a means to his goal, Brecht arrived at the concept of "alienation" (*verfremdungs*)—distancing the audience from the stage events emotionally so it can view them critically. To achieve alienation, Brecht adopted many conventions that had not been previously used but, through Brecht's influence, have since become common:

- Brecht exposed the theatrical means.
- Brecht urged his performers to present characters rather than fully identify with them.
- Brecht often set the action of his plays in other times and places.
- Brecht allowed theatrical elements to contrast one another and thereby make independent contributions to the thought that the production might generate.
- Brecht used captions, songs, and other structural devices to draw attention to the construction of events.

Brecht reminded the audience members that they were in a theatre by calling attention to the theatre's means (which formerly had been concealed to support a theatrical illusion). He insisted that lighting instruments be left unmasked, that scenery be fragmentary (merely sufficient to indicate place), that musicians be visible (sometimes on stage), and that when objects were suspended, the ropes supporting them be clearly visible.

Brecht sometimes advised his actors to present their characters rather than *become* the characters (as Stanislavsky wished). To help actors achieve distance from their roles, Brecht advised them in rehearsal to speak of their characters in the third person. For example, an actor might verbalize a character's action saying, "He crosses the stage and says…" Brecht viewed the actor's job as being that of a reporter who remains objective and critical while telling a story. Such practices marked a conscious break with those that had long dominated the stage.

Brecht sought to achieve alienation by distancing the story either through time or place. According to Brecht, most historical drama treats its subjects from a present-day point of view, thereby creating the impression that conditions, having always been the same, are unchangeable. Brecht, contrarily, sought to make the differences between past and present readily apparent so the audience would recognize that, because the world has changed, it can still be changed if we do not like conditions as they now exist.

Brecht further sought alienation through his handling of the various theatrical elements. He opposed the notion (championed by Wagner and embraced by most of Brecht's contemporaries) that the most effective theatrical production is a synthesis of all the arts, each element reinforcing the others in a fully unified work. Brecht called this practice wasteful because through it each element repeats in its own way what is being done by all of the others. Instead, he advocated that each element make its own comment

and hoped that disparity among elements would encourage the audience to assess the varying comments. For example, Brecht's songs often set ironic or disillusioned lyrics to light-hearted tunes; the disparity between melody and words was intended to make the listener more critically aware of the song's implications.

Brecht adopted a number of structural devices to create alienation. Rather than have one scene flow smoothly into another, he used captions (projected on screens), songs, or other devices to emphasize breaks in the action. In some of his plays, captions were also used at the beginning of scenes to summarize the content of the scene to follow; instead of focusing on the suspense of what is going to happen, Brecht wanted the audience to focus on the social implications of the events. Instead of wondering

Bertolt Brecht's *Mother Courage* as produced by the American Repertory Theatre. Directed by János Szász; scene design by Csaba Antal; costume design by Edit Szücs; light design by John Ambrosone.

Richard Feldman

what will happen, the audience should critically examine how and why the events happen.

Although these conventions may suggest that Brecht was didactic, he was also intent on entertaining. His stories have many complications and reversals and are leavened with songs and other devices intended to capture and hold attention. In fact, Brecht the storyteller so often subverts Brecht the ideologue that many theatregoers remain oblivious of his desire to provoke social change. Brecht's concept of alienation is often misinterpreted as a demand that spectators be continuously distanced from the events. In actuality, Brecht engages the audience empathetically and then, through some device (such as a song), creates the distance needed to evaluate what has been experienced during the empathetic moments. Thus, there is a continuing alternation of empathy and distance (much like that created through the alternation of episodes and choral odes in Greek drama). One might also get the impression from reading Brecht that settings and costumes played little role in his productions. But, though scenery was restricted in quantity, in Brecht's theatre it was always designed and executed with great care; each piece was meticulously crafted and sometimes intricately detailed. The costumes often looked used and worn, in accordance with the character and situation, but many were elegant. The overall effect was one of considerable richness.

Brecht called his theatre epic because he thought it had more in common with epic poetry (in which dialogue and narration alternate and in which time and place are quickly transformed) than with the dramatic traditions that had dominated the theatre since the Renaissance. Of Brecht's many plays, the best known are *The Threepenny Opera* (1928), *Mother Courage and Her Children* (1938–1939, produced 1941), *Life of Galileo* (1937–1939, produced 1943), *The Good Person of Setzuan* (1938–1943, produced 1943), and *The Caucasian Chalk Circle* (1944–1945, produced 1948). Let us look at *The Good Person of Setzuan* as an example of Brecht's epic drama.

THE GOOD PERSON OF SETZUAN

Like many of his major plays listed above, Brecht wrote and rewrote *The Good Person of Setzuan* while living in exile before and during World War II, thereby creating a larger gap between the play's composition and its first production. The play is a parable in which Brecht distances his audience by setting it in China. Brecht's prologue establishes the epic nature of the play. In it, narration and dialogue are mingled and time and place are telescoped. The prologue demonstrates the irony that permeates the piece: the water seller, Wong, having assured the Three Gods, who have come to earth looking for a good person, that everyone is waiting to receive them, can find no one who will give them lodging except the prostitute, Shen Te. In addition, the prologue establishes the situation: The gods find the good person for whom they have been searching—Shen Te—and enjoin her to remain good. When she objects that she cannot be good unless she has the financial security that will permit her to refuse evil, the gods are unmoved, declaring that they "can't meddle in questions of economics." Herein Brecht suggests that not only is economic need the root of evil (because it forces people to do things that are wrong merely to survive) but also that the solution to human problems is not to be found in divine injunctions.

The scenes following the prologue show Shen Te buying a small shop to support herself, only to have greedy relatives and hangers-on take advantage of her goodness. When she falls in love with the penniless Yang Sun, who wishes to become a pilot, Shen Te gives him money she needs to pay her bills. On the verge of ruin, she disguises herself as a male cousin, Shui Ta, who suppresses humanitarian feelings and demands that those who want assistance must work—on his capitalistic terms. Thereafter the action is devoted to the conflict between good and evil as seen in the protagonist's two personae. Shui Ta appears for short intervals at first, but eventually takes over and becomes a capitalist boss who exploits workers and does whatever is needed to survive. The other characters suspect that Shui Ta has killed Shen Te. When the gods return disguised as judges before whom Shui Ta is brought, he reveals to them privately not only that he is Shen Te but also that she is pregnant and must provide for her child. But the gods can only admonish Shen Te to be good and to disguise herself less often as Shui Ta. The play ends with Shen Te's dilemma unresolved. An epilogue suggests that it is up to the audience

Bertolt Brecht's *The Good Person of Setzuan* as produced at the American Repertory Theatre. The costumes in the background reflect the influence of Beijing Opera, China's major theatrical form. Directed by Andrei Serban; costumes by Catherine Zuber.

Richard Feldman

to find a way out, presumably by changing the economic system.

The Good Person of Setzuan alternates short and long scenes. The short scenes serve two purposes: to break up the action and to comment on the long scenes used to develop the action. Brecht makes no attempt to create the illusion of everyday reality. For example, when Wong says he will find a place for the gods to spend the night, he suggests the attempt by circling the stage and pantomiming knocking on imaginary doors that are slammed in his face. This approach allows Brecht to telescope events and to eliminate transitions. Brecht's structural techniques are explained in part by his belief that scenes should be clearly separated as one means of creating alienation. He also insisted that it should be possible to express the social content of each scene in one sentence and that all parts of the scene should be clearly related to this statement.

Brecht oversimplifies characters because he is principally concerned with social relationships. Many of the characters in *The Good Person of Setzuan* are designated by their social functions, such as Wife, Carpenter, or Policeman, rather than by names. Brecht did not intend to portray well-rounded individuals but rather to interpret social forces. Therefore, the action does not exist to reveal character; rather, character exists to reveal social attitude. The only character who seems concerned about morality is Shen Te; the plot progresses in large part through the series of choices she makes about dilemmas created by economic conditions. The other characters are primarily concerned with attaining selfish goals or (in the case of the gods) sustaining a dogmatic view.

Today, many of our most familiar theatrical conventions (no front curtain to hide the stage, the use of fragmentary scenery and visible lighting instruments, and other practices that call attention to the theatrical medium) derive in large part from Brecht, although Brecht's intention of provoking social change is often ignored.

Artaud and the Theatre of Cruelty

Another strain of theatre in the 1920s and 1930s focused on forces quite different from those Brecht emphasized; it was concerned with those impulses buried in the unconscious mind. The most influential representative of this strain was Antonin Artaud (1896–1948), whose views, like those of Brecht, were not immediately accepted but, like Brecht's, became influential after his death. Whereas Brecht thought the key to improving the human lot lies in transforming external circumstances, Artaud thought the key lies in confronting internal divisions.

Artaud for a time was a member of the surrealist movement, which flourished during the 1920s. *Surrealism* emphasized one aspect of Freud's teachings: the importance of the unconscious. According to the surrealists, significant truths are those deeply buried in the psyche, suppressed by the conscious mind. In order to expose these "truths," the conscious mind must be subverted. The surrealists promoted dreams, automatic writing, and stream of consciousness as paths through which images, ideas, and experiences buried in the subconscious could escape the conscious mind's control and rise to the surface, where the insights they offered could be utilized. Surrealism made its greatest impact in painting, best known through the work of Salvador Dalí, in which familiar objects are used in unfamiliar ways, juxtaposed with unrelated objects, or placed in "dream landscapes" to create visual metaphors that stimulate the imagination and lead to new perceptions. Artaud eventually broke with the surrealists, but his experience with them was crucial to his work both in theatre and in film.

Artaud expressed his major ideas about theatre in a series of essays collected in *The Theatre and Its Double* (1938). According to Artaud, the theatre in the Western world has been restricted to a narrow range of human experience, primarily the psychological problems of individuals or the social problems of groups. Artaud considered such theatre insignificant because it failed to touch the most important influences on human behavior, those buried in the unconscious. But if these influences remain buried and unconfronted, they lead to divisions within a person (and between people) and ultimately lead to hatred, violence, and disaster. Artaud believed that if theatre were used properly, it would free people from destructive impulses. As he put it, "The theatre has been created to drain abscesses collectively."

Artaud was certain that his goals could not be reached through appeals to the rational mind (Brecht's approach) because the conscious mind has been conditioned to sublimate and ignore the very things that need to be examined. Thus, he argued, it is necessary to subvert the audience's defenses to provoke a visceral response. Artaud sometimes referred to this as a "theatre of cruelty," not because it was physically cruel but because it forced the audience, against its wishes, to confront itself on its deepest level of being. Because he considered the conventions of the established theatre to be directed to the conscious mind, he proposed to replace them with a "new language of the theatre." Believing that the proscenium-arch theatre creates a barrier between performers and spectators, he proposed replacing it with large, undivided spaces such as barns, factories, airplane hangars, and warehouses. Within these spaces he wanted to locate acting areas in corners, overhead on catwalks, and around the walls so as to place the audience in the midst of the action.

Artaud wanted to do away with scenery altogether and replace it with symbolic costumes and properties. In discussing lighting, he wrote of a "vibrating, shredded" effect with pulsating changes (comparable to strobe lighting). He favored great variety in sound, ranging in volume from a whisper to a factory at peak production; he advocated using the human voice

Practitioners & Theorists

PETER BROOK AND THE THEATRE OF CRUELTY

Although Artaud's theories had already influenced some directors and critics, they did not attract wide attention in England and America until Peter Brook began to experiment with them in the early 1960s.

In 1963 Brook, assisted by Charles Marowitz and with support from the Royal Shakespeare Company, selected a group of twelve actors with whom they worked throughout the 1963–1964 theatre season. Through exercises they experimented with sound (made with their voices, on their bodies, and with objects), movement, rhythm, and pantomime; they sought to replace clichéd solutions with innovative, non-realistic means of expression. They also sought to replace the typical pattern of beginning-middle-end development with discontinuous or simultaneous scenes. They performed a "Collage *Hamlet*" with sequences from Shakespeare's text rearranged, lines from different scenes juxtaposed, characters dropped or blended, and discontinuous fragments inserted. A five-week public showing of the group's work was presented under the title "Theatre of Cruelty." Though what the group did deviated in many ways from Artaud's ideas, critics began to equate Artaud with Brook's experiments, especially following his 1964 Royal Shakespeare Company production of *Marat/Sade* (1964) by Peter Weiss. The play is set in an insane asylum in which the inmates enact a play; Brooks's staging made extensive use of Artaudian techniques and became one of the most influential productions of the 1960s. In both England and America (where its awards included a Tony for Best Play and Best Director), this production was hailed as a practical application of Artaud's theories. With the success of this production, Artaud became widely known for the first time.

not primarily for speech but for yelps, cries, and varied emotional and atmospheric effects. He considered these innovative means capable of bypassing the conscious mind. As he put it, "Whereas most people remain impervious to a subtle discourse... they cannot resist effects of physical surprise, the dynamism of cries and violent movements, visual explosions, the aggregate of tetanizing effects called up on cue and used to act in a direct manner on the physical sensitivity of the spectators." These conventions were to be coupled with stories of mythical proportions and implications. The ultimate purpose was to break down the audience's defenses, drag suppressed impulses to the surface, and force the audience to face and deal with those things that, if unacknowledged, create hatred and violence.

Post–World War II European Drama and Theatre

Though mostly written prior to World War II, the ideas of Brecht and Artaud took root in the 1950s and 1960s where they exhibited considerable influence on theatre, first in Europe and then in the United States. Perhaps because Europe had suffered so much devastation and been subjected to so many atrocities, its postwar mood was much more serious than that of America. In Germany, Brecht's establishment of the Berliner Ensemble in East Berlin provided a home for his socially conscious plays. Likewise,

Marat/Sade as produced by American Repertory Theatre under the direction of János Szász. Scene design by Riccardo Hernandez; costume design by Edit Szücs; lighting by John Ambrosone.

Max Frisch (1911–1991), author of *Biedermann and the Firebugs* (1958), and Friedrich Duerrenmatt (1921–1990), author of *The Visit* (1956), wrote plays dealing with corruption and the moral responsibility of the individual. Although German drama differed from its French counterpart in tone, the drama of both nations drew upon a similar set of questions regarding the very foundations of truth and values.

In France, questions regarding truth, values, and moral responsibility were pursued by a group of philosophers known as the existentialists. Jean-Paul Sartre (1905–1980), the best-known existentialist, denied the existence of God, the validity of fixed standards of conduct, and the possibility of verifiable moral codes. He concluded that because none of the institutions (church, state, society) from which we have taken our standards can prove the correctness or necessity of those standards, human beings are "condemned to be free" (that is, people deprived of absolute standards are

condemned to choose individually the values by which they will live). He insisted that unquestioning conformity to values established by others is immoral, whereas choosing (and living by) one's own values is to define oneself as a moral being. Sartre's views were persuasive because they came at a time when many Nazis were seeking to escape punishment for war crimes by arguing that they had merely obeyed German laws or carried out their government's policies. The crucial question was, which takes precedence: law and policy (no matter how perverted) or individual moral values? Many Nazis were convicted on the premise that the individual should refuse to obey unjust or inhuman demands, even legal ones. This conclusion, which reflects Sartre's, has been used since then to justify protests of all kinds (nonviolent and violent) against governmental policies as well as local authorities and various institutions.

Albert Camus (1913–1960), another existentialist philosopher and writer, concluded that our

Three characters discover that "hell is other people" when they are confined eternally with each other in Jean-Paul Sartre's *No Exit*. Pictured is the American Repertory Theatre production of Sartre's play; translated by Stuart Gilbert; direction and scene design by Jerry Mouawad; costumes by Rafael Jaen; lighting by Jeff Forbes.

T. Charles Erickson

situation is absurd because the human longing for clarity and certainty is met with, and forever thwarted by, the irrationality of the universe into which we have been thrown; it is absurd also because we can neither rid ourselves of the desire for order nor overcome the irrationality that stands in the way of order. Camus reasoned that the only recourse is to choose one's own standards and live by them. Both Sartre and Camus were convinced that we can examine our situation and make decisions that permit us to act meaningfully in accordance with those decisions. Both also wrote plays that set their ideas into dramatic action. Among Sartre's plays, the best known are *The Flies* (1943) and *No Exit* (1944); among Camus's plays, the best known are *Caligula* (written 1938, produced 1945) and *The Just Assassins* (1949). Although their ideas broke from tradition, their plays expressed them using traditional dramatic structure: showing a protagonist facing a problem, pursuing it through a set of complications to a point of crisis, and making choices that permit a clear resolution.

Absurdist Drama

A group of playwrights emerged in France around 1950 who accepted the views of Sartre and Camus about the human condition,

but unlike those two writers, these playwrights believed that making rational and meaningful choices was impossible in an irrational universe. For them, the world consisted of chaos and lack of order, logic, or certainty, and their plays embodied this vision in a structure that abandoned cause-and-effect relationships for associational patterns reflecting a world that is irrational and in which truth is unknowable. The critic Martin Esslin (1918–2002) came to label drama containing this set of characteristics and viewpoint *absurdist* (owing to Camus's description of the human condition as "absurd"). Esslin's book *Theatre of the Absurd* (1961) describes the work of the playwrights that he considered to be absurdist, and thus, unlike the earlier modernist movements *absurdism* is an arbitrary category created by a critic rather than an organized movement created by artists consciously working together toward a goal.

Among the absurdist playwrights, who included Eugene Ionesco (1909–1994) and Jean Genet (1920–1986), the most influential was Samuel Beckett (1906–1989). Beckett's play *Waiting for Godot* (1953) brought him and absurdist drama international recognition. Let us briefly examine *Waiting for Godot* as representative both of his work and of absurdist drama.

WAITING FOR GODOT

The basic plot of *Waiting for Godot* is fairly simple. During Act I, Vladimir and Estragon, two tramps in ragged clothes, wait for Godot—someone they claim as an acquaintance but would not recognize if they saw him. While waiting, they meet Pozzo and Lucky, two men who have a master-servant relationship; Pozzo commands Lucky and controls him through a long rope tied around Lucky's neck. After sharing some time with the tramps, Pozzo and Lucky leave. A boy arrives and tells the tramps that Godot will not come today but will certainly come tomorrow. Estragon and Vladimir declare their intention to leave but remain motionless. The events of Act II parallel those of Act I with small variations. Pozzo is now blind and cannot remember having met the tramps before, and Lucky, who entertained them the day before by reciting his philosophical thoughts is now mute. When Pozzo and Lucky leave, the boy appears again and delivers the same message: Godot will not come today but will surely come tomorrow. The tramps again declare their intent to leave but do nothing. The events do not lead to a resolution. We never learn who Godot is. We never learn whether or not he will come or what might happen if he did. The end effect is a sense of circularity that advances the play's major themes, which are common in most of Beckett's plays: loneliness, alienation, codependency, the inadequacy of language, and the absence of objective meaning.

Ian McKellen, as Estragon, and Patrick Stewart, as Vladimir, in a 2009 production of *Waiting for Godot* at London's Theatre Royal Haymarket. Directed by Sean Mathias, the critically acclaimed production set box office records and was revived in 2010 (with Roger Rees replacing Stewart) and toured to Australia, New Zealand, and South Africa.

The loneliness and alienation of human beings is embodied visually in the stark setting. There is only the suggestion of a road and tree, whose fragile boughs do not seem strong enough to support the weight of a human body. Beckett shows human beings isolated in a symbolic wasteland, cut off from all but the most minimal human contact, passing the time as best they can while waiting doggedly or hoping desperately for something that will give meaning to the moment or to life itself.

In his plays, Beckett increasingly reduced the scope of action and means to those absolutely essential for projecting his vision. This limited scope of action intensifies the importance of the gestures, stage business, pauses, and language he has scripted in his plays. Their form, structure, and mood cannot be separated from their meaning. They explore a state of being rather than develop an action. Perhaps more than those of any other dramatist, Beckett's plays embody the absurdist vision and methods.

Post–World War II American Drama and Theatre

World War II disrupted theatrical activity in many countries around the world, and in war-ravaged Europe it motivated reassessment of values and theatrical practices. This reassessment of values and theatrical practices would occur in America as well, but not until somewhat later than it did in Europe. This seems due to a number of factors that led to an atmosphere of complacency and optimism rather than critical introspection: the United States was geographically removed from the fighting, the economy in the United States boomed in the post-war years, and the war's outcome promoted the United States to "super power" status. These factors may explain why theatre and drama in America

changed little in the years immediately following World War II. Modified realism continued to be the major approach in theatrical production, and psychological realism, derived from Stanislavsky, its dominant acting style. This production approach reached its peak in Elia Kazan and Jo Mielziner's stagings of the plays of Arthur Miller and Tennessee Williams.

Psychological realism dominated the plays of the postwar period. The two major dramatists were Arthur Miller (1916–2005) and Tennessee Williams (1911–1983). Miller remains best known for his early plays *All My Sons* (1947), *Death of a Salesman* (1949), and *The Crucible* (1953). *All My Sons* is an Ibsenesque drama about a manufacturer of airplane engines who has put profit above the safety of wartime pilots. *Death of a Salesman* focuses on Willy Loman, an unsuccessful businessman who sacrifices personal happiness in a failed pursuit of material success. *The Crucible* explores the hysteria surrounding the seventeenth-century Salem Witch Trials and suggests parallels with Senator Joseph McCarthy's communist witch-hunts of the 1950s. In his major plays, Miller focuses on conflicting values and the moral choices individuals make within a given social setting.

While Tennessee Williams has a diverse body of work, he is best known for *The Glass Menagerie* (1945), *A Streetcar Named Desire* (1947), and *Cat on a Hot Tin Roof* (1955). A largely autobiographical work, *The Glass Menagerie* is a "memory" play in which the protagonist Tom (Williams's surrogate) recalls scenes from his home life with a lingering sense of guilt for having abandoned his sister. The success of that play was followed by *A Streetcar Named Desire*, a powerful drama pitting the contrasting culture of Blanche DuBois, a fading Southern belle, against Stanley Kowalski, a primal, almost animalistic, member of the urban working class. Along with Marlon Brando's definitive portrayal of Stanley, the Actors Studio's reputation was enhanced by Kazan's direction of several of Miller and Williams's plays, on which he collaborated with designer Jo Mielziner. Kazan

Practitioners & Theorists

THE ACTORS STUDIO

For over sixty years professional actors have had a home away from home—the Actors Studio—where they could explore their craft in private and take risks they might not take so easily in public. In 1947, the Actors Studio was founded by Robert Lewis, Elia Kazan, and Cheryl Crawford, all former members of the Group Theatre, to provide its members an ongoing opportunity to develop their craft. Studio membership is highly selective and follows a rigorous audition process. Once admitted, there are no fees or tuition and the membership is life-long. The members serve as a group of nurturing peers who encourage and support one another's growth.

Awareness of the studio's work grew quickly after Marlon Brando, an Actors Studio member, captured the public's imagination with his portrayal of the inarticulate, uneducated, and assertive Stanley Kowalski in Tennessee Williams's *A Streetcar Named Desire* (1947), directed by Kazan. Brando's impact was enormous, not only affecting acting style but also contributing greatly to the influence of the Actors Studio and its version of the Stanislavsky system, usually referred to as "the Method." This approach, which concentrated on the actor's belief in the truth of the dramatic moment, could give scenes considerable psychological intensity. A frequent criticism of the Method, however, was that actors using it often neglected the technical skills needed to externalize internal feelings. The Actors Studio has described many of the criticisms of its work as misunderstandings perpetuated by outsiders who have little practical notion of serious actor training.

Today the Actors Studio has homes in New York City and West Hollywood. Current members include Phillip Seymour Hoffman, Robert De Niro, Laura Dern, Jack Nicholson, Dustin Hoffman, Sally Field, Christopher Walken, Marissa Tomei, and many others who became widely known, especially through their film roles.

Al Pacino and Marisa Tomei, featured here in the 2003 production of Oscar Wilde's *Salome*, are lifetime members of the Actors Studio.

Joan Marcus/UPI Photo Service/Newscom

and Mielziner established the production style that dominated the American theatre from the late 1940s until the 1960s. This style combined psychological realism in acting and directing with simplified, skeletal settings that permitted fluid shifts in time and place. Let us look more closely at a play that is representative of both the period and of the Kazan-Mielziner approach to staging.

CAT ON A HOT TIN ROOF

Tennessee Williams's *Cat on a Hot Tin Roof* is a play about mendacity—deception and lying, both to oneself and others. Although divided into three acts, the action is continuous; each act takes up precisely where the preceding one left off. The play, then, has a late point of attack, and the amount of exposition about past events is considerable, although skillfully worked into the action.

The occasion that has brought all of the characters together is Big Daddy's sixty-fifth birthday, which coincides with the results of Big Daddy's clinical tests for cancer. Big Daddy and Big Mama are told that he merely has a spastic colon, news that puts them in a highly celebratory mood though based on a lie. The others know that Big Daddy is dying, and because he is a multimillionaire who has not made a will, they are concerned with who will inherit his wealth. The obvious candidates are Big Daddy's two sons. The elder, Gooper, a corporation lawyer, is married to Mae and has five children. They covet Big Daddy's wealth and spend most of their time in transparent attempts to ingratiate themselves or to discredit Gooper's younger brother, Brick. A former football star and sports announcer, Brick has become an alcoholic. He and his wife Maggie have no children; he is as indifferent to his father's wealth (and everything else) as Gooper is fixated on it. Throughout the play Brick walks with the aid of a crutch, having broken his ankle the night before while

Arthur Miller's *Death of a Salesman*, 1949. Lower level, Lee J. Cobb as Willy and Mildred Dunnock as Linda; upper level, Arthur Kennedy as Biff and Cameron Mitchell as Happy. Directed by Elia Kazan; designed by Jo Mielziner.

Eileen Darby Images, Inc

Jason Patric and Ashley Judd in the 2003 Broadway revival of Tennessee Williams's drama, *Cat on a Hot Tin Roof*, directed by Anthony Page; scene design by Maria Bjornson; costumes by Jane Greenwood; lighting by Howard Harrison; sound by Christopher Cronin.

Sara Krulwich/The NeRedux Picturesw York Times/Redux

attempting to jump hurdles. Both the crutch and the constant resort to alcohol are symbolic of what Williams calls Brick's "spiritual disre-pair," born out of his disgust with mendacity.

But if Brick has no interest in Big Daddy's wealth, his wife does. Maggie, who comes from a far less wealthy family than Brick, describes herself as "consumed with envy and eaten up with longing." Her description of her position as that of "a cat on a hot tin roof" gives the play its title. Maggie sees having a child by Brick as her only hope of obtaining Big Daddy's wealth. Unfortunately for her, Brick refuses to touch her because of her role in the death of his best friend Skipper, who destroyed himself after Maggie accused him of being in love with Brick.

The play concentrates primarily on three characters: Maggie, Brick, and Big Daddy. Big Daddy's situation is the primary motivator of the action, and it is he who forces Brick to acknowl-edge his responsibility in Skipper's death. Brick's

withdrawal and inaction are a primary spur for others who throughout the play seek to provoke him into action.

The first act is devoted almost entirely to Maggie and Brick as she tries to make him understand their precarious position in relation to Big Daddy's wealth. Because Brick has abdi-cated any concern for life and because they have no children, they are in danger of being disin-herited altogether or having to accept whatever Gooper may choose to dole out to them. Brick refuses to cooperate in her desire to be pregnant. The only time he shows anything more than indifference comes when she (or Big Daddy) insists that they talk about Skipper.

The second act is devoted primarily to Brick and Big Daddy. Much of this act is taken up with Big Daddy trying to work up to a serious talk with Brick. During these preliminaries we find out much about Big Daddy who, begin-ning in poverty, has made himself rich through his own efforts. He makes it clear that he dis-likes Gooper but that he does not want what he has accumulated to be wasted. Big Daddy sets out, therefore, to find out why Brick drinks, and he ultimately forces Brick to acknowledge that when, in a phone conversation, Skipper confessed his love, Brick had hung up on him. (Though Williams himself was homosexual, for his character Brick, the thought that he and Skipper may have loved each other is disgust-ing and psychologically paralyzing.) Big Daddy says that it was Brick's unwillingness to face this situation with his friend, rather than Maggie's accusations, that caused Skipper's death. Hurt by the truth, Brick in retaliation reveals the truth about Big Daddy's cancer tests. The act ends with both men denouncing mendacity and those who practice it.

The final act is taken up with a gathering of all the characters except Big Daddy, dur-ing which they reveal the truth to Big Mama. Gooper and Mae try to coax Big Mama into approving papers Gooper has had drawn up about authority over the property. She refuses, and Maggie takes control by announcing that she is pregnant. Gooper and Mae accuse her of lying, but later Maggie attempts to make the lie true by depriving Brick access to alcohol until he makes love to her.

Maggie's final line of the play asserts her love for her husband, as does Big Mama's last line to Big Daddy. Both Big Daddy and Brick respond to these declarations of love by saying, "wouldn't it be funny if that was true," thereby underscoring the difficulty to discern the truth in a world so full of mendacity.

There is an alternative third act to *Cat on a Hot Tin Roof*, written at the insistence of Elia Kazan, the original director of the play on Broadway. Kazan thought that Big Daddy was too powerful a character not to reappear in the

Maggie and Brick square off in the Hartford Stage production of *Cat on a Hot Tin Roof*. Directed by Michael Wilson; scene design by Geoff Cowie; costume design by David C. Woolard; and lighting design by Rui Rita.

third act (in Williams's original script Big Daddy appears only in the second act) and that Brick should undergo significant change as a result of his confrontation with Big Daddy in the second act. In the original Broadway version, Big Daddy does appear in the third act, although primarily to show that he favors Brick and to ask that a lawyer be sent for so he can make a will. In both versions, Big Daddy is later heard offstage howling in pain as the cancer ravages him. In the alternative version, Brick does show change. Early in the act he suggests that Maggie arrange for him to go to a treatment clinic, and later, when Gooper and Mae accuse Maggie of lying about being pregnant, he defends her and subsequently appears to acquiesce to her demands. The overall effect of the Broadway version is to make the play far more positive than Williams wished. He stated that no conversation, "however revelatory, ever effects so immediate a change in the heart or even the conduct of a person in Brick's state of spiritual disrepair." The disagreement between Williams and Kazan illustrates the power that directors may have over a script and how they can persuade playwrights to make changes, even ones with which they do not agree. Initially, Williams published the play with both third acts, inviting readers and future producers to decide which third act they preferred. Later, for a 1974 revival, Williams combined aspects of the two third acts to create yet another version of his ever-popular play.

The Development of American Musical Theatre

Although the modified realism of American spoken drama has received more serious study, the musical was the most popular theatrical form in the United States during the twentieth century. Music and theatre have been intertwined for many centuries. The choral passages of Greek drama were sung and danced; the majority of the lines in Roman comedy were accompanied by music; the Italians developed wholly sung opera; and Shakespeare included songs in some of his plays. The eighteenth century introduced a number of popular musical forms, including ballad opera and comic opera, and the nineteenth-century theatre used music to underscore melodrama's action. When the plays did not require music, some type of musical entertainment was usually included as an additional entertainment.

Even so, the form now known as musical theatre did not begin to emerge as a distinct type until the late nineteenth century. Early examples of musical theatre usually emphasized the romantic appeal of faraway places or exotic situations; the stories were primarily excuses for songs and ensemble choral numbers, often sung and danced by beautiful young women. Around World War I, a change occurred when ballroom dancing and ragtime music, both then in vogue, were introduced into musicals; with them came more familiar characters and surroundings. Nevertheless, the storyline remained relatively unimportant, and the emphasis continued to be on spectacular settings, songs, dances, and chorus girls (a pattern that continues in many Las Vegas musical entertainments to the present day).

The relationship between music and story as well as the use of songs to convey and develop psychological motivation did not begin to be truly significant until the late 1920s. Beginning with Jerome Kern and Oscar Hammerstein's *Show Boat* (1927), the American musical took shape as a theatrical entertainment that integrated a coherent story, believable characters, song, music, and dance. *Of Thee I Sing!* (1931), a musical satirizing politics and politicians, with music by George and Ira Gershwin and a libretto by George Kaufman and Morrie Ryskind, was the first musical to be awarded a Pulitzer Prize for Drama.

By 1940, the musical had become distinctively American and perhaps America's most significant contribution to world theatre. The American musical had emerged as a coherent integration of story, music, and dance. *Oklahoma!* (1943), by Richard Rodgers and Oscar Hammerstein II, furthered this integration and set the standard for the "book musical" of the period (musicals wherein songs and dances seemed a logical extension of the libretto's dramatic action). The extended ballet at the end of its first act demonstrated that musical theatre, which already contained conventions far from realistic (breaking into song or dance in public and being joined by others) has particular flexibility in assimilation of modernist influences. Signifying the influence of this musical, Richard Rodgers and Oscar Hammerstein II were awarded a special Pulitzer Prize for *Oklahoma!* in 1944. Rodgers and Hammerstein continued their success with *Carousel* (1945), *South Pacific* (1949), *The King and I* (1951), and *The Sound of Music* (1959). Several other composers and authors in the post–World War II period followed the lead of Rodgers and Hammerstein, among them Alan Jay Lerner and Frederick Loewe with *Brigadoon* (1947) and *My Fair Lady* (1956); Frank Loesser with *Guys and Dolls* (1950); and Leonard Bernstein, Arthur Laurents, and Stephen Sondheim with *West Side Story* (1957). Overall, the period of 1943–1968 became known as The Golden Age of the American Musical.

The popularity of the musical is probably attributable to its multiple appeals. The musical and choreographic elements, sources of pleasure in their own right, can also facilitate storytelling. For example, the lyrics of songs contribute to clarity by expressing emotional response and intention directly, much as soliloquies and asides did in earlier drama. Music, through such conventions as the reprise (the repetition of musical phrases or fragments of lyrics), can connect or recall moments separated in time. Furthermore, music assists in condensing time, as when a song or musical passage is used to show quickly a progression

Oklahoma! is often credited as one of the first musicals to fully integrate story in a meaningful way with all its visual, aural, and kinetic aspects. Pictured here is its Broadway revival. Directed by Trevor Nunn; choreographed by Susan Stroman; scene and costume designs by Anthony Ward; lighting by David Hersey.

Joan Marcus

The "rumble" scene between the rival gangs, the Jets and the Sharks, in West Side Story; composed by Leonard Bernstein; book by Arthur Laurents; lyrics by Arthur Laurents and Stephen Sondheim. Note the chain-link fence and the painted background, which visually modify the realism of the scene to create a mood and a sense of monumentality to the events. Directed and choreographed by Jerome Robbins; scene design by Oliver Smith; lighting by Jean Rosenthal.

The Billy Rose Theatre Collection, the New York Public Library for the Performing Arts, the Astor, Lenox and Tilden Foundation

of events that in actuality occurs over a long period. For example, in *My Fair Lady*, the speech lessons that alter the flower seller Eliza's accent so she can pass as a duchess are condensed primarily into one song, "The Rain in Spain." In addition, music establishes mood and builds expectation. Even before the action begins, an overture establishes the general mood of the work to follow, and thereafter music helps to establish the appropriate emotional tone and, through modulations in tempo, key, and volume, to build individual scenes and the work as a whole.

A musical usually provides considerable visual stimulation. Scenic, costume, and lighting designers typically are offered wide scope for their talents in musical productions. There are usually several changes in time and place and a large cast (often with much doubling), which require multiple sets and costumes. Dance usually plays a large role, commenting on the action

Julie Andrews, as Eliza Doolittle, and Rex Harrison, as Henry Higgins, in the original 1956 Broadway production of *My Fair Lady*, the Alan Jay Lerner and Frederick Lowe musical that is based on George Bernard Shaw's play *Pygmalion*.

Pictorial Press Ltd/Alamy

and forwarding the story much as the songs do. Considering all of these appeals, it is not surprising that the musical has long been among the most popular of theatrical experiences.

Summary

The modernist era resulted in an explosion of artistic experimentation. The different modernist artistic movements often existed simultaneously and challenged each other for supremacy. While most of them originated in Europe, to varying degrees each gradually exerted influence on American theatre. The diversity of these theatrical forms raised awareness that no single correct approach to theatrical production exists and that each artist is free to offer his or her vision of truth and human experience no matter how eccentric. Absolutist notions were largely denied but not wholly abandoned.

In many ways, absurdism extended the relativist view as far as it could go because it implied that we have no way of proving or disproving the validity of any position. Whereas Brecht suggested that, by examining and weighing arguments, we can arrive at rational conclusions about the changes needed to make the world more just, Beckett suggested that the very notion of rational choice is a delusion. That works embodying such polar visions were often presented in the same theatre for the same audience indicates how varied theatrical experiences had become in the postwar era. Similarly, though elitist critics favored the avant-garde, the most popular mode in mainstream theatre continued to be a modified form of realism as well as musicals. The fact that works as disparate as *The Importance of Being Earnest*, *Death of a Salesman*, *Waiting for Godot*, and *Oklahoma!* all continue to be frequently produced indicates the continuing influence of the modernist era and the diversity of its modes of expression.

THEATRE IN A BROAD CONTEXT

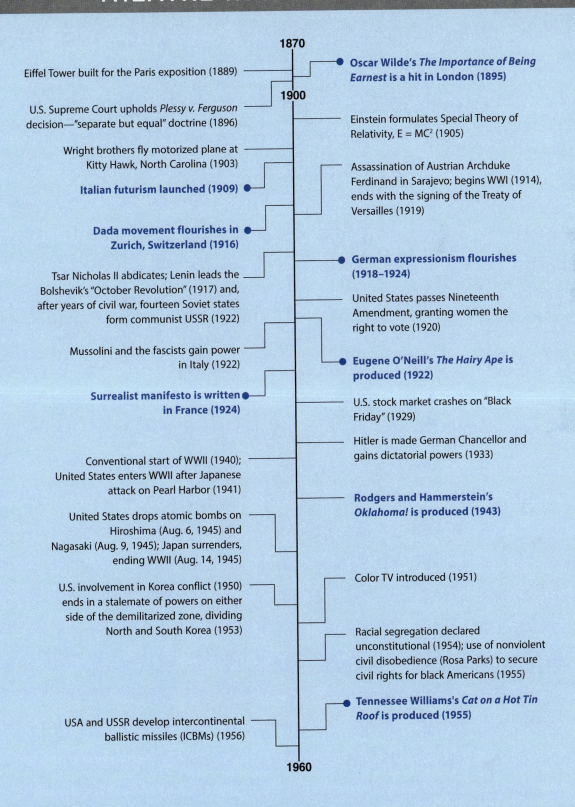

1870

Eiffel Tower built for the Paris exposition (1889)

● **Oscar Wilde's *The Importance of Being Earnest* is a hit in London (1895)**

1900

U.S. Supreme Court upholds *Plessy v. Ferguson* decision—"separate but equal" doctrine (1896)

Einstein formulates Special Theory of Relativity, $E = MC^2$ (1905)

Wright brothers fly motorized plane at Kitty Hawk, North Carolina (1903)

Italian futurism launched (1909) ●

Assassination of Austrian Archduke Ferdinand in Sarajevo; begins WWI (1914), ends with the signing of the Treaty of Versailles (1919)

Dada movement flourishes in Zurich, Switzerland (1916) ●

● **German expressionism flourishes (1918–1924)**

Tsar Nicholas II abdicates; Lenin leads the Bolshevik's "October Revolution" (1917) and, after years of civil war, fourteen Soviet states form communist USSR (1922)

United States passes Nineteenth Amendment, granting women the right to vote (1920)

Mussolini and the fascists gain power in Italy (1922)

● **Eugene O'Neill's *The Hairy Ape* is produced (1922)**

Surrealist manifesto is written in France (1924) ●

U.S. stock market crashes on "Black Friday" (1929)

Hitler is made German Chancellor and gains dictatorial powers (1933)

Conventional start of WWII (1940); United States enters WWII after Japanese attack on Pearl Harbor (1941)

Rodgers and Hammerstein's *Oklahoma!* is produced (1943)

United States drops atomic bombs on Hiroshima (Aug. 6, 1945) and Nagasaki (Aug. 9, 1945); Japan surrenders, ending WWII (Aug. 14, 1945)

Color TV introduced (1951)

U.S. involvement in Korea conflict (1950) ends in a stalemate of powers on either side of the demilitarized zone, dividing North and South Korea (1953)

Racial segregation declared unconstitutional (1954); use of nonviolent civil disobedience (Rosa Parks) to secure civil rights for black Americans (1955)

● **Tennessee Williams's *Cat on a Hot Tin Roof* is produced (1955)**

USA and USSR develop intercontinental ballistic missiles (ICBMs) (1956)

1960

The Guthrie Theatre is part of the regional theatre movement that helped to decentralize theatre in America. Pictured is the Guthrie Theatre's production of Shakespeare's *The Two Gentlemen of Verona*. As directed by Joe Dowling, the action of Shakespeare's play is set within a 1950s television studio during a live broadcast. Scene design by Ricardo Hernandez; lighting design by Christopher Akerlind; costume design by Ann Hould Ward.

T. Charles Erickson

[Because of decentralization and subsidization] Good theatre is available throughout the country—some of it truly exceptional in quality—and without question, it is providing forums to communities that were not available four decades ago. ... [T]his is an extraordinary achievement in a very short time.

—Peter Zeisler, "Seize the Moment," *American Theatre* (September 1994)

Decentralization and Subsidization

New Directions

World War II disrupted theatrical activity in many countries around the world, and almost everywhere it motivated reassessment of values and theatrical practices. In many countries reassessment led to decentralization of the theatre, which often was accomplished through financial assistance in the form of subsidization. In America, the decentralization of theatre—from the 1950s through the 1980s—took a somewhat different path than it did in Europe. However, both in America and in Europe this decentralization gave rise to new voices being heard and new artistic directions being explored.

European Decentralization and Subsidization

Subsidization is as old as the theatre. It began with the Greeks and remained the primary means of supporting performances until the Renaissance, when the theatre became a commercial venture. Even thereafter, many rulers subsidized the theatre. For example, the king of France provided at least some financial support to all of the companies in Paris during the seventeenth century; and it was by his decree that the Comédie Française was created in 1680. The world's first national theatre, the Comédie Française has continued to the present day and has received governmental subsidies throughout its more than three-hundred-year history. Seeking to emulate France, the Scandinavian countries, Russia, and most of the small German states (Germany was not united until 1870) founded state-subsidized theatres in the eighteenth century. Most of those theatres still survive and are so geographically dispersed throughout northern and eastern Europe that the countries in those areas were not faced, as France, England, and America were following World War II, with the need to decentralize their theatres.

In 1958 when President Charles de Gaulle launched a decentralization of the arts in France stating that it was "every citizen's right to culture," France had four state theatres—all were located in Paris. In order to cultivate theatrical activity throughout its nation, the government began to establish dramatic centers in cities throughout France. Implementing this goal required money, much of which came from government subsidies. The French chose to subsidize theatre (and the arts as a whole) not as a form of national charity, but as an investment in the nation's creativity, one which the French believe has paid valuable dividends. Today, there are more than forty national drama centers, two hundred fifty theatre companies with state contracts, and around six hundred subsidized theatre companies in France.

The Germanic and Scandinavian countries have long considered state or municipal funding for the arts a cultural responsibility like that for education. Although these governments do not underwrite all of a theatre's expenses, they own the theatre buildings and have subsidized as much as 80 percent of the theatre's operating expenses, making it possible to keep ticket prices relatively low. The subsidized companies usually offer seasons of representative plays from the past in combination with new or recent plays. Through the 1980s, the theatre staffs (including directors, designers, and actors) were employed on renewable contracts, complete with pension plans and other benefits comparable to those for workers in industry and government. (Each of these countries also has privately owned and operated theatres run much like Broadway theatres are in America.) These were the

companies and practices that many theatre workers in England and America looked to as models.

England, unlike continental European countries, had never awarded government subsidies on the premise that theatre is a business that must be self-supporting. But during World War II, the government had funded performances intended to build the morale of military troops and factory workers. When the war ended, financial support for the arts was continued through the Arts Council of Great Britain. The Council was created to decide which organizations should receive funds. Government funding increased after 1948, when Parliament authorized local authorities to devote a percentage of their tax revenues to the arts. More than fifty cities and towns in Great Britain came to subsidize theatres. Among these provincial theatres and theatre festivals, none grew more rapidly and became as influential as the Stratford Festival in Stratford-upon-Avon.

Although the origins of the Stratford Festival can be traced to 1879, when it became the home of an annual summer festival of Shakespeare's plays, it gained tremendous prestige and popularity in the years following World War II. By 1961 it had been given a new name and charter as the Royal Shakespeare Company (RSC) and grew from national to international prominence. The RSC leased the Aldwych Theatre in London as a

Chekhov's *The Three Sisters* produced in 1952 in Rome by Teatro Eliseo.

Mondadori/UIG/Universal Images/Age Fotostock

second base so that the company could perform year-round. Between 1964 and 1975, when the RSC was performing in Stratford, the Aldwych hosted the World Theatre Season; major theatre companies from around the world performed there in limited engagements, providing a cross-fertilization of drama and theatre practices that greatly diversified and enriched British theatre and drama. Meanwhile, the RSC was now performing a diversified repertory of plays that featured Shakespeare and new British playwrights of the time like Harold Pinter and Tom Stoppard. Peter Brook, one of the world's finest directors, was associated with the RSC during the 1960s and staged some of its most influential productions, among them his 1964 production of *Marat/Sade* (which critics labeled an example of Artaud's Theatre of Cruelty and which drew wide attention to Artaud's ideas for the first time in England and America) and his 1970 production of *A Midsummer Night's Dream* (which utilized circus and acrobatic techniques). The RSC eventually dropped its practice of maintaining a London theatre, although it still takes some of its Stratford productions to London and throughout England on tour. Thanks in large part to government subsidy and support, the RSC ranks among the world's best companies and is recognized as a leader in Shakespearean performance.

The move to decentralize British theatre was balanced to some extent by Parliament's decision to subsidize the formation of a National Theatre in 1949, although numerous challenges delayed its opening for many years. The National Theatre was inaugurated in 1963 as a company led by Laurence Olivier (then regarded as England's foremost actor), but it did not move into its permanent home on the south bank of the Thames river until 1976. The National Theatre has the most elaborate performance facilities in England, with three performance spaces (a thrust-stage theatre, a proscenium-arch theatre, and a flexible theatre). In addition to offering over twenty productions each year at its London site, the National Theatre has toured productions across England and internationally. In recent years, the National Theatre has supplemented

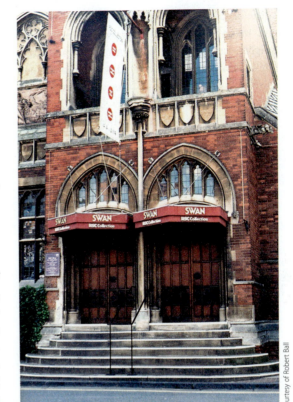

Courtesy of Robert Ball

The Royal Shakespeare Company theatre complex in Stratford-upon-Avon currently contains a large traditional proscenium-arch theatre and a more intimate thrust performance space. A £100 million renovation of the facilities was completed in 2010. The renovation enhanced the thrust stage and improved the audience's experience by creating better foyers, shops and audience facilities, an expanded bar and restaurant as well as new spaces for platform performances, talks, and concerts.

its governmental subsidy through a number of special partnerships with corporations to provide low-price tickets, particularly for older and younger audiences. This practice has proved quite successful. In 2008, for example, patrons under the age of eighteen accounted for more than 12 percent of the National Theatre's audience of over a million people. Its repertory of world drama and its overall excellence have made it a major force in world theatre.

A third subsidized English group, the not-for-profit English Stage Company (better known as the Royal Court Theatre) was founded in 1956 and made its mark by championing new playwrights writing for a noncommercial audience. These new playwrights created works that helped to revitalize British drama. Prior to its production of John Osborne's *Look Back in Anger* (1956), the postwar English theatre had been devoted primarily to revivals or innocuous, "proper" dramas. Osborne's play—an attack on the English class system and traditional values—was a slap in the face of "respectability." It brought a new audience into the theatre and inaugurated a new school of writers (the "angry young men").

Within a brief time, the tone of English theatre shifted as the speech and attitudes of disaffected groups brought new vigor to the stage. Among the playwrights produced by the Royal Court was Edward Bond, whose *Saved* (1965) would prove instrumental in changing British censorship practices that had been in existence for over two hundred years. England's Lord Chamberlain had long held the right to determine which plays were fit for public performance. The Lord Chamberlain refused to license *Saved* in part because of a scene in which a baby is stoned to death in its carriage. The Royal Court produced Bond's play by temporarily reforming itself as a private, members-only club. The Lord Chamberlain prosecuted and won its case, but the Royal Court and Bond

refused to relent. In 1967 they produced Bond's next "unapproved" play, *Early Morning*, which portrays Queen Victoria as having a lesbian affair with Florence Nightingale. This forced Parliamentary hearings and the Licensing Act, which had allowed the censoring of plays since 1737, was abolished. The Royal Court continues to produce the work of new, challenging playwrights and is partially supported by a government subsidy through the Arts Council.

The decentralization of British theatre continues, as do questions about the English government's subsidization of theatre. In 2006 the Arts Council sponsored a national debate, bringing together groups in twenty different regions of England from all ranges of society to discuss issues related to the arts and public funding. Whether or not public funding for the arts should exist was not a contentious issue. Instead, the debate was over who should be funded and who should make that determination. Should most of the public funding go to well-known institutions (such as the Royal Shakespeare Company and the National Theatre) or to smaller groups in different areas of the nation? Should members of the general public have a say on the committees that determine which groups will be funded? Should funding go to individual artists? Ongoing debates over these questions will continue to shape British theatre's decentralization and subsidization.

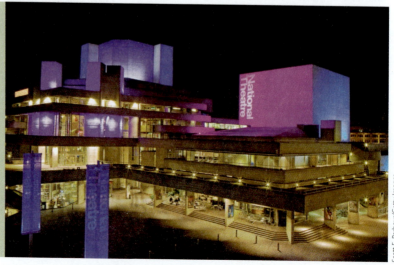

The National Theatre in London combines its governmental subsidy with corporate partnerships to underwrite its performance programs and support other initiatives. For example, as part of a renovation to improve its energy efficiency, as seen here, the National Theatre has replaced much of its exterior illumination with more environmentally friendly LED lighting.

Scott E. Barbour/Getty Images

American Regional Theatres

The conviction that theatre must be entirely self-supporting persisted longer in the United States than anywhere else. The government had financed the Federal Theatre during the 1930s, primarily because it wanted to reduce unemployment. After the Federal Theatre came to an end in 1939, no further government assistance was given until the mid-1960s. However, market forces, the aspirations of emerging theatre artists, corporate foundations, and civic leaders (who saw the potential of live theatre to enhance their communities) combined to further the decentralization of American theatre.

In the late 1940s Margo Jones (1911–1955), having codirected the triumphant 1945 Broadway production of *The Glass Menagerie* by the then little-known playwright Tennessee Williams, opened a regional theatre in Dallas that became a prototype for American regional theatres. Jones's theatre (Theatre '47) championed the works of new playwrights and presented important world drama of the past. Jones was devoted to the creation of theatre independent of Broadway and its commercial goals. Her theatre also departed from the use of a proscenium arch and surrounded the stage with spectators in an arena theatre configuration (further treatment of theatre configurations may be found in Chapter 11).

In addition to Margo Jones, Nina Vance (Houston's Alley Theatre) and Zelda Fichlander (Washington D.C.'s Arena Stage) were pioneers in the regional theatre movement. During the 1950s, these and other companies emerged, struggled to survive, and ultimately received a major boost from the Ford Foundation, which in 1959 made large grants to several companies that had succeeded in winning local support. Thus, the major impetus for decentralization in America came from individuals supported by private rather than governmental subsidy.

Decentralization received another boost in 1963 with the opening of the Guthrie Theatre in Minneapolis. Tyrone Guthrie, then one of the world's foremost directors, selected Minneapolis over established theatre centers as the site for his company, and funds were raised locally to construct a new building for it. The publicity surrounding this theatre aroused considerable interest (or envy) in other cities. Something approaching a boom in the construction of new arts centers followed. But this boom might not have been possible without the combined efforts

T. Charles Erickson

The founding of regional theatres, like the Alley Theatre (Houston, Tex.), helped to make theatre accessible across the country. Pictured is the Alley Theatre's production of *Eurydice* by Sarah Ruhl, a revisionist telling of the Greek myth in which Orpheus retrieves Eurydice from death; directed by Gregory Boyd; lighting by Rui Rita; scene design by Hugh Landwehr; costumes by Alejo Vietti.

of individual donors and corporate sponsors as well as local, state, and federal assistance.

In 1965, with the establishment of the National Endowment for the Arts (NEA), the United States joined the majority of other developed countries who had long believed that an enlightened government should provide financial support for the arts. Like England's Arts Council, the NEA dispensed federally appropriated funds to arts groups throughout the United States. In its first year of operation, the NEA had only $2.5 million (slightly more than one cent for each person living in the United States) to distribute among all the arts. At its peak in 1993–1994, the NEA's budget was $170.2 million (about sixty-eight cents per capita). But by 1998, its appropriation had shrunk to $98 million. (That same year the French government devoted approximately $2.3 billion annually to subsidize the arts.) Along with the creation of the NEA, the federal government encouraged states to establish arts councils, and in turn the states encouraged cities and communities to form their own councils.

Tax laws also encouraged corporations and foundations to make grants to arts organizations by making all or part of the grants tax deductible. Such grants and subsidies made it feasible for resident theatres to be established throughout the country. These companies are linked through

Society, Art & Culture

SUBSIDIZATION AND THE NEA

Although the National Endowment for the Arts had faced some opposition from time to time, it seemed secure until 1989, when some members of Congress introduced legislation to place strictures on the type of art that could be subsidized; others campaigned to abolish the NEA altogether. Defenders of the NEA argued that the new proposals would impose censorship on the arts, endanger the freedom of expression guaranteed by the Constitution's First Amendment, discourage innovative and challenging art, and advocate officially approved standards for art not unlike those of communist eastern Europe. Supporters of the proposed strictures responded that, "this is not a question of censorship. This is a question of whether the American people should continue to subsidize this art with their hard-earned money."

The issues involved in this controversy have not been resolved. On one side, some oppose all subsidies for the arts, believing that art is a commodity that must compete in a free market and that if it deserves support, it will find it. On the other side, some argue that market forces are historically short-sighted (most art now considered "great" was unpopular at the time of its creation), and that they would reduce artistic innovation and unfairly favor the economically privileged (those who could afford to experience and participate in arts that others could not). For many, the underlying conflict seemed to be a question of majority values versus the equal opportunity for freedom of expression.

In 1998, the Supreme Court upheld a 1990 law specifying that in making awards the NEA should take into account "general standards of decency and respect for the diverse beliefs and values of the American public." For many, this seemed a defeat for freedom of expression; others hailed it as a victory for majority values. The ruling settled little, especially because the justices who supported it indicated that the ruling was advisory rather than compulsory and neither defined "general standards of decency" nor indicated who should make such decisions.

Actors Theatre of Louisville (Ky.) and the Humana Foundation partner to present the Humana Festival of New Plays. Pictured is *War of the Worlds*, a play by Anne Bogart, Naomi Lizuka, and the SITI Company, which premiered at the twenty-fourth annual Humana Festival.

the Theatre Communications Group (TCG), which was created in 1961 with funds supplied by the Ford Foundation. TCG serves as a centralized source of information for more than five hundred not-for-profit professional theatres and provides a forum where common problems can be discussed and solutions sought.

Today, federal, state, and local governments appropriate funds to subsidize the arts. The sums are not large, but that they exist at all marks a major change in American attitudes toward the arts, one that has not gone unchallenged by those who believe that the government should have no role in the arts. The existence of more than five hundred not-for-profit theatres may make theatrical conditions appear more stable than they are. Few of these theatres could exist without financial support from governments,

corporations, foundations, or private donors in addition to the revenue they generate through ticket sales. Although the government funding awarded through grants may be small, it is nonetheless very important; studies indicate that each federal grant dollar attracts more than six dollars from private and corporate donations. Unlike many European theatres, for which ongoing governmental support is assured, American theatres receive grants for periods ranging from one to five years and they have no assurance that their grants will be renewed. Consequently, most not-for-profit theatres in the United States devote much of their time to developing grant proposals and soliciting support. Unable to make firm, long-range plans, they must be prepared to alter their programs if support is not forthcoming. Nevertheless, it is subsidization that has made possible the decentralization of the American theatre.

Most regional theatres have two theatre spaces, a larger venue for more well-known works and then a second stage for smaller, less commercial productions. In the process they offer a season of plays that intermingles classics with new or recent works. They do not seek long runs and can afford to take greater chances than Broadway does. They have become attractive to playwrights who wish to avoid reshaping their plays to fit the demands of Broadway producers. Several (among them the Actors Theatre of Louisville) now offer festivals of new plays each year. The regional theatres now offer a two-way street to New York; new plays that are successful at a major regional theatre might be selected for New York productions, while the recent hit plays of New York typically then get produced at regional theatres. Likewise, the regional theatre movement has helped decentralize the talent as many actors, directors, and designers work both in New York and in the regional theatres.

The successful decentralization of theatre in America through its regional theatres has proven Margo Jones prophetic when she said, "in inspiring the operation of thirty theatres like ours, the playwright won't need Broadway." Playwright Steven Dietz serves as an example of the success possible beyond Broadway. Though never having had a Broadway production, Dietz is annually one of the most produced playwrights in America and has had his worked produced in nearly twenty countries and ten languages. With over thirty plays—including *God's Country* (1988), *Halcyon Days* (1991), *Trust* (1992), *Lonely Planet* (1993), *Handing Down Names* (1994), *Private Eyes* (1996), *Dracula* (1996), *Still Life with Iris* (1997), *Inventing van Gogh* (2004), and *Becky's New Car* (2008)—Dietz has written on a variety of subjects in very different tones. Compare, for example, *God's Country*, a chilling drama that treats the northwestern white supremacist group called

"The Order," with the quickly shifting frames of self-deception in the comic thriller *Private Eyes*. One common feature among Dietz's many plays is his clever use of suspense to engage and maintain audience interest. Dietz also creates characters that, whether the tone of the play is serious or comic, audiences can easily identify with and care about. These features may partially explain why his plays are so widely produced.

Off-Broadway and Off-Off-Broadway

While the regional theatre movement was underway across America, a different type of decentralization was taking place at the traditional center of professional theatre in the United States—New York City. Two major factors contributed to the creation of Off-Broadway, an umbrella term given to performance venues just outside of the traditional New York City theatre district: production costs on Broadway and the creative aspirations of theatre practitioners. The cost of producing a play on Broadway included renting and maintaining a large theatre, providing scenery, costumes, lighting, and stage properties, as well as hiring union personnel. Broadway theatres were "union houses" that required the employment of union stage performers, members of Actors Equity, and union stagehands, members of the International Alliance of Theatrical Stage Employees (IATSE). At the same time that production costs were increasing, theatre faced increased competition from television. To minimize their financial risk, investors tended to produce plays and musicals with sufficient mass appeal to achieve long runs and thereby defray initial expenses. Although this practice minimized risk, it arguably led to predictable material being chosen for the stage; material that had little chance of offending or confusing anyone. It was under these conditions that some theatre artists in the 1950s sought an outlet for their creativity beyond the confines of Broadway. Theatrical groups found out-of-the-way buildings where low production costs permitted them to offer plays less likely to appeal to Broadway audiences. Most groups, working in buildings never intended for theatrical purposes, experimented with spatial arrangements unlike those in Broadway's proscenium theatres. Many Off-Broadway companies played to small audiences because theatres seating more than two hundred persons had to adhere to fire and safety provisions more stringent than the companies would have been able to meet. Performing to smaller crowds for fewer consecutive performances in less expensive venues allowed these groups to take greater risks. These ventures marked the beginning of Off-Broadway.

Off-Broadway proved so attractive that about fifty groups performed there during the 1950s. Of these, the most important was the Circle in the Square, which won critical acceptance both for itself and for Off-Broadway when in 1952 it achieved resounding success with Tennessee

Williams's *Summer and Smoke*, a play that had previously failed on Broadway. In more recent years, notable Off-Broadway theatres have included the Manhattan Theatre Club and Playwrights Horizons, both of which provide a venue for new and established playwrights.

By the 1960s, Off-Broadway had become so successful that theatrical unions insisted on stricter working conditions and higher wages. As a result, production costs rose until the advantages originally offered by Off-Broadway largely disappeared. This prompted those who wanted to exercise the full range of their creativity to develop Off-Off-Broadway—in still more out-of-the-way spaces where unions were largely ignored (though most unions eventually approved a special Off-Off-Broadway contract with conditions less restrictive than those in Off-Broadway contracts).

Of the early Off-Off-Broadway groups, one of the most important was the La MaMa organization, founded in 1961 by Ellen Stewart (1919–2011). La MaMa emphasized new plays and provided a place free from restrictions (except those imposed by its limited funds) where dramatists could see their plays performed. By 1970,

Sara Krulwich/The New York Times/Redux

Engaged, a rarely produced play by W. S. Gilbert (one-half of the comic operetta writing team of Gilbert and Sullivan), might not have sufficient marketing appeal to be produced on Broadway. But today Off-Broadway offers appropriately sized venues for such works that have merit if not mass appeal. *Engaged* by W. S. Gilbert in the Theatre for a New Audience Off-Broadway production; directed by Doug Hughes; sets by John Lee Beatty; costumes by Catherine Zuber; lighting by Rui Rita; sound by Aural Fixation.

La MaMa was presenting more plays each season than all of the Broadway theatres combined. Although these plays varied enormously, many were determinedly innovative, defying and altering accepted notions of dramatic effectiveness. This free-ranging experimentation in playwriting also extended to directorial techniques. Tom O'Horgan was the most successful of La MaMa's directors. He subsequently directed *Hair*, *Lenny*, and *Jesus Christ, Superstar* on Broadway, using the approach he had perfected at La MaMa, which seemingly owed much to Artaud: extensive use of nonverbal vocal sound, overamplification of sound, highly varied lighting (including strobe), oversized effigies or symbolic stage properties, and the "physicalization" of almost every moment. His productions were colorful and uninhibited. When La MaMa toured abroad, it seemed so innovative that it was asked to establish branches in various countries, thereby helping to spread the Off-Off-Broadway model internationally. Today, La MaMa owns a space with three theatres and remains an incubator of new plays.

In addition to Off-Broadway and Off-Off-Broadway, New York theatre was transformed via the creation of two institutional not-for-profit theatre companies: the New York Shakespeare Festival/Public Theatre and Lincoln Center. Joseph Papp (1921–1991) founded the New York Shakespeare Festival Theatre in 1954 and soon persuaded municipal authorities to let him stage plays free of charge in Central Park. This program became so popular that in 1962 the city built the Delacorte Theatre there. In 1967, Papp acquired the former Astor Library on the edge of Greenwich Village and transformed it into the Public Theatre with five performance spaces. Not only does this organization maintain a heavy production schedule, composed of Shakespeare's plays, revivals, and new plays, but also it provides performance space for many other companies. Several of its productions, most notably *A Chorus Line*, moved to Broadway and garnered Tony Awards. Now headed by Artistic Director Oskar Eustis, the New York Shakespeare Festival/Public Theatre remains an influential force in New York theatre.

The New York Shakespeare Festival's production of Shakespeare's *Measure for Measure*. Directed by Mary Zimmerman; scene design by Dan Ostling.

Tom O'Horgan's 1971 staging of Julian Barry's *Lenny*, based on the life of the comedian Lenny Bruce. The fifteen-foot puppets represent such popular-culture figures as Little Orphan Annie, Boris Karloff, and the Lone Ranger. The musicians are dressed as bandaged accident victims. Scenery by Robin Wagner; costumes by Randy Barcello.

Photo by Martha Swope

In 1960 plans were announced for the Lincoln Center for the Performing Arts, with venues for ballet, opera, concerts, and theatre. The theatre portion was initially envisioned as a pseudo-National Theatre with a permanent repertory company. For many years, financial difficulties plagued the company. However, guided by the motto "Good Plays, Popular Prices" Lincoln Center was reestablished in 1985 and has become one of New York's foremost producers, staging new plays and revivals as well as large-scale productions such as Tom Stoppard's *The Coast of Utopia* trilogy and *War Horse*, works that had originated at England's National Theatre. As with the Public, Lincoln Center has won numerous Tony Awards and transfers successful shows to Broadway, with the profits directed back into the company to support other projects. In 2012, Lincoln Center opened a small studio theatre to complement its two existing stages.

Broadway, Off-Broadway, Off-Off-Broadway, and the institutional not-for-profit theatres all play an important role in offering a diversity of theatrical experiences in New York. The distinctions between the types of work offered at each type of venue are based on a combination of prospective audience and economic factors. By union contracts, a Broadway theatre has five hundred or more seats, Off-Broadway between hundred and four hundred ninety-nine, with Off-Off-Broadway having ninety-nine seats or less.

Alternative Theatre Groups

Some of the individuals who formed Off-Off-Broadway theatres were interested not only in finding a creative outlet for their talents but

Society, Art & Culture

THEATRE ACROSS AMERICA

New York still attracts the greatest attention as a theatrical center, but many other cities also have thriving theatre communities. Seattle has twelve theatres where actors work under Actors Equity contracts. These include the Seattle Repertory Theatre, a Contemporary Theatre, Intiman Theatre, and the Seattle Children's Theatre. In addition to the Equity companies, there are numerous others covering a wide range of interests and appeal to audiences.

Los Angeles claims to have more than two hundred fifty theatre companies, presenting more than one thousand shows per year. These include a few major companies, such as the Mark Taper Forum and South Coast Repertory Theatre, but the majority are small ninety-nine-seat houses, a size that permits them to operate under Equity waiver contracts that offer performers little pay.

Chicago is estimated to have as many as two hundred theatre companies at any one time. These companies have a strong pool of actors available from the more than fourteen hundred members of Actors Equity who live in Chicago. The city government recognizes the value of theatre and has helped to finance the upgrading of several theatres, including $18.8 million for the new home of the Goodman Theatre (founded in 1925), noted for giving many now-famous theatre artists their start (among them David Mamet). The Steppenwolf Theatre Company has launched the career of many notable actors (including Gary Sinise, John Malkovich, and Laurie Metcalf). Other notable Chicago theatres include the Court Theatre, Victory Gardens, and Second City (a comedy revue theatre that helped to develop the talents of John Belushi, Dan Aykroyd, Bill Murray, Alan Arkin, and countless others). There are also several theatres that give voice to the concerns of various audience constituencies: Congo Square Theatre (African American), Teatro Vista (Latino), Rasaka (Asian), Babes with Blades (feminist), and About Face (gay and lesbian).

Other major cities that support a lively theatre scene include Minneapolis, San Francisco, Boston, Denver, Philadelphia, Atlanta, Washington, Houston, and still others too numerous to discuss.

Many smaller cities have long-standing theatre companies of excellent quality with unique missions to serve their audiences. For example, The Perseverance Theatre in Juneau, Alaska (a community of thirty thousand accessible only by plane or boat), hosts Alaskan Native performance festivals, educational outreach programs, and special projects with Alaskan artists, and performs new and classical plays both in Juneau and throughout the state on tour.

also in using the power of theatre as a means of social, political, or artistic change. Social historians have characterized the 1960s as a period of great upheaval across America, in Europe, and elsewhere. In the United States, this upheaval may have begun in the mid-1950s with the civil rights movement, but it quickly extended to a reaction against traditional attitudes regarding conformity to social norms (dress, sexual behavior, gender role, speech, etc.). As the 1960s progressed, this social revolution took on an increasing political dimension as the antiwar movement protesting America's military involvement in Vietnam escalated. In fact, theatre played an active role in the social and political upheaval of the 1960s. The decentralization of theatre in America had encouraged new voices that were now using theatre as a means to urge others to recognize and address what they believed were social, economic, or political problems. Although mainstream theatre remained primarily a commercial enterprise, the new voices exploring alternatives to the commercial stage were moving American theatre in new directions that would yield significant changes in theatre practices and conventions.

During the 1960s, the Living Theatre, more than any other Off-Off-Broadway theatre organization, epitomized rebellion against established

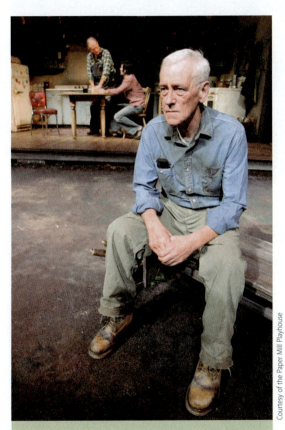

Courtesy of the Paper Mill Playhouse

Michael Healy's *Drawer Boy* demonstrates the increased decentralization of the American Theatre. Although the play has been frequently produced across America, it never played on Broadway. Pictured here is John Mahoney in the Paper Mill Playhouse production of the play, reprising his performance from an earlier production by Chicago's Steppenwolf Theatre Company.

authority in all of its aspects: values, behavior, language, dress, theatrical conventions. When Judith Malina and Julian Beck founded the Living Theatre in New York City, it was devoted to poetic drama. However, as Malina and Beck became influenced increasingly by Brecht, Artaud, and anarchist theory, it grew into a company focused on radical social and political change. In 1964, its theatre having been closed for failure to pay taxes, the Living Theatre left the United States and until 1968 toured Europe, where it gained a large and enthusiastic following, especially among disaffected young people. In 1968, the Living Theatre returned to the United States with the repertory it had created during its exile.

The most extreme of the Living Theatre's pieces was *Paradise Now* (1968). It began with actors circulating among the spectators denouncing strictures on freedom (to smoke marijuana, travel without a passport, to go nude in public, and the like). Thereafter during the performance, both spectators and actors roamed the auditorium and stage indiscriminately; many removed their clothing and some smoked marijuana—in other words, many of the strictures they denounced were defied. The performance continued for four or five hours with several scenes proceeding simultaneously throughout the theatre. Actors provoked some spectators into voicing opposition and then overrode them, often by shouting obscenities or even spitting on them; at the end, the company sought to move the audience into the streets to continue the revolution begun in the theatre. Its aggressive behavior, combined with its anarchistic politics, won the Living Theatre enormous notoriety while their performance style challenged the boundary between art and life. They treated space and time as real, and actors played themselves rather than characters. Likewise, actors wore their own clothing instead of costumes, and the subject matter, contemporary social and political issues, was pursued through improvised confrontations rather than through a predetermined text.

Trinity Mirror/Mirrorpix/Alamy

The Living Theatre's production of *Paradise Now*, during which the actors mingled with the audience, urged them to remove their clothing (which many did), attacked (even spat on) those who seemed to oppose them, and in general used performance to urge revolutionary change in society.

The Living Theatre also participated in two important changes made by theatre groups during the late 1960s: the introduction of obscene language and nudity. Although obscene language and simulated nudity were common features of early Greek comedy and late Roman mimes, neither had been considered acceptable in legitimate theatrical performances since the fall of Rome. But during the 1960s, the rebellion against accepted attitudes and assumptions that had begun with the civil rights movement gradually passed over into other areas. Demonstrations, then common, usually involved the deliberate public violation of some convention or law considered unwarranted or unjust. Continued assaults on the conventions of polite behavior, and the inability of authorities to prevent violations, gained tolerance of behavior previously considered unacceptable.

After a change in the law, nudity and obscenity first came to Broadway in 1968 in the musical *Hair*, a plea for tolerance of alternative lifestyles. In contrast, the Living Theatre abused spectators who had paid to see its performances but did not agree with their opinions. Rather than being entertained, these spectators were subjected to physical and political intimidation. Why, then, did audiences attend? Novelty and notoriety probably attracted many, whereas others probably came out of sympathy for the group's political goals and defiance of authority; still others probably applauded the group's use of the theatre for purposes other than diversionary entertainment and for insisting on the responsibility of theatre to play an active role in social change. By the early 1970s, however, the group, probably because of its excesses, had lost most of its following. Still, its influence continued.

By the 1970s, though the limits of permissibility were vague, almost any subject, behavior, or manner of speaking was potentially acceptable in the theatre.

Although the most radical, the Living Theatre was not the only group seeking to change society through theatre. Among these, two of the most effective were the Bread and Puppet Theatre (founded in New York City in 1961), which used both actors and giant puppets to enact parables (often based on the Bible) that denounced war and the futility of materialism, and the San Francisco Mime Theatre (founded in 1966), which performed satirical pieces promoting civil rights, equality for women, and various other causes. The Bread and Puppet Theatre and the San Francisco Mime Theatre were also two among many theatres that sought to attract audiences by breaking down the distinctions between high art and popular culture. They borrowed freely from *commedia dell'arte*, festivals, parades, circuses, and variety theatre in their efforts to form a more tolerant and accepting society. Both groups were also recipients, for a time, of limited state and NEA funding.

Joseph Chaikin (previously a member of the Living Theatre) founded The Open Theatre (1963–1974) in New York City. Chaikin had shared the Living Theatre's concerns for social consciousness and change but became more focused on redefining theatre's aesthetics and on actor training. Chaikin's work, which was grounded in theories of role-playing and theatre games, made a number of contributions in these areas. Two of the most significant were "collective creation" and "transformation." Transformation was a constantly shifting reality in which the same performer assumes and discards roles or identities as the context changes. Reality was treated not as fixed but as ever-changing,

AP Photo/Craig Line

After several years of operation in New York City, the Bread and Puppet Theatre relocated to Vermont. Bread and Puppet shared its fresh baked bread with audiences at every performance, believing that community is built through sharing and that art, like bread, is a basic necessity of life.

implying that because reality is not fixed, we can reshape ourselves and our society into what we would like them to be. The Open Theatre's scripts, which sought to reveal fundamental moral and social patterns buried beneath troubling contemporary events or preoccupations, usually evolved from its workshops in close collaboration with its playwrights. After selecting a topic of interest, the actors, through improvisations, explored the potentials of situations and characters; the playwright then chose and shaped the discoveries that seemed most effective into a written script. One of the Open Theatre's most successful collaborations was with Jean-Claude van Itallie on *The Serpent* (1969), in which the assassinations of Martin Luther King Jr. and John F. Kennedy are interwoven with the story of Adam and Eve and other biblical events. Written as a ritualized ceremony, the play explores the human struggle between freedom of choice and obedience to external authority. An open-ended work, *The Serpent* invites the audience to find connections between the Book of Genesis's archetypal stories and modern American society. Another successful collaboration resulted in Megan Terry's *Viet Rock* (1966), which (with scenes that moved quickly between battlefields, congressional hearings, and family life) ridiculed bureaucratic justifications of the war in Vietnam and praised the simple pleasures of life that war disrupts and destroys. Such collective creation, explored by several theatres in the 1960s and 1970s, continues to be practiced by some groups.

None of these groups was dedicated to commercial success. Their goals in making theatre were social, political, and artistic. Their explorations broadened the notion of what could be considered theatre as well as its possible practices and conventions. They all had limited resources. Most never controlled a theatre building and had to perform wherever they could. But what they lacked in financial resources they compensated for in innovation and ingenuity. They were practicing what Jerzy Grotowski (1933–1999), director of the Polish Laboratory Theatre in Wroclaw, Poland, called "poor theatre."

Poor and Environmental Theatres

Grotowski believed that theatre should not try to compete with movies and television; instead it should emphasize what makes theatre unique: the direct and immediate interaction between actor and audience. Rather than a technologically rich theatre, Grotowski sought to create one in which everything not absolutely necessary would be eliminated; he called his approach "poor theatre."

Because of the actor's central role in performance, Grotowski devoted much of his attention to actor training. He coupled intensive physical exercises with training designed to remove the performer's psychological inhibitions; he also sought to develop the actor's voice as an instrument capable of exceeding all normal demands. Ultimately, he wished actors to surpass so completely the spectators' expectations as to arouse a sense of magic. In performance, each actor wore only one costume; if their character's status changed or if they played another role, then the actor changed his or her physicality and not the costume. Likewise, in lieu of traditional scenery, a limited number of functional props might be rearranged in nonrepresentational ways. Any music had to be produced by the actors themselves. The performers, deprived of all nonessential and technological aids, had to depend entirely on their own resources.

Grotowski worked in a space that was reconfigured for each production, with a limited number of spectators and an actor-audience spatial relationship determined by the show's content. For example, *Kordian* (1962), which takes place in an insane asylum, was staged in a large room throughout which double-decker beds were spaced irregularly; audience members sat on some of the beds, whereas others were used by actor-patients, and the action, which took place in and around the beds, placed the spectators in its midst, allowing them to function as passive inmates or observers. For *The Constant Prince* (1967), in which the title character patiently accepts mistreatment and suffering, the theatre was arranged so that all of the spectators looked down into a space that resembled a hospital teaching theatre where, as Grotowski put it, psychic surgery takes place (see illustration).

Grotowski viewed theatre as the modern equivalent of a tribal ceremony, and his goal was to create a ritualized, communal experience. He searched scripts for archetypal patterns of human behavior independent of time and place and developed them (often severely changing the original script) to make both actors and audience confront themselves spiritually. His goals resembled Artaud's, though his means differed markedly. During the late 1960s, Grotowski became a major influence on theatre in Europe and America. His company performed widely, and he conducted workshops for various other theatres and for some of the world's most prominent directors. His influence was further disseminated through his book *Towards a Poor Theatre* (1968). Although few others attempted to restrict resources as severely as he did, many groups adapted his approach to staging and actor training. In the 1970s, Grotowski moved away from theatre into other explorations only partially related to theatre.

In America, Richard Schechner, having examined various contemporary practices including those of the "poor" theatres, sought to describe the conventions of an approach to performance that he labeled "environmental theatre." Some of these conventions concern the performance space. "The event can take place either in a totally transformed space or in a 'found' space," Schechner wrote. In other words, space may be adapted to make it appropriate to the action, or a suitable space not requiring alteration may be found (for example, a production depicting war as a game might be performed in a gymnasium or on a playground). "All the space is used for performance; all the space is used for the audience."

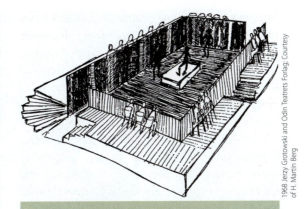

1968 Jerzy Grotowski and Odin Teatrets Forlag; Courtesy of H. Martin Berg

Arrangement of the performance and audience spaces for Grotowski's production of *The Constant Prince*.

That is, the way in which the total space can be used is entirely flexible; any part of the space may be used by performers or spectators, or performers and spectators may be intermingled.

Other conventions relate to what is performed. Schechner wrote: "A text need be neither the starting point nor the goal of a production. There may be no text at all." Unlike traditional performances (which seek to embody an existing dramatic text), in environmental theatre, performance takes precedence over text and may be entirely improvisational, leaving no text behind once the performance ends. During a performance, "focus is flexible and variable"—that is, a production need not be shaped by the traditional assumption that all spectators must be able to see the same thing at the same time. Instead, several scenes may be going on simultaneously in various parts of the space; spectators are free to choose which they will watch.

Environmental theatre blends categories long treated as distinct during performance: acting space and nonacting space (stage and auditorium); performer and spectator; text and performance; sequentiality and simultaneity. It challenges conventions previously considered necessary for effective theatrical production and enjoyable audience experience, suggesting how easy it is to confuse the theatre's essence with its prevailing conventions.

Notice the actor-audience relationship in the flexible theatre space used for The Performance Group's production of Brecht's *Mother Courage.*

Courtesy of Richard Schechner

Multimedia, Happenings, and Performance Art

Even as the "poor" theatres restricted their means, other theatres emphasized the very elements (electronic and spectacular) that the poor theatres sought to eliminate. As early as 1964 Marshall McLuhan, mass-communication theorist, argued that, as electronic media have replaced the printed page as our primary mode of communication, we have become increasingly adept at processing multiple and concurrent stimuli (we watch on television events going on halfway around the world as we simultaneously carry on conversations in our living rooms). McLuhan concluded that we no longer require messages to be received in orderly sequence or one at a time.

Electronic media affected the theatre by creating the desire to make the representation of place in the theatre as transformable as it is in film and television. One result was to reduce the amount and specificity of built scenic elements (because of the time required to shift full-stage sets). Another was to encourage experimentation with "multimedia"—combinations of elements from several media. The best-known multimedia experimentation was done by the Czech designer Josef Svoboda. Around 1958, Svoboda began work on two projects—Polyekran (multiple screen) and Laterna Magika. Polyekran used filmed images entirely but sought to overcome the "visual paralysis" of a single screen by hanging screens of different sizes at various distances from the audience, projecting different images on each, and changing the images at varying time intervals—thus creating a dynamic visual field and giving the audience a choice of images to watch. Laterna Magika used motion pictures in combination with live actors. Often the performers in the film and on the stage were the same, and at times a live performer seemed to emerge from the screen.

In 1959, Svoboda began to incorporate elements from these experiments into the staging of drama. He also experimented with devices for moving scenic units and platforms in ways intended to make the stage instantly transformable both in configuration and visual appearance. Some of his productions used closed-circuit television, with some scenes performed in a studio miles from the theatre and projected onto screens hung above a stage on which other live scenes were being acted. Closed-circuit television was also used to project close-up images of the actors' faces on screens during moments of crisis. Such experiments by Svoboda and others popularized several practices: using projected still pictures on multiple screens as a scenic background; interjecting filmed sequences into the dramatic action; manipulating the volume, direction, or quality of stereophonic sound; and using closed-circuit television in multiple ways.

These developments are related to others then occurring in the visual arts. Stimulated by dissatisfaction with restrictions imposed by the media in which they worked (for example, two-dimensionality), painters sought to overcome the restrictions by such devices as gluing three-dimensional objects onto paintings. Sculptors, to overcome the static nature of their medium, attached motors to sculptures to make them move or used light to vary the appearance. Out of such experiments eventually came *happenings*, pioneered by composer John Cage and painter Allan Kaprow. Kaprow believed that in addition to the art objects on display, the space and all those who attend must be considered essential parts of the total artistic experience. For his first happening in 1959, Kaprow divided a gallery into three compartments: In each were several types of visual art and a number of individuals who repetitively performed assigned tasks, while images were projected onto various surfaces, including human beings; meanwhile taped music and sound effects were played. All of those who attended were expected to carry out instructions handed them as they entered. Subsequent happenings varied, but most were multimedia events that had common characteristics with implications for theatrical performance:

- They broke down barriers between the arts and mingled elements.

- They shifted emphasis away from creating a product to participating in a process.

- They sought to provide an experience rather than present a message or meaning.

Josef Svoboda's multimedia design for an adaptation of Maxim Gorki's *The Last Ones* at the National Theatre, Prague. The various fragmentary set pieces at stage level permit multiple scenes to be played simultaneously or in sequence against projections seen at the rear of the stage.

- They shifted emphasis from the artist's intention to the participants' awareness.
- They often made each participant a partial creator of the event.

Many aspects of happenings and environmental theatre recall futurism and the dada movement.

Over time, happenings passed out of vogue. But the artistic impulse that had prompted them remained and resurfaced in the 1970s as *performance art*. Performance art may intermingle borrowings from (any or all of) visual arts, dance, music, video, and theatre. It may be scripted or improvised. It may or may not make use of props and costumes. Often a solo performance, it also may use multiple performers. It may be highly personal or confrontational, and it often explores issues of sexuality, violence, and power in ways that challenge marketplace values, governmental authority, and the way the media manipulate perceptions (especially of the body as object and commodity). Perhaps the essence of performance art is that there are no rules about what is allowed.

The major creators of performance art originally came from the visual arts, dance, or music; they were attracted to performance art in part

Sara Krulwich/The New York Times/Redux

The New York Metropolitan Opera's 2008 production of Berlioz's *Damnation de Faust* used a complex system of computers, infrared cameras, digital projectors, and scrim to create a multimedia interactive performance. The technology allowed the nuances of the live performance—performers' movements, voices, and orchestra dynamics—to trigger and shape video projections that dominate the setting's visual appearance. Holger Förterer, who designed the software that controls the technology, has dubbed it "augmented reality" (as opposed to "virtual reality"). The production, and others like it, demonstrate how far technology has come since Svoboda's early experiments and suggests the potential of such technology to create the visual dynamism of film while maintaining the immediacy of live theatre. The production was directed by Robert Lepage.

because it disregarded boundaries among the arts, thereby greatly expanding the means of expression. Theatre artists originally found performance art less attractive, perhaps because theatre has always combined elements from various other arts and because performance art tended to de-emphasize story/text and to use performers not as actors but as narrators or as objects to be manipulated spatially.

Broadway and Musicals after Subsidization

Decentralization and subsidization altered the character of Broadway, which had been the primary producer of new plays in America before the mid-1960s. After the establishment of the NEA and regional theatres, Broadway came to premiere plays less and less frequently, choosing instead to present new plays that had been successful in regional, Off-Broadway, Off-Off-Broadway, or British theatres. Revivals of plays that had been successful on Broadway in the past were also sometimes produced. This practice of avoiding entirely new plays that had no successful record of attendance may have lessened financial risk but did not eliminate it, in part because audiences were not always eager to attend productions of plays with ticket prices ranging from $50 to over $100.

The situation was somewhat different for musicals, which remained Broadway's favorite fare; most of the productions that originated on Broadway were musicals, but many musicals also were tried out first elsewhere. Until around 1968, the type of musical that achieved dominance during and following World War II continued. Some of the best were *Funny Girl* (1964) by Jule Styne; *Hello, Dolly* (1964) and *Mame* (1966) by Jerry Herman; *Cabaret* (1966) by John Kander; and *Sweet Charity* (1966) by Sy Coleman.

But beginning in 1968, the musical underwent significant change. The crucial production was *Hair* (1968) with its rock music, limited story, single setting, "hippie" dress, strobe lighting, highly amplified sound, and promotion of alternative lifestyles. *Hair* was also the first Broadway production to include nudity and obscene language. It broadened what might be used as subject matter for a musical and explored

Although "happenings" are no longer in vogue, their spirit of communal creation remains in group events like the Burning Man Festival. Held each year in late August in the Black Rock Desert of Northern Nevada, the festival brings together hundreds of people to participate in acts of self-expression, culminating in the burning of a giant wooden effigy, the Burning Man.

HECTOR MATA/AFP/Getty Images

different ways dance and music might be used to convey thought and dramatic action. Several musicals using the rock idiom followed; perhaps the most successful was *Godspell* (1974) by Stephen Schwartz. Other innovations to the American musical included Michael Bennett's *A Chorus Line* (1975), which features a chorus as the principal character and uses a presentational style in which dancers auditioning for a chorus job tell their personal stories. *A Chorus Line* became one of the longest-running shows in Broadway's history, continuing until 1990. Meanwhile, the older type of musical continued sporadically in such works as *Annie* (1977) by Charles Strouse, and *La Cage aux Folles* (1983) by Jerry Herman.

Perhaps the most successful innovator of the American musical since the 1940s has been writer/composer Stephen Sondheim. Early in his career, Sondheim contributed to Golden Age musicals, writing the lyrics for *West Side Story* (1957) and *Gypsy* (1959), and the music and lyrics for *A Funny Thing Happened on the Way to the Forum* (1962). Starting in 1970, Sondheim took musicals in new directions as he experimented

with various approaches: *Company* (1970) had no chorus and used the principal performers in the song-and-dance sequences; *Pacific Overtures* (1976) borrowed conventions from Japanese theatre; *Sweeney Todd* (1979), based on a nineteenth-century melodrama, was operatic in its use of music throughout; *Sunday in the Park with George* (1983) took its inspiration from a painting by Georges Seurat and used counterpoint to great effect; *Into the Woods* (1987) deconstructed familiar fairy tales. Almost all of these depart from the upbeat optimism of previous American musicals; they offer ironic and melancholic views of human behavior and social values and avoid happy endings. Sondheim changed musicals in part by making the songs and music much more complex. Rather than writing songs that express an unambiguous emotion or point of view, as was typical in earlier musicals, Sondheim writes lyrics and music that are filled with inner tensions that suggest unacknowledged conflicts or hidden desires and reveal multiple possibilities of meaning. Subtext is a significant element in his lyrics and music, contributing to the sense

The much praised revival of *Cabaret*, which featured Alan Cumming as the provocative Emcee. Directed by Sam Mendes; costumes by William Ivey Long; sets by Robert Brill; lighting by Peggy Eisenhauer and Mike Baldassari.

Joan Marcus

of ironic acceptance characteristic of much of Sondheim's work. Sondheim's work also epitomizes the divide between critical and popular tastes: He has won eight Tony awards (more than any other composer), but none of his post-1970 shows has lasted even two years on Broadway.

While the musical has traditionally been seen as an American art form, the most popular musicals on the Broadway stage in the 1970s and 1980s were imported from England. Andrew Lloyd Webber, with *Jesus Christ, Superstar* (1971), *Evita* (1976), *Cats* (1981), and *Phantom of the Opera* (1986), became the most commercially successful composer of musicals. At nearly eighteen years, *Cats* was the longest-running Broadway musical, until it was eclipsed by *Phantom of the Opera*, which has been running since January 26, 1988. Webber's work was joined by other imports by way of the London stage, among them *Les Misérables* (1985) and *Miss Saigon* (1989) by the Frenchmen Alain Boublil and Claude-Michel Schönberg. Meanwhile the strength of the American musical was mostly represented through revivals—among them *Gypsy, Guys and Dolls, Damn Yankees, Carousel, Chicago, Cabaret, The Pajama Game*, and *Sweeney Todd*. As discussed in Chapter 9, the American musical would reemerge in the mid-1990s.

Les Misérables ran on Broadway for 6,680 consecutive performances between 1987 and 2003, and it has been produced all over the world. In London, *Les Misérables* has been running since October 8, 1985, and in 2010, a new 25th anniversary production, pictured here, premiered in London before touring the world.

A New Generation of American Playwrights

Although after 1960 Arthur Miller and Tennessee Williams continued to write, they were overshadowed by a new generation of playwrights, among them Edward Albee, Neil Simon, Lanford Wilson, David Mamet, Terrence McNally, Christopher Durang, and Sam Shepard.

At the beginning of his playwriting career, Edward Albee grabbed the public's attention with biting dialogue and experimental theatrical forms, evident in his one-act plays *The Zoo Story* (1958) and *The Sandbox* (1960). During the 1960s, Edward Albee reinvigorated American drama and became the most honored American playwright, especially after the 1962 production of *Who's Afraid of Virginia Woolf?*. The play explores the destructive psychological relationship of a husband and wife who are held together by an intense love–hate relationship that is painfully abrasive to them and those around them. During a night of drinking and sadomasochistic games, they strip away their illusions and face the harsh realities of their lives. It was recommended for the Pulitzer Prize, but the final committee objected to the play's vulgarity and sexual themes and opted not to award a prize that year. Thus far, Albee has written over thirty plays and received three Pulitzer Prizes for drama: *A Delicate Balance* (1967), *Seascape* (1975), and *Three Tall Women* (1994). More recently, his Tony Award–winning play *The Goat, or Who I Sylvia?* (2002) tells the story of a long-married couple confronting the husband's love affair with a goat.

While Albee was the most critically acclaimed American playwright of the 1960s, that decade saw the rise of America's most commercially successful post-war playwright—Neil Simon. Many of his early comedies such as *Barefoot in the Park* (1963), *The Odd Couple* (1965), *Plaza Suite* (1968), and *The Sunshine Boys* (1972) were also made into successful films. His critical stature rose in the 1980s via an autobiographical trilogy comprised of *Brighton Beach Memoirs* (1983), *Biloxi Blues* (1985), and *Broadway Bound* (1986); these were soon followed by his Pulitzer Prize–winning play *Lost in Yonkers* (1991). Simon's more than thirty plays cover a range of topics, but many of his most successful ones revolve around marital conflict, sibling rivalry, adolescence, or the fear of aging. With sharp dialogue, Simon blends comedy with more serious moments to craft plays that have attracted a wide audience.

Lanford Wilson (1937–2011) began his career in the Off-Off-Broadway theatre. Among his many plays are *Balm in Gilead* (1965), *Hot L Baltimore* (1973), *Tally's Folly* (1979, Pulitzer Prize), *The Fifth of July* (1978), *Burn This* (1987), and *Redwood Curtain* (1982). The storyline in Wilson's plays is minimal; the focus is on character relationships and the eventual revelation of hidden feelings, disappointments, and hopes. Wilson's compassionate treatment of the misfits and rejects of society marks him as a particularly humane contemporary playwright.

In the 1970s and 1980s, David Mamet rose to prominence. In works such as *American Buffalo* (1975), *Glengarry Glen Ross* (1984, Pulitzer Prize), and *Speed-the-Plow* (1988), Mamet depicts the debasement and distortion of human beings by the materialistic goals of American society as epitomized in its business dealings. Other plays, among them *Sexual Perversity in Chicago* (1974), explore the inability to make personal commitments and establish satisfying relationships. *Oleanna* (1992), set in a university, treats contemporary issues of "political correctness" and sexual harassment. *The Cryptogram* (1995) traces the disintegration of trust within a family, while *November* (2007) comically treats an amoral president trying to save his political skin at any cost before an upcoming election. Mamet has also written for television (*The Unit*) and film (*The Postman Always Rings Twice* (1981), *The Verdict* (1982), *Wag the Dog* (1997) and *Hannibal* (2001)).

While Terrence McNally's playwriting career began in the 1960s, he did not achieve significant success until the late 1980s. Starting with *Frankie and Johnny in the Claire de Lune* (1987), McNally enjoyed a string of critical and commercial successes including *The Lisbon Traviata* (1989), *Lips Together, Teeth Apart* (1991), *A Perfect Ganesh* (1993), *Love! Valor! Compassion!* (1994, Tony Award), *Master Class* (1995, Tony Award), and the book for the musicals *Kiss of the Spider Woman* (1992, Tony Award), *Ragtime* (1997, Tony Award), and *The Full Monty* (2000). McNally also attracted considerable notoriety for his play *Corpus Christi* (1998), a work that depicts Jesus and his disciples as gay men living in modern-day Texas.

Christopher Durang has written numerous plays that take serious subjects and treat them so outrageously that they comically underscore the absurdity of modern life. Durang, who studied playwriting at the Yale School of Drama, has served as the Co-Chair of the Playwrights Program at the Julliard School since 1994. His plays include *Sister Mary Ignatius Explains It All for You* (1979), which lampoons Catholic dogma and hypocrisy; *Beyond Therapy* (1981), which ridicules psychotherapists as more in need of help than their patients; and *The Marriage of Bette and Boo* (1985), which treats a dysfunctional family, alcoholism, and its disastrous effects on subsequent generations. Other plays include *The Actor's Nightmare* (1981), *Baby with the Bathwater* (1983), and *Laughing*

Sierra Boggess, left, and Tyne Daly in a scene from the Manhattan Theatre Club's 2010 revival of Terrence McNally's Tony Award-winning *Master Class*, the story of opera singer Maria Callas.

AP Photo/Boneau-Bryan/Brown

Wild (1987). More recent works include *Mrs. Bob Cratchit's Wild Christmas Binge* (2002), a revisionist take on *A Christmas* Carol, and *Why Torture I Wrong, and the People Who Love Them* (2009).

Sam Shepard has been among the most prolific and provocative of contemporary American playwrights. He began his writing career in 1964 in the Off-Off-Broadway theatre and for many years thereafter turned out a large number of plays, among them *Chicago* (1965), *Mad Dog Blues* (1971), and *The Tooth of Crime* (1973), without revising the scripts because he considered it dishonest to change what he had originally written. In the mid-1970s, he altered this view and wrote his most successful plays, including *Curse of the Starving Class* (1977), *Buried Child* (1979, Pulitzer Prize), *True West* (1980), *Fool for Love* (1983), and *A Lie of the Mind* (1985). Recent, somewhat less successful plays include *Simpatico* (1993), *The Late Henry Moss* (2000), *The God of Hell* (2004), *Kicking a Dead Horse* (2007), and *Ages of the Moon* (2009). Although there is much variety in Shepard's work, a number of motifs recur: attempts to escape or deny the past, the cowboy and the West as basic American myths, the family as a battleground, and characters caught between empty dreams and an insubstantial reality. Let us look at Shepard's most produced play, *True West*.

TRUE WEST

True West is a tightly focused work, dominated by the intense interactions between two brothers. The younger brother, Austin, is an Ivy League–educated screenwriter, while the older brother, Lee, is a petty thief and drifter. Over the course of the play, each brother finds himself wishing he were in the other's place.

The entire play is set in the kitchen of their mother's home 40 miles east of Los Angeles. Austin is house-sitting while their mother is in Alaska. After an absence of five years, Lee has arrived unexpectedly and is viewed as a distraction by Austin who is struggling to write and sell a screenplay to Hollywood producer Saul Kimmer. The opening scene establishes each brother's character and the tense relationship between them. Lee does not fit in the modern, suburban world, but prides himself on being self-reliant. In contrast, with his wife, kids, house, and car, Austin is living the traditional American Dream. Looming over the brothers is the ghostly presence of their father, an alcoholic living somewhere in the Arizona desert. In addition, the threat of violence continually percolates under the scene with Lee informing Austin that if Austin won't lend him his car, "then I'll just take the damn thing."

The second scene further develops the characters. Lee battles against feeling inferior and resents any show of charity by Austin. At the same time, at different points in the play, Lee expresses his own condescending attitude towards Austin's art and lifestyle; when Austin argues that being a Hollywood writer is a lot of work, Lee responds: "What's the toughest part? Deciding whether to jog or play tennis?" While Lee pokes fun at Austin, Lee also envies what his brother has. Reflecting his conflicted nature, in the second scene, Lee talks about how suburbia kills the soul, yet he also wishes he had grown up in an idealistic suburban home.

While the majority of the play is simply the two brothers, the third scene injects an outside presence, Saul Kimmer, who serves as the catalyst for the overt conflict between the brothers, as they compete for his attention and money. As agreed upon, Lee is away while Austin pitches his screenplay idea to Saul, who responds very favorably. While everything seems to be falling in Austin's favor, Lee returns early (carrying a stolen television) and proceeds to steal some of Saul's attention away from Austin. Lee starts to pitch Saul his own idea for a modern Western, and Saul suggests that Austin write an outline for the story.

The fourth scene involves Austin writing out Lee's story idea, but he is only doing it so that he can get his car keys back from Lee. More importantly, by working together the brothers start to reveal the ways in which they fantasized about the other's life. Lee says: "I always wondered what'd be like to be you." Austin finds this ironic, because Austin always pictured Lee out having adventures, "And I used to say to myself, 'Lee's got the right idea. He's out there in the world and here I am. What am I doing?'" This envy, or wonderment at each other's very different life, foreshadows the role reversals that will occur during the second act.

When Act Two opens the brothers' fortunes have been reversed. While playing golf, Lee won a bet with Saul that has resulted in Saul taking on Lee's screenplay project while dropping Austin's. Besides having Saul's attention, Lee is now in a position to hand out favors, saying he convinced Saul to let Austin write the screenplay; but instead of any sense of cooperation, there is only sibling rivalry. Though Austin is desperate (calling his own project his "only shot"), he refuses to help Lee write his screenplay.

In scene seven there is a literal reversal of the play's opening, as now Lee is the one at the typewriter, while Austin is the one steadily drinking. Likewise, while Lee now views himself as a screenwriter, Austin considers taking up Lee's former occupation of being a petty thief, but Lee doubts whether Austin would be able to steal even something as simple as a toaster. The scene also involves a deeper discussion of their absent father. Lee continues to state that he wants to help their father, but Austin still harbors deep

Philip Seymour Hoffman, left, and John C. Reilly starred in the 2000 Broadway production of *True West*. Every third performance the actors alternated who played the character Austin (on left) and who played Lee.

AP Photo/Joan Marcus

resentment, knowing their alcoholic father will never change his ways and that Austin will never win his father's favor.

By scene eight, the downward spiral of their lives is visually evident on stage. While Austin polishes all the toasters he has stolen, Lee is destroying the typewriter with a golf club while also burning pages of his would-be screenplay. Both men are extremely drunk, the stage is littered with empty beer cans and whiskey bottles, and the plants that Austin was supposed to take care of are dead. As the scene progresses, Lee dumps the contents of the kitchen drawers on the floor and eventually rips the phone off the wall. The play's opening image of middle-class suburbia has devolved into a garbage dump of chaos. Amidst this scene of domestic disintegration, Austin declares his desire for a new beginning, to go with Lee into the desert. While Lee cannot understand why Austin would want to leave his life, Austin concludes: "There's nothing real down here, Lee! Least of all me!" Austin's pursuit of the American Dream has left him hollowed out. But instead of Austin's romanticized vision of a life of freedom in the desert, Lee reveals that he lives there out of necessity, that he is ill-equipped for normal society. At the end of the scene, as the fractured lives nearly explode into a violent confrontation, they instead settle on a deal: If Austin writes the screenplay, Austin can go with Lee into the desert (with Lee keeping all the money).

The final scene opens in the bright light of day, with the brothers' stark reality now fully evident. Shepard's stage directions indicate that "the stage is ravaged," creating the image of "a desert junkyard." Both brothers are dripping sweat, with Lee roaming the stage bare-chested, kicking at the debris and occasionally pouring beer on himself while Austin frantically scribbles at their screenplay. When their mother returns home unexpectedly, the illusion of their situation is gradually stripped away. As Lee backs

out of their screenplay deal, Austin viciously attacks Lee, choking him with the phone cord. After a violent struggle, Lee appears to be dead. But before Austin can leave, Lee gets to his feet and blocks Austin's exit. As the brothers face off, the lights change and they "now appear to be caught in a vast desert-like landscape." Then before the action can be resolved, the lights fade to black.

The ambiguous ending suggests that Shepard is more interested in posing questions than in answering them. While the plot engages the audience, they are ultimately left pondering the psychology of the characters and the questions of identity (both personal and cultural) that they raise. The title *True West* evokes multiple images, suggesting the traditional terrain of cowboys, open spaces, freedom, self-made law, and the gunfights one might find in a Hollywood Western. (Some critics see the play's ending as a pseudo-contemporary Western, with the characters facing off in a duel-like fashion.) In the play, the characters suggest that the mythic old West has died; as Lee says, "Built up? Wiped out is more like it." Later, when Saul says that Lee's screenplay shows "the real West," Austin retorts, "There's no such thing as the West anymore! It's a dead issue! It's dried up." Instead of cowboys roaming the prairie, Austin suggests that the West is now freeways, smog, colored TVs, and Safeway supermarkets. It is also Hollywood, the call of the big screen, the place that can make you a star, which has become its own American Dream. However, when Austin says "There is nothing real down here," he might be critiquing Hollywood as superficial, a place made of surfaces and illusion. In part, the play deals with the myth of the American West, an image that helps to define the American character, but the play suggests that that myth is no longer viable.

True West also engages with another central component of the American mythos—the family. As with the West, the image of family does not live up to its ideal. Instead of the desired, supportive loving family, there is tension, rivalry, and violence. Lee's statement that family members are most likely to kill each other foreshadows the climatic confrontation, and by the play's end, their mother no longer recognizes her home. Traditionally, the home and family are realms of safety and security, but in this play, dysfunction is carried to an extreme, and the neatly organized suburban home that opens the play is left in chaotic ruins at its end.

True West also subtly explores issues of money, power, and dominance as the brothers battle for control. At the outset, Lee has physical power, while Austin has power from intellect and social position. Then each has power through Saul, that is, through connections with those in positions of power. Access to power includes access to money, which is a form of and a means to identity; it lets one act. Money helps put people into roles and out of them; the presence or absence of money helps dictate the choices available to a person. From Austin's perspective, the money from the screenplay could turn Lee's life around, offering the security of a home or a ranch. Likewise, when Lee becomes a screenwriter he views himself as "legitimate" because he is "on salary." To some degree, money offers access to identity and status. On the other hand, while Lee sees money as the way to save their alcoholic father, Austin aptly notes that more than money is needed to change a person.

While the play engages with all these themes, it is also a character study. Shepard has stated: "I wanted to write a play about double nature, one that wouldn't be symbolic or metaphorical or any of that stuff. I just wanted to give a taste of what it feels like to be two-sided. It's a real thing, double nature. I think we're split in a much more devastating way than psychology can ever reveal." In the play, the issue of individual identity comes to the forefront when Austin says, "[Saul] thinks we're the same person." The play deals with two people who are very different, yet it also suggests that these contrasting roles and identities may be found inside all of us. The desire to be our own boss may conflict with our desire for a comfortable income. The desire for freedom battles with the desire for security and safety. In one sense, Lee and Austin are two sides of one personality as they embody impulses that tempt us, desires between which we must often choose.

Looking at the production history of Shepard's play also offers an apt summary of the ways in which American theatre decentralized after World War II, while fostering a strong degree of interdependence between New York and the regions. From 1974–1984, Shepard was playwright-in-residence at the Magic Theatre in San Francisco, and they premiered *True West* in 1980. The success of the play at that regional theatre led to a New York production at Joseph Papp's Public Theatre starring Tommie Lee Jones (Austin) and Peter Boyle (Lee). In 1982, Chicago's Steppenwolf Theatre revived the play with the then relatively unknown John Malkovich (Lee) and Gary Sinise (Austin). Again the regional success fostered a New York production, but this time it was the entire Steppenwolf production in an Off-Broadway venue, where it ran for two years and through multiple casts. In 2000, *True West* was again staged in New York, but this time on Broadway; the added twist was that every third performance the actors Phillip Seymour Hoffman and John C. Reilly alternated who played Austin and who played Lee. This production earned multiple Tony nominations. Highlighting the enduring popularity of the play and the diversity of production opportunities, recent productions of *True West* include a one weekend New York showcase production (2010), a three-week Off-Off-Broadway run (2012), and a staging at Actors Theatre of Louisville (2012), one of the premier regional theatres.

Summary

During the years following the end of World War II, the theatre underwent many changes. Perhaps the most significant change was the decentralization of theatre (which saw the establishment of permanent companies where there previously were none). Throughout Europe this decentralization was made possible through governmental subsidies. Governmental subsidies played an important role in America, particularly in attracting corporate and local support, but not as singularly forceful a role as they did in Europe. Still, as theatre moved in new directions it gave rise to new voices. Many of these new voices in the 1960s and 1970s were focused on using the theatre as a means of social and political change. Others were more interested in expanding the artistic landscape of what theatre can be. Together they questioned individual values and social conventions as well as challenged established practices and conventions. These challenges came to affect almost every aspect of theatre beginning in the 1960s and accelerating thereafter.

THEATRE IN A BROAD CONTEXT

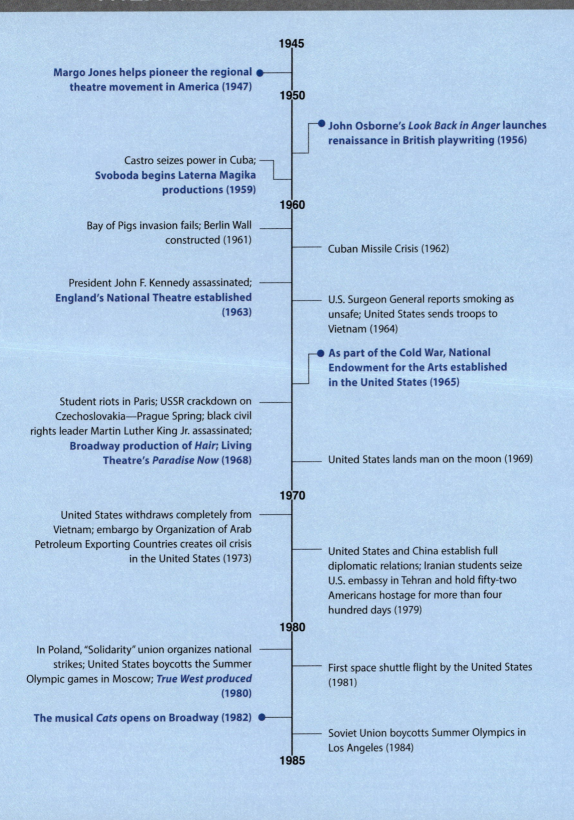

1945

Margo Jones helps pioneer the regional theatre movement in America (1947) ●

1950

● John Osborne's *Look Back in Anger* launches renaissance in British playwriting (1956)

Castro seizes power in Cuba; **Svoboda begins Laterna Magika productions (1959)**

1960

Bay of Pigs invasion fails; Berlin Wall constructed (1961)

Cuban Missile Crisis (1962)

President John F. Kennedy assassinated; **England's National Theatre established (1963)**

U.S. Surgeon General reports smoking as unsafe; United States sends troops to Vietnam (1964)

● **As part of the Cold War, National Endowment for the Arts established in the United States (1965)**

Student riots in Paris; USSR crackdown on Czechoslovakia—Prague Spring; black civil rights leader Martin Luther King Jr. assassinated; **Broadway production of *Hair*; Living Theatre's *Paradise Now* (1968)**

United States lands man on the moon (1969)

1970

United States withdraws completely from Vietnam; embargo by Organization of Arab Petroleum Exporting Countries creates oil crisis in the United States (1973)

United States and China establish full diplomatic relations; Iranian students seize U.S. embassy in Tehran and hold fifty-two Americans hostage for more than four hundred days (1979)

1980

In Poland, "Solidarity" union organizes national strikes; United States boycotts the Summer Olympic games in Moscow; *True West produced* (1980)

First space shuttle flight by the United States (1981)

The musical *Cats* opens on Broadway (1982) ●

Soviet Union boycotts Summer Olympics in Los Angeles (1984)

1985

Contemporary theatre has become increasingly diverse. That diversity is reflected in its makers—an ever more inclusive array of playwrights, designers, and performers—its practices and conventions, and the subjects it treats. *Next to Normal* is perhaps the first Broadway musical to seriously treat mental illness and its effects on a family. Tony Award–winning musical score by Tom Kitt; book and lyrics by Brian Yorkey; direction by Michael Greif; musical staging by Sergio Trujillo; sets by Mark Wendland; costumes by Jeff Mahshie; lighting by Kevin Adams; sound by Brian Ronan.

America has always been a culture of more ethnic diversity than any in the West, and singularly, it has been for centuries the land where people have come to escape their own histories and cultures, even as they cling fiercely to those values and symbols left behind.
—Bonnie Marranca, "Preface," *Interculturalism and Performance*

Contemporary Theatre and Its Diversity

Cultural Diversity

During 2010, more than 1,800 not-for-profit theatres scattered throughout the United States presented approximately 16,000 productions and more than 160,000 performances. Total attendance was over 31 million. Over 500 of these theatres were professional not-for-profit theatres and 74 of them were members of the League of Resident Theatres (LORT), which primarily hire artistic personnel who belong to the professional unions representing actors, directors, and designers. These theatres contributed approximately $1.9 billion to their local economies. An additional 12 million people attended a Broadway theatre performance in 2010; it is estimated that Broadway contributed over $11 billion to the New York City economy that year. While these statistics demonstrate that theatre is a multibillion dollar industry that has a significant amount of activity beyond New York, they cannot capture the artistry or diversity of expression found in American theatre since decentralization began.

Americans have long accepted the notion that the United States is a "melting pot" without always acknowledging that many groups, because of skin color or ethnicity (African, Asian, Native American, and some Latino/Hispanic), have been denied full absorption into the mainstream where "whiteness" and European cultural values have been accepted as the norm. Still others—women, gays and lesbians, the economically deprived, and the physically disadvantaged—have been denied equity for other reasons. Since the 1960s, most of these groups have rebelled against marginalization and have asserted their determination to have their worth acknowledged and their needs met in the theatre. But some of these groups have come to question the desirability of absorption into the "melting pot" if that means denying or abandoning their own cultures, traditions, and aesthetic sensibilities. They have argued that, instead of trying to achieve homogenization, America would be better if it acknowledged, accepted, and valued differences. Efforts to implement these ideas have done much to diversify the American theatre both through plays by and about various groups and through theatres devoted to or sensitive to their needs. Although transculturalism, the back-and-forth movement between cultures, is slowly becoming the paradigm for a new generation of theatre makers and audiences, this new model was made possible by a prior generation of theatre artists determined to have their voices be heard and their concerns be recognized. In part, this chapter looks, from a cultural and historical perspective, at a variety of groups who participated in this process.

African American Theatre

A Raisin in the Sun (1959) by Lorraine Hansberry (1930–1965) explored most of the themes that would be significant in subsequent African American drama: integration versus separation of the races; inequities and injustices inflicted on African Americans; aspirations for the good life and the obstacles to achieving one's potential; and maintaining dignity in the face of overwhelming circumstances. Hansberry's domestic drama won wide critical acclaim in the postwar period and was the first play by an African American woman to be presented on Broadway, where it won the New York Drama Critics Circle Award. Inspired by a Langston Hughes poem, this play about the dreams and struggles of a black family living in Chicago raises issues about American society that remain to be answered satisfactorily.

African American playwrights have grown in visibility and black producing organizations have greatly increased since *A Raisin in the Sun* was first produced. Among the early playwrights, one of the most important was Amiri Baraka (LeRoi Jones), who set out to develop a black aesthetic. In 1966 he founded Spirit House in Newark, where he promoted a separatist black society and a theatre devoted to the credo "By us, about us, for us." Among his best-known plays are *Dutchman* (1964) and *Slave Ship* (1967). Another important African American theatre was the New Lafayette Theatre, founded in Harlem in 1967, which sought to provide leadership for black theatres in America through an information service and *Black Theatre Magazine*. Because of dissension within the company, it came to an end in 1973.

The most durable of the companies was the Negro Ensemble Company (NEC), founded in New York in 1967 by Douglas Turner Ward. Since its founding, the NEC has produced a wide range of plays dealing with African American themes. In addition to providing a venue for writers, it also helped launch the careers of performers such as Phylicia Rashad, Denzel Washington, and

Slave Ship by Amiri Baraka (LeRoi Jones) as produced by the Chelsea Theatre gave its audiences a visceral experience of slavery's horrors through its startling use of light and sound in an intimate setting.

Courtesy of Chelsea Theatre

Samuel L. Jackson; the latter two appeared in the NEC's production of Charles Fuller's *A Soldier's Play* (1981), which won the Pulitzer Prize. While the company has had periods of severe economic difficulties, in 2012 the NEC marked its forty-fifth anniversary, and throughout its history, via full productions and staged readings, it has helped develop over two hundred new plays.

Other African American companies have been established throughout the United States. Among these, some of the best are the Crossroads Theatre Company in New Brunswick, New Jersey; the Lorraine Hansberry in San Francisco; the St. Louis Black Repertory Company; Penumbra Theatre Company in St. Paul; the Oakland (CA) Ensemble Theatre; Jomandi Productions in Atlanta; the New Federal Theatre in New York; and the Providence Black Repertory Company in Rhode Island. There are also a number of black theatre festivals and conferences celebrating African American drama and theatre and discussing common issues.

The upsurge in African American theatrical activity provided a corresponding increase in opportunities for actors, directors, and playwrights (a second wave will be examined later). Among the playwrights and directors who took advantage of these new opportunities was George C. Wolfe. Wolfe first gained wide recognition for his play *The Colored Museum* (1986), a series of eleven exhibits about African American life that combine satire and anger. He next wrote a musical, *Jelly's Last Jam* (1991), which traces the career of jazz musician Jelly Roll Morton; the show was nominated for eleven Tony Awards. He then conceived and directed the popular musical *Bring in 'Da Noise, Bring in 'Da Funk* (1996) for which he earned his second Tony Award for directing; he had previously won in 1993 for directing Tony Kushner's *Angels in America*. Wolfe also served as head of the New York Shakespeare Festival/Public Theatre (1993–2005), where he directed the critically acclaimed premiere productions of the musical *Caroline or Change* (2004) by Tony Kushner (book) and Jeanine Tesori (musical score), and *TopDog/Underdog* (2001) by Suzan-Lori Parks.

While Wolfe has begun to direct films [among them HBO's *Lackawanna Blues* (2005)], he has also periodically returned to the stage, directing the Tony Award–winning revival of *The Normal Heart* in 2011.

Lloyd Richards (1919–2006) gained fame for his direction of the original Broadway production of Lorraine Hansberry's *A Raisin in the Sun*. From 1979 to 1991 he served as the artistic director of the Yale Repertory Theatre and as dean of the prestigious Yale School of Drama. Richards was not only a gifted director, but an astute developer of emerging playwrights through his position, from 1968 to 1999, as artistic director of the National Playwrights Conference at the Eugene O'Neill Theatre Center. Richards is credited with having helped to develop the playwriting talents of Wendy Wasserstein, Christopher Durang, Lee Blessing, David Henry Hwang, and August Wilson. Richards's long-standing collaboration with Wilson began in 1984, when he directed Wilson's *Ma Rainey's Black Bottom*. Richards went on to direct the world premieres of Wilson's *Fences* (1985), *Joe Turner's Come and Gone* (1986), *The Piano Lesson* (1987), *Two Trains Running* (1990), and *Seven Guitars* (1995).

No African American playwright has been more influential and successful than August Wilson (1945–2005). His first success came in 1984 with *Ma Rainey's Black Bottom*, about African American musicians in the 1920s in Chicago. Through his "Century Cycle" (see box) of ten plays, Wilson documented and examined the African American experience throughout each decade of the twentieth century. Wilson's project stemmed from his belief that you must know your past, so you can understand the present, and build a better future. While dealing with racial issues, unlike some earlier African American dramatists, Wilson only occasionally explores the theme of black rage at white oppression but rather concentrates more on African American identity and quests for fulfillment and dignity. Nevertheless, Wilson feels deeply the need for separate African American theatres and has stimulated much discussion about this issue. Let us look at *Fences* as an example of Wilson's work.

FENCES

Set in 1957, *Fences* occurs on the brink of the civil rights movement. The protagonist, Troy Maxson, is a 53-year-old family man who struggles with the psychological wounds of his past. Raised by a firm disciplinarian father, Troy left home at age 14 and moved north. Trying to survive led to his being a petty thief and landing in prison for 15 years. Coming out of prison, Troy met and married Rose; had a child, Cory; and enjoyed success as a star baseball player in the Negro Leagues before becoming a garbage man. Throughout the play, Troy harbors deep resentment over having been denied the opportunity to play Major League Baseball, as racial integration did not occur until 1947.

Fences shares similarities with Arthur Miller's *Death of a Salesman* as both examine a hardworking family man who struggles to find his place in society. In *Fences*, Troy lives on the underside of the American Dream, and as much as anything he is a survivor. He takes pride and refuge in his family; it has been his salvation, but it has also left him stagnant. He believes his chief duty is to provide for his family. While his sense of responsibility is admirable, Troy does not provide his son the kind of love and approval that he seeks.

In addition to wanting his father to like him, Cory needs his father's approval to accept a football scholarship. While Troy champions hard work and self-determination, he is psychologically wounded by the opportunities he was denied. He fails to see the ways in which society is changing, that sports would be a means to a college education for his son. When he forces his son to quit football and work a job at the grocery store, he effectively kills his son's major dream.

At the top of Act Two, Troy reveals to Rose that not only has he been having an affair with Alberta, but that she is pregnant. Coming from a family where everyone is a half brother or sister, Rose values fidelity and is deeply wounded.

Joan Marcus

Denzel Washington (right) and Viola Davis (left) starred in the 2010 Broadway revival of *Fences*. Directed by Kenny Leon, the production received ten Tony Award nominations, winning for Best Revival of a Play as well as Best Actor (Washington) and Best Actress (Davis).

For Troy, the affair has been his escape from his problems and his chance to revive his dormant life. In turn, Rose notes that in their 18 years of marriage, she has sacrificed her hopes and dreams, but that she has stayed ever loyal and supportive of him. Ultimately, Alberta dies while giving birth to a baby girl. When Troy returns with the illegitimate child, Rose is faced with a painful choice, but decides that the innocent child should not be punished. She tells Troy: "From right now…this child got a mother. But you a womanless man." As in *Death of a Salesman*, an extramarital affair causes a son to lose respect for his father. In their final confrontation, Troy kicks Cory out of the house, but unlike his own father, Troy does not physically beat his son when he could.

The final scene of the play leaps forward 7 years to the day of Troy's funeral (another echo of *Salesman*). Cory has become a Marine corporal and has returned home for the first time since their fight. Still resenting his father, Cory initially refuses to attend the funeral; however, Rose urges forgiveness and Cory relents after she tells him: "Your daddy wanted you to be everything he wasn't…and at the same time he tried to make you into everything he was. I don't know if he was right or wrong…but I do know he meant to do more good than he meant to do harm." Through the sum of his strengths and his weaknesses, his success and failures, Troy is a man who commands our attention and respect.

In some of his other works, Wilson incorporates elements of the supernatural, but *Fences* is rooted firmly in the realist tradition and its focus on family issues—husband–wife dynamics, father–son relationships, infidelity, and parental

Practitioners & Theorists

AUGUST WILSON'S CENTURY CYCLE

August Wilson wrote a play set in each decade of the twentieth century; eight of the ten plays won a New York Drama Critics Circle Award for Best New Play. All of them, except *Ma Rainey*, are set in the Hill District of Pittsburgh, where Wilson was born. Wilson compared his approach to writing individual plays as "working in collages" (wherein one shifts and reorganizes accumulated material until arriving at an overall pleasing composition) and said he thought of his ten plays as "all one work." Here is a list of Wilson's plays specifying the decade in which they are set and the year they were first produced:

Play	Decade of action	Year First Produced
Gem of the Ocean	1900s	2003
Joe Turner's Come and Gone	1910s	1986
Ma Rainey's Black Bottom	1920s	1984
The Piano Lesson	1930s (Pulitzer Prize Winner)	1987
Seven Guitars	1940s	1995
Fences	1950s (Pulitzer Prize Winner)	1985
Two Trains Running	1960s	1990
Jitney	1970s	1982
King Hedley II	1980s	1999
Radio Golf	1990s	2005

responsibilities—marks it as his most mainstream. In addition to winning four Tony Awards, the original 1987 Broadway production grossed $11 million in its first year, which was then a record for a nonmusical. Likewise, a 1997 production in Beijing by an all-Chinese cast further suggested the ways in which *Fences*, while firmly rooted in the African American experience, stretches across cultures to express the human condition. Wilson once said: "I think my plays offer (white Americans) a different way to look at black Americans. For instance, in *Fences*, they see a garbage man, a person they don't really look at, although they see a garbage man every day. By looking at Troy's life, white people find out that the content of this black garbage man's life is affected by the same things—love, honor, beauty, betrayal, duty. Recognizing that these things are as much part of his life as theirs can affect how they think about and deal with black people in their lives." Ultimately Wilson's work shows us both our similarities and our differences. Likewise, his career shows an artist who is specifically African American while also mainstream. By the time of his death in 2005, Wilson had secured his place as one of the five best American playwrights of all time.

TopDog/Underdog as produced by the Hartford Stage Company with K. Todd Freeman as Booth (standing) and David Rainey as Lincoln. Directed by Amy Morton; scene design by Loy Arcenas; costume design by Nan Cibula-Jenkins; lighting by Kevin Rigdon. To save on costs, this was a coproduction between Chicago's Steppenwolf Theatre and Houston's Alley Theatre; after performing in those two cities, the production moved to the Dallas Theatre Center and then Hartford Stage.

T. Charles Erickson

Latino Theatre

The first play known to have been staged in what is now the United States was performed by Spanish soldiers near El Paso in 1598. But it was not until the late nineteenth century that Spanish-language theatre became common, first in California, then in Texas, and, by the early twentieth century, in all of the territories bordering Mexico. From 1918 into the 1930s, Los Angeles supported five professional Spanish-language theatres, and professional companies toured widely throughout some parts of the country. During the 1930s, economic depression and the inroads of film ended most of this activity, although amateur theatres continued to fill the need. All of these developments made little impact on the dominant white and English-speaking culture, which remained largely oblivious to them.

Not until the 1960s did Latino theatre begin to make an impression on the wider American consciousness, first through the work of El Teatro Campesino, a bilingual Chicano company founded by Luis Valdez in 1965. Valdez was very successful in calling attention to the plight of migrant workers in California and winning public support for them during a strike by grape pickers. Valdez later turned to writing plays about the heritage and lives of contemporary Mexican Americans. He achieved his greatest popular success with *Zoot Suit* (1978), which mingled traditional Mexican musical forms with Living Newspaper techniques in a play based on an actual case of injustice against a group of young Mexican Americans during World War II. *Zoot Suit* became the first Latino play produced on Broadway and was then made into a film. Valdez's other works include *Los Vendidos* (*The Sellouts*) (1967), *I Don't Have to Show You No Stinking Badges* (1986), and the film *La Bamba* (1987).

El Teatro Campesino inspired other Latinos to use theatre as a means of cultural expression. Currently in the United States there are

Edward James Olmos starred in Luis Valdez's *Zoot Suit*, which premiered at the Mark Taper Forum before becoming the first Latino play produced on Broadway in 1979.

Universal/Everett Collection

more than one hundred Latino theatre groups—Chicano, Puerto Rican, Cuban, and other categories. Some of the best known of these are Repertorio Español and the Puerto Rican Traveling Theatre, both in New York; and El Teatro Campesino, El Teatro de la Esperanza, and the Bilingual Foundation of the Arts in California. A large number of cities maintain Hispanic American theatre groups and some, including Miami and Chicago, host international festivals of Chicano and Latino theatre.

Among the Latino playwrights who have made a significant mark on the contemporary American theatre are the playwrights Marie Irene Fornes and Nilo Cruz, the Puerto Rican–born playwright José Rivera, and Octavio Solis. Maria Irene Fornes, a Cuban-born American who began writing plays in 1965, has never achieved wide popular recognition. However, she has won six Obie Awards for Off-Broadway and Off-Off-Broadway productions including

Fefu and Her Friends (1977) and *The Conduct of Life* (1985); the latter draws parallels between political subjugation and the subjugation of women in Latin America. She has also mentored several young Hispanic playwrights, among them Cuban exile Nilo Cruz, who credits Fornes with giving him his start as a playwright. The two met in 1988 in Miami, and Fornes encouraged him to join the now-defunct INTAR Hispanic Playwrights-in-Residence Laboratory in New York. Cruz has said, "I come from the Irene Fornes school, you don't write a play about an idea—you write a play about characters." When Cruz's play *Anna in the Tropics* was awarded the 2003 Pulitzer Prize for drama, it was only the second play to have ever been so awarded before being staged in New York; it was also the first time a Latino

playwright won. Cruz's plays typically focus on characters whose dignity and creative potential are at odds with the repressive circumstances in which they live. His other plays include *A Park in Our House* (1995), *Two Sisters and a Piano* (1998), *Lorca in a Green Dress* (2003), and *Beauty of the Father* (2006).

José Rivera has gained considerable attention for his plays *Marisol* (1992), *Cloud Tectonics* (1995), *Sueño* (1998, his adaptation of Calderon's Spanish Golden Age drama *Life Is a Dream*), and *References to Salvador Dalí Make Me Hot* (2000). Several critics have noted that Rivera's use of realistic and fantastic elements existing alongside each other reflects the magic realism of Gabriel Garcia Márquez. Recently, Rivera has worked as screenplay writer, and his *Motorcycle Diaries* was nominated for a 2005 Academy Award. One of

T. Charles Erickson

Nilo Cruz's Pulitzer Prize–winning play *Anna in the Tropics* as produced by the McCarter Theatre, featuring Jimmy Smits (center, dressed in white). Directed by Emily Mann; scene design by Robert Brill; costumes by Anita Yavich; lighting by Peter Kaczorowski; sound by Dan Moses Schreier.

his most recent plays is *Boleros for the Disenchanted*, which was performed in regional theatres across America in 2008 and 2009.

Octavio Solis has written over a dozen plays and although his plays are not limited to characters and issues particular to the Latino-American community, they resonate deeply within that community. Let's examine one of his most recent plays, *Lydia*.

LYDIA

Solis wrote *Lydia* on a commission by the Denver Center Theatre. The play's popularity has resulted in professional productions throughout the country and *Lydia* was a finalist nominee for the American Theatre Critics Association prize for the best new play originally produced outside of New York City. Critics have compared Solis's play to modern classics by Arthur Miller and Eugene O'Neill.

Lydia is set in El Paso, Texas, during the early 1970s. Solis has chosen to set many of his plays in El Paso, where he was born and raised. As an American city bordering Mexico, Solis has called El Paso "a crucible of cultures." This border-city setting is especially appropriate for the characters in *Lydia* because, as Solis has put it, they are caught "between two ways of being, two ways of life." Similarly, his characters speak in English and Spanish as well as in regional mixtures of the two. The play tells the story of a family shattered by an accident. The accident took place three days before Ceci's *quinceañera*— a celebration coinciding with a young woman's fifteenth birthday and often viewed as a right of passage in Hispanic cultures. The accident left Ceci brain damaged. That accident happened two years before the play's action begins and we witness its effects upon the Flores family.

Solis grabs our attention quickly. Ceci lies on a mattress in the living-room and introduces her *familia* in accosting poetic images. Claudio, Ceci's father, is a "[b]roken man drowning in old *rancheras* and TV." Claudio has detached himself from the family; when he is not working or sleeping, he watches television or listens to old records with headphones on. Ceci's mother, Rosa, "a beautiful woman losing beauty by the day," has decided to stop giving Ceci her medication, placing her faith in God to heal Ceci. Ceci's oldest brother, Rene, is an "elder volcano" who spends his evenings getting drunk and getting into fights. Ceci's other brother, "sad-boy Misha," is something of a writer and a poet. Her relationship with Misha is the closest she has with a family member. Ceci understands that they are "[a]ll sad and wounded cause of somethin'. Somethin' that broke," but as she gets closer to identifying what that something is her speech degenerates into incomprehensible babble. Solis has introduced us to the characters and shown us that Ceci retains a vibrant spirit locked inside her uncommunicative body all in the first few minutes of the play. The remainder of the opening scene reveals how the family functions.

Next we meet the two characters from outside the family who play important roles in the action: Alvaro, Ceci's cousin, who has returned from Vietnam to work for the U.S. Border Patrol, and the play's title character, Lydia. Rosa has decided to return to work and she hires Lydia, an illegal Mexican immigrant, to do domestic chores and help care for Ceci. Lydia quickly forms a special relationship with Ceci. When Alvaro visits the family wearing his Border Patrol uniform, there is considerable tension. Just as the tension seems to dissipate, Lydia emerges with Ceci, who wears her *quinceañera* dress. Lydia tells us that Ceci has told her that she wanted to wear the dress for Alvaro and to dance with him. Alvaro and Ceci dance, during which Ceci loses control of her bladder and wets herself. She refuses to let go of Alvaro until Rene tears Ceci from him. Alvaro leaves and when Claudio enters, he is furious at the sight of Ceci wearing the ruined dress that once symbolized hopes of a happy future but now painfully reminds him of

Lydia by Octavio Solis in its world premiere performance at the Denver Center Theatre under the direction of Juliette Carrillo.

Denver Center Theatre Company

all that has been lost. In order to protect Lydia, Misha claims it was he who dressed Ceci. Claudio turns his rage on Misha and not only gives him a terrible beating but also blindly socks Rosa in the eye when she tries to intervene. The ending to the first act involves Ceci telling us of a dream she has in which Lydia gives Claudio the love he lacks, love that might help heal him. As Ceci speaks, we see Lydia approach Claudio, remove his headphones, and the two of them begin to make love while Rene watches from the shadows.

Lydia acts as the catalyst of the play's action. She brings passion back into the family, and with it all the joys and harm that passion can cause. It is difficult not to compare the two young women and see in Lydia the young woman Ceci might have become if not for the accident. Lydia acts as a kind of *curandera* (a healer) who seemingly reads Ceci's thoughts and eventually reveals long-kept secrets about the accident. Their relationship and Ceci's poetic speeches open the otherwise realistic action of the play to a magical, spiritual dimension.

Act Two begins with a scene that might be a dream or a memory of Ceci's in which she is much younger, playing with Misha, Rene, and Alvaro, as if they were ants and she were their ant-queen. In this fantasy, Rene and Alvaro kiss. Meanwhile, Rene ridicules Misha's crush on Lydia, referring to her as whore. Alone with Ceci, Misha shares his feelings for Lydia with Ceci, who gives responses we can hear and understand even though Misha cannot.

Later, Alvaro returns. At first, the action flashes back to the day of the accident. We see Alvaro and Ceci interact. Ceci wants to be close to Alvaro and begs him to let her come with him on a "guys' night out" he and Rene are planning. Alvaro refuses. The action seamlessly segues into the present. Claudio asks Alvaro what really happened on the night of the accident, but Alvaro does not provide an answer. The long-kept secrets surrounding the accident are only revealed in a still later scene in which a drunken Rene is railing at Alvaro and Lydia interjects that Ceci knows what happened on the night of the accident. Then, through Lydia (although we hear Ceci directly), the other characters learn that Ceci had hidden away on the backseat floor of the car to secretly join Alvaro and Rene. We learn that Ceci overheard Rene and Alvaro having a sexual encounter in the parked car. Livid by this discovery, Ceci revealed herself and began berating them. With Ceci still yelling at them, striking Rene in the head with her flailing fists, Rene started the car and drove off. When Rene turned his head back to apologize to Ceci, the car struck a pole and Ceci was sent flying through the windshield. Now that the truth is out, Rosa orders Rene out of the house, and he leaves never to return. Misha asks Lydia if Rene's accusations about her having an affair with Claudio were true. Lydia does not answer this question, but Alvaro, under orders from Rosa, removes Lydia for deportation.

The next day when Claudio asks what has happened to Lydia, Rosa suggests that she turned her over to Immigration and reminds him that he, too, lacks proper papers. Claudio asks Rosa for the truth about Rene and Alvaro and Ceci on the night of the accident, but she does not tell him. The play ends with a final scene between Misha and Ceci. Although Ceci's brain is damaged, Ceci's body has all the normal hormonal urges of a young woman. Desperate for physical affection, she places Misha's hand under her dress. He resists this and she cries. Ultimately, a type of exchange seemingly takes place in which Ceci is allowed the love she craves and Misha absorbs the poetry within her soul before, swallowing a metal pull-tab from a can of beer, Ceci dies.

Critics have written about the play's frank and what some may find shocking approach to sexuality. Still, no aspect of the play has raised more controversy than its ending.

Asian American Theatre

Lydia by Octavio Solis in its world premiere performance at the Denver Center Theatre under the direction of Juliette Carrillo.

Denver Center Theatre Company

Asian Americans have also made their mark on contemporary drama and theatre. Asians first came to America in large numbers when Chinese workers were imported in the mid-nineteenth century to help build railroads. Those who remained usually clustered within cities such as San Francisco, New York, Chicago, Los Angeles, and Seattle. In some of these cities, theatres were established to cater to Asian audiences. San Francisco, for example, maintained a Beijing Opera company until the 1940s. World War II, the Korean War, and the Vietnam War tended to make Americans more aware of Asian cultures and to increase the immigration of Asians to the United States.

When white dramatists initially depicted Asian Americans, they often reduced Asian Americans to a few stereotypes: dutiful houseboy, inscrutable detective, wise Confucian patriarch, treacherous dragon lady, or submissive Asian doll-bride. Rebelling against these stereotypes, around 1965 Asian Americans began to write their own plays and found their own theatres. Some of the most important of the companies were the East West Players, founded in Los Angeles in 1965 but now centered in New York; the Asian Exclusion Act, founded in Seattle in 1973 and later renamed the Northwest Asian American Theatre Company; the Asian American Theatre Workshop, founded in San Francisco in 1973; and the Pan Asian Repertory Theatre, founded in New York in 1977.

Today, in addition to clusters of Asian American theatres on the East and West Coasts, several midwestern cities maintain Asian American performing arts groups. One of these is Theatre Mu, which blends Asian and Western artistic forms (both ancient and contemporary) to give voice to the experience of the Asian American culture and community.

Several Asian American playwrights have played an important role in development of Asian American drama and theatre. Though now more acclaimed for his fiction writing, Frank Chin was the first Asian American playwright to have his work staged in a mainstream New York theatre; his *Chickencoop Chinaman* (1971), satirizing both self-stereotyping and media stereotyping,

Society, Art & Culture

SHOULD WE WRITE ONLY ABOUT OUR OWN CULTURE?

In debates over multiculturalism, an ongoing issue concerns whether playwrights should (or can effectively) write about cultures other than their own. Writers from minority cultures are especially subject to pressure, often being accused of betraying their heritage when they write critically about it or choose to write about some group other than their own. As Margo Jefferson, an African American critic for the *New York Times*, comments, minority dramatists are often told "that they should not wash dirty linen in public. … Put a diverse audience in a theater to see a play set in a particular ethnic, racial or sexual world, and it's clear that the audience members closest to that world feel that outsiders have no right to invade it with their responses."

August Wilson, the African American playwright, felt strongly that he must write about his own culture: "I am more and more concerned with pointing out the differences between blacks and whites as opposed to pointing out similarities. … We have different ideas of justice and morality. … blacks have been all too willing and anxious to say that we are the same as whites."

On the other hand, Ping Chong, a major Asian American performance/video artist, playwright, and director, argues:

> I'm not going to let myself be ghettoized as an Asian-American artist. I'm an American artist…we cannot lose sight of the fact that we all live in a society where we have to coexist. It doesn't mean that I have to like your culture. But we have to be sensitive to each other's cultures. I think it extremely naive to think that no one but Asians can write about Asians. It would simply be another point of view. I do make shows about white characters even though I didn't grow up Anglo. Does that mean I shouldn't write about them?… I believe it is important to be inclusive; a free society should allow for a multiplicity of views.

Some members of specific cultures believe that their experience is so complex that no outsider can understand or represent it adequately. They may also resent having aspects of their cultural heritage "appropriated" by outsiders who incorporate it into their own works without acknowledging its origins or who distort it through lack of understanding. Daryl Chin, an Asian American critic, writes, "These debates [over multiculturalism] are about feelings of disenfranchisement and exclusion. … The reason the debates are so painful is that they strike at the very heart of who people think they are."

and *The Year of the Dragon* (1974) were produced by the American Place Theatre. Another prominent Asian American dramatist is Philip Kan Gotanda, whose first work, *The Avocado Kid or Zen in the Art of Guacamole*, a rock musical, was presented by the East West Players in 1979. His other works include *A Song for a Nisei Fisherman* (1980), *The Dream of Kitamura* (1982), *The Wash* (1985), *Yankee Dawg You Die* (1988), *Fish Head Soup* (1991), *Day Standing on Its Head* (1993), and *The Ballad of Yachiyo* (1995).

The best-known Asian American dramatist is David Henry Hwang, who first came to prominence in 1980 with his Obie-winning play *F.O.B.* (which stands for "fresh off the boat"). The play explores the contrasts and conflicts between established Asian Americans and newly arrived immigrants. His subsequent plays include *The Dance and the Railroad* (1981), *Family Devotions* (1981), and *The Golden Child* (1996). Hwang's best-known play is *M. Butterfly* (1988), which focuses on race, gender, and politics and suggests that Westerners view "Orientals" (both individuals and nations) as submissively "feminine," willing to be dominated by the aggressive, "masculine" West. Hwang fuses this perception with a real-life story in which a French diplomat carried on a twenty-year relationship with a Beijing Opera performer of female roles (and a spy for the Chinese government) without recognizing that the performer was male. With *M. Butterfly*, Hwang became the first Asian American playwright to win the Tony Award. One of Hwang's more recent plays, *Yellow Face* (the title refers to the practice of Caucasian performers playing Asian characters in thickly applied yellow makeup) is a satirical comedy on how perceptions of race play a role in art, commerce, and politics. *Yellow Face* premiered in 2007 at the Mark Taper Forum in Los Angeles in connection with the East West Players. The play was subsequently produced at the Public Theatre in New York and garnered Hwang his third Obie Award in 2008. Hwang's career, which began focused on plays about the Asian American experience, has expanded over time to include numerous subjects and interests. In addition to plays, Hwang has long been an active writer of books for musicals and opera. His opera and musical theatre credits include the books for the Philip Glass opera *1,000 Airplanes on the Roof* (1988), revisions for Disney's Broadway musical *Aida* (2000), Disney's Broadway musical *Tarzan* (2006, music and lyrics by Phil Collins), and

Korean American contemporary playwright Young Jean Lee satirizes African American identity politics in her recent play, *The Shipment*. Ms. Lee, who has also lampooned Asian Americans in her *Songs of the Dragons Flying to Heaven*, uses irreverent comedy to provoke cross-cultural dialogue concerning how various ethnic groups unconsciously process experience through a racial filter.

Sara Krulwich/The New York Times/Redux

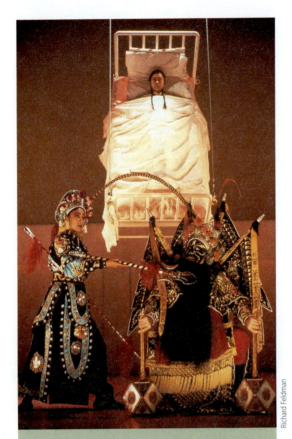

Richard Feldman

***The Woman Warrior**, adapted by Deborah Rogin from the work of Maxine Hong Kingston. Directed by Sharon Ott; scene design by Ming Cho Lee; costume design by Susan Hilferty; lighting by Peter Maradudin.*

Nationalist government; *Question 27, Question 28* (2003), which treats the experience of Japanese American women detained in American internment camps during World War II; *The Long Season* (2005), a musical love story about Filipino immigrants in Alaska; and *Ameriville* (2012), a work that mixes hip hop, jazz, poetry, spoken word, and other forms as it examines American society in the aftermath of Hurricane Katrina.

A number of other prominent Asian American playwrights, including Julia Cho and Elizabeth Wong, have been able to alternate between writing plays that particularly appeal to Asian American stages and ones for predominantly Caucasian stages and audiences. Playwright and director Rick Shiomi, who leads Minneapolis's Theatre Mu, believes that the emerging trend for Asian American drama (and for that of other minorities) involves "crossover" works that "will be part of a larger American canon that's going to be much more mixed." Theatre critic Sarah Lemanczyk sees this new trend in Asian American drama as stemming from globalization, the increasing influence of Asian nations, and the West's growing awareness of Asian culture.

Native American Theatre

the revised libretto for a revival of Rogers and Hammerstein's *Flower Drum Song* (2002).

Another prolific Asian American dramatist in recent years has been Chay Yew. Yew, who long served as the artistic director of both the Asian American Workshop in Los Angeles and the Northwest Asian American Theatre in Seattle, has had his plays produced throughout America as well as Malaysia, Singapore, and the United Kingdom. Yew's plays include *A Language of Their Own* (1995), part of a trilogy on being gay and Asian; *A Winter People* (2002), an adaptation of Chekhov's *The Cherry Orchard*, but set in 1935 mainland China during the last days of its

There have been few Native American theatre groups. The first all-Native American company, the Native American Theatre Ensemble, was founded by Hanay Geiogamah in 1972. With support from the La MaMa company in New York, it presented plays based on myths and contemporary life with the aim of building pride in the Native American heritage. Geiogamah is also one of the founders of Project HOOP (Honoring Our Origins and People), which seeks to use theatre and native performance to enrich education of Native Americans. Geiogamah's plays include *Body Indian* (1972) and *49* (1982). In recent years, Geiogamah (now a professor of literature and film and a member of the American Indian Studies Center at UCLA) has transformed his company into the American Indian Dance Theatre, with nineteen members drawn from a dozen tribes. Among the company's most ambitious works is *Kotuwokan* (1998), a dance-drama about a young Indian's attempt to find his way in the present-day world.

The American Indian Community House in New York has long served as a community center for Native Americans living in New York and has maintained a performing arts program that has sought to revive authentic Native American rituals and performance traditions.

The Denver Center Theatre's production of *Black Elk Speaks*, dramatized by Christopher Sergel, based on the book by John G. Neihardt. Directed by Donovan Marley.

Spiderwoman Theatre, founded by three Native American sisters, was the first all-female Native American group in the United States. Another successful Native American company is Naa Kahidi [Clan House] Theater in Alaska, which has performed its adaptations of Tlingit myths at numerous theatre festivals in the United States and Europe. Other Native American performers include Elvira and Hortensia Colorado, whose *Walks of Indian Women—Aztlan to Anahuac* (1988) traces the history of Native American women since pre-Columbian times. Recently, the plays of Native American playwright William S. Yellow Robe Jr. have cast a critical eye on the problems facing contemporary Native Americans: the destructiveness of alcohol and chemical addiction, conflicts between traditional Native and popular cultures, problems associated with the rapid rise of casinos on Native American lands, and unemployment. His plays include *Sneaky* (1987), *Better-n-Indins* (2005), and *Grandchildren of the Buffalo Soldiers* (2005).

Theatre by and for Women

Women, representing as they do roughly one-half of the world's population, cannot on one level be considered a minority. Nevertheless, throughout the theatre's history they have been relegated to a minor position. Although written about in ancient Greece, for example, they did not themselves either write plays or act in them. In England they were not permitted to appear on the stage until 1661, and though prominent as actresses thereafter, seldom did they write plays or attain positions of power in the theatre until recently. In the twentieth century, women began to write plays more frequently, although even those sufficiently successful to have won Pulitzer Prizes (among them Susan Glaspell, Zoe Akins, and Mary Chase) have largely disappeared from memory. Only gradually have women come to be accepted as directors and heads of theatre companies.

Changes have come about primarily through concern for women's rights, which date back to at least the nineteenth century but were given new energy by the civil rights movement that accelerated in the 1960s. Many women have been concerned primarily with gaining equal rights within the existing system; others have perceived such a clear difference between men (characterized as competitive, aggressive, and violent) and women (seen as cooperative, nurturing, and pacifistic) that they have advocated replacing male with female values. Still others have seen themselves as members of an oppressed group within a white, male, Eurocentric society and have sought alliances with other groups who have been comparably marginalized because of such factors as ethnicity, economic class, or sexual orientation. These differences have influenced plays written by women.

Beginning in the 1970s, a number of theatres were formed to present the work of feminist writers. Some of the most important of these have been The Looking Glass Theatre, New Georges, Six Figures Theatre Company, Voice and Vision, Woman Seeking..., Spiderwoman Native American Theatre, and the Women's Project and Productions, all in New York; Chrysalis Theatre in Northampton, Massachusetts; Perishable Theatre Women's Playwriting Festival in Providence, Rhode Island; Horizons Theatre in Arlington, Virginia; The Oh Sooo Politically Correct Players and The Theatre Conspiracy in Washington, D.C.; Red Hen Productions in Cleveland, Ohio; Footsteps Theatre Company in Chicago; Root Wym'n Theatre Company in Austin, Texas; Brava! For Women in the Arts and Women's Will in San Francisco; the Latina Theatre Lab in Oakland, California; and the Omaha Magic Theatre. Multiple national festivals of women's theatre have been held in the United States each year. Over the past few decades, the number of theatres devoted to addressing the needs and concerns of women and to providing greater opportunities for women in the performing arts has grown considerably.

Some female playwrights have written almost exclusively for feminist theatres and have not sought a broader audience. Others have won recognition in mainstream theatres. Among the first wave of the latter group are Marsha Norman, Beth Henley, Wendy Wasserstein, and Paula Vogel (a more recent second wave of female playwrights will be treated later in this chapter). Other prominent contemporary female playwrights include Constance Congdon, Sarah Ruhl, Tina Howe, Lisa Loomer, Josephina Lopez, Theresa Rebeck, and Naomi Wallace.

Marsha Norman's first play, *Getting Out*, was voted the best new play by the American Theatre Critics Association in 1977. She is probably best known for *'night, Mother*, winner of the Pulitzer Prize in 1983, in which a woman, having lost all desire to live, matter-of-factly announces to her mother her plan to commit suicide and carries it out. Norman has gone on to write several plays as well as the book and lyrics for the Broadway musicals *The Secret Garden* (1991, Tony Award for Best Book) and *The Red Shoes* (1993) and wrote the libretto for the Broadway musical adaptation of *The Color Purple* (2005).

Beth Henley gained early critical acclaim for her play *Crimes of the Heart*, winner of the Pulitzer Prize in 1981. The play, which focuses on the lives of three sisters, begins with the news that the youngest sister has shot her husband because, as she puts it, "I didn't like his looks." Henley followed this success with several other plays, including *The Miss Firecracker Contest* (1984), about colorful characters in small southern towns. Her more recent plays include *Impossible Marriage* (1998) and *The Jacksonian* (2012).

Wendy Wasserstein (1950–2006) is best known for *The Heidi Chronicles*, winner of the 1989 Pulitzer Prize and the first play by a female

Society, Art & Culture

CREATING THEATRE OUTSIDE THE BOX

Today's theatre is more diverse than many people imagine. Individuals who, in another time, might not have been considered possible theatre makers are creating theatre that challenges their abilities and the preconceptions others may have about who can do theatre and the purpose of theatre in society. In short, these theatre practitioners are thinking and playing "outside the box."

The United States has dozens of theatre groups and festivals in which senior citizens actively participate. Some of these use a "reader's theatre" format, which requires only minimal movement and no memorization of dialogue. Others perform fully staged musicals. Stagebridge is one of America's longest standing senior theatres. Located in Oakland, California, it is dedicated to providing opportunities for older adults to use theatre as a way to bridge generations. Since its founding in 1978, Stagebridge has performed for over 300,000 people. Its company, which consists of over one hundred performers and volunteers (whose average age is seventy), performs short plays and musicals and also gives workshops at senior facilities and centers as well as engages in intergenerational literacy programs with children. In addition to Stagebridge and other theatre companies for seniors, each year festivals of senior theatre are presented across America.

Scores of programs have arisen that provide performance opportunities for children and adults with physical and developmental impairments. For example, the "Dramatically Able" program, operated by the Wild Swan Theatre in Ann Arbor, Michigan, provides teachers with theatre games and performance activities to exercise verbal and nonverbal communication skills, increase awareness of oneself and others, and encourage creativity. The National Theatre Workshop of the Handicapped (NTWH) is a theatre training institute for adults with physical disabilities. NTWH offers training in almost all aspects of theatre and brings together disabled and able-bodied actors and playwrights to collaborate on creative performance projects. In 2009 SENSE Theatre began in Sacramento, California, as a theatrical program designed to improve the social and emotional functioning of children with autism and related neurodevelopmental disorders.

The National Theatre of the Deaf (NTD) is one of the oldest and best-known theatre groups involving individuals with a physical impairment. NTD produces professional-quality theatre that links American Sign Language to the spoken word in a diverse repertory of world drama. Since its inception in 1967, NTD has performed in all fifty states and has conducted over thirty international tours. It received a Tony Award for theatre in 1977, and in 1986 became the first American theatre company to perform in the People's Republic of China. Some company members also crossed into the mainstream as Linda Bove became a regular on *Sesame Street*, while Phyllis Frelich won a Tony Award for *Children of a Lesser God* (1980).

T. Charles Erickson

The National Theatre of the Deaf production of *Curiouser and Curiouser*, adapted from Lewis Carroll's *Through the Looking Glass*.

to win the Tony Award. The play's action begins in the mid-1960s and ends in the late 1980s as it traces changes in the political and personal life of the title character. As Heidi develops a feminist consciousness, she comes to see the ways in which the women's movement both has and has not fulfilled its promises. Wasserstein's other plays include *Uncommon Women and Others* (1977), *Isn't It Romantic* (1983), *The Sisters Rosensweig* (1992), and *An American Daughter* (1997).

Paula Vogel, who began writing plays in the 1970s, began to draw mainstream attention with her play *The Baltimore Waltz* in 1992. Winner of an Obie Award, this imaginative play mixes comedy with a tragic undertone as the lead character's brother dies of AIDS. Her plays include *Desdemona, A Play about a Handkerchief* (1979), *The Oldest Profession* (1981), *And Baby Makes Seven* (1984), *The Mineola Twins* (1996), and *The Long Christmas Ride Home* (2003). In addition to her own work, Vogel has influenced American theatre via her teaching. As a professor of playwriting at Brown University, her students have included Nilo Cruz, Lynn Nottage, Quiara Alegría Hudes, and Sarah Ruhl (all of whom are discussed later). As a playwright Vogel is best known for *How I Learned to Drive*, which won the Pulitzer Prize in 1998. Let us look at that play as an example of Vogel's work and of a contemporary play by a woman.

HOW I LEARNED TO DRIVE

First produced in 1997, *How I Learned to Drive* draws a parallel between learning to drive a car and learning how to navigate one's way through life from adolescence to maturity. The play's sections are given such headings as "Idling in the Neutral Gear," "You and the Reverse Gear," and "Driving in Today's World." This parallel is particularly meaningful to the play's central character, Li'l Bit, who was taught to drive by her uncle—a pedophile who used her driving lessons as an opportunity to seduce her.

How I Learned to Drive is not organized linearly. Rather it looks at various moments in the protagonist's life, moving easily back and forth from one time period to another as they become relevant to her feelings or anxieties. It ranges from the time when Li'l Bit is eleven until she is approximately forty years old. Memory or an association of ideas primarily triggers the shifts in time. Li'l Bit and Uncle Peck are the only complex characters. The others, of which there are many, are played by three actors designated as Male Greek Chorus, Female Greek Chorus, and Teenage Greek Chorus, who fill in wherever needed. The use of a few performers playing multiple supporting roles reduces the cast size needed to produce the play; more importantly, they focus our attention on the two main characters, they form the social context for various scenes, and their speeches introduce considerable explanatory and background information. Through them we find out much about the family life that surrounds Li'l Bit and Uncle Peck, including the way the family members tease Li'l Bit about her body and in the way they talk to her about sex. In contrast, Peck seems to genuinely care for her and his attention helps her to feel special and appreciated. The family is also somewhat insensitive in their treatment of Peck. Li'l Bit and Uncle Peck are both more or less socially isolated and spend considerable time together. The family never seems to suspect that anything unusual is going on between them.

Both Li'l Bit and Uncle Peck are damaged people. They want and need love but there are too many warped experiences in their way. Vogel treats Peck somewhat sympathetically, but she also includes a past for the character that suggests his behavior is part of an ongoing pattern, that he has also molested a nephew. In addition, Uncle Peck was probably molested as a child and as much as he claims to love Li'l Bit, he cannot let go of his compulsion to seek physical intimacy with her. Li'l Bit falls into a pattern of behavior after she leaves home that indicates her need for

Sara Krulwich/The New York Times/Redux Pictures

How I Learned to Drive in its 2012 New York revival, starring Elizabeth Reaser as Li'l Bit and Norbert Leo Butz as Uncle Peck. Directed by Kate Whoriskey; scene design by Derek McLane; costumes by Jenny Mannis; lighting by Peter Kaczorowski.

love but that is ultimately self-destructive. It is Li'l Bit who finally finds the strength to separate herself completely from Uncle Peck. Peck ultimately drinks himself to death while Li'l Bit tries to adjust herself to a life in which she cannot find a satisfying unity of body and mind. While she is still damaged, the ending suggests forgiveness.

How I Learned to Drive requires very little scenery. Two chairs may be used to represent the car, the most important prop, and also to indicate a dining room at home or a restaurant and other locations. The place of the action is the mind and memory. The play sweeps away most concrete details to focus on the thoughts, desires, and feelings of guilt in its central characters.

How I Learned to Drive is especially unusual in its depiction of a pedophile. Though deeply flawed, Peck is not condemned or stereotyped as a crafty, unloving criminal. Both Li'l Bit and Uncle Peck arouse sympathy. Typifying the complexity Vogel seeks, in an interview for the 2012 New York revival, she stated: "It's about the gifts we receive from the people who harm us." It is Vogel's ability to cut through stereotypes and show us the human side of frailty that marks most of her plays.

Richard Feldman

How I Learned to Drive as produced by the American Repertory Theatre (Cambridge, Mass.), featuring Debra Winger as Li'l Bit and Arliss Howard as Peck. Directed by David Wheeler; scene design by J. Michael Griggs; costumes by Viola McKenthuen; lighting by John Ambrosone.

Gay and Lesbian Theatre

Contemporary plays that focus on gay and lesbian characters are actively shaping the landscape of the American theatre. The works of award-winning playwrights Terrence McNally, Tony Kushner, and Moisés Kaufmann, for instance, are among the most produced in the country, and have helped normalize representations of gay and lesbian relationships on stage. Likewise, recent successful musicals such as *Spring Awakening* (2006) and *The Book of Mormon* (2011) deal openly with the topic of homosexuality in society. Indeed, many strides have been made in recent decades to create a theatre community more inclusive of LGBTQ (lesbian, gay, bisexual, transgender, queer) concerns.

The public presence of gay and lesbian theatre is a relatively recent phenomenon. Although homosexuality has been an occasional topic in drama since the Greeks, there were laws against the overt depiction of homosexuality onstage until the late 1960s. Mart Crowley's *The Boys in the Band* (1968), the first play on Broadway specifically about gay men, is often said to have marked a turning point in the acceptability of plays about homosexuality, although all of its characters were still treated as doomed or irrevocably unhappy. Following the Stonewall riots in 1969 (when a group of homosexuals, reacting to years of intimidation in New York, attacked police who were raiding a gay bar), advocates of "gay pride" encouraged greater openness in plays and productions about gay life.

One of the best-known exponents of gay theatre was Charles Ludlam (1943–1987), head of the Ridiculous Theatrical Company from 1967 until his death and author of several plays, among them *Bluebeard* (1970), *Camille* (1973), and *The Mystery of Irma Vep* (1984), which parodied familiar literary genres and the absur-

dities of art and life. Ludlam acted in his own plays, often playing several roles, most of them female. Similarly, Harvey Fierstein won mainstream acceptance for his *Torch Song Trilogy* (1981) and for cowriting the musical *La Cage aux Folles* (1983), both of which were made into films.

In the 1970s, gay theatre companies were formed in major cities throughout the United States. These theatres played an important role in promoting a sense of identity and addressing the concerns and interests of those within the gay, lesbian, and bisexual communities. In 1978, a Gay Theatre Alliance was formed to link gay theatre companies. In New York at this time, Café Cinno and La MaMa Theatre Club produced some of the most well-known plays dealing with LGBTQ issues. As is the case with all theatre companies formed during that time, some of the companies have since closed, while others have remained in operation, and new companies have formed. For example, New York's TOSOs (The Other Side of Silence), founded by Stonewall riot participant Doric Wilson in 1974, suspended operations after several years and then reopened in 2005 as TOSO II. The WOW (Women One World) Cafe in New York remains one of the oldest and most prominent theatres devoted to the concerns of women, particularly lesbians.

In 1985, GLAAD (the Gay and Lesbian Alliance Against Defamation) was formed to combat defamatory media coverage and representations of gays and lesbians stemming from the onset of the AIDS epidemic. Since then, GLAAD has had a powerful impact on the stage and screen representations of gays and lesbians. Today, most major American cities contain theatres that specifically address gay and lesbian audiences or host gay and lesbian theatre festivals. For example, Theatre Rhinoceros, formed in 1977, remains an important producer of gay and lesbian theatre in San Francisco, and Act Out Productions sponsors the Columbus National Gay and Lesbian Theatre Festival in Ohio.

Beginning in the 1980s, the AIDS crisis generated numerous plays about the LGBTQ community, including Larry Kramer's *The Normal Heart* (1985) and William Hoffman's *As Is* (1985). Later AIDS-themed plays include Cheryl West's *Before It Hits Home* (1991), Terrence McNally's *Lips Together, Teeth Apart* (1991), and Paul Rudnick's *Jeffery* (1993). These are just a few of dozens of theatrical works created in the midst of the crisis that explored the damage AIDS was inflicting on the gay community.

Though few plays focusing on lesbian relationships have made their way into the mainstream, lesbianism has been a topic in drama for decades. Lillian Hellman's *The Children's Hour* (1934), for instance, centers on the story of two women accused of being in a sexual relationship. While Hellman is often critiqued for her unsympathetic portrayal of lesbian identity, others have

been celebrated for their nuanced treatment of lesbian relationships. Jane Chambers's *Last Summer at Bluefish Cove* (1980), Holly Hughes's *The Well of Horniness* (1983), and Diana Son's *Stop Kiss* (1998) are among the most acclaimed plays that explore lesbian themes. Less visible in the mainstream, several feminist theatre collectives of the 1970s also focused on lesbian issues. The Lavender Cellar in Minneapolis, Red Dyke Theatre in Atlanta, and The Lesbian Feminist Theatre Collective of Pittsburgh, used theatrical art to make personal and political statements about the inequality lesbian women were facing in society.

Playwright Tony Kushner has been a pioneer in advancing discussions of LGBTQ issues in the theatre. Kushner became the most praised American playwright of the 1990s for his *Angels in America: A Gay Fantasia on National Themes,*

Joe Mantello, left, as Ned Weeks and John Benjamin Hickey as Felix Turner in the 2011 Tony Award-winning revival of Larry Kramer's *The Normal Heart* (1985), one of the first plays to focus on the AIDS crisis.

AP Photo/The O and M Co., Joan Marcus

an epic work consisting of two parts, *Millennium Approaches* (1991) and *Perestroika* (1992); each part won the Tony Award for Best Play, while *Millennium Approaches* also won the Pulitzer Prize. The two parts, which require several hours to perform, treat not only AIDS but also the crisis that faces America as concern for self overwhelms the needs of others, even loved ones. Throughout the world *Angels in America* was one of the most produced plays of the 1990s, marking it as one of the most celebrated American plays written in the last fifty years. Let us take a closer look at *Millennium Approaches*, a complete play in itself that is often studied and performed without *Perestroika*.

ANGELS IN AMERICA, PART I: MILLENNIUM APPROACHES

Angels in America is both an intimate treatment of the lives of two couples and a sweeping portrayal of America near the end of the twentieth century. The first of these couples, Louis and Prior, are two gay men dealing with the reality of the AIDS crisis in 1985 New York. When Prior notices lesions developing on his body, Louis is unable to cope with the fact that his partner is dying. Their struggle to continue their relationship raises profound questions about the nature of caretaking and what it means to love another human being.

Joe and Harper are a Mormon husband and wife whose relationship is also deteriorating. Throughout the play, Joe tries to reconcile his repressed gay identity with his belief in a church doctrine that condemns homosexuality. Joe is an idealistic and ambitious conservative who wants to live a decent and "correct" life. Harper consistently confronts Joe about the problems in the marriage, but she, too, is privately suffering. In an effort to escape her unhappiness, Harper self-medicates with Valium.

While the play often explores the lives of these couples realistically, Kushner also introduces nonrealistic elements throughout the drama: Harper speaks to "Mr. Lies" in her Valium-induced hallucinations, an Angel descends from the ceiling to discuss the coming of the new Millennium, Prior converses with his dead ancestors, and Roy Cohn is confronted by the ghost of accused traitor Ethel Rosenberg, whom he boasts to have successfully lobbied to execute. These moments of heightened theatricality have inspired many critics to discuss the "Brechtian" elements of Kushner's work. Like Brecht's plays, *Angels* comments on society by making audiences aware of theatrical artifice and nonrealism.

Kushner's *Angels* is an issue-oriented play that theatricalizes social problems and politics. The character Roy Cohn is based on the historical figure of the same name who fought for the causes of 1980s Reagan conservatism while hiding his homosexuality. In the play, Cohn's ruthless self-serving personality is contrasted with Joe's naïve idealism. By the end of *Millennium Approaches*, Joe and Roy are both trapped by larger forces that are out of their control. White liberalism is also critiqued in the play, most notably through the character of Belize, a gay black nurse, who confronts Louis's ignorance of racial issues.

Angels continues to speak to a new generation of theatre artists because of the human characters, gay and straight, that populate the world of the play. Though it deals explicitly with politics, *Angels* is not a polemical diatribe against a particular doctrine, but a consideration of the flaws of human beings living in 1980s America. Ultimately, the play offers hope that the new millennium may bring human transformation and spiritual grace.

Performance Art Since 1990

The major creators of performance art originally came from the visual arts, dance, or music; they were attracted to performance art

The climactic final scene in Tony Kushner's *Angels in America: Millennium Approaches* features the appearance of The Angel, played in the Broadway production by Ellen McLaughlin; Prior Walter played by Stephen Spinella. Directed by George C. Wolfe; scene design by Robin Wagner; costume design by Toni-Leslie James; lighting by Jules Fisher.

in part because it disregarded boundaries among the arts, thereby greatly expanding the means of expression. Many theatre artists originally found performance art less attractive, perhaps because theatre has always combined elements from various other arts and because performance art tended to de-emphasize story/text and to use performers not as actors but as narrators or as objects to be manipulated spatially. Still, others have found liberation in the power of performance art to generate provocative new images and to convey different perspectives. Perhaps the most influential force in American performance art today is P.S. 122, an organization based in New York.

For several years now, however, the label "performance art" has been extended by some to include solo theatre pieces by such performers as Eric Bogosian, Spalding Gray (1941–2004), John Leguizamo, and Anna Deavere Smith. Several artists have also blended theatre, dance, and performance art; among the most notable of them are Laurie Anderson, Pina Bausch (1940–2009), Martha Clarke, Ping Chong, and Meredith Monk. Aspects of performance art have also been appropriated by music videos and other media adaptations. Because of these alterations and expansions, some critics insist that performance art in the 1990s was swallowed up by theatre and entertainment media on the one hand and the commodity-driven art world on the other. Other critics see performance art as a grassroots performance form that opposes the commoditization of art and the individual.

Richard Foreman writes, directs, and designs the scenery for works that often straddle the boundaries some critics have drawn between performance art and theatre. Pictured is his play *Benita Canova*, as presented by the Ontological-Hysteric Theatre (New York).

T. Charles Erickson

Certainly the performance art of the twenty-first century differs significantly from that of the 1970s, and the term has been applied to so many diverse activities that it has lost specificity. Nevertheless, "performance art" continues to indicate the contemporary tendency to break down barriers between the arts and to help us understand that "performance" can take many forms.

Postmodernism

The ideas and practices of environmental theatre and performance art are related to postmodernism, a label that is imprecise but one that suggests major changes from modernism. Most of these changes involve the breakdown of clear-cut categories. With modernism, the crucial battles had involved absolute versus relative standards and values. The triumph of relativism meant that artists did not have to work in the same style; each could choose the one that seemed most appropriate. In the theatre, directors came to consider each production a problem requiring its own stylistic solution. In addition, many new styles (symbolism, expressionism, surrealism, and the like) enlarged the available choices. Once a stylistic choice was made, however, there was still unity of production as the director sought to shape every aspect to fit that mode. For modernists, there were many stylistic categories, but each was clearly differentiated.

Postmodernism melded categories by ignoring or deliberately violating differentiations and breaching the boundaries between the arts, as in performance art and multimedia; by breaking down the barriers between spectator and performance space, as in environmental theatre; and by removing distinctions between audience and performers, as in happenings. Postmodernists ignored previous distinctions between popular and high culture and often intermingled them, as in the 1987 production of *The Comedy of Errors* (at New York's Lincoln Center) in which the Flying Karamazov Brothers (a comic juggling team) not only played key roles but also incorporated juggling and acrobatics into Shakespeare's play. Postmodernism also blurs distinctions between dramatic forms, as does a good deal of contemporary drama.

Postmodernism is eclectic and referential. It mingles elements from disparate styles, periods, or cultures. Postmodernist architecture is recognizable in large part because of the combination within single buildings of various stylistic motifs and forms from the past. The imitative use of prior forms is sometimes referred to as "pastiche" and it applies to texts as well as spatial and visual forms. Postmodern pastiche evokes a form or text, stripped from its original context or function, and places it into a relationship with other forms or other texts. For example, in 2007 a San Diego company staged *Caliban's Island*, mixing Shakespeare's *The Tempest* with an episode of *Gilligan's Island* and Robert Browning's *Caliban upon Setebos*. Whereas some might say that mingling such a sampling of texts is a distortion of each individual work, the postmodern view is that each of the works is already "intertextual," a weaving together of various texts. For example, Gonzolo's speech in Shakespeare's *The Tempest* (II.i. 148–57), gives Gonzolo's vision for the island's governance. This speech paraphrases Florio's 1603 translation of Montaigne's essay "On Cannibals" (penned in 1580) and Montaigne's essay owes much to Peter Martir's *De Orbe Novo* (1511).

Postmodernists argue that every work is already a tapestry of prior texts and ideas woven together; rather than treat forms or texts from the past as relics to be honored, postmodernists often treat them as cultural debris to be played with, recombined into new expressions, or surfaces to be skimmed.

Many aspects of postmodernism came together in the theatre pieces of Robert Wilson, among them *Einstein on the Beach* (1976), *CIVIL warS* (1984), *Time Rocker* (1997), and many more. In these pieces, Wilson borrowed from several media, cultures, and historical periods. Although some of Wilson's pieces have included spoken portions, many did not have texts in the traditional sense. They were essentially visual pieces, enhanced by music and sound, in which juxtaposed visual images appeared, disappeared, grew, diminished, and metamorphosed over time. Time was an important element; typically,

it was slowed until movement became almost imperceptible, permitting every detail to be experienced; different elements within a scene progressed at different tempos. Because the performance aspects of visual image, time, sound, and movement were of equal, if not greater, importance than scripted dialogue, it has been difficult for others to restage Wilson's work. Many of his pieces were very long, from four to twelve hours; one lasted seven continuous days and nights. Likewise, the scale of some of his pieces was very large. For example, *CIVIL warS* contained many segments, one each staged in West Germany, the Netherlands, Italy, France, Japan, and the United States. It included such disparate historical figures as Abraham Lincoln, Karl Marx, Frederick the Great, Voltaire, and a Hopi Indian tribe, as well as wholly invented present-day and fictional characters. It was intended to reflect all types of conflicts (public and private) that interfere with human relationships. Utilizing twelve languages, *CIVIL warS* was not meant for an audience from any single culture.

According to Wilson, there is nothing to understand in his pieces, only things to experience, out of which each spectator constructs his or her own associations and meanings. Some spectators have been infuriated or bored by the length and lack of clear-cut intention in Wilson's pieces, but some critics have called him the most innovative and significant force in contemporary theatre. Wilson has expanded into directing plays and operas by established playwrights, among them Shakespeare's *King Lear*, Euripides's *Alcestis*, Wagner's *Parsifal*, Büchner's *Danton's Death*, and Ibsen's *When We Dead Awaken*. Even when he has staged classical texts, however, Wilson has avoided using visual elements to merely illustrate what is in the text. Instead, he has sought to suggest other dimensions through imagery related (not literally but perhaps thematically) to the text. He has also collaborated with others in creating new pieces. Among these are *The Black Rider* (1990), on which he collaborated with

Richard Feldman

A segment of Robert Wilson's *CIVIL warS* at the American Repertory Theatre. Design by Robert Wilson with collaborators Tom Kamm and Jennifer Tipton. The tall figure at right is Abraham Lincoln; at left, an owl; at center back, King Lear carrying Cordelia. Most critics and scholars judge *CIVIL warS* to exemplify postmodernism.

singer/musician Tom Waits, and *Sonnets* (2009), based on twenty-four of Shakespeare's sonnets, on which he collaborated with singer-songwriter Rufus Wainwright.

Postmodern Influences on Interpretation and Design

Postmodernism has influenced directing in several ways, perhaps most significantly by altering attitudes about the director's relationship to the playwright and the script. Modernists assumed that the director's task is to translate the playwright's script faithfully from page to stage. This assumption incorporated another: the director can determine a playwright's intentions through a meticulous analysis of the script. Postmodernists, on the other hand, argue that there can be no single "correct" interpretation of a text because words do not convey precisely the same meanings to everyone. Furthermore, once a work is finished, its creator's statements about its meanings have no more authority than anyone else's because the text, not the author, elicits the responses and interpretations. Such arguments free a director or a designer to interpret a script as he or she thinks appropriate even if this interpretation is at odds with the playwright's. These views also encourage directors to propose new interpretations of well-known plays. In fact, in recent times, directors have often been judged by the novelty (sometimes more than by the aptness) of their interpretations. Some directors have argued that many classics have come to be so revered that we can see them with a fresh eye only in radical reinterpretations.

Most radical reinterpretations have involved plays by authors long dead. But since the 1980s, some directorial decisions have elicited strong objections from living authors. In 1984, Samuel Beckett threatened to withdraw his *Endgame* from production at the American Repertory Theatre in Cambridge, Massachusetts, because the director, JoAnne Akalaitis, had relocated the action to a derelict subway station and cast some black actors in roles traditionally played by white performers. In 1994, Beckett's estate forced the closure of an English production of his *Footfalls* because it did not adhere to Beckett's stage directions. In both instances, although not a single word of either play's dialogue had been cut, Beckett's complaint was that the director had moved beyond interpretation to construct a new meaning by altering the play's visual content. In another instance, Arthur Miller successfully sued the Wooster Group, a New York company directed by Elizabeth LeCompte, forcing it to remove, in a piece called

L.S.D. (1984), portions of *The Crucible* to illuminate contemporary attitudes about hallucinogenic drugs by juxtaposing them against attitudes about witchcraft in colonial New England as shown in Miller's play. The Wooster Group had previously incorporated portions of Thornton Wilder's *Our Town* into a piece called *Route 1 & 9* (1981) and juxtaposed them with a black-face vaudeville routine and a pornographic film. The group's idea was to comment on Wilder's idyllic view of America in which ethnic groups and sex are ignored, as are the industrial wastelands through which run the two highways that give the piece its title. Some critics have suggested that if a director or a theatre company wishes to distort or change the meaning of a play, why not simply elect to produce a different play or write an entirely new one? Directors who resist this view usually argue that the appropriation of a well-known work is essential to a revisionist message or that as creative artists, they should be allowed to interpret works as they see fit. Radical reinterpretations that use a play as raw material to make new statements may or may not be postmodern in style, but they reflect the influence of contemporary theory and thought on theatrical production.

Richard Feldman

The 1984 American Repertory Theatre (A.R.T.) production of Samuel Beckett's *Endgame* as directed by JoAnne Akalaitis; scene design by Douglas Stein; lighting by Jennifer Tipton. Beckett threatened to withdraw A.R.T's permission to perform his play because he deemed the interpretation a distortion of his work.

Designers have also claimed their rights as interpretive artists. Before postmodernism, scene designers, for example, typically sought to meet the practical needs of a particular play and to support the director's interpretation of it. Modernism encouraged scene designers not only to suggest the location called for by the play, but also to render that location within a particular style and to selectively distort reality to convey mood, theme, and pertinent psychological forces. However, the function of scene design generally remained akin to the illustration of a story. Influenced by postmodernism, some scene designers have exerted their role as cocreators of the play's action and others have begun to explore the possibilities of scene design that seemingly bears only an incidental relationship to the play.

The influence of postmodernism and other contemporary thought on interpretation and design raises important questions. Where is meaning found and who creates it, the author or the reader? What is the place of a play script in performance? Does that written script guide the form its performance should take or is it as malleable an element as acting, scenery, costumes, or lighting? Are directors and designers justified in reshaping (even radically altering) a script to suit their own vision? Should a playwright's preferences be honored even after audience tastes and staging conventions have changed? What is the role of the contemporary director (principal creative artist, as in film, or servant of the script)? None of these questions can be answered definitively, but they have created heated debate.

Julio Donoso/Sygma/Corbis

Another contemporary theatre trend involves the intercultural application of theatrical conventions from various cultures. Pictured is a rehearsal of *Mahabharata,* **directed by Peter Brook (standing) at his International Center for Theatre Research in Paris. The nine-hour play is adapted from the Sanskrit epic; the cast featured actors from sixteen countries and the play was performed in both English and French versions.**

Contemporary British Drama

The post–World War II decentralization of British theatre and the renaissance in British playwriting launched by John Osborne's *Look Back in Anger* (1956) created a fertile environment for playwrights, initially led by Harold Pinter, Tom Stoppard, and Peter Shaffer, then followed by Caryl Churchill, David Hare, and others.

Harold Pinter (1930–2008) was awarded the Nobel Prize for Literature in 2005. Also an actor, a director, and a political activist, he wrote over thirty plays, including *The Birthday Party* (1957), *The Homecoming* (1964), *Old Times* (1970), and *Remembrance of Things Past* (2000). Many of these plays have common characteristics:

The action usually involves a small group of people and takes place in a single room; all of the events could occur in real life (sometimes the situations and dialogue suggest naturalism); nevertheless, they create a sense of ambiguity and menace, primarily because the motivations of the characters are never clarified. Because Pinter believes that people use speech more to conceal than to reveal their attitudes and feelings, we often have to guess why they act as they do. Pinter is known as "the master of the pause"; it is during the pauses and silences in his plays that we often glimpse the unspoken subtext.

Another of England's great playwrights is Tom Stoppard. Born in Czechoslovakia to Jewish parents who fled their home country just ahead of the Nazis, Stoppard and his surviving family moved to England after World War II. Stoppard first won recognition with his award-winning *Rosencrantz and Guildenstern Are Dead* (1967),

Robbie Jack/Corbis Entertainment/Corbis

The action of Tom Stoppard's *Arcadia* alternates between the early 1800s and the present, until the final scene (pictured here) when both time periods share the stage. Along with *Angels in America*, *Arcadia* was the most produced contemporary play of the 1990s and has enjoyed frequent revivals in recent years.

a play that focuses on two minor characters from *Hamlet* who sense that important events are going on around them but who die without ever understanding the action of which they have been an insignificant part. In his subsequent plays, among them, *Travesties* (1974), *The Real Thing* (1982), *Arcadia* (1993), *The Coast of Utopia* (2002), and *Rock 'n' Roll* (2006), he continues to combine verbal wit and highly imaginative action with complex ideas about contemporary perceptions of reality. Of his eleven major plays, nine have won a Best New Play Award in either London or New York. An outspoken human rights activist, Stoppard is also an accomplished screenwriter whose 1998 film *Shakespeare in Love* won an Academy Award for best screenplay.

Peter Shaffer first achieved success in the late 1950s and early 1960s, but is now best known for *Equus* (1973) and *Amadeus* (1979); both plays won the Tony Award and ran for over one thousand performances on Broadway. *Equus* focuses on a psychologist who must determine why a teenage boy blinded six horses. In the process, the play questions how living a normal life can also deaden the spirit and passion that should be a part of human life. *Amadeus* uses a rival composer, Salieri, to tell the story of opera composer Wolfgang Amadeus Mozart. After very successful runs in London and New York, the play was turned into an Academy Award–winning film.

Caryl Churchill first rose to prominence in the 1970s with *Vinegar Tom* (1976) and *Cloud Nine* (1979); the latter has the first act set in colonial, Victorian Africa, with the second act (using the same characters) set a hundred years later in contemporary London. It also uses cross-gender casting to explore the way social expectations impact gender roles. Other plays include *Top Girls* (1982), *Serious Money* (1987), *Mad Forest* (1990), *The Skriker* (1994), and *A Number* (2002). Churchill's plays are as creative in form as they are varied in content. She has used songs, poststructural word-play, rhym-

ing couplets, sparse realistic dialogue, and surrealistic long monologues. She has sometimes treated time as fluid or twisted rather than linear. While her style is constantly evolving and responding to her subject matter, her interests are consistent. She has stated that her primary concerns are issues of "power, powerlessness, and exploitation."

Other major British playwrights of the era include Alan Ayckbourn, Michael Frayn, and David Hare. Initially considered the "British Neil Simon," Ayckbourn has had a long, distinguished career filled with a diversity of plays including *The Norman Conquests* (1973), *A Chorus of Disapproval* (1984), and the inter-related plays *House* and *Garden* (1999) in which the same cast simultaneously performs two different plays in two different theatres. Michael Frayn is best known for *Noises Off* (1982), a very popular farce that is structured as a play-within-a-play, and *Copenhagen* (1998), a Tony Award–winning drama about a meeting between nuclear physicists Niels Bohr and Werner Heisenberg. After writing for Britain's small experimental theatres, Hare moved into mainstream theatres via works such as *Plenty* (1978) and *The Secret Rapture* (1988). He continued with works such as *Skylight* (1995), *Amy's View* (1997), *The Judas Kiss* (1998), and *Stuff Happens* (2004). Hare's major plays often focus on the issue of how the desire to gain and maintain power and wealth undermine and destroy personal integrity, shared values, and concern for the common good.

While the above playwrights were still active, in the 1980s and early 1990s, the lack of new playwrights led some observers to believe that British playwriting had stagnated. A sudden jolt occurred in the 1990s by a group of young, confrontational playwrights who created what became known as "In-Yer-Face Theatre," plays marked by shocking, graphic (violent or sexual) content. Some of the notable writers include Sarah Kane (1971–1999) with her plays *Blasted* (1995) and *Psychosis 4:48*

(1999); Mark Ravenhill with his plays *Shopping and F***ing* (1996) and *The Cut* (2006); and Patrick Marber with *Dealer's Choice* (1995) and *Closer* (1997).

The most successful of the new generation of playwrights has been Martin McDonagh. Born in London to Irish parents, McDonagh set his early plays in rural Ireland. These include *The Beauty Queen of Leenane* (1996), *A Skull in Connemara* (1997), *The Lonesome West* (1997), *The Cripple of Inishmaan* (1997), and *The Lieutenant of Inishmore* (2001). His plays consistently mix black humor with violence and brutality. In *Pillowman* (2003), set in a nonspecified totalitarian state, a writer of horror stories is interrogated after several local children have been murdered in ways that seem to have been inspired by his gruesome and imaginative stories. *A Behanding in Spokane* (2010) marked his first play set in the United States, and concerns a man trying to locate the hand he lost twenty-five years ago. McDonagh's film work includes writing and directing the Academy Award–winning short film *Six Shooter* (2005), the Academy Award–nominated *In Bruges* (2008), and *Seven Psychopaths* (2012).

Martin McDonagh's *The Lieutenant of Inishmore* as produced at the Alley Theatre under the direction of Gregory Boyd; set and lighting by Kevin Rigdon; costumes by Judith Dolan.

T. Charles Erickson

Contemporary Musical Theatre

By the late 1980s British imports dominated musical theatre on Broadway and, after a string of flops, many critics began to question whether revivals of American musicals and foreign imports were enough to ensure the future of the Broadway musical. However, in the mid-1990s several factors helped to revitalize the musical and Broadway:

- Dynamic new musicals attracting new audiences

- Renovation of the 42nd Street area and Disney's entrance as a producer of Broadway musicals

- Musicals based on films and pop music

The appearance of dynamic new musicals helped revitalize the form and attract new audiences to Broadway. *Rent* (1996), by Jonathan Larson, uses rock music as it adapts Puccini's opera *La Bohème* (1896) to life among the young on New York's lower East Side. It tells the story of a group of struggling young artists living under the specter of AIDS as they cope with their disappointments and revel in their capacity for love.

It achieved great popularity (fanned by the death of the author on the eve of the musical's premiere) and won a number of prestigious awards. *Bring in 'Da Noise, Bring in 'Da Funk* (1996)—conceived and directed by George C. Wolfe with several collaborators—used tap dancing to evoke the history of African Americans.

Another important factor in the revival of the musical (and Broadway theatre) was the 42nd Street Development Project, which transformed an area of urban blight into something resembling the showplace of Broadway that it was in the early twentieth century. At great expense, the Disney Corporation refurbished the New Amsterdam Theatre, the Livent corporation remodeled and linked two theatres to create the Ford Center, and the New Victory Theatre was revived as a theatre for young audiences. With newly refurbished buildings to support theatrical activity and the removal of striptease clubs, the 42nd Street area became more "family friendly." The Disney Corporation enhanced this image by producing stage versions of its animated films, *Beauty and the Beast* (1994) and *The Lion King* (1997), which attracted large audiences, including families who did not ordinarily attend Broadway. *The Lion King* also won high critical praise and numerous awards for its design and directing (by Julie Taymor).

The turn of the century brought with it a musical treating an unlikely subject as well as a megahit musical that set Broadway records for its awards and ticket prices. *Urinetown* (2001) is a satirical musical that treats a rebellion by the people of a major city forced, because of a prolonged water shortage, to use only public toilets, for which they must pay a corporation sizable fees. Violators of the policy, created by officers of the corporation and enforced by local politicians and the police, are reportedly sent to "Urinetown," a place from which no one has ever returned. *Urinetown* mocks not only capitalism and political corruption,

but also the happy endings typical in many Broadway musicals. At the end of the story, the rebellion succeeds after many sacrifices and all restrictions and fees are removed. This quickly leads to a water-shortage crisis in which many die from the lack of fresh water, while others kill the heroine who lifted the restrictions. This unlikely Broadway musical garnered the 2002 Tony Awards for Best Direction, Best Book, and Best Musical Score. Meanwhile, *The Producers* (2001), a musical based on Mel Brooks's 1968 film of the same name, broke long-standing Broadway box office records when it sold over $3 million worth of tickets in a single day. The popularity of the show also led to the creation of a select number of "premium seats," which sold at a top price of $480. The story concerns two theatrical producers who scheme to get rich by overselling interests in a Broadway flop but face disaster when the terrible, pro-Nazi musical they produce unexpectedly turns out to be a hit. *The Producers* set another record when it won an unprecedented twelve Tony Awards in 2001.

Broadway producers have long sought musicals based on material familiar to the general public. A number of musicals derived from films and pop music familiar to the baby-boomer generation appeared. Among them were *The Full Monty* (2000), *Hairspray* (2002), *Mamma Mia* (1999, based on the music of the pop group ABBA), *Movin' Out* (2002, based on the music of Billy Joel), and *Jersey Boys* (2005, based on the music and life of Frankie Valli and The Four Seasons). Other successful musicals based on somewhat less familiar material include *Wicked* (2003, based on Gregory Maguire's novel *Wicked: The Life and Times of the Wicked Witch of the West*), and *Spring Awakening* (2006, based on the 1891 German play of the same title by Frank Wedekind). Meanwhile, a handful of entirely original musicals have proved successful, including *Avenue Q* (2003), an adult-themed musical that incorporated

The musical *Wicked* is based on Gregory Maguire's novel *Wicked: The Life and Times of the Wicked Witch of the West*, which offers a very different look at the land of Oz and the characters made popular in the film, *The Wizard of Oz*. Pictured here are Idina Menzel (right) as Elphaba and Kristin Chenoweth as Glinda. Music and lyrics by Stephen Schwartz; book by Winnie Holzman; directed by Joe Mantello; choreography by Wayne Cilento; scene design by Eugene Lee; costume design by Susan Hilferty; lighting by Kenneth Posner; sound by Tony Meloa.

Sara Krulwich/The New York Times/Redux Pictures

Sesame Street-style puppets; *The 25th Annual Putnam County Spelling Bee* (2005), which incorporated audience participation; *The Drowsy Chaperone* (2006); *In the Heights* (2007); and *Next to Normal* (2008). More recently, Trey Parker and Matt Stone, the creators of the animated comedy *South Park*, joined with Robert Lopez (one of the cowriters of *Avenue Q*) to create the controversial but highly successful musical *The Book of Mormon* (2011); the show

won nine Tony Awards and throughout its first year played to over 100 percent capacity as it grossed over $66 million.

Despite critics constantly predicting the impending demise of the American musical, numerous new musicals are touted each season as being under development for Broadway production. Likewise, the 2011–2012 Broadway season recorded a record $1.14 billion in ticket sales and an audience of 12.33 million people.

The Broadway production of *In the Heights* features an innovative score of hip-hop and popular Latin music as it follows the adventures and struggles of characters in New York City's Dominican American neighborhood of Washington Heights. Book by Quiara Alegría Hudes; music and lyrics by Lin-Manuel Miranda; directed by Thomas Kail; choreographed by Andy Blankenbuehler; scene design by Anna Louizos; costumes by Paul Tazewell; lighting by Howell Binkley.

The Next Wave of Contemporary American Playwrights

There are a number of new voices in American drama, many of them once considered marginal, that fully exemplify the increasing crossover and diversity of contemporary theatre. They are of varied religious backgrounds and cultural heritages; some are straight, some are gay; and many are of racially diverse ancestry. Some of these playwrights studied their craft at prestigious Ivy League schools known for their drama programs; others, like Tracy Letts, never finished college. Examined as a group, these playwrights suggest the increasing diversity, depth, and complexity of American drama.

The critical and popular success of Suzan-Lori Parks perhaps marks how far African American playwrights have come in gaining mainstream acceptance. Parks's early plays include *The Death of the Last Black Man in the Whole Entire World* (1990), *The America Play* (1994), and *In the Blood* (1999). In 2002, Parks became the first female African American dramatist to win the Pulitzer Prize for drama with her play, *TopDog/Underdog*. Between its New York staging and regional theatre productions it became the most successful play by an African American female since Ntozake Shange's *for colored girls who have considered suicide/when the rainbow is enuf* (1975).

Parks's most recent works include *365 Days/365 Plays* (2006, a year-long project in which she wrote a short play every day for a year), *The Book of Grace* (2010), and a musical adaptation of the opera *Porgy and Bess* (2011).

Richard Greenberg, a graduate of Princeton and the Yale School of Drama, achieved his first critical success with *Life Under Water* (1985) while he was still a student at Yale. Many of Greenberg's plays explore issues of loneliness, misunderstandings, and the inability to connect. Believing that "time is something that can be tinkered with," Greenberg often distorts and overlaps time in the over twenty-five plays he has written. These include *Eastern Standard* (1988), *Night and Her Stars* (1995), *Three Days of Rain* (1997), an adaptation of August Strindberg's *The Dance of Death* (2003), *The Violet Hour* (2003), and the 2003 Tony Award–winning play *Take Me Out,* which treats the "coming out" of a homosexual major league baseball player. Greenberg's more recent plays include *The American Plan* (2009) and *Our Mother's Brief Affair* (2009).

Lynn Nottage was born and raised in Brooklyn. She has written many plays since her first play, *Poof* (1993), was selected as the cowinner of the National Ten-Minute Play Contest. Her subsequent plays include *Crumbs from the Table of Joy* (1995), *Intimate Apparel* (2003), *Fabulation* (2005), and *Ruined* (2008). *Ruined*, which is set in the Democratic Republic of the Congo during its civil war, focuses on the horrors of war inflicted upon women and the various ways they are "ruined" by human brutality. Nottage, who is known for doing meticulous research on the subjects of her plays, traveled to Africa to interview Congolese refugees to collect stories for the play, which received the 2009 Pulitzer Prize for Drama. Among her many awards and recognitions, Nottage received a 2007 MacArthur Genius Award and the National Black Theatre Festival's August Wilson Playwriting Award. Besides her work as a writer, she is a teacher and a long-time social activist. Nottage, who is a graduate of Brown University and the Yale School of Drama, has said, "I want people to know that my story, that of the African-American woman, is also the American story."

Chicago-area playwright Tracy Letts was a founding member of the critically acclaimed but now defunct Bang Bang Spontaneous Theatre. Since 2002 Letts has been an ensemble member of the Steppenwolf Theatre Company, working regularly as an actor and, with increasing success, as a playwright. His first play, *Killer Joe* (1993, screenplay 2012), is a violent black comedy about a young man who hires an assassin to kill his mother and is then faced with unexpected violence from the killer. Letts's other plays include *Bug* (1996, screenplay 2007); *Man from Nebraska* (2003), a Pulitzer Prize finalist; and *August: Osage County*, winner of the 2007 Pulitzer Prize for Drama and winner of the 2008 Tony Award for Best Play.

Naomi Iizuka was born in Tokyo and spent her youth in various countries all over the world (life experience that seems to have significantly influenced her perspective and writing). A graduate of Yale, she has written over twenty plays, including *And Then She Was Screaming* (1990), *Crazy Jane* (1992), *Tattoo Girl* (1994), *Skin* (1995), *Polaroid Stories* (1997), *36 Views* (2001), *At the Vanishing Point* (2004), *Anon(ymous)* (2006), *Hamlet: Blood in the Brain* (2006), and *Ghostwritten* (2009). Iizuka, whose American Latina mother (of Cuban and Spanish extraction) met her Japanese father in America, has said that, "In terms of being an Asian American writer, I'm mixed race. I think there are issues about being racially mixed that are different than for people who are Japanese-American, or Korean-American, or Chinese-American in background.... I think a lot of people look at me and don't know what they're seeing. There are issues that people who are of mixed heritage deal with that are complicated in terms of finding their home in a specific ethnic group." These complications seem to surface in her plays, which explore themes of identity, cultural archetypes, the tenuous nature of perception, and the fluidity of truth.

Sara Krulwich/The New York Times/Redux

Tracy Letts's *August: Osage County*, which *New York Times* theatre critic Charles Isherwood called "flat-out, no asterisks and without qualifications, the most exciting new American play Broadway has seen in years." Produced by the Steppenwolf Theatre Company in Chicago, the production was later moved to a Broadway theatre. Directed by Anna D. Shapiro; sets by Todd Rosenthal; costumes by Ana Kuzmanic; lighting by Ann G. Wrightson; sound by Richard Woodbury; music by David Singer.

Tony Kushner, best known for *Angels in America* (discussed earlier in the chapter), has had many successes, including *A Bright Room Called Day* (1987). He is known for frequent revisions (even after a play is published) and for spending years on a given text. For example, Kushner began writing his play, *Homebody/Kabul*, in 1997. Set in London and Afghanistan at the end of the 1990s, *Homebody/Kabul* tells the story of a lonely and overmedicated British housewife whose obsession with Afghan culture and history leads her to travel to Kabul, only to find that there's a great deal more to comprehending the culture than reading an out-of-date guidebook. Kushner finished the play a few months prior to the September 11, 2001, terrorist attacks.

The play proved almost prophetic and struck a particularly responsive chord with New York City audiences. Kushner's other plays include a number of adaptations [such as *Stella* (1987) based on a play by Goethe, and *The Illusion* (first version 1988) based on a play by Pierre Corneille], and a musical—*Caroline, or Change* (2002). Kushner confronts a variety of contemporary concerns, challenging his audience to consider whether or not a person can achieve a sense of belonging in modern times.

Trained as a musician throughout her childhood, Quiara Alegría Hudes is a playwright who has found success independently and in collaboration on musicals. She wrote the book for *In the Heights* (2007), a Tony Award–winning musical about the adventures and struggles of characters in New York City's Dominican American neighborhood of Washington Heights. The score features hip-hop, salsa, merengue, and soul music. Hudes's plays include *Yemaya's Belly* (2005) and *26 Miles* (2009), as well as three works now informally known as "The Elliot Trilogy," a critically acclaimed look at an American soldier and his Puerto Rican family. *Elliot, A Soldier's Fugue* (2007), a finalist for the Pulitzer Prize, focuses on a young Marine deciding whether to do a second tour of duty in Iraq. *Water by the Spoonful* (2011) focuses on his return from that war as he struggles to find his place in society; the play won the 2012 Pulitzer Prize, making her the first Latina playwright to do so. The final play in the trilogy, *The Happiest Song Plays Last*, is scheduled to open in April 2013 at Chicago's Goodman Theatre. A graduate of Brown University with a master of fine arts degree (MFA) in Drama, she studied with Paula Vogel. Hudes has said she draws

inspiration from her family's background and experiences. Her mother emigrated from Puerto Rico as a child. Hudes's father was Jewish, but the couple divorced when Hudes was a child and she grew up with her grandmother, her mother, her Puerto Rican stepfather, and her Jewish aunt, who was a musician and influenced Hudes's early career. As Hudes has said, "It's easy to see why I became a writer in a family like that—what are you going to do, not tell the story?"

Sarah Ruhl, another one of Paula Vogel's playwriting students at Brown University, has enjoyed much success. Her plays include *Late: a cowboy song* and *Eurydice* (both in 2003—the latter being a revisionist take on the Orpheus myth in which the female character plays an active rather than a passive role); *The Clean House* (2004), for which Ruhl received the Susan Smith Blackburn award and was a Pulitzer Prize finalist; and *Dead Man's Cell Phone* (2007), a widely

Sara Krulwich/The New York Times/Redux

Bruce Norris's play *Clybourne Park* (2010) won the Pulitzer Prize, Tony Award, and Olivier Award. Playing off Lorraine Hansberry's *A Raisin in the Sun* (1959), the first act is set in 1959, while the second act is in 2009; the setting is the house that the Younger family wishes to buy in Hansberry's play, and then the same house fifty years later. Thus, the play looks at housing desegregation as well as gentrification.

produced play about technology and the disconnect people experience while living in the digital age. She made her Broadway debut in 2009 with *In the Next Room (or The Vibrator Play)*, for which she was again a Pulitzer Prize finalist as well as a Tony Award nominee. Ruhl's plays are often described as quirky, as the rules of time and space are flexible in the worlds she creates and her characters frequently address the audience directly. Ruhl is also the recipient of a 2006 MacArthur Genius Award.

Summary

As this chapter indicates, theatre has become increasingly diverse. This chapter has examined a number of groups (categorized by ethnicity, gender, and sexual orientation) that have created drama and theatre responding to their concerns. Some of the artists discussed were deliberate in choosing to create expressions from their point of view as an alternative to the "mainstream." Those artists challenged the broader society through theatre that expressed the perspectives of their communities. Over time, some of these artists gained mainstream recognition and acceptance.

Recently some scholars and critics have argued that since the end of the Cold War, with the explosion of online culture and the increasing interconnectedness caused by globalization, our world has moved beyond traditional boundaries of national, ethnic, and sexual identity thereby affecting the separatism of theatre by and for distinct communities. Transculturalism, the back-and-forth movement between cultures, is slowly becoming the paradigm for a new generation of theatre makers and audiences. This may arise from a desire to exert personal freedoms beyond the potentially narrow confines of a specific identity or from the discovery that problems often stem not from the failure to understand one's own culture but rather from the failure to understand other cultures. Whatever the cause, the contemporary theatre seems (as always) to be in a period of transition as it holds onto the past with one hand even as it extends the other hand to grasp the future.

THEATRE IN A BROAD CONTEXT

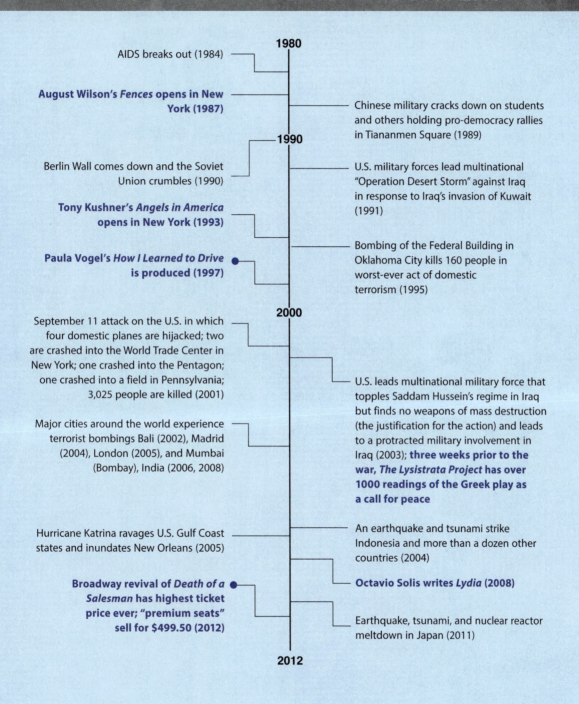

1980

AIDS breaks out (1984)

August Wilson's *Fences* opens in New York (1987)

Chinese military cracks down on students and others holding pro-democracy rallies in Tiananmen Square (1989)

1990

Berlin Wall comes down and the Soviet Union crumbles (1990)

U.S. military forces lead multinational "Operation Desert Storm" against Iraq in response to Iraq's invasion of Kuwait (1991)

Tony Kushner's *Angels in America* opens in New York (1993)

Paula Vogel's *How I Learned to Drive* is produced (1997)

Bombing of the Federal Building in Oklahoma City kills 160 people in worst-ever act of domestic terrorism (1995)

2000

September 11 attack on the U.S. in which four domestic planes are hijacked; two are crashed into the World Trade Center in New York; one crashed into the Pentagon; one crashed into a field in Pennsylvania; 3,025 people are killed (2001)

Major cities around the world experience terrorist bombings Bali (2002), Madrid (2004), London (2005), and Mumbai (Bombay), India (2006, 2008)

U.S. leads multinational military force that topples Saddam Hussein's regime in Iraq but finds no weapons of mass destruction (the justification for the action) and leads to a protracted military involvement in Iraq (2003); **three weeks prior to the war, *The Lysistrata Project* has over 1000 readings of the Greek play as a call for peace**

Hurricane Katrina ravages U.S. Gulf Coast states and inundates New Orleans (2005)

An earthquake and tsunami strike Indonesia and more than a dozen other countries (2004)

Broadway revival of *Death of a Salesman* has highest ticket price ever; "premium seats" sell for $499.50 (2012)

Octavio Solis writes *Lydia* (2008)

Earthquake, tsunami, and nuclear reactor meltdown in Japan (2011)

2012

Traditional African theatre performance often relies heavily on dance, storytelling, drumming, and ritual. Here, a stilt dancer, in the Dogon tradition, performs for Mali villagers. Stilt dance is a traditional performance form in many parts of Africa. Towering above others, the stilt dancers are thought to be able to act as intermediaries with the gods, interceding with them to bring favorable rains or other blessings to the village.

[This is] an assertion of the necessity for all those concerned with the contemporary theatre—in any role—to be sensitive to and aware of theatre worldwide. … We are acknowledging the dynamic interaction of performance traditions from all cultures in present day theatre.
—The Cambridge Guide to World Theatre

Asian and African Theatre

The performance traditions we have examined so far have been confined primarily to European and American theatre. But the theatre varies widely from one culture to another, as is readily apparent if we turn our attention to theatre in Asia, Africa, and other regions of the world. In this book it is not possible to look at all the variations. Consequently, we have chosen to consider some aspects of theatre in Asia and Africa. The examples must be limited, since the variations found on those two continents are numerous indeed.

Theatre in Japan

At about the time the medieval religious cycles were flourishing in Europe, a very different kind of theatrical experience was being offered halfway around the world in Japan. There, Noh theatre was perfected and codified so thoroughly that it is still performed today much as it was over five hundred years ago. It came into being in isolation from Western theatre and represents a wholly distinct theatrical tradition.

To understand Noh theatre we need to look at the political and cultural context out of which it developed. During the sixth century A.D. the Buddhist religion arrived in Japan from India and China. With it came a written language and many nonnative arts and crafts. In the seventh century an emperor gained power over Japan and took ownership of all land. For some four hundred years Japan flourished under this system, but by the twelfth century the emperor had lost most of his political power. In 1192 he ceded his secular authority to a *shogun* (military dictator), although he retained his status as a near-god in the religious realm. The shogunate became hereditary, although new families won possession of the title from time to time. Japan was ruled in this manner until 1867, when American intervention led to the downfall of the shogunate and the return of power to the emperor.

Under the shogunate, Japan developed a strict social hierarchy. The highest class was the *samurai* (warriors), with the shogun at their head. Below them were three other classes (each with subcategories): merchants; artists and craftsmen; and farmers and peasants. Each rank had a specified code of behavior and mode of dress. Japanese life became highly structured and formalized. In 1338 the Ashikaga family gained control of the shogunate and retained it for the next two hundred fifty years. One of its goals was to eliminate foreign cultural influences and develop native art forms. Of the native forms, Noh was to enjoy special favor.

Noh Theatre

The most significant developments in Noh theatre began around 1375. At this time, the shogun took the Noh performer and dramatist Kiyotsugu Kan'ami (1333–1384) and his son Zeami Motokiyo (1363–1444) under his patronage and granted them samurai status in his court. Working within this refined atmosphere, these two men gave Noh its characteristic form. Zeami, greatest of Noh dramatists, wrote approximately fifty of the two hundred fifty plays that still make up the active Noh repertory. He also defined Noh's goals and conventions. All the plays in the present Noh repertory were written more than four hundred years ago and are still performed much as they were when written. Noh is thus essentially a product of the fourteenth, fifteenth, and sixteenth centuries.

The major influence on Noh's view of the world was Zen Buddhism, which teaches that ultimate peace comes through union with all being, that individual desire must be overcome, and that nothing in earthly life is permanent. Noh plays typically have as protagonists ghosts, demons, or obsessed human beings whose souls cannot find rest because in life they were devoted to worldly honor, love, or other goals that keep drawing them back to the physical world and its imperfections.

Noh dramas are classified into five types, according to the principal character:

- God plays
- Warrior plays
- Women plays
- Madness plays
- Demon plays

Noh theatre masks are traditionally made of wood, painted, and handed down for many generations. Whereas there are only five basic types of mask (aged, male, female, deities, and monsters), there are many variations within these types. Pictured is a mask for the female character in *The Shrine in the Fields*.

Fedor Selivanov/Shutterstock.com

Traditionally, a program is made up of one play of each type performed in the order given here. These make up a pattern that shows, in the first play, the innocence and peace of the world of the gods; then, in the next series of three plays, the fall, repentance, and possibility of redemption for human beings; and finally, the glory of defeating the forces that stand in the way of peace and harmony.

Each Noh script is short (often shorter than a Western one-act play) and does not emphasize storytelling. The dialogue serves primarily to outline the circumstances that lead up to, and culminate in, a dance. Above all, Noh is a musical dance-drama that evokes an emotional state and mood. Most of the lines (written partly in verse and partly in prose) are sung or intoned. Even the brief spoken passages are recited in a stylized manner. Ordinary speech is used only when a player comes on stage between the parts of a two-part piece to summarize the first part.

The performers can be divided into three groups: actors, chorus, and musicians. The actors are trained from childhood and expect to devote twenty or more years to perfecting their craft. The five hereditary schools of Noh performance have handed down their traditions and conventions since the fifteenth century. There are two divisions of actors: those who play the secondary character, the *waki*, and the *waki*'s followers (whose function is to introduce the drama and lead the main character toward the climactic moment), and those who play the *shite*, the main character, and his or her followers. Two other types of actors also appear in Noh: *kyogen*, actors whose primary skill is in performing the short comic plays that are presented on the same bill with Noh plays but who appear in Noh in the role of commoners, peasants, and narrators; and *kokata*, child actors who, as students, play children or minor roles.

The chorus is composed of from six to ten members (each play specifies the number to be used in that play). They sit at one side of the stage throughout and sing or recite many of the *shite*'s lines (especially while the *shite* is dancing) or narrate events. Each play requires two or three drummers and one flute player. No other instruments are ever used. The drummers, in addition to playing their instruments, punctuate the performance with a variety of vocal sounds. There are two stage attendants, whom the audience is supposed to ignore—one to assist the musicians, the other to assist the actors in changing or adjusting costumes or masks and to bring on or remove stage properties as needed. All of the performers and assistants are male.

The *shite* and his companions wear masks of painted wood, many of them passed down for generations. Costumes are rich in color and design, based on the official dress of the fourteenth and fifteenth centuries. Most garments are made of elaborately embroidered silk. Each character has its traditional costume, headdress, hand properties, and positions on stage. The chorus, musicians, and attendants wear stiff shoulder boards and divided skirts, the traditional dress of the samurai.

Masked performer of the Noh Theatre accompanied by musicians. The performer is Kanze Kiyokaze, headmaster of the Kanze Noh School, which traces its roots back to Noh's founder Kan'ami. He is performing at Tokyo's National Noh Theatre in the main role of an old man in Zeami's *Akoyanomatsu*.

The Yomiuri Shimbun via AP Images

The Noh stage, standardized for almost four hundred years, is raised about three feet. The two principal areas, the stage proper (*butai*) and bridge (*hashigakari*), are both roofed like the shrines from which they are descended. Four pillars, each with its own name and use, support the roof of the *butai*. By the upstage-right pillar (*shitebashira*, or principal character's pillar), the actor pauses upon entering to tell the character's name and background. While reciting this speech, the actor faces the downstage-right pillar (*metsukebashira*, or gazing pillar). The downstage-left pillar (*wakibashira*) marks the place where the *waki* sits when not directly involved in the action. The upstage-left pillar (*fuebashira*, or flute pillar) marks the flute player's position.

The stage is divided into three areas, although none is separated architecturally, except by the pillars (see photo). The largest area, the main stage, is enclosed by the four pillars and is about eighteen feet square. Back of the upstage pillars is the rear stage (*atoza*), where the musicians and attendants sit. To stage left of the main stage is the *waki-za*, where the chorus kneels on the floor in two rows.

There are two entrances to the stage. The principal one, the bridge, is a railed walkway about six feet wide and forty feet long leading from the mirror room, where the actors prepare for their entrances. In front of the bridge three live pine trees symbolize heaven, earth, and humanity. The bridge is used as an entrance for the musicians and for all important characters. The other entrance, the "slit," or "cut-through," door (only about three feet high and located upstage left) is used by the chorus and the stage assistants. The rear walls of the stage and bridge are made of wood. Painted on the wall behind the orchestra is a pine tree and on the stage-left wall, bamboo, reminders of the natural scenery that formed the background in the earliest years of Noh. There is

A Noh stage. At left, the bridge; at center rear, the pine tree painted on the back wall; at right, the *waki-za* (the area used by the chorus). The four upright pillars define the principal acting area. Notice the temple roof above the stage.

Hulton Archive/Getty Images

no other scenery in the Noh theatre. A few stage properties are used, usually miniature skeletal outlines of boats, huts, shrines, and the like, typically made of bamboo. These are set in place and removed as needed by the stage attendant.

The audience views the performance from two sides: in front of the main stage and facing the stage from alongside the bridge. The theatres used today hold three hundred to five hundred people. Although they are now indoor structures, they retain many outdoor features: The shrine-like roof of the stage is retained in its entirety under the ceiling of the auditorium, and lighting simulates the even distribution of outdoor light.

Every element of performance is strictly controlled by conventions that have been established for centuries. Rather than encouraging innovation, Noh seeks to perfect and preserve an art form. Let us look more closely at a Noh play, *The Shrine in the Fields* (c. 1400).

THE SHRINE IN THE FIELDS (NONOMIYA)

The Shrine in the Fields (*Nonomiya*) is usually attributed to Zeami. It belongs to the third category (woman play) and is based on episodes from one of the most famous of Japanese novels, *The Tale of Genji* (c. 1021). In the novel, Lord Genji is the lover of Lady Rokujo (she is called Miyasudokoro in the play) but after a time neglects her. During a festival, attendants of Lord Genji's wife publicly humiliate Lady Rokujo when they push her carriage out of the procession and disable it. Humiliated, she decides to leave the capital and go to Nonomiya, where her daughter is being prepared to become the priestess of Ise, the sun goddess. While at Nonomiya, Lady Rukujo is visited by Lord Genji, who brings her a branch of *sakaki* (a sacred evergreen tree) as a sign of his trustworthiness and begs her to return with him.

Shrine gate   Straw hut

Retreat   Grave mound   Large board hut

Well curb with *susuki*   Plum tree stand   Carriage

© Cengage Learning 2014

Pictured here are some standard Noh stage properties. In contrast to western theatre's frequent emphasis on illusionism, Noh theatre relies on simplicity and suggestion.

Although she does not, she is forever after tormented by her humiliation and sense of loss. Lord Genji's visit and Lady Rokujo's response to it are the emotional focus of *The Shrine in the Fields*.

Each Noh play is set in a specific season of the year, named early in the drama, and the mood and imagery of the entire play must be in keeping with that season. In *The Shrine in the Fields* the time is late autumn, the seventh day of the ninth month, the day on which Lord Genji visited Lady Rokujo at Nonomiya. The mood throughout is one of melancholy and bittersweet longing.

As is typical in Noh drama, the introductory scene compresses time and place: An itinerant priest (the *waki* or secondary character) travels—almost instantaneously—from the capital to Nonomiya, where his curiosity is aroused by the seemingly perfect preservation of the shrine although it has long been abandoned. When the ghost of Miyasudokoro (the *shite*) appears in the guise of a village girl, he questions her about the shrine and herself, and gradually it becomes apparent that there is something mysterious about both her and the place. The first portion of the play occurs at dusk, and when the moon (a symbol of Buddha) appears, she vanishes and then returns dressed as the Miyasudokoro of long ago, having changed both mask and costume. As she recalls the festival at which she was publicly disgraced, her emotion builds, and she prays that the attachments that forever draw her back to this place will leave her.

As in all Noh plays, the climactic moment is expressed in dance. The script does little to indicate the length of the dance, which continues in performance for several minutes. In this final portion of the play, the conflicting attractions of this world and the next are symbolized by the ghost's passing back and forth through the gate of the shrine. At the end, the freeing of her soul is indicated by her departure from the "burning house," a metaphor for the world. In Buddhist teaching, enlightened persons are counseled to leave the world as willingly as they would flee a burning building.

In Noh, a number of devices distance the spectator from the play. The language is stylized throughout; most of the passages are intoned or sung; the lines of dialogue are divided in ways that differ markedly from the practices typical of Western drama, so that a single thought may be divided between the *shite* and *waki* or between a character and the chorus; the *shite* sometimes speaks of himself or herself in the third person; and the chorus frequently speaks the lines of both the *waki* and the *shite*. In addition, numerous quotations from or allusions to earlier literary works are embedded in the text.

For *The Shrine in the Fields* the basic appearance of the stage is altered only by the addition of a stylized gate and brushwood fence, and the only property of any significance is the sprig of *sakaki* that Miyasudokoro places at the shrine gate (as Lord Genji had done long ago). During the performance the chorus are seated at stage left, while the musicians and stage attendants are seated at the rear; all are visible throughout, each becoming part of the visual picture.

The Shrine in the Fields does not seek to tell a story or to develop character so much as to capture a mood, to distill a powerful emotion, and to express an attitude about the physical world and human existence.

Other Traditional Japanese Theatre Forms

Japan developed two other traditional theatre forms: Bunraku and Kabuki. Bunraku, in which puppets represent the characters, came to prominence in the seventeenth century. The puppets went through many changes. Originally they were only heads with drapery representing the body; later, hands and feet and then movable eyes, movable eyebrows, and jointed and movable fingers were added. Eventually the puppets were doubled in size to their present height of three or four feet and elaborately costumed.

Three handlers, who are visible to the audience, operate each puppet. One handler manipulates

Puppet handlers work their craft in a Bunraku performance of *1,000 Cherry Trees* in Osaka, the city where Bunraku originated.

Michael S. Yamashita/Corbis

the head and right arm; a second, the left arm; and a third, the feet. A narrator, seated stage left on a platform with the *samisen* player, tells the story, speaks the dialogue, and expresses the feelings of each puppet. Musical accompaniment is provided by a *samisen* (a three-stringed instrument with a skin-covered base that can be both struck and plucked) and occasionally other instruments of lesser importance. The stage itself is long and shallow. Unlike Noh, Bunraku represents all locales scenically, and the scenery is changed as the action requires. Bunraku is probably the most complex puppet performance in the world.

The major writer of plays for Bunraku was Chikamatsu Monzaemon (1653–1724), Japan's greatest playwright. He wrote many kinds of plays but is best known for his five-act history plays and his three-act plays on contemporary life. He was admired above all for his plays about the double suicides of lovers, his sensitive characterizations, and beautiful language.

Kabuki, long the most popular of the traditional forms, also first appeared in the seventeenth century. More open to change than the other forms, it has borrowed many of its plays and conventions from Noh and Bunraku but has adapted them to its own needs. Originally, Kabuki

was performed on a stage resembling that used for Noh. But as time passed, it underwent many changes and today bears little resemblance to the Noh stage. The Kabuki stage is now framed by a proscenium opening about ninety feet wide but only about twenty feet high. The auditorium is correspondingly wide and shallow, with all seats facing the stage. A raised walkway (the *hanamichi*) connects the stage to the back of the auditorium. Most important entrances and exits are made along this walkway, and some major scenes are played there. Thus, some of the action occurs in the auditorium in the midst of the audience.

Unlike Noh, Kabuki uses a great deal of scenery, although the settings are not meant to be fully illusionistic. White floor mats are used to represent snow, blue mats to indicate water, and gray mats the ground. Relatively realistic buildings are depicted frequently, but the entry gates to houses are often removed by stage assistants when no longer needed. These and other conventions call attention to the fictional nature of the performance. Alterations to sets, changes of props, and adjustments to costumes are made in full view of the audience by stage attendants; by convention these stage attendants are treated as invisible.

The arrangement of a Kabuki theatre as shown in this c. 1745 color inked woodblock print.

Masanobu, Okumura/The Art Gallery Collection/Alamy

Most Kabuki plays are divided into several acts made up of loosely connected episodes that emphasize highly emotional incidents. The climactic moment in many scenes is reached in a highly stylized pose (the *mie*) struck and held by the principal character; the moment is often accompanied by the rhythmic pounding of wooden clappers. Actors in heroic or villainous roles are offered numerous opportunities to demonstrate their skill through these *mies*, which are greatly admired by Japanese audiences. The most popular Kabuki play is Takedo Izumo's *Chushingura* (1748), the eleven acts of which require a full day to perform. A play about honor and revenge, it tells how forty-seven faithful samurai avenge the wrongs done to their master.

Song and narration are important to Kabuki. Those plays adapted from Noh or Bunraku retain many conventions of the original forms. Therefore, in some plays a narrator or chorus performs some passages. Since the Kabuki actor never sings, passages that must be sung require a chorus. An orchestra, the composition of which varies according to the origin of the play, accompanies much of the action. The orchestra often includes flutes, drums, bells, gongs, cymbals, and strings, although the most essential instrument is the *samisen.*

Kabuki acting is a combination of stylized speaking and dancing. Almost all movement borders on dance, distilling the essence of emotions and action into stylized postures, gestures, and movements. Similarly, the spoken lines follow conventionalized patterns of intonation. Roles are divided into a small number of types: loyal, good, and courageous mature men; villains; young men; comic roles (including comic villains); children; and women. The female roles are called *onnagata*. All roles, including the *onnagata*, are played by males. Like Noh, actor training in Kabuki takes many years and is primarily a hereditary profession. Each family has an elaborate system of stage names, some of them so honored that they are awarded (in elaborate public ceremonies) to those considered undisputed masters of their art.

Kabuki actors do not wear masks, but some roles use boldly patterned makeup to exaggerate the musculature of face or body. Each role also has its traditional costumes, some so heavy (up to fifty pounds) that stage attendants must assist the actors in keeping them properly arranged.

Although Kabuki is highly conventionalized, it includes many elements that resemble, though in exaggerated form, Western usages, perhaps most notably in scenery and lighting, melodramatic stories, and emotional acting. Consequently, Kabuki is the Japanese form that appeals most to Westerners, and many modern

Japanese actor Ebizo Ichikawa XI performs as Spirit of the Wisteria in "Fuji Musume," a famous classic dance from Kabuki theatre. Ebizo Ichikawa XI is the heir apparent of a Kabuki dynasty stretching back thirteen generations.

Bruno Vincent/Getty Images

European and American directors have borrowed Kabuki conventions for productions of Greek and Shakespearean tragedies (perhaps most notably the Théâtre du Soleil in Paris). Westerners usually understand Japanese conventions only in a general way, and much of what they find attractive they have learned from the Kabuki-derived conventions used in Japanese films about samurai, especially those directed by Akira Kurosawa (1910–1998). Of all the Japanese forms, Noh remains the least understood in the West. Though some may not fully comprehend them, Japanese theatrical conventions serve as a reminder that the theatrical experience can vary widely from one culture to another and that the kinds of theatre with which one may be most familiar today do not exhaust theatre's immense and diverse range of possible forms.

Modern Japanese Theatre

By the late nineteenth century, some Japanese scholars, directors, and playwrights became interested in Western drama. It was probably most admired and studied in Japanese universities, where plays by Shakespeare, Ibsen, Shaw, Chekhov, Strindberg, and others were studied and sometimes performed. Japan's best-known playwrights who were influenced by Western forms include Kobo Abe (1924–1993) and Yukio Mishima (1925–1970); the latter also wrote Kabuki plays and modern Noh plays. Writing plays of the Western type has flourished in recent decades, and the Japan Playwrights Association has published a ten-volume anthology of plays in the Western style from the 1950s through 1990s. Some contemporary playwrights include Juro Kara, Minoru Betsuyaku, and Masakazu Yamazaki.

Among contemporary Japanese directors, the best known is Tadashi Suzuki, who established his own company, the Suzuki Company of Toga. There he developed a disciplined acting method that synthesized the martial arts, Kabuki, and Noh techniques. He staged several productions that were seen in the United States and Europe, some of them adaptations of Greek myths. Many American theatre departments have begun to offer training in the Suzuki method, described in his *The Way of Acting* (1993). In 1992, in collaboration with the American director Anne Bogart, he established the Saratoga (N.Y.) International Theatre Institute (SITI).

Practices & Styles

SANKAI JUKU *AND* BUTOH

Butoh is an avant-garde performance form that originated in Japan during the turbulent 1960s. In the 1960s, a new generation of Japanese struggled with the questions concerning conformity and social values even as the effects of radiation from the atomic blasts at Hiroshima and Nagasaki lingered. A rebellious dance drama or performance art response to these tensions, Butoh was initially often called *ankoku butoh* ("dance of darkness") because of its use of grotesque imagery and explicit sexuality to address the mystery of an existence precariously balanced between creation and self-destruction. In the late 1960s, Butoh became a rallying point for avant-garde artists in the ongoing underground countercultural movement in Japan.

Founded in 1975, Sankai Juku, a "second-generation" Butoh company led by Amagatsu Ushio, has achieved resounding international fame; they have performed around the world in over forty countries. The all-male company of performers, often dressed only in robes or *sarong*-like garments, use white rice powder to cover their shaven heads and near-nude bodies. Sankai Juku's Butoh performances use slow-motion, repetitive movement patterns, and selective isolations of body parts. These movements can be executed so slowly that, at times, it may seem as if the performers are statues. This intense stillness and the slow, ritualized movement patterns are juxtaposed by sharp movements, cries, and facial expressions that may convey intense pain, surprise, or ecstasy. The scene design for Sankai Juku performance often presents a stark landscape. This, in combination with evocative lighting, strange music, and the appearance and movements of the performers, conveys a surreal quality to the audience.

The work of Amagatsu Ushio and Sankai Juku expresses many of the typical tensions found in earlier Butoh, while surrounding them in a mood of calm and serene detachment suggestive of Zen Buddhism.

JOEL SAGET/AFP/Getty Images

Ushio Amagatsu's Japanese Butoh company, Sankai Juku, at a performance in Paris.

Yukio Ninagawa, another internationally famous Japanese director, has done many productions of Western and Japanese plays. He brought Mishima's modern Noh plays to Lincoln Center in 2005 and he has staged numerous Japanese versions of Shakespeare in England.

In the past twenty years Japan has built more than two dozen performance halls. Within Japan, contemporary entertainment forms are more popular than the traditional ones, but Japan is determined to support and maintain its dramatic heritage.

Theatre in China

Records of performance in Chinese territories can be traced back to 1767 B.C. After 1000 B.C. there are references to secular entertainments at court, and by 200 B.C. emperors were keeping thousands of entertainers at court who performed what was called the "hundred plays" because of the great diversity of the entertainments. One Chinese emperor established a school to train performers and, according to legend, at one time it included 11,409 students. However, a fully developed drama did not begin to emerge until about 1000 A.D. The first major period of Chinese drama came during the Yuan Dynasty (1279–1368), and about seven hundred titles of Yuan plays have survived. The most complex literary plays were written during the Ming Dynasty (1368–1644). Plays from this period might have as many as fifty or more acts, each with its own title. In the opening act, a secondary character sets forth the author's purpose and explains the story. Succeeding acts introduce many plot strands, all of which are happily resolved in the final scene. Probably the most admired play from the Ming Dynasty is *The Peony Pavilion* (c. 1600) written by Tang Xiansu (1550–1616). In fifty-five acts, it tells a story of a girl who pines her life away for a lover she has seen only in a dream. When he finally appears at her grave, she is resurrected. This play was presented in its entirety (for the first time anywhere) at Lincoln Center in New York in 1999. Although such plays were very popular with readers, they did little to vitalize the theatre.

It was not until the nineteenth century that what has come to be called Beijing Opera emerged as a dominant and truly theatrical form. Beijing Opera is a hybrid that evolved from several regional forms brought to Beijing in 1790 to celebrate the emperor's eightieth birthday. Many of these regional companies remained in Beijing and amalgamated with others to create the most widely known Chinese theatrical form—Beijing Opera. It is a theatrical rather than a literary form. Instead of a single work, an evening's performance is usually made up of a series of selections from longer works. These are intermingled with acrobatic displays. A text is merely an outline for a performance and the author is not even listed on the program. All the plays end happily, and each troupe has its own version of the plays they perform.

The traditional Chinese stage was an open platform, usually almost square, covered by a roof supported by lacquered columns. The stage was equipped only with a carpet, two doors

Beijing Opera performers wear elaborate costumes as shown here.

Tan Kian Khoon/Shutterstock.com

in the rear wall (the one on stage right for all entrances and that on stage left for all exits) between which hung a large embroidered curtain. In the beginning, the theatre was based on the layout of teahouses, but in the twentieth century Western-style auditoriums became the standard. The only permanent properties were a wooden table and a few chairs that could be rearranged quickly to indicate a change in place or function. Other conventions include using a wall painted on a blue cloth to represent a fort, city gate, or mountain pass; a whip indicating that the actor is riding a horse; and many others that are recognized immediately by the audience. Through such conventions, many places and actions are indicated. Throughout the performance, assistants help the actors with their costumes and rearrange the stage as needed. The audience is expected to ignore these stagehands. The musicians also remain in full view and play a strong role in all performances.

On the relatively bare stage, the actors appear in lavish and colorful costumes and speak, sing, and move according to rigid conventions. In Beijing Opera, the roles are divided into four main types: male, female, painted face, and comic. The male roles (*sheng*) are subdivided into old men (*lao sheng*), young men (*xiao sheng*), and warrior types (*wu sheng*). Actors playing these roles wear simple makeup and (except for young heroes) beards. Female roles (*dan*) are subdivided into the quiet and gentle (*qing yi*), the vivacious or dissolute (*hua dan*), warrior maidens (*wu dan*), and old women (*lao dan*). The painted face actors (*jing*) have brilliant and elaborate patterns painted on their faces. They include warriors, bandits, courtiers, officials, gods, and other supernatural beings. The comic actors (*chou*) speak an everyday dialect and are free to improvise and tell jokes. They wear white makeup around their eyes and combine the skills of a mime and an acrobat. Except for the clowns, characters render their lines in an extremely stylized manner.

Movement is also highly stylized, and gestures have been fully codified. Methods of walking or running vary with each role. There are about three hundred standard costume items, each intended to describe its wearer's character type, age, and social status through color, design, ornament, and accessories. The complex conventions of Beijing Opera require long and rigorous training, which lasts from six to twelve years. Eventually training becomes very specialized as teachers decide which kind of role the student should master.

The Chinese government spent over $400 million to complete its titanium and glass-covered Grand National Theatre in Beijing. The structure, which is said to resemble a giant egg floating on a shallow man-made lake, is entered through an underwater transparent walkway connected to the shore.

After the Communists assumed control in China in 1949, Beijing Opera was subjected to reform and many plays were forbidden. Not until the 1980s and the rejection of the "Cultural Revolution" were traditional plays performed once more; in many instances they were revised to fit the Communist ideal.

During the twentieth century, Western drama came to be admired by many in China but it never became a major force. The most important of the playwrights who were influenced by Western writers was Cao Yu (1910–1996), who wrote about contemporary social problems in *Thunderstorm* (1933) and *The Bridge* (1945). A number of Chinese directors and playwrights have achieved recognition within China since 1949. Prominent directors of spoken drama include Ming Jinghui and Lin Zhaohua, while notable playwrights include Wu Han, Zong Fuxian, Lao She, and Sun Huizhu. In addition, Gao Xingjian won acclaim in China and then internationally. He writes more in the vein of absurdism and the avant-garde, traits seen in works such as *Bus Stop* (1983) and *The Other Shore* (1986); the latter was highly critical of the Communist government and led to Xingjian emigrating to France where he won the Nobel Prize for Literature in 2000.

China has also begun to build major theatrical complexes similar to those in the West. Opened in 1998, the Grand Theatre in Shanghai cost about $150 million and includes a main auditorium seating 1800 and two smaller halls (seating six hundred and two hundred). It is one of Asia's most advanced theatrical structures. In the large auditorium, the main stage, rear stage, and two side stages can be rotated, raised, or lowered; its orchestra pit accommodates one hunderd and twenty instrumentalists. Opened in 2007, the Grand National Theatre in Beijing cost over $400 million. The egg-shaped building, four hunderd and thirty feet long and one hundred and thirty-five feet high, includes an opera house, a concert hall, and a theatre. It will be interesting to see how these new buildings affect theatrical production in China.

Other Asian Countries

There are many other countries in Asia, each with its own performance traditions, but Japan and China are the best known for their theatrical forms. In India a wide variety of entertainments can be traced back at least two thousand years, and between the first and ninth centuries A.D. drama written in Sanskrit reached an advanced stage before it declined. A number of plays have survived from that period and are available for study. Under British rule from the eighteenth to the twentieth century, India produced diverse types of plays too numerous to trace in detail. The number of languages that are still common in India makes for varied dramatic forms, each of which tends to be popular in specific parts of India.

Other parts of Southeast Asia are noted especially for their work with puppets. For several centuries much of Southeast Asia has been dominated by Muslim standards, which discourages drama being performed by human actors. But where human performance has been frowned on, performance using puppets has been more easily accepted. Puppetry has flourished in many parts of Southeast Asia, and shadow puppetry has been particularly popular in Indonesia.

Wayang Kulit

One of the most distinctive forms of Asian theatre is performed via shadow puppets. In Indonesia shadow puppetry is called *wayang kulit*. It uses flat puppets, ranging from six inches to three feet in size, made of leather (traditionally from the hide of water buffalo). The puppets are cut and perforated to create intricate patterns of light and shadow when their images are cast onto the screen. The performances of *wayang kulit* enact dramas based on particular sections of the great Hindu epics the *Mahabharata* (c. fourth century B.C.) and the *Ramayana* (c. fifth or fourth century B.C.). In most places this form of theatre maintains a spiritual aspect and the puppeteer, called a *dalang*, is not only a performance artist but also a spiritual figure. The *dalang* sits between a light source (traditionally a torch or hanging oil lamp) and the screen. The closer the *dalang* moves the puppet toward the screen, the more clearly the shadow of its outline appears. The entire performance is accompanied by a *gamelan*, a gong-chime musical ensemble composed of different types of xylophones, percussion and stringed instruments, flute, and singers.

All the puppets used during a single performance (usually no more than fifty) are manipulated by a single *dalang* who delivers the dialogue (much of it improvised) and narrative passages, sings songs, and inflectionally cues the musicians. It requires great vocal flexibility to suggest so many different characters in a single performance and a strong command of the story and all its characters. In some traditional performances, the *dalang* holds a small wooden striker between his toes and calls forth the character's spirit into the puppet by knocking on the box or stand holding the puppets. This procedure is sometimes referred to as "waking" the puppets

and it may last several seconds or several minutes. Characters are differentiated by the size, shape, costume, and color of the puppets as well as by the quantity and arrangement of their perforations. Typically, the amount of perforations made to the puppet suggests its status; low-class characters have very few perforations, while gods have many. In performance, puppets with numerous perforations seem to flicker into corporeal existence as the *dalang* brings them into the action.

Traditional *wayang kulit* performances last from around 8:30 P.M. until sunrise. The different parts of the action relate to the passing hours. First, a problem or situation is established followed by an intrigue, usually in the stronghold of the hero's enemies. Then, the hero appears accompanied by clownish servants (this phase of the action usually takes place around midnight). The action reaches its crisis in a battle fought by the hero against powerful enemies. Finally, the conflict is resolved and ends in the triumph of the hero over the forces of evil (as the dawn overcomes the night).

Because Asia's cultural sensibility honors tradition, Asian theatre forms have proven less susceptible to change over time than those in America and Europe. However, there remains considerable diversity in Asian theatrical forms.

Pictured are two puppets used in *wayang kulit* performances. The more intricately perforated puppet is the god Vishnu. Note the differences between this puppet and the other, which represents an earthy comic figure.

Courtesy of Robert Ball

Theatre in Africa

Europeans and Americans remained largely ignorant of African performance traditions until the twentieth century. Nevertheless, African performance activities had through the centuries been numerous—religious rituals, festivals, ceremonies, storytelling, and various kinds of celebrations—and had been woven into daily life. These varied widely from one part of Africa to another. When Europeans took control of most of the continent, they brought their own ideas about theatre and tried to establish them there. The presence of the colonialist heritage and indigenous forms created a wide spectrum of performance in Africa. Nevertheless, it is difficult to generalize about theatre in Africa because there are more than eight hundred local languages in use, and local traditions do not always travel well from one part of Africa to another.

During the late nineteenth century, European countries, acting on agreements reached in international conferences, divided up most of Africa among themselves and thereafter sought to impose their languages, governmental forms, and ideas about effective theatre practices on the territories they controlled. Nevertheless, indigenous forms and performance conditions persisted alongside the European forms that were imported. Because little was recorded about the native traditions prior to the twentieth century, Europe and America's knowledge of African theatre has remained limited.

European observers tended to emphasize the linguistic elements of indigenous performances, even though those aspects were often the least important. In contrast, in traditional African performances, "languages" other than words, especially drumming and dance, often communicated more to African audiences than words did. Additional important "languages" include

Society, Art & Culture

AFRICA IN FOUR QUESTIONS

Take a quiz to test your knowledge of Africa in four quick questions—the answers are included below.

1. How big is Africa?
2. How many people live in Africa?
3. What percentage of Africa's population depends on agriculture for its living?
4. What is the most common cause of death in Africa today?

1. Africa contains over 20 percent of the world's land mass—1,700,000 square miles (roughly three times the size of the United States).
2. Approximately 1 billion people live on the African continent or about 14 percent of the world's population. More than 70 percent of Africa's population is under the age of twenty-five.
3. Approximately 65 percent of Africa's population makes their living from agriculture. However, nearly 50 percent of all Africans live on less than $1 a day.
4. AIDS; AIDS has hit strongest in sub-Saharan Africa where the average life expectancy is 46, compared to 68 in North Africa.

visual imagery, symbolism, gesture, mask, and costume. African performances had traditionally occurred in spatial arrangements quite different from those of European theatres, but the Europeans usually sought to impose the proscenium arch stage on African performances. In traditional African performances, direct audience participation was usually expected. It was accepted that the dancing, music, and song would induce such communal responses as clapping in rhythm, singing refrains, repeating phrases, or making comments. Dancing and music were important elements in most indigenous performances.

It would be impossible to treat theatrical performance in every country on the African continent, since there are close to fifty states. Those in North Africa are dominated by Arab languages and customs; those south of the Sahara Desert are highly diverse. In addition to indigenous languages, much of today's theatre in Africa uses English, French, or Portuguese, depending upon which European country occupied and imposed its

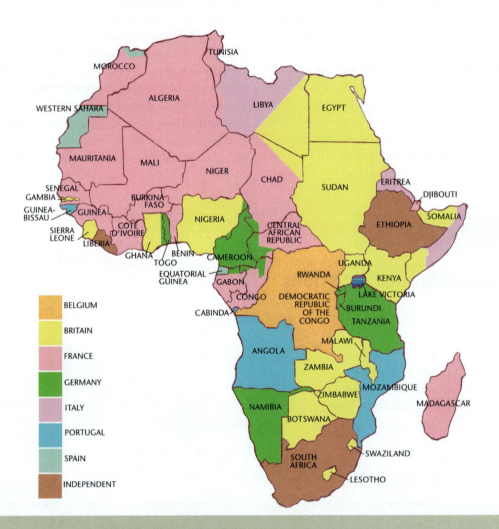

Melissa Gaspar

Africa: Its Colonial Past and Present-Day Countries. Color areas illustrate European colonization and control of Africa up to 1914 (see color key provided). Names of current African nations and their borders are designated in black. Most African countries did not gain independence until the 1960s, and the lingering effects of European colonization continue to affect Africa to the present day.

demands on the native populations. Most countries still have been unable to rid themselves of their colonial past, though many attempt to do so.

Performance in Nigeria

In looking at contemporary conditions, we have chosen to begin with Nigeria, the most populous African country, as well as one diverse in language groups and performance conditions. It includes more than two hundred fifty ethnic groups, of which the most important are the Hausa, Yoruba, Ibo, and Fulani. Public performance has long been important as a medium of expression and communication, and different types of performance are given throughout the country and throughout the year. One of the major Yoruba festivals was (and is) the *egungun*, in which sacrifices were offered and petitions for blessing and prosperity were addressed to the dead. A "carrier" was selected to gather up the accumulated evil of the community and carry it away in a canoe. Some aspects of this ceremony are still common in Nigeria.

The most popular contemporary theatrical form in Nigeria is Yoruba opera (now usually called Yoruba Traveling Theatre). It was developed primarily by Hubert Ogunde, who in 1946 established a professional company (the first in modern Nigeria) with which he toured thereafter. The form consisted of an opening glee (or rousing musical number), followed by a topical and satirical story with dialogue, songs, and dances, ending with another glee. The emphasis was on entertainment but there was always a clear moral message. Ogunde created some thirty-eight operas. His company was tremendously popular and imitated. By 1981 there were some one hundred twenty Yoruba companies. Since then, they have increasingly turned to television, films, and videos, so much so that live performances have greatly declined. (The Yoruba Traveling Theatre is very similar to the Concert Parties in its neighboring country, Ghana.)

English language plays also became common from around 1900 and drama was introduced into the schools founded by the English colonial government or by religious organizations that were seeking to convert Nigerians to Christianity. English-language theatre flourished, especially after 1960, when Nigeria was granted independence. Some of the country's major playwrights include John Pepper Clark, Ola Rotimi (1938–2000), and Femi Osofisan. But the dominant playwright has been Wole Soyinka, especially since 1986 when he became the first African to be awarded the

Courtesy of Eckhard Breitinger

Aspects of the colonial past sometimes appear in contemporary African drama and theatre. Here, in *Guest of Honor*, the associations between the past and present form a political statement as the Head Waiter (Alex Muluku) welcomes the audience to his Africa.

Society, Art & Culture

IN WHAT LANGUAGE SHOULD WE WRITE?

One of the most controversial questions in Africa today concerns the language in which plays should be written or performed. Because so many tribal languages are spoken by the various groups within each country, the language of the former colonial power (most commonly English or French) is the only one shared (though not always fully understood) by all the groups. Consequently, much of the drama is written in European rather than African languages. One powerful movement insists that native languages should always be used if Africa is ever to escape its colonial past.

> The moment you write in English you assume a readership who can speak and read English, and in this case it can only mean the educated African elite or the foreigners who speak the language. This means that you are precluding in terms of class the peasantry or the workers in Africa who do not read or understand these foreign languages.

> — Ngugi wa Thiong'o, Interview in *"Mother Sing for Me,"* by Ingrid Bjorkman (London, 1989) 3.

Courtesy of Eckhard Breitinger

"Woyigira" Mujama (the "Dirty Man" Reformed) as performed by Uganda's Katanga Theatre Group, Kampala, Uganda.

Nobel Prize for Literature. This has not kept him from being punished by a government that has imprisoned him and threatened him with death for his opposition to certain government policies. After 1994, Soyinka largely gave up writing plays to devote his time to human rights activities. One of his most recent plays, *King Baabu* (2001), premiered at the National Arts Theatre in Lagos. *King Baabu* is an adaptation of Alfred Jarry's grotesque comedy *Ubu Roi* (1896) and takes satirical aim at African dictators who have sacrificed their people to enrich themselves. Among his other plays are *The Lion and the Jewel* (1959), *A Dance of the Forests* (1960), *Madmen and Specialists* (1970),

and *Death and the King's Horseman* (1975). Let us look at one of his plays, *The Strong Breed* (1964).

THE STRONG BREED

The dramatic and staging conventions used in *The Strong Breed* are much the same as those found in European and American theatres. Consequently, there are few uses that seem strange to an American reader. The difference from European and American drama lies primarily in the subject matter and its treatment, which strongly reflects the *egungun* traditions, but placed in a modern context. In *The Strong Breed*, the dramatic action focuses on a ritual that can be found in many societies throughout time—the selection and expulsion of a scapegoat who will take all the problems of the village on himself and carry them away. Eman, a new resident of the village, mistakenly believes that the ritual is observed here as it was in his own community, where a carrier willingly allows the troubles and cares of the village to be loaded onto a symbolic vessel and placed on his head so he can carry it down the river and thereby cleanse the community, making way for happiness and prosperity in the new year. This ritual is of primary importance to the residents of this village and most of the play is devoted to making certain that a carrier can be found to take the village's troubles before a new year begins. In the village Eman has left, the carrier was honored for his strength, courage, and wisdom. However, in the village to which Eman has recently come, the carrier himself becomes the object of loathing and is driven from the village permanently. Consequently, only outsiders are chosen as carriers; they are drugged and hypnotized so they appear happy to receive the beatings, curses, and other forms of abuse heaped upon them.

It is never made clear why Sunma, who seems to be in love with Eman, does not tell him of the difference in customs here, not even when a girl dragging an effigy appears and lures a simpleton into the bush where he can be captured and prepared for the ritual. Eman is so unsuspecting that he even gives the girl one of his garments to put on the effigy. In the action that follows, through a series of flashbacks, we learn that Eman is a descendant of a long line of carriers (the strong breed) and that he has left his own village because he had been devastated when his wife died in childbirth. As in Greek tragedy, Eman finds that he cannot escape his destiny—to be a carrier. Beginning to understand the situation in which he has placed himself, he tries to escape from the villagers but they become increasingly desperate

as midnight approaches and they have no one to carry away the year's burdens. In their panic, the villagers kill Eman but when they realize what they have done, most are filled with shame. They begin to doubt the traditions they have been taught and turn away from their leaders. Change seems to lie ahead though it comes too late for Eman.

The Strong Breed develops a number of themes common in Soyinka's plays: the need to balance the traditional and the modern; the habit of following custom and mistaken beliefs unquestioningly; and the special individual, who through dedication and vision awakens the people and leads them toward better ways, even though he may become a victim of the society he seeks to benefit. Soyinka's plays form a bridge between traditional and contemporary performance.

South Africa

The indigenous peoples of South Africa are Khoisans, Zulus, Basutos, Xhosas, Swazi Ndebeles, Pondos, and other smaller groups (several of which are often grouped together as Bantus). Europeans began to covet South Africa during the seventeenth century. Around 1650 the Netherlands began to encourage Dutch immigrants to settle there. By 1815 the English also began to gain control over much of the territory and thereafter there was a struggle between the Dutch, the English, and native groups. The discovery of diamonds in 1867 and gold in 1886 led to the Boer Wars, which by 1902 the English had decisively won. By the 1880s, most of the native peoples were confined to territories not unlike the reservations the United States government set aside for Native Americans. The English and Afrikaaners (mostly descendants of northwestern Europeans) eventually joined in 1910 to form the Union of South Africa. The government drew increasing international criticism after 1950 when it established the doctrine of apartheid (the Afrikaans word for "apartness"), a law requiring separate white and nonwhite residential areas. As a result, South Africa essentially became a police state for blacks wherein much of the black population was moved into townships, best described as shantytowns. They could work in cities but could not live there. In 1990, the government agreed to start dismantling apartheid, and in 1994, the country's first democratic elections led to Nelson Mandela, a black lawyer, becoming president. The process of democratizing South Africa continues with Jacob Zuma as its current president.

During apartheid, several groups in South Africa wrote and produced plays that attacked the injustices of apartheid laws and the ways in which various groups were unjustly treated. Perhaps the most influential playwright and performer to come out of Afrikaans theatre is Pieter-Dirk Uys. In addition to writing plays, he performed as a satirical drag character, Evita Bezuidenhout, who highlighted the ridiculousness of apartheid. Other Afrikaaner playwrights included Bartho Smit (1924–1986) and Adam Small. Black African writers and performers who attained popularity during apartheid included Gibson Kente (1932–2004), Mbogeni Ngema, Maishe Maponya, and Matsemala Manaka, all of whom have become very popular in South Africa and in several other countries.

The most famous South African dramatist is Athol Fugard. He has been writing about South African issues since 1959. His autobiographical play *Master Harold and the Boys* (1982) dramatizes how the once close relationship between Harold, the son of a tearoom's owner, and the establishment's black head waiter is destroyed by the racial arrogance and privilege taught to Harold. Some of Fugard's other plays include *The Blood Knot* (1961), *Sizwe Bansi is Dead* (1975, cowritten with John Kani and Winston Ntshona), *The Road to Mecca* (1984), *My Children! My Africa!* (1989), and *Sorrows and Rejoicings* (2001), which evaluates post-apartheid South Africa. The film version of Fugard's novel *Tsotsi* (1980), which treats the relationship between poverty and gang activity in the former townships, won the Academy Award for Best Foreign Film in 2006. In 2011, Fugard won a Special Tony Award for Lifetime Achievement in Theatre.

Pitcho Womba Konga, Congolese creator and promoter of hip-hop culture (L), and Mali actor and writer Habib Dembele (R) perform in *Sizwe Bansi Is Dead* by Athol Fugard, John Kani, and Winston Ntshona in a production directed by Peter Brooks and performed during the sixtieth Avignon International Theatre Festival.

Society, Art & Culture

THEATRE OF THE STRUGGLE

In 1976 the Market Theatre, cofounded by Barney Simon (1932–1995), began performing plays in a former produce market in Johannesburg. It became known throughout the world as South Africa's "Theatre of the Struggle." The struggle was against the racist policies of South Africa's apartheid government.

Although there were other theatres using their stages to produce anti-apartheid plays, the Market Theatre was one of the first to circumvent a 1965 law that forbade racially mixed casts and audiences. When the Market Theatre drew the attention of South Africa's security police, its producers reminded police of an obscure law; buildings open to all races prior to segregation were allowed to remain so as long as their exterior had not been altered. Because the market had been open to all and the exterior of its 1912 building had never been altered, it was allowed to remain desegregated. At a time when South African blacks and whites could not live on the same street and socialization with one another was frowned on, the Market Theatre staged Shakespeare's *Othello* with an interracial cast. Still, black artists risked arrest whenever they broke governmentally mandated curfews (for blacks) to attend rehearsals or performances. Among the plays premiered at the Market Theatre were Percy Mtwa's *Bopha* (1986), in which a black policeman charged with upholding the apartheid laws must deal with his activist son, and Percy Mtwa, Mbongeni Ngema, and Barney Simon's *Woza Albert!* (1981), which dramatizes how Jesus might respond if he returned to apartheid South Africa and how the government might respond to him.

Since the end of apartheid, the Market Theatre has become a sprawling center for the arts. This has revived old criticisms leveled at the theatre by some South Africans. The Market Theatre's location in the center of urban Johannesburg separated it from the townships, and its close relationship to the Johannesburg City Council seemed to some as if the theatre was collaborating with the very forces those on its stages were decrying. The Market Theatre has been awarded considerable financial assistance to develop its facilities, while all-black theatres with fewer resources have had to fend for themselves. However, few deny that the theatre played an important role in the struggle against apartheid. In 2006 the Market Theatre celebrated its thirty-year anniversary by remounting its 1984 production of Barney Simon's *Black Dog*, a gripping and controversial anti-apartheid play.

The abolishment of apartheid left South Africa with many challenges, among them the role of the arts in a culture that had long been split along racial lines. Apartheid had established a duality of culture; European theatrical traditions mainly practiced in state-supported institutions within white urban areas, and indigenous and highly political theatre practiced in rural areas and the townships. Although the post-apartheid government developed policies to transform its former cultural institutions on a national level, many claim that the agencies responsible for implementing these policies lack sufficient funding, experience, and political will to do so. Matters came to a head when, in 2004, the Minister of Arts and Culture dissolved the board of the National Arts Council (NAC)—the head agency overseeing the transformation process. For its part, the NAC has claimed that some of the nine regional provinces have failed to establish funding mechanisms envisioned in the national arts policy. Since then the National Arts Council has been reorganized, but critic Robert Greig's questions concerning the problem remain: "Is the National Arts Council propping up provinces that can't get their act together and fund artists who live there? Or, by contrast, is it funding rich, urbanized provinces to the detriment of artists everywhere?" Although the South African government has built centers for the arts in cities, such as Johannesburg, some claim that these state-funded theatres support a conservative approach to the arts, offer only token support for indigenous performance, and fail to support innovative works that grapple with the economic, social, and political challenges most South Africans face.

Still, the role of theatre as a powerful force to unite the divisions in South Africa's culture seems undeniable. This potential is seen in the Grahamstown Festival, an annual showcase of the best theatre productions from all over the country, where approximately five hundred theatre events are presented.

North Africa

As we have seen, ancient Egyptian rituals were among the earliest performance modes that we know about. Subsequently, the areas across North Africa bordering onto the Mediterranean became well known as active areas for theatrical entertainments in the Hellenistic and Roman eras. Then, in the seventh and eighth centuries, Muslim influence spread throughout North Africa and gradually Arabic became the accepted language and Islam the official religion. Because these cultures disliked theatrical performance, it was not until the nineteenth century (when Egypt was under English domination) that theatrical companies began to appear. After 1870, European-style productions began to be

available. Singing and dancing were the most important elements and all roles were played by men.

Tawfig al-Hakim (1898–1987), who wrote some eighty plays, was among the most important Egyptian dramatists of the early twentieth century. His *The People in the Cave* (1933) was the opening production of the Egyptian National Theatre in 1935. In the late 1960s, the popularity of theatre gradually was replaced by film and television, of which Egypt is the primary supplier to the Arabic world. Since 1990, Egypt has promoted the annual Cairo International Festival of Experimental Theatre.

Other North African countries (among them Morocco, Algeria, and Tunisia) came under the domination of France and French theatre. Morocco and Tunisia regained independence in 1956; both have since founded national theatres, and their playwrights have for the most part tried to create an Arab form of drama. None of these North African theatres has gained a strong reputation.

Other African Countries

Other African countries with extensively developed performance traditions include Ghana, Tanzania, Uganda, Kenya, Togo, Sudan, Ethiopia, Sierra Leone, Senegal, Mali, and the Ivory Coast. Unfortunately we can not discuss each of these. African theatre is still handicapped by its colonialist heritage. Rather than judging it by European and American practices, it would probably be best to admire its broad range of theatrical activities, most of which, considering the enormous number of ethnic and linguistic divisions within Africa, understandably appeal to limited and local but often enthusiastic audiences.

THEATRE IN A BROAD CONTEXT

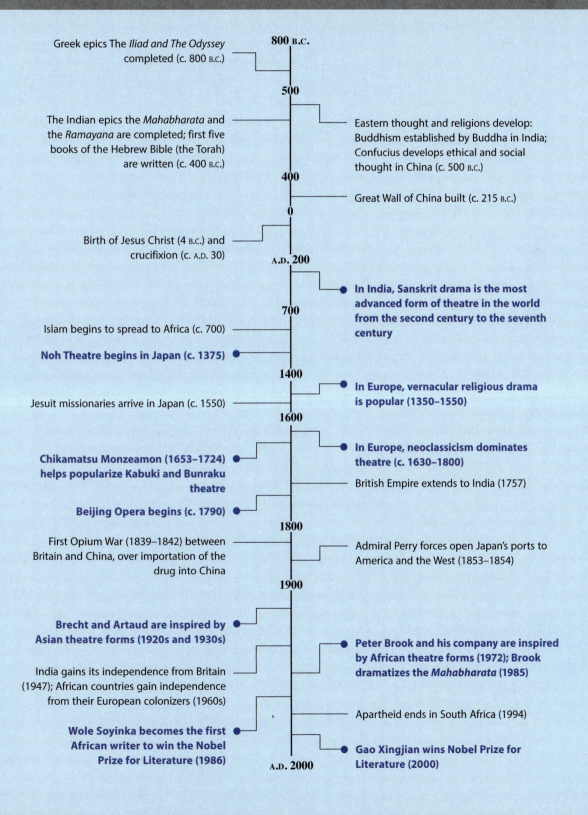

Greek epics The *Iliad* and *The Odyssey* completed (c. 800 B.C.)

800 B.C.

500

The Indian epics the *Mahabharata* and the *Ramayana* are completed; first five books of the Hebrew Bible (the Torah) are written (c. 400 B.C.)

Eastern thought and religions develop: Buddhism established by Buddha in India; Confucius develops ethical and social thought in China (c. 500 B.C.)

400

Great Wall of China built (c. 215 B.C.)

0

Birth of Jesus Christ (4 B.C.) and crucifixion (c. A.D. 30)

A.D. 200

In India, Sanskrit drama is the most advanced form of theatre in the world from the second century to the seventh century

700

Islam begins to spread to Africa (c. 700)

Noh Theatre begins in Japan (c. 1375)

1400

Jesuit missionaries arrive in Japan (c. 1550)

In Europe, vernacular religious drama is popular (1350–1550)

1600

Chikamatsu Monzeamon (1653–1724) helps popularize Kabuki and Bunraku theatre

In Europe, neoclassicism dominates theatre (c. 1630–1800)

British Empire extends to India (1757)

Beijing Opera begins (c. 1790)

1800

First Opium War (1839–1842) between Britain and China, over importation of the drug into China

Admiral Perry forces open Japan's ports to America and the West (1853–1854)

1900

Brecht and Artaud are inspired by Asian theatre forms (1920s and 1930s)

Peter Brook and his company are inspired by African theatre forms (1972); Brook dramatizes the *Mahabharata* (1985)

India gains its independence from Britain (1947); African countries gain independence from their European colonizers (1960s)

Apartheid ends in South Africa (1994)

Wole Soyinka becomes the first African writer to win the Nobel Prize for Literature (1986)

Gao Xingjian wins Nobel Prize for Literature (2000)

A.D. 2000

Epilogue to Part 2

In Part 2, we have looked at several varieties of theatrical experience. Although those we have examined are important, they do not exhaust the possibilities. Several others from the theatre's long past might justifiably have been selected for study.

The theatre is always in flux. It seems likely that the versions with which we are now familiar will change as conditions alter. We can only speculate about what these alterations will be, although we can be sure they will come. Changes are not always welcome, but they are necessary because theatre can remain vital only by reflecting the dynamics of the culture within which it exists.

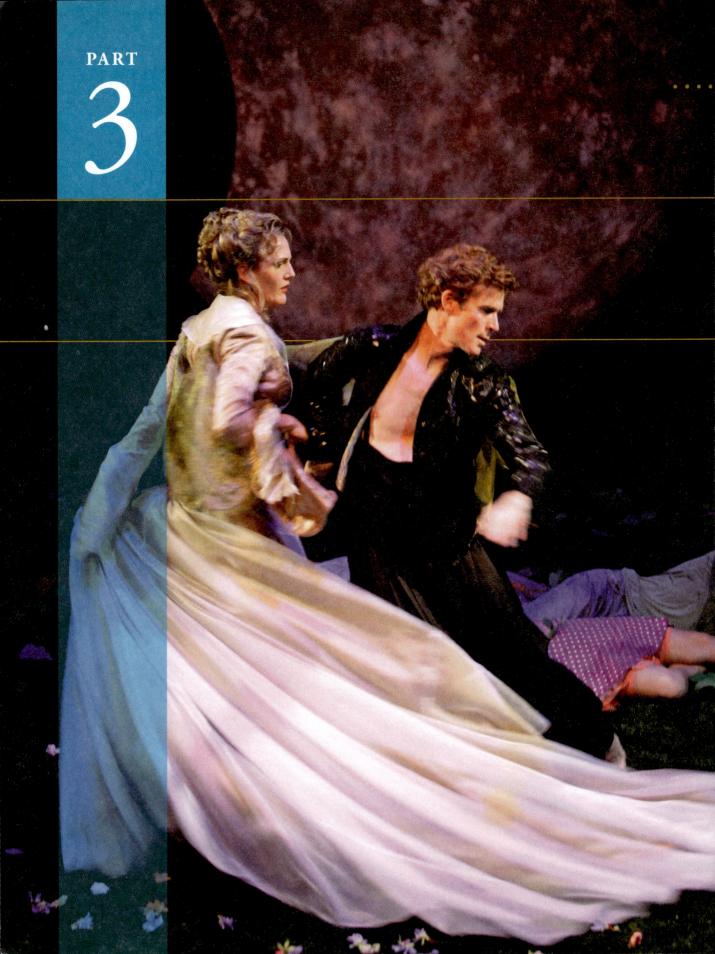

PART

3

Theatrical Production

In parts 1 and 2, we discussed how theatrical conventions and practices vary widely from one period to another and from one culture to another. So far, we have looked at the theatre from theoretical and historical points of view in an attempt to understand the nature of theatre and varieties of theatrical experience. We will now examine how the theatre functions today.

What follows is an overview of the purposes, principles, materials, and working methods of each of the theatre arts—the varied processes involved in the creation of a production. The primary focus is on typical procedures, although important variations are noted. Topics explored include types of theatrical spaces and how they influence production, production design, and the work of playwrights, dramaturgs, producers, directors, actors, and designers (scenery, costume, lighting, and sound). Taken together, these topics provide an overview of theatrical production today.

The elements and principles of design are put to use in order to create a storybook world for Dr. Seuss' *How the Grinch Stole Christmas!* under the direction of Matt August; scene designs by John Lee Beatty; costume designs by Robert Morgan with makeup design by Angelina Avallone; lighting by Pat Collins.

T. Charles Erickson

The elimination of stage–auditorium dichotomy is not the important thing—that simply creates a bare laboratory situation, an appropriate area for investigation. The essential concern is finding the proper spectator–actor relationship for each type of performance and embodying the decision in physical arrangements.
—Jerzy Grotowski, *Towards a Poor Theatre*

Theatrical Space and Production Design

Because the essence of theatre lies in the interaction of performers and audience assembled in the same place at the same time, the physical space in which a performance occurs is a crucial element in the theatrical experience. Like other elements, the theatrical space can be organized in several ways, each with its own potential and limitations.

The Influence of Theatrical Space

Three basic characteristics of any theatrical space influence both audience response and the way in which production elements are used:

- Degree of formality
- Size
- Configuration or arrangement of the actor-audience relationship

The degree of formality that a theatrical space possesses influences audience expectations and their responses. An elaborate theatre building with carpeted lobbies and auditorium, fixed comfortable seating, and complex theatrical technology creates a different set of expectations than does a theatrical space improvised in a warehouse, where the audience sits on the floor, wooden platforms, or folding chairs, and in which the technology is minimal. The former suggests refinement, permanence, and extensive resources; it may arouse expectations of elaborate design, skilled acting, and polished productions. The latter suggests roughness, temporariness (perhaps a deliberate break with tradition), and limited resources; it may arouse expectations of experimentation and the need for imagination to supply what can only be suggested. The audience may also assume that the degree of formality suggests that certain types of responses are more appropriate than others and thereby affects the way in which they respond to staged events. Adult audiences may be less likely to scream and shout in an ornate and elaborately decorated theatre than in a warehouse theatre or an outdoor theatre with informal seating arrangements.

The size of the theatrical space also exerts an influence. Very large spaces may make it difficult for all members of the audience to see and hear all that the performers are doing or saying; small details are likely to go unnoticed, stage business may be simplified or enlarged, spectacle may be given increased emphasis, and sound may require amplification. More intimate spaces permit greater subtlety in the use of voice, gesture, and facial expression, as well as the effective use of greater detail in costumes and properties. Intimate spaces generally are now preferred over large ones, in part because the close-ups and sound tracks used in television and film have conditioned audiences to expect to see and hear everything clearly. The influence of size (overall scale) on the total theatrical experience accounts for many of the differences among theatres of the past and present. A Greek theatre holding fifteen thousand people inspired performance conventions quite different from those used in today's theatres intended for a few hundred.

Finally, the arrangement or configuration of theatrical space is an important influence. Not only does it define the physical relationship of the performer to the audience, but also it shapes how production elements (scenery, costumes, lighting, and so on) can be used. There are four common physical arrangements of the actor-audience relationship:

- **Proscenium Arch Stage.** The acting area is placed at one end of the space with all of the spectators facing it.
- **Thrust Stage.** The acting area is surrounded on two or three sides by the audience.
- **Arena Stage.** The acting area is completely surrounded by the audience on all sides.
- **Flexible Space.** The relationship of acting and audience areas is variable and flexible.

Overall, then, theatrical space creates an environment that influences the theatrical experience. Let us look more closely at the four basic configurations or arrangements of the actor-audience relationship and their influences.

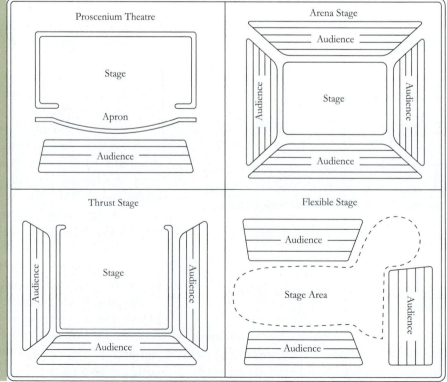

Four arrangements of theatrical space: proscenium, thrust, arena, and flexible. Flexible space, as the name implies, can take many forms: the audience and performers can remain separated or be intermingled; the configuration can also change during the course of a performance.

Proscenium Theatre

Stage

Apron

Audience

Arena Stage

Audience

Audience · Stage · Audience

Audience

Thrust Stage

Audience · Stage · Audience

Audience

Flexible Stage

Audience

Stage Area

Audience

Audience

Drawing by David Betts

The Proscenium-Arch Stage

Probably the most familiar type of theatre is still that with a raised stage framed by a proscenium arch, although other types have become increasingly common. The proscenium arch clearly marks the division between stage and auditorium, although some part of the acting platform may extend forward of the proscenium (this extension is called the *apron* or *forestage*). In the auditorium, all of the seats may be on the same level (though usually with the floor raked upward toward the rear to improve the view of the stage), or there may be one or more balconies. In the proscenium theatre, the stage is designed to be seen from the front only. This affects the director's grouping of actors to create stage images and the means used to achieve emphasis and subordination. It also affects the actors' bodily positions, movement, gestures, and use of voice and speech. Because the stage action is oriented in one direction, the designer frequently uses the back and sides of the stage for the scenery, entrances, and exits. The scenery may be as tall as the designer wishes and the space allows, and it may consist of few or many units. The only fundamental restriction is that audience's view not be obstructed. The lighting designer needs to be concerned with giving three-dimensionality to actors and objects as perceived from the auditorium.

The proscenium stage is usually equipped with a curtain that may be used to conceal or reveal the playing space (although today this curtain is infrequently used). The stage ordinarily has an overhead system of ropes or cables, pulleys, and battens that permit drapes or scenic pieces to be raised into the space above the stage or lowered to stage level. This overhead system is typically called a *fly system* because offstage operators "fly" drapes or scenery in or out of the audience's view as framed by the proscenium arch opening. This system may be designed to operate manually or electronically. Usually there is offstage space on either side (called *wings*) to permit the shifting and storing of scenery. There also may be other machinery for shifting scenery:

- Hydraulic or pneumatic lifts
- Elevators (allowing portions of the stage and its scenery to be lowered or raised)
- Turntables or revolves (allowing portions of the stage to be revolved)

T. Charles Erickson

An example of a proscenium-arch stage configuration used for the Hartford Stage Company's production of *Dividing the Estate* by Horton Foote; directed by Michael Wilson; scene design by Jeff Cowie; lighting by Rui Rita; costumes by David C. Woolard.

However, such complex machinery is not commonplace because of its cost.

In the proscenium theatre, the action and scenery are usually farther from the audience than in other types of theatres. There may be an orchestra pit or forestage between the first row of seats and the acting area. Because scenery and costumes typically are not viewed at close range, they may be less precisely detailed than in other types of theatres. Likewise, because it is typically seen from only one side, scenery used within the proscenium-arch stage may require only its front side to be completed.

The Thrust Stage

In a theatre with a thrust stage, the seats are usually arranged around three (or occasionally two) sides of the performance space. The thrust stage brings the audience and performers into a more intimate performer-audience relationship than does the proscenium theatre because more of the audience is closer to the action than is possible in a proscenium theatre of the same size. The thrust stage also normally lends a more three-dimensional quality to the acting area than

does the proscenium stage. However, because the action is viewed from three sides, the director, actors, and designers need to consider how the action will be perceived from three directions simultaneously rather than, as in the proscenium theatre, only one.

The thrust stage discourages realistic spectacle of the type made possible by the proscenium-arch stage. Tall scenery must be kept to the rear of the performance space so as not to interfere with sightlines. Although some thrust stages are backed by an area equipped with a fly system like that of a proscenium stage, extensive use of scenic effects there may divide audience attention between the action taking place on the main stage and scenic effects taking place at the back of the stage. Many thrust theatres make no provision for flying scenery, drops, or curtains above the main performance space, although lighting instruments are usually mounted in recesses in the ceiling or on a grid above the stage. Generally, furniture, properties, and scenery are shifted by hand on a thrust stage. Some furniture or properties may be mounted on wheeled platforms and moved on and off the stage from the rear of the platform. A few thrust stages have some portions mounted on hydraulic lifts, and there may be several traps in the stage floor.

The thrust stage of the Guthrie Theatre in Minneapolis has long been considered one of the finest in the country. When they built a new theatre complex in 2006, they created an adaptation of their legendary thrust stage; as pictured here, it seats 1,100 spectators, all within sixty feet of the stage. The complex also contains a 700-seat proscenium theatre and a 200-seat flexible-seating "black box" theatre.

John Doman/KRT/Newscom

The Arena Stage

The typical arena theatre is simply an open space left at floor level in the middle of the auditorium. In some arena theatres, the floor of the performance area can be raised or lowered in segments to provide variety in levels or to differentiate locales. The seating is usually a stepped arrangement on four sides of the acting area. In some theatres of this type, the seats are not permanently installed, and the arrangement may be varied at will, but in others comfortable armchair seating of the kind typical of proscenium theatres is used.

Because the arena stage provides a three-dimensional playing area, the director, actors, and designers must be concerned with expressiveness from every angle. In an arena stage, the costumed actors, lighting, furniture, and properties usually play a more significant role in characterizing mood, time, and place than does the scenery because these aspects do not obscure the audience's view. The scene designer may use a few open structures, such as trellises and pavilions through which the audience can see, but ordinarily the scene designer depends more on furniture, properties, and treatment of the stage floor. Provision is seldom made for flying scenery, although a few architectural fragments may be suspended overhead. Occasionally, multileveled settings are used, but they must be constructed so that the audience can clearly see the action on all levels. Screens for projections are sometimes hung at various spots over the acting area, over the audience, or around the walls (the same image may be projected on different screens simultaneously so that all members of the audience can see it), but usually the scene designer must suggest locale, period, mood, and style with a few scenic elements.

Because there is no curtain, all changes are made either in full view of the audience or in semidarkness. Shifting is usually done by hand. Many arena theatres have passageways between the seating areas or passageways running under the seating and opening onto the acting area; these latter passageways are known as *vomitoria* or more simply as "voms." These serve as exits and entrances for actors and as means of getting scenic units or properties on and off the stage. Most arena stages are relatively small and intimate. However, because spectators view the production elements from multiple angles, this stage configuration makes special demands on the director's staging and on the production's design to visually communicate from every angle.

Flexible Space

In a flexible stage, the space relationship of performer to audience is flexible and variable—an arrangement that may change from one production to another or even during the same performance. In such an arrangement, spectators and actors may be intermingled in multiple playing and seating areas, or the place of performance may shift, as when scenes are played at various sites along a procession route (as in medieval theatre or in some contemporary street theatre), or there may even be a different audience for each scene or at each site, although the configuration of the theatrical space may not have changed. A flexible space may be indoor or outdoor, small or large, but its flexibility is usually made possible by the absence of permanently structured seating and stage areas.

Although most theatrical performances seek to have all members of the audience see and hear the same things at the same time, those using the intermingled arrangement often enlist multiple foci. Some spectators may be watching one scene while others are watching another, or spectators may be able to choose which scenes they will watch, moving about in the space in order to see the scene that has attracted their attention. Sometimes performers may ask spectators to participate in the action, to move or to assist with some task. In other instances, the distinctions between performers and spectators remain clear, and the space each group occupies remains distinct; in still others, performers and spectators share a single, common space. The key is flexibility in the use of all theatrical elements.

An arena stage provides considerable intimacy, as shown here in a production at the Arena Stage, Washington, D.C.

Nic Lehoux/VIEW Pictures Ltd/Alamy

Society, Art & Culture

THEATRE ARCHITECTURE

In *The Shapes of Our Theatres*, Jo Mielziner (1901–1976) writes, "All theatre interiors consist of two essential areas: one is 'the auditorium,' which is designed specifically for the audience; the other, designed for the production, we know as 'the stage.' …Independently they have no life; together they produce a living theatre. It is therefore the sensitive interrelationship of the two that makes a theatre design either a success or a failure."

In the twentieth century, however, many persons have objected to the dichotomy between auditorium and stage and have sought means to bridge them. Laszlo Moholy-Nagy (1895–1946) writes, "Stage and spectator are too much separated, too obviously divided into active and passive, to be able to produce creative relationships and reciprocal tensions. It is time to produce a kind of stage activity that will no longer permit the audience to be silent spectators." He suggested building auditoriums with "suspended bridges and drawbridges running horizontally, diagonally, and vertically"; segments of the stage capable of moving toward the spectators to create effects similar to those of close-ups in film; runways that extend completely around the seating area; and other devices that place the spectator in a dynamic relationship with the action.

Marvin Carlson concludes in his *Places of Performance* (1993) that, as a result of twentieth-century experiments with theatrical space, "Never before in history has a public had available for its consideration" so many diverse "physical spaces in which theatre today may be presented. … In addition to this huge selection of historical spaces, the twentieth century has produced experimental directors who have explored the possibilities of an almost infinite variety of nontraditional spaces," streets, parks, woodlands, factories, warehouses, and "all manner of public and private buildings."

The intermingling of performers and audiences became more frequent during the 1960s when there was a movement to reject theatre buildings altogether. Some argued that, like museums and concert halls, theatres discourage all except a cultural elite. These innovators sought instead to take performances into parks, streets, and other places where theatrically unsophisticated spectators might discover the theatre. Instead of a building with permanent structures dedicated for performance, they advocated the use of flexible or "found" space, either adapting a production to fit existing areas or altering existing areas to fit the needs of the production. Others adopted a flexible space arrangement out of financial necessity or convenience since it requires only an open space without fixed seating or stage.

Today, many regional and university theatres have a flexible space, usually in addition to a proscenium or thrust stage. Often referred to as a "black box" (because it is basically a bare room with black walls), it is most frequently used for productions with limited or special appeal—nontraditional works or performance modes, new or untested plays, low-budget or student productions. These theatres allow for different stage configurations to be erected for specific productions or for the theatrical space to remain wholly flexible.

The variety of audience-performer configurations is great, but all can be reduced to one or some combination of the four basic types of theatrical space. Experimentation with performance spaces reminds us that theatre does not require a permanent structure built especially for it and that all spatial arrangements are merely ways of facilitating the interaction of performers and audiences.

Earthquakes in London was produced at London's National Theatre and used a flexible space that intermingled audience and performers. Audience members sat on stools along the elevated catwalk and stood in the open floor areas. The seemingly black area in the photo also was seating, extending along both sides of the performance space. The far right and left contained elevated performance spaces that were like mini proscenium-arch spaces for some scenes.

Auxiliary Spaces

In addition to the performance space, theatre buildings usually have a number of auxiliary spaces. Several of these are intended to serve the audience—lobby, restrooms, corridors, exits, and refreshment stands. Others are spaces for theatrical personnel, such as box office and other work space. The amount and type of work space provided in theatres varies widely.

Many theatres, especially those on Broadway, as well as many of those used by low-budget companies, do not include a full range of facilities for the construction of scenery and costumes, nor do they contain storage for equipment or properties not currently in use. Broadway productions are rehearsed elsewhere, costumes and scenery are built in studios far removed from the theatre, and backstage space is often minimally equipped. Broadway theatres host productions rather than serve as the

Practices & Styles

THEATRE FACILITIES AND AUXILIARY SPACES

A well-designed, self-contained theatre (one with facilities for preparing productions as well as performing them) will include all or most of the following:

- **Scene shop**: A space for the construction, assembly, and painting of scenery as well as storage for equipment, materials, and finished scenery when not in current use.
- **Property room or shop**: A space for the storage of furniture and bulky props. Large theatres may also have a specialized space for the construction, modification, or repair of stage properties.
- **Costume shop**: A space for the construction and alteration of costumes as well as facilities for their laundry, dyeing, cleaning, and pressing.
- **Costume storage**: A space to store costumes or costume pieces so that they may be altered or modified for future use.
- **Light shop**: A work space for lighting personnel.
- **Lighting storage**: A storage space for lighting accessories, spare parts, equipment, and instruments.
- **Control booth(s)**: A space for lighting and sound control board operators during the performances. Ideally, control booths have a full view of the stage and a monitor system so that booth personnel may see and hear the performance as well as communicate with offstage personnel.
- **Rehearsal room(s)**: A room or rooms with space approximating that of each stage space the theatre operates.
- **Dressing rooms**: Rooms with appropriately lighted mirrors for the application of makeup, restrooms, and showers for the performers and crew.
- **Green room**: A space for the performers to relax before or between scenes and for performers and crew members to assemble to receive instructions or notes.
- **Business offices**: A box office for taking ticket requests, dispensing tickets, and securing funds; and additional office space for personnel such as dramaturgs, business managers, and artistic directors.

permanent home of a company. Many small companies, such as Off-Off-Broadway groups, even if they are permanent, often function in very limited facilities. Regional and university theatres usually have more extensive facilities.

Using the Theatrical Space

Normally, in planning a production, little is done to shape the audience and its space. Most directors assume that the audience space of the theatre in which they will be working is fixed—as is the case in the majority of theatres. Although directors must take into account the auditorium's size, shape, sightlines, acoustical properties, and the physical relationship created between audience and performers, most tend to view these factors as given and unchangeable circumstances. However, some theatrical spaces are designed so that their overall arrangement and audience-actor relationship can be easily altered. In these instances, directors may shape the audience space to suit their production.

Jerzy Grotowski, director of the Polish Laboratory Theatre, made audiences an integral part of his production design. For each production, he had a specific number of spectators in mind (never more than one hundred), and he would permit no more than that number to attend. He also sought to induce the audience to participate in the action unselfconsciously. In his 1964 production of *Doctor Faustus*, Grotowski organized the space like a banqueting hall. The audience, treated as friends invited to share Faustus's last meal before the Devil claims his soul (to whom he had sold it many years earlier), sat at the tables, while the action took place on, under, and around the tables. The German director Peter Stein staged several productions in film studios or gutted and rearranged theatre spaces. In his 1977 production of *As You Like It*, the court scenes took place in one studio. For the Forest of Arden scenes, the audience passed through a tunnel to reach another studio in which bleacher-style seating had been erected along the sides. Scenic units, among them a large, live beech tree, a small field of wheat, and a pond filled with water, provided various locations for the action. The Living Theatre often encouraged the audience and actors to use the same space indiscriminately, thereby forcing some spectators to become unwilling participants in the action.

Grotowski's arrangement of the space for *Doctor Faustus*. The dark figures represent performers; the lighter figures, spectators. Faustus is seated at the smaller table at top.

1968 Jerzy Grotowski and Odin Teatrets Forlag; courtesy of H. Martin Berg

The arrangement of the actor–audience relationship influences how the audience perceives the action. (*Above*) The production team for the American Repertory Theatre's production of *Romeo and Juliet* used a variation of a thrust stage configuration, which placed the audience on two opposing sides for their production of the play. (*Below*) Fabric runners and chandeliers were added to the basic stage space to designate lanes of performance space and characterize the play's party scene where Romeo meets Juliet. Directed by Gadi Roll; scene design by Riccardo Hernandez; costume design by Kasia Maimone; lighting by D. M. Wood.

T. Charles Erickson

T. Charles Erickson

But these are atypical approaches. Directors may try to predict the makeup of the audience and how it is likely to respond, but for the most part they conceive of the audience members as reactors who come to see a production created for them. Normally, the director lets others (through publicity, news releases, and other means) attract as large an audience as possible to the space being used for the production.

Production Design

Although the theatrical space greatly influences the performance and the audience's response to it, the director, actors, and designers select and shape aural and visual signs (within the performance space) to arouse a set of desired audience responses. But the possibilities—in terms of the way one shapes these signs, how skillfully one coordinates them, and how spectators respond to this shaping—are so numerous that the results can seldom be fully controlled. Nevertheless, each production has an overall design—a collaborative assemblage of its many parts.

The audience members perceive a production's overall design through what they hear and see. Sound designers use sound effects and music to convey mood, enhance dramatic tension, and suggest various associations to the audience. Scene, costume, and lighting designers address their work to shape the audience's visual perceptions. However, it is important to remember that directors and actors also make use of visual and aural aspects. The performers' vocal delivery of the dialogue (inflectional patterns, volume, rhythm, and rate) shapes information about character relationships, motivations, emotions, and overall meaning. Likewise, the director's composition of the actors on stage (how much space they use and how they relate to each other as well as to the stage settings, costumes, and properties) communicates messages quite apart from or in conjunction with the spoken dialogue.

Elements and Principles

Six elements of visual design serve as basic building blocks from which scene, costume, and lighting designers construct various images or patterns:

- Line
- Shape
- Space
- Color
- Texture
- Ornamentation

Designers may use these basic elements in very different ways depending on the meaning they wish to communicate and the response to it they wish to elicit. The basic principles of design help them use the visual elements effectively:

- Harmony
- Balance
- Variety
- Proportion
- Rhythm
- Emphasis

Theoretically, how audiences respond depends on how these aspects of design have been shaped. The various theatre artists primarily use the elements and principles of design to create meanings they hope the audience will perceive.

Typically, designers use the principle of *harmony* to ensure that individual aspects of the stage picture (the setting, the costumes, the properties, and lighting relating to it) all relate as parts of a whole image. If monotony is to be avoided, however, *variety* is also needed. Variation in the visual elements (line, shape, space, color, texture, and ornamentation) is therefore selectively applied to achieve an overall image with both variety and harmony. Likewise, different forms of *balance* may be used to create the desired level of stability for the stage picture. The even distribution of mass

Principles of design can be seen at work in the creation of this production of Shakespeare's comedy *Much Ado About Nothing* at the Alley Theatre. Note how proportion has been distorted to create giant fruit, the shape and color of which are somewhat reflected in that of Hero's skirt (center). Directed by Scott Schwartz; scene design by Walt Spangler; costumes by Fabio Toblini; lighting by Michael Gilliam.

T. Charles Erickson

created by symmetrical balance, for example, typically conveys the appearance of formality or stability, whereas asymmetrical balance (which depends on an uneven distribution of mass) typically conveys informality, casualness, or even chaos. *Proportion* involves the comparative scale of each part to all the others and selectively may be used to create a variety of impressions. For example, a door disproportionately large in relation to the rest of the setting visually implies its significance. Similarly, the manipulation of proportion in a costume may do much to change an actor's appearance and possibly convey a visual message about the character the actor portrays. All designs use *emphasis* to selectively focus audience attention. The entrance of a woman wearing a canary yellow dress, for example, into a gathering of others wearing muted earth tones lends her emphasis by way of contrast. All of the visual elements of design may be shaped by *rhythm*. Lines and shapes may be repeated, thereby suggesting visual motifs; the size and number of objects onstage (as well as their relative placement to each other) gradually may be changed to suggest a sense of spatial or temporal progression; gradations in color (hue, saturation, and value) may lead the eye from one point to another; changes in texture and ornamentation may convey a sense of flow and change; and the movement of the actors may generate feelings of urgency or calm.

Our brief treatment of the principles of design and how they may be used to shape visual design elements barely scratches the surface of their immense possibilities. Significant study and practice is needed to wield these principles and elements in creative and meaningful ways. Although in such a general discussion the elements and principles of design may seem abstract, they are manifested concretely during every moment of a performance.

Collaboration and the Designers' Process

One of the major challenges of production design arises from the need to coordinate individually conceived parts (in acting, directing, scenery, costumes, lighting, and sound) to create a whole capable of eliciting desired responses and interpretations. Preparing a theatrical production involves the combined efforts of many artists. A common interpretation or goal is usually required for individual artists to coordinate their efforts on various aspects of the production into a cohesive experience for the audience. This process generally requires much communication and collaboration,

Practitioners & Theorists

JULIE TAYMOR AND COORDINATED PRODUCTION DESIGN

Julie Taymor (1952–) has achieved an enviable reputation for her coordinated production designs. The *New York Times* critic Mel Gussow writes of her 1996 production of *Juan Darién*, "The play draws its power from the symbiosis of design, movement and music, melding diverse performance art forms and transforming the stage into a living theatrical organism."

Taymor's ability to coordinate successfully the various aspects of production design may be credited to a number of factors. She has training in movement, highly developed skills in the visual arts, and considerable experience in conceiving and developing new theatre pieces. Taymor began her formal training in 1969 at L'École de Mime Jacques LeCoq in Paris, which emphasizes the physicalization of character and emotion. With LeCoq she also began work with masks, a convention that she has used often in her work as a director and designer. In 1971 Taymor apprenticed with Joseph Chaikin's Open Theatre and Peter Schumann's Bread and Puppet Theatre (both companies were developing new theatre pieces through group discussion and improvisation). The Open Theatre emphasized the actor's movement, whereas the Bread and Puppet Theatre emphasized puppets as "moving sculptures" made from found materials. In 1974 she traveled to eastern Europe, Japan, and Indonesia to study puppetry, dance, and the visual arts. She remained in Indonesia until 1978, perfecting her use of puppetry, dance, and masks.

When Taymor returned to the United States, she quickly established a reputation as an outstandingly creative visual artist. She designed sets and/or costumes for productions at Baltimore's Center Stage, La Mama, the New York Shakespeare Festival, and other Broadway, Off-Broadway, and regional theatres. Her sets, costumes, masks, and puppets for the American Repertory Theatre's 1984 production of *King Stag* garnered special praise.

Taymor is the recipient of a Guggenheim Fellowship and a "genius" grant by the MacArthur Foundation. Her costume design and direction for the Broadway musical *The Lion King* (1998) won her lavish praise and two Tony Awards. Taymor has also expanded into directing films, including *Titus* (1999), *Frida* (2002), and *The Tempest* (2010). Taymor also continues to develop and direct new works for the stage. She was the original director of the musical *Spider-Man: Turn Off the Dark* (2010) which features music and lyrics by Bono and The Edge and a book by Taymor and Glen Berger.

The American Repertory Theatre production of Carlo Gozzi's *King Stag* was fancifully stylized through its use of costumes, masks, and puppetry designed by Julie Taymor. Directed by Andrei Serban; scene design by Michael Yeargan; lighting by Jennifer Tipton.

CAMERA PRESS/Nigel Norrington/Redux

but the manner or style in which this takes place varies depending on the individual artists within the production team, the available time, and other constraints that may affect their efforts. The common basis of their collaboration is the play itself and the interpretative focus that will guide the creative choices artists make for a particular production of it. (Chapter 13 includes a treatment of the director's preparations and early process. Here we will concern ourselves with the designers' preparations and early processes.)

Most designers begin their preparations by familiarizing themselves with the play. Initially, they may read through the play to gain an intuitive feel for it, taking note of their emotional reactions and perhaps specific images that the play evokes. In subsequent readings, the designers try to understand the play as a total structure—its action, characters, themes, language, meaning—because the production design needs to reflect or enhance all of these elements. As designers continue to study the play, they focus increasingly on clues about specific requirements of the play and its overall style. During this process, they accumulate information of various sorts from the play.

Although the play is the primary source of information, designers may also use information from other sources. Scene designers may wish to know about decorative motifs, architectural styles, furnishings, and favorite color schemes in use during the period of the play's action. Costume designers may need to determine what clothing was in use at the time of the play's action (characteristic silhouettes, typical textures and materials, dominant colors, ornamental motifs, usual accessories). The designers may also need to be familiar with the manners and customs of the time in order to understand why, when, and how garments or furniture were worn or used. They may wish to explore the stage setting and costuming conventions for which the play was originally written or that were in use when the play takes place. Lighting designers may wish to research the quality of light found in the various locations indicated in the play just as sound designers may wish to explore the soundscapes of these locations. All of the designers may wish to understand the political and social contexts out of which the play came, or they might undertake a variety of other explorations, depending upon the production concept.

Practitioners & Theorists

APPIA ON HIERARCHY IN PRODUCTION DESIGN

Many persons have commented on the relative importance of the elements that make up a production. Adolphe Appia (1862–1928), one of the twentieth century's major theoreticians of the theatre, had strong convictions about hierarchy in production design:

> The first factor in staging is the interpreter, the actor. The actor carries the action. Without him there is no action, hence no drama. Everything must be subordinated ... to this element—which takes first rank hierarchically ... the body is alive, moving and plastic; it has three dimensions. Space ... must conform to his plastic form, his three dimensions. What else is there: Light! ... Like the actor, light must become active; ... it must be put to the service of ... the actor's dramatic and plastic expression. ... Here is our normally established hierarchy: the actor presenting the drama, three-dimensional space at the service of the actor's plastic form, light, giving life to both.

—Adolphe Appia, "Actor, Space, Light, Painting"

Although the designers may not incorporate all they learn into their designs, the fuller understanding they have gained of the play and its context may stimulate their imaginations.

Before they make sketches, plans, and plots (perhaps before they have even begun to study the play and its context in detail), the designers meet with the director and one another to discuss the play and the interpretive focus for their production of it. The director may use an initial meeting to elicit ideas from the designers and to ask them to participate in formulating this focus. Many directors explain a production concept they have already formulated to the designers at an initial meeting but remain open to suggestions or to making alterations in the concept. The process of collaboration is unique to each group and situation, but communication, respect, and a certain degree of trust are always vital components of an effective collaborative process. A clear production concept or interpretive focus—a framework of the intended meaning or the type of experience the production team wishes the audience to have—provides a common purpose. However it evolves, an interpretive focus must be decided on before the designers can work together effectively and avoid working at cross-purposes. Because the work of each designer impinges on that of the others, each designer must be sensitive to the ideas and needs of the others.

In *The Illusion*, Tony Kushner's adaptation of Pierre Corneille's seventeenth-century play about love, loss, and redemption, the action moves fluidly not only over time and space but also through different layers of reality. This poses special challenges for its production team. Pictured here is the Hartford Stage Company production directed by Mark Lamos; scene design by John Conklin; costumes by Martin Pakledinaz, lighting by Pat Collins.

T. Charles Erickson

The designers may require other information before they begin work. Because each type of stage yields different challenges and opportunities for the designers, the type of stage (proscenium, thrust, arena, etc.) on which the play will be performed is a primary concern for the designers. Although the theatre's architecture usually predefines the type of stage, some theatres are designed with the capacity to alter the arrangement of the playing space and the resulting performer-audience relationship. Designers also need to know if the director has any special demands (specific floor plan needs such as space for dances or fight scenes, particular costume pieces, and any special lighting or sound effects the director will require, etc.). Moreover, the designers need to know what budget and time constraints apply and what equipment and personnel are available. After they understand the constraints within which they must work—the script, the production concept, the performance space, the budget, and the personnel—the designers are ready to proceed.

Although each visual and aural element, considered in isolation, is capable of projecting a message and evoking a response, in actuality these elements are seldom wholly separated from each other. In theatrical production, most are present simultaneously, and their relationships change continually as the action develops. Over time each individually created sign or message is modified by others that combine to form the total effect. A theatrical production is therefore a group creation and the collaboration of the various artists who create it is vital to its effectiveness. The ways in which theatre artists in each area of theatrical production contribute to the overall impact of a theatre performance are explored in the chapters that follow.

Many new plays, like *Lydia* by Octavio Solis, go through a careful process of revision even after their initial production. *Lydia* was modestly revised after its premiere production at the Denver Center Theatre and again after this production at the Yale Repertory Theatre; directed by Juliette Carrillo; sets by Andrew Boyce; costumes by Amanda Seymour; lighting by Jesse Belsky; fight direction by Rick Sordelet; with original music by Chris Webb.

Carol Rosegg

[A] play in a book is only the shadow of a play and not even a clear shadow of it. ... The printed script of a play is hardly more than an architect's blueprint of a house not built or built and destroyed.

—Tennessee Williams, Afterword, *Camino Real*

Playwriting and Dramaturgy

In the contemporary theatre, although a play is typically the beginning point of a production, its creator, the playwright, is often the theatre artist most removed from the process of play production. It has not always been so. Greek playwrights usually staged their own works. Shakespeare and Molière both wrote plays for the companies in which they acted, apparently knew in advance who would play each role, and were undoubtedly involved in staging their plays. But since the nineteenth century, playwrights have usually worked in isolation—not knowing, while writing, who would act in their plays or if they would be able to find someone willing to produce their scripts. Only a few playwrights today have close ties to theatre organizations. Even those writers fortunate enough to have directors or theatres to collaborate with them on developing scripts usually work alone until the script has reached a point where input from others can be helpful. Thus, the initial stage of writing is typically a personal and isolated process.

The Playwright

The source of inspiration for a play cannot be foreseen. It may be a newspaper article, a personal experience, a criminal act for which the motives are unclear, or almost any other source, because the possibilities of drama are ever-present and because almost anything has the potential to stimulate a dramatist's imagination. Each writer has a view of the world or a range of interests that make some subjects more attractive than others. Samuel Beckett was preoccupied with the human predicament in an unknowable universe, whereas Henrik Ibsen was concerned with personal and social morality in an explainable universe. Although both sought to write truthfully, their interests drew them to widely differing subjects, just as their perceptions about human beings and the human condition caused them to treat their subjects distinctively.

The working methods of playwrights also vary widely. Bertolt Brecht began with an outline and then elaborated on it. Victorien Sardou (the most successful French dramatist of the nineteenth century) wrote the climactic scene first and then worked backward from it. Henrik Ibsen made numerous notes about situations and characters, often over a period of years, before actually beginning a play. Paula Vogel, before forming a general plot outline, plays music that she associates with some aspect of the play over and over as she begins the writing process. Sam Shepard has said that he begins with a visual image and starts writing without knowing where it will lead. In some instances, plays have been written with the aid of group improvisations. The playwright may present an outline, situation, or idea to a group of performers who then improvise on this material; as story, movement, and dialogue develop, the dramatist selects and shapes what seems most effective until a finished work has emerged. As these variations suggest, there are many different working methods, and writers discover and follow those procedures that work best for themselves.

The mechanics of playwriting also differ from one writer to another. (Basic structural patterns, form, and style are discussed in Chapter 3.)

Beckett did most of his writing by hand in bound notebooks. Some writers compose at a computer; others talk into tape recorders. However they proceed, writers seldom arrive at the final version of a script in the first draft. It is sometimes said that plays are not written but rewritten. Some writers spend years refining a script. For example, August Wilson's first draft of *Ma Rainey's Black Bottom* did not include Levee and the other band members, although in his final version of the play these characters are essential to its conflict. On the other hand, Sam Shepard long refused to revise at all on the grounds that to do so would be like lying because it would deny what he had originally set down.

Practitioners & Theorists

YASMINA REZA

Yasmina Reza (1959–) has made a career of writing plays that often explore intellectual arguments and concepts only to peel them back, exposing the ridiculousness of human beings and their relationships.

Reza, who began as an actress in the French theatre and who writes in French, achieved critical success with her very first plays, *Conversations after a Burial* (1987) and *Winter Crossing* (1990). Both plays received the Molière Award (the French equivalent of England's Olivier Award and America's Tony Award) for Best Author. She gained wider popular recognition with her play *Art* (1994), which has been translated and performed in over thirty languages and which received Molière, Olivier, and Tony awards for Best Play. The catalyst of *Art* is a large, nonfigural, white-on-white painting that generates arguments among three long-time friends about the nature and purpose of art. Over time we see their arguments stem as much (if not more) from the deeply hidden tensions and resentments between them than from their feelings about the painting. Reza's *Life X 3* (2000) takes a basic situation and presents three variations on it, each possessing unique nuances. Reza's most recent play, *God of Carnage* (2006), premiered in Zurich and received the Nestroy-Theatre prize for the best German-language performance of the season, the Olivier Award for Best New Comedy (2009), and the Tony Award for Best Play (2009). In *God of Carnage*, polite society proves a thin veneer as the meeting between two sets of parents to discuss a playground altercation between their children quickly gives way to bitter infighting. As the characters quickly shift alliances (couple versus couple, women versus men, and even husbands and wives in temporary alliance with each others' partners), it becomes clear that everyone is out for themselves and that adult confrontations are handled no more maturely than those of children.

Perhaps because her plays contain a great deal of humor as they portray human beings as laughable, critics have labeled Reza's plays comedies or farces; she resists this categorization. "My plays have always been described as comedy but I think they're tragedy. They are funny tragedy, but they are tragedy. Maybe it's a new genre."

Because plays are intended for the stage, most writers need to see their work performed before they can be sure they have accomplished what they intended. Lines that look effective on paper may sound contrived when spoken. A playwright needs to be certain that the dialogue places the emphasis of a speech at just the right point, that the rhythms are effective when spoken aloud, that speeches make their intended points, that the vocal patterns are appropriate to each character, and that the interaction among characters seems believable. A playwright usually also seeks to make sure that the dramatic action is clear, that revelations create the intended effect, that tension mounts, relaxes, and builds to a climax. In summary, the dramatist must create a play that is effective in performance and not merely on the page.

In the course of developing a script, the playwright needs and can get various kinds of help. An initial step may involve a reading of the play aloud by one or more people (preferably a different person for each character). This not only allows the playwright to hear his or her work, but because others who are present may voice their reactions, it also helps the playwright to get some sense of how an audience responds to the script. Whereas this type of reading usually provides the playwright a basis for revisions, it also creates a problem that every playwright must ultimately deal with: assessing the validity of others' responses. Many listeners

A read-through of a new play at the National Playwrights Conference in the Barn Theatre of the Eugene O'Neill Theatre Center in Waterford, Conn.

A. Vincent Scarano; courtesy of the Eugene O'Neill Theatre Center may volunteer advice, but advice from one source often contradicts advice from another. In the end, the playwright must decide which responses are valid or helpful. After revisions have been made, the next step may be a staged reading, in which performers, usually with scripts in hand and after some rehearsal, speak the dialogue and walk through the stage action. After assessing the play as presented and the audience's responses, the playwright usually makes further revisions.

Some playwrights are fortunate enough to have new works commissioned by a theatre as was the case with Octavio Solis's *Lydia* or to work as a resident playwright such as Sam Shepard's position with San Francisco's Magic Theatre when they produced *True West*. Others may be members of a playwrights' workshop where scripts can be worked on over a period of time in a process that includes multiple opportunities for rehearsed readings or performances. The Eugene O'Neill Theatre Center in Waterford, Connecticut, is one organization providing this kind of help. Each summer it selects from hundreds of applicants a few playwrights to be in residence for its National Playwrights Conference in which their new works are developed with the help of directors, performers, select critics, and audiences. In the past, all the plays were given a very quick and simple production using modular, gray scenic units and assorted properties. More recently, under the leadership of Wendy Goldberg, the conference's artistic director, the individual needs of each play have been assessed. The conference, which has always maintained a

Sara Krulwich/The New York Times/Redux

Hope Davis and Jeff Daniels in the Broadway production of *God of Carnage* by Yasmina Reza (translated by Christopher Hampton); directed by Matthew Warchus; sets and costumes by Mark Thompson; lighting by Hugh Vanstone.

balance of very experienced playwrights and less experienced ones, also has a theatre-for-youth pilot program, an international playwright residency in collaboration with Ireland's Abbey Theatre, and educational outreach programs.

Ultimately, full production is the playwright's goal. In New York, several organizations, including the La MaMa Experimental Theatre Club and the Manhattan Theatre Club, assist dramatists to develop their plays through fully mounted productions. One of the most active of these is Playwrights Horizons, which was founded over thirty-five years ago to "support and develop the work of contemporary American playwrights, composers, and lyricists." It has presented works by over three hundred fifty playwrights. Its productions have garnered numerous awards, including six Tony Awards and five Pulitzer Prizes, for its playwrights. Plays are revised and rehearsed, given a limited number of performances, reworked (sometimes over several years), and performed again. Each season Playwrights Horizons presents at least four new plays or musicals in its mainstage season and one or two new works in its studio series. (Studio-series productions are presented on a smaller scale than those produced for the mainstage season.) In addition, Playwrights Horizons offers twenty to twenty-five readings of new plays each year, awards commissions for the early development of new works, and also operates a film-development program with Steven Spielberg's Amblin Entertainment. Few organizations maintain such an ambitious ongoing development program for new plays.

Courtesy of the Philadelphia Theatre Company

The Laramie Project, a collaboratively written play by Moisés Kaufman and members of the Tectonic Theatre Project, as produced by the Philadelphia Theatre Company. The play treats the death of Matthew Shepard, a gay college student who was brutally beaten, tied to a fence, and left there to die. Tectonic company members developed the play from hundreds of hours of taped interviews with Laramie residents. They were given additional support by the Denver Center Theatre, the New York Theatre Workshop, and the Sundance Theatre Lab.

In recent years, regional theatres have played an increasingly prominent role in granting playwrights fully mounted productions. The Denver Center Theatre and Actors Theatre of Louisville have been particularly supportive of the creation and development of new plays. Each year, in addition to commissioning new plays from established playwrights, the Denver Center Theatre hosts its Colorado New Play Summit. The summit typically produces two world premieres in addition to providing staged readings of three to four new plays and holding panels on issues related to new play development and production. The Humana Festival of New American Plays hosted by the Actors Theatre of Louisville performs fully mounted productions of at least four full-length new plays as well as presenting a series of short plays (from 1979 to 1989 these were winners of a national one-act play contest, and since then the winners of a national ten-minute play contest). Since its inception, more than seventy-five thousand scripts have been submitted and considered for inclusion in the Humana Festival and over three hundred plays representing the works of over two hundred writers have been produced. Critics and producers from the United States and abroad attend the Colorado New Play Summit and the Humana Festival of New American Plays, which may greatly help playwrights gain subsequent performances for their works.

Once a new play has been produced at one regional theatre and been deemed to have merit, it frequently gains production at another. The intervals between separate professional regional theatre productions of a new work are usually used to revise the play. Among the plays that have gone through this process are Wendy Wasserstein's *The Heidi Chronicles*, August Wilson's *The Piano Lesson*, Tony Kushner's *Angels in America*, and Paula Vogel's *How I Learned to Drive*, all of which won Pulitzer Prizes. Most of the plays now seen on Broadway have profited from some comparable developmental process before being presented there.

Despite the many efforts to assist playwrights in developing new plays, the number of writers who actually obtain such assistance is relatively small. Many playwrights complete their plays without the benefit of staged readings or workshop performances. However it comes into being, the written work will probably seem only partially complete to its author unless it is fully realized through a stage performance; this requires finding a producer. Playwrights frequently send copies of their plays to various resident theatres, but because these theatres often receive several hundred unsolicited plays each year, they may not read all of them. Some theatres refuse to accept any unsolicited manuscripts. Playwright Allan Katz humorously drew attention to this

How I Learned to Drive went through a long developmental process that included staged readings and workshops. It was developed at the Perseverance Theatre in Alaska before moving to New York. After winning the Pulitzer Prize in 1998, it was produced all across America. Pictured here is the 2012 New York revival, starring Elizabeth Reaser and Norbert Leo Butz.

Sara Krulwich/The New York Times/Redux

situation: "I recently wrote to a number of the most prestigious theaters in New York informing them that because they've repeatedly refused to accept my new play for consideration I've decided to kill myself. Lincoln Center Theater was the first to respond. They said they don't accept unsolicited suicide notes." Many theatre organizations request that playwrights send only a one-page summary and a small excerpt of the unsolicited play; other theatres refuse to read any unsolicited plays. Thus, despite playwrights' efforts, some plays are never produced. In fact, relatively few new plays receive fully staged productions in professional theatres.

Practitioners & Theorists

PLAYWRIGHTS ON PLAYWRITING

Many playwrights do not find it easy to talk about how they work. They may do so in a general way but are usually aware that approaches to writing are enormously variable. Here, some playwrights describe their working process.

Sarah Ruhl: "For me the work emerges out of the ordinary. I mean, of course work emerges out of extraordinary moments of loss and ecstasy and all that, but it also emerges from day-to-day observations, having time to stare out the window. And I think that many, many people right now are losing the ordinary, we're so plugged in all the time."

August Wilson: [On writing *The Piano Lesson*] "I just started writing a line of dialogue and had no idea who was talking. … Someone says something to someone else, and they talk, and at some point I say, 'Well, who is this?' and I give him a name. But I have no idea what the story line of the play is. It's a process of discovery."

Marsha Norman: "I'm a purist about structure. … In plays you have eight minutes at the beginning in which to let the audience know what's at stake, who this is about and when they can go home. I think audiences get real nervous if you don't do that."

David Henry Hwang: "[I]n some ways rehearsal is the worst time to rewrite because you're under a lot of time pressure. If you've spent a year with a play, there's something absurd about rewriting the whole thing in four weeks."

George Bernard Shaw: "Only geniuses can tell you exactly what is wrong with a scene, though plenty of people can tell you something is wrong with it. So make a note of their dissatisfaction; but be very careful how you adopt their cure if they prescribe one."

Wendy Wasserstein: "I rewrite endlessly. … [I]f you write comedy, sometimes you can be forcing the comedy by overwriting it. You're trying to make it funny, as opposed to letting the characters speak for themselves."

Arthur Miller: "The very impulse to write, I think, springs from an inner chaos crying for order, for meaning, and that meaning must be discovered in the process of writing or the work lies dead as it is finished."

The difficulties of finding a producer and making contractual arrangements are so complex that most writers prefer to work through an agent. Securing an agent is not easy because agents make their living from a percentage (usually 10 percent) of each client's earnings and therefore choose to represent only those they consider potentially successful. Agents can be of great help, nevertheless, because they understand the legal and financial aspects of producing and can help to place plays and negotiate contracts.

A producer who is interested in a play may purchase an option on it, which gives the producer the exclusive right to the play for a specified period of time. If the producer decides to stage the play, a contract is drawn up. The Dramatists Guild, an organization to which most playwrights belong and that seeks to protect the rights of playwrights by establishing professional and contractual standards for its members, sets forth the typical provisions of such contracts. The writer seldom relinquishes television, film, amateur, or foreign rights to the producer because these may eventually be far more financially rewarding than the initial production. The contract usually specifies that the writer must be available for consultation and revisions throughout the rehearsal period, conditions that most playwrights are eager to meet.

During rehearsals, many changes to the written text may be made. Some of these may result from work with a new-play dramaturg (a process discussed later in this chapter). The director, as the artist (next to the writer) most fully involved in maximizing the play's theatrical effectiveness, often makes suggestions for revisions. When based on mutual respect, the playwright–director relationship can be very productive. But sometimes directors make demands that writers think unjustified. When Tennessee Williams's play *Cat on a Hot Tin Roof* was first presented on Broadway, its director, Elia Kazan, cajoled Williams into rewriting the final act. Williams was so unhappy with the results that when he published the play, he included both his preferred version and the one he had written to please Kazan. Producers may also suggest or demand revisions thought to increase the play's box-office appeal or to keep down costs. Although playwrights' contracts state that they need not make changes they consider undesirable, they often accede to changes rather than risk cancellation of the production or denial of future productions. Many playwrights now prefer to work in regional or Off-Broadway theatres because such organizations are much more sensitive to the writer's wishes than is Broadway, where the sums of money invested make producers less willing to take chances.

Playwrights often revise new plays right up to opening night. Many theatres now have a series of preview performances to which tickets are sold (often at slightly reduced prices) but from which

Director and playwright Mary Zimmerman adapts classical myths into riveting plays. Her *Metamorphoses* originated at the Lookingglass Theatre in Chicago before being produced at a number of regional theatres and eventually on Broadway. Zimmerman's latest play, *Argonautika*, compresses the epic adventures of Jason and Medea into a two and a half hours. The play treats Medea (pictured here in white) as an innocent victim of love. Scene design by Daniel Ostling; costumes by Ana Kuzmanic; lighting by John Culbert.

T. Charles Erickson

critics are usually excluded. Previews supposedly permit the playwright and the production team to assess audience response for use in fine-tuning the script and production before the official opening and critics write published reviews. Further rewriting may be done following the initial production, but most playwrights feel the need to put this experience behind them and go on to new projects. Nevertheless, a playwright may continue to rework a script over many years and through several productions. Tennessee Williams, late in his career, wrote new versions of many of his earlier plays.

The Dramaturg

Many theatres now have a dramaturg (sometimes with assistants) on their staff. Although the acceptance of a dramaturg as a valued member of a theatre has grown considerably in recent years, the role of the dramaturg is still not widely understood. This is partly because the duties and working procedures of the dramaturg differ widely from one theatre organization to another.

The dramaturg is not a recent innovation. In Europe the position is usually traced back to Gotthold Ephraim Lessing, an eighteenth-century German playwright and critic. In 1767, upon being asked by the newly created Hamburg National Theater to serve as its resident playwright, Lessing declined but proposed instead that he become its in-house critic, offering advice on the selection of plays, critiquing the company's productions, and publishing a journal through which he might influence public taste by setting forth his theories about the nature and purposes of drama. His offer was accepted and, although the Hamburg National Theater lasted only two years, Lessing's work there established a precedent for later companies. The function he fulfilled later became standard in the many government-owned and subsidized theatres of Germany and elsewhere in Europe. Only gradually did it find favor in English-speaking theatres, in which it has gained increasing acceptance as a valuable position that serves a useful function.

Fundamentally, a dramaturg acts as an internal critic within a particular theatre. The dramaturg examines artistic choices and raises questions concerning their effectiveness in respect to a theatre's immediate and long-range goals. This fundamental description is sometimes divided into two basic functions: finding, developing, or shaping plays (literary management), and working with directors on specific productions of plays (production dramaturgy).

Lydia Diamond adapted Toni Morrison's novel, *The Bluest Eye*, into a stage play with the assistance of Steppenwolf Theatre Company dramaturg and director of New Play Development, Ed Sobel. The play treats, as does the novel on which it is based, perceptions of beauty and their relation to racism.

T Charles Erickson

Literary Management

In the United States, the person who helps a theatre find, develop, or shape plays is often called a literary manager. The literary manager's duties may vary considerably from one company to another, but they almost always include reading new scripts. Almost every not-for-profit professional theatre is inundated annually with new plays that playwrights hope will be produced. Literary managers read, or arrange for others to read, these plays. They choose those few that appear to have sufficient potential to warrant further consideration by the company. Because the volume is usually great, many companies will read only those plays submitted by agents or recommended by people whose judgments they trust.

Literary management may also include new-play development. This involves working with playwrights to help them realize the full potential of their scripts. (This process is sometimes taken over by the director or producer, but, because it is a dramaturgical function, it is discussed here.) New-play development is a delicate process because it is not so much a matter of advising writers what they should do or demanding that they make certain changes as it is helping writers clarify for themselves what they are seeking to do and finding means to do it. Literary managers sometimes describe to the writer what they find in the text and ask if that is what was intended. If it is not, then discussions may help the writer clarify what he or she is seeking to do and why it is not coming through. This process, or some variation of it, may go on over a long period—before a play has received a reading, following readings of a play before an audience, during and following workshops in which a director and performers work on the play, and during and following partially or fully mounted productions of the play. The goal is to help authors realize as fully as possible the vision they set out to embody.

Although some type of new-play development has probably existed since the beginning of theatre, current practices vary considerably from those typically used earlier in the twentieth century, when producers often demanded changes intended primarily to increase the play's box-office appeal, or when directors requested changes based on their ideas about theatrical effectiveness, or when starring performers demanded changes that would enhance their roles or make their roles more attractive. Such practices have not disappeared, but it is now more common, especially in not-for-profit theatres, for those working with playwrights to be most concerned with helping the writer achieve the full potential of a script. For this reason, most playwrights prefer to work with one or a series of not-for-profit theatres.

But the old practices have not wholly disappeared, and not all playwrights are enthusiastic about "play development" based on reactions from others. Bruce Miller of Theatre IV in Richmond, Virginia, likens much play development to "a room of strangers who tell the playwright how to rewrite their play." Susan Jonas, dramaturg for the Classic Stage Company in New York, summarizes some of the adverse responses to new-play development: "There is a great deal of criticism directed against the way that new play development is done in this country. Many charge that in the process, dramaturgs and others do a lot of damage trying to normalize the play, using their own preconceived notions of play structure." The playwright's original impulse, which gives a distinctive quality and focus to the play, can become muddied by following the well-meaning advice from others with different perspectives. The playwright must learn which reactions are helpful. A.R. Gurney, one of America's most successful playwrights, has also voiced concern about too many people getting involved in reworking a play: "I think in this country we're committed to developing plays, and many plays I've seen have been rewritten too much. ... [Y]ou can almost see that too

Practices & Styles

PLAYWRITING AS COLLABORATIVE PROCESS

Concern with "new-play dramaturgy" has in recent years served to remind us that the theatre, including playwriting, is a collaborative process, although all of those involved may not be equal partners. In the afterword to the published version of his *Angels in America, Part Two: Perestroika* (1992), Tony Kushner writes:

The fiction that artistic labor happens in isolation, and that individual talents are the sole provenance of artistic accomplishment, is politically, ideologically charged and, in my case at least, repudiated by the facts. While the primary labor on *Angels* has been mine (defensively, nervously, I hasten to shore up my claim to authorship), over two dozen people have contributed words, ideas, structures to these plays. … Had I written these plays without the direct and indirect participation of my collaborators, the results would be entirely different and much the poorer for the deprivation—would, in fact, never have come to be.

Although Kushner graciously acknowledges the contribution of his collaborators, he may "nervously" assert his claim to authorship because of recent disputes between playwrights and dramaturgs over ownership and compensation.

Lynn Thomson, the dramaturg for the late Jonathan Larson's *Rent* (1996), sued the playwright's estate on the grounds that her contributions to the play's development were worth 16 percent of Larson's royalties. Although Federal Court Judge Lewis Kaplan ruled in favor of Larson's estate, he expressed his belief that Thomson's dramaturgy had played an important role in the "radical transformation of *Rent* from an unproducible work in development into a critically and commercially viable play." However, the judge denied her claim because there had been no contractual arrangement between Larson and Thomson. Legal disputes between dramaturgs and playwrights are rare, but Kaplan's decision does underscore the positive effect of collaboration even as it raises questions about where the credit (and payment) to one person should stop and to another begin.

Rent, Jonathan Larson's rock musical adaptation of Puccini's opera *La Bohème*, was the subject of a lawsuit from the production dramaturg, Lynn Thomson, who claimed to have written a sizable portion of the script.

ArenaPal/Topham/The Image Works

many hands have been on the play. The individual voice is gone."

Literary managers are also usually involved in helping to select a company's season of plays. This usually involves keeping informed about and reading new plays that have been presented elsewhere, especially in the United States and Europe, as well as finding plays from the past that seem particularly relevant to current interests and issues. In considering plays for production, one of the dramaturgical duties of a literary manager is to ask of any play proposed for production this three-part question: Why this play for this audience at this time? Unless compelling answers can be offered, there seems little reason to produce a play.

The literary manager, or the production dramaturg, may also be involved in the selection and preparation of a particular version of a play. If a play was originally written in another language, for example, the challenge of selecting the most effective translation arises. The literary manager usually examines all of the available translations of foreign language plays and (in consultation with the director) assesses their relative effectiveness. If none is satisfactory, a new translation may be required. If the literary manager is qualified, he or she may make a new translation. More often, the producing theatre commissions someone thought particularly appropriate to make the translation. Plays from the past, even those in English, often pose comparable problems because they may include obsolete phrases, outmoded social customs, or unfamiliar ideas. Sometimes the dramatic or theatrical conventions that shaped a play are barriers to present-day production. The chorus in Greek tragedy almost always creates special challenges for modern productions, as do plays from other cultures. Decisions must be made about how these challenges may be successfully met in a production intended for the theatre's present-day audience. Sometimes the answer is to adapt the play, a task that may fall to the literary manager or to someone selected by the literary manager and director.

Production Dramaturgy

Production dramaturgy is concerned with specific productions. The production dramaturg works most closely with the director but may also work with designers and other members of a production team, as well as with those concerned with publicity, programs, and outreach. The production dramaturg's work used to be (and often still is) considered the responsibility of the director. Some directors refuse to work with dramaturgs because they prefer to do this work themselves or because they view the dramaturg as usurping one of their functions. The director–dramaturg relationship works best when it is grounded in mutual respect and a desire to explore fully how to make the written text come to life on stage. If disagreements arise, the dramaturg usually retreats to performing only those functions the director specifically requests.

The production dramaturg does not make decisions but helps the director make them by asking questions or supplying information crucial for clarifying the goals of the production and the interpretation of the play. For example, dramaturgs may research the author's life and writings in an effort to understand more fully the concerns that have shaped the play. They may also explore the period or cultural environment in which the play takes place or in which the author lived. They may bring to light what critics have written about the play or what reviewers have said about previous productions. They may examine still other sources to increase the director's understanding of the play and the context out of which it came.

Dramaturgs usually attend rehearsal often. The dramaturg may discuss with the director what he or she was trying to achieve, the disparities between the director's intentions and what the dramaturg saw on the stage, and possible reasons for the differences. These and other

Practitioners & Theorists

DRAMATURGS ON DRAMATURGY

What is a dramaturg? There is no easy answer because what dramaturgs do varies so widely from one company to another. Here are some attempts to describe dramaturgy and the role of the dramaturg.

Mark Bly (senior dramaturg and director of new play development, Alley Theatre): "When pressed for a definition of what it is that I do as a dramaturg, both in a rehearsal hall and in the theater at large, I generally answer, 'I question.' … On individual projects, the dramaturg can be that artist who functions in a multifaceted manner helping the director and other artists to develop and shape the sociological, textual, directing, acting, and design values."

Liz Engelman (former president of the Literary Managers and Dramaturgs of the Americas): "The joke is the dramaturg doesn't prescribe, but asks questions. So you don't say 'Your play sucks!' You say, 'Why does your play suck?' Then it's up to them to figure out why."

Michael Lupu (senior dramaturg, Guthrie Theatre, Minneapolis): "Simply stated, dramaturgs— that is, individuals holding such a paid or unpaid position in a theatrical institution—are not necessarily indispensable. But dramaturgy—that is, a complex creative, intellectual activity inherent within the universe of drama and theater—is indispensable. There is sufficient proof that bringing a play to life on stage can happen without the involvement of a dramaturg. For practical purposes, though, the production will fail or will not happen at all if dramaturgy is blatantly ignored."

Robert Brustein (former artistic director of the American Repertory Theatre, Cambridge, Mass.): "The most delicate and difficult function of all remains that of internal critic—finding a way to communicate your views about particular productions, and about the conduct of the theatre, without arousing the defensiveness of the artistic director or hurting the feelings of the company…. As the humanist in the woodpile, it is the dramaturg who must act as the conscience of the theatre, reminding it of its original promise, when it threatens to relax into facile, slack, and easy paths."

types of feedback can assist directors in clarifying and realizing their interpretation of the play.

Dramaturgs often have some responsibility for educating the audience. They may supply information about the play, its past, this production, or other matters that will help those who do publicity to make the play more attractive and accessible to an audience. They may also have some responsibility for the printed program (especially if it includes materials that support and elaborate on the interpretation given the play). If the theatre has an outreach program that takes productions into schools or brings student audiences to the theatre, the dramaturg may have responsibility for assembling auxiliary materials to prepare the audience or make the

Pictured here is the world premiere of *The Laramie Project* at the Denver Center Theatre featuring (left to right) John McAdams, Barbara Pitts, Greg Pierotti, Amanda Gronich, and Mercedes Herrero.

Dan McNeil; courtesy of the Denver Center Theatre

experience more meaningful. The dramaturg may also be responsible for "talk back" sessions (discussions between theatre personnel and audiences) following performances.

Overall, then, the dramaturg serves a critical and advisory function, assists in articulating the production team's vision of the production, seeks to help clarify and refine that vision during rehearsals, seeks to prepare audiences for experiencing the production most fully, and helps in evaluating the results after the production ends.

Because dramaturgs are involved in the work of every member of the production team, it is often difficult to separate the dramaturgical from other functions, especially those of the director.

Although the playwright and the dramaturg serve different functions in the theatre, their work often converges. The playwright is concerned with creating a play, whereas the dramaturg is concerned with ensuring that the final version of the play realizes the playwright's intentions and that those intentions are embodied on the stage.

Hamish Linkater, left, and Alan Rickman in the 2011 Broadway premiere of Theresa Rebeck's *Seminar*, a comedy about aspiring novelists who sign up for classes with a celebrated fiction writer, played by Rickman. Directed by Sam Gold.

Directing is psychology. It's about how to work with other human beings. It's also the art of inducing a psychological effect on a group of people who have come into a theatre to experience that effect. In your mind you're saying to yourself: "What do I want the audience to feel?" From there it's a process of moving toward that feeling with actors, designers, etc., yet allowing yourself to discover the unexpected along the way.

—Mark Lamos in *The Director's Voice*, ed. Arthur Bartow

Directing and Producing

Although directors have ultimate responsibility for the artistic aspects of productions, they depend on playwrights to provide the plays and producers to secure the necessary resources. The director works with the performers and designers to transform the playwright's work into a particular stage treatment using the resources (money, space, and personnel) the producer makes available. Thus, although the functions of playwright, producer, and director are distinct, they entwine on a practical level. The way they come together varies from one situation to another, but, whatever the starting point, the three functions—writing, producing, directing—ultimately meet in production.

The Producer

Producers have the financial and managerial tasks of making productions available to the public. Although they may not make artistic decisions directly, they nevertheless influence artistic decisions through their willingness or unwillingness (or ability or inability) to meet the requests of the playwright,

director, and other artists. Producers in the Broadway theatre are often accused of placing financial considerations above artistic integrity, but it is their job to stay within a budget, to recover the investment made in the production, and, if possible, to earn a profit. Someone must carry out the producer's functions, because otherwise productions would never reach the stage.

Although almost all producers have the same basic responsibilities, the specific conditions governing their work vary from one type of organization to another. The producer's responsibilities are most clearly defined in the Broadway theatre. Today, producers of Broadway shows usually are organizations, a group of individuals, or consortia who raise the necessary capital and carry out the other functions of a producer. In return, they receive payment for these services plus a large percentage of any profit. Production costs on Broadway typically run into millions of dollars, and success is unpredictable. Therefore, producers usually have to seek financial backing from many people or groups because few individuals are willing to assume all of the financial risk. Producers usually approach prospective investors with a proposed budget that covers expenses up to opening night, weekly operating expenses after the show opens, and a statement about how profits will be divided. Sometimes it takes months, even years, to raise the money needed for a production. Each production is usually capitalized as a corporation or partnership to limit the financial liability of investors.

After producers raise the necessary capital, they negotiate contracts with all of the personnel who will be involved. This process can be difficult, because eleven different unions may be involved—those representing dramatists, directors and choreographers, performers, musicians, stagehands, wardrobe attendants, press agents and managers, treasurers, ushers and doorkeepers, porters and cleaners, and engineers. Producers also rent space for auditions and rehearsals, lease a theatre for performances, arrange for publicity, and facilitate ticket sales. They are responsible for administering the payroll, keeping financial records, and making reports to investors at specified intervals. Occasionally, productions return very large profits, but a production can run for two or three years and never recover its original investment because the weekly expenses on a large show may consume most of the income from ticket sales, leaving little to repay the money spent before the production opened. The producers are also responsible for closing a show at the end of its run.

The producer's responsibilities are less clearly defined in other situations. Most professional resident companies are ongoing not-for-profit organizations that present a number of plays each year. They often own a theatre or perform in one owned by a municipality or arts organization or in a space leased for an extended period. Although each production has its own budget within the theatre's total budget, such theatre companies are more concerned with financing the ongoing institution than with a single production. Most companies of this type have an artistic director, who is concerned primarily with staging, and a managing director (or producing director), who is concerned with financing and marketing. Both are typically involved in raising money, establishing policy, and choosing the repertory. There is also a board of directors, which must be consulted about many issues that concern the organization's well-being and that may assist in raising funds. Because resident professional companies cannot support their activities entirely from box-office receipts, much time is spent pursuing grants or soliciting contributions. As not-for-profit organizations, they are eligible for grants from foundations, the National Endowment for the Arts, state and local arts councils, corporations, and private donors. Although this form of organization distributes the producer's responsibilities somewhat differently than is the norm on Broadway, these duties must still be performed, and the managing director or business manager usually assumes a large portion of them.

In community theatre, the organization itself usually serves as the producer, and volunteers carry out many of the duties under the supervision of the organization's officers and board of directors. Some of the duties may be delegated to an individual (president or treasurer) or to a committee. Many community theatres hire only a director and a designer-technician because the purpose of such organizations is to provide an outlet for the talents of people for whom theatre is an avocation.

In educational theatre, the producer's functions may be divided among several people. Usually, the school owns the performance space, and individuals on its payroll in other capacities do most of the supervisory work. The chair of the department or the director of theatre may have responsibilities that combine those of the artistic and managing directors of a resident company. Some theatre programs have a paid business manager who is responsible for keeping accounts, making purchases, running the box office, and handling publicity. In many small schools, the director of each play may have to assume many of the producer's tasks.

Practices & Styles

PRODUCING NEW *HAIR*

Predicting which plays and musicals will enjoy broad-based appeal can be a tricky business, as evinced by the recent 2009 Broadway revival of *Hair: The American Tribal Love-Rock Musical*.

When *Hair* was first produced at Joe Papp's Public Theatre in 1967, its use of nudity and profanity on stage, its freewheeling dramatic structure, its antiwar sentiments, and its rebellious attitude toward all sorts of social restrictions made the musical seem to many an authentic voice of its time. The Public Theatre sold the rights to *Hair*, which was moved to Broadway in 1968, where it acquired a new director (Tom O'Horgan) and again proved commercially successful. However, when the musical was revived on Broadway in 1977, it already seemed dated and the production was short-lived. It seemed then that this time capsule of the 1960s counterculture was too embedded in its time to survive unearthed of its milieu.

However, when the Public Theatre celebrated the fortieth anniversary of the musical by producing it at the Delacorte Theatre in Central Park, it proved again successful with audiences. Producers were again interested in mounting a Broadway revival. This time the Public Theatre did not sell its rights to the production; instead, the theatre agreed to a partnership in which they would maintain equal say on artistic and business matters but would not financially back the production. It took several months for sufficient financial backing to emerge. Potential investors were understandably concerned that *Hair* might not be able to "recapture the magic" it created in a park, where many of the audience receive free tickets, when produced in an enclosed Broadway theatre with individual tickets costing from $40 to $300. After several months passed without attracting sufficient investors, a change was made in its lead producers and *Hair* underwent a modest trimming of its budget. Finally, the production went into rehearsals amidst a major casting change and media speculation concerning the viability of *Hair*'s future.

The new Broadway production opened in March of 2009 and not only produced advance ticket sales in excess of $6 million but received glowing reviews and a Tony Award for Best Revival of a Musical. Aside from the excellence of the production, producer Jeffrey Richards credits nostalgia and changing demographics with the production's financial success: "When *Hair* first came out, it never did much business with people over 50. And now the people who saw it the first time are coming back—and many of them are over 50, of course, so we have them as well as the younger generations."

Hair: The American Tribal Love-Rock Musical at the Delacorte Theatre in New York's Central Park as directed by Diane Paulus, featuring (left to right) Tommar Wilson, Will Swenson, and Bryce Ryness.

Ari Mintz/Newscom

Regardless of the type of organization, then, tasks are much the same, though who performs them and the procedures may vary. In all cases, financial support must be provided, contractual arrangements made, space and personnel provided, publicity for productions disseminated, tickets sold, and bills paid. The producer is concerned with the business of show business.

The producer is also often involved in choosing the plays to be produced. On Broadway, it is the producer who selects the play. Often the director and designers are not even contacted until after this basic decision has been made, although increasingly producers bring to Broadway productions that have been successful in regional theatres, Off-Broadway, or abroad (principally London).

Most permanent organizations present a season composed of several plays. In choosing a season of plays, the group may take the following into consideration:

- The variety of periods and forms being offered
- The production requirements of each play (including cast size, and scenic, costume, and lighting demands)
- The total cost in relation to the organization's budget and projected income
- The tastes of local audiences and probable box-office appeal

During the play-selection process, advice may be sought from a number of sources. (Much of this work may involve a literary manager or dramaturg, as discussed in Chapter 12.)

Professional organizations deal directly with living authors or their agents in negotiating arrangements to produce plays. Amateur production rights are usually handled by play agencies, such as Samuel French or Dramatists Play Service. A play under copyright (which continues for the lifetime of the author plus seventy years) may not be performed without written permission (usually in the form of a contract) from the copyright owners or their authorized agent. Such contracts require that royalties be paid for each performance. Older plays may not require payment if their copyrights have expired, but recent translations or adaptations of older plays may be copyrighted even if the original copyright has expired.

Once the script is selected and production contracts are negotiated, the process of mounting the play begins.

The Director

Just as the producer is concerned with the financial aspects, the director is concerned with the artistic aspects of production. Ordinarily, the director

- decides upon an interpretation of the script and a production concept that will shape its staging.
- casts and rehearses with the performers.
- works with the designers.
- integrates all of the elements into a finished production.

In the first of these functions, the director may work closely with a dramaturg, if one is available, or may choose to work alone.

Analyzing and Studying the Play

Regardless of working procedures or personnel, the starting point for most productions is a play. Even at this beginning point in the process, many questions face the director: What is the basic story? If the play is a foreign work, what translation is best suited to the production? How might the play's events and their arrangement affect a live audience? Should portions of the script be cut? Should certain scenes be transposed? What is the significance of the play's time and setting? Should these be altered? To answer these questions effectively, the director first needs to understand the play thoroughly on its own terms.

A full understanding of a play usually requires some form of analysis. There is no standard way to analyze a play (one way is described in Chapter 3). Most directors begin by reading the play several times to become familiar with its overall qualities. They may note its structural pattern of preparation, complication, climax, and resolution. Some directors divide a script into short segments (units or beats) defined by the entrance or exit of characters or by major changes in the characters' motivations. They then examine the function of each segment in relation to those that precede and follow it as well as in relation to the play as a whole. Some directors may also note their emotional reactions to certain moments in the play or images that these moments inspire.

They may define the "through line" (or "spine") of the action that holds the play together and determines its overall thrust—its themes, point of view, and implications. The director studies all of the characters to understand their individual functions in the play and the challenges and opportunities they pose for the performers who play the roles. The director may note scenic, costume, and lighting requirements in order to work intelligently with the designers. Through such study, the director becomes aware of the opportunities and challenges a play's production poses.

Directors also typically consult other sources so as to understand better the author's point of view and other concerns that may have shaped the play. They may explore the cultural environment depicted in the play and the context from which it emerged. They may also read what critics have written about the play or what reviewers have said about previous productions. They may examine still other sources to increase their understanding of the play. All of this may be

Most directors seek relevancy when selecting a play to direct. They typically ask themselves "Why do this play *now*?" Initially produced on Broadway in 1947, Arthur Miller's *All My Sons* raises issues of personal and social responsibility through the story of a man who profited from the sale of defective warplane parts, which resulted in the death of American pilots. Director Simon McBurney's 2008 revival of Miller's play came at time when irresponsible banking and investment scandals rocked America's economy. McBurney's production featured (from left to right) Patrick Wilson, John Lithgow, Katie Holmes, Dianne Wiest, and Christian Camargo. Scenery and costumes by Tom Pye; lighting by Paul Anderson.

Sara Krulwich/The New York Times/Redux

crucial in shaping the director's interpretation of the play and its theatrical production.

If the play is new or in development, the director may work directly with the playwright. This can simplify the director's task, because the playwright may be able to answer many questions the director may have about the play. However, it may also complicate the director's work if what the playwright says he or she intended is not, in the director's opinion, clearly embodied in the play. In the latter case, although the director may suggest revisions, most contracts specify that the playwright cannot be required to alter the play. Still, in an atmosphere of mutual trust and respect, most dramatists welcome insights that the director and the rehearsal process may offer, and they frequently revise a new play right up to opening night (or occasionally throughout the play's preview performances).

After studying the play, the director decides upon an interpretation that accounts for the significance of the play's dramatic action and defines the focus of the production. The director may distill his or her interpretation of the play into a production concept: a short statement that conveys the director's vision for the production. Whether phrased as a metaphor, an action that takes place over the duration of the performance, or as a philosophical statement, a production concept basically defines the focus of the production by articulating what the director will try to realize on stage and communicate to the audience. The concept then becomes an organizational tool for the production team, who will use it as a guide in making the numerous choices about the staging, design, and acting for this particular production of the play.

Approaches to Directing

There are as many approaches to directing a play as there are directors. Still, three basic types of approach may be described as the two extremes of a continuum and a center point.

- The literal approach
- The translation approach
- The auteur approach

After careful study of Shakespeare's *Twelfth Night,* director David Warren chose to draw pointed contrasts between the play's serious and comedic moments in the Long Wharf Theatre's production. In this early scene the production drew special attention to the seriousness of Viola's plight as she finds herself alone on the coast of a strange country after a storm and shipwreck have separated her from her twin brother. Scene design by James Youmans; costumes by Toni-Leslie James; lighting by Peter Maradudin.

T. Charles Erickson

The literal approach stems from the belief that a play is a finished and self-disclosing artifact and that the director serves the playwright by transferring the play as literally as possible from page to stage. Directors who accept this notion of their function usually retain the time and place specified in the text and closely (though not necessarily slavishly) follow the playwright's prescriptions about staging. Just as a literal translation of a play from one language to another may distort the spirit of the original, an overzealously literal production may fail to project a play's essential qualities, especially if the play is from the past or written for another culture with conventions that differ markedly from those familiar to the audience.

The translation approach stems from a view of directors as translators whose goal is to capture the spirit of the play, although to do this they may depart from the playwright's specifications. This second approach is now the most

Practitioners & Theorists

DIRECTORS ON DIRECTING

Directors have different notions about their function in respect to how they work with others. Here are the thoughts of several prominent European directors on the director's role in creating theatre.

Adrian Noble (England): "I tend to give the actors quite a strong conceptual line on a play because I feel people respond better to a firm framework. ... I think my job is to work very hard beforehand on the text, and then with the designer, and then with the leading actors, involving them very definitely with the thinking behind the production and the very, very strong idea of it that I have. Once they've grasped the idea they have tremendous freedom within it."

Peter Stein (Germany): "The function of the director is not that of the father, but perhaps that of the elder brother. ... A director's approach should always depend on what is needed for the play. I find that the best stage dynamic comes if I am accepted as a brother who has very good eyes."

Ariane Mnouchkine (France): "I'm like a midwife. I help to give birth [to the production]. The midwife doesn't create the woman, and she's not the husband. But still, if she's not there, the baby is in great danger and might not come out. I think a really good director is that. Let's say I am a good director when I don't fail to be that."

Giorgio Strehler (Italy): "The undeviating search for the truth of the text, the painstaking search for the dramatic work of art, these are the essential tasks of the director. ... The problem is the excessive emphasis given to the director's role. ... Directors have contributed much to the invention of the modern theatre, but they have also often given a skewed image of what 'Theatre' is."

common, although the way it is applied varies widely from one director to another and even from one production to another. Directors using this approach usually search for a metaphor, dominant theme, or set of conventions that will define the focus—the directorial or production concept—that will shape the production.

A Soviet director, Nikolai Okhlopkov, shaped his production of *Hamlet* around the metaphor of the world as a prison, using a setting composed of cell-like cubicles in which various scenes were played. Perhaps a more common practice is to base a production on an analogy rather than a metaphor, suggesting that the action in a play is analogous to that of another time and place. For example, Orson Welles set *Macbeth* in Haiti, replacing the witches with voodoo priests. Other directors have relocated the action of *Troilus and Cressida* (which is set during the Trojan War) to the American Civil War. Of course, unless carefully formed, the use of a metaphor or analogy can reduce a play's complexities by rigidly limiting its focus.

Peter Brook shaped his widely admired production of *A Midsummer Night's Dream* around a central motif: the potentials and dangers of love. The fantasy scenes in the woods became dreamlike demonstrations to Theseus and Hippolyta, who are about to be married, of the effects of misunderstandings between lovers and about love. To underscore these connections, Brook used the performers cast as Theseus and Hippolyta to also play Oberon and Titania (their parallels in the fantasy world). Most earlier productions of the play had exploited the opportunities for visual spectacle offered by Theseus's court and the enchanted wood. Brook used the same set throughout—a white box (with front and top removed) devoid of decoration. The stage was treated as a space where the fundamental human relationships in Shakespeare's play could be isolated and examined, rather than as a space to illustrate the locales indicated in its story. Most earlier productions had emphasized the magical aspects of the fairy world and had sought to make Puck's flying convincingly real. For the fairy magic, Brook substituted stage and circus magic. Trapezes were used for

A scene from the 1959 premiere of Jean Genet's *The Blacks* produced at the Théatre de Lutèce in Paris, directed by Roger Blin, one of France's most internationally admired directors.

Akg-images/Newscom

the flying scenes, and characters on the trapezes performed tricks of stage magic such as keeping plates spinning on sticks. Bottom, rather than being transformed into an ass, became a clown with a red rubber ball for a nose. Thus, the magic was translated from fairyland into a context more familiar, though no less magical, to a modern audience. Despite his visual substitutions, Brook altered none of the play's words. His goal was to make audiences consider the implications of certain human relationships rather than concentrate on the spectacle and fantasy.

Ariane Mnouchkine, working with the Théâtre du Soleil in Paris, has used conventions borrowed from Asian (especially Indian and Japanese) theatre in several productions of Shakespeare's history plays and Greek tragedies. She believes that the formalized conventions of Asian theatre can illuminate the repetitive, ritualized power struggles in these plays. Because these conventions are unfamiliar to her Western audience, they draw attention to themselves and encourage the audience to see the more familiar dramatic actions in a fresh light. Mnouchkine's attempt is to "reinvent the rules of the game by which everyday reality is portrayed, revealing it not to be familiar and unchangeable, but astonishing and capable of transformation."

ArenaPal/Topham/The Image Works

Shakespeare's *A Midsummer Night's Dream* as performed by the Royal Shakespeare Company under the direction of Peter Brook. From left to right are Alan Howard as Oberon, Sara Kestelman as Titania, and John Kane as Puck. Rather than illusionism, Brook employed a conscious theatricality as the action occurred in a set that looked like a bare, white, empty box, complemented by vibrantly colored costumes. He also incorporated circus motifs such as trapezes being used for flying scenes and having Bottom's transformation into an ass being depicted via a clown-like red rubber ball for a nose. Scenic and costume design by Sally Jacobs.

Other variations on the translation approach could be cited, but their shared assumption is that fundamental patterns of meaning may be hidden beneath the surface detail of a play. Furthermore, the audience may more fully grasp a play's significance through artistic choices that reveal these deeply embedded patterns. Although this approach can be effective, if ineptly applied, it can distort the play (even without changing a word of its dialogue) by calling attention to bizarre staging rather than illuminating the play's themes and implications through innovative choices.

A third approach to directing places less emphasis on the written play. Using this approach, directors may begin with the play but feel free to reshape it as they see fit. A director who treats the script as raw material to be reshaped for his or her own purposes is sometimes called an *auteur* (French for "author") because the director is considered the principal creative force. Taken to its most extreme expression, this approach to directing virtually eliminates the playwright (or at least the distinctions between writer and director). Although the auteur approach is the least common approach, a few directors have achieved startling results using it.

The Polish director Jerzy Grotowski often began with well-known plays, uncovered what he considered to be basic (archetypal) patterns of human behavior in them, and then reshaped the plays (through cutting, rearranging, and relocating scenes for his own purposes), to provoke his audience's self-examination and self-recognition. Perhaps his best-known and most radical reshaping of a play involved Wyspianski's *Akropolis*, one of Poland's most revered classics, set in the royal palace at Cracow on the Feast of the Resurrection. During the action, the walls' tapestries come to life and enact what amounts to a history of Western civilization, at the end of which the resurrected Christ leads all of the figures in a procession to liberate Europe from its past errors. Grotowski saw the play as treating

Mary Zimmerman wrote and directed *Metamorphoses* (pictured here as produced by the Circle in the Square Theatre), having adapted Ovid's novel into a play that collided classical sources and contemporary images. Scene design by Dan Ostling; costumes by Mara Blumenfeld; lighting by T.J. Gerckens.

Courtesy of Dan Ostling

hopes and fantasies that had been destroyed by World War II and the Nazi concentration camps. He reshaped the play so that rather than stressing the possibility of redemption, it depicted "the cemetery of our civilization." The setting became an extermination camp at Auschwitz, and its characters prisoners who, during the course of the play, build cremation ovens and occasionally, in their nightmares, perform scenes based in a distorted way on those in Wyspianski's play. At the end they march into the ovens they have built, following a lifeless figure representing Christ. In such an approach the director's vision overrides the playwright's, and the original script becomes material to be shaped (just as acting, lighting, scenery, and costumes are).

In Robert Wilson's early theatre pieces, the written scripts are inadequate as bases for productions by others. Wilson usually lays out each piece as a storyboard. A master board shows at a glance the development of the entire piece. Wilson elaborates each segment in detailed storyboards before realizing them on stage. So tightly entwined is the play with its manner of visual expression that some of Wilson's pieces can properly be said to exist only in their performances. Similarly, performance artists often conceive their pieces as performances rather than as written drama, thereby making it difficult to separate their persona or performance style from the written text; consequently, others may find it quite difficult to stage their works.

Regardless of the approach, directors have to work with others in transforming their vision into reality because at least some production tasks must be delegated to others. The discussion that follows will undoubtedly make directing seem far more rational and precise than it is. Although most directors begin with a reasonably clear idea of what they wish to accomplish, they also make discoveries through their interactions with designers and performers that provide new insights into the play and alter their initial plans. Where directors ultimately arrive may be different from (and more rewarding than) their original destination. But such discoveries are unpredictable, and we must be content with a look at some typical working procedures that directors use.

The Director and the Designers

Some directors (among them Robert Wilson and Julie Taymor) also serve as their own designers, but that is unusual. Because the creation of production designs is a lengthy process, the director meets as early as possible with the designers to discuss the play and the production concept. The director may have already formed his or her vision for the production, or it may evolve out of such discussions. However it is arrived at, if the designers and the director are not to work at cross-purposes with each other, the production's focus should be clear to everyone involved. Directors should also relate any specific demands they may have, such as the shape of the set, the need for multiple levels, the placement of entrances, specific mood lighting, garments with specific features, and so on.

After the initial meetings, designers must be allowed time to conceive their designs. (Chapters 15–17 provide a fuller discussion of various approaches and procedures used to create production designs.) Then, at subsequent meetings, the designs are considered and a number of questions are usually explored. Do the designs adequately project the production concept? Do they fit the play's action, mood, theme, and style? How do the designs for each aspect (scenery, costumes, lighting, and sound) complement and support each other? Will scenic and costume pieces functionally serve the uses the director has planned for the production's staging? If costume or scenery changes must occur during performance, will the proposed designs permit these changes without undue delays? Can the designs be achieved within the production's budget, personnel, and time constraints? Consideration of such questions during the planning stages can prevent problems and costly last-minute changes. The designs are revised until the director and designers are all satisfied.

After the designs are approved, although there may be regular production meetings, each artist works more or less independently until the final rehearsals. In the meantime, the director's prime task becomes casting and rehearsing the performers.

Shakespeare's *Love's Labor's Lost* is given a new twist by director Michael Kahn at The Shakespeare Theatre in Washington, D.C. Kahn's 2007 production set the action in the 1960s and translates the capriciousness of Shakespeare's young aristocrats into more familiar terms for a contemporary audience. Scene design by Ralph Funicello; costumes by Catherine Zuber; lighting by Mark Doubleday.

Auditions and Casting

Audition procedures and methods vary. One is the "open call," which purportedly allows all of those interested to audition. But even open calls usually restrict access in some way. For example, in professional theatres, the casting call may be open only to those who can prove that they are professional actors (members of the stage union for performers, Actors Equity, or performers who can otherwise document their professional status). If there are many applicants, some may be eliminated on the basis of their résumés or preliminary interviews and never actually audition. Even those granted auditions may have only a short time (one to two minutes is typical) in which to demonstrate their suitability. Under

such circumstances, choices may be made on the basis of personal or physical attributes rather than on proven ability.

Many professional producing organizations increasingly depend on casting directors to save them time by creating a small pool of likely candidates. These casting directors sift through résumés, confer with agents, conduct initial auditions, and call on their own memories or DVDs of the performers' previous work. This pool of prescreened candidates is then usually auditioned thoroughly by the director, often in consultation with the casting director, producer, or playwright. The casting process usually progresses from open to closed (or "call-back") auditions. During the latter type, the prospective actors in the narrowed field are generally given

camera press/Nigel Norrington/Redux

Cross-cultural or conceptual casting was used for the 2008 Broadway revival of *Cat on a Hot Tin Roof*, which featured an all-black cast led by James Earl Jones as Big Daddy. Pictured here is the 2009 London version of that production, with Jones, right, and Adrian Lester, left, as Brick. The play, originally set in the 1950s, was set some fifteen years later to make the context of a black plantation owner more believable, but no other substantial changes were made to the play. Director Debbie Allen explained that her casting choice proved the play's universality and lent a new perspective to the play.

more time to demonstrate their suitability for the roles and may be called back several times.

Some directors or producing organizations ask performers to present previously prepared audition material. Frequently actors are asked to perform two short, contrasting monologues unrelated to the play being cast. Sometimes actors are able to study the play being cast and read a passage from it as an audition piece. The director may ask actors to read material they have not previously seen, then give explanations and ask the actors to read the same material again with these instructions in mind. Through

this method, called "cold readings," directors try to evaluate the actor's flexibility and quickness in assimilating direction. Some directors use improvisations or other methods to test the actor's imagination, inventiveness, or physical agility.

Many factors determine final casting. Some roles demand specific physical characteristics (such as being shorter or taller than others) or a particular vocal quality. The director must also consider the emotional range of each role and the actor's potential to achieve this range. Characters often need to be paired or contrasted (in romantic situations, for example), and casting

Practices & Styles

NONTRADITIONAL CASTING

Once considered extremely controversial, different forms of nontraditional casting have become increasingly accepted. "Nontraditional casting" implies casting performers in roles for which, in the past, they might not have been considered. There are many approaches to this kind of casting including colorblind casting, cross-cultural casting, and conceptual casting.

"Colorblind" casting ignores race and ethnicity and casts performers solely on the basis of their talent and suitability to a role. Although such casting has become relatively common in many professional companies and university theatres, it is still questioned when it leads to mixed-race family groups or when it seems to deny social realities. Some observers argue that colorblind casting shifts the question of minority underrepresentation away from the failure of new plays to include minority characters. Others charge that colorblind casting allows cultural differences to be ignored by absorbing representatives of other cultures into the dominant white, Eurocentric culture.

"Cross-cultural" or "conceptual" casting often involves changing the race or ethnicity of some or all characters to bring a new perspective to a play. For the Shakespeare Theatre's 1997 production of *Othello*, director Jude Kelly cast Othello and Bianca with white performers and all of the remaining characters with African American ones. Some critics complained that the casting made the play's lines referring to skin color ridiculous (Desdemona's skin was clearly not "alabaster" nor was Othello's "black"). Others claimed that this controversial "photo negative" casting emphasized the status of Othello and Bianca as "outsiders" to the play's Venetian society and focused attention on the social dynamic of racism that isolates whoever is in the minority. Ironically, historically the role of Othello has more often than not been cast with a white performer, who affects a black character, in an all-white cast.

Issues related to nontraditional casting are not restricted to race and ethnicity. They also extend to differently abled performers and failures to cast them, even in roles that include characters with those qualities. Because issues related to casting reflect divisions within American society, they are not likely to be resolved until those divisions are completely healed and greater diversity—and its representation on stage—is embraced.

must answer this need. The director must also look at the cast as a whole and assess the way the performers will look and work together. After weighing all of the factors, the director eventually chooses the performers who seem most capable of embodying the qualities he or she is seeking.

Working with the Actors

After casting is completed, the director works to mesh actors with their roles and the dramatic action to bring the script to life on the stage. The director supervises rehearsals, but a director is not a dictator. Actors bring their own insights, many of which may be novel or provocative. Most (though not all) directors are willing to discuss the actors' responses and are sufficiently flexible to adopt those that improve the initial plans. Most directors attempt to create an atmosphere free from unnecessary tensions in which the actors may explore and develop their roles. The director needs to be tactful and understanding because each actor faces unique challenges and may have

Performers depend on the director to assist them with constructive feedback on their work. Pictured here, Lisa Peterson gives feedback to the performers who make up the modern-dress chorus in Ellen McLaughlin's version of Sophocles's *Oedipus* at the Guthrie Theatre.

T. Charles Erickson

favorite working methods. Some actors take criticism gracefully in the presence of others, but others may become argumentative or so embarrassed that they find it difficult to continue.

Throughout the rehearsal process, the director assesses the actors' work and makes suggestions for improvements. Because actors cannot see their work from the audience's point of view, they rely upon the director to do this service for them. Effective directors are usually sensitive listeners and observers, critics, disciplinarians, teachers, and friends. Ultimately, they are the audience's surrogate because they try to shape the performance in ways that will be most effective for those who will see it.

The Director's Means

The director's means include the entire resources of the theatre: the script; the physical and psychological capacities of the actors; the stage space, scenery, and properties; costumes and makeup; lighting; and sound. Because each of these elements is discussed elsewhere in this book, the focus here is on the director's work with the actors to shape stage images, movements, gestures, and stage business and to focus voice and speech.

Stage Images

Each moment of a performance may be thought of as an image that sends a message to the audience. The director needs to be aware of visual composition not merely to create beautiful stage pictures but, more important, to form images that convey the situation, emotional content, and character relationships. (In actuality, these images operate in conjunction with the lines and movements of the actors, but left to chance, they can inadvertently contradict the text and lead to audience confusion.) The director uses various devices of visual composition to emphasize what is most important and to subordinate other parts. These devices will be described first as they relate to the proscenium stage and later as they are modified for other types of stage arrangements or configurations.

One of the most important controls over emphasis and subordination is the position of the performers on stage. Certain bodily positions are more emphatic than others. For example, all other factors being equal, the performer most fully facing the audience will be the most emphatic. Similarly, height can be used to achieve emphasis because, if all other factors are equal, the actor most elevated will be the most emphatic. To vary and control height, the director may have actors stand, sit, kneel, lie down, or mount steps or platforms. The director may also control emphasis by the placement of actors within the stage space or through the creation of spatial relationships. When, for example, a single actor on one side of the stage opposes a large group of actors on the other side, the single actor gains emphasis. Emphasis may also be created through visual focus—as when all of those on the stage look at the same person or object, thereby directing the audience's attention to a specific point. Other ways of gaining emphasis

include costume (one example of which would be a brilliantly colored garment amid drab clothing), lighting (using, for example, a spotlighted area while other areas are relatively dark), and scenery (placing an actor in a doorway or against a piece of furniture, for example, to strengthen the visual line). Directors seldom depend on a single source of emphasis; several are often used simultaneously, especially when emphasis needs to be divided among several characters, each requiring differing degrees of emphasis.

When one moves from the proscenium to the thrust stage (which is viewed from three sides) or the arena (which is viewed from four sides), the means to create visual emphasis are more limited. The impact of visual composition lessens when not all of the audience views it from the same vantage point. For example, bodily position

T. Charles Erickson

Staging lends emphasis and can create meaningful juxtapositions, as seen here in the Syracuse Stage production of *The Diary of Anne Frank*. Directed by Timothy Bond; scene design by Marjorie Bradley Kellogg; costumes by Lydia Tanji; lighting by Les Dicket.

becomes relatively meaningless because actors facing one part of the audience may have their backs turned to another. For much the same reason, stage area loses much of its effectiveness because nearness to one part of the audience may be distance from another part. But most of the other devices apply. Nevertheless, in thrust and arena theatres it is difficult to compose visual images that are expressive from every angle. The director must therefore construct images from a variety of angles throughout the performance so that no part of the audience is neglected.

The way devices for achieving emphasis are used depends greatly on the stage setting. The placement of doors and furniture encourages some compositional patterns and impedes others. The absence of furniture in settings for many period plays (for example, *Oedipus Rex* and most of the scenes in *Hamlet*) rules out the detailed routine of daily life that is typical in such modern plays as *A Doll's House*. The type of play also affects composition. For example, many of the visual devices appropriate to a farcical *commedia dell'arte* script such as *The Servant of Two Masters* might be out of keeping with an expressionistic play such as *The Hairy Ape*.

Some directors consider stage images the legacy of a time when the "picture-frame" stage was the only type in use, and they argue that its conventions have been invalidated by more recent stage forms. Others believe that concern for visual composition leads to a self-conscious or unnatural positioning of performers on stage. They argue that if the performers understand the dramatic situation, they will instinctively group themselves properly. Flexible (or variable) stages pose the greatest problem to the creation of effective stage images because several scenes may proceed simultaneously in various parts of a space shared by both spectators and performers. This use of theatrical space rejects the traditional view that each moment of a performance should have a major focal point to which every spectator's attention is directed and that should be visible and audible to every member of the audience. However, despite the flexible theatre's use

of multiple focal points, every individual scene, even if simultaneously performed with others, creates visual messages, planned or not.

Many objections to the deliberate use of stage images concern the possibility that these compositions will draw attention to themselves and distract attention from the play's action. No doubt poorly conceived or inappropriate compositions may have this effect. But one cannot deny that the stage images that continually form, dissolve, and transform as the audience watches are a major component of any production and that they embody meaning. Therefore, although there may be controversy over the way this element is to be approached, its importance is undeniable.

Movement, Gesture, and Business

Although particular images are important, the dominant impression of a performance is one of movement—flow, change, and development. Consequently, movement is among the director's most powerful means of expression. Movement serves many functions.

- It gives emphasis because it catches the eye and directs attention.
- It helps define character and mood.
- It clarifies situation through its tempo and quality.
- It may provide contrast and build scenes to a climax through its type, size, and tempo.
- It provides variety.
- It may indicate dramatic type or style.

Directors work with actors to make sure that their movements focus audience attention on important stage business as well as to assist the performers in making their characterizations distinct. For example, an elderly person normally uses fewer and slower movements than a young person, just as a nervous or angry person moves differently from a casual or relaxed person.

Directors may also help performers to shape their movements in order to clarify dramatic situations. Highly emotional scenes normally incite more movement (and more rapid and sharply defined movement) than do quiet moments. Movement may be used to build scenes to a climax, to provide contrast, and to establish tempo. Gradually increasing the amount and size of movement can create a sense of growing confusion, conflict, or development and change. Contrast in movement from one scene to another can point up differences in the play's mood, tempo, and situation, as well as provide variety. Finally, directors may wish to use the performer's movement to reinforce the play's genre or dramatic style. The movement called for by *Oedipus Rex* is typically more stately and formal than that called for by *Cat on a Hot Tin Roof*. For plays that depart from

realism, such as *The Hairy Ape*, deliberately distorted or stylized movement may be called for.

Movement can be divided into three main types: from place to place, gesture, and business. Each type may be dictated by the script or invented by the director or the performers. Many movements (such as entering, exiting, dancing, or lighting lamps) may be specified in stage directions or dialogue. On the other hand, many older plays include no stage directions, and all movement must be deduced. When devising stage movement, most directors take their cues from the script so that the movement not only provides variety but also embodies the desires and responses of the characters and therefore appears motivated. Character relationships and emotional connotations are among the most common motivators of movement—feelings of

West Texas A&M University, *The Resistible Rise of Arturo Ui* by Bertolt Brecht; Royal C. Brantley, Director; Anne C. Madlock, Costume Designer; Jarod Roberts, Scene Designer; Tim Cummings, Lighting Designer; Shawn D. Irish, Photographer

Directed by Royal C. Brantley, pictured here is a production of Bertolt Brecht's *The Resistible Rise of Arturo Ui*, a satirical allegory about Adolf Hitler's rise to power in Nazi Germany. In this scene the audience's attention is focused via multiple means: the main character is elevated above the others; he faces front (versus everyone else in profile or with backs to the audience); he is clothed in a different color (that also contrasts with his immediate background); and he has multiple characters pointing in his direction. Were one of the downstage characters to turn and face the audience, he or she could gain focus via the contrast.

love, anger, and eagerness normally move characters toward each other, whereas disgust, fear, and reluctance separate them. Movement from place to place is the broadest type that directors use in working with the performers.

Gesture, facial expression, and bodily attitude, which together create what is commonly called body language, are of special importance for achieving subtlety and clarity. Gesture normally involves only the hands and arms, but at times the torso, head, feet, or legs may be used gesturally. Gesture can provide a subtle means of gaining emphasis. For example, a gesture by a performer who is about to speak is usually sufficient to shift attention to that performer at the right moment. Gesture can also convey basic psychological traits. A great many spontaneous gestures may suggest an uninhibited, outgoing personality, whereas few and awkward gestures may suggest the opposite. Bodily attitude—stiffly upright, slumping, relaxed, and so on—is an especially useful means for conveying emotional attitudes or immediate reactions. So is facial expression, which, though it is not always visible in a large auditorium, is a supplementary aid in conveying a character's response.

Another kind of movement, stage business, involves physical activities such as filling and smoking a pipe, arranging flowers, wrapping packages, eating and drinking, dueling, and so on. Stage business is frequently prescribed by the script, but it may also be invented by the director or performers to clarify action or enrich characterization. Stage business must be carefully timed to make appropriate points and coordinate with dialogue to avoid diverting attention from important lines or action.

In recent years, several nontraditional uses of movement, gesture, and business have become common. Although most stage movement attempts to re-create believable human behavior, some directors may use nonrealistic movement to stylize the production or to physicalize abstract ideas or for still other purposes. Performers may writhe on the floor in tangled masses, crawl about the set, and perch on various structures. Movement in general has become more uninhibited, and the range of acceptable movement has been considerably extended.

Voice and Speech

The director's means also include the voice and speech of the performers. Just as innovative movement has become important, so, too, has nonverbal vocal sound. In nonrealistic plays, directors may use voice to create dissonance, modulations ranging from the loudest to the softest, cries, yelps, and so on. Nevertheless, the director is still most commonly concerned with voice as a medium for language or song. (Because voice and speech are more fully the performer's concern, they are discussed at greater length in Chapter 14.) The director needs to understand voice and speech thoroughly in order to use them effectively and to coach performers intelligently. In using voice and speech, the director has four main concerns:

- The dialogue should be audible and comprehensible to the entire audience.

- The performers' vocal qualities—that which distinguishes any two sounds of like duration, pitch, and volume from each other, such as breathiness or nasality—should be appropriate to their characters.

- The inflectional pattern and volume of the performers should be appropriate not only to their characters but also to specific situations and the meaning of their lines.

- The tempo and rhythm of the performers' dialogue should vary appropriately in accordance with the changing dynamics of the action.

The director's means are varied and, although discussed separately here, they are applied simultaneously in the theatre, first one and then another being given primacy. Through such continuous adjustments, the director seeks to achieve clarity in motivation, action, and meaning, in addition to creating that underlying and indefinable sense of excitement that characterizes theatrical performance at its best.

ANNE BOGART

Few contemporary directors are as noted for their work with performers on controversial productions as is Anne Bogart, who helped to popularize an acting technique called *viewpoints*. The technique, which was first articulated by choreographer Mary Overlie, grew out of postmodern dance improvisations and breaks down time and space—the two dominant elements of movement that performers deal with—into several categories. Bogart and others have expanded this technique into a training method that allows performers to generate bold nonrealistic physicalizations while working as an ensemble. Bogart uses viewpoints in her staging to encourage her audience to see familiar plays or subjects in a new light.

Bogart's directing work can be divided into several basic areas. She has created theatrical profiles of significant artists and thinkers. Bogart has provided a provocative combination of Andy Warhol interviews/writings with Dante's *Inferno* in her *Culture of Desire* (1997), playfully reworked Brecht's theories and criticism in *No Plays No Poetry* (1988, for which she won an Obie Award), and explored the creative imagination of Orson Welles's *War of the Worlds* (a 1999 production based on the 1938 radio play). Bogart has also created new approaches to familiar or classic plays. In a 1984 production, she set the musical *South Pacific* in a clinic for emotionally disturbed war veterans. Her 1982 adaptation of *A Streetcar Named Desire* was set in a German club whose members take turns playing scenes from the play; there were ten Stanleys and twelve Blanches (one of them a man). Third, Bogart has conceived and directed wholly new plays. Her play *Cabin Pressure* (1999) examines a theatre audience's experience of suspense and anticipation. Finally, she directs the new plays and operas of others, among them Paula Vogel's *Baltimore Waltz* (1992), for which Bogart was awarded her second Obie.

In 1992, she cofounded with Tadashi Suzuki, the Japanese director and acting theorist, the Saratoga International Theatre Institute (SITI), the goal of which is to "revitalize the theatre from the inside out"; SITI has conducted acting workshops and symposia and has presented plays directed by Bogart and Suzuki. Her work was featured at the Actors Theatre of Louisville's 10th Annual Classics in Context Festival: Modern Masters—Anne Bogart. She has also authored a book on directing and currently serves as the head of the graduate directing program at Columbia University in New York.

Bogart's directing provokes strong, conflicting responses. Because she often adapts or radically stages well-known plays or subjects grounded in our cultural past, her work can seem iconoclastic. As the *New York Times* theatre critic Mel Gussow has pointed out, "Depending on the point of view, [Anne Bogart] is either an innovator or a provocateur assaulting a script."

SITI performers embody esoteric critics in a scene from Anne Bogart's world premiere production of *Cabin Pressure* at the Humana Festival of New American Plays. During the scene, the performers pushed this table holding microphones closer and closer to the audience as they spoke, creating an intimidating cacophony of voices. Directed by Anne Bogart; settings by Paul Owens; costumes by Walt Spangler; lighting by Mimi Jordan Sheridan.

Courtesy of Actors Theatre of Louisville. Photo by Richard C. Trigg

Rehearsing the Play

Rehearsals can seldom be held under conditions approximating those of performance. In most cases, the scenery, costumes, lighting, and properties are not available until the final days, and the rehearsal space is seldom the stage on which the play will be presented. Therefore, the director and performers must rely heavily on imagination during rehearsals.

The typical rehearsal space is a large room (at least as large as the stage) on the floor of which the ground plan of the set is outlined with tape. If there is more than one set, each is indicated with different colored tape. Chairs and tables, as well as improvised doors and levels, help the performers become familiar with the setting. Temporary properties that approximate those to

be used in performance are necessary if there is complex stage business, such as serving a meal or fighting a duel. Similarly, rehearsal garments may be needed for plays in which unusual headdresses, hoopskirts, and other unfamiliar features or accessories will appear.

In order to plan rehearsals effectively, the director needs to know how much time will be available. In the nonprofessional theatre, performers are usually available for rehearsal only in the evenings for three or four hours and for a period of four to six weeks. In the professional theatre, a rehearsal period of three to four weeks is typical, with performers available for approximately eight hours each day. A group that evolves its own scripts may require months to prepare a performance. Whatever the situation, the director ascertains the approximate number of hours available for rehearsals and plans a schedule to

Acclaimed French director Ariane Mnouchkine in rehearsal in 1970 with her company Théâtre du Soleil. Their theatre is located in a former munitions factory in the Vincennes area of eastern Paris.

Jean-Pierre Couderc/Roger-Viollet/The Image Works

use the time to maximum advantage. Because all problems cannot be worked on simultaneously, the director divides the schedule into progressive phases.

Any generalized discussion of the rehearsal process makes it seem more standardized than it usually is because rehearsals are shaped to meet the particular demands of each play. However, the typical rehearsal process involves the following phases:

- Read-throughs and "table work"
- Staging or "blocking"
- Working with the performers
- Shaping the performance
- Integrating all the other elements of the production (scenery, costumes, lighting, sound, and so on)

The amount of time devoted to reading, discussing, and studying the play varies with the director, with the complexity of the script, and with the experience of the cast. During this period, the director may explain the production concept and clarify the main objectives toward which everyone should be working. Sometimes these early rehearsals are referred to as "table work" because they may involve group reading and study done around a table. However, some directors choose to devote time during the early rehearsals to group activities (such as improvisations and theatre games) intended to familiarize the performers with each other, lessen inhibitions, encourage trust, and otherwise prepare the performers for the work ahead. Whatever method is chosen, early rehearsals usually strive to familiarize the actors with each other, the play they will perform, their roles, and the function of their roles within the play.

Staging, or blocking, establishes each performer's movements from place to place and each performer's bodily position at each moment. For example, an actor might be asked to enter up center, cross slowly to a sofa down left, and stand facing front. Initially, most directors are concerned only with large patterns of movement; subtleties and refinements come later. When the blocking for one segment is finished, the director moves on to the next, repeating the process until the entire play is blocked. Many directors believe that the initial blocking is merely tentative, and they adjust it as rehearsals proceed. When this is the case, the performers should be made aware that they must be prepared to adjust to changes as they occur. Some directors believe that blocking should evolve out of character relationships

Persephone by Noah Haidle as directed by Nicholas Martin for the Huntington Theatre (Boston); scene design by David Korins; costumes by Jenny Mannis; lighting by Ben Stanton. Note how the blocking—in combination with costumes, scenery, and lighting—creates mood and dramatic tension.

T. Charles Erickson

and the performers' sense of their roles—a collaborative process among performers and director, which takes longer to develop. Regardless of how the blocking is achieved and when it is set, once it is set, the performers should understand where and when they are to move.

After the play is staged, time is typically devoted to deepening the performers' understanding of their lines and blocking. For each act, the director may specify the date by which the performers should have their lines memorized. As with blocking, there is disagreement about the best time for performers to memorize lines (early or after the performers are thoroughly familiar with the roles). However, it is generally acknowledged that it is difficult for performers to achieve subtle characterizations or to build scenes properly if they must continually consult their scripts. During this phase, the director helps the performers to incorporate their lines and movements as clear expressions of the characters' desires, actions, and relationships. Typically, the director focuses the performers' attention on one segment or scene at a time to clarify the characters' motivations and define their relationships within each segment. A single scene may be repeated many times as these working sessions continue. This allows the performers the repetition needed to memorize their lines and movements as well as a clearer grasp of their specific motivations for what they say and do. If the performers have difficulties, the director may ask them questions or structure improvisations that stimulate responses and attitudes that can then be adapted to the scripted situation. Whatever the process used, it is important that the performers understand who their characters are, what they are doing, why they are doing it, and how they relate to one another.

With musicals, the director's task becomes especially complex during this and later phases of rehearsals. For musicals, a choreographer normally creates and rehearses the dances separately, just as the musical director rehearses the singers and chorus separately (normally with only piano accompaniment). The director must eventually integrate songs and dances into the whole and devise the transitions that lead smoothly from spoken lines into song and from stage movement into dance.

The next phase of rehearsals usually is dedicated to ensemble playing and shaping the action for an overall effect. At this time, the director fine-tunes transitions between scenes, timing, and the proper emotional dynamics needed to support the progression of scenes. Some directors may go over the same scene repeatedly to achieve the proper timing or intensity, just as they may adjust the pacing of scenes for the sake of variety, but typically the director now works with the performers on progressively larger segments of the action. If the director has not previously allowed the performers an uninterrupted "run-through" of the entire play, almost all directors include at least one at this point in the rehearsal process.

The final phase of rehearsals integrates all of the elements of production. Frequently, this is the first time the performers have rehearsed in the actual performance space with the scenery, lighting, and sound (including, in musicals, the full orchestra) that will be used in performance. Likewise, it is often the performers' first opportunity to rehearse in their costumes and makeup. As might be expected, many adjustments are typically made during these final rehearsals. It is usual to have at least one rehearsal to work out problems with lighting levels and cues, costume and scene changes, sound, music, and properties. This is usually called a "technical rehearsal." Technical rehearsals are then followed by at least two or three dress rehearsals intended to approximate as nearly as possible the conditions of performance. During these rehearsals, difficulties are noted and attempts are made to correct them before the next rehearsal. Some directors invite several people to dress rehearsals to get indications of probable audience response and to prepare the performers for a larger audience. In the professional theatre, preview performances function as a series of additional dress

Richard Feldman

Jonathan Miller (right) directing actors in a production of the eighteenth-century comedy *The School for Scandal* **at the American Repertory Theatre.**

that these assistants perform can vary widely from theatre to theatre, as can their titles, but their work is of vital importance. One assistant may takes notes from the director during rehearsals about points to discuss with the performers, designers, or technicians. This individual may also post notices and keep everyone informed of things they need to know. Another assistant may act almost like a secondary director: attending production conferences, serving as liaison with designers, and coaching or rehearsing scenes with the performers. Typically called the assistant director, this individual performs whatever tasks are assigned by the director. Depending on the size or complexity of the production, there may be more than one assistant director.

Perhaps the most indispensable of the director's assistants is the stage manager. The stage manager is responsible for running the show at each performance and, during the rehearsal period, for compiling the promptbook, which becomes the blueprint for performances. In the professional theatre, the stage manager may organize and run auditions and, after the show opens, may rehearse the performers if necessary. The stage manager is the director's surrogate during performances, charged with seeing that everything functions as the director intended.

rehearsals, after each of which changes may be made. The changes are then tried out on other audiences until the play opens.

When the play opens, the director's job is considered to be complete, although many directors come back at intervals to revitalize performances. By opening night a production promptbook has been compiled; it records the blocking, stage business, lighting cues, sound cues, and everything that is required to run the show as the director intended.

The Director's Assistants

The director may have one or more assistants who can fulfill a variety of functions. The tasks

Thinking about the Director's Work

Today, not only are approaches to directing varied, but so, too, are the plays and the theatrical conventions available. When we attend the theatre, our experiences may also be varied. We may find ourselves confronted with the commonplace and boring, the exotic and puzzling, the novel and exciting, or some combination of these. Such variety often makes it difficult to respond intelligently. Here is a list of questions that may help the theatregoer assess the director's contributions.

1. Was there an identifiable production concept, unifying metaphor, or interpretational approach? If so, what was it, and how was it manifested in the production? To what effect?

2. How closely did the production adhere to the play? Did the production alter time, place, or other aspects of the play? If so, how? To what effect? If not, how did this production make—or fail to make—the play relevant to its audience?

3. How did the director's casting choices influence the production?

4. What effect did the performer-audience arrangement or configuration have on the performance? Did the director's staging take advantage of this relationship? If so, in what ways?

5. Did the director's staging clearly convey the action? How was the staging used to clarify character relationships or emphasize important actions?

6. Did the director's staging create any memorable images or visualizations? If so, which? What overall effect

did these have on the production as a whole?

7. Was there appropriate variety in mood and tempo? Did the action, as a whole, build to a climax or have a discernible pattern or shape? What effect did this have on the audience?

8. Did the production make use of any unusual conventions? If so, which? To what effect?

9. Were the production design elements (scenery, costumes, lighting, sound) coordinated to support the action and the production concept? If not, what aspect seemed out of place or inconsistent with the rest? Did the director make any specific use of the design elements? With what effect?

10. Overall, did the production achieve its apparent goals? If not, where did it fall short? With what overall results?

Other questions could be posed, and many of them will arise as other areas of production are examined in the chapters that follow.

Kevin Spacey as the title character in Shakespeare's *Richard III*, as directed by Sam Mendes. In addition to acting, since 2003 Spacey has served as the Artistic Director of London's Old Vic Theatre Company. They produced *Richard III* in London in 2011 and then brought that production to the Brooklyn Academy of Music in 2012.

Acting is the art of saying a thing on the stage as if you believed every word you utter to be as true as the eternal verities of life; it is the art of doing a thing on the stage as if the logic of the event demanded that precise act and no other; and of doing and saying the thing as spontaneously as if you were confronted with the situation in which you were acting for the first time.

—John Barrymore (a legendary American actor, known best for his performance as Hamlet)

Acting

Of all theatre practitioners, the actor most nearly personifies the stage for the general public, perhaps because the actor is the only theatre artist the audience normally sees. The actor's function is to embody characters that otherwise exist only in the written word and the imagination. What the performers say and do and the way they interact with each other and their surroundings creates a play's action. The script may provide the blueprint; the designers, the visual context; and the director, the overall focus; but it is the living presence of the actor that is most essential to the audience's theatrical experience.

Actors are among the few artists (along with dancers and singers) whose basic means of expression cannot be separated from themselves; they must create roles by using their own bodies and voices. The director, designers, and playwright can sit in the auditorium and watch what they have created, but stage performers can never completely separate themselves from what they are creating. Even a filmed stage performance violates the essence of stage acting: the moment-by-moment interaction of the live performer and the live audience. In films, scenes are almost always shot out of sequence and over a span of several weeks or months; the actors have only a general notion of how the scenes

will fit together; typically film actors do not see the scenes in sequence until the film is ready for release months later. Even then, the performance they (and the public) see has been given much of its shape by the film's editor. Audience response cannot alter or influence what happens during a screening. All of these factors do not make the screen actor's job less difficult than the stage actor's, but they do make it different. Stage actors play scenes in the order specified by the script and complete the entire play at each performance. They must be fully aware of how the action develops, and they must shape their performances to increase and relax tension, vary tempo, create appropriate emphases, and build the action to a climax. They prepare for these tasks through many rehearsals with a director, whose critical advice and editing shape the total production, but it is the actors who must re-create the performance each time—and for a new audience, whose immediate feedback continuously influences that performance.

In many ways, acting is an extension of everyday human behavior. Almost everyone speaks, moves, and interacts with others. We also play many roles during the course of a day, adjusting to changing contexts: home, business, school, recreation, and so on. Perhaps it is not surprising, then, that it is not always easy to convince would-be actors that rigorous training is necessary. Nevertheless, acting requires carefully honed skills because the ability to use behavior expressively in the theatre differs from the ability to function adequately in daily life.

Acting skill is a mixture of three basic ingredients: innate ability (a special talent for acting), training, and practice (or experience). Talent is perhaps most essential, but usually it is not enough in itself; it needs to be nurtured and developed through extensive training and repeated application in performance.

The Actor's Training and Means

In acting training, not all aspects of process can be addressed simultaneously. Therefore, different aspects of acting (voice, movement, scene study, and so on) are singled out for specialized attention even as attention is being paid to the interrelationship of the various parts. Ultimately, the goal is to integrate all of the parts into a seamless whole.

The Actor's Instrument

Just as it takes musicians many years of training and practice to master their instruments, actors spend years mastering their instrument. However, unlike musicians, the instrument that actors learn to master is themselves: their body, voice, imagination, concentration, and psychological responsiveness. As the actor's primary means of communicating, the body and voice need to be flexible, disciplined, and expressive. Flexibility is needed so the actor can express physically or vocally a wide range of attitudes, traits, emotions, and responses. But flexibility alone is not sufficient; actors must also be able to control body and voice at will, and such control comes only through understanding, practice, and discipline.

AP Photo

Paul Robeson, playing Yank, the title character in a 1931 London production of Eugene O'Neill's *The Hairy Ape.*

Actors typically begin by learning how the body and voice operate physiologically. They then proceed to explore how their own body and voice habitually function. If one can discover what one's usual body alignment is, how one is breathing, what one's sources of tension are, and so on, one is then in a position to work toward expanding one's range of expressiveness as well as gaining control over one's physical and vocal instrument. The initial goal is to eliminate inhibiting tensions so one can move freely and effortlessly and achieve a resonant, flexible voice; the ultimate goal is control over both body and voice for expressive use in performance.

Because the body and voice are integral parts of a total system that includes psychological forces, it is difficult to achieve physical and vocal freedom and expressiveness without some concern for the psychological processes that may create tension or block creative expression. One popular means of dealing with these has been through improvisational

Practitioners & Theorists

ACTORS' THOUGHTS ABOUT ACTING

Many well-known actors have been quite articulate about their profession. Here are a few excerpts.

Willem Dafoe (a member of the Wooster Group and well-known screen actor): "I think that all the characters I play are basically me. I believe that under the right set of circumstances we're all capable of anything, and that acting allows the deepest part of your nature to surface—and you're protected by the fiction as it happens."

Laurence Fishburne (contemporary actor who frequently performs for both stage and film): "There's no feeling like the feeling one gets from performing live. It's really exhilarating, it's really thrilling, and it's always scary … it's always dangerous."

Joseph Chaikin (leading actor of the Open Theatre): "Only when [the actor] is awake to the whole event of the piece, rather than just his part, and his interest in what is told in the piece is immediate … can his work be organized to each performing situation. What he learns is how to live through the situation each time, instead of just repeating the results. [Otherwise] his performance is without the most essential acting dimension—that of being there and inhabiting the play as it's performed."

Fiona Shaw (leading contemporary British actress, speaking of her performance as Electra): "Literature, I think, is humanity's dialogue with itself and an actor is the interpreter of the text of the writer, who is tapping the soul of who we all are. The best one does is to give it expression— the key being one's own grief that reveals a very dark pool of basic grief that everybody has. In the end, I suspect, that dark pool is a very similar pool to everybody else's pool."

Judi Dench (one of England's major actresses and 1999 Oscar winner for her role in *Shakespeare in Love*): "What I like is doing as many different things as possible in the theatre at the same time. I like being in a repertoire of four or five plays. … You're kept very much on your toes. … It's like a permanent first night and that keeps it very alive; doing a play eight times a week is a killer."

theatre games designed to break down inhibitions, build self-confidence, and foster trust in fellow performers. Other exercises have been borrowed from a variety of sources, both Western and Asian, most of which treat inner impulses, body, and voice as interrelated processes. Therefore, to work on any one of these is to help the others. The goal is to develop a sensitive, skilled, and expressive instrument that the actor can control.

In addition to mastery of body and voice, actors usually seek more specialized training in dancing, fencing, singing, and other skills that increase their ability to play a wide range of roles in a variety of theatrical forms.

Observation and Imagination

Actors require highly developed powers of observation and imagination. Because human beings learn about each other in large part through observation, actors need to develop the habit of watching other people (for example, the dominant behavioral patterns of various personality types or age groups). Although observed behavior may not always be directly transferable to the stage, it can be drawn on in creating convincing characterizations.

Actors must also develop imagination in order to "feel their way" into the lives of others and into fictional situations. The imagination grows when fed by a few particular details or circumstances. For this reason many actors start improvisations or scene work by identifying the *given circumstances* that they are working with: the basic who, what, when, and where that constitute the situation. An actor's imagination also requires specificity to transform the stage world into one that compels belief. To behave believably, the actor handling a plastic pistol imaginatively particularizes it with the properties of a real one (its weight, texture, and deadly potential). Similarly, to embody the character's attitudes convincingly, the actor must imaginatively endow the objects, places, and people with the emotional significance and value they hold for the character. Most imagination techniques are based on behaving as if the fictional world were true. However it may be approached and developed, imagination plays a fundamental role in believable acting.

Concentration

No matter how well actors have mastered the basic skills, they are unlikely to use these skills effectively onstage unless they have also learned to control, shape, and integrate them as demanded by the script and the director. Control is usually achieved only through daily practice and disciplined effort over a long period.

One mark of control and discipline is concentration—the ability to immerse oneself in the situation and to shut out all distractions. Before actors rehearse or perform, they must clear their minds of unrelated personal concerns in order to adopt those of their characters. During rehearsals, actors may need to tune out peripheral noise. They must be able to remain focused on the scene, despite interruptions by the director, and make ongoing adjustments. Well-developed concentration is also required during performance. No matter how often they have performed the roles, actors should make each moment seem as if it were happening for the first time. To create this illusion, actors must concentrate on what is developing around them—not in a general way but on the specific speeches, gestures, and movements of others in the scene—and must respond with the appropriate level of intensity at the appropriate moment.

Basic Stage Vocabulary and Conventions

Over the centuries, actors have developed certain ways of doing things onstage because they have proven more effective than others. Many routine tasks have been reduced to a set of conventions that actors are expected to know. Directors take for granted that actors are familiar with these conventions and give many instructions in a kind of stage shorthand.

Among the basic conventions is the division of the stage into areas, which facilitates giving directions. The term *upstage* indicates the area toward the rear of the stage, and *downstage* refers to the area toward the front of the stage. These terms date from the time when the back of a raked stage actually did slope upward away from the audience and downward toward it. Stage right and stage left refer to the actor's right and left when facing the auditorium. The stage floor may also be spoken of as though it were divided into squares, each with its own

Practices & Styles

APPLYING IMAGINATION AND OBSERVATION

All actors use their imaginations and powers of observation to create believable characters with whom they frequently have little in common. However, few actors have the opportunity to test their skills while facing the challenge of playing complex nonhuman characters. Veteran actor André De Shields faced such a challenge in playing a 350-pound gorilla named Graham who is trained to communicate in American Sign Language in Mark Medoff's play *Prymate* (2003).

To prepare for the role, De Shields studied gorillas by reading about them, observing them in zoos and on film, and speaking with a gorilla-behavior specialist. He learned to imitate the dozens of specific sounds that gorillas make, the manner in which they shift their attention every ten to fifteen seconds (because gorillas have a strong sense of peripheral vision, they seldom directly focus on one object for long), and the manner in which they communicate affection or warn others off their territory. He wanted to make certain that his physical actions as Graham were accurate and specific, even though doing so was physically very taxing. Once De Shields had a thorough knowledge of how gorillas communicate and move, he sought to understand why Graham acts as he does and how he might perceive different objects, actions, and events. De Shields then built an imaginative bridge between himself and his 350-pound gorilla character.

De Shields has played a wide variety of roles on Broadway and throughout America's regional theatres including Willy Loman in *Death of a Salesman*, Vladimir in Samuel Beckett's *Waiting for Godot*, and one of the amateur male strippers in *The Full Monty* on Broadway. He originated the role of Graham at Florida State University before playing the part on Broadway. In addition to the physical rigor and psychological savvy needed to create the character, De Shields also needed great personal courage because he believed that some would find the image of a black man playing a gorilla offensive and potentially racist. But "if you want to explode a stereotype, you don't avoid it," he explained in an interview with the *New York Times*. "You face it down."

André De Shields plays a 350-pound gorilla, and Phyllis Frelich plays the anthropologist who teaches him to use American Sign Language in the Broadway production of Mark Medoff's *Prymate*.

Sara Krulwich/The New York Times/Redux Pictures

designation: *up right, up center, up left, down right, down center, down left.*

Actors are also expected to be familiar with stage vocabulary that relates to the position of their bodies. *Full front* means facing the audience; *one-quarter* indicates a quarter-turn away from the audience; *one-half* or *profile* means a 90-degree turn away from the audience; *three-quarter* means a 135-degree turn away from the audience; and *full back* means turned completely away from the audience.

Other terminology may supplement designations of area and bodily position. To *open up* means to turn slightly more toward the audience; *turn in* means to turn toward the center of the stage; *turn out* means to turn toward the side of the stage. Two actors are sometimes told to *share a scene*, meaning that both should play in the one-quarter or profile position so that they are equally visible to the audience. To *give stage* means that one actor gives the dominant stage position to another by facing away from the audience more than the other actor does. In most scenes, emphasis shifts frequently from one character to another, and the actors may constantly be giving and taking the stage according to who needs to be most emphatic at a specific moment. To *focus* means to look at or turn toward a person or object so as to direct attention there. Actors may also be told to *dress the stage* (that is, move to balance the stage picture). Experienced actors make such movements unobtrusively and almost automatically.

Similarly, experienced performers are expected to be able to emphasize or subordinate stage business and dialogue. An actor may need to *lift* (to draw attention to) a line of dialogue that will be particularly important later. Simi-larly, an actor may need to *plant* (to make sure the audience notices) an object (such as a letter) in an earlier scene that will be important later in the play. The actor may make sure it is noticed early on in many different ways. For example, the actor may hesitate, start to put it one place, then select the final spot. Conversely, some actions need to be *masked* or *cheated*, away from the audience. Eating, for example, must be faked to a large degree, because actors can seldom eat the actual food or the amount indicated by the script in the time provided. Unless stage business or dialogue needs to be emphasized or subordinated in some particular way, actors normally strive to make their movements and line deliveries natural, unobtrusive, and appropriate to the moment-by-moment action of the play.

Scene Study

While actors are involved in gaining control over themselves as instruments, they are simultaneously involved in scene study, based on either scripts as a whole or scenes from scripts. This involves close attention to dramatic action and how it develops. Most actors learn to break scenes into beats or units of action. These are based on alterations in motivation or a change in tactics by a character or some other change such as the entrance or

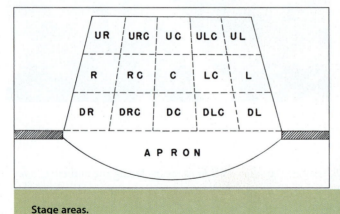

Stage areas.

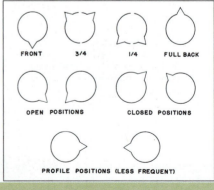

Performer positions.

exit of a character. Actors also note changes in tempo and mood and so on. This study is usually preliminary to rehearsing the scenes with other actors. Over time, actors typically study and enact scenes from a wide variety of plays—past and present. This allows them to gain the broadest possible experience in multiple dramatic forms and styles. Scene study and its embodiment in performance (both in the classroom and in fully mounted productions) ultimately bring together all of the elements of actor training.

From Training to Performing

Prior to the twentieth century, would-be actors usually learned on the job. First, they had to be accepted into a company as "utility" actors, roughly equivalent to being apprentices. They then played small roles in a variety of plays and observed the more experienced and established actors closely. Training was essentially a mixture of observation and trial and error. After a few years, young actors discovered the types of roles to which they seemed best suited and settled into that "line of business," usually for the rest of their careers. But in the late nineteenth century, when resident companies were driven out of existence by touring productions (usually cast in New York with experienced actors), would-be actors were deprived of their traditional training ground. Although some acting schools had existed before this time, the demise of the resident companies was the principal spur to the founding of actor-training programs in the United States. In the twentieth century, actor training gradually gained a foothold in colleges and universities, which have now become the principal trainers of actors, although there are still many actor-training studios, especially in large cities. Today, resident theatre companies have become prominent in the United States again, and most of them employ actors who are graduates of universities or other training programs. A few resident companies even have their own schools.

Most training programs stage productions to provide students opportunities to apply what they are being taught. Today's training programs retain

Performers Ethan Hawke and Sinead Cusack are seen here in Tom Stoppard's new translation of Anton Chekhov's *The Cherry Orchard*; directed by Sam Mendes. Hawke and Cusack regularly take on both film and stage projects to enrich their acting careers.

Sara Krulwich/The New York Times/Redux

some features of the earlier apprentice system, although in today's schools learners often play major roles that in professional companies would be cast with experienced professionals. Some theatre programs in colleges and universities provide highly specialized training for actors in which education about the other aspects of the theatre are only minimally covered. Others provide more comprehensive training, believing that if actors are familiar with all aspects of theatrical production (scenery, costumes, and lighting), they will be better able to utilize these elements in their performances. All training schemes, old or new, attempt (though often in quite different ways) to stimulate and integrate the three foundations of artistic skill: talent, training, and practice.

A would-be actor may complete training programs and receive a degree or certificate, but there are no exams or boards as there are for lawyers and doctors to certify an actor's readiness to practice the profession. Certification, such as it is, comes from being cast in professional productions. The decision to become a professional actor takes enormous courage because the number of aspirants greatly exceeds the number of jobs. Although there are now more acting jobs in the nation's resident companies than in New York's theatres, many theatre companies still hold auditions and do some of their casting in New York. Though it is possible to be an actor and live in one of the many cities that support professional companies, aspiring stage actors still tend to gravitate to New York, just as aspiring film and television actors gravitate to Los Angeles. Chicago, Minneapolis, Seattle, and a few other cities have managed to remain largely independent of both New York and Los Angeles.

Wherever actors live or wish to work, they all face the problem of being cast. This is true even for members of Actors Equity Association, the professional actors' union. Less than one-quarter of Equity's members are ever employed at the same time, and fewer than 20 percent make their living solely from acting. For most actors, the chances of being cast are improved greatly if they have an agent, whose job it is to help them get employment and whose own income depends on their clients' success. However, the most influential agents only take on new clients with proven earning potential. Despite the odds against success, many people persist, and enough are sufficiently successful to encourage others to try. Nevertheless, aspiring actors must be prepared to accept rejection as part of their lives. Many, perhaps most, aspiring actors spend more time working as waiters or in temporary office jobs while they make the rounds of auditions than they do performing for pay on the stage. Patience and persistence are necessary attributes of would-be actors.

Most of the procedures involved in casting have already been discussed in Chapter 13. Let us assume that the actor is one of those lucky enough to have been cast and is now ready to create a role.

Creating a Role

Each time actors undertake a new role, they are faced with a number of tasks. Perhaps the most basic is to understand the role. (One approach to analyzing the script and the role is described in Chapter 3.) It is usually helpful to look at the role in relation to four levels of characterization.

1. Biological: What does the script reveal about the character's gender, age, physical appearance, and condition of health?

2. Sociological: What does the script reveal about the character's profession, social class, economic status, family background, and standing in the community?

3. Psychological: What does the script reveal about the character's attitudes, likes, dislikes, general emotional makeup, motivations, and goals?

4. Ethical: What does the script reveal about the character's system of values and choices when faced with crises and conflicts?

Because a character may have been given many traits, it is also helpful to determine which among these traits are necessary within the dramatic action. Such inquiries form a broad base for further explorations.

The actor also needs to examine how the role relates to all of the others in the play. What does the character think of each of the others? How does the character present himself or herself to each of the other characters? What does each of the others think of the character? What is the function of each of these variations within the dramatic action?

The actor needs to understand the script's themes, implied meanings, and overall significance, which demands not only attention to observable relationships among characters and ideas but also sensitivity to subtext—the emo-

tional undercurrents, unexpressed motivations, and attitudes that inform the underlying meaning of their lines. Many plays, notably those by Anton Chekhov and Harold Pinter, depend heavily on subtext because the characters cannot or will not directly address the problems or feelings that lie just beneath the surface. In such scripts, the actor must make the audience sense these unstated elements or else the action will lose much of its power.

The actors also need to examine their roles in relation to the director's interpretation of the script (the production concept). They may wish

Practitioners & Theorists

BRECHT AND GROTOWSKI ON ACTING

Directors frequently comment on acting because the actor is the primary material they use to embody their interpretations of scripts. Some directors have envisioned a distinctive purpose for the theatre, which places particular demands on the actor. Bertolt Brecht envisioned the "epic theatre," where the actor's job was to observe human relations with a scrutiny that shows them to be changeable rather than naturally fixed. Jerzy Grotowski envisioned the "poor theatre," where the actor's mission was to create a unique encounter with the spectators without relying on other theatrical means. Here are statements about acting by Brecht and Grotowski.

Bertolt Brecht (one of the twentieth century's major playwrights and directors, explaining the kind of acting he sought for his epic theatre): "The actor does not let himself be transformed into the man he presents so that nothing of himself is left. He is not Lear, Harpagon, or the good soldier Schweik—he is 'showing' them to an audience. … Giving up the idea of complete transformation, the actor brings forward his text, not as an improvisation, but as a quotation. … In this sort of acting, where the transformation of the actor is incomplete, three devices can contribute to the alienation of the words and actions of the person presenting them: adoption of the third person, adoption of a past tense, and the speaking of stage directions and comments. … Through this threefold process the text is alienated in rehearsal and in general will remain so in performance."

Jerzy Grotowski (Polish director who exerted great influence on the training of actors beginning in the 1960s): "One must not think of the spectator while acting. … If the actor has the spectator as his point of orientation, he…will be offering himself for sale. … A sort of prostitution … at the same time, he must not neglect the fact of the public … he must act vis-à-vis with the spectators … he must … do an act of extreme yet disciplined sincerity and authenticity. He must give himself and not hold himself back, open up and not close in on himself in a narcissistic way. … The most important thing for me … is to rediscover the elements of the actor's art."

to talk with the director about their reactions to the interpretation and how it affects their roles; some may even try to persuade the director to alter the production concept. Ultimately, however, the actors must make their roles fit whatever interpretation is being used to shape the production.

Psychological and Emotional Preparation

In addition to understanding the script and the way a role fits into the total concept, the actors must be able to project themselves imaginatively into the world of the play, the specific situations, and their individual characters' feelings and motivations. An actor who has difficulty doing this may need to experiment with ways of inducing empathetic involvement. One method, borrowed from Stanislavsky, is to employ *emotion memory* (searching in one's own past for a parallel situation, recalling the emotion felt at that time, and using that emotion in acting the present scene). Another method is to search out people similar to the character and find out more about their situation and feelings. For example, an actor playing a hospital worker may come to understand the character's attitudes and frustrations more fully by

Actors from many countries come together in Peter Brook's company in the Bouffes du Nord Theatre in Paris. Brook believes that by assembling an international group of performers, who share their different training, performance traditions, and techniques, the company may transcend any one language or style of performance. Pictured here are William Nadylam and Antononio Figeroa in a scene from *A Magic Flute*, Brook's version of Mozart's opera.

Elliott Franks /eyevine/Redux

spending time in a hospital and participating in or observing what goes on there. The most typical method is the use of improvisations and theatre games to explore, in collaboration with other actors, multiple feelings about, and responses to, situations similar to those in the script. Such explorations may be necessary in many different scenes during the preparation or rehearsal process.

Many American acting training programs also borrow three important psychological concepts from the Stanislavsky system: objectives, obstacles, and actions. An *objective* is the goal or result characters are striving to accomplish in a given beat, scene, or play. In other words, an objective is what a character wants. The *obstacle* is what prevents characters from achieving their objectives. The *actions* are the methods or tactics characters use to achieve an objective. Through a process of script analysis and discussion with the director, actors make choices about the most appropriate objectives, obstacles, and actions. For instance, in *Angels in America*, Roy Cohn's objective in Act Three, Scene Five might be to convince Joe to accept the job in Washington, D.C. This is a reasonable objective because Roy needs someone to help him from being disbarred. One obstacle to

his objective is that Joe is reluctant to do anything unethical. The actions the actor playing Roy chooses to use could vary greatly, but may include the following: to intimidate Joe, to plead for mercy, to threaten him, to humiliate Joe, or to enlighten him on the realities of the political world. None of these is necessarily correct because an actor's work is inherently collaborative and must complement the director's approach to the script in a specific production context. Though training programs may differ in the exact terminology they use to describe these Stanislavsky-based concepts, professional directors often expect actors to be able to analyze what their characters want, how the characters are going to get what they want (using which actions), and what is preventing them from achieving their goals.

Movement, Gesture, and Business

Whether the director specifies much of the actors' movement or, at least initially, lets the actors position themselves and move about as their responses impel them, actors need to feel comfortable with their blocking and movement.

Many plays make intense emotional demands on the performers. Yet even in the most tempestuous whirlwind of emotion, performers need to maintain a center of calm and control over their actions. Seen here (left to right) are Jennifer Sternberg as Mag and Maureen Silliman as Maureen in the climactic scene from Martin MacDonagh's *The Beauty Queen of Leenane* as produced by the Two Rivers Theatre Company under the direction of Jonathan Fox.

T. Charles Erickson

Actors should tell the director if they do not. Most discrepancies can be settled if the actor and director discuss the character's motivations, relationship to other characters in the scene, and the function of the scene. If actors and directors can agree on these points, they can also usually agree on how these points are to be enacted.

Even if the director specifies much of the movement, the actor still must fill in many details—the character's walk, posture, bodily attitudes, and gestures. (For a discussion of movement and its purposes, see Chapter 13.) Actors may find it helpful to approach physical characterization in three steps:

1. Identify the character's physical traits as described within the text and required by the action and note any changes that occur during the play.

2. Assess which of a character's physical traits need to be dominant in any given unit or beat.

3. Work for physical distinctiveness through greater specificity—within the limits established by the script, role, and production concept.

It is sometimes helpful to think of a play as though it had no dialogue; actors would then physically have to convey their situation, motivations, and emotional responses. This approach, if followed fully, would probably lead to an overabundance of movement (and overacting), but used in the preparatory stages it can stimulate the actors' imagination and provide the actors with a number of choices to explore. It may also require actors to execute each movement precisely, helping them avoid vague, indefinite, and confusing movement. Whatever approach is used, the actor's goal is to create a physical characterization that is appropriate to the play and the production—clear, expressive, and distinct.

Particular plays may require specialized movement skills. If, for example, the action for a play is set in a particular period or place wherein

In Anna Deavere Smith's one-woman show *Let Me Down Easy*, the actress embodies over two dozen distinct characters. As *New York Times* theatre critic Charles Isherwood put it, "Ms. Smith is so meticulous in her attention to the details of voice, language and physical bearing that give people definition ... that the ample use of costumes, props and sets is probably superfluous." Seen here is one of Smith's male characters.

T. Charles Erickson

specific social conventions affect physical behavior, posture, or mannerisms, the performer may need to adopt them in his or her physical characterization. Likewise, a convincing illusion of violence on stage (such as a stabbing, shooting, or fistfight) requires specialized movement skills as well as careful planning and timing. Sometimes a fight choreographer is employed to make the action convincing, safe, and a fitting expression of each participating performer's character.

Vocal Characterization

Although actors cannot radically change their dominant vocal traits during a rehearsal period, they may, if they have well-trained voices, modify their vocal patterns considerably for purposes of characterization. The variable factors in voice are pitch, volume, and quality, each of which may be used to achieve many different effects. Typically, the voice is used to speak lines in a manner that evokes or defines emotions, ideas, or situations. The voice is also sometimes used as a type of sound gesture or as a way to create mood through nonverbal dissonances, harmonies, or rhythmical effects.

The variable factors of speech are articulation, duration, inflection, and projection (or audibility). *Articulation* involves the production of sounds, whereas *pronunciation* involves the selection and combination of sounds. A person may articulate sounds clearly but mispronounce words, just as a person may know how to pronounce a word but articulate sounds so imprecisely as to be unintelligible. The well-trained actor should be able to speak clearly or to alter articulation and pronunciation to suit character and situation. One of the most memorable features of Meryl Streep's roles is her vocal characterizations, achieved through control over articulation, pronunciation, and quality.

Duration refers to the length of time assigned to any sound, *inflection* to rising and falling pitch. Both duration and inflection are used to stress some syllables and subordinate others. Without proper stress, words may be unrecognizable. (Try, for example, shifting stress from the first to the second syllable of *probably*.) *Duration* also refers to the number of words spoken per minute. Slowness can create the impression of laziness, old age, or weakness, whereas a rapid rate may suggest tension or vivacity. Inflection (change in pitch) is one of the principal indicators of meaning. Surprise, disgust, indifference, and other reactions may be indicated by tone of voice, and the alteration of inflection can often completely change the meaning of a line or transform a statement of fact into a question. Duration and inflection play key roles in dialects (regional "accents"). Vocal coaches often counsel those working on a southern accent, for example, to end sentences on a rising inflection and to maximize the duration of vowel sounds.

In performance, actors should be both audible (which depends on projection or volume) and intelligible (which depends primarily on articulation and pronunciation) because the audience needs both to hear and to understand what the characters are saying. Actors must also be concerned with *vocal variety* (which may be achieved through alterations in any of the variable aspects of voice and speech). Nothing is more deadening than hearing all lines delivered at the same pace or intensity. Vocal variety is more easily achieved if the actor clearly understands the situation and motivations because any change in thought or feeling triggers changes in volume, pitch, or quality, as well as in the variable factors of speech.

Memorization and Line Readings

A task that every actor faces is memorization. It is usually helpful to memorize speeches and movements simultaneously because they reinforce each other. Furthermore, because blocking is done in relation to specific speeches, this conjunction ultimately becomes fused in the memory.

Memorization is aided by a few simple procedures. Because it is impossible to memorize everything at once, the script may be broken into beats and mastered one at a time. In each, the actors must ultimately not only learn their own lines but also memorize *cues* (the words or actions of others that immediately precede and trigger their lines) as thoroughly as they memorize their own lines. Before trying to memorize specific lines, it is helpful to study the sequence of ideas or shifts in emotion and tone—the overall development of the beat. Familiarity with sequence and a thorough understanding of the meaning and purpose of each line in a beat are the greatest aids to memorization. (The actual process of memorization requires going over the lines many times, usually while someone else keeps an eye on the script as a check on accuracy as well as to provide the appropriate cues.)

Once the actors have memorized or have become very familiar with their lines, they begin to color their understanding of the lines through the controllable factors of voice and speech to form distinctive line readings. Often these line readings are developed without conscious effort, but the actors must be concerned with timing, pacing, and pauses. They must make sure that speeches, especially long ones, build properly, that their line readings create a sense of spontaneity and conviction, and that their readings are appropriate to character, emotion, and situation.

Refining the Role

The foundation work (understanding the role; psychological and emotional preparation; movement, gesture, and business; vocal characterization; memorization) proceeds simultaneously with rehearsals, some of it in isolation, much of it with the director and other actors. In the early phases, different approaches to a scene or aspects of character may be tried and abandoned. Eventually, the major decisions are made, the movement and vocal patterns become clear, and the lines are committed to memory. There follows a period of refining and perfecting the role and integrating it into the whole performance.

This phase is difficult to describe because it varies with each actor, role, and production. Typically, much of the time is spent on deepening one's understanding of motivations and

Mickey Solis and Annika Boris as the title characters in the American Repertory Theatre's highly stylized production of *Romeo and Juliet*. Directed by Gado Roll.

T. Charles Erickson

relationships. Other concerns during this phase are complex business, precise timing, pacing, and variety. Actors must define each step of their characters' journeys throughout the action to ensure that it builds appropriately.

No single role (except in those plays with one character) is complete in itself. It is sometimes said that performing in a play is not acting so much as reacting. The director usually works to achieve the sense of give-and-take, cooperation, and mutual support that characterizes ensemble playing. The goal is a seamless whole rather than a series of separate performances; it can be reached only if all actors are willing to subordinate themselves to the demands of the production. Ensemble playing depends on the actors' awareness of each other's strengths and weaknesses, where they will get support, and where they need to compensate for another's weakness.

Dress Rehearsals and Performance

Not until dress rehearsals are actors usually able to work with all properties, settings, costumes, makeup, and stage lighting. Frequently, this is also the first time they have been able to work on the stage that will be used for performances. Thus, dress rehearsals may be occasions of considerable stress and exciting discoveries.

Of special importance to actors are their costumes because they affect not only appearance but also movement and gesture. Actors should find out everything they can about their costumes in advance of dress rehearsals—how a garment may enhance some moments or restrict others, what its possibilities are for use in stage business, and so on. If stage garments will be significantly different from clothing they normally wear, actors are typically provided suitable rehearsal garments early in the rehearsal process. Even if resources or budgets make this impossible, actors should consider from the beginning of rehearsals how they might use their costume and how it might affect their performance. Actors should also give thought to their makeup well before the dress-rehearsal period begins. Although the costume designer may also design the actor's makeup, especially when it is complicated or stylized, the actor should know at least what effects are desired and understand generally how to create them.

Because actors typically rehearse with reasonable facsimiles of the properties they will use in performances, their adjustment to the actual properties is much easier. Still, actors should expect or request extra time to deal

with specialty props, such as pyrotechnics (guns that fire blanks, confetti cannons, and so on). Experienced actors understand that every aspect of the production—costumes, scenery, properties, lights, and sound—affects their performance and how it will be perceived by the audience. Consequently, they try to gain a working understanding of these aspects and are patient as they are integrated into the production.

T. Charles Erickson

The Huntington Theatre's production of *The Rivals*, by Richard Brinsley Sheridan, drew praise from critics for its actors' ability to embody the desires of the characters as if they were their own. Directed by Nicholas Martin; scene design by Alexander Dodge; costumes by Michael Krass; lighting design by Dennis Parichy.

Performance is the ultimate goal. The better prepared the actors are, the more confident they will feel on opening night, although it is a rare actor who does not experience some nervousness—which, because it increases alertness, may be turned to advantage. Some actors feel a letdown after opening night and must guard against diminished effectiveness during the following performances. Long runs create special dangers because the actors may begin to perform mechanically due to fatigue or overfamiliarity with their roles. The best guards against such letdowns are concentration and reminders that each performance is the first for this particular audience. Ultimately, performance offers the actor one of the best opportunities for learning because the ability to affect or control an audience's responses is a major test of acting skill.

Thinking about the Actor's Work

When we attend the theatre, our attention is focused primarily on the characters because it is through them that the action develops. But what the actors who play the characters do and say is based on the dramatist's script, just as the interpretation and overall production concept are decided by the director. What actors wear is provided by the costume designer; the stage environment is created by the scenic designer; and much of the mood and emphasis is created by the lighting and sound designers. In such a cooperative venture, it is not easy to isolate the actors' contributions. Perhaps that is as it should be because usually the director's goal is to create a unified whole rather than a collection of easily distinguishable parts.

Nevertheless, even if we cannot determine precisely what is to be attributed to each production element, we often are impelled to make the attempt. Here are some questions that may help us assess the actors' performances and estimate their contributions to the production:

1. Were actors and roles adequately meshed? Were some actors more effective than others? In what ways? How did this affect the action of the play?

2. How did the type of space in which the performance took place affect the actors' tasks? With what results?

3. Were the actors audible? Understandable? Were the vocal characterizations suited to the roles? Were there actors whose voices noticeably enhanced or detracted from their performances? In what ways?

4. Were the physical characterizations suited to the roles? Were there actors whose movement or gestures noticeably enhanced or detracted from their performances? In what ways? How extensively were movement and stage business used? Did they have distinctive qualities? If so, what was the result?

5. Were some actors more effective than others in conveying their characters' psychological attributes and motivations? If so, how and with what effect?

6. Were the relationships among the characters clear? Were some actors more effective than others in creating clear and convincing relationships? If so, how and with what effect?

7. Were any special skills (such as dancing, singing, fencing, dialects, or accents) required of any of the actors? If so, how effectively were the demands met? With what effect on the production?

8. Did the actors make any special use of costume, scenery, properties, or lighting? If so, in what ways and with what effect?

9. Did the actors achieve a sense of "the first time"? Did they work together effectively as an ensemble? If so, with

what effect? If not, what interfered? With what result?

10. Overall, were the themes and implications of the play clear? Was the clarity or lack of it attributable to the acting? Script? Directing? Visual design? Total production?

Most of these questions cannot be answered precisely, not only because some of the needed information may not be available but also because, even if the information were available, responses would be at least partially subjective. Answers to each question are likely to vary widely from one audience member to another. Nevertheless, trying to answer these questions as they relate to specific productions or performances focuses attention on the processes and results of acting and will encourage detailed attention to actors' performances.

Tony Cisek's scene design for George Bernard Shaw's *Heartbreak House* at the Two Rivers Theatre Company features a towering accumulation of household furniture and debris from a ship (including one of the ship's guns) at the rear of the theatre's thrust stage. The play is set in the home of Captain Overshot, a former sea captain turned munitions inventor, and ridicules the English gentry and their complacency in the months leading up to World War I. Directed by Aaron Posner; costume design by Olivera Gajic; lighting design by F. Mitchell Dana.

A stage setting has no independent life of its own. Its emphasis is directed toward the Performance. In the absence of the actor it does not exist. … The actor adds the one element that releases the hidden energy of the whole. Meanwhile, wanting the actor, the various elements which go to make up the setting remain suspended … in an indefinable tension. To create this suspense, this tension, is the essence of the problem of stage designing.
—Robert Edmond Jones, *The Dramatic Imagination*

Scene Design

The scene designer is concerned with the organization and appearance of the performance space. The designer defines and characterizes the space, arranges it to facilitate the movement of the actors, and uses it to reinforce the production concept or interpretive focus.

The Functions of Scene Design

Scene design serves many functions.

- Scene design delineates the performance space.
- Scene design helps communicate the world of the play.
- Scene design organizes the acting space (creates a floor plan).
- Scene design characterizes the acting space and in doing so may reinforce the production style, its interpretive focus, and pertinent themes.
- Scene design creates mood and atmosphere.

Scene design defines the performance space by establishing distinctions between onstage and offstage. Through the use of flats, drapes, platforms, floor treatments, and other means, designers delineate the acting space. In arena and thrust theatres, the layout of audience seating itself may outline the acting space. In a flexible space, acting space and audience space may be intermingled. Designers also use *masking* to obscure people, objects, or portions of the stage not meant to be seen by the audience. Masking may be accomplished in many ways (primarily through drapes and flats), but the amount of masking depends on the type of stage, the needs of the production, and its style.

Scene design organizes the acting space by creating a floor plan that shapes movement, composition, character interaction, and stage business. The location of exits and entrances, the placement (or absence) of furniture, the presence or absence of steps, levels, and platforms—all the elements of the setting and their arrangement—are among the greatest influences on blocking, visualization, and movement. A setting can be organized in many different ways; arranging it to maximum advantage for a specific production requires careful and cooperative planning by the designer and the director.

T. Charles Erickson

Pictured is James Youmans's scene design for *Night of the Iguana* by Tennessee Williams at the Guthrie Theatre (Minneapolis). Youmans's design visually characterizes the performance space and provides (in conjunction with the lighting) a strong sense of mood. The production was directed by John Miller-Stephany; lighting design by Marcus Dillard; costumes by Matthew J. LeFebvre.

Scene design visually characterizes the acting space. How it does so often depends on the interpretive focus of the production, its style, or the themes the production team wishes to emphasize. If, for example, the production team wishes to emphasize the social and environmental factors that shape the behavior of the characters, it may be desirable to represent locales realistically. If this is the case, the designer will probably select architectural details, furniture, and decorations that clearly indicate a specific period and locale. For example, the designer might create a setting for *A Doll's House* that suggests a room in a Norwegian house around 1880. Conversely, if the production team wishes to emphasize the timelessness of the action, the scene designer might create fragmentary settings with only enough pieces to estab-lish the general character of the locale. Another approach might rely largely on visual motifs and theatrical conventions from the era when the play was written. A setting for *Tartuffe*, for example, might use decorative motifs and a wing-and-drop setting that reflects the age of Louis XIV. Or the interpretive focus of a production may shift the time and place of the action to emphasize an idea or dynamic. For example, if the creative artists producing *Hamlet* decide to translate the play's violence and power dynamics into an American Mafia context, the scene designer will need to make particular choices about how to characterize the performance space in a way that reinforces the concept.

Another way of characterizing the space is to treat it as flexible and nonspecific, a common

T. Charles Erickson

Eugene Lee's scene design for the world premiere of *Coming Home* by Athol Fugard provides both the interior and exterior spaces required by the play with a single setting. Note how floor treatment, levels, and the minimal exterior stone wall help to designate particular spaces. *Coming Home* was directed by Gordon Edelstein at the Long Wharf Theatre; lighting design by Stephen Strawbridge.

practice for plays with actions divided into many scenes and set in many places, as is typical in most of Shakespeare's plays. To represent each place realistically would require a large number of sets as well as a great deal of time to change them, thereby interrupting the continuity, rhythm, and flow of the action. On the other hand, to play all of the scenes on the flat floor of an undecorated stage might become monotonous. A common solution is an arrangement of platforms, steps, and ramps that breaks up the stage space, that provides several acting areas that can be used all together or isolated singly through lighting, and that can be localized as needed through the addition of a few well-chosen properties, pieces of furniture, banners, or images projected on screens, or through other means.

However the scene designer chooses to characterize the performance space, that characterization makes a visual statement that affects how the audience perceives the play's action. For example, in a play about war, the game of chess has been used as a metaphor, with the stage floor laid out in black and white squares and the characters costumed to suggest chess pieces. The settings for *The Hairy Ape* may incorporate images that suggest the dehumanization of individuals.

Scene design is only one part of a total design, which includes costumes, lighting, acting, and all the other elements of a production. It should evolve in consultation with those responsible for the other parts of the whole. It is not, as a painting is, complete in itself; it cannot be judged entirely by appearance because it should not only look appropriate but also function appropriately.

The Scene Designer's Skills

Scene designers need a variety of skills, many of them pertinent to other arts, especially architecture, painting, interior design, and acting. Like architects, scene designers conceive and build structures; they sculpt space and must be concerned with its function, size, organization, construction, and visual appearance. Also like architects, they must be able to communicate their ideas to others through sketches, scale models, and technical drawings that indicate how each element will look when completed.

Scene designers, in some aspects of their work, use skills similar to painters; for example, one of the designer's primary ways of communicating with the director and other designers is through sketches and drawings. During preliminary discussions of a production, designers usually make numerous sketches to demonstrate possible solutions to design problems; before these designs are given final approval, they usually are made into scenic models. In addition to making sketches showing entire settings, designers also make painters' elevations—scale drawings of each piece of scenery showing how it should finally appear. Depending upon the situation, designers may be called upon to paint (or supervise others who paint) the scenery they have designed.

In other aspects of their work, scene designers use the skills of an interior decorator because many sets are incomplete without furniture, rugs, drapes, pictures, and decorative details. In creating appropriate interiors, designers also need some of the actor's skills because they must understand the characters who inhabit the spaces and whose tastes have dictated the choice of furnishings and decorative features.

In order to create settings that reflect a specific period or place, scene designers must be familiar with the history of decorative motifs (the use of line, color, and pattern to adorn), decorative arts (including the furniture and accessories of various times and cultures), and the history of architectural styles. In stage settings, such details not only reflect a specific period or place but also indicate the economic status and tastes of the characters. A knowledge of art history also allows designers to draw upon various visual styles. They may wish, for example, to create a setting done in the surrealistic style of Salvador Dalí or one that uses a particular artist's color palette. Designers also benefit from a knowledge of stage history so that they may (when appropriate) draw on the theatrical conventions of other times, places, or cultures to connect the play with its original context or to otherwise enhance the production concept.

Michael Yeargan's scene design for Beth Henley's *Ridiculous Fraud*, as directed by Lisa Peterson at the McCarter Theatre. Note how the designer enhances the interior and exterior (augmented by Peter Kaczorowski's evocative lighting design) with a few decorative details.

T. Charles Erickson

It is useful for scene designers to understand construction techniques and scene painting. Although it has become standard practice for technical directors and others to determine how scenery will be built and painted, the designer's awareness of these practical considerations can be invaluable in assisting others to realize their ideal within the constraints of time, materials, and labor. Designers should also be familiar with new materials and technologies and their potential for design purposes. Computer literacy has become increasingly important for scene designers.

Most designers now use computer-assisted design or drafting programs to help them in creating or communicating their designs. These programs allow the designer to revise their drafting more quickly (with great accuracy). Three-dimensional animation programs can help the designer communicate to others how multiple sets, or parts of them, may move. However, though computer-assisted design and architectural programs are useful tools for designers, such programs have their limitations and cannot replace the designer's artistic skills and judgment.

Practitioners & Theorists

THE ART OF SCENE DESIGN

The scenic designer is not only an expert in the practical skills of theatre but an artist whose work functions collaboratively in theatrical production. Below are thoughts from designers that highlight the importance of the artistic aspects of scenic design.

John Conklin (Scenic Designer, 2011 NEA Opera Honors Ceremony Tribute): "I think the greatest quality that any artist or anybody in the world can have is curiosity." (On Scene Design): "You have to see everything together and see what it does. Not what you told it to do and not what you thought it was going to do—see what it does … unlike architecture or painting, it gets thrown away at the end, which I think is so wonderful. It does not exist without the performance and it only exists in memory."

Josef Svoboda (Czech scenic designer): "My great fear is that of becoming a mere 'décorateur' … true scenography is what happens when the curtain opens and can't be judged in any other way."

Pamela Howard (British stage designer and author of *What is Scenography?*): "Scenography—the creation of the stage space—does not exist as a self-contained art work. Even though the scenographer may have studied fine art and be by instinct a painter or a sculptor, scenography is much more than a background painting for the performers, as has often been used in dance. Scenography is always incomplete until the performer steps into the playing space and engages with the audience. Moreover, scenography is the joint statement of the director and the visual artist of their view of the play, opera or dance that is being presented to the audience as a united piece of work."

Adolphe Appia (Swiss designer, architect, and theatre theorist): "In every work of art there must be a harmonious relationship between feeling and form, a perfect balance between the idea which the artist wishes to express and the means he uses to express it."

Working Plans and Procedures

There is no standard way of moving through the design process. After having studied the play and discussed the production approach with the director and other designers, most designers make many tentative, preliminary sketches as a means of thinking through possibilities. Some designers make a scale model of the empty performance space on which they explore different arrangements of scenic pieces. Others use computer animation programs to generate virtual models for this purpose. Most designers generally think in terms of how they will use design elements—line, shape, space, color, texture, and ornamentation—to express and support the dominant qualities of the dramatic action or the production's interpretive focus.

However they work, designers eventually arrive at preliminary designs to present at a conference with the director and the other designers. (Design decisions involve not only how the settings function as acting spaces but also how they relate to costume and lighting designs and the total "look" of the production.) Through a process of reaction and revision, tentative agreement is reached, but before the designs are finalized, they must be rendered in a manner that conveys how the sets will look on stage. Some scene designers create perspective color sketches to serve this purpose. Others construct three-dimensional scale models that show in miniature how each set will look when completed. (It is not unusual for directors to ask for either a color sketch or a scale model, although in many situations both are expected.) Scene designers must also supply floor plans (drawn to scale) that show the layout of each set on the stage.

After the designs have been approved, the next step is to make working drawings. The number and type of drawings needed vary from one type of organization to another. For example, in a permanent company that maintains a stock of scenic units, it may be unnecessary to make working drawings of every flat and platform because some of the units may be pulled from stock. In the Broadway theatre, every piece is usually built new by union workers who insist on precise drawings for every detail. In addition to perspective sketches, floor plans, and scale models, the designer may have to provide some or all of the following:

- Rear elevations—drawings of each unit as seen from the rear, which indicate the type of construction, materials, and methods to be used in assembling it. This job is often performed by the technical director.

- Front elevations—drawings of each unit as seen from the front that show each unit in two dimensions from the front, with indications of such features as molding, baseboards, and platforms.

- Side elevations—drawings that show units in profile, indicating the thickness and shape of each unit.

- Detailed individual drawings—drawings that show the methods by which complex units are to be built.

- Painters' elevations—drawings that show how the unit should be painted.

With the exception of the perspective sketches, all of the plans are drawn to scale so that the exact size of any object may be determined. In addition to the drawings listed here, designers may need to provide special plans showing how the scenery is to be shifted and how it is to be stored during performance when it is not on stage.

Once the plans are completed, the construction phase can begin. Although designers may not be directly involved in building the scenery, they must approve all work to ensure that it conforms to the original specifications.

HAMLET

Scene designer Robert Schmidt's preliminary sketch for a production of Shakespeare's *Hamlet* at the Alabama Shakespeare Festival. Note (below left) the colored scale model of the design and (below right) the design after being constructed.

MING CHO LEE

Ming Cho Lee is often said to be the most influential of contemporary American scene designers. Born in China, he learned landscape watercolor before coming to the United States in 1949. After studying at Occidental College and UCLA, he went to New York, where he became an assistant to Jo Mielziner, then America's foremost scene designer. Most of Lee's early work was done for groups with limited budgets, among them the New York Shakespeare Festival, for which he was principal designer from 1962 until 1972. During these years, Lee developed the style that was to influence many other designers—abandoning the use of pictorial, painted scenery in favor of defining the space with scaffolding built from metal pipes or wood and combining them with fragments of scenery (usually heavily textured) suggesting collage. Although by 1980 Lee's designs had become more realistic, he is still usually associated with a spare, elegant, minimalist style. He has continued to experiment with innovative materials and multimedia. Though he has seldom worked on Broadway, his influence there is strong because many of its designers are graduates of Yale University's School of Drama, where Lee is head of design training. Each spring for several years, Lee has hosted the Stage Design Portfolio Review, an exhibition of work by student designers from throughout the country at which Lee and a number of other leading designers discuss and offer critiques of the students' designs. This has become a major showcase for young designers seeking to enter the profession.

Lee prefers to work in regional or repertory companies because he feels that is where collaboration is most respected ("the regional theatre atmosphere invites you to behave as part of a family"), whereas on Broadway stars, directors, or producers exert too much control. Lee considers his strengths as a designer to be his sense of proportion and his understanding of the demands and restrictions of various kinds of theatrical space—arena, thrust, or proscenium. Some of his most successful work has been for arena and thrust stages. In 2006 he was awarded the Helen Hayes Tribute honoring outstanding lifetime achievement in scene design. Lee's recent scene designs include *Stuff Happens* for the Mark Taper Forum (in Los Angeles), and *A Christmas Carol* for the McCarter Theatre (Princeton, N.J.).

Basic Scenic Elements

A combination of changing tastes, rising costs, improved materials, and new equipment has steadily diminished the desire for full-stage, realistic settings. The majority of settings today are composed of a few set pieces and stage properties; they tend to be fragmentary and evocative rather than completely representational, many being wholly abstract. However, traditional stagecraft practices still play a major role in most settings and the built pieces (though fewer in number) are usually constructed according to time-tested procedures or variations on them.

Designers use a few basic kinds of scenic units: soft, framed, and three-dimensional. Designers need to understand each kind of scenic unit at their disposal—as well as the physical materials available for construction of the units—so they can combine them creatively into expressions that are both evocative and practical. Let us look briefly at each type.

Ming Cho Lee's setting for John Osborne's *The Entertainer* at the Guthrie Theatre (Minneapolis). The play draws parallels between the decline of music-hall entertainers and the British Empire. Although the play indicates a number of different locations, Lee's design uses a single setting to suggest all of the locations and provides poignant commentary through the figures of the lion (symbol of the empire) and the female figure (a music-hall showgirl dressed in the colors of the British flag, representing Britannia).

Soft-Scenery Units

Soft-scenery units are typically made of unframed cloth. Usually suspended from overhead, they provide a large area of scenery that can easily be moved or folded up and stored when not in use. The following are among the most common soft-scenery units:

- Drops
- Draperies
- Scrim
- Cycloramas

Drops are used to enclose settings at the back and to provide surfaces on which scenes can be painted. A drop is made by sewing together enough lengths of canvas or cloth to create an area of the desired size. Typically, the cloth is attached to a batten at the top for support and to another at the bottom to keep it stretched and free from wrinkles. A drop may also have portions cut out so that another drop or object is visible behind it, thereby creating apparent depth and distance. Drops can be raised into or lowered from the fly space above the stage; they can also be rolled up and stored when not in use.

Draperies may be hung parallel to the proscenium on either side of the stage in a series from front to back in order to mask the sides of the stage in the manner of wings. They may be any color. Black draperies are sometimes used to surround the acting area or to create an enclosing void for a fragmentary setting. Draperies may also be made of canvas or muslin; they may be dyed, or they may have scenes (such as a forest or a distant city) painted on

Michael Yeargan's setting for the recent revival of August Wilson's *Joe Turner's Come and Gone* uses a combination of hard and soft scenic pieces. The scrim upstage both serves as a projection surface for color and clouds and reveals the silhouetted forms of smokestacks behind it. The play is set in and around a boarding house and Yeargan's design emphasizes the transitory status of the characters by placing them wall-less against the vast expanse of nature and impending change.

them and be hung in folds to create stylized backgrounds.

Scrim, a specialized curtain made of gauze, appears opaque when lighted only from the front but is transparent when lighted from behind. It can be hung in folds or stretched tightly. It may be used initially as a background for a scene and then become transparent to show another scene behind the first one; it may be used for the appearance and disappearance of ghosts and apparitions; and it can create the effect of seeing a scene through fog, mist, or the haze of memory.

A *cyclorama* is a neutral, undecorated surface that surrounds the stage area on three sides.

To avoid the appearance of seams, it is a continuous, tightly stretched curtain suspended on a U-shaped pipe curving around the back and sides of the stage. Its perceived color may be changed through lighting. It is used to represent the sky, to give the effect of infinite space, and to allow the maximum use of stage space without the need for numerous masking pieces. It is also used as a surface for projections (such as moving storm clouds or abstract, symbolic patterns).

Soft-scenery units are used more extensively on proscenium stages than on thrust or arena stages, where less masking is needed and where scenic units are more likely to interfere with sightlines.

Framed Units

Some units are framed to make them self-supporting. They are usually relatively small in comparison with soft-scenery units but can be combined to create larger surfaces. The following are the basic framed units:

- Flats
- Doors and windows
- Screens

A *flat* is a wooden or metal frame covered by a relatively flat surface (either stretched cloth or a thin sheet of wood) that can be painted or treated texturally. Flats of almost any width or height can be made, but as they become larger, they become less stable, thereby requiring additional support from above or below the stage. Flats may be constructed in a variety of forms, but three basic types are typical: flats without an opening (for walls, etc.); flats with an opening (for doorways, windows, etc.); and flats specifically cut or pieced together to simulate a particular silhouette (such as trees or distant vistas). Most flats have smooth edges so that they can be combined to create larger units, such as the walls of a box set or the exterior of a castle. Occasionally, drops are framed on all four sides.

Doors are often used in conjunction with flats, but, because doors are a moving piece of hard scenery used by actors, they require special attention. The door itself is an expressive object often needing trim and ornamentation, but it is the action of the door's movement in conjunction with the stationary flat that raises a challenge. Because flats are not normally stabilized structures in the manner of actual walls, when a door is opened its weight may subtly flex the opening of the flat. This may make the subsequent closing of the door difficult. If the door is to be slammed shut by a performer, the entire structure into which it is set will need to be specially constructed so as not to wave back and forth. Because the use of freestanding or suspended forms has increased in contemporary theatre, doors sometimes need to be framed without being attached within a flat. This again requires special attention to its installation. The same is true of windows and other suspended or freestanding units used by performers.

Screens have become increasingly used as a surface on which to project still or moving

Jeff Cowie's scene design for *Dividing the Estate* by Horton Foote as directed by Michael Wilson at the Hartford Stage Company is an interior composed of a variety of framed scenic units; lighting design by Rui Rita; costumes by David C. Woolard.

T. Charles Erickson

pictures. Screens may be used alone or with other screens. They may rest on the floor or, more commonly, be suspended above the stage. They may be rigged so that they can be raised, lowered, or moved laterally during a performance; they may be of any shape or size and made from almost any material—wide-mesh netting, translucent plastic, textured cloth, and so on. Some of these surfaces blur images, some give texture, and some permit images to bleed through onto other surfaces. On some screens, images can be projected only from the front; and on others, only from the rear. Screens can be used for projected slides or moving images; they may also be used to show offstage or onstage live scenes transmitted to the screens by way of closed-circuit television. There is a wide range of uses for screens, although some options require more advanced technology than is available in many theatres.

Three-Dimensional Units

Because they are relatively flat surfaces, soft and framed scenic units are often considered two dimensional (although all scenic units are three dimensional). Other units, however, especially those that support considerable weight, are widely categorized as three dimensional. These most commonly include:

- steps
- ramps
- platforms
- columns
- trees and rocks
- fragmentary architecture

Extensive use of three-dimensional units is most common on proscenium stages or in flexible spaces, but they may also be used sparingly on thrust and arena stages. Three-dimensional objects or fragments of architecture may be suspended above a thrust or arena stage to suggest what is not shown. How one constructs these various types of scenic units is beyond the scope of this discussion; such processes are described fully in books on scenic practices.

Materials and Methods

For a long time, scenery was made of wood and cloth. Today, a wider variety of materials are used to construct stage scenery. A variety of substitutes for wood may be used. Steel, aluminum, and other metal alloys offer greater strength and support than the same amount of wood but weigh more and have less flexibility. Steel can be cut and bent to hold different shapes, but this process requires special skills and equipment. Fiberglass (treated with chemicals to make it pliable) may be molded into rocks and other shapes and allowed to harden, creating lightweight pieces capable of supporting heavy loads. Styrofoam and urethane may be incised to create the three-dimensional forms of moldings, bricks, and carvings, or sculpted to create figurines and other properties otherwise difficult to construct. Such chemically formed or treated materials, however, must be used carefully to avoid toxic poisoning from fumes emitted when the materials are subjected to heat or other chemicals. Safety devices, such as respirator masks that filter out harmful fumes or particles, have been developed to protect those who work closely with such materials. Vacuform molds, in which one can duplicate in plastic almost any shape (including armor, swords, and small scenic units), have also become common. However, the selection of materials and methods always depends on the particular circumstances (space, labor, budget, and so on) and on the desired function and effect.

Assembling and Painting Scenery

The initial stages of scenery construction usually occur in a scene shop. Although in certain instances scenery may be built in the performance space, more often it is built in

Practitioners & Theorists

MICHAEL YEARGAN

Michael Yeargan got his start as a scene designer quite early in life. His fourth-grade music teacher took Yeargan's class on field trips to the opera, then assigned the students follow-up projects, one of which was to re-create scenes from the opera in shadow boxes made from shoeboxes. Yeargan says, "I loved it, and I'm still doing it today." A graduate of the Yale School of Drama, Yeargan now teaches Stage Design there to a new generation of theatre makers while he also creates scene designs for professional theatres and opera companies. Yeargan's New York theatre credits include the scene designs for *South Pacific*, *Cymbeline*, *Awake and Sing!*, *Seascape*, *The Light in the Piazza*, and *A Lesson from Aloes*. His design credits for opera include companies from all over the world, including the New York Metropolitan Opera, the Welsh National Opera, London's Royal Opera House, Théâtre du Châtelet (Paris), the Frankfurt Opera, Opera Australia, and the San Francisco Opera. In addition, he regularly contributes scene designs for plays at a number of regional theatres, including the American Repertory Theatre in Cambridge, Massachusetts, where his credits include *King Stag*, *Six Characters in Search of an Author*, *Long Day's Journey Into Night*, and *The Threepenny Opera*.

Although he travels the world designing scenery, Yeargan regularly returns to his home state of Texas to work at The Dallas Theatre Center, the Houston Grand Opera, and the Dallas Opera. This two-time Tony winner (Best Scenic Design of a Musical in 2005 for *The Light in the Piazza* and in 2008 for *South Pacific*) prefers the quiet of his studio to the public spotlight. "I just won the Drama Desk award … when they called out my name, I panicked. Winning the Tony is even worse."

Asked in an interview about the design process, Yeargan said, "I think that everyone assumes that you read a play as a set designer and say, 'OK, he says that the window's over here and the door's over there,' and you just kind of do what's written, which I don't think is ever the case." Dallas Theater Center artistic director Richard Hamburger has said of Yeargan, "He's totally unpretentious and serves plays with joyful abandon and humility."

shops adjoining the stage or, as is the case for Broadway productions, built in scenic studios far removed from the theatres in which the performances will occur. Regardless of where the construction takes place, after basic units (flats, door frames, doors, steps, platforms, and the like) are constructed (or brought from storage), they are usually combined into larger units (the walls of a room, a door frame and door, platforms and steps, and so on). The way the pieces are assembled depends partially on whether the scenery must be transported from one place to another, whether it must be shifted during the performance, or whether it must be stored during the run of the production. Once erected, scenery for single-set shows may not need to be moved until the production closes. Such sets are typically assembled with permanent joining methods (which provide ample stability), whereas multiple sets may require temporary joining methods so that scenic units may come apart and be moved quickly. Finally, the scenery is painted.

The ultimate objective in most scene painting is the illusion of a particular form or material.

Joan Marcus

Pictured here is a 2010 Yale Repertory Theatre production of *Battle of Black and Dogs*. Set at a construction site, most of the action occurs on the main level; however, the scene design, by Riccardo Hernandez, also allowed audiences to look at a level beneath the flooring for action that occurred down there. Directed by Robert Woodruff, with lighting by Stephen Strawbridge.

To accomplish this, after the scenery has been painted with priming and/or base coats to ensure a flat neutral surface, a variety of other painting techniques are then applied. These techniques include the following:

• Lining

• Blending

• Stenciling

Lining is frequently used to make a flat surface appear dimensional by replicating shadow and highlight. For example, lining may be used to suggest changes of dimension on a piece of trim surrounding a door or along the cornice of a wall.

Blending lends the appearance of texture by applying three or more tones of a color on a surface. The contrast, resulting from the use of different tones, gives the color greater depth. The degree of contrast one creates depends upon the effect desired. Wet-blending (applied while the paints are still wet) or dry-blending may be done; although these procedures differ, they accomplish the similar goals of lending greater depth and texture to a surface. Perhaps the most common blending techniques include *spattering*, *sponging*, *scumbling*, and *dry-brushing*.

Spattering involves flicking small drops of paint from a brush onto the base coat with one color that is slightly lighter and a second that is slightly darker than the base coat. This technique creates the illusion of raised and receding surfaces. *Sponging* involves dipping a natural sponge in paint and patting it on the surface of the base coat. Although effective, sponging is a very time-consuming technique when large surface areas must be treated. *Scumbling* involves simultaneously applying and blending more than one shade of paint on the same surface to give a mottled effect. *Dry-brushing*, as the name implies, involves taking a relatively dry brush dipped in a small amount of paint and brushing it lightly over a surface so that the paint beneath is still somewhat visible. This technique may be applied to create shading, streaking, general texture, or more specific effects.

Stenciling is often used to create the repetition of a motif in an interlocking pattern (as is the case when creating the illusion of wallpaper). A pattern is cut into specially designed paper or plastic, the pattern is then set against the surface to be painted, and when paint is applied and the stencil is removed, the desired pattern is left upon the surface.

All of the scene-painting techniques described (and only the most common ones have been treated) may be applied in combination with others. Some combination of scene-painting techniques is typical in the painting done for any one scene design. Most scene designers are accomplished scene painters and they may choose to supervise or participate in the scene painting for their designs. Often, shops will employ scenic artists to paint the scenery. Even when scene designers do not participate in the scene-painting process, they still create painter's elevations and approve the finished painting before it is moved or transported to the stage on which it will be used.

A variety of scene painting techniques were used to create the illusion of marble flooring, aged and weathered stonework, wood, stucco walls, and a daytime sky to complete Alexander Dodge's scene design for *The Miracle at Naples* at the Wimberly Theatre (Boston).

T. Charles Erickson

Shifting Scenery Onstage

Whereas a single setting may not require shifting, multiple settings need to be planned so that their individual units can be disassembled quickly and quietly, moved easily, and stored economically. Several methods are used in shifting scenery: manual, flying, wagons, revolves, and elevators.

The least sophisticated method involves *manual* scene shifting. Using this method, one or more stagehands move each part of a set to some prearranged storage space offstage and bring the elements of a new setting onstage. It requires breaking the setting into small units. Because manual shifting can be used on any stage, however simple or complex, a designer can always rely on it, though a large crew of stagehands may be required to make it efficient.

Another common method of shifting is *flying*—suspending scenic elements above the stage and raising or lowering them as needed. Flying requires a counterweight system composed of battens, lines, and pulleys. Weights sufficient to counterbalance whatever is being flown must be carefully placed into the system. With an adequate counterweight system, a single stagehand can easily raise and lower scenic elements of enormous size and weight. Newer flying systems use electrically controlled winches without counterweights and often provide greater flexibility.

Another common device for shifting scenery is the *wagon* (a platform on casters). The larger the wagon, the more scenery it can accommodate, but many stages do not have sufficient wing space to store or maneuver large wagons. Some stages have permanently installed tracks that guide wagons on and off stage with precision, but such a system has limited flexibility. Wagons can be used singly, in pairs, in groups, or in combination with other shifting devices. The primary advantage of the wagon is that it permits heavy or complex scenic pieces to be shifted more efficiently than by hand.

A *revolving stage*, or *turntable*, is another device for shifting scenery. It may be a permanent feature cut into the stage floor with a supporting central pivot or a low circular platform that sits on castors atop the stage floor created for a

Neil Prince's scene design for *The Umbrellas of Cherbourg* at the Two Rivers Theatre Company satisfied the musical's need for multiple locations with a revolving stage framed by (and containing) vertical translucent units.

T. Charles Erickson

specific production. A turntable usually bears the weight of two or more settings simultaneously; the individual sets are placed so that each faces the circumference of the circle. Scene changes are made by revolving the stage until the desired setting faces the audience. In the meantime, settings that face the backstage area may be changed for later use. Because of the tremendous weight they normally bear, most turntables are moved by electric motors.

Still another shifting device, the *elevator stage*, raises and lowers segments of the stage. In some theatres, portions of the stage may be lowered to a basement, where scenery is mounted and then raised to stage level. In other theatres, the stage is divided into several sections, each mounted on its own elevator lift that can be

raised, lowered, or tilted; these sections can then be used in combinations that create platforms, ramps, or a variety of levels without the need of building and shifting such units in the usual manner. Theatres in which the stage proper is fixed may have a lift that raises and lowers the orchestra pit, so that it can be set below stage level for musicians, raised to the auditorium level and used for audience seating, or raised to stage level for use as a forestage.

Seldom is a single method of shifting exclusively used. Most often, two or more methods are used in conjunction. Designers need to know which methods are available to them and decide which will be used for each unit that must be moved. These decisions are important because audiences may become impatient with delays

T. Charles Erickson

As designed by Riccardo Hernandez and directed by Rebecca Taichman, when love returns to Olivia's heart in the McCarter Theatre's production of *Twelfth Night* by William Shakespeare, the stage is transformed to convey her feelings. Hernandez's scene design makes use of multiple projections along with a staggering shower of rose petals to achieve a stunning effect. Lighting design by Christopher Akerlind; costumes by Miranda Hoffman.

Practices & Styles

ACTION AND SPECTACLE

Designers create settings that are appropriate to the play but also provide spectacle through the settings' visual variety and appeal. Can a spectacular design overwhelm a production? What is the proper relation between spectacle and action? Is it different for every play? Here, some of America's most successful scene designers address these questions.

Heidi Ettinger (designer for regional theatres as well as Broadway plays and musicals, among them *'night Mother*, *Into the Woods*, *The Secret Garden*, and *Smokey Joe's Cafe*): "If 'spectacular' means extremely theatrical, then it's all for the good. On the other hand, if it means just a lot of scenery decorated to within an inch of its life, then I don't find 'the spectacle' particularly appealing. But the design for *Les Misérables* … it was spectacular in that it created a truly theatrical event, an event that couldn't be reproduced in any other media."

Robin Wagner (designer for rock concert tours of groups like the Rolling Stones and for such Broadway plays and musicals as *Lenny* [see page 207], *A Chorus Line*, *Angels in America* [see page 251], and others): "How do you draw an event as opposed to the objects that make an event? … Theatre design is not about painting or sculpture, it's about life, which is the very essence of theatre. … You have to be extremely careful not to snuff out the life of a script visually, because the design is a very powerful instrument. Vision is the strongest sense that a person has and what is there will either support or drown that which has to live in it."

Marjorie Bradley Kellogg (designer for numerous regional theatre companies, many of which perform in thrust or arena spaces): "When I was studying Michelangelo, I was taught that one of the great things about his sculptures was that they seemed to be made from the inside out, rather than from the outside in. There is a form there and he was just taking away all the outside junk. That's what positive and negative space is about—the statue is positive and the rest of the marble around it is the negative space. What we tend to think when we look at scenery is that the scenery itself is the positive, whereas what's really positive is the space contained within the scenery. It's positive because that's what the actors are going to be moving through."

caused by lengthy scene changes, and such delays can destroy the rhythm of a production. Today, extremely complicated settings that demand exacting precision in their shifting and coordination with other effects may use computers programmed to orchestrate the total effect. Few theatres now try to hide scene shifts from the audience. Efficiency and speed are the primary concerns.

Set Decoration and Properties

Even after the sets are assembled onstage, they are incomplete without set decoration and properties. These elements, though part of the design, are not structural parts of the setting.

Set decoration and properties include such items as banners, coats-of-arms, window draperies, furniture, pictures, and books—anything that completes the setting. Properties may be subdivided into *set props* and *hand props*. The former is a property either attached to the setting or functioning as a part of the design. The latter is used by the actor in stage business. The designer is always responsible for selecting and designing set props and may also select the hand props. Directors frequently make specific requests regarding hand props because of their intimate connection with the acting. Responsibility for obtaining both types may be assigned to a property master and crew, who may buy, rent, or construct props to the designer's or director's specifications. If the theatre maintains a stock of previously used props, items may be pulled and adapted for reuse. However obtained, set decoration and properties are necessary to complete the design.

Technical Rehearsals, Dress Rehearsals, and Performances

Even after the settings are complete, they must be integrated with the other elements that make up the total production. Typically, this is accomplished during technical and dress rehearsals. A *technical rehearsal* focuses attention on elements other than acting (although typically at least portions of all scenes are performed) so that the various designers and technicians can see if the "technical" elements—in this case, scenery (including scene shifts, properties, and all stage business involving properties)—are available and are functioning properly both separately and as parts of the whole. Any difficulties revealed by a technical rehearsal are corrected as quickly as possible so that dress rehearsals (in which costumes and

makeup are added if they were not included in the technical rehearsals) can proceed as nearly like performances as possible. In complex productions, more than one technical rehearsal may be needed to make certain that all necessary adjustments have been made (including the levels and cues for lighting and sound). Thorough preproduction planning is necessary because it is very difficult to make major changes in scenery at this late point.

Dress rehearsals allow the scene designer to view the settings in use by the actors and stagehands (under conditions that approximate performance). The designer must be available for consultation and changes until the play has opened. On opening night, responsibility for the scenery passes to the stage manager and the stage crews.

The Scene Designer's Assistants and Coworkers

Many people aid the scene designer. In the professional theatre, designers are usually members of the United Scenic Artists Union, and they are usually assisted by members of this or other unions. Designers who routinely work for Broadway and regional theatres often employ one or more assistants who make working drawings, construct models, search for furniture and properties, act as a liaison between the designer and the scenic studios that construct the scenery—anything the designer may request. In some regional and nonprofessional theatres, the *technical director* is likely to perform many of these functions.

The technical director's job may be independent of the designer's and of equal status. When a permanent organization produces several shows a year, the designer's job may be divided into its artistic and practical aspects. The designer may

Technical rehearsal for the Long Wharf Theatre's production of *Let Me Down Easy*; directed by Stephen Wadsworth; scene design by David Rockwell; costume design by Anne Hould-Ward; lighting by David Lander; sound design by David Budries. During technical rehearsal, production staff members sometimes sit in the house to observe the action from the audience's viewpoint. Note the tables loaded with lighting and sound monitors as well as notepads, scattered cups, tissues, and personal effects.

then conceive the designs, do the drafting, and create the model, while the technical director may be responsible for the technical drawings, building, and assembly. The technical director may also purchase all materials, supervise construction, and be responsible for the crews who run the shows.

In the professional theatre, all people involved in the construction, assemblage, painting, and shifting of scenery are usually members of a union. In other types of organizations, this work is undertaken by assigned or volunteer helpers under the supervision of the designer, the technical director, or a scene shop supervisor. In all types of theatres, during performances the heads of stage crews operate under the supervision of the stage manager. Their duties include the efficient movement and accurate placement of scenery and properties during the performance as well as the maintenance of scenery and properties during the run of the show.

The designer's assistants frequently go unnoticed by the public because little is done to draw attention to them. Often, and especially in the professional theatre, their names do not even appear in the programs. Nevertheless, they are indispensable members of the overall production team; without them the scenery would not be built and painted and could not function efficiently or be shifted during performances.

Thinking about the Scene Designer's Work

The range of scenic design in today's theatre is great. It may be realistic or abstract. It may incorporate or intermingle elements from almost any period, style, culture, or set of conventions. It is a field that continues to change. The recent rise in the use of projections in performance, for instance, has expanded the medium of scenic design and the necessary training of scenic designers. The following questions focus attention on crucial aspects of scenic design as an aid to understanding more clearly the designer's contribution to the performance, no matter the situation or mode in which the designer works.

1. How did the type of space in which the production was performed affect the designer's work? How did the

designer take advantage of the space's potential and cope with its limitations?

2. Did the scenery define the performance space? If so, in what ways and through what means? If not, with what effect?

3. How did the floor plan affect the action? Were there multiple levels? If so, how did they relate to each other, and how were they used? Were there specific entrances and exits? If so, how did their placement affect the action? Did the arrangement of furniture (or other elements) enhance or inhibit action? How did the overall arrangement affect movement and visual composition?

4. What sorts of scenic units (soft, framed, three-dimensional, or other) were used, and how did these affect the overall setting? Was the setting realistic? Fragmentary? Abstract? What was the overall effect?

5. Were sets (or any parts) changed during the performance? If so, by what means? How long did the changes take? How did the varied settings affect the mood, tension, and tempo?

6. What characteristics did the scenery embody? What did the scenery convey about the characters? Socioeconomic conditions? Period? Locale? How did it affect the play's tone, mood, and atmosphere?

7. Were there any unusual scenic features? Projected images? Highly distinctive effects? If so, how did they affect the performance?

8. How did the scenery relate to the costumes, lighting, and sound? Did these elements enhance and complement one another? If so, how? If not, in what ways? With what results?

9. Did the setting suggest any specific interpretation of the play? If so, what interpretation? How did the setting convey this interpretation? If it did not, what was the result?

10. How did the scenery contribute to (or detract from) your experience of the production as a whole? What would have been lost if the scenery had been eliminated?

The relevance of each question may vary according to the particular production and setting. There are no absolute answers to many of the questions because responses are inevitably subjective. But so are most responses to art of whatever kind. Nevertheless, formulating answers to these questions forces us to go beyond our usual cursory reaction to scenery and to examine it and its function in production more specifically and critically.

Sheri Rene Scott costumed as the evil sea-witch, Ursula, from *The Little Mermaid*. Music by Alan Menken; lyrics by Howard Ashman and Glenn Slater; book by Doug Wright, based on the Hans Christian Andersen story and the Disney film. Costume designer Tatiana Noginova used the appearance of tentacles and fish scales to help create the character. The wig, as shown here, was designed by David Brian Brown, who wired and styled it to make it look as if the character is underwater. Directed by Francesca Zambello; choreography by Stephen Mear; sets by George Tsypin; lighting by Natasha Katz; sound by John Shivers.

The transformation of the human body, its metamorphosis, is made possible by the costume, the disguise. Costume and mask emphasize the body's identity or they change it; they express its nature or they are purposely misleading about it; they stress its conformity to organic or mechanical laws or they invalidate this conformity.
—Oskar Schlemmer, *Man and Art Figure*

Costume Design and Makeup

The costume designer is concerned primarily with the visual appearance of characters, but an actor's costume may also affect how the actor moves and feels. Whereas the scene designer helps to define the stage environment within which the action develops, the costume designer helps to define the characters that exist within that environment. Thus, the work of the scene designer and costume designer interacts and needs to be coordinated carefully.

The Functions of Costume Design

Costume design serves several functions.

- Costume design helps to define the characters and their relationships as well as establish their relative importance.
- Costume design helps to establish time and place.
- Costume design helps to suggest mood and atmosphere.

- Costume design may alter performers' appearances and movements.
- Costume design often reinforces changes in the dramatic action and the production's style and interpretive focus.

Primarily, costume design defines the characters and their relationships; it helps performers and audiences understand who the characters are and how they relate to one another. Costumes usually indicate gender and may reflect age (by adhering to stereotypical notions of what is appropriate to each age group). Costumes may also reflect a character's psychology through what an individual character chooses to wear, especially when those choices depart from the norm. It may establish the characters' social and economic status by distinguishing between lower and upper classes, between rich and poor, or between more and less affluent members of the same group. It may identify occupation (nurse, soldier, policeman) or lifestyle (conservative middle class, fashionable leisure class, disaffected youth).

In addition to conveying information about individual characters, costume design can also establish or clarify relationships between characters. For example, in Shakespeare's history plays, in which warring factions are significant, members of the same faction can be related to each other and contrasted with members of rival factions through the line, texture, or color of their costumes. Costume color schemes can also be used to show sympathetic relationships (through compatible colors) or antagonistic relationships (through clashing or contrasting colors) among characters. Changes of costume are often used to indicate changes in a character, an alteration in the relationship among characters, or the passage of time. Costume may also establish the relative importance of characters in the action. Major characters can be made to stand out from minor ones by manipulating any or all of the elements and principles of design. For example, Hamlet is given emphasis in part through his insistence on wearing black (the color of mourning), whereas the others are dressed in colors more appropriate to festivities following the wedding of Gertrude and Claudius.

Costume design often helps to establish time and place. If the production team is using a realistic approach, the costumes may be based on the clothing worn at the time of the dramatic action (fifth century B.C., Shakespeare's lifetime, present day, and so on); they may indicate a particular country or region (ancient Rome, seventeenth-century France, southwestern United States); a particular kind of place (throne room, battlefield, hospital, farm); or a time of day or occasion (casual morning at home, formal dance).

Costumes (more so than setting and lighting) are likely to retain some realistic qualities because they are worn by actors who must be able to move effectively and appropriately in them and because actors usually draw on real-life behavioral patterns in building their characterizations. Nevertheless, costumes do not always adhere to realistic standards. They may embody a metaphor, symbol, or allegorical concept. For example, in the medieval play *Everyman*, a character called Death summons the title character to his grave; Everyman then tries unsuccessfully to persuade several of his companions (Beauty, Strength, and Goods among them) to accompany him. The costumes need to capture the essence of each character as indicated by its name. On the other hand, a production of *Hamlet* utilizing

the metaphor of the world as prison may embody this perception in more subtle and varied ways.

Costumes may reflect mood and atmosphere. The high-class attire of the characters in *The Importance of Being Earnest* not only suggests a certain level of formality, but may also suggest an atmosphere of frivolous excess (see illustration on page 164). Conversely, the ragged and threadbare clothing worn by Vladimir and Estragon in most productions of Beckett's *Waiting for Godot* may work in conjunction with the setting to suggest a bleak mood of diminished expectations (see illustrations on pages 22 and 186).

Costumes may help establish a particular style. In *The Hairy Ape*, the fashionable people

Jess Goldstein's costumes for *The School for Scandal* at the McCarter Theatre (Princeton, N.J.) help to establish the action as taking place in the late 1700s, among the gentry class. Directed by Mark Lamos; scene design by Michael Yeargan; lighting design by Stephen Strawbridge.

T. Charles Erickson

on Fifth Avenue are dressed like marionettes to reinforce their mechanical behavior. Costumes may reflect formalized conventions or a level of exaggeration, as they do in *commedia dell'arte*.

Costume can alter an actor's appearance as well as affect an actor's movement. By manipulating line and proportion, the costume designer can make a plump actor appear more slender or a thin actor stouter. Boots may disguise an actor's thin legs; color and ornament can draw attention to an actor's good features and away from weaker ones. Costume also can be used to make a handsome actor plain or misshapen. And, as in many children's plays, actors may be transformed into animals, trees, or fantastic creatures. Light, flexible, and close-fitting garments (such as leotards) allow the actor to move and gesture freely, whereas heavy garments (with bustles, trains, and the like) may slow down and restrict movement and gesture. Garments may be designed to help determine the amount, type, and overall pattern of movement and stage business.

Costume may underline the development of the dramatic action through costume changes. A

Practitioners & Theorists

THE ART OF COSTUME DESIGN

Like scenic designers, costume designers are artistic collaborators whose work is central to the creation of a unified production. Several prominent costume designers discuss how effective costume design is not just about the mastery of technique.

Susan Mickey (professional costume designer and professor of design): "Designers are the authors of the visual narrative in a performance. Furthermore the work of a costume designer fundamentally seeks to answer one question: Who are we? An enormous series of choices are made by the designer in order to accomplish a costume on stage and the details in each choice lend credibility to the design. The goal is to make the honest choice each and every time."

Robert Edmond Jones (Broadway designer): "Each element has its own particular relation to the drama and plays its own part in the drama. And each element—the word, the actor, the costume—has the exact significance of a note in a symphony. Each separate costume we create for a play must be exactly suited both to the character it helps to express and to the occasion it graces."

William Ivey Long (five time Tony Award–winning costume designer): "I describe my job as basically helping someone become someone else."

Rosemary Ingham (costume designer and author of numerous books on theatrical design): "Designing in the theatre is intellectual and imaginative, practical and poetic, mechanical and magical."

Barbara and Cletus Anderson (professional designers and authors of *Costume Design*): "Good costume designers must know a tremendous number of things about a great many subjects. They need to know about drama as literature and as a performing art, and about the physical makeup of the theatre. They must understand people and what makes them tick. They need to know about drawing and painting and the history of art. …"

Pictured are Daniel Radcliffe as Alan and Lorenzo Pisoni as Nugget in Peter Shaffer's *Equus*, a play that treats a young man's obsession with horses. Atop the platform shoes, the performer's height and movement is altered. The metal and leather headgear forms the shape of a horse's head without restricting the actor's vision. Finally, the soft brown pants and form-fitting body stocking (with overlay) suggest the coloration of a horse. Scene and costume design by John Napier; directed by Thea Sharrock; lighting design by David Hersey.

Sara Krulwich/The New York Times/Redux

movement from happiness to sorrow or alterations in a character's fortunes, age, or sense of well-being may be underscored by changes in what the character wears. Costume may create both variety and unity because characters are not only individuals but also parts of a whole. Although each costume may be distinctive in some way, each must fit the total visual style of the production. Thus, costume design plays an important role in reinforcing a production's style and interpretive focus.

The Costume Designer's Skills

Costume designers need a variety of skills, many of which are pertinent to other professions (for example, fashion design, visual art, tailoring, sewing, dramatic literature, psychology, social and cultural history, and acting). Like the fashion designer, the costume designer

Practitioners & Theorists

CATHERINE ZUBER

Catherine Zuber was born in London but makes her home in the United States. She holds a Master of Fine Arts degree from the Yale School of Drama, where she studied scenic design with Ming Cho Lee and costume design with Jane Greenwood. Zuber has designed costumes for many regional theatres, among them Center Stage in Baltimore, where she designed costumes for Ibsen's *Ghosts*. In this production, Zuber applied the type of boned ribbing often used for period corsets to the outside of the leading female character's dress in order to convey a sense of the character's confinement. Because the garment and the boning were dark in color, many members of the audience may not have consciously noticed this detail, but Zuber believes it helped the actress to identify and convey this aspect of her character. Zuber has also served as the resident costume designer at the American Repertory Theatre, where she designed costumes for dozens of productions including *The Good Woman of Setzuan* and *The Cabinet of Dr. Caligari*. Catherine Zuber has earned a reputation as a designer who does exhaustive research: "For some projects, you have to be a sociologist. ... Your task is to examine in close detail what is authentic, always keeping in mind that truth is stranger than fiction. Every shoe, every tie, every shirt collar needs to express the time and place." But Zuber uses her research as a way to support and strengthen her creative choices rather than as a "museum approach" to design. She enjoys that, as an artist, she is sometimes called upon to "invent a world." (See illustrations on pages 35, 123, 170, 181, 205, 342, 431, and below, for examples, of Zuber's work.)

Zuber's artistry has earned her wide critical acclaim and several prestigious awards including several Drama Desk Awards, an Obie Award for Sustained Excellence in Costume Design, the 2004 and 2005 Lucille Lortel Awards for Outstanding Costume Design, the 2005 and 2008 Tony Awards for Best Costume Design of a Musical (*The Light in the Piazza* and *South Pacific*), and the 2006, 2007, and 2010 Tony Awards for Best Costume Design of a Play (*Awake and Sing*, *The Coast of Utopia*, and *The Royal Family*).

Catherine Zuber's costumes transform actors into giant lizards for Edward Albee's *Seascape*. Directed by Mark Lamos; scene design Michael Yeargan; lighting design by Peter Kaczorowski.

Joan Marcus

creates garments for particular types of people to wear for particular occasions or purposes. In creating garments, both types of designers keep in mind gender, social and economic class, activity, climate, and season, as well as stylistic qualities. But unlike fashion designers, costume designers must work within circumstances dictated by the script, director, performance space, and budget. Fashion designers establish fashions; costume designers use fashions. Costume designers must be able to project themselves into any period and create garments not only for present-day fashions but also for those of other eras.

Because they communicate their ideas to others through sketches, costume designers must develop skills like those of the visual artist. They use sketches to indicate their preliminary ideas about individual costumes and the overall look of the production. Some costume designers now use computers to generate sketches. However produced, sketches facilitate discussion of the costumes, their relationship to the other visual elements, and their appropriateness to character, dramatic action, and production context. Costume designers must also be able to render their final designs in color.

Although costume designers are not always involved in the construction of the garments they have designed, they often draw upon their knowledge of cutting, draping, patterning, and sewing in their designs. Their sketches indicate how garments are shaped and contain details that inform the cutter, draper, or tailor how the garment should be built. Such information is essential for making patterns from which the garments will be constructed. Because costume designers also specify the material to be used, they need to be familiar with various fibers (cotton, wool, linen, silk, synthetic fibers) and the characteristics of each. Such information permits designers to choose cloth for appearance, durability, specific use, cost, and other pertinent factors. Designers must also be knowledgeable about weaves, textures, and other qualities because these are important to the overall appearance of a costume.

Courtesy of the American Conservatory Theatre

Costumes may identify the period in which the action takes place, but they must also help to define the characters. Seen here are Elizabeth Raetz as the innocent Cécile and Lisa Bruneau as the worldly Merteuil in costumes by Deborah Dryden for Giles Havergal's adaptation of *Les Liaisons Dangereuses* at San Francisco's American Conservatory Theatre.

Costume designers must be well grounded in social and cultural history (including the visual arts, dance, and theatre) because clothing reflects the mores, standards of beauty, and stylistic preferences of period and place. The more designers know about daily life, occupations, class structure, and favorite pastimes of a society, the better prepared they will be to design garments that reflect the status and function of a character within a specific culture. Because much of our information about clothing of the past comes from painting and other visual arts, a knowledge of art history is helpful. Some productions draw on theatrical conventions that were in use when the play was written; consequently, knowledge of theatre history, especially the history of theatrical costuming, may be useful to the designer.

Above all, costumes need to be suited to the characters who wear them. Costume designers must be able to analyze characters in the same way actors do, in terms of each role's significant traits, psychological motivations, feelings, and functions within the dramatic action.

Working Plans and Procedures

After the costume designer has studied the play and met with the director and other designers to discuss the production approach, the costume designer begins to create a scheme for the costumes. Because there are usually several characters and because they appear in many scenes in many combinations, the designer typically creates an action chart, makes preliminary sketches, and examines them in various combinations to see how they fulfill the needs of individual scenes, whether they sufficiently reflect the progress of the dramatic action, and how the costumes fit together as a group. There is usually a series of design meetings at which the designers show their sketches and research and begin to discuss their design approach. Through a process of reactions and revisions with the director and other designers, an agreement is eventually reached. After revisions, the designs are rendered in color. The costume designer then begins to fully develop the designs.

The costumer's working drawing is a color sketch for each costume (although the same basic design may be used for several characters if they are part of a group—soldiers, for example, or members of a mob in which everyone wears variations of the same clothing). This sketch shows the lines and details of the costume as seen from the most distinctive angle. If there are

OVERCOAT WITH VENT FOR RIDING
LOW-HEELED VICTORIAN BOOTS
3-PIECE SUIT WITH VEST

MADAME ARCATI
BLITHE SPIRIT
AMERICAN PLAYERS THEATRE. 2011

*REMOVES JACKET AND ADDS HELMET FOR SEANCE

Devon Painter

Costume designer Devon Painter's rendering for the American Players Theatre production of *Blithe Spirit* depicts the character Madame Arcati at two different points in the play. The art of costume design requires an ability to reflect and reinforce a character's psychological transformation through specific changes to the costume.

unusual features, the details are shown in special drawings (usually in the margins of the sketch); if the front, back, and sides of a garment all have distinctive features, the costume is usually shown from each of these angles. Samples of the materials to be used in constructing the garment may be attached to each drawing.

Most costume designers use a *costume chart* to communicate their broad organization of the characters' costumes at a single glance (see Table 16.1). It briefly identifies what each character wears in each of the scenes in which he or she appears. Sometimes color samples of each garment are included so that the range of colors and the overall color scheme can quickly be conveyed. The chart can also be used as the basis for more detailed *dressing lists*. These lists remind the actors (and those who may assist them) which costume pieces they wear in each scene. (Note how much more detail is provided in Table 16.2 than in the broad costume chart in Table 16.1.) The costume chart and dressing lists are tools that communicate the designer's intentions and help keep the costumes organized for running the production efficiently.

Realizing the Designs

Costumes may be borrowed, rented, assembled from an existing wardrobe, or newly made. When costumes must be borrowed, designers look for garments that fit their needs, although they often must accept clothing that is less than ideal. Borrowed clothing can be altered only slightly because usually it must be returned in the same condition as when it was borrowed.

TABLE 16.1   A DOLL'S HOUSE COSTUME CHART

Character	Act 1	Act 2	Act 3
Nora	**1** Gray wool jacket and skirt + outerwear (Removes outerwear during act)	**2** Outfit **1** – gray jacket + and blouse	**3** Tarantella outfit (After quick-change) **4** Pale blue suit + Outerwear
Delivery Boy	**1** Brown and maroon outfit + outerwear		
Porter	**1** Black suit	**1**	
Helene (The Maid)	**1** Black dress with white apron	**1**	**2** Nightgown and shawl
Torvald	**1** Black "working" outfit (Later adds outerwear, and then removes it)	**2** Trousers, shirt and frock from **1** + maroon tie and gold vest	**3** White tie and tails with party mask (Later removed)
Mrs. Linde	**1** Distressed burgundy jacket & skirt + outerwear (Removes outerwear during act)	**1**	**1**
Dr. Rank	**1** Gray wool 3-piece frock suit (Adds outerwear during act)	**2** Outfit **1** + green vest and green/black tie	**3** Black tie and tails
Anne-Marie (Children's Nurse)	**1** Navy dress	**1**	
Ivar (One of Nora's sons)	**1** Gray knickerbockers and jacket		
Emmy (Nora's daughter)	**1** Gold wool dress with striped pinafore		
Bob (Nora's other son)	**1** Blue suit with gold tie		
Krogstad	**1** Dark gray suit + brown outerwear	**1**	**1**

Courtesy of Margaret Mitchell

TABLE 16.2   DRESSING LIST OR CARD FOR NORA IN *A DOLL'S HOUSE*

Costume 1	Costume 2	Costume 3	Costume 4
Chemise	**Remove:**	**Remove all except:**	**Remove all except:**
Corset w/garters	Gray wool jacket	Corset, chemise	Corset, chemise
Corset cover	**Add:**	**Add:**	and petticoat
Petticoat 1	Black/maroon blouse,	Petticoat 2	**Add:**
Bustle pad	Black/maroon jacket	Fishnet stockings	Brown stockings
Black stockings		Black satin pumps	Brown pumps
Black boots		Red/black skirt	Pale blue skirt
Gray wool jacket		Black embroidered bodice	Pale blue jacket
Gray wool skirt		Jet necklace	Brown coat
Black wool cape		(All rigged for quick change)	Brown hat
Black hat, maroon flowers		Wig 2	Black gloves
Black gloves		Black shawl	
Gold/onyx earrings			
Wig 1			
Wedding ring			

Courtesy of Margaret Mitchell

Through the imaginative use of accessories and ornamentation, however, much can be done to alter the appearance of a garment.

Costumes from rental houses vary considerably. Some larger rental agencies buy the costumes from a Broadway or road show when it closes and rent these costumes as a group. Other houses employ staff designers who create costumes for frequently produced plays. In other cases, costume houses assemble a variety of costumes for each period, and from this stock the most appropriate garments are selected for any given show. When costumes are rented, the costume house assumes many of the designer's functions. The director and costumer may give detailed explanations of their interpretation of the play and request specific colors and kinds of garments, but they ultimately may not get precisely what they wanted. Rented costumes typically arrive at the theatre only in time for one or two dress rehearsals, and there is seldom time to obtain replacements or make more than minor changes. Even groups that normally make their own costumes usually rent some articles (such as military uniforms and men's tailored period suits) that are difficult or costly to construct.

Permanent theatre organizations that make their own costumes usually maintain a wardrobe of items from past productions. In this way, a large stock of garments is built up over time. If garments are to be taken from stock, the play is sometimes designed with these in mind. The costumer knows what is available and can choose carefully. Existing costumes in the theatre's own wardrobe can be remade or altered to fit new conceptions.

Edward Hibbert in a costume fitting for his portrayal of the strong-minded British matriarch Lady Bracknell in *The Importance of Being Earnest* at the Long Wharf Theatre.

The procedures and working conditions for creating new costumes vary from one kind of organization to another. In the Broadway theatre, the producer contracts with a costume house to make the costumes. The designer must approve the finished costumes but has little to do with the work beyond attending fittings. The designer does not need to supply patterns or cutting, stitching, and fitting directions because the costume house provides these services. In nonprofessional and academic theatres, designers may need to supervise construction of their designs. If so, they must be skilled in pattern drafting, draping, and fitting. Again, whether or not they supervise the construction, designers should understand the techniques used to carry out designs so they will know what effects can be accomplished and by what means.

Regardless of who makes the costumes, standard procedures are involved in the final realization of the costume designer's sketches.

- Accurate measurements of all the actors are taken.

- Necessary materials are secured or purchased and modified as needed.

- Draping decisions are made and/or patterns are drafted as guides for cutting and shaping the materials. Frequently "mock-ups" are made with inexpensive fabric.

- The material is cut and the parts basted (sewn loosely with large stitches) together.

- Actors are called for a fitting with the designer or one of the designer's assistants.

- The garments are stitched and any desired ornamentations are added.

- A final fitting takes place to ensure that the finished garment fits, looks, and functions as planned.

Many new costumes need to look worn, faded, or tattered. Such garments may need to be *distressed* (that is, treated in ways analogous to overpainting in scenery). They may be washed several times; may be rolled up wrinkled to get a rumpled look; may be sprayed with paint, dye, or bleach to achieve fading or staining; may have the nap worn off the cloth with brushing in strategic places to indicate wear; or may be subjected to a variety of other processes to produce the desired effect.

The Costume Designer and the Actor

Edward Hibbert plays Lady Bracknell in the finished costume for *The Importance of Being Earnest* at the Long Wharf Theatre. Directed by Doug Hughes; scene design by Hugh Landwehr; costumes design by Paul Tazwell; lighting by Donald Holder.

T. Charles Erickson

Costume designers and actors need to cooperate because each supplements and extends the work of the other. Whenever possible, designers try to consider the unique physical aspects of each actor when planning costumes. They must keep in mind the movement demanded of the actor in a particular production. It is difficult, for example, to climb high steps in a tight skirt, and an actor who must fence may be seriously endangered by billowing shirt sleeves, although these garments may enhance movement in other situations.

For their part, the actors are responsible for exploring the potentials and limitations of the costumes they will wear. Unfamiliar garments may seem awkward initially, but if actors recognize that the clothes in each period emphasize qualities that were admired at that time and allow movements that were then socially useful, beautiful, or desirable, they may use those qualities more effectively. For example, the sleeves of a man's fashionable coat in the eighteenth century would not allow the arms to hang comfortably at the sides (they had to be bent at the elbows and held away from the body), whereas the modern suit coat is cut so the arms are most comfortable when hanging at the sides (outward and upward movements are restricted). Both garments reflect attitudes about appropriate male behavior and consequently encourage some movements and inhibit others. If designers understand the relationship between cut and movement, they can help the actors get the feel of the period by making their garments from authentic period patterns.

The designer can also aid the actors by proper attention to shoes and undergarments. The height of the heel exerts considerable effect on stage movement (high-heel shoes throw the weight forward onto the balls of the feet, whereas flat shoes shift weight toward the heels). Similarly, undergarments affect movement. Hooped crinoline petticoats, for example, will not allow the same freedom of movement as modern underclothing. Corsets can force the body into certain configu-

rations and inhibit action. If costumes encourage appropriate movement, they can be of enormous help to the actor. For optimum effectiveness, however, the actor and director must be willing to explore the possibilities of garments and allow sufficient time for rehearsal in them.

Makeup

Traditionally, makeup has been considered the actor's responsibility. However, in many situations today, the actor's makeup is at least initially the product of design and collaboration. In the professional theatre, the costume designer often conceives of the actor's makeup as a part of the design, especially when a very stylized or complex makeup is required. After the makeup design has been shown to them, professional actors generally apply it themselves. Because actors in the nonprofessional theatre are typically less experienced or adept with makeup than their professional counterparts, the design and application of makeup are sometimes delegated to the costumer, director, or another skilled person. Although the way makeup is handled varies widely, it is treated here in conjunction with costuming because of its close connection with the actor's appearance.

Makeup can serve several functions:

- Characterize—convey age, state of health, race, and basic attitude, such as grumpiness or cheerfulness

- Aid expressiveness—emphasize facial features and make them more visible to the audience

- Restore color and form that are sometimes diminished by stage lighting

- Indicate performance style, as in expressionist plays, where distorted makeup may indicate distorted ideas or behavior, or in Kabuki or Chinese Opera

When the makeup for a production is designed and supervised by one person, it is

T. Charles Erickson

Michael Krass's costume design takes center stage in the Huntington Theatre (Boston) production of *The Rivals*. The design uses selective exaggeration to support the play's comic tone. Directed by Nicholas Martin; scene design by Alexander Dodge; lighting design by Dennis Parichy.

Practitioners & Theorists

WILLIAM IVEY LONG

William Ivey Long became involved in theatre, in part, because his parents were involved in doing theatre at The Lost Colony and at the Carolina Playmakers (now the Playmakers Repertory Theatre) in Chapel Hill, North Carolina. Growing up around theatre, Long remembers his childhood home so full of fabric and costumes that they had to clear off the dining room table to eat meals. He had early experiences as a props master and technical director before receiving his undergraduate degree in history at The College of William and Mary. Long then studied art history at the University of North Carolina and eventually studied scene design at the Yale School of Drama under Ming Cho Lee. But when Long first moved to New York City after graduating from Yale, he spent his time working with a clothing couturier and making a collection of historical dolls, not designing scenery or costumes. Eventually, his friends convinced him that he should return to theatre and he did. Since then, Long has designed costumes for over fifty Broadway and Off-Broadway plays and musicals, including *Six Degrees of Separation*, *Miss Saigon*, *Lend Me a Tenor*, *The Marriage of Bette and Boo*, *Contact*, and *The Frogs*, as well as revivals of *Cabaret*, *Guys and Dolls*, *Chicago*, *Private Lives*, and *The Homecoming*. (See an example of his costume designs on pages 29 and 218.) He has also designed the costumes for opera productions all over the world, for the Rolling Stones's *Steel Wheels* rock concert tour, for a Siegfried and Roy Las Vegas show, and for numerous dance performances. In the process, he has won five Tony Awards for Best Costume Design (1982 for *Nine*, 1992 for *Crazy for You*, 2001 for *The Producers*, 2003 for *Hairspray*, and 2007 for *Grey Gardens*) and been inducted into the Theatre Hall of Fame.

usually coordinated through a *makeup plot* (sometimes supplemented by sketches). The plot is a chart recording basic information about the makeup of each character: the base color, liners, eye shadow, and powder; special features, such as a beard or enlarged nose; and any changes to be made during the performance. The plot serves both as a guide for applying makeup and as a check on how the makeup of each actor relates to that of all the others. Sometimes a sketch of each actor's face is made to show how the makeup is to be applied.

Types of Makeup

Makeup effects may be achieved in two basic ways: through painting and through added plastic, prosthetic, or three-dimensional pieces. Painting involves the application of color, high-

lights, and shadows to the face or other parts of the body. Plastic makeup includes the addition of such items as false noses, warts, beards, and wigs.

Painted makeup may be divided into four categories:

- Age makeup
- Straight or character makeup
- Racial/ethnic group makeup
- Special painted effects

Age makeup is of concern only when actors are to play characters whose age differs significantly from their own. Various age groups typically have distinct coloration, highlights, shadows, and lines. These are usually evident on the face as well as on the hands and other visible parts of the body, which must all be made up appropriately or they may destroy the illusion

Referring to the makeup designer's drawing posted on the mirror, a performer applies her makeup with precision prior to a performance of *KÀ*, one of Cirque du Soleil's long-running shows in Las Vegas.

created by facial makeup. A straight makeup uses the actor's own basic characteristics without altering them significantly. A character makeup is one that markedly changes the actor's appearance. The change may involve making the actor seem fatter or coarser or more lean and wizened, or it may emphasize some distinctive facial feature (such as a thin, sharp nose or large, soulful eyes). Racial/ethnic makeup emphasizes characteristic skin coloration, eye shapes, and hair color and texture, along with other traits that differentiate Asian, Polynesian, Indian, African, Caucasian, and other subgroups. Special painted effects include clown makeup, distortions for stylistic reasons, and decorative designs painted on the face (such as tattoos and the markings used by some tribal peoples). The materials needed for these and other effects, as well as those required for the most basic stage makeup,

are available from manufacturers and makeup supply houses. Almost all makeups begin with a base. However, the base alone is likely to make the actor's face appear flat and uninteresting. Therefore, lines, highlights, and shadows are applied over the base. The effects that can be achieved by painting with makeup are almost endless.

Nevertheless, significant transformations in an actor's appearance are most frequently accomplished with three-dimensional elements. For example, a change in the shape of the nose and the addition of a beard and bushy eyebrows can mask an actor's features more completely than painting can. The shape and size of the nose can be changed through prosthetics, usually made from plastics or rubber latex that can be molded into the desired shape. Similar prosthetic pieces can simulate fleshy jowls, a jutting chin, a

T. Charles Erickson

Costume designer Junghyun Georgia Lee uses exaggerated wigs to convey the artifice of French seventeenth-century high society in *The Misanthrope* at the Yale School of Drama.

Minneapolis Star/ZUMA Wire Service/Alamy Limited

Effective make-up, including the use of prosthetics, is crucial to the success of converting the animated movie *Shrek* into a stage musical.

protuberant forehead, large warts or scars, and other protrusions. They are attached to the face with liquid adhesive and may be removed and reapplied as needed.

The addition of facial hair and wigs, or alterations to performers' own hair, can also aid in significantly transforming their appearance. Some actors can grow beards and mustaches on demand, but these can also be made or purchased. However, purchased facial hair pieces may not precisely match a particular actor's hair color or fit well. Facial hair pieces may also be made by ventilation. In this process, strands of hair pieces are tied with specialized needles onto a tightly woven net, measured, and precisely cut to fit a specific actor to achieve the desired effect. Ventilated hair pieces have the advantage of precision and durability because the entire piece can be applied with liquid adhesive, taken off, and reapplied many times without damage. The appearance of the actor's hair can be changed significantly through styling and coloring, but wigs may be required for extreme changes or rapid switches. Wigs are now so readily available that they often provide the easiest means of altering hair color and style. Wigs made from materials other than human or plastic hair are seldom satisfactory if a realistic effect is sought. For stylized wigs, various materials may be used: hemp, yarn, confetti, strips of paper, and so on. Baldness can be simulated with a "bald wig." Finally, hair coloration may be altered with dye, although this can be longer lasting than is sometimes desired.

Costume and makeup aid the actor's transformation into the character, although in productions that do not seek realistic effects, makeup may not be used at all; the actor is said to be "presenting" the character rather than attempting to "be" the character, and consequently there is no need to disguise the actor's own appearance. Nevertheless, makeup is still used in the majority of stage productions and completes the visualization of the character that costume design seeks to achieve.

The Costume Parade, Dress Rehearsals, and Performances

When the costumes are finished, some theaters have a *dress parade*, during which every costume for the play is viewed sequentially so that the actors may appear in the correct combinations, in the appropriate costumes, and under lights simulating those to be used in performance. The actors may be asked to perform characteristic actions or special business to make sure the costumes are fully functional. The dress parade allows the designer and director to evaluate the costumes without the distractions of a performance. Problems are noted and corrected before dress rehearsals begin. In the Broadway theatre, the dress parade is held at the costume house; in other organizations, it is usually held onstage. It is normally supervised by the costume designer.

After problems are corrected, the costumes are moved to the dressing rooms in the theatre to be used for the performances. If no dress parade is held, its functions must be accomplished during the technical rehearsals. Dress rehearsals allow the costumes to be seen under conditions as nearly like those of performance as possible. There should be few changes at this time, but any that are necessary need to be made quickly so the actor is not faced with new details on opening night. In most situations, the designer's work is considered complete after opening night.

The Costume Designer's Assistants

The costume designer needs several helpers. In the professional theatre, costume designers usually are members of the United Scenic Artists Union, and their helpers may be members of this or other unions. The designer's assistant, usually a younger member of the United Scenic Artists, may make sketches, search for appropriate materials, supervise fittings, act as liaison with the costume shop and other theatre workers, or undertake any other assigned task.

Pattern drafters, drapers, cutters, tailors, stitchers, and fitters make the costumes. For Broadway productions, these workers usually are union members who work at a professional costume house. In regional theatres some of this work may be done by union members, but much of it is not. In the nonprofessional theatre, almost all of this work is done by volunteer or student labor, although frequently a paid staff person supervises the construction and maintains the theatre's wardrobe.

When the costumes are finished, a wardrobe supervisor takes charge and is responsible for seeing that costumes are ready for each performance.

T. Charles Erickson

Stylized application of makeup along with a body suit and matching gloves help turn Icelandic film and stage actor Stefán Karl—best known for playing Robbie Rotten on Nickelodeon's *LazyTown*—into the Christmas-hating Grinch for *Dr. Seuss' How the Grinch Stole Christmas!* Costume design by Robert Morgan; makeup design by Angelina Avallone; directed by Matt August; scene design by John Lee Beatty; lighting by Pat Collins.

The costumes may need to be mended, laundered, cleaned, or pressed. In long-run productions, garments are replaced when they begin to look shabby. During performances, the wardrobe supervisor is responsible to the stage manager.

Dressers help actors into and out of costumes. The number of dressers depends on the size of the cast and the number and rapidity of costume changes. Sometimes actors need little or no help, but quick changes and complicated garments may require more than one dresser for a single actor. There should be enough dressers to avoid delays, keep performances running smoothly, and ensure that the costumes are in good condition at all times.

Thinking about Costume and Makeup

The range of costume and makeup in today's theatre is great. Each may be treated realistically or nonrealistically; each may reflect closely what is indicated by the script or deviate markedly from the script's specifications; or each may be largely ignored (with performers wearing their own clothing and no makeup). Costumes and makeup may make strong stylistic or interpretational statements, or they may be so unobtrusive as to be practically unnoticed. In all

Photo by Roger Mastroianni

No costume is truly complete until an actor infuses it with the life of the character. Here, Steve Tague plays Hamlet in *Hamlet* at the Great Lakes Theater Festival (Cleveland, Ohio) in costume designer Star Moxley's subtle but richly textured costume.

cases, the important issues concern why the specific choices were made and how they affect the production. The following questions may contribute to a fuller understanding of choices and their results in the use of costume and makeup.

1. Did the type of space in which the production was staged permit close-range viewing of costumes and makeup? Were details easily visible? What was the overall effect of the space on costumes and makeup?

2. What, if any, specific period, style, or production concept did the costuming convey? If it did so, which? How closely did the approach adhere to the script? If it departed significantly from the script, in what ways did it do so? With what effect?

3. How were the costumes and makeup used to characterize each role? Did they distinguish characters by clarifying specific occupations or professions? Socioeconomic status? Lifestyles? Age of characters? Taste? Psychological traits? If so, through what means? If not, what was the effect? Were some character traits ignored? If so, which and with what result?

4. Did costumes clarify character relationships? If so, how? With what results? If not, how did they fail to do so? With what results? Did they create appropriate emphasis and subordination? If so, through what means? If not, what prevented them from doing so?

5. Did the costumes enhance or inhibit the performers' movements and business? In what ways? With what results?

6. How were the costumes and makeup used to enhance or alter the actor's appearance? Was this done appropriately in terms of the role? Was the actor's overall physical appearance effective (or ineffective) for the role? In what ways was the effectiveness (or ineffectiveness) attributable to costume and makeup?

7. Were there costume or makeup changes? How did they relate to developments in the dramatic action or alterations in the character's situation or attitudes?

Did the changes in costume or makeup clarify the developments? If so, in what ways? If not, why not?

8. Were there any unusual, unexpected, or highly distinctive costumes or makeup? What features or means served to create these effects? Did the distinctiveness enhance or detract from the overall effect?

9. How did costumes and makeup relate to scenery and lighting? Did they enhance and complement each other? If so, how? If not, in what ways? With what results?

10. Overall, how did costume and makeup contribute (or fail to contribute) to the total production?

The relevance of these questions will vary according to the particular production and play. To answer some of the questions about every costume or for the entire cast would be too time consuming; for other questions, adequate answers may require information available only to those actually involved in the creation of the costumes and makeup. Nevertheless, attempts to answer parts or all of these questions require us to look closely at costumes and makeup and to evaluate their contributions to a theatrical production.

Lighting in the Hartford Stage Company's production of Tennessee Williams's *A Lovely Sunday for Creve Coeur* not only provides visibility, it also provides texture and directs focus. The high-intensity sidelight draws the viewer's eye to the women standing (left). Lighting design by Rui Rita; directed by Michael Wilson; scene design by Jeff Cowie; costumes by David C. Woolard.

T. Charles Erickson

[L]ighting is the audience's guide to the story, and to what the production is doing. Light can confuse or clarify the issue. … Good lighting requires that the light complement the action of the script, score or choreography. Lighting that is imposed on a production, no matter how jazzy or flashy, works against the production as a whole.

—Jennifer Tipton (award-winning lighting designer)

Lighting and Sound Design

Lighting makes the other elements of theatrical production visible. But it does much more because it plays a major role in creating mood and atmosphere, in emphasizing visual elements, and in blending the entire stage picture. Stage lighting often escapes conscious notice because it is intangible, the sources are often hidden, and it is visible only when it strikes a reflecting surface. Consequently, lighting is often ignored unless it is clearly inadequate or overtly executed. Nevertheless, how light is controlled has a significant, though often subtle, effect on the audience's perception of a performance.

Sound also makes its greatest contribution when it is designed for careful integration with the production as a whole. Because, like lighting, sound depends on electronic means, it is treated here at the end of this chapter's section on lighting design.

The Controllable Qualities of Light

Lighting designers achieve their goals by manipulating the four controllable qualities of light:

- Intensity (or brightness)
- Distribution
- Color
- Movement

Intensity depends primarily on the number of lamps used and their wattages. It may be increased or decreased in several ways: through the use of dimmers to decrease or increase brightness; through the number or types of instruments focused on the same area or object; through the distance of instruments from what is being lighted (brightness diminishes with distance); and through the presence or absence of color filters. Selective intensity, when used in combination with the other controllable qualities of light, greatly affects the audience's perception of mood and helps to direct their attention.

Distribution refers to both the placement of the light source and the area that it illuminates. Lighting instruments may be mounted almost anywhere in the theatre: in the auditorium, above the stage, on the floor, on vertical or horizontal pipes, or on stands. The direction from which light approaches a subject determines its dimensionality and has great impact on the overall lighting effect. A carefully

Jon Linstrum's lighting design for *Shockheaded Peter*, a darkly comic musical based on Heinrich Hoffmann's nineteenth-century cautionary children's book *Struwwelpeter* (Slovenly Peter), captured the distorted reality of Hoffman's stories through his dramatic use of uplighting and sidelighting. Scene design by Julian Crouch and Graeme Gilmour; costumes by Kevin Pollard; sound by Mic Pool and Roland Higham.

planned distribution of light allows the designer to use frontlighting, backlighting, crosslighting, downlighting, or uplighting, separately or in various combinations. All light may be directed at one area, or it may be distributed equally or unequally over the entire stage. The lighting designer uses the carefully planned distribution of light to enhance the stage compositions created by the director and the actors, thereby reinforcing the dramatic action.

The use of color in lighting is substantially different than the use of color in scenery or costumes because the primary colors of light are different from the primary colors of pigment. In light, they are red, green, and blue, which, when mixed together, produce white. By contrast, the red, blue, and yellow of pigment mix to black. The visible spectrum of light is divided into colors (red, orange, yellow, green, blue-green, blue, and violet), each of which is distinguishable from the others because it is composed of light waves of a unique length. We attribute color to objects because of their capacity to absorb some wavelengths and to reflect others. In stage lighting, filters control the appearance of color through the principle of

selective transmission known as *subtractive color mixing*. Each color filter permits certain wavelengths of light to pass through and restricts others. A blue filter, for example, screens out or diminishes other color wavelengths allowing only those necessary to create that specific hue of blue to pass through. Filtering the light reduces the amount of light that reaches the stage. To avoid unwanted distortions, light from a number of color sources may need to be mixed, thereby employing the principle of *additive color mixing* (mixing different colored light together to produce achromatic white light). For example, a yellow dress illuminated with a highly saturated blue light will appear green on stage, and a red dress illuminated with a highly saturated green light will appear black. Lighting designers therefore may focus multiple instruments, often with multiple different colors, on each part of the stage to ensure control over not only intensity but also color. Other types of color mixing are also possible and used to produce various tints, shades, hues, saturations, and intensities.

Movement refers to perceptible alterations in any of the controllable qualities. The principal

A change in lighting can create a dramatic shift in mood even though all the major pieces of scenery remain unchanged, as in these two moments from the Guthrie Theatre's production of *The Glass Menagerie* by Tennessee Williams. Lighting design by Jane Cox; scene design by Richard Hoover; costumes by Ann Hould-Ward; directed by Joe Dowling.

T. Charles Erickson

device for creating a sense of movement is a lighting cue. A lighting cue occurs when a lighting control board, or console, triggers some lamps to be brightened and others dimmed, thus creating a shift of intensity, color, and/or distribution on stage. Another form of movement occurs when lighting instruments are physically manipulated by an operator, as is the case when a follow spot tracks an actor's movements. Automated or "intelligent" lighting instruments can be programmed to illuminate different areas of the stage from varying angles and to change their color and texture filters remotely. All of these means allow light to change moment by moment in accordance with the shifting moods and the development of the dramatic action. Its ability to move and change continuously makes lighting the most flexible of the production elements.

Practitioners & Theorists

FEMALE PIONEERS IN STAGE LIGHTING

Jean Rosenthal and Tharon Musser have been among the most influential lighting designers in America. Rosenthal (1912–1969) is often said to have created the field of lighting design. When she began working in the theatre (first with Orson Welles and John Houseman in the Federal Theatre Project in 1936), lighting was still the province of the scenic designer or master electrician. From 1938 until her death, Rosenthal was lighting designer (as well as production supervisor) for the Martha Graham Dance Company; perhaps because light was such an essential element in Graham's pieces, Rosenthal was able to perfect lighting as a distinct artistic statement and creator of a strong sense of mood. Largely because of Rosenthal's pioneering example, lighting design after World War II came to be recognized as a specialized field. Among Rosenthal's numerous designs for the Broadway theatre, the best known are *West Side Story* (see illustration on page 193) and *The Sound of Music*. Rosenthal's book *The Magic of Light* (1972) sums up her views on stage lighting.

Tharon Musser (1925–2009) was a graduate of Berea College and the Yale School of Drama. Musser did most of her early lighting work for dance companies, especially José Limon's. Her first major Broadway assignment was José Quintero's production of O'Neill's *Long Day's Journey into Night* in 1956. She went on to design for several repertory companies, among them the American Shakespeare Company, and for over one-hundred Broadway productions. Musser won three Tony Awards (in 1972 for *Follies*, in 1976 for *A Chorus Line*, and in 1982 for *Dreamgirls*). She is also credited with several innovations in lighting practice, perhaps most notably computerized lighting, which she introduced to Broadway in *A Chorus Line* (1975). In 2003 Musser was honored with the Ruth Morely Designing Woman Award for her many achievements in stage lighting.

Musser believed that mastery of technical skills alone is insufficient preparation for a young lighting designer. Instead, she strongly advocated a liberal education as the foundation for further training. She argued that art history courses are more valuable than lighting courses because although the lighting designer must attain adequate technical training, ultimately that training will be ineffective unless it is combined with a vision that creates paintings with light. She urged young designers to work in regional and summer stock theatres because of the variety of experience those theatres offer and because they permit young designers to try out—in a short span of time—many ideas that help to develop craft into art.

The Functions of Lighting Design

Lighting designers selectively shape the controllable qualities of light to fulfill the various functions of light design:

- Provide appropriate visibility
- Sculpt dimensionality
- Reinforce and create stage compositions
- Enhance mood and atmosphere
- Support style and production concept
- Reinforce the action

A minimum level of visibility is essential if the performance is to be seen. Having achieved this basic function, one must consider how lighting affects our perception of dimensionality (mass and form). A three-dimensional structure will appear flat if all of its surfaces are evenly lighted. Conversely, its shape will be revealed or emphasized by light that varies markedly from one surface to another. Thus, the lighting designer can define or alter apparent shape, dimension, and depth by manipulating the light's distribution, intensity, and color. This ability to influence perception of mass and form, often referred to as *modeling*, is among the lighting designer's most potent means of creating mood, atmosphere, and stylistic traits.

Lighting aids in reinforcing and creating stage compositions. It can selectively reveal or conceal some parts of the stage (or scene). By directing the eye to the most important elements, it creates emphasis on those areas or objects and minimizes importance of others using *selective focus*. On the proscenium stage, the acting (or foreground) areas are usually more brightly lighted than the background. Additionally, the intensity at stage level (where the action takes place) is usually greater than on the upper parts of the set, helping to keep the audience's attention on the performers.

Perhaps one of lighting design's most important functions is to enhance mood and atmosphere. Bright, warm light is associated with gaiety and well-being; cool light, with somberness. Glaring white light may create a sense of starkness or clinical probing, whereas low-intensity lighting with many areas of shadow may create an atmosphere of mystery or threat. It is impossible to specify precisely the effect of each use of lighting because our response is determined by the total context and not merely by the lighting.

Lighting may be used to support the style or the production's concept. If the stylistic goal is realism, the lighting may establish the source of the light (sun, moon, lamps, firelight) and let the source motivate intensity, distribution of light and shadow, color, and movement. Light may reflect the time of day, weather conditions, or season, and it may suggest the play's period through the lighting fixtures used on stage. If the style is not realism, the source of the light and the way it is handled may suggest that as well. Visible light sources may be used to distribute light evenly over the entire stage, establishing the performance space itself (rather than some fictional locale) as the place of the dramatic action. For an expressionistic play, light from very low or sharp angles may be used to distort facial features, or saturated colors may be used to indicate the dominant emotion. The production's concept or interpretive focus may be supported by the ways in which light is controlled, the logic this control establishes, and its compositional focus.

Finally, lighting reinforces the action by reflecting the dominant feeling of each scene and the changes in mood, time, and atmosphere from one scene (or location) to the next. Changes in lighting may also underscore the rhythmical patterns of scenes and changes in rhythm from one scene to another.

Although it serves many functions, lighting is among the most abstract of theatrical means. It works through suggestion and association rather than through concrete references (as scenery, costumes, and acting usually do). Many lighting designers believe their designs to

THE ART OF LIGHT DESIGN

Often overlooked by theatregoers (there was not a Tony Award for lighting design until 1970, twenty-three years after costume and scenic design), the artistic contributions of the lighting designer can be central to the way a production communicates its meaning. Several renowned lighting designers discuss their art.

Donald Holder (Tony Award–winning lighting designer of *The Lion King*): "One of the jobs of a lighting designer is to be an illusionist, to convince the audience that they're someplace special. The job for me as the lighting designer for *The Lion King* was to create a luminous world, a magical, vibrant world filled with light that evoked the majesty of the Serengetti, the majesty of natural light in Africa."

Richard Pilbrow (internationally renowned lighting designer and author of *Stage Lighting Design: The Art, The Craft, The Life*): "Modern lighting creates a world of light that enwraps the actor, linking him with his environment. Lighting provides the glue that joins all elements of the production together and thus helps to underline for the audience the full emotion and meaning of the play."

J. Michael Gillette (lighting designer and author of *Designing with Light*): "In lighting design, just as in literature, the concepts of good and evil are often associated with light and darkness. When a scene is lit with dark and murky shadows, most people instinctively react with a sense of foreboding."

Frances Reid (lighting designer and author of *Stage Lighting Handbook*): "Stage lighting is not an exact science. It is science in the service of performing art. Rules are few, if indeed there are any. Provided that the lighting works with the other elements in the production to enable author and actors to communicate with their audience, virtually anything goes."

be most effective when they work in harmony with the other production elements, whether the audience is consciously aware of the light or not.

The Lighting Designer's Skills

Lighting designers need a variety of skills, many of them pertinent to other professions, such as visual artist, electrical or optical engineer, computer programmer, display designer, electrician, social and cultural historian, and stage director.

Like other theatre designers, lighting designers need skills like those of the visual artist because they communicate through visual means. They must have an understanding of elements of design and principles of composition in order to create a unified design idea. Lighting designers may demonstrate their preliminary ideas by making many drawings, then render their final designs as sketches that emphasize light and shade—gradations in intensity, dominant direction, distribution—as well as color. Lighting designers must also be able to draft various

T. Charles Erickson

Davy Cunningham's lighting design for *Translations* by Brian Friel as produced by the McCarter Theatre under the direction of Garry Hynes. Note how Cunningham's lighting works in cooperation with Francis O'Connor's setting and costumes.

scale drawings of the stage and auditorium to show the mounting positions of lighting instruments and the areas they are to light. Today, most designers use computers to generate these drawings.

Like electrical engineers, lighting designers need to understand physics and electronics because they work with complex instruments and control boards operated by electricity. They need to know how the equipment works as well as the physical principles involved, so that they can make maximum use of the resources and avoid their inefficient and dangerous misuse. Like optical engineers, lighting designers need to understand the principles of optics and light because they manipulate the variable properties of light when they use lamps, lenses, reflectors, color filters, and other

equipment. The fuller their understanding of the principles and properties of light, the greater their potential for using light effectively for artistic purposes. Although lighting designers work in a more restricted and specialized sphere than electrical and optical engineers, all use the same base of information. Advances in computer technology have created sophisticated, automated lighting instruments, and today's lighting designers occasionally require computer programming skills in order to use this technology effectively.

In the application of skills, lighting designers have much in common with display designers, who create tableaus for major retail storefront windows and tradeshows, because both use the intensity, distribution, direction, and color of light to focus attention on important elements

Practitioners & Theorists

JENNIFER TIPTON

Jennifer Tipton is one of today's most admired lighting designers. Her influence is evident not only through her work as a designer but also through her teaching at the Yale University School of Drama—many of her former students have gone on to distinguished careers in lighting design for Broadway and regional theatres. Tipton has designed for dance, opera, and theatre and has won awards for her excellence in lighting all three. Her lighting designs for dance—among them designs for Paul Taylor, Twyla Tharp, Robert Joffrey, and Mikhail Baryshnikov—have earned her two Bessie Awards in New York and an Olivier Award in London. In theatre, she has designed for Broadway productions, the New York Shakespeare Festival, and many regional companies (including the American Repertory Company, the Goodman Theatre, and the Guthrie Theatre). Her designs have won her numerous awards, including two Tony Awards (the first for Andrei Serban's 1977 production of *The Cherry Orchard* and the second for Jerome Robbins's *Broadway* in 1989). In 2001, Tipton was awarded the Dorothy and Lillian Gish Prize of $250,000 for her work in lighting design. She is also the recipient of the Jerome Robbins Prize, a 2005 lifetime achievement award for her outstanding contributions to design, and, in 2008, a MacArthur Genius Grant. Tipton is especially known for her work with avant-garde companies and innovative directors such as Robert Wilson, Peter Sellars, and JoAnne Akalaitis. (Examples of Tipton's lighting designs may be seen on pages 254, 255, and 309.)

and to blend the elements into a whole that creates the appropriate mood. The lighting designer's work is usually more complex than the display designer's, however, because in the theatre one is telling an evolving story within a space that is used continuously by live, moving actors, whereas in a display the artist usually lights a fixed picture or one in which movement is created by electronically programmed elements.

Although lighting designers may not perform the physical labor required to realize their designs, they must know what has to be done and supply the information needed by those who actually do the tasks. Consequently, like the stage electrician, designers must know what instruments are available; what each can do; what types of lamps, electrical cable, connectors, and the like are needed; where instruments are to be mounted and plugged in; and a host of other details. The designer's practical knowledge must be as extensive as the stage electrician's, although the designer may not be as skilled at installing and operating the equipment.

Lighting designers should be grounded in social and cultural history (including the visual and performing arts) because they often must know what role light played in various periods in the past. They need to be aware of what illuminants (candles, oil, torches, gas, and so on) were available in each period, how each was used, and what qualities of light each generated (so they can re-create or adapt these illuminants for their work as desired). Although today lighting designers normally work entirely with electrical light, they frequently must create the effects of other illuminants. Designers also need to know the conventions that governed stage lighting in each era of theatre history, in case a production requires these.

Multidirectional lighting, torches, and fog combine to create a strong mood and evoke the historic period for Shakespeare's *Cymbeline*. Lighting design by Marcia Madeira; directed by Larry Carpenter; scene design by John Falabella; costumes by David Murin.

Lighting designers take an approach more nearly like that of the director than that of any other theatre artist because they, like the director, shape the action in time and space. Lighting designers must be attuned not only to the overall needs of each scene but also to each moment as it develops to most effectively communicate the story being told on stage. Light is the most flexible of all theatrical means, being instantaneously and continuously variable. Consequently, the lighting designer needs to work closely with the director to be certain that how the design shapes time and space serves the goals of the production.

The Lighting Designer's Working Procedures

Lighting designers are in a somewhat different position from that of other theatre artists. Because lighting is seen as it is reflected by the actors, costumes, setting, and performance space, the lighting designer's work is codependent on what is created by others. This means that frequently lighting designers must adjust their work to enhance that of others rather than proceeding independently. For example, the color of costumes or scenery can be drastically affected by the colors chosen by the lighting designer. Lighting designers can make general plans but until the floor plan and setting are agreed upon, they cannot make firm decisions about the placement and direction of lighting instruments, and until the movement pattern of each actor is established, they cannot know precisely how the light needs to be distributed. Firm color choices must also wait until the costume and scene designers have made their decisions. Lighting design therefore seldom becomes as fixed as other design elements do during the initial phases of preproduction planning.

Like the other designers, lighting designers should be able to convey their ideas about how the stage should look during performances. The device most frequently used by lighting designers to convey this is *value sketches*. These sketches emphasize mood and atmosphere or light and shadow. The number and type of sketches depend upon the complexity and variety of the lighting to be used. Instead of sketches (or in addition to them), lighting designers sometimes use a *lighting score* that breaks the play into scenes or units and indicates the time of day, source of light, overall brightness, the desired mood, color, and any other lighting factors that will affect the action. Some lighting designers use computer simulations to show how the production will look when lighted. Value sketches, lighting scores, and computer simulations all serve as a basis for discussion with the production team about the how the controllable qualities of light may best enhance the production.

Lighting designers usually attend several rehearsals to become familiar with the movement patterns and to understand the director's intentions. Increasingly, designers also try out and perfect aspects of their lighting designs (especially color mixing or automated lighting effects) in a laboratory or use computer simulations before implementing them. However lighting designers work, they usually do not arrive at fully developed designs until shortly before the instruments are to be hung and focused.

Organizing the Distribution of Light

Although value sketches and lighting scores communicate how the lighting should look in terms of mood, atmosphere, and quality, the lighting instruments must still be precisely chosen and placed to achieve these effects. Lighting designers use two primary working plans to organize the distribution of light: *light plots* and *instrument schedules*.

Light plots can be divided into two types: floor plans and centerline sections. The floor-plan plot is drawn to scale and shows, as seen from a top view, the layout of the stage, scenery, and the auditorium. On this plot are indicated the type, size, and position of each instrument and the area it will light. The centerline section, also drawn to scale, shows the vertical arrangement (from a side view) of the stage, scenery, and auditorium, and the type, size, and position of each instrument and the area it will light. Together these plots show the horizontal and vertical distribution of the light sources. Some designers make a separate light plot for each setting and then a composite plot showing all of the settings simultaneously in order to see how the lighting for each scene relates to that of all of the others. (See illustration on the following page.)

Light plots also take into consideration the three principal types of stage lighting: area light, general illumination, and special effects. Area light is confined to a relatively small and very specific portion of the stage. It is used principally for illuminating acting areas, which demand the greatest emphasis and usually require variety in intensity, color, and distribution. The principal sources of specific illumination are *spotlights*.

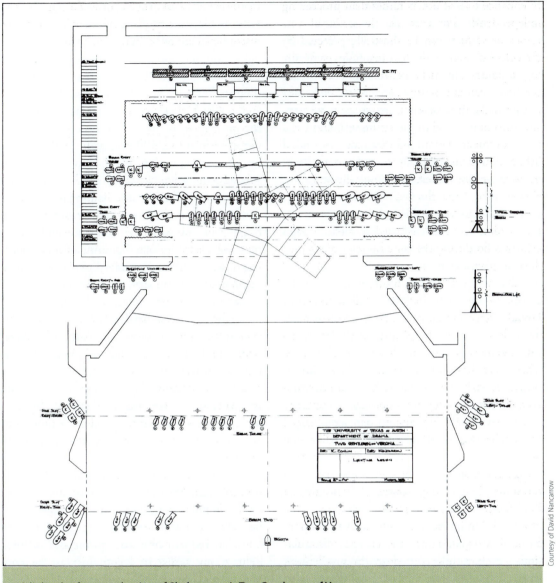

A light plot for a production of Shakespeare's *Two Gentlemen of Verona*.

Spotlights combine the reflector of the light source with one of several types of lens that help concentrate and disperse a beam focused on a specific area. But because a single light can illuminate only a small segment of the stage, lighting designers usually divide the total acting space into several smaller areas. Each area is then lighted separately. At least one light is focused on each area from each side to strike it at an angle of forty-five degrees both horizontally and vertically. More typically, several instruments (mounted at varying levels and angles) are focused on each area. The lighting for each area should overlap into adjacent areas to avoid distracting variations in brightness and darkness as actors move about the stage.

Where instruments are mounted to achieve the desired distribution depends in part on the type of stage. In the proscenium theatre, acting areas on the apron of the stage cannot be lighted effectively from behind the proscenium arch, and therefore some instruments typically are mounted in the auditorium—in ceiling apertures, in vertical apertures at the sides, or on the front of a balcony. Upstage areas are normally lighted by instruments hung behind the proscenium arch—on pipe battens suspended over the stage at intervals from front to back, on vertical pipes at either side of the stage, on stands, or on the floor. In the arena theatre, all instruments are usually mounted above the acting area and audience or on vertical pipes located where they will not interfere with sightlines or movement on and off stage. Because performances are viewed from four sides, the acting areas must be lit from all directions. On the thrust stage, most of the instruments are mounted over the acting area, but there may be a space upstage of the main performance space where others are hung. Because the action is normally seen from two or three sides, lighting on thrust stages is usually a hybrid of the techniques used for a proscenium and arena stage. In flexible or variable performance spaces, the instruments may be mounted almost anywhere in the performance space provided they do not obstruct sightlines or movement throughout the space.

General illumination spreads over a much larger space than area light. General illumination is most fully exploited on the proscenium stage, where it serves three functions: to light the background elements (cyclorama, ground rows, drops) not illuminated by spotlights; to blend acting areas and provide a smooth transition from the higher intensity of the acting areas to the lower intensity of the background; and to enhance or modify the color of settings and costumes. Although general illumination cannot be confined to small areas, its direction can be partially controlled. For example, borderlights may be hung above the acting area and pointed downward or tilted in one direction. Striplights and floodlights may be suspended on battens above the stage, mounted on

vertical stands, or placed on the floor. On the arena stage, general illumination plays a minor role because usually there is no background to light, and the specific illumination covers the entire acting space. On the thrust stage, general illumination depends heavily on the specific architectural structure and scenic choices for the upstage areas. In flexible or variable spaces, the need for general illumination is determined by the configuration of the space for each specific production.

Special effects are out-of-the-ordinary demands—among them fires, rainbows, fog, bright rays of light (to simulate sunlight or moonlight), explosions, lightning, strobe lights, and "black" light (ultraviolet light used to pick out specially treated substances on a dark stage).

In making light plots, each type of light (area, general, and special effects) is considered separately and then as a part of the total unit. The location of all lighting instruments is indicated on the plots.

A wide array of lighting instruments and accessories are available to the lighting designer, who must understand their properties and principles in order to select the appropriate equipment needed to create the desired effects. For example, although both ellipsoidals and fresnels may be considered spotlights because each combines a reflector with a convex lens, fresnels use a thin, specially designed convex lens that reduces heat absorption and diffuses light evenly across its beam. Just as the type of lens may change the properties of light an instrument emits, so too may the type of reflector used. There are also a variety of automated lighting instruments that may be programmed to change their focus and their color filters or to create specific patterns of light and shadow on cue from a remote control board. Likewise, there are numerous accessories that can shape the pattern of light and shadow. Among the most common of these are *gobos* (etched metal or glass filters) that selectively block some light from reaching the stage so that patterns of light and shadow are created. For example, one may simulate a forest on stage by using

Specific illumination pops the characters out from the general color wash covering the rear and sides of the stage in Mimi Jordan Sherin's lighting design for *Two Sisters and a Piano* by Nilo Cruz. Scene design by Mark Wendland; costumes by Anita Yaich; directed by Brian Kulik.

T. Charles Erickson

gobos of branches and leaves. Suffice it to say that each instrument and accessory may serve a different purpose depending on its basic properties and how it is used. Therefore, lighting designers must understand the basic properties of each type of lighting instrument in order to select the proper instrument to create the effect they wish.

After the light plots are completed, an instrument schedule is made. This is a spreadsheet that lists each lighting instrument with its specifications (type, wattage, lens, reflector, lamp, and any other pertinent information), mounting position, color filter, area lighted by it, control channel, circuit into which it is plugged, and dimmer to which it is connected. The schedule summarizes all of the technical information needed for acquiring and setting up lighting instruments.

Setting the Lights, Rehearsals, and Performances

Typically, the performance space is not available for work on lights until a few days before technical and dress rehearsals. Using the light plots and instrument schedule as guides, the master electrician and electrics crew mount each instrument in the location specified by the light plot. The indicated light filter is added, the instrument is plugged into the proper circuit, and it is then connected to the designated dimmer. The instruments may be focused tentatively at this time; final focusing may have to wait until the other production elements are added.

TABLE 17.1   LIGHTING INSTRUMENT CHART

Inst#	Instrument	Position	Focus	Lamp	Circuit	Dimmer	Color	Notes
1	6316 Ellipsoidal	2nd Ante-Pro.	Down-R	1k	202	4	R54	
2	6316 Ellipsoidal	2nd Ante-Pro.	Down-L	1k	203	5	R54	
1	ETC Source 4	1st Ante-Pro.	Center-R	575w	120	1	R60	
2	ETC Source 4	1st Ante-Pro.	Center-C	575w	125	2	R60	
3	ETC Source 4	1st Ante-Pro.	Center-L	575w	123	3	R60	Leaf Gobo
1	VL6	1st Electric	Variable	400w	7	10	Variable	Programmed by Lynn
2	VL6	1st Electric	Variable	400w	14	17	Variable	Programmed by Lynn
3	639 Ellipsoidal	1st Electric	Center-L	1k	1	11	R64	
4	639 Ellipsoidal	1st Electric	Center-L	1k	3	16	R60	
5	639 Ellipsoidal	1st Electric	Center-C	1k	2	14	R60	
6	639 Ellipsoidal	1st Electric	Center-C	1k	4	20	R62	
1	639 Ellipsoidal	2nd Electric	Up-L	1k	27	28	R64	Leaf Gobo
2	639 Ellipsoidal	2nd Electric	Up-L	1k	29	29	R64	Leaf Gobo
3	6"" Fresnel	2nd Electric	Up-R	750w	24	22	R62	2"" Top Hat
4	6"" Fresnel	2nd Electric	Up-R	750w	30	23	R62	2"" Top Hat
1	6"" Fresnel	3rd Electric	Center-R	750w	44	37	R73	Barndoor
2	6" Fresnel	3rd Electric	Center-R	750w	46	36	R73	Barndoor
1	Par 64	4th Electric	Down-R	1k	54	46	R08	
2	Par 64	4th Electric	Down-R	1k	58	50	R80	
3	Par 64	4th Electric	Down-R	1k	56	48	R08	

Courtesy of Robert Ball

To expedite these procedures, a number of aids may be used to avoid the need to refer constantly to light plots or instrument schedules. Sometimes at each instrument position the information about the instrument type, circuit, and so on is noted on a piece of tape and attached at the spot where the instrument is to be mounted. Other times the information about all of the instruments to be hung on a particular batten is indicated on a single note card. Each designer and/or master electrician usually has his or her shortcuts for making the complex process of mounting and focusing instruments more efficient. Although most of the work is done by others, the lighting designer or an assistant is usually available to answer questions or to clarify plans.

Setting and focusing instruments can be time consuming because it is difficult to confine light precisely. Unwanted lines, shadows, and bright patches may appear; and when the same instruments must be used to light more than one scene or set, an ideal adjustment for one may not be ideal for the others. This process may go on for hours, even days, until the desired results have been achieved.

Cue sheets indicate when lighting shifts occur throughout the production and often

Three lighting designers (Brian MacDevitt, Kenneth Posner, and Natasha Scott) coordinated their efforts for the three parts of Tom Stoppard's trilogy *The Coast of Utopia*. Pictured here is a scene from the first play, *Voyage*. Lighting not only awed opening-night audiences, who reportedly gasped when the lighting revealed what appeared to be a skating rink with an image of St. Basil's Cathedral suspended above it, but also allowed for faintly ghosted images upstage to enrich the scene's action. Lighting design by Brian MacDevitt; scene design by Bob Crowley and Scott Pask; costumes by Catherine Zuber; music and sound by Mark Bennet; directed by Jack O'Brien. The three lighting designers, two scene designers, costume designer, and director all won Tony Awards for their work. With additional wins for Best Play, Featured Actor, and Featured Actress, *The Coast of Utopia's* seven Tony Awards are the most for a non-musical.

Sara Krulwich/The New York Times/Redux

provide a brief description of the desired lighting conditions on stage. The light cues are then recorded into a computerized light-board.

Lighting is usually integrated with the other elements for the first time during technical rehearsals. Alterations may be required at that time, and further adjustments may be made during and after dress rehearsals. This is a crucial time in the lighting designer's work because many decisions that determine the final design are not definitively made until these rehearsals. The lighting designer can be called on to compensate for other less flexible aspects of production because it is easier to adjust lights than to make a new costume or to repaint a set at this point in the production process. Some productions, especially those on Broadway, have a number of preview performances, after each of which some adjustments may be required. After a production officially opens, responsibility for maintaining the integrity of the lighting design passes to the electrics crew.

The Lighting Designer's Assistants

In the professional theatre, the lighting designer is usually a member of the United Scenic Artists Union, as is the assistant designer (if there is one). The assistant may make sketches and light plots, compile instrument schedules, locate the necessary equipment, and act as liaison between the lighting designer and the rest of the production staff, as well as aid in programming lights and supervising their installation.

The lighting crew installs, operates, and maintains all lighting equipment and shifts electrical equipment that must be moved during scene changes. The highest ranking member of the lighting crew is the master electrician (sometimes called the lighting supervisor). The master electrician works closely with the designer when equipment is being installed and instruments adjusted. After the show opens, the master electrician must see that all materials are properly maintained and must check before each performance to ensure that everything is in working order. These technicians report to the stage manager. In the professional theatre, lighting crew members and master electricians are usually members of the International Alliance of Theatrical Stage Employees union (IATSE). In the nonprofessional theatre, crews are usually students or volunteers.

The Increasing Role of Sound Design

Although sound has always played an important role in theatrical production, it is the most recent design area to be recognized as its own independent art. Historically, many have viewed the theatrical use of sound as primarily the craft of recording and playing pre-existing sounds or reinforcing live sound through amplification. However, this view has undergone radical change. In 1986 the stagehands' union (IATSE) chartered its first sound design chapter, and in 1993 it gained acceptance for a standard labor contract for Broadway and Broadway-tour sound designers. In 1991 John Gromada was awarded an Obie (an award given for excellence in Off-Broadway theatre) for sound design for the New York production of *Machinal*. In the fall of 1993, the Yale School of Drama for the first time admitted sound designers to its design program

rather than (as previously) to its technical crafts division. Tony Awards were not given for "Best Sound Design of a Play" and "Best Sound Design of a Musical" until 2008. These developments in effect recognized sound as the fourth design discipline (along with scenery, lighting, and costume) and reflect that a more complex use of sound has become typical in many professional theatre productions.

Some maintain that this growing recognition owes to the development of digitized sound that, in conjunction with computers, permits designers to create and manipulate sound waves, not merely record or amplify them. As avant-garde opera and theatre director Peter Sellars has said, "We are beyond the era of sound effects. Sound is no longer an effect, an extra." Sound designer James Lebrecht has been asked to design effects as abstract as "the sound of shimmering light reflecting off a swimming pool at night." Such a request suggests that an effective sound design goes well beyond the basic physics involved and demonstrates the increasing tendency to explore and use sound's aesthetic possibilities as an integral aspect of production design.

Sound may be divided into three categories: verbal (the actors' voices), nonverbal (music and abstract sound), and realistic (sound identifiable by recognizable sources). Because the first category has already been discussed in the chapters on directing and acting, little need be said about it here.

The Functions of Sound Design

Sound may fulfill any of four main functions:

- Evoke mood and atmosphere
- Reinforce the action
- Reinforce the performers' voices
- Support the production's style or comments on the action

A mood or atmosphere of gaiety or somberness can be evoked by music, just as mystery or strangeness can be evoked by abstract hollow sounds. Environmental sounds, such as birds singing, may be used to suggest a quiet pastoral scene. Thunder and rain may be used to set the mood for an impending murder.

Sound may reinforce the action by preparing the audience for present or future events or by suggesting offstage events. Gunshots, crashing dishes, doorbells, telephones, and similar sounds may prepare for onstage action or indicate offstage occurrences. Certain identifiable noises may establish the time of day (a rooster crowing is usually associated with daybreak) or season of the year (sleigh bells are usually associated with winter), just as others may place the action outdoors, indoors, in the country or city, or near a specific location such as a railroad or river.

Sound may be live or recorded. But in either case, it may be amplified. The actors create live sound, but whether or not it is amplified usually depends on the size of the auditorium or, in the case of musicals, whether the singing voices need to be amplified to be heard above the musical accompaniment. However, the sound designer may also choose to amplify one or more of the performers' voices for a special effect. Live orchestras are seldom amplified. Most nonmusical dramas do not demand music, but recorded music is often added to underscore an effect, to establish the appropriate mood before the performance begins, or to bridge scenes and cover scene changes.

Sound may comment on the action by giving audiences clues about the response sought by the director. Lugubrious music played during a long pathetic speech can make a comic or

Sara Krulwich/The New York Times/Redux

Although sound design has only recently become fully recognized as a fourth design discipline, sound has long been recognized as an integral component of musical theatre. Seen here is the 2009 Broadway revival of *West Side Story*, which transplants Shakespeare's *Romeo and Juliet* to the world of mid-1950s New York street gangs. Sound design by David C. Woolard.

satirical comment, or the clashing of cymbals may heighten a pratfall. Thus, sound may be used as an additional element that by contrasting or heightening the stage action makes a comment upon it.

The Sound Designer's Working Methods and Resources

The sound designer usually begins by closely examining the play for opportunities to use sound effectively. Some opportunities may be obvious; stage directions may call for the sound of a glass windowpane being smashed, or one character may mention that "the six o'clock train is right on time." However, most opportunities to use sound are less obvious and demand the careful consideration of the designer in consultation with the director. For example, if two characters remain onstage while four or five others exit to play cards in a room offstage, the decision whether or not we hear any of the sounds from this offstage game may add an important nuance or prove distracting.

Most sound designers use their study of the play and their imaginations to develop a *sound score*. The score provides the following information:

- The function for each intended sound cue
- When the cue should be heard
- The cue's duration (how long it should be heard)
- The origin of the sound (live, recorded, etc.) and what will need to be recorded or used to make the sound
- The intended treatment of the sound (whether it needs to be distorted, enhanced, and so on)

After creating the sound score, the sound designer may present it to the director and to the other designers for discussion and refinement.

The sound designer then begins to collect sounds to meet the needs of the sound score. The designer may need to research specific effects, music, or environments called for in the play to ensure that the appropriate sounds are selected. Although a wide range of effects is available commercially in sets of recordings labeled "sound effects libraries," these do not always meet the needs of a production. Synthesizers or digital samplers can produce almost any sound, but to achieve the desired quality, some sounds may need to be created live or recorded from a live source. Once the intended sounds are found or created, they typically are recorded and uploaded into a computer to be edited and enhanced as desired. Computer technology can be used to alter a recorded sound's duration, pitch, and reverberation, as well as to change its quality by rewriting its digital signature. Sounds can be mixed, fused, and adjusted by a number of other techniques to produce almost any desired effect. Likewise, the range of recording equipment has increased so that most organizations now own some type of recording equipment that allows them to create the effects most appropriate to their needs. In the professional theatre, a playlist approximating the sound that is planned for the production is often used for some rehearsals, allowing sound designers to evaluate the effectiveness of their designs and to make ongoing adjustments. An audio technician or engineer sometimes assists the designer during this process of collecting, recording, and modifying sound.

The designer then creates a *sound plot*, which is similar to the sound score but much more detailed in its organization. It designates a letter or number for each cue, specifying its function, its script page, its duration, its playback system (digital player, computer, or whether it will be made live), and its source direction (the speaker or speakers it should be played through and their location). On the basis of these decisions, the designer creates a digital playlist (as it will be used in the production). Sound must then be integrated into the production with all appropriate information written into the stage manager's promptbook. Cue sheets are usually created for the personnel who will operate the sound board during the performances. During technical and dress rehearsals, sound levels and lengths of cues may need to be adjusted and the playlist altered to reflect these changes. Backup files are made in case anything should happen to the original. After the production opens, the sound designer's work is considered to be ended, and responsibility for the execution of the sound design passes to the stage manager and sound board operator.

Effective execution of a sound design requires a sound system of high quality. Some groups have only the simplest of recorder/playback units, whereas others have very elaborate systems. An effective system allows all of the controllable factors of sound—pitch (or frequency), quality (or timbre), volume (or amplitude), direction, and duration—to be varied in relation to each other and in accordance with the demands of the production. Complete flexibility in direction, for example, requires a series of speakers located at various spots on the stage and in the auditorium so that a sound (such as that of an airplane) can begin on one side, seem to approach, pass overhead, and pass out of hearing on the other side. Effective placement and control are made more complex by the acoustics of the space in which sound may reverberate or be reflected off various surfaces.

Mixed-Media Productions

Mixed- (or multi-) media productions may combine elements from several media, but characteristically they mingle live action (which may include dance) with projected still or moving pictures and stereophonic sound and music.

Several factors may explain the popularity of multimedia, but perhaps the most important of these are contemporary changes in artistic taste and audience perception. Influenced by film, television, and our interaction with computers, many of us expect time, place, and focus to shift rapidly, without delays. This being the case, many playwrights have begun to write accordingly. In general, the result has been a more fluid treatment of the stage space. Significant advances in computer and other electronic technology have been adapted for theatrical use, making it possible to program many effects and to control them with great precision. For these reasons, traditional settings have been largely supplanted by those created with a few built pieces combined with effects created through light and sound. The stage has become technologically more complex, while stage settings have become less illusionistic.

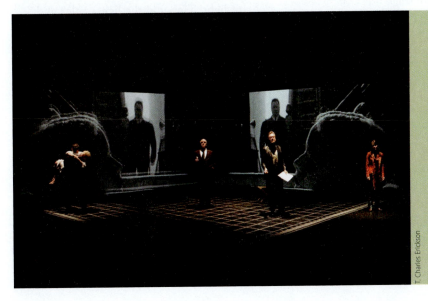

T. Charles Erickson

The action in Terry Johnson's *Hitchcock Blonde* moves fluidly between the late 1950s (as Alfred Hitchcock shoots his film *Psycho*) and the late 1990s (as a film professor and ardent Hitchcock fan has an affair with one of his female students). The Alley Theatre's production of the play (seen here) used multiple projection screens to incorporate still and moving images to support the play's action. Directed by Gregory Boyd; scene, sound, projection and costume design by William Dudley; lighting by Chris Parry.

A notable feature of multimedia productions has been the liberal use of projected images, often of still pictures, frequently several shown simultaneously on a number of screens. The images may be fragments of the same picture, or each may be unlike the others. All are usually chosen for their appropriateness to the mood or theme of the piece; some may suggest comparisons between the dramatic events and those of other times and places. For example, a production of Shakespeare's *Troilus and Cressida*—which takes place during the Trojan War—might project images of wars in various periods and places, thereby suggesting the similarity of all wars. Filmed sequences may also be used in various ways. Footage of real events may be used to supply a context for a play's action; filmed sequences using the play's actors may be interjected into the action to give it greater scope; or filmed sequences and live sequences may be coordinated. Closed-circuit television can be used to project onto large screens close-ups of the actors' faces, portions of the action, or even of the audience.

In these and other ways, multimedia productions, which depend heavily on the work of the lighting, sound, and scenic designers, have enlarged the scope of theatrical design and probably will continue to do so as new technology is developed and adapted to stage use.

Thinking about Stage Lighting and Sound

Stage lighting is among the most difficult production elements to evaluate because it usually attracts attention not to itself but to the actors, scenery, costumes, or directing. Unless we have difficulty seeing, are distracted by shadows on the actors' faces, are annoyed by glare, or are fascinated by some beautiful or spectacular lighting effect, we may not think about the lighting. Yet light is an essential production element both for the sake of artistry and for the sake of visibility. Sound is perhaps more immediately noticeable, but how and when it is used can have a profound effect on emotional response to a stage moment and our understanding of its significance. Our attention to the lighting and sound choices made by their designers can enhance our understanding of any theatrical production. The following questions may contribute to a fuller understanding of stage lighting and sound.

1. How did the type of theatrical space used for the production (proscenium, arena, thrust, flexible) affect the use of lighting?

2. What overall approach governed the lighting and sound? Did they suggest recognizable sources? Were they used to suggest a specific time of day, period, or place? If so, how? With what effect? Were the lighting and sound dictated by stylistic or interpretational considerations? If so, what were the results?

3. How did lighting and sound affect (or help to create) mood and atmosphere? Did mood and atmosphere change? If so, how? With what results?

4. How effectively did the lighting designer use the controllable qualities of light? How did the light's color and intensity affect your perception of costumes and scenery? How did the distribution of light on stage affect your focus and attention? Did the designer use direction (frontlighting, downlighting, backlighting, crosslighting) to emphasize certain areas and features or to de-emphasize others? With what effect?

5. Was sound and lighting used to underscore or reinforce the development of the dramatic action or in some way clarify the production concept or its interpretive focus? If so, how? With what results?

6. Were there any unusual lighting or sound effects? If so, which and with what results? Did these call undue attention to themselves at any point? If so, how?

7. How did the lighting enhance or fail to enhance the acting, scenery, costumes, and makeup? Was it unified with all the other elements?

8. How did the sound enhance or fail to enhance the acting, lighting, and scenery? Was it unified with the other elements? Was sound used to comment upon the action? If so, in what ways? With what results?

9. Overall, how effectively did lighting contribute to the total production?

10. Overall, how effectively did the sound contribute to the total production?

The relevance of each of these questions may vary with the particular production and play. Furthermore, some of these questions may not be answerable because there is not adequate information or because the lighting and sound cannot be isolated from other production elements or the total context. Nevertheless, attempting to answer some or all of these questions can make us examine lighting and sound more closely and lead us to appreciate more fully their contributions to theatrical production.

Afterword

Throughout the course of this book, we have looked at theatre from several angles:

- We addressed the basic characteristics of theatre as entertainment and as an art form.
- We examined approaches to evaluating performances.
- We analyzed the way plays are written and structured.
- We explored some of the different ways in which the theatrical experience has varied in the past and the way it continues to change in the present.
- We discussed how each of the theatre arts functions today and how all are combined to create the performances we see in the theatre.

Taken together, these explorations provide a foundation for a fuller understanding and appreciation of theatre.

But a foundation is just that—something to build on rather than a finished structure. What one chooses to do with the foundation is as important as the foundation itself. It can be abandoned, or it can be a basis for further growth. Whether your understanding and appreciation of theatre will continue to develop depends upon continued engagement with the form, whether it be as a practitioner helping to create the work of art, as a reader exploring the history and drama, or as an audience member perceiving the theatrical event. All are essential facets of the art form and each can be a rewarding experience for those interested in exploring the human condition.

Glossary

absurdist drama A term used to describe certain plays of the post–World War II period. The writers of these plays believed that the human condition is absurd because the desire for clarity and order is met only by the irrationality of the universe, thus making rational or meaningful choice impossible. Absurdist plays abandoned the logic of cause-to-effect relationships for associational patterns reflecting the illogical nature of the human situation. Two of the most prominent absurdist playwrights were Beckett and Ionesco.

agon In Greek Old Comedy, a debate over the merits of the "happy idea."

alexandrine French verse form containing twelve-syllable lines, divided into two six-syllable hemispheres, with each pair of adjacent lines rhyming.

antagonist The primary opponent of the leading character in a dramatic action.

arena stage Type of theatre with audience seating on all sides of the performing space; also known as theatre-in-the-round.

art for art's sake A late nineteenth-century movement, which asserted that the only functions of art were to intensify experience and to provide sensuous pleasure. In this respect it challenged the scientific outlook of realism and naturalism, their focus on contemporary subjects, and their tacit agenda for social change.

auteur approach A directorial approach in which the director treats the script as raw material to be reshaped for his or her own purposes or even constructs a new script through an intermingling of texts.

auto sacramentales Short plays produced in Spain between 1500 and 1700 that combined characteristics of morality and cycle plays. Characters included human, biblical, supernatural, and allegorical figures (Fortune, Grief, Beauty, Sin, etc.), who at times intermingled in stories that could be drawn from any source as long as they supported the value of the sacraments and church doctrine.

backdrop *See* **drop**.

backstage The areas beyond the visible performance space, especially the workspaces of the backstage personnel, such as stage crews and technicians.

balance A design principle that allows the relationships between objects and performers on stage to be manipulated for a desired effect; forms of balance include symmetry, asymmetry, radial, and axial balance.

batten A pipe suspended above the stage by lines that permit it to be raised or lowered; scenic pieces or lighting instruments may be hung from it. Battens are attached to the top and bottom of drops to keep the cloth stretched and free of wrinkles.

blending Scene painting technique that suggests the appearance of texture by applying three or more tones of a color on a surface.

blocking The placement and movement of the actors on stage moment by moment, usually planned by the director.

border A short curtain or piece of painted canvas hung parallel to the front of the stage and in a series from front-to-back, used to mask the overhead space. Striplights mounted behind the borders are called borderlights.

box set A setting or set that fully encloses the acting space on three sides like the walls of a room, resembling a box with one side removed.

bruitisme A form of "noise music" (based on the sounds of everyday life) popular with the Italian futurists.

Bunraku A Japanese form of doll or puppet theatre.

butai The primary acting area in the Japanese Noh theatre, which includes areas associated with the four pillars (*shitebashira, wakibashira, fuebashira, metsukabashira*) and specific characters and functions.

Butoh An avant-garde performance form that originated in Japan during the turbulent 1960s. Initially called *ankoku butoh* ("dance of darkness") because of its use of grotesque imagery and explicit sexuality to address the mystery of an existence precariously balanced between creation and self-destruction.

character makeup Application of makeup intended to markedly alter one or more of an actor's natural facial features.

characterization That which delineates a person or differentiates that person from others, typically operating on four levels: physical, sociological, psychological, and moral.

choregus A wealthy citizen in ancient Greece who helped finance the training and costuming of the chorus. One *choregus* was chosen for each competing dramatist at the City Dionysia festival.

chorus In Greek drama, a group of actors who spoke, sang, and danced in unison; the choral songs and dances, usually commenting on the action, separated the play into episodes.

chou The comic characters in Chinese opera.

City Dionysia The principal Athenian festival (held in honor of the god Dionysus) at which plays were performed.

climactic plot structure An arrangement of a play's events wherein, typically, scenes build sequentially in a cause-to-effect relationship from inciting incident to the climax or resolution.

climax The highest point of interest or suspense, typically the moment that determines the outcome of a play's action.

colorblind casting Casting that ignores race and ethnicity and casts performers solely on the basis of their talent and suitability to a role.

comedy A form of drama based on some deviation from normality in action, character, or thought treated as to arouse laughter or ridicule and that ends happily.

commedia dell'arte A type of performance that emerged in Italy during the sixteenth century. Starting from a scenario that merely outlined the situation, complications, and outcome, the actors improvised the dialogue and action. Each actor always played the same stock character, who wore his or her distinctive costume and mask. The most popular characters were the *zanni*, or comic servants, whose contrivances served both to create and resolve complications. *Commedia* companies played throughout Europe and enjoyed great popularity everywhere until the middle of the eighteenth century.

complication Any new element that can potentially change the direction of a play's dramatic action.

conceptual casting Changing the race or ethnicity of some or all characters to bring a new perspective to a play (also sometimes referred to as "cross-cultural casting").

conventions Theatrical and dramatic practices, devices, and procedures that are mutually understood and accepted by both theatre practitioners and audiences. Things seldom happen in the theatre precisely as they would in life, but audiences easily overlook and accept these deviations if they understand the conventions being used. When initially introduced, a convention may be misunderstood; it gains acceptance through continued usage. Some common conventions are Shakespeare's use of soliloquies, characters breaking into song or dance in the midst of a scene in musicals, and the rapid and visible changes that shift the action from one locale to another in many kinds of plays.

costume chart A broad organizational chart used to indicate what costumes and accessories each actor will wear in each scene. It may also be used by costume crews as a guide for dressing the actors during performances.

crew The backstage personnel who assist in mounting and running a production. There are usually separate crews for scenery, costumes, properties, lighting, and sound.

crisis The final turning point in the action of a play, usually brought about by the revelation of those things that have been partially or entirely unknown by one or more of the principal characters.

cue The words, actions, or other prearranged indications that serve as signals for actors to go on to their next line or action, or for lighting, sound, or other crew members to execute some agreed-upon change.

cue sheet A list of prompts for any changes in lights, sounds, or other production elements during the course of a performance. Cue sheets also indicate the changes to be made, along with any other information needed to carry out the appropriate action.

cycle plays In the Middle Ages, a series of short plays dramatizing events drawn from the Bible, often extending from the Creation to Doomsday.

cyclorama Any arrangement of cloth or other material (including plaster) that curves around the rear of the stage and partially down the sides. Usually neutral in color, it is often lighted to represent the sky or used as a projection surface.

Dada An early twentieth-century movement that sought to replace logic, reason, and unity in art with change and illogicality.

dalang The performer who speaks the dialogue and manipulates the shadow puppets used in *wayang kulit. See **wayang kulit**.*

dan Female roles in Chinese opera; divided into quiet and gentle females (*qing yi*); vivacious or dissolute females (*hua dan*); warrior maidens (*wu dan*); and old females (*lao dan*).

decorum A principle supporting French neoclassic drama that suggested characters should behave in a manner appropriate to their social status, gender, and ethnicity.

dénouement (French meaning "unraveling" or "untying") The final portion of a play, it extends from the crisis to its end. It may resolve the conflict, make sense of the various strands of action, answer the questions raised earlier, or solidify a theme.

deus ex machina A Greek term meaning "the god from the machine," referring to the common practice of flying in a god to resolve a difficult dramatic situation. Later it came to mean the use of any unprepared-for and unexpected means of resolving an action. *See* **machina**.

dimmer A device for altering the flow of electrical current and thereby selectively changes the intensity of particular lighting instruments.

discovery The introduction of information or revelations of sufficient importance to raise a complication.

distressed Costume practice of making clothing used and worn (similar practice may be applied to scenic units and stage properties).

dramatic action Not only what the characters do but also why they do it, in relation to some question, problem, or theme that forms the central focus of the play as a whole.

dramaturgy A theatre's internal critic who, depending upon the theatre, may perform any of the following tasks: assist in selecting plays and translations, work developmentally with playwrights on new plays, work with the production team as a research specialist or offer advice on production choices, and prepare programs, articles, and other supplementary materials for the public.

dress parade A procedure used by the costume designer to make certain that costumes have been completed as designed and function appropriately. For each scene, the actors don their costumes, appear together, and perform characteristic actions under lights simulating those that will be used in performance.

dressers Wardrobe personnel responsible for assisting actors with costume changes during performances.

dressing lists or **dressing cards** Lists (often on index cards) of all the costumes and accessories worn by each performer and used by dressers or the performers to ensure that all the correct items are worn in the appropriate scenes.

dress the stage When applied to performers, a request that the performer move to balance the stage picture. When applied in the context of scene design, a request to add decorations or objects appropriate to the environment that will complete the visual illusion.

drop A hanging unit made of lengths of cloth sewn together and attached at the top to a batten that supports it and to another at the bottom that keeps it stretched and free of wrinkles. Scenes of various sorts may be painted on drops. Drops usually serve as backgrounds (backdrops) for the action.

dry-brushing Scene-painting technique that involves taking a relatively dry brush dipped in a small amount of paint and brushing it lightly over a surface so that the paint beneath is still somewhat visible.

eccyclema The platform, rolled or pushed out through the central doorway of the ancient Greek skene, used typically to display the corpses of characters slain offstage.

egungun A traditional Nigerian New Year's ceremony that ends with the sins of the community being loaded onto a "carrier" who cleanses the village by taking them away.

elevations Scene designers' two-dimensional scale drawings that communicate detailed information to others regarding the appearance and construction of each scenic unit; these typically include front, rear, and side views as well as the desired paint treatment.

emotion memory The practice of searching in one's past for a parallel situation, recalling the emotion felt at that time, and using that emotion in acting the present scene.

emphasis Focus typically achieved through some form of contrast.

English aestheticism *See* **art for art's sake**.

environmental theatre A type of performance, especially during and after the 1960s, in which acting and audience space may be intermingled to achieve interaction between spectators and performers.

epic theatre A theatrical form, usually associated with Bertolt Brecht, that emerged in the 1920s. Brecht sought to distance ("alienate") spectators emotionally in order to help them more objectively watch and judge what they saw. Ultimately Brecht hoped his audiences would relate what they saw in the theatre to conditions in society and then seek to alter the sociopolitical system. Brecht called his theatre "epic" because the alteration of dialogue and narration, with its frequent shifts in time and place, had more in common with epic poetry than with traditional drama.

episodic plot structure An arrangement of a play's events wherein its scenes jump from one to the next, often separated by time or place, without necessarily building a cause-to-effect relationship between them.

existentialism A philosophical position that gained popularity following World War II, especially through the writings of Jean-Paul Sartre, and carried over into playwriting by Sartre and Albert Camus. The argument of the existentialists was that there are no longer any certainties and that human beings are condemned to choose their own values and to live by them, whether or not these values are accepted by others.

exposition The setting forth of information about events, characters, and the present situation that precede the play's point of attack. Typically, exposition is most abundant in the opening scene, where it is used to clarify the situation, establish the identity and relationship of the characters, and set forth the present situation, although it may occur throughout the play.

expressionism An artistic movement that flourished, especially in Germany, from around 1910 to about 1924. Believing that the industrial age had turned human beings into machine-like creatures, expressionism sought to undermine materialist values and create "the new man," who would reshape the world in accordance with the needs of the human spirit. Expressionist drama made extensive use of distortion and grotesque imagery to portray the present human condition. Expressionism found its way into American drama, as in O'Neill's *The Hairy Ape*.

farce A type of comic, secular drama that usually emphasizes situation over character or idea. Coincidence, misunderstanding, ridiculous violence, and rapid pace are its typical ingredients.

flat A basic scenic unit composed of a covered frame existing in various types, the most common being wall, door, or window flats; two or more of which may be joined to create a larger scenic surface.

flying or **fly system** A method of shifting scenery in which scenic elements may be suspended overhead and lowered into or raised out of audience view as needed. *Flying* also refers to the raising and lowering of performers by cables attached to a body harness.

footlights A row of striplights mounted at floor level at the front of the proscenium stage or around the outer edges of a thrust stage.

French scenes The division of a printed play into new scenes with each entrance or exit of a character. French drama long used this organization of dramatic action to indicate an alteration in the motivations or focus created by the change of characters on stage.

front elevations Drawings of each scenic unit as seen from the front.

front of the house That part of the theatre forward of the stage and the activities and persons associated with it: audience, ushers, box office, and the like. Often used as the opposite of **backstage**.

futurism A movement launched in early twentieth-century Italy that glorified the speed and energy of the machine age and sought to replace traditional art forms with new ones. These new forms included "synthetic" drama, which compressed into a moment or two the essence of a full-length play, the use of simultaneously staging different scenes or events in different parts of the performance and audience spaces, and various attempts to induce confrontational audience/performer interaction.

gas table The controlboard for a lighting system that uses gas as the illuminant.

general illumination Stage lighting that spreads over a relatively large area, serving one or more of three functions: (1) lighting all background areas not illuminated by spotlights; (2) blending the acting areas together and providing a smooth transition between the high intensity of the acting areas and the lower intensity of the background; (3) enhancing or modifying the color of settings and costumes.

gesamtkunstwerk A German term meaning "master artwork," usually associated with the opera composer Richard Wagner. Wagner believed that a theatre production should create a unified illusion and that all choices should be filtered through a single consciousness to achieve this unified effect.

given circumstances The basic who, what, when, and where that constitute the dramatic situation.

give stage A term used to ask one actor to give the dominant stage position to another by facing away from the audience more than the other actor.

glee A rousing musical number and the opening number in Yoruba opera.

gobo A thin template made of metal or glass into which a pattern is generally cut that, when inserted directly into the lighting instrument's focal point, projects a pattern of shadows by obstructing some portion(s) of the light.

green room A room in the theatre where all of the actors and crew members can assemble to relax or receive instructions.

habit à la romaine The usual costume worn by actors playing Greek or Roman heroes in neoclassical theatre; a stylized adaptation of Roman armor, tunic, and boots.

hanamichi A raised gangway or walkway that connects the front of the stage to the back of the auditorium; important entrances and much of the action take place on this gangway.

hand props *See* **properties**.

happenings Multimedia performance events, pioneered by visual artists in the 1950s and 1960s, that sought to (1) break down the barriers between the arts and between performers and spectators, (2) shift emphasis from creating a product to participating in a process, and (3) shift emphasis from communicating an artist's intention to enhancing the participant's awareness.

hashigakari In the Noh theatre, a long bridge leading from the dressing room to the stage; used as the principal entrance for actors and musicians.

hell mouth In medieval theatre, a specific mansion representing Hell and often portrayed as the mouth of a beast.

inciting incident An occurrence that sets the main action of a play in motion.

independent theatre movement A trend that began in the 1880s and continues to the present, originating because major theatres would not produce certain new plays, either because of indifference or because official censors would not license the plays for production. Independent theatres, which could avoid censorship by performing only for their subscribers, were able to introduce and gain acceptance for many new plays. In the twentieth century, variations on this original plan have been used whenever the theatre has been unresponsive to new forms of writing or production. Twentieth-century independent theatres have been labeled little theatres, art theatres, fringe theatres, alternative theatres, Off-Broadway, Off-Off-Broadway, and so on.

instrument schedule A chart used by lighting designers that lists each lighting instrument with its specifications (type, wattage, lens, reflector, lamp, and any other pertinent information), mounting position, color filter, the area it lights, the circuit into which it is plugged, and the dimmer to which it is connected.

intermezzi Interludes between the acts of Italian court drama that acted as elaborate compliments suggesting parallels between some mythological figure and the person in whose honor the festival was being given. Eventually, the spectacular appeals of *intermezzi* were absorbed into opera.

interpretive focus The central or most significant meaning that the director and production team wishes to convey in relation to a play, story, or scenario. This focus serves as a common understanding that guides subsequent decisions in respect to staging and design choices.

jing Chinese opera characters represented in part by elaborate patterns painted on the actors' faces.

Kabuki The most popular of the traditional Japanese theatrical forms; it uses highly stylized settings, acting, costumes, and makeup in its performance of melodramatic stories.

komos An exit to feasting and revelry.

kyogen Japanese short farces performed as interludes between Noh plays.

laterna magika A multimedia form popularized by Josef Svoboda and others that incorporated film and live actors in an interactive manner.

lazzi Improvised comic stage business or routines based on character type and situation.

lift When used in the context of acting, the practice of drawing an audience's attention to a particular line or piece of information through its delivery by the actor.

light plots These come in two basic types: floor plans and section plots. A floor plan–oriented light plot shows, as seen from a top view, the layout of the stage, the setting, and the auditorium. On this plot are indicated the type, size, and position of each lighting instrument and the area it will illuminate. Section plots show the layout of the stage, the setting, the auditorium, and lighting positions from a side view. Taken together, these plots show the horizontal and vertical distribution of the light sources in conjunction with the stage setting and auditorium.

limelight The first effective spotlight, consisting of a hood equipped with a reflector, lens, and a column of calcium (lime) onto which hydrogen and oxygen were directed, along with a gas flame. The flame heated the lime to incandescence, creating an extremely bright light. Its frequent use as a follow spot gave rise to the phrase, "in the limelight."

lines of business The division of acting into a few categories defined by the character types they included. Until the late nineteenth century, an actor was employed in terms of his or her line of business. Actors usually began their careers as utility actors and played supernumerary roles until they discovered the character type for which they were best suited. Most actors then continued in that line of business for the remainder of their careers.

lining Scene painting technique used to make a flat surface appear dimensional by replicating shadow and highlight.

literal approach One of three basic directorial approaches in which the director serves the playwright by transferring the play as literally as possible from page to stage.

liturgical drama The incorporation of drama into or performed in conjunction with the church service or liturgy.

liturgical play A play incorporated into or performed in conjunction with the church service or liturgy.

Living Newspaper A form that developed within the Federal Theatre Project, financed by the U.S. government during the 1930s to relieve unemployment. Each Living Newspaper treated a single pressing problem (such as slum housing) and advocated social reform and corrective legislation to solve the problem. The Federal Theatre Project ended in 1939 when Congress, offended by the partisan stance of the Living Newspapers, refused to appropriate funds to continue it.

ludi A Roman term, literally meaning "games," that referred to the religious festivals at which theatrical performances were given.

machina A cranelike device used to simulate flying in the Greek theatre. *See deus ex machina.*

magic if A key aspect of Stanislavsky's system through which actors project themselves into the world of the play; actors imagine how they might feel or act if they were a particular character in a particular situation.

major dramatic question The most significant question raised by the inciting incident; a question that, typically, will be pursued throughout most of the play.

makeup plot A chart recording basic information about the makeup of each character.

mansion The basic scenic structure in the medieval theatre used to represent locale. As many mansions as were needed to indicate the locales of a play's action were present simultaneously on platforms or wagons. After the place of the action was indicated by associating it with a specific mansion, the performers used as much of the adjoining platform space as was needed for the action. *See* **platea**.

masking The use of hard or soft material to obscure people, objects, or portions of the stage not meant to be seen by the audience.

masks An acting practice that hides (or "cheats") an action from the audience's view.

melodrama A form of drama, especially associated with the nineteenth century, based on a clear distinction between good and evil. Typically a virtuous protagonist seeks to overcome seemingly insurmountable threats created by a villain. Suspense is created and increased until the last moment, when the villain is punished and the protagonist rescued and rewarded. Melodrama often incorporates elaborate spectacle and originally used music to create mood and to underscore emotional responses.

messenger scene A standard part of Greek tragedy used to describe violent events that have taken place offstage. Greek sensibilities forbade enacting scenes of violence onstage. *See* **eccyclema**.

mie A highly stylized pose struck and held by a principal character in Japanese Kabuki.

modernism An umbrella term for a wide range of artistic styles that broke from the traditional relationship of fidelity between perception and representation. Modernism valued imaginative and formal artistic innovation over accurate renditions of recognizable subjects.

morality plays In the late medieval theatre, plays of an allegorical nature that treated the spiritual trials of ordinary persons.

naturalism A late nineteenth-century form of extreme realism whose chief spokesman was Emile Zola. The naturalists argued that plays should be a slice of life that demonstrates the effects of heredity and environment. Naturalism was the first artistic movement to treat working-class characters with the same seriousness accorded the middle and upper classes by earlier movements. In the twentieth century, naturalism is often used as a label for plays that seek to re-create the details of everyday life, especially its seamy side.

naumachia A staged or mock sea battle; one of the most spectacular of the Romans' theatrical entertainments.

neoclassicism The set of rules, conventions, and beliefs that dominated much drama and theatre from the Renaissance to the end of the eighteenth century. Neoclassicism recognized only two legitimate forms of drama (tragedy and comedy), arguing that the two forms should never be mixed. Tragedy should treat serious stories of kings and nobles, whereas comedy should treat the domestic world of the middle or lower classes. According to the neoclassicists, plays should be written in five acts, observe the unities of time, place, and action, and uphold poetic justice in their endings.

neocolonialism The residue of attitudes, practices, and power structures left over from occupation/domination by foreign states/cultures; especially noteworthy in (but not restricted to) Africa and parts of Asia.

new stagecraft A term used in the United States for its early assimilation of European modernist innovations. Simplification and suggestion were the hallmarks of this trend, which valued the ability of scene design to evoke mood and stimulate the imagination more than its ability to create a detailed reproduction of the real world.

onnagata Female roles played by male actors in Japanese Kabuki theatre.

open-up A term used to ask a performer to turn slightly more toward the audience.

orchestra The "dancing place"; in ancient Greek theatre, the main performance space in which the chorus sang and danced.

overpainting Any modification of the base coat; overpainting is used to simulate textures, materials, decorations, or conditions.

pageant wagon In the medieval theatre, a platform on wheels that each play was mounted on and moved from one playing place to another, thereby achieving processional staging.

panorama A scenic element in the nineteenth-century theatre; a continuous scene painted on a long expanse of canvas that could remain fixed or be rigged to move, giving the effect that characters, though remaining on stage, were moving from one place to another.

parabasis In Greek Old Comedy, choral passage addressed directly to the audience and most frequently filled with advice on civic or other contemporary problems.

parodoi The spaces at either side of the orchestra between the *skene* and the auditorium in the Greek theatre, used primarily as entrances and exits for the performers, especially the chorus.

parodos The processional entrance of the chorus in the Greek theatre.

performance art A contemporary type of presentation, often by a solo performer, that typically intermingles elements from various arts. Performance art usually encourages spectators to derive from the presentation whatever is meaningful to them.

plant Something an actor does to make sure the audience notices an object (such as a letter) in an earlier scene that will be important later in the play.

platea In the medieval theatre, an undifferentiated stage space in front of the mansions.

plot The arrangement of a play's incidents or the overall structure of its action. Thus, it differs from story, which may have begun long before the play begins.

point of attack The moment within the overall story wherein the playwright begins his or her treatment of events.

poor theatre A phrase, introduced by Jerzy Grotowski, to identify a type of theatre that discards all technological aids not essential to theatrical performance. Grotowski concluded that there are only two essential theatrical elements: the actor and the audience.

postmodernism A term used to describe certain contemporary artistic tendencies, among them the blurring of distinctions between dramatic forms and the mingling of elements from disparate styles, periods, and cultures.

producer The person responsible for financing a production, making contractual arrangements with those involved, leasing a theatre, publicizing the show, selling tickets, and handling all other aspects relating to the business and managerial side of theatrical production.

production concept Sometimes called the directorial concept; a metaphor, dominant idea, or set of conventions used by a director to shape a production; also referred to as an interpretational focus.

promptbook A copy of the script in which the blocking and stage business of the actors, cues for lighting and sound, and all other information needed by the stage manager have been entered.

properties Onstage objects of two types: (1) set properties, required to complete or decorate the set, and (2) hand properties, used by the actors in their stage business.

proportion A design principle that involves the comparative scale of each part to all the others and may selectively be used to create a variety of impressions.

proscenium arch An architectural feature that frames a stage opening to keep spectators from seeing around or over the stage setting.

protagonist The principal character in a dramatic action.

realism An attempt in writing and production to represent characters and events as they are observed in real life. Scattered attempts at realism are found throughout theatre history, but, as a movement, realism emerged in the 1850s, grounded in the scientific outlook and the belief that human behavior can best be explained in terms of hereditary and environmental influences. Realists argued that because we can know the real world only through direct observation, playwrights should write only about the society around them as objectively as possible.

rear elevations Drawings of each unit as seen from the rear that indicate the type of construction, materials, and methods to be used in assembling it.

regional theatre Term used to designate ongoing not-for-profit theatres throughout the United States. Such theatres are sometimes called resident theatres.

repertory The total group of plays a company chooses for presentation. A repertory company is one that alternates performances of several productions.

Restoration The period in English history following the restoration of Charles II to the throne in 1660, extending to about 1700. In theatre, the period is noted for its comedy of manners, which focused on the amoral behavior and witty verbal exchanges of the idle upper class.

revolving stage A circular platform or segment of the stage floor mounted on a central pivot. When it is revolved, one setting comes into view as another moves out of sight.

romanticism A dramatic style that emerged during the early nineteenth century and rejected the strictures imposed by neoclassicism. Romanticism favored infinite variety over standardized norms of neoclassicism and glorified the writer as a genius who operated beyond the limitations of stultifying rules.

samisen A three-stringed musical instrument used as the primary accompaniment in Japanese Bunraku theatre.

satyr play A short comic or satiric play that followed each set of three tragedies at the City Dionysia in Greece. Its chorus was composed of satyrs (half-man, half-goat creatures), and its story usually poked fun at some Greek myth.

scaenae frons The façade enclosing the back and sides of the stage in the ancient Roman theatre. It served as background for all types of plays.

scrim A curtain or drop made of gauzelike fabric. When lighted only from the front, it appears opaque. When lighted from the back, it appears translucent.

share a scene A term used to ask two performers to play in the one-quarter or profile position so that they are equally visible to the audience

sheng Male roles in Chinese opera; divided into young men (*xiao sheng*); old men (*lao sheng*); and warriors (*wu sheng*).

shite The principal character and his followers in Japanese Noh theatre.

side elevations Drawings that show scenic units in profile, indicating the thickness and shape of each unit.

sightline The line of vision from any audience seat to any point on stage. Often used to indicate how much of the stage action can be seen from any part of the house.

skene The scene house in the Greek theatre; literally meaning a hut or tent, the word probably derives from the structure used originally as an offstage place where actors could change costumes. It is the source of our word "scene."

soliloquy A speech given by a character who is alone on stage; generally expresses a character's inner thoughts through this convention.

sound score Provides the reason for each intended sound cue and approximates when it should be played, its duration, as well as information about its source, its playback, and any special treatment it may need.

spattering Scene painting technique involving flicking small drops of paint from a brush onto the base coat with one color that is slightly lighter and a second that is slightly darker than the base coat.

specific illumination Stage light confined to a limited area, usually produced by spotlights.

sponging Scene painting technique that involves dipping a natural sponge in paint and patting it on the surface of the base coat.

spoken decor Locale established through character speech rather than representation scenically.

spotlight A lighting instrument composed of metal housing, reflector, lamp, and lens designed to illuminate restricted areas with a concentrated beam of light. The major types of spotlights are plano-convex, fresnel, and ellipsoidal.

stage business Detailed action performed by the actor, such as filling and smoking a pipe or setting a table; often prescribed by the script but may be invented by the actors or the director to clarify or enrich action or characterization.

stage house The stage and all of the space above it to the roof.

stage manager The individual responsible for running the show during performances, making sure that everything functions as intended.

stenciling Scene painting technique often used to create the repetition of a motif in an interlocking pattern.

stock characters Easily recognizable broad character types.

straight makeup Application of makeup intended to make visible or enhance an actors natural facial features without significantly altering them.

striplight A lighting instrument composed of a series of lamps usually mounted in a rectangular trough and used for general illumination. There are three basic types of striplight: (1) footlights, mounted in the floor at the front of the stage; (2) borderlights, hung from battens above the stage in a series from front to back; and (3) miscellaneous striplights, used to light backings, the cyclorama, or other scenic elements.

Sturm und Drang A German term, meaning "storm and stress," used to identify a group of German playwrights who wrote serious plays that experimented with bold subjects and dramatic form in the late eighteenth century.

subplots Events or actions of secondary interest that often provide contrast to or commentary on the main plot.

subtext Unstated motivations, ideas, or tensions beneath the surface of a play's text. Sometimes the subtext is more important than the text.

summer stock Companies that perform only during the summer, typically in resort areas, and produce a series of plays.

supernumeraries Extra characters with nonspeaking roles.

surrealism A movement, especially in the 1920s, emphasizing the importance of the unconscious. Believing that the most significant truths are those buried in the unconscious, surrealists sought to release these suppressed forces by exploring dreams, automatic writing, and stream-of-consciousness.

symbolism A movement that emerged in the late nineteenth century, symbolism was the first of several that sought to counter the influence of realism and naturalism. Rather than seeking truth through direct observation of the world around them, symbolists argued that truth can only be intuited and that these intuitions can be expressed only indirectly through symbols.

talk-back sessions Discussions between theatre personnel and audiences following performances.

technical director A position found primarily in resident and educational theatres, the technical director is usually responsible for implementing the designer's plans: purchasing materials; supervising the building, assembling, and painting of sets; and overseeing the crews that run the shows.

technical rehearsal One of the final rehearsals, usually immediately preceding dress rehearsals, devoted primarily to making sure that all of the technical elements (scenery, costumes, makeup, lighting, sound, and properties) are ready and are functioning as planned.

theatre of cruelty Antonin Artaud's label for the type of performance he advocated to force audiences to confront the violent impulses suppressed within their unconscious minds. Although he acknowledged that such confrontations might be cruel, Artaud thought them necessary to overcome violence and divisiveness if the theatre is to fulfill its goal of "draining abscesses collectively." Little heeded during his lifetime, Artaud later exerted major influence on theatrical practice, especially during the 1960s.

theatre-in-the-round *See* **arena stage**.

theatron The "seeing place"; in ancient Greece, the slope upon which the audience sat to see the plays performed, and the origin of our word "theatre."

thrust stage Type of theatre with audience seating arranged around three, or occasionally two, sides of the performance space.

tragedy A form of drama that presents a serious action and maintains a serious tone (although there may be moments of comic relief). The protagonist is usually one who arouses our sympathy and admiration but who encounters disaster through the pursuit of some goal, worthy in itself, conflicting with another goal or principle.

translation approach Currently the most common directorial approach in which the director tries to capture the spirit of the play, although to do so may depart from the playwright's specifications.

trap An opening in the stage floor that allows performers to appear or special effects to materialize from beneath the floor.

turn-in A term used to ask a performer to turn toward the center of the stage.

turn-out A term used to ask a performer to turn toward the side of the stage

unities Neoclassicism demanded that three unities be observed: unity of time (which usually was interpreted to mean that all events should occur within twenty-four hours); unity of place (which typically required that the action occur in the same place); and unity of action (which typically required that there be only one plot). Most other movements have considered unity of action necessary, although interpreting it more liberally than the neoclassicists, but have rejected the unities of time and place.

viewpoints An improvisational technique that grew out of postmodern dance, which Anne Bogart and others have expanded into a training method that allows performers to generate bold nonrealistic physical expressions while working as an ensemble.

waki The secondary character and his followers in Japanese Noh theatre.

wayang kulit The performance form and term for leather puppets that a *dalang* manipulates in a shadow puppet performance.

well-made play Term used to describe logically constructed plays following the pattern of careful exposition and preparation, a series of complications that creates growing suspense and builds to a climactic moment, after which all-important questions are resolved. Although most of these features can be found in plays from the time of the Greeks onward, the term "well-made play" is associated with Eugène Scribe, the popular nineteenth-century French playwright who reduced these traditional playwriting techniques to a formula. Although "well-made play" is now often used condescendingly, Scribe's practice has supplied the pattern for much realistic playwriting since his time.

willing suspension of disbelief Samuel Taylor Coleridge's description of the audience's complicity in accepting stage events; although we know that the events of a play are not real, we agree for the moment not to disbelieve them.

wings From the Renaissance onward, a major scenic element consisting of pairs of flats set up parallel to the front of the stage and arranged in a series from downstage to upstage. They were used in conjunction with two other major scenic elements: drops or shutters (flats that met at center back) used to enclose the rear of the stage, and borders used to complete the scene overhead. Today, the term is primarily used for the offstage space on either side of the stage.

Yoruba opera (or Yoruba Traveling Theatre) The most popular form of entertainment in Nigeria. It includes an introduction composed of song and dance, followed by a topical play, and concluding with another section of song and dance. It is very similar in form to the Concert Party of neighboring Ghana.

zanni The servants of the *commedia dell'arte*; origin of the word "zany."

Bibliography

This bibliography lists some of the many important books on theatre. The divisions correspond to those in the text. All works are in English.

Part One: Foundations

Chapter 1
The Nature of Theatre

Brook, Peter. *The Empty Space.* New York: Avon Books, 1968.

Esslin, Martin. *The Field of Drama: How the Signs of Drama Create Meaning on Stage and Screen.* New York: Methuen, 1987.

Lahr, John, and Jonathan Price. *Life-Show: How to See Theatre in Life and Life in Theatre.* New York: Viking Press, 1973.

Rozik, Eli. *The Roots of Theatre: Rethinking Ritual and Other Theories of Origin.* Iowa City: University of Iowa Press, 2002.

Schechner, Richard. *Performance Theory.* New York: Routledge, 1988.

Shepherd, Simon. *Drama/Theatre/Performance (The New Critical Idiom).* New York: Routledge, 2004.

Styan, J. L. *Drama, Stage and Audience.* New York: Cambridge University Press, 1975.

Turner, Victor. *From Ritual to Theatre: The Human Seriousness of Play.* New York: Performing Arts Journal Publications, 1982.

Wilson, Glenn. *The Psychology of the Performing Arts.* London: Croom Helm, 1985.

Chapter 2
The Audience and Criticism

Bennett, Susan. *Theatre Audiences: A Theory of Production and Reception.* New York: Routledge, 1997.

Blau, Herbert. *The Audience.* Baltimore: Johns Hopkins University Press, 1990.

Esslin, Martin. *An Anatomy of Drama.* New York: Hill & Wang, 1976.

Kauffmann, Stanley. *Theatre Criticisms.* New York: Performing Arts Journal Publications, 1984.

Lahr, John, and Jonathan Price. See under Chapter 1.

McConachie, Bruce. *Engaging Audiences: A Cognitive Approach to Spectating in the Theatre (Cognitive Studies in Literature and Performance).* Basingstoke, U.K.: Palgrave/Macmillan, 2008.

Styan, J. L. See under Chapter 1.

Vena, Gary. *How to Read and Write about Drama.* New York: Arco, 1988.

Chapter 3
The Play

Barry, Jackson G. *Dramatic Structure: The Shaping of Experience.* Berkeley: University of California Press, 1970.

Beckerman, Bernard. *Dynamics of Drama: Theory and Method of Analysis.* New York: Knopf, 1970.

Esslin, Martin. *The Field of Drama.* New York: Methuen, 1987.

Fergusson, Francis. *The Idea of a Theatre.* Princeton, N.J.: Princeton University Press, 1949.

Grote, David. *Script Analysis.* Belmont, Calif.: Wadsworth, 1985.

Hayman, Ronald. *How to Read a Play.* New York: Grove Press, 1977.

Heffner, Hubert. *The Nature of Drama.* Boston: Houghton Mifflin, 1959.

Pfister, Manfred, and John Halliday. *The Theory and Analysis of Drama (European Studies in English Literature).* New York: Cambridge University Press, 1991.

Scanlan, David. *Reading Drama.* Mountain View, Calif.: Mayfield, 1988.

Styan, J. L. *The Elements of Drama.* New York: Cambridge University Press, 1960.

Part Two: Varieties of Theatrical Experience

Banham, Martin, ed. *Cambridge Guide to Theatre.* Cambridge: Cambridge University Press, 1995.

Brockett, Oscar G., and Franklin J. Hildy. *History of Theatre*, 10th ed. Boston: Allyn and Bacon, 2007.

Carlson, Marvin. *Theories of the Theatre: A Historical and Critical Survey, from the Greeks to the Present,* rev. ed. Ithaca, N.Y.: Cornell University Press, 1994.

Duerr, Edwin. *The Length and Depth of Acting.* New York: Holt, Rinehart and Winston, 1962.

Izenour, George C. *Theatre Design.* New York: McGraw-Hill, 1977.

Laver, James. *Drama: Its Costume and Decor.* London: Studio Publications, 1951.

Leacroft, Richard, and Helen Leacroft. *Theatre and Playhouse: An Illustrated Survey of Theatre Building from Ancient Greece to the Present Day.* London: Methuen, 1984.

Oenslager, Donald. *Stage Design: Four Centuries of Scenic Invention.* New York: Viking Press, 1975.

Oxford Companion to the Theatre, 4th ed. London: Oxford University Press, 1983.

World Encyclopedia of Contemporary Theatre. 6 vols. London: Routledge, 1994–2001.

Chapter 4
Festival Theatre: Greek, Roman, and Medieval Theatre Experiences

Arnott, Peter D. *Greek Scenic Conventions in the Fifth Century B.C.* Oxford: Clarendon Press, 1962.

———. *Public and Performance in Greek Theatre.* London: Routledge, Chapman and Hall, 1989.

Beacham, Richard C. *The Roman Theatre and Its Audience.* Cambridge, Mass.: Harvard University Press, 1992.

Beare, William. *The Roman Stage: A Short History of Latin Drama in the Time of the Republic,* 3d ed. London: Methuen, 1963.

Bevington, David. *From Mankind to Marlowe: Growth in Structure in the Popular Drama of Tudor England.* Cambridge, Mass.: Harvard University Press, 1962.

Bieber, Margarete. *The History of the Greek and Roman Theater,* 2d ed. Princeton, N.J.: Princeton University Press, 1961.

Chambers, E. K. *The Mediaeval Stage.* 2 vols. Oxford: Clarendon Press, 1903.

Craik, Thomas W. *Revels History of Drama in English.* Vol. 2, *1500–1576.* New York: Barnes & Noble, 1980.

———. *The Tudor Interlude: Stage, Costume, and Acting.* Leicester, U.K.: University of Leicester Press, 1958.

Duckworth, George E. *The Nature of Roman Comedy.* Princeton, N.J.: Princeton University Press, 1952.

Dugdale, Eric. *Greek Theatre in Context (Greece and Rome: Texts and Contexts).* Cambridge: Cambridge University Press, 2008.

Gertsman, Elina, ed. *Visualizing Medieval Performance: Perspectives, Histories, Contexts.* Surrey, U.K.: Ashgate Publishing, 2008.

Green, J. R. *Theatre in Ancient Greek Society.* New York: Routledge, 1994.

Hunter, R. L. *The New Comedy of Greece and Rome.* New York: Twayne, 1985.

Kitto, H. D. F. *Greek Tragedy,* 2d ed. London: Methuen, 1950.

Kolve, V. A. *The Play Called Corpus Christi.* Stanford, Calif.: Stanford University Press, 1966.

Nicoll, Allardyce. *Masks, Mimes and Miracles.* New York: Harcourt Brace Jovanovich, 1931.

Ogden, Dunbar. *The Staging of Drama in the Medieval Church.* Newark: University of Delaware Press, 2002.

Pickard-Cambridge, A. W. *The Dramatic Festivals of Athens,* 2d ed. Rev. by John Gould and D. M. Lewis. Oxford: Clarendon Press, 1968.

Potter, Robert. *The English Morality Play: Origins, History and Influence of a Dramatic Tradition.* London: Routledge and Kegan Paul, 1975.

Sommerstein, Alan. *Greek Drama and Dramatists.* New York: Routledge, 2002.

Tydeman, William, Michael J. Anderson, and Nick Davis, eds. *The Medieval European Stage 500–1550.* Cambridge: Cambridge University Press, 2001.

Vince, Ronald W. *Ancient and Medieval Theatre: A Historiographical Handbook.* Westport, Conn.: Greenwood Press, 1984.

———. *A Companion to the Medieval Theatre.* Westport, Conn.: Greenwood Press, 1989.

Walton, J. Michael. *Living Greek Theatre: A Handbook of Classical Performance and Modern Production.* Westport, Conn.: Greenwood Press, 1987.

Webster, T. B. L. *Greek Theatre Production,* 2d ed. London: Methuen, 1970.

Wickham, Glynne. *Early English Stages, 1300–1660.* 3 vols. New York: Columbia University Press, 1959–1979.

Wiles, David. *Greek Theatre Performance.* Cambridge: Cambridge University Press, 2000.

Chapter 5
Creating a Professional Theatre: Elizabethan England, Italian Commedia dell'Arte, and Seventeenth-Century France

Andrews, Richard. *Scripts and Scenarios: The Performance of Comedy in Renaissance Italy.* Cambridge: Cambridge University Press, 1993.

Astington, John N. *English Court Theatre, 1558–1642*. Cambridge: Cambridge University Press, 1999.

Barroll, J. L., et al. *Revels History of Drama in English*. Vol. 3, *1576–1613*. New York: Barnes & Noble, 1975.

Beckerman, Bernard. *Shakespeare at the Globe, 1599–1609*. New York: Macmillan, 1962.

Bentley, Gerald E. *The Profession of Dramatist in Shakespeare's Time, 1590–1642*. Princeton, N.J.: Princeton University Press, 1971.

———. *The Profession of Player in Shakespeare's Time, 1590–1642*. Princeton, N.J.: Princeton University Press, 1984.

Bjurstrom, Per. *Giacomo Torelli and Baroque Stage Design*. Stockholm: Almqvist and Wiksell, 1961.

Bradley, David. *From Text to Performance in the Elizabethan Theatre: Preparing the Play for the Stage*. New York: Cambridge University Press, 1992.

Cairns, Christopher, ed. *Scenery, Set, and Staging in the Italian Renaissance*. Lewiston, N.Y.: Edwin Mellen Press, 1996.

Callaghan, Dympna. *Shakespeare without Women*. New York: Routledge, 2000.

Clubb, Louise G. *Italian Drama in Shakespeare's Time*. New Haven, Conn.: Yale University Press, 1989.

Duchartre, Pierre L. *The Italian Comedy: The Improvisation, Scenarios, Lives, Attributes, Portraits and Masks of the Illustrious Characters of the Commedia dell'Arte*. Trans. by R. T. Weaver. London: Harrap, 1929.

Graves, R. B. *Lighting the Shakespeare Stage, 1567–1642*. Carbondale, Ill.: Southern Illinois University Press, 1999.

Gurr, Andrew. *Playgoing in Shakespeare's London*. Cambridge: Cambridge University Press, 1987.

———. *The Shakespearean Playing Companies*. Oxford: Oxford University Press, 1996.

Hewitt, Barnard, ed. *The Renaissance Stage: Documents of Serlio, Sabbattini, and Furttenbach*. Coral Gables, Fla.: University of Miami Press, 1958.

Howarth, W. D., et al., eds. *French Theatre in the Neo-Classical Era, 1550–1789*. Cambridge: Cambridge University Press, 1997.

Ingram, William. *The Business of Playing: The Beginning of the Adult Professional Theater in Elizabethan London*. Ithaca, N.Y.: Cornell University Press, 1993.

Knutson, Roslyn L. *Playing Companies and Commerce in Shakespeare's Time*. Cambridge: Cambridge University Press, 2001.

Lawrenson, T. E. *The French Stage in the XVIIth Century: A Study in the Advent of the Italian Order*, rev. ed. Manchester: Manchester University Press, 1984.

Lea, Kathleen M. *Italian Popular Comedy: A Study of the Commedia dell'Arte, 1560–1620*. 2 vols. Oxford: Clarendon Press, 1934.

Lough, John. *Paris Theatre Audiences in the Seventeenth and Eighteenth Centuries*. London: Oxford University Press, 1957.

McCarthy, Gerry. *The Theatres of Molière*. London: Routledge, 2002.

Mittman, Barbara G. *Spectators on the Paris Stage in the Seventeenth and Eighteenth Centuries*. Ann Arbor, Mich.: UMI Research Press, 1984.

Mongredien, Georges. *Daily Life in the French Theatre in the Time of Molière*. London: Allen and Unwin, 1969.

Nicoll, Allardyce. See under Chapter 4.

Oreglia, Giacomo. *The Commedia dell'Arte*. New York: Hill & Wang, 1968.

Orgel, Stephen, and Roy Strong. *The Theatre of the Stuart Court: Including the Complete Designs ... Together with Their Texts and Historical Documentation*. 2 vols. Berkeley, Calif.: University of California Press, 1973.

Orrell, John. *The Human Stage: English Theatre Design, 1567–1640*. New York: Cambridge University Press, 1983.

Schwartz, Isidore A. *The Commedia dell'Arte and Its Influence on French Comedy in the Seventeenth Century*. Paris: H. Samuel, 1933.

Scott, Virginia. *Molière: A Theatrical Life*. Cambridge: Cambridge University Press, 2000.

Stern, Tiffany. *Rehearsal from Shakespeare to Sheridan*. New York: Oxford University Press, 2000.

White, John. *The Birth and Rebirth of Pictorial Space*, 2d ed. London: Faber & Faber, 1967.

Wickham, Glynne. See under Chapter 4.

Wickham, Glynne, et al. *English Professional Theatre, 1530–1660*. Cambridge: Cambridge University Press, 2000.

Wiley, W. L. *The Early Public Theatre in France*. Cambridge, Mass.: Harvard University Press, 1960.

Chapter 6
From Romanticism to Realism

Antoine, André. *Memories of the Théâtre Libre*. Trans. by Marvin Carlson. Coral Gables, Fla.: University of Miami Press, 1964.

Bentley, Eric. *The Playwright as Thinker: A Study of Drama in Modern Times*. New York: Reynal, 1946.

Bogard, Travis, et al. *Revels History of Drama in English*. Vol. 8, *American Drama*. New York: Barnes & Noble, 1977.

Booth, Michael R. *English Melodrama.* London: Herbert Jenkins, 1965.

Booth, Michael, et al. *Revels History of Drama in English. Vol. 6, 1750–1880.* New York: Barnes & Noble, 1975.

Carter, Lawson A. *Zola and the Theatre.* New Haven, Conn.: Yale University Press, 1963.

Davis, Tracy. *Actresses as Working Women: Their Social Identity in Victorian Culture.* New York: Routledge, 1991.

Donohue, Joseph W. *Theatre in the Age of Kean.* Oxford: Blackwell, 1975.

Glasstone, Victor. *Victorian and Edwardian Theatre.* Cambridge, Mass.: Harvard University Press, 1975.

Grimsted, David. *Melodrama Unveiled: American Theatre and Culture, 1800–1850.* Chicago: University of Chicago Press, 1968.

Hunt, Hugh, et al. *The Revels History of Drama in English. Vol. 7, 1880 to the Present Day.* New York: Barnes & Noble, 1978.

Innes, Christopher. *A Sourcebook on Naturalist Theatre.* New York: Routledge, 2000.

Koller, Ann Marie. *The Theatre Duke: Georg II of Saxe-Meiningen and the German Stage.* Stanford, Calif.: Stanford University Press, 1984.

McConachie, Bruce A. *Melodramatic Formations: American Theatre and Society, 1820–1870.* Iowa City: University of Iowa Press, 1992.

McCormick, John. *Popular Theatres of Nineteenth-Century France.* New York: Routledge, 1993.

Meisel, Martin. *Realizations: Narrative, Pictorial, and Theatrical Arts in Nineteenth-Century England.* Princeton, N.J.: Princeton University Press, 1983.

Moi, Toril. *Henrik Ibsen and the Birth of Modernism: Art, Theater, Philosophy.* Oxford: Oxford University Press, 2006.

Moynet, Jean-Pierre. *French Theatrical Production in the Nineteenth Century.* Binghamton, N.Y.: Max Reinhardt Foundation, 1976.

Quinn, Arthur H. *A History of the American Drama from the Beginning to the Civil War,* 2d ed. New York: Appleton-Century-Crofts, 1943.

———. *A History of the American Drama from the Civil War to the Present Day,* 2d ed. New York: Appleton-Century-Crofts, 1949.

Rowell, George. *The Victorian Theatre,* 2d ed. London: Oxford University Press, 1979.

Southern, Richard. *Changeable Scenery: Its Origin and Development in the British Theatre.* London: Faber & Faber, 1952.

Stein, Jack M. *Richard Wagner and the Synthesis of the Arts.* Detroit, Mich.: Wayne State University Press, 1960.

Stephens, John R. *The Profession of the Playwright: British Theatre, 1800–1900.* London: Cambridge University Press, 1992.

Chapter 7
Modernism and Its Effect: 1885–1960

Appia, Adolphe. *The Work of Living Art and Man Is the Measure of All Things.* Coral Gables, Fla.: University of Miami Press, 1960.

Artaud, Antonin. *The Theatre and Its Double.* Trans. by Mary C. Richards. New York: Grove Press, 1958.

Bablet, Denis. *The Revolution of Stage Design in the Twentieth Century.* Paris: Amiel, 1977.

Braun, Edward. *The Director and the Stage: From Naturalism to Grotowski.* New York: Holmes and Meier, 1982.

Brecht, Bertolt. *Brecht on Theatre.* Trans. by John Willett. New York: Hill & Wang, 1965.

Brockett, Oscar G., and Robert R. Findlay. *Century of Innovation: A History of European and American Theatre and Drama since 1870,* 2d ed. Boston: Allyn and Bacon, 1991.

Brustein, Robert. *The Theatre of Revolt: An Approach to Modern Drama.* Boston: Little, Brown, 1964.

Clurman, Harold. *The Fervent Years: The Story of the Group Theatre in the Thirties.* New York: Hill & Wang, 1957.

Craig, Edward Gordon. *On the Art of the Theatre,* 2d ed. Boston: Small, Maynard, 1924.

Davis, Hallie Flanagan. *Arena.* New York: Duell, Sloane and Pearce, 1940.

Deak, Frantisek. *Symbolist Theater: The Formation of the Avant Garde.* Baltimore: Johns Hopkins University Press, 1993.

DiPietro, Cary. *Shakespeare and Modernism.* Cambridge: Cambridge University Press, 2009.

Gordon, Mel. *Dada Performance.* New York: PAJ Publications, 1987.

Gorelik, Mordecai. *New Theatres for Old.* New York: Samuel French, 1940.

Greene, Naomi. *Antonin Artaud: Poet without Words.* New York: Simon & Schuster, 1970.

Innes, Christopher. *Avant-Garde Theatre 1892–1992.* New York: Routledge, 1993.

Kirby, Michael. *Futurist Performance.* New York: Dutton, 1971.

Larson, Orville K. *Scene Design in the American Theatre, 1915 to 1960.* Fayetteville: University of Arkansas Press, 1989.

Melzer, Annabelle. *Latest Rage the Big Drum: Dada and Surrealist Performance.* Ann Arbor, Mich.: UMI Research Press, 1980.

O'Connor, John, and Lorraine Brown, eds. *Free, Adult, Uncensored: The Living History of the Federal Theatre Project.* Washington: New Republic Books, 1978.

Patterson, Michael. *The Revolution in German Theatre, 1900–1933.* London: Routledge and Kegan Paul, 1981.

Roose-Evans, James. *Experimental Theatre: From Stanislavsky to Peter Brook*, new rev. ed. London: Studio Vista, 1984.

Shafer, Yvonne. *American Women Playwrights, 1900–1950.* New York: Peter Lang, 1995.

Styan, J. L. *Max Reinhardt.* Cambridge: Cambridge University Press, 1982.

Volbach, Walther. *Adolphe Appia, Prophet of the Modern Theatre.* Middletown, Conn.: Wesleyan University Press, 1968.

Willett, John. *Expressionism.* New York: McGraw-Hill, 1970.

———. *The Theatre of Bertolt Brecht.* New York: New Directions, 1959.

Chapter 8
Decentralization and Subsidization: New Directions

Beauman, Sally. *The Royal Shakespeare Company.* New York: Oxford University Press, 1982.

Berkowitz, Gerald M. *New Broadways: Theatre across America, 1950–1980.* Totowa, N.J.: Rowman & Littlefield, 1982.

Bigsby, C. W. E. *A Critical Introduction to Twentieth-Century American Drama. Vol. 2, Williams/Miller/Albee.* New York: Cambridge University Press, 1984.

Biner, Pierre. *The Living Theatre*, 2d ed. New York: Horizon Press, 1972.

Boardman, Gerald. *American Musical Comedy: From Adonis to Dreamgirls.* New York: Oxford University Press, 1982.

Brockett, Oscar G., and Robert R. Findlay. See under Chapter 7.

Brook, Peter. *The Shifting Point: Forty Years of Theatrical Exploration, 1946–1987.* New York: Harper and Row, 1988.

Brustein, Robert. *Revolution as Theatre: Notes on the New Radical Style.* New York: Liveright, 1971.

Burian, Jarka. *The Scenography of Josef Svoboda.* Middletown, Conn.: Wesleyan University Press, 1971.

Cook, Judith. *The National Theatre.* London: Harrap, 1976.

Croyden, Margaret. *Lunatics, Lovers and Poets: The Contemporary Experimental Theatre.* New York: McGraw-Hill, 1974.

Esslin, Martin. *The Theatre of the Absurd*, rev. ed. New York: Doubleday, 1969.

Findlater, Richard. *Twenty-Five Years of the English Stage Company.* London: Methuen, 1981.

Gorelik, Mordecai. See under Chapter 7.

Goldberg, Roselee. *Performance Art: From Futurism to the Present*, rev. ed. New York: Abrams, 1988.

Gottfried, Martin. *Broadway Musicals.* New York: Abrams, 1979.

Grotowski, Jerzy. *Towards a Poor Theatre.* New York: Simon & Schuster, 1968.

Hirsch, Foster. *A Method to Their Madness: The History of the Actors Studio.* New York: Norton, 1984.

Itzin, Catherine. *Stages in the Revolution: Political Theatre in Britain since 1968.* New York: Methuen, 1981.

Kerensky, Oleg. *The New British Drama: Fourteen Playwrights since Osborne and Pinter.* New York: Taplinger, 1979.

Kirby, Michael. *Happenings.* New York: Dutton, 1965.

Kolin, Philip C., ed. *American Playwrights since 1945: A Guide to Scholarship, Criticism, and Performance.* Westport, Conn.: Greenwood Press, 1989.

Kostelanetz, Richard. *The Theatre of Mixed Means.* New York: Dial Press, 1968.

Kumiega, Jennifer. *The Theatre of Grotowski.* London: Methuen, 1985.

Pasolli, Robert. *A Book on the Open Theatre.* Indianapolis: Bobbs-Merrill, 1970.

Patterson, Michael. See under Chapter 7.

Roose-Evans, James. See under Chapter 7.

Segel, Harold B. *Twentieth-Century Russian Drama.* Baltimore: Johns Hopkins University Press, 1993.

Styan, J. L. *Modern Drama in Theory and Practice.* 3 vols. New York: Cambridge University Press, 1981.

Chapter 9
Contemporary Theatre and Its Diversity

Abramson, Doris E. *Negro Playwrights in the American Theatre.* New York: Columbia University Press, 1969.

Aronson, Arnold. *American Avant-Garde Theatre: A History.* New York: Routledge, 2000.

Betsko, Kathleen, and Rachel Koenig. *Interviews with Contemporary Women Playwrights.* New York: Beech Tree Books, 1987.

Bradby, David. *Director's Theatre.* New York: St. Martin's, 1988.

Brater, Enoch, ed. *Feminine Focus: The New Women Playwrights.* New York: Oxford University Press, 1989.

Brockett, Oscar G., and Robert R. Findlay. See under Chapter 7.

Byrd Hoffman Foundation. *Robert Wilson: Theatre of Images.* New York: Byrd Hoffman Foundation, 1984.

Case, Sue-Ellen. *Feminism and Theatre.* New York: Routledge, 1988.

Chinoy, Helen K., and Linda Jenkins, eds. *Women in American Theatre,* 2d ed. New York: Theatre Communications Group, 1987.

Clum, John M. *Acting Gay: Male Homosexuality in Modern Drama.* New York: Columbia University Press, 1992.

DeJongh, Nicholas. *Not in Front of the Audience: Homosexuality on Stage.* New York: Routledge, 1992.

Everett, William, ed. *The Cambridge Guide to the Musical.* Cambridge: Cambridge University Press, 2008.

Eyre, Richard, and Nicholas Wright. *Changing Stages.* New York: Knopf, 2001.

Hill, Errol, ed. *The Theatre of Black Americans.* 2 vols. Englewood Cliffs, N.J.: Prentice Hall, 1980.

Huerta, Jorge. *Chicano Theatre: Themes and Forms.* Ypsilanti, Mich.: Bilingual Press, 1982.

Kanellos, Nicolas. *A History of Hispanic Theatre in the United States: Origins to 1940.* Austin: University of Texas Press, 1990.

Marowitz, Charles. *Prospero's Staff: Acting and Directing in the Contemporary Theatre.* Bloomington: Indiana University Press, 1986.

Marranca, Bonnie. *The Theatre of Images* [Robert Wilson, Richard Foreman, Lee Breuer]. New York: Drama Book Specialists, 1977.

Pottlitzer, Joanne. *Hispanic Theatre in the United States and Puerto Rico.* New York: Ford Foundation, 1988.

Roose-Evans, James. See under Chapter 7.

Sanders, Leslie C. *The Development of Black Theatre in America: From Shadows to Selves.* Baton Rouge: Louisiana State University Press, 1988.

Seller, Maxine S., ed. *Ethnic Theatre in the United States.* Westport, Conn.: Greenwood Press, 1983.

Shank, Theodore. *American Alternative Theatre.* New York: Grove Press, 1982.

Shyer, Laurence. *Robert Wilson and His Collaborators.* New York: TCG, 1989.

World Encyclopedia of Contemporary Theatre. See under Chapter 3.

Chapter 10
Asian and African Theatre

Allain, Paul. *The Art of Stillness: The Theatre Practice of Tadashi Suzuki.* Basingstoke, U.K.: Palgrave/Macmillan, 2003.

Banham, Martin., ed. *A History of Theatre in Africa.* Cambridge: Cambridge University Press, 2004.

———. *African Theatre: Playwrights and Politics.* Bloomington: Indiana University Press, 2001.

———. *The Cambridge Guide to African and Caribbean Theatre.* Cambridge: Cambridge University Press, 1994.

Barber, Karin, et al. *West African Popular Theatre.* Bloomington: Indiana University Press, 1997.

Bowers, Faubion. *Japanese Theatre.* New York: Hermitage House, 1952.

Brandon, James R. *The Cambridge Guide to Asian Theatre.* Cambridge: Cambridge University Press, 1993.

Breitinger, Eckhard, ed. *Theatre and Performance in Africa.* Bayreuth: Bayreuth University Press, 1997.

Cavaye, Ronald, Paul Griffith, and Akihiko Senda. *A Guide to the Japanese Stage: From Traditional to Cutting Edge.* London: Kodansha International, 2005.

Etherton, Michael. *The Development of African Drama.* London: Hutchinson, 1982.

Gibbs, James. *African Theatre: Playwrights and Politics.* Bloomington: Indiana University Press, 2001.

Gibbs, James. *Wole Soyinka.* London: Macmillan, 1986.

Gray, John. *Black Theatre and Performance: A Pan-African Bibliography.* Westport, Conn.: Greenwood Press, 1990.

Fraleigh, Sondra Horton. *Dancing into Darkness: Butoh, Zen, and Japan.* Pittsburgh: University of Pittsburgh Press, 1999.

Hironaga, Shuzaburo. *Bunraku: A History of Japanese Puppet Theatre.* Osaka: Bunrajyza Theatrem, 1959.

Komparu, Kunio. *The Noh Theatre: Principles and Perspective.* New York: Weatherhill, 1983.

Kruger, Loren. *The Drama of South Africa: Plays, Pageants, and Publics since 1910.* New York: Routledge, 1999.

Leiter, Samuel L. *The Art of Kabuki: Plays in Performance.* Berkeley: University of California Press, 1979.

———. *New Kabuki Encyclopedia.*, rev. ed. Westport, Conn.: Greenwood Press, 1997.

Mrazek, Jan, ed. *Puppet Theater in Contemporary Indonesia: New Approaches to Performance-Events.* Ann Arbor: University of Michigan Press, 2001.

Ngugi Wa Thiong'o. *Decolonizing the Mind: The Politics of Language in African Literature.* Portsmouth, N.H.: Heinemann, 1986.

Obafemi, Olu. *Contemporary Nigerian Theatre.* Bayreuth: Bayreuth University Press, 1997.

Ortolani, Benito. *The Japanese Theatre: From Shamanistic Ritual to Contemporary Pluralism*, rev. ed. Princeton: Princeton University Press, 1995.

Powell, Brian. *Japan's Modern Theatre: A Century of Change and Continuity.* London: Curzon Press, 2002.

Rubin, Don, ed. *The World Encyclopedia of Contemporary Theatre. Vol. 3, Africa.* New York: Routledge, 1997.

Sakanishi, S. *Kyogen.* Boston: Marshall Jones, 1938.

Scott, A. C. *The Kabuki Theatre of Japan.* New York: Collier, 1966.

Suzuki, Tadashi. *The Way of Acting.* New York: Theatre Communications Group, 1986.

World Encyclopedia of Contemporary Theatre. See under Chapter 3.

Part Three: Theatrical Production

Chapter 11
Theatrical Space and Production Design

American Theatre Planning Board. *Theatre Check List: A Guide to the Planning and Construction of Proscenium and Open Stage Theatres.* Middletown, Conn.: Wesleyan University Press, 1969.

Burris-Meyer, Harold, and Edward C. Cole. *Theatres and Auditoriums*, 2d ed. with supplement. Huntington, N.Y.: Krieger, 1975.

Cogswell, Margaret, ed. *The Ideal Theater: Eight Concepts.* New York: American Federation of Arts, 1962.

Green, Peter Arthur. *Design Education: Problem Solving and Visual Experience.* London: Batsford, 1974.

Howard, Pamela. *What Is Scenography?* London: Routledge, 2002.

Ingham, Rosemary. *From Page to Stage.* Portsmouth, N.H.: Heinemann, 1998.

Izenour, George C. *Theatre Design*, 2nd ed. New Haven, Conn.: Yale University Press, 1997.

Jones, Robert E. *The Dramatic Imagination.* New York: Meredith, 1941.

Maier, Manfred. *Basic Principles of Design.* New York: Van Nostrand Reinhold, 1977.

Mielziner, Jo. *Shapes of Our Theatres.* New York: Clarkson N. Potter, 1970.

Schubert, Hannelore. *Modern Theatre Buildings: Architecture, Stage Design, Lighting.* New York: Praeger, 1971.

Sommer, Robert. *Design Awareness.* San Francisco: Rinehart Press, 1972.

Chapter 12
Playwriting and Dramaturgy

Cardullo, Bert, ed. *What Is Dramaturgy?* New York: Peter Lang, 1995.

Cohen, Edward M. *Working on a New Play: A Play Development Handbook for Actors, Directors, Designers, and Playwrights*, 2d ed. New York: Limelight Editions, 2004.

Cole, Toby. *Playwrights on Playwriting.* New York: Hill & Wang, 1961.

Dramatists Sourcebook. New York: Theatre Communications Group (frequently updated).

Jonas, Susan, et al., eds. *Dramaturgy in American Theater: A Source Book.* Fort Worth, Tex.: Harcourt Brace, 1997.

Packard, William. *The Art of the Playwright.* New York: Thunder Mouth Press, 1997.

Savran, David. *In Their Own Words: Contemporary American Playwrights.* New York: TCG, 1988.

Smiley, Sam. *Playwriting: The Structure of Action.* Englewood Cliffs, N.J.: Prentice Hall, 1971.

Spencer, Stuart. *The Playwright's Guidebook: An Insightful Primer on the Art of Dramatic Writing.* New York: Faber and Faber, 2002.

Ullom, Jeffrey. The *Humana Festival: The History of New Plays at Actors Theatre of Louisville.* Carbondale: Southern Illinois University Press, 2008.

Chapter 13
Directing and Producing

Ball, William. *A Sense of Direction: Some Observations on the Art of Directing.* New York: Drama Book Publishers, 1984.

Bartow, Arthur. *The Director's Voice: 21 Interviews.* New York: TCG, 1988.

Bloom, Michael. *Thinking Like a Director.* New York: Faber and Faber, 2001.

Bogart, Anne. *A Director Prepares: Seven Essays on Art in Theatre.* New York: Routledge, 2001.

Bradby, David. See under Chapter 9.

Braun, Edward. *The Director and the Stage: From Naturalism to Grotowski.* New York: Holmes and Meier, 1982.

Clurman, Harold. *On Directing.* New York: Macmillan, 1972.

Cohen, Robert, and John Harrop. *Creative Play Direction*, 2d ed. Englewood Cliffs, N.J.: Prentice Hall, 1984.

Cole, Toby, and Helen K. Chinoy, eds. *Directors on Directing*, rev. ed. Indianapolis: Bobbs-Merrill, 1963.

Delgado, Maria M., and Paul Heritage, eds. *In Contact with the Gods? Directors Talk Theatre.* Manchester: Manchester University Press, 1996.

Farber, Donald C. *From Option to Opening: A Guide for the Off-Broadway Producer,* rev. 4th ed. Wolfeboro, N.H.: Longwood, 1989.

———. *Producing Theatre: A Comprehensive Legal and Business Guide,* 2d ed. New York: Limelight Editions, 1997.

Hauser, Frank, and Russell Reich. *130 Lessons in Leadership from the Director's Chair.* New York: Walker & Company, 2008.

Hodge, Francis, and Michael McLain. *Play Directing: Analysis, Communication, and Style,* 7th ed. Boston: Allyn and Bacon, 2009.

Jones, David R. *Great Directors at Work: Stanislavsky, Brecht, Kazan, Brook.* Berkeley: University of California Press, 1986.

Langley, Stephen. *Theatre Management in America, Principles and Practice: Producing for Commercial, Stock, Resident, College and Community Theatre,* rev. 2d ed. New York: Drama Book Publishers, 1990.

Newman, Danny. *Subscribe Now! Building Arts Audiences through Dynamic Subscription Promoting.* New York: TCG, 1983.

O'Neill, R. H., and N. M. Boretz. *The Director as Artist.* New York: Harcourt Brace, 1987.

Shagan, Rena. *The Road Show: A Handbook for Successful Booking and Touring in the Performing Arts.* New York: ACA Books, 1984.

Shevtova, Maria, and Christopher Innes. *Director/Directing.* Cambridge University Press, 2009.

Thomas, James. *Script Analysis for Actors, Directors and Designers.* Boston: Focal Press, 1992.

Whitmore, Jon. *Directing Postmodern Theatre: Shaping Signification in Performance.* Ann Arbor: University of Michigan Press, 1994.

Wills, J. Robert, ed. *The Director in a Changing Theatre.* Palo Alto, Calif.: Mayfield, 1984.

Chapter 14
Acting

Benedetti, Robert L. *The Actor at Work,* 10th ed. Boston: Allyn and Bacon, 2008.

Berry, Cicely. *Voice and the Actor.* London: Virgin, 1993.

Chaikin, Joseph. *The Presence of the Actor: Notes on the Open Theatre, Disguises, Acting and Repression.* New York: Theatre Communications Group, 1991.

Cohen, Robert. *Acting Professionally: Raw Facts about Careers in Acting,* 7th ed. Basingstoke, U.K.: Palgrave/Macmillan, 2009.

Cole, Toby, and Helen K. Chinoy, eds. *Actors on Acting: The Theories, Techniques, and Practices of the Great Actors of All Time as Told in Their Own Words,* 4th ed. New York: Crown, 1995.

Hagen, Uta. *Respect for Acting.* New York: Macmillan, 1973.

Harrop, John, and Sabin Epstein. *Acting with Style,* 2d ed. Englewood Cliffs, N.J.: Prentice Hall, 1989.

Lessac, Arthur. *The Use and Training of the Human Voice.* New York: Drama Book Publishers, 1987.

Lewis, Robert. *Advice to the Players.* New York: Theatre Communications Group, 1989.

Machlin, Evangeline. *Speech for the Stage.* New York: Routledge, 2003.

McGaw, Charles J., Larry D. Clark, and Kenneth L. Stilson. *Acting Is Believing,* 8th ed. New York: Wadsworth, 2003.

Potter, Nicole. ed. *Movement for the Actor.* New York: Allworth Press, 2002.

Spolin, Viola. *Improvisation for the Theatre,* rev. ed. Evanston, Ill.: Northwestern University Press, 1983.

Stanislavsky, Constantin. *An Actor Prepares.* Trans. by Elizabeth Reynolds Hapgood. New York: Theatre Arts Books, 1936.

———. *Building a Character.* Trans. by Elizabeth Reynolds Hapgood. New York: Theatre Arts Books, 1949.

———. *Creating a Role.* Trans. by Elizabeth Reynolds Hapgood. New York: Theatre Arts Books, 1961.

Yakim, Moni, with Muriel Broadman. *Creating a Character: A Physical Approach to Acting.* New York: Applause, 1993.

Chapter 15
Scene Design

Arnold, Richard L. *Scene Technology,* 3d ed. Englewood Cliffs, N.J.: Prentice Hall, 1994.

Aronson, Arnold. *American Set Design.* New York: Theatre Communications Group, 1985.

Bablet, Denis. *Stage Design in the Twentieth Century.* New York: Amiel, 1976.

Bay, Howard. *Stage Design.* New York: Drama Book Publishers, 1974.

Bellman, Willard F. *Scenography and Stage Technology: An Introduction.* New York: Harper and Row, 1977.

Burdick, Elizabeth B., et al., eds. *Contemporary Stage Design.* Middletown, Conn.: Wesleyan University Press, 1975.

Corey, Irene. *The Mask of Reality: An Approach to Design for the Theatre.* Anchorage, Ky.: Anchorage Press, 1968.

Davis, Tony. *Stage Design.* Crans-Pres, Celigny, Switzerland: RotoVision, 2001.

Howard, Pamela. See under Chapter 11.

Jones, Robert Edmond. See under Chapter 11.

Koltai, Ralph. *Ralph Koltai: Designer for the Stage.* London: Nick Hern Books, 2006.

Larson, Orville K., ed. *Scene Design for Stage and Screen: Readings on the Aesthetics and Methodology of Scene Design for Drama, Opera, Musical Comedy, Ballet, Motion Pictures, Television and Arena Theatre.* Westport, Conn.: Greenwood Press, 1976.

Mielziner, Jo. *Designing for the Theatre.* New York: Atheneum, 1965.

Oenslager, Donald. *Scenery Then and Now.* New York: Norton, 1936.

Parker, W. Oren. *Sceno-Graphic Techniques.* Carbondale: Southern Illinois University Press, 1987.

Parker, Oren, R. Craig Wolf, and Dick Block. *Scene Design and Stage Lighting*, 9th ed. Boston: Wadsworth, 2008.

Payne, Darwin. *The Scenographic Imagination*, 3d ed. Carbondale: Southern Illinois University Press, 1993.

Pecktal, Lynn. *Designing and Drawing for the Theatre.* New York: McGraw-Hill, 1995.

Smith, Ronn. *American Set Design 2.* New York: Theatre Communications Group, 1991.

Sporre, Dennis J., and Robert C. Burroughs. *Scene Design in the Theatre.* Englewood Cliffs, N.J.: Prentice Hall, 1990.

Chapter 16
Costume Design and Makeup

Anderson, Barbara, and Cletus Anderson. *Costume Design.* New York: Holt, Rinehart and Winston, 1984.

Barton, Lucy. *Historic Costume for the Stage.* Boston: Baker's Plays, 1935.

Corey, Irene. *The Face Is a Canvas: The Design and Technique of Theatrical Makeup.* New Orleans: Anchorage Press, 1990.

Richard Corson, James Glavan, and Beverly Gore Norcross. *Stage Makeup*, 10th ed. Boston: Allyn and Bacon, 2009.

Emery, Joy S. *Stage Costume Techniques*, 2d ed. Englewood Cliffs, N.J.: Prentice Hall, 1992.

Ingham, Rosemary, and Liz Covey. *The Costume Designer's Handbook: A Complete Guide for Amateur and Professional Costume Designers.* Portsmouth, N.H.: Heinemann, 1992.

———. *The Costume Technician's Handbook*, 3rd ed. Portsmouth, N.H.: Heinemann, 2003.

Motley [design firm]. *Designing and Making Stage Costumes.* London: Herbert Press, 1992.

Payne, Blanche. *History of Costume from the Ancient Egyptians to the Twentieth Century.* New York: Harper and Row, 1965.

Pecktal, Lynn. *Costume Design: Techniques of Modern Masters.* New York: Back Stage Books, 1993.

Russell, Douglas. *Costume History and Style.* Englewood Cliffs, N.J.: Prentice Hall, 1983.

———. *Stage Costume Design: Theory, Technique and Style*, 2d ed. Englewood Cliffs, N.J.: Prentice Hall, 1985.

Smith, C. Ray, ed. *The Theatre Crafts Book of Makeup, Masks, and Wigs.* Emmaus, Penn.: Rodale Press, 1974.

Chapter 17
Lighting and Sound Design

Ballou, Glen, ed. *Handbook for Sound Engineers.* Indianapolis: H. W. Sams, 1987.

Bellman, Willard F. *Lighting the Stage: Art and Practice*, 3d ed. New York: Broadway Press, 2001.

———. *Scenography and Stage Technology.* See under Chapter 14.

Bergman, Gosta M. *Lighting in the Theatre.* Totowa, N.J.: Rowman & Littlefield, 1977.

Briggs, Jody. *Encyclopedia of Stage Lighting.* Jefferson, N.C.: McFarland and Company, 2008.

Burian, Jarka. See under Chapter 8.

Collison, David. *Stage Sound.* New York: Applause Theatre Books, 1990.

Essig, Linda. *Lighting and the Design Idea.* New York: Harcourt Brace, 1997.

Gillette, J. Michael. *Designing with Light*, 5th ed. New York: McGraw-Hill, 2007.

Jones, Robert E. See under Chapter 11.

Jones, Tom Douglas. *The Art of Light and Color.* New York: Van Nostrand Reinhold, 1973.

Kaye, Deena, and James LeBrecht. *Sound and Music for the Theatre: The Art & Technique of Design*, 3rd ed. St. Louis, Mo.: Focal Press, 2009.

Keller, Max. *Light Fantastic: The Art and Design of Stage Lighting.* Munich: Prestel Verlag, 1999.

Leonard, John A. *Theatre Sound.* New York: Routledge, 2001.

McCandless, Stanley R. *A Method of Lighting the Stage.* New York: Theatre Arts Books, 1984.

Moody, James L. *The Business of Theatrical Design.* New York: Allworth Press, 2002.

Palmer, Richard H. *The Lighting Art: The Aesthetics of Stage Lighting Design*, 2d ed. Englewood Cliffs, N.J.: Prentice Hall, 1994.

Parichy, Dennis. *Illuminating the Play: The Artistry of Lighting Design.* Portsmouth, N.H.: Heinemann, 2009.

Parker, W. Oren, and R. Craig Wolf. See under Chapter 15.

Rosenthal, Jean, and Lael Wertenbaker. *The Magic of Light.* Boston: Little, Brown, 1972.

Warfel, William B. *The New Handbook of Stage Lighting Graphics*, rev. ed. New York: Drama Book Publishers, 1990.

Warfel, William B., and Walter R. Klappert. *Color Science for Lighting the Stage.* New Haven, Conn.: Yale University Press, 1981.

Watson, Lee. *Lighting Design Handbook.* New York: McGraw-Hill, 1990.

Index

A

A Contemporary Theatre (ACT), 208
ABBA, 260
Abbey Theatre, 319
Abe, Kobo, 277
About Face, 208
Abraham, 87
Absurdist drama, 185–87
Across the Universe, 309
ACT. *See* A Contemporary Theatre (ACT)
Act Out Productions, 248
Acting. *See also* Actors
  action and, 362, 368, 372
  actor's instrument and, 356, 358
  actor's thoughts about, 359
  audience and, 361, 371, 372
  Brecht on, 365
  business and, 367–68
  costumes and, 371
  director and, 152–53, 360, 365–66, 368, 370, 372
  dress rehearsals and, 371–72
  gesture and, 367–68
  Grotowski on, 365
  line readings and, 369–70
  movement and, 367–68
  observation/imagination and, 360, 372
  performing/performance and, 363–72
  professional theatre and, 102
  rehearsals and, 357, 360, 367, 369, 371–72
  stage vocabulary/conventions and, 360–62
  training and, 356–70
  vocal characterization and, 369
Acting companies, 102–4, 106
Acting Company, 175
Acting space, 214, 375
Action
  acting and, 362, 368, 372
  defined, 40–41, 367
  dramatic (*see* Dramatic action)
  production design and, 310
  theatrical space and, 299, 300
Actor Prepares, An, 158
Actors. *See* Acting; Performers/performance
Actors Equity, 204, 208

Actors Equity Association, 364
Actor's Nightmare, The, 221
Actors Studio, 187, 188
Actors Theatre of Louisville, 204, 225, 320, 350
Adding Machine, The, 172
Additive color mixing, defined, 418
Adler, Stella, 177
Aeschylus, 65, 70
Aestheticism, 162–63
African American playwrights, 262–63
African American theatre, 230–31
  costume design and, 408, 410
  criticism and, 343
  director and, 153–55, 342–47
  lighting and, 426, 430
  LORT and, 229
  makeup and, 410
  modernism and, 165
  professional theatre and, 102
  Russian theatre and, 158
African theatre, 268, 269, 283–91
Agamemnon, 70
Age makeup, defined, 409
Agent, playwriting and, 322
Ages of the Moon, 222
Agon, defined, 77
Aida, 241
Ajax, 70
Akalaitis, JoAnne, 255, 424
Akerlind, Christopher, 76, 196, 390
Akins, Zoe, 243
Akoyanomatsu, 271
Akropolis, 340
al-Hakim, Tawfig, 290
Alabama Shakespeare Festival, 381
Albee, Edward, 218, 220, 401
Alcestis, 70, 253
Aldwych Theatre, 198–99
Alegría, 14
Alekseev, Konstantin Sergeevich, 157–58
Alexander the Great, 43, 77
Alexandrine, 131
Alice in Bed, 162
Alienation, 178–81
All My Sons, 187, 335
Allegorical concept, 398
Allegory, 49
Allen, Debbie, 343
Alley Theatre, 27, 201, 259, 308, 327, 435

Alternative theatre groups, 207–12
Amadeus, 258
Ambrosone, John, 162, 179, 184
America Play, The, 262
American Buffalo, 220
American Conservatory Theatre, 151, 402
American Daughter, An, 246
American Indian Community House, 243
American Indian Dance Theatre, 243
American Indian Studies Center, 243
American Laboratory Theatre (New York), 177
American musical, 191–94, 217–19
American Plan, The, 263
American Player's Theatre, 403
American playwrights, 220–22
American regional theatres, 201–4
American Repertory Company, 424
American Repertory Theatre, 123, 162, 179, 181, 184, 185, 254, 255, 306, 309, 327, 354, 370, 387, 401
American Shakespeare Company, 420
American Sign Language (ASL), 245, 361
American theatre, 175–77, 183–85, 203, 208, 229, 269, 286–87
American Theatre Critics Association, 237, 244
Ameriville, 242
Amplitude, 435
Amy's View, 258
And Baby Makes Seven, 246
And Then She Was Screaming, 263
Anderson, Barbara, 399
Anderson, Cletus, 399
Anderson, Laurie, 251
Anderson, Maxwell, 177
Anderson, Paul, 335
Anderson, Susan, 162
Andrews, Julie, 194
Andronicus, Livius, 78
Angels in America, 249–51, 264, 320, 325, 367, 392
Ankoku butoh, defined, 278
Anna in the Tropics, 236
Annie, 218
Anon(ymous), 265
Antal, Csaba, 179
Antigone, 70

Antoine, André, 152, 155, 167
Antony and Cleopatra, 34
Appia, Adolphe, 165–67, 310, 379
Apprentices, 86, 102, 106
Apron, defined, 299
Arcadia, 258
Arcenas, Loy, 234
Architettura, 113–14
Arditti, Paul, 20
Arena stage, 298, 301, 312, 382, 384
Arena Stage (Washington, D.C.), 201, 302
Arena theatre, 375, 428
Argonautika, 322
Aristophanes, 77
Aristotle, 40, 43, 44
Arkin, Alan, 208
Arms and the Man, 156
Arp, Hans, 169
Art, 316
"Art for art's sake," 162–63
Art history, 378, 402–3
Artaud, Antonin, 182–83, 199, 206, 209, 213, 291
Articulation, 369
Artistic director, 332
Art(s), 10–17, 21–22
  censorship and, 11
  defined, 10, 15–17
  performance, 214–17, 250–52
  visual (*see* Visual arts)
Arts Council of Great Britain, 198, 200, 202
As Is, 249
As You Like It, 16, 305
Ashikaga family, 270
Ashman, Howard, 396
Asian American theatre, 239–42
Asian American Theatre Workshop, 239
Asian American Workshop, 242
Asian Exclusion Act, 239
Asian theatre, 269–82, 291, 339
Asides, 49, 143
Assistants
  costume designer's, 412–13
  director's, 353, 354
  lighting, 431–32
  scene designer's, 393–94
At the Vanishing Point, 265
Atlanta Shakespeare Company, 57
Atoza, defined, 272